CONSTRUCTION ARBITRATION AND ALTERNATIVE DISPUTE RESOLUTION

This book provides comprehensive, rigorous and up-to-date coverage of key issues that have emerged in the first quarter of the 21st Century in transnational construction arbitration and alternative dispute resolution (ADR).

Covering four general themes, this book discusses:

- the increasing internationalisation of dispute resolution in construction law;
- the increasing reliance on technology in the management of construction projects and construction arbitration/ADR;
- the increasing prominence of collaborative contracting in construction and infrastructure projects;
- the increasing importance of contractual adjudication such as dispute boards in construction and infrastructure projects;
- the increasing prevalence of statutory adjudication mechanisms across the world; and
- the greater incidence of investment disputes and disputes against States and State entities over construction and infrastructure concessions and agreements.

Tapping into their substantial expertise in practice and in research, the contributor team of senior practitioners and academics in the area of construction law and dispute resolution provide readers with information that balances an intellectually rigorous academic contribution against the backdrop of real concerns raised in practice.

Construction Arbitration and Alternative Dispute Resolution is an invaluable resource for practitioners in the field, academics in arbitration and construction law, and post-graduate students in construction law and dispute resolution.

Renato Nazzini is Professor of Law and Director of the Centre of Construction Law and Dispute Resolution at King's College London and partner at LMS Legal LLP, London. He is an international arbitrator, counsel and construction specialist with experience in common law and civil law jurisdictions in Europe, Asia, Africa and America and has acted, as arbitrator or counsel, under most international rules, including the ICC, the LCIA, the UNCITRAL and the Milan Chamber of Commerce (CAM) Rules. He is a member of the ICC Arbitration and ADR Commission, Italy, a member of the ICC Task Force on Dealing with Corruption Issues in International Arbitration and a member of the Board of the International Construction Law Association and of Africa Construction Law.

I0894591

CONSTRUCTION PRACTICE SERIES

Series editors: Philip Britton and Phillip Capper

Construction Contract Variations
Michael Sergeant and Max Wieliczko
Holman Fenwick Willan LLP

Adjudication in Construction Law
Darryl Royce

Delay and Disruption in Construction Contracts
Fifth Edition
Edited by Andrew Burr

The Law of Construction Disputes
Second Edition
Cyril Chern

Construction Insurance and UK Construction Contracts
Third Edition
Roger ter Haar QC, Marshall Levine and Anna Laney

Construction Law
Second Edition
Julian Bailey

International Contractual and Statutory Adjudication
Andrew Burr

Remedies in Construction Law
Second Edition
Roger ter Haar QC

Professional Negligence in Construction
Second Edition
Ben Patten and Hugh Saunders

Litigation in the Technology and Construction Court
Adam Constable QC, Lucy Garrett QC and Calum Lamont

Chern on Dispute Boards
Practice and Procedure
Fourth Edition
Cyril Chern

The Law of Construction Disputes
Third Edition
Cyril Chern

Construction Arbitration and Alternative Dispute Resolution
Theory and Practice around the World
Edited by Renato Nazzini

For more information about this series, please visit:
www.routledge.com/Construction-Practice-Series/book-series/CPS

CONSTRUCTION ARBITRATION AND ALTERNATIVE DISPUTE RESOLUTION

THEORY AND PRACTICE AROUND THE WORLD

EDITED BY RENATO NAZZINI

informa law
from Routledge

First published 2022
by Routledge
2 Park Square, Milton Park, Abingdon, Oxon OX14 4RN

and by Routledge
605 Third Avenue, New York, NY 10158

Routledge is an imprint of the Taylor & Francis Group, an informa business

© 2022 selection and editorial matter, Renato Nazzini; individual chapters, the contributors

The right of Renato Nazzini to be identified as the author of the editorial material, and of the authors for their individual chapters, has been asserted in accordance with sections 77 and 78 of the Copyright, Designs and Patents Act 1988.

All rights reserved. No part of this book may be reprinted or reproduced or utilised in any form or by any electronic, mechanical, or other means, now known or hereafter invented, including photocopying and recording, or in any information storage or retrieval system, without permission in writing from the publishers.

Trademark notice: Product or corporate names may be trademarks or registered trademarks, and are used only for identification and explanation without intent to infringe.

British Library Cataloguing-in-Publication Data
A catalogue record for this book is available from the British Library

Library of Congress Cataloging-in-Publication Data
Names: Nazzini, Renato, editor.
Title: Construction arbitration and alternative dispute resolution : theory and practice around the world / edited by Renato Nazzini.
Description: Milton Park, Abingdon, Oxon [UK] ; New York, NY : Routledge, 2021. | Series: Construction practice series | Includes bibliographical references and index.
Identifiers: LCCN 2021015083 (print) | LCCN 2021015084 (ebook) | ISBN 9780367710064 (hardback) | ISBN 9781003155973 (ebook)
Subjects: LCSH: International commercial arbitration. | Construction industry—Law and legislation. | Construction contracts. | Arbitration and award.
Classification: LCC K2405.B84 C66 2021 (print) | LCC K2405.B84 (ebook) | DDC 343.07/8624—dc23
LC record available at https://lccn.loc.gov/2021015083
LC ebook record available at https://lccn.loc.gov/2021015084

ISBN: 978-0-367-71006-4 (hbk)
ISBN: 978-0-367-74074-0 (pbk)
ISBN: 978-1-003-15597-3 (ebk)

Typeset in Times New Roman
by Apex CoVantage, LLC

CONTENTS

PART III GOOD FAITH AND COLLABORATIVE DISPUTE RESOLUTION

PART IV CONTRACTUAL ADJUDICATION: DISPUTE BOARDS IN INTERNATIONAL CONSTRUCTION DISPUTES

PART V STATUTORY CONSTRUCTION ADJUDICATION: A GLOBAL PERSPECTIVE

DETAILED CONTENTS

PART III GOOD FAITH AND COLLABORATIVE DISPUTE RESOLUTION

PART IV CONTRACTUAL ADJUDICATION: DISPUTE BOARDS IN INTERNATIONAL CONSTRUCTION DISPUTES

NOTES ON THE CONTRIBUTORS

David Arias
David Arias is a partner in the international arbitration practice at Herbert Smith Freehills. He has more than 30 years of experience in dispute resolution, serving as counsel and arbitrator in more than 150 cases in venues across Europe, America and Africa. He is a professor of procedural law and arbitration, and he has chaired the IBA Arbitration Committee and the Club Español del Arbitraje, of which he is Honorary President.

Christian Aschauer
Christian Aschauer is Professor of Austrian Arbitration Law and International Arbitration at the University of Graz and an Independent Arbitrator based in Vienna. He has been conducting arbitrations under the rules of many institutions, including in particular the ICC, SCC, VIAC and LCIA, and is a member of the Council of the Milan Chamber of Arbitration.

Julian Bailey
Julian Bailey is a solicitor and partner at White & Case LLP, London, and adjunct professor of law at Hamad bin Khalifa University, Doha, Qatar. He is the author of *Construction Law* (3rd ed, 2020).

Matthew Bell
Dr Matthew Bell is Senior Lecturer and Co-Director of Studies for Construction Law at Melbourne Law School, The University of Melbourne. He is Professional Support Lawyer (part-time) to the Construction and Major Projects Group of Clayton Utz, and previously a construction lawyer at Clayton Utz (based in Melbourne) and at Clifford Chance (based in London).

Olivier Caprasse
Specialised in arbitration, Professor Olivier Caprasse (Universities of Liège and Brussels) is a member of the Brussels Bar. Author of more than 130 publications (mainly in arbitration and corporate law), he has seated as chair, co-arbitrator or sole arbitrator in more than seventy national and international arbitrations (ICC, Cepani, AFA, Geneva Chamber of Commerce and Industry, CACI, SCC, ad hoc, Uncitral) and has represented clients in numerous arbitrations. He has been a member of the ICC Court since 2016.

Shouyu Chong

Shouyu Chong, LLM (corporate and financial services law, National University of Singapore) is a PhD candidate at the Centre of Construction Law and Dispute Resolution, King's College London (KCL); a visiting lecturer at the Dickson Poon School of Law, KCL; and a research fellow at the Singapore International Dispute Resolution Academy, Singapore Management University. He researches and consults on private international law and cross-border dispute resolution mechanisms, and is a co-author (with Nadja Alexander) of *The Singapore Convention on Mediation – A Commentary* (Wolters Kluwer, 2019). His research on the Singapore Convention on Mediation is published internationally and has been cited widely.

Michael Cottrell

Michael Cottrell, LLB, MSc, is a senior associate in the London office of Pinsent Masons LLP, specialising in international dispute resolution and arbitration. Michael's practice is focused primarily on the energy and infrastructure sectors, where he acts for contractors, employers and states on disputes arising out of large, complex projects, but also encompasses investor-state dispute settlement. Michael has represented clients in both commercial and investment treaty arbitration proceedings, including as advocate, under various institutional rules. Michael acted on one of the recent leading cases on state immunity before the Privy Council.

Taner Dedezade

Taner Dedezade (www.dedezade.co.uk) is a barrister, with over 20 years' experience, practising from Corbett & Co (www.corbett.co.uk), specialising in the resolution of international construction and engineering disputes, mostly concerning projects based on FIDIC contracts. He is also a FIDIC-accredited trainer and has delivered numerous lectures and workshops all round the world through Cornerstone seminars (https://www.cornerstone-seminars.com/) and for the King's College MSc. He was awarded the FIDIC trainer of the year 2020 and was invited by FIDIC to provide online Top-up Training to the FIDIC President's List of Adjudicators.

James Doe

James Doe is Co-Global Head of the construction disputes practice at Herbert Smith Freehills. James' expertise is with major infrastructure, construction and engineering projects, with a particular focus on complex process engineering, power plants and oil and gas related projects. James' practice is predominately international and he has a wealth of experience working with clients from around the globe, in particular those from the Middle East, Europe and Asia.

Duncan W Glaholt

Duncan W Glaholt, C. Arb., is the founder of the leading Canadian construction law firm Glaholt Bowles LLP in Toronto. He has been named one of Canada's leading construction lawyers and arbitrators in Who's Who Legal, Chambers Guides, Lexpert/American Lawyer Media 'Leading 500 Lawyers' and other similar publications. Mr Glaholt is certified as a Specialist in Construction Law by the Law Society of Ontario and has been awarded the Ontario Bar Association Award of Excellence in construction law in 2014.

Mr Glaholt is a founding fellow and past president of the Canadian College of Construction Lawyers, a fellow of the American College of Construction Lawyers and a fellow of the International Academy of Construction Lawyers. In addition to his practice as an advocate, he sits nationally and internationally as a mediator, arbitrator, dispute review board chair, adjudicator, court appointed monitor and referee of construction industry disputes. Mr Glaholt is the author, co-author and editor of a number of construction industry publications and is an adjunct professor at the University of Toronto Faculty of Law.

Nicholas Gould

Nicholas Gould is a partner in the specialist construction, engineering and energy law firm, Fenwick Elliott LLP, where he conducts a mix of international dispute resolution and non-contentious work. He is a solicitor-advocate, chartered surveyor, accredited adjudicator and CEDR lead mediator. He sits as arbitrator and on dispute boards. He acts for contractors, employers and governments in the building, construction, engineering, infrastructure, transport, energy, oil and gas, and process engineering sectors. Nicholas is a visiting professor at King's College London and Vice President of the ICC's Arbitration Commission. He is President Elect of the DRBF and past Chairman of the Society of Construction Law.

Shy Jackson

Shy Jackson is a partner at Bryan Cave Leighton Paisner, a solicitor advocate, a fellow of the Chartered Institution of Arbitration and a fellow of the Chartered Institution of Civil Engineering Surveyors. He specialises in construction law and his practice covers advising clients on complex construction and engineering projects in the UK and internationally, including in litigation, arbitration, adjudication and other forms of ADR.

Sean Kelly

Sean Kelly is a special counsel with the Construction and Major Projects Group of Clayton Utz based in Melbourne, Australia. He acts for local and international clients regarding claims and dispute resolution on complex construction and infrastructure projects.

Malik Laazouzi

Malik Laazouzi is Professor of Law at Paris 2 – Panthéon-Assas University. Founder of the LL.M. AWArDS, he focuses on international and investment arbitration and on international litigation. He has co-authored a book dedicated to the law of international contracts and holds the yearly column on investment arbitration in the French *Revue de l'arbitrage*.

Robbie McCrea

Robbie McCrea is a lawyer specialised in international infrastructure projects and disputes. He has more than a decade of experience working on projects around the world, and has represented clients in litigation and all forms of ADR including many dispute boards. Robbie has regularly written and given talks on industry issues such as the FIDIC forms of contract, dispute boards and arbitration issues.

Renato Nazzini

Renato is Professor of Law and Director of the Centre of Construction Law and Dispute Resolution at King's College London and partner at LMS Legal LLP, London. An experienced arbitrator and counsel in international arbitration, he has a wide industry knowledge, from construction, oil and gas, and infrastructure to IT and digital, from pharmaceuticals to consumer goods and has acted under most international rules, including the ICC, the LCIA, the UNCITRAL and the Milan Chamber of Commerce (CAM) Rules. A dually qualified English solicitor and Italian advocate, he understands and navigates the different approaches across common law and civil law jurisdictions and is able to resolve effectively and pragmatically complex substantive and procedural problems. Aware of the multi-cultural dimension of many international disputes, he has worked across Europe, Africa, Asia and America. He is a member of the ICC Arbitration and ADR Commission, Italy, a member of the ICC Task Force on Dealing with Corruption Issues in International Arbitration, and a member of the Board of the International Construction Law Association and of Africa Construction Law. Renato published seven books and more than one hundred articles and book chapters on international arbitration or competition law and is general co-editor or member of the editorial board of five leading international journals. He has been visiting professor at the University of Turin, the University of Zurich and FGV of San Paulo, Brazil. He holds two PhDs, one from the University of London and another from the University of Milan, and is a regular speaker at conferences around the world.

James Pickavance

James Pickavance is a partner at Jones Day and leads the construction and infrastructure practice in London. He has experience of all major forms of dispute resolution, advising public bodies and corporations on domestic and international, single or multi-jurisdictional disputes across a range of industry sectors, but in particular energy, major infrastructure and commercial development. He is a visiting fellow at King's College London. He has authored over forty articles and wrote the leading textbook, *A Practical Guide to Construction Adjudication*.

Maud Piers

Maud Piers is Associate Professor of Law at University of Ghent, Belgium, where she focuses her research and teaching on international arbitration law, ADR, and technology and dispute resolution. She regularly acts as an arbitrator and is the Vice-President of the Belgian Center of Arbitration and Mediation (Cepani). She was also the founder and is currently an editor (and former editor-in-chief) of b-Arbitra, which is the first Belgian Review for Arbitration.

Erik Schäfer

Erik Schäfer, attorney at law (DE), is partner of COHAUSZ & FLORACK, a Düsseldorf boutique firm focussing mainly on all aspects of protecting and commercially exploiting technology and intellectual property. His main areas of practice are arbitration, matters with a technical 'flavour', especially IP and IT. Since 1994 he has been acting either as counsel or arbitrator in national and international arbitration proceedings. He is a trained mediator. Erik works in English, Spanish, French and German language.

Patricia Shaughnessy

Patricia Shaughnessy, Stockholm University, specialises in international disputes and commercial law. She is a member of the ICC Court of Arbitration and until recently, served as the Vice-Chair of the Board of the SCC Arbitration Institute, having been a Board member since 2005 and a member of the committees drafting the SCC Rules. She was a government-appointed expert on the revisions to the Swedish Arbitration Act. She acts as an arbitrator, expert and consultant. She served as a US Supreme Court fellow and practiced law for ten years in the US.

Maxime Tecqmenne

Maxime Tecqmenne is a research assistant in European Union law and arbitration law at the University of Liège (ULiège). He obtained a master's degree in law from the University of Liège in 2018.

Toh Chen Han

Toh Chen Han (BA (Hons) Jurisprudence, Oxon) is a partner of Pinsent Masons MPillay LLP. He is the Immediate Past Chair of the Society of Construction Law (Singapore), a fellow of the Singapore Institute of Arbitrators, and a contributing editor of the Singapore Journal and Construction Law, and Singapore's leading construction law textbook, *Law and Practice of Construction Contracts* (Chow Kok Fong, 2018).

TABLE OF CASES

Germany

Hong Kong

India

International Chamber of Commerce

International Centre for Settlement of Investment Disputes

International Court of Justice

Iran

Italy

Jersey

Malaysia

Namibia

Netherlands

Permanent Court of Arbitration

Poland

Singapore

South Africa

Stockholm Chamber of Commerce

Sweden

Switzerland

Ukraine

United Arab Emirates

United Kingdom

United States

TABLE OF LEGISLATION

TABLE OF INTERNATIONAL TREATIES AND CONVENTIONS

TABLE OF ARBITRATION RULES

CHAPTER 1

Introduction

Renato Nazzini

1.1 This book builds upon the discussion we had at a conference held at the Centre of Construction Law and Dispute Resolution at King's College London in June 2019. The debate centred on key dispute resolution themes that would be crucial for the construction industry in the first half of the 21st Century. However, the book is not simply a collection of the papers given at the conference. All the speakers have substantially reworked and expanded their contributions and the book includes chapters by authors who did not participate in the conference.

1.2 This is the second book that the Centre publishes in the Lloyd's Arbitration Law Library based on a dynamic and interactive research methodology that brings together academia, legal practice and industry.[1] Research themes are discussed and selected at the Centre, in light of our ongoing projects and interaction with the industry. Then, the chosen themes are debated at a conference, which allows us to test assumptions, reasoning and conclusions, and obtain feedback from a wider audience. Following the conference, further research and analysis are carried out and our findings are published in a book aimed at practitioners, academics and students around the world.

1.3 Our method is always to look at problems globally. The Centre is based in London, a stone's throw from the Royal Courts of Justice, and it is only natural that often our starting point is English law. But the commercial and technical problems facing the construction industry today are not purely domestic but global. Therefore, as the previous book, this book also addresses questions on an international level, comparing different approaches and solutions, and identifying emerging trends that defy national boundaries.

1.4 This time we identified six main themes. The first is the internationalisation of dispute resolution. Internationalisation may take place in two ways. It may occur by a process of spontaneous convergence across jurisdictions adopting the same or similar approaches to resolving a given legal problem. Or it may happen by an international treaty or other binding instrument. In the first part of the book, we discuss one example of each approach. The problem of the law governing the arbitration agreement is an example of spontaneous convergence, at least in part.[2] The Singapore Convention on Mediation is an

1 The first is R Nazzini (ed), *Key Themes in International Construction Arbitration* (London, Informa 2017).

2 Under Article V(1)(a) of the New York Convention, enforcement of an arbitral award may be refused if the arbitration 'agreement is not valid under the law to which the parties have subjected it or, failing any indication thereon, under the law of the country where the award was made'. However, both in the interpretation of the Convention and beyond the scope of application of Article V(1)(a) there is ample room for spontaneous convergence (or indeed divergence) across jurisdictions: see R Nazzini, 'The Problem of the Law Governing the Arbitration Clause between National Rules and Transnational Solutions', in this book.

example of internationalisation by treaty and its impact on, and use by, the construction industry will certainly be topical for many years to come.

1.5 The second theme is the impact and use of artificial intelligence ('AI') in dispute resolution. This has two aspects: the implications of the use of AI (and other new technologies) during the procurement and execution of the project for dispute resolution and the use of AI in dispute resolution itself. Needless to say, all those involved in a construction project from the procurement stage to the 'bitter end' of arbitration or litigation cannot afford to ignore how new technologies will change the world as we know it.

1.6 The third theme is good faith and collaborative dispute resolution. Under this broad heading, the authors discuss good faith from substantive and procedural perspectives, comparing common law and civil law approaches to the problem. This is an area in which more convergence is certainly desirable and probably achievable through appropriate contract drafting. If the parties do wish to make use of dispute avoidance and dispute resolution techniques based on collaboration and good faith rather than adversarial procedures, they should be strongly encouraged to incorporate such techniques in their contracts and train the project teams to make effective use of these techniques.

1.7 The fourth theme is contractual adjudication or Dispute Boards. In this field, there have been significant developments in the past few years, not least the 2017 edition of the FIDIC suite of contracts. This section is likely to be of great interest to all practitioners in the field.

1.8 As our fifth theme, we decided to provide a strong comparative analysis and overview of statutory adjudication regimes across the world. This will provide a unique insight into the similarities and differences of how adjudication works, from the United Kingdom to Singapore, from Canada to New South Wales (and other Australian jurisdictions).

1.9 Last but not least, we look at the risks and traps of contracting with the State in the 21st Century and how to avoid them.

1.10 This book will be of interest to construction practitioners worldwide. It is yet one more example of the commitment of the Centre of Construction Law and Dispute Resolution to the study of how best to resolve construction disputes in a way which is both practical and truly international. It is part of a continuing endeavour that would not be possible without our dedicated staff at the Centre, our visiting professors and visiting fellows, all the authors of this book and the continuing support of our publisher. To all I express my unreserved gratitude.

Professor Renato Nazzini PhD FCIArb
Director, Centre of Construction Law and Dispute Resolution
King's College London
London-Rome, 28 June 2021

PART I

THE INTERNATIONALISATION OF CONSTRUCTION DISPUTE RESOLUTION

CHAPTER 2

The problem of the law governing the arbitration clause between national rules and transnational solutions

Renato Nazzini

Introduction

2.1 Parties rarely choose the law applicable to the arbitration clause.[1] This frequently gives rise to complexities. The obvious solution – but one that, for some reason, is not yet prevalent – is for arbitration clauses to make an express choice of the law applicable to the clause itself. It is difficult not to endorse this solution. If the parties choose the law applicable to the arbitration clause, in all but rare cases, such a choice will be given effect by arbitrators and courts. The determination of the law applicable to the arbitration clause will not be problematic. And this is the end of the matter.

2.2 However, the existence of a drafting solution does not mean that the analysis of the legal solution in the absence of clear drafting on the point is unnecessary. The first reason is, quite simply, that not all arbitration clauses have an express choice of law provision concerning the law applicable to the clause itself. Indeed, this is currently the case for the vast majority of arbitration clauses. And even when there is general awareness of the need for such a choice, there will no doubt still be some arbitration clauses without an express choice of law provision concerning the clause itself because, for example, the parties could not agree on such a law or simply due to neglect or forgetfulness. After all, there is an enormous amount of literature on arbitration clauses and how to draft them. And yet there are still problematic clauses that give rise to disputes. The perfect world of perfectly drafted contracts with perfectly drafted arbitration clauses does not yet exist. So problems arise.[2]

2.3 The second reason is that the study of the law applicable to the arbitration clause provides fertile ground for an analysis of the transnational dimension of international arbitration, that is, of the way in which international arbitration interacts with multiple

1 In this chapter, the phrases 'arbitration clause' and 'arbitration agreement' will be used interchangeably. An arbitration agreement may be an arbitration clause but may also be a stand-alone agreement. Certain issues discussed in this chapter are relevant only to arbitration agreements that are in the form of clauses in a wider contract (eg, the question whether a choice of law of the main contract extends also to the arbitration clause) while others are relevant to stand-alone arbitration agreements as well (eg, the question of the jurisdiction most closely connected with an arbitration agreement). This will be apparent in the discussion.

2 The problem may arise in several procedural contexts: see L Collins, 'The Law Governing the Agreement and Procedure in International Arbitration in England' in J Lew (ed), *Contemporary Problems in International Arbitration* (Dordrecht, Martin Nijhoff 1987) 127. Furthermore, different laws may govern these different aspects of the arbitration agreement. For a useful explanation of the various nuances see K P Berger, 'Re-examining the Arbitration Agreement: Applicable Law – Consensus or Confusion?' in Albert Jan van den Berg (ed), *International Arbitration 2006: Back to Basics?* ICCA Congress Series No 13 (Montreal 2006) (The Hague, Kluwer Law International 2007) 301, 303–306.

national legal systems and multiple national legal systems interact with each other in framing internationally accepted solutions to legal problems. This chapter contributes to this debate by examining the problem of the law applicable to the existence, validity and effectiveness of the arbitration clause when there is no express choice of such a law.[3] Its aim is to set out a framework for the development of a possible 'transnational'[4] solution to the problem so that convergence and predictability can, with time, be achieved.

2.4 Perhaps most importantly, the law governing the arbitration clause may be crucial to resolving disputes in the construction sector and lack of clarity thereof may give rise to significant uncertainty and costs. Consider the following examples:

a A subcontract is governed by Qatari law. Disputes are to be referred to arbitration in Geneva. Claimant wishes to join the employer in a dispute with the subcontractor. Whether the arbitration clause is governed by Swiss law or Qatari law may well be material.

b A joint venture agreement is governed by Nigerian law. Disputes are to be referred to arbitration in London. One joint venture partner commences arbitration, and the other objects to the jurisdiction of the arbitral tribunal. Should the tribunal apply Nigerian law or English law to the determination of the validity of the arbitration clause?

c There is a major explosion at a power plant. The owner-employer claims under the relevant insurance policy, and the insurer pays up. The EPC contract between the owner-employer and the EPC contractor is governed by Brazilian law, but disputes are to be referred to arbitration in London. Is the alleged right of the insurer to claim directly against the ECP contractor in London arbitration proceedings governed by Brazilian or English law?

d A contract for the construction of an offshore facility in Sweden is governed by Swedish law, but disputes are referred to arbitration in London. Disputes arise that sound in contract and in tort, and there is an issue concerning the scope of the arbitration clause. Is the admissibility of evidence of pre-contractual negotiations to construe the arbitration clause to be governed by English law (inadmissible) or Swedish law (admissible)?

This chapter is structured as follows. First, it explains why a separate inquiry into the law governing the arbitration clause is necessary and discusses the implications of such a separate inquiry. Second, it reviews three possible approaches to determining the law governing the arbitration clause, namely (1) the application of the law chosen by the parties to govern their substantive rights and obligations; (2) the application of the law of the seat of the arbitration; and (3) the application of 'transnational' rules. Finally, conclusions are drawn.

3 This chapter builds upon R Nazzini, 'The Law Applicable to the Arbitration Agreement: A Transnational Solution?' (2016) 2 International and Comparative Law Quarterly 681 and a later chapter published by the author in R Nazzini (ed), *Key Themes in International Construction Arbitration* (London, Informa 2018) 5.

4 For the purposes of this chapter, it is proposed to give the adjective 'transnational' the widest possible (negative) meaning of anything that is different from the application of national rules applicable to domestic arbitration. The term 'transnational' is probably more correct than the widely used 'international' because 'international' arbitration is, in fact, an arbitration that transcends the boundaries of one given national legal system but is still governed by a set of national laws.

The need for a separate inquiry into the law governing the arbitration clause

2.5 It is trite that a complex matrix of laws applies in international commercial arbitration. Generally, the expressions 'applicable law', 'proper law' and 'governing law' are used as synonymous and interchangeable. In arbitration, the applicable law has three main aspects: (1) the law governing the substance of the dispute (*lex causae* or substantive law); (2) the law governing the arbitration clause itself; and (3) the law governing the proceedings (*lex arbitri*). Thus, in the *Channel Tunnel* case, Lord Mustill famously explained:[5]

> It is by now firmly established that more than one national system of law may bear upon an international arbitration. Thus, there is the proper law which regulates the substantive rights and duties of the parties to the contract from which the dispute has arisen. Exceptionally, this may differ from the national law governing the interpretation of the agreement to submit the dispute to arbitration. Less exceptionally it may also differ from the national law which the parties have expressly or by implication selected to govern the relationship between themselves and the arbitrator in the conduct of the arbitration: the 'curial law' of the arbitration, as it is often called.

While Lord Mustill considered it exceptional for the law applicable to the arbitration clause to be different from the law applicable to the substantive rights and duties of the parties, it is now well established that these two laws may be different and that, whether in the end they are different or not, a separate inquiry into the law applicable to the arbitration clause itself is necessary.[6] Three reasons may be given for this proposition.

2.6 The first is theoretical and is perhaps the least persuasive. The idea is that the arbitration agreement possesses its own specific nature and the nature of the arbitration agreement determines which law applies to it. So, if the nature of the agreement is procedural, it would follow that the law of the seat, as the curial law of the arbitration, should apply to the arbitration agreement. If the nature of the agreement is substantive, this would lead to the conclusion that the substantive law governing the main contract should apply to the arbitration agreement too. This approach does not solve the problem of the law applicable to the arbitration clause but mutates it into a different question, that of the nature of the arbitration clause itself. And this is, of course, a question on which there is no consensus among scholars[7] and which the arbitral tribunals and courts, quite rightly, generally do not address. It is submitted that these metaphysical conjectures are not an efficient way of resolving the problem at hand. The arbitration agreement is, certainly, a contract and, as such, is subject to conflict of laws analysis as any other contract.

5 *Channel Tunnel Group Ltd v Balfour Beatty Construction Ltd* [1993] 1 All ER 664, 682, [1993] AC 334, 357–358.

6 P Bernardini, 'Arbitration Clause: Achieving Effectiveness in the Law Applicable to the Arbitration Clause' in A van den Berg (ed), *Improving the Efficiency of Arbitration Agreements and Awards: 40 Years of Application of the New York Convention*, ICCA Congress Series No 9 (Paris 1998) (The Hague, Kluwer Law International 1999) 197.

7 According to some commentators, for example, the nature of the arbitration agreement is both substantive and procedural, which is rather unhelpful as a guide to determining the law applicable to the agreement itself: see Bernardini, 'Arbitration Clause: Achieving Effectiveness in the Law Applicable to the Arbitration Clause' 199–200 and J Lew, 'The Law Applicable to the Form and Substance of the Arbitration Clause' in A Jan van den Berg (ed), *Improving the Efficiency of Arbitration Agreements and Awards: 40 Years of Application of the New York Convention*, ICCA Congress Series No. 9 (Paris 1998) (The Hague, Kluwer Law International 1999) 114, 117.

The question is why the determination of the law applicable to the substantive rights and duties of the parties does not automatically, and without more, apply to the arbitration clause as it does to all clauses in the contract.

2.7 The second reason rests on the doctrine of separability, according to which the arbitration clause must be treated as a separate contract from the main agreement, particularly for the purpose of assessing its existence, validity and effectiveness.[8] If the arbitration clause is separate from the main contract, so the argument goes, then the law applicable to it may be different from the law governing the substantive rights and duties of the parties. Insofar as the proposition is that the law applicable to the arbitration clause *may* be different from the law governing the main contract, it is difficult to disagree with it.

2.8 Separability can today be considered a general principle of international commercial arbitration[9] and, in any event, the arbitration clause, even from a purely contractual perspective, has its peculiar scope and function, which justify a separate inquiry into the applicable law. This does not mean, however, that the arbitration clause must be treated as a completely stand-alone contract. The doctrine of separability means that the existence, validity and effectiveness of the arbitration clause must be assessed independently of the existence, validity and effectiveness of the main contract. For other purposes, for example, assignment, the arbitration clause continues to be considered an integral part of the main contract.[10] Thus, 'the autonomy of the arbitration clause and of the principal contract does not mean that they are totally independent one from the other'.[11] In the UK Supreme Court case of *Enka v Chubb*, Lord Hamblen and Lord Leggatt, with whom Lord Kerr agreed, explained this idea clearly. Separability does mean that an arbitration clause should always be treated as a separate agreement for the purpose of determining its governing law. But it does mean that an arbitration clause may more readily than other clauses be governed by a different law from that which applies to the main contract.[12]

2.9 The third reason in favour of a separate inquiry is that, in the body of international and domestic arbitration law, special rules apply to the arbitration agreement, which does, therefore, have its own legal regime different from that of the main contract. Most importantly, Article II(1)-(2) of the New York Convention on the Recognition and Enforcement of Foreign Arbitral Awards ('New York Convention') sets out the requirement that, in order to be recognised by the Contracting States, an arbitration agreement must be 'in writing'. This requirement applies regardless of the formal requirements applicable to the main contract. Article V(1)(a) of the same Convention provides that a ground on which a court of a Contracting State may refuse recognition and enforcement of an award is that 'the agreement referred to in Article II ... is not valid under the law to which the parties have subjected it or, failing any indication thereon, under the law of the country where the

8 *Fiona Trust v Privalov* [2007] UKHL 40, para 17; *Hecht v Busiman's* 4 July 1972, 99 Journal du Droit International (1972) 843 (French Supreme Court); *Prima Paint Corp v Flood & Conklin Mfg Co* 388 US (1967) 395, 403–404.

9 JF Poudret and S Besson, *Comparative Law of International Arbitration* (London, Sweet & Maxwell 2002) 258; J Lew, L Mistelis and S Kröll, *Comparative International Arbitration* (The Hague, Kluwer Law International 2003) 106.

10 *Hussman (Europe) Ltd v Al Almeen Development and Trade Co* [2000] 2 Lloyd's Rep 83, para 1.

11 Y Derains, 'ICC Arbitral Process: Part VIII. Choice of Law Applicable to the Contract and International Arbitration' (1995) 6(1) ICC Intl Ct Arb 10, 16–17.

12 *Enka Insaat Ve Sanayi AS v OOO Insurance Company Chubb* [2020] UKSC 38 (*Enka v Chubb*), paras 40–42.

award was made'. In this way, Article V(1)(a) sets out a conflict of laws rule specifically applicable to the arbitration agreement.[13]

2.10 Furthermore, it is not uncommon for domestic legislatures to provide their own conflict of law rules for determining the law governing the arbitration agreement. Article 178(2) of the Swiss Federal Private International Law Act provides that '2 As regards its substance, an arbitration agreement is valid if it conforms either to the law chosen by the parties, to the law governing the subject-matter of the dispute, in particular the law governing the main contract, or to Swiss law.' Similarly, Article 6 of the Arbitration (Scotland) Act 2010, provides that

> [w]here (a) the parties to an arbitration agreement agree that an arbitration under that agreement is to be seated in Scotland, but (b) the arbitration agreement does not specify the law which is to govern it, then, unless the parties otherwise agree, the arbitration agreement is to be governed by Scots law.

There are numerous other examples of domestic legislation making provision on this issue.[14] In many common law jurisdictions, the matter is addressed in case law and doctrine.[15] Arbitral tribunals have also consistently recognised that the arbitration agreement may be subject to a distinct legal regime.[16]

2.11 Thus, there is little doubt that a separate inquiry into the law applicable to the arbitration agreement is needed, if such a law is disputed, and it cannot be automatically assumed that the law governing the substantive rights and duties of the parties applies also to the arbitration agreement, even when such an agreement is a clause in a wider contract. The next question is how to determine which law applies to the arbitration agreement. The answer could be found, quite easily, in Article V(1)(a) of the New York Convention, which sets out a conflict of laws rule specifically applicable to the arbitration agreement. The same rule is adopted in Articles 34(2)(a)(i) and 36(1)(a)(i) of the UNCITRAL Model Law on International Commercial Arbitration 2006 ('Model Law'), on applications for setting aside the award at the place of the arbitration and on enforcement of domestic and foreign awards, respectively. As the majority of the UK Supreme Court held in *Enka v Chubb*, there is a strong argument, based on consistency, to the effect that this very same rule applies to determining the law governing an arbitration agreement, including not only its validity but also its scope, across the board and regardless of the procedural setting, pre- or post-award, or whether the issue arises with respect to a domestic or foreign arbitration.[17]

---

13 Similar wording is used in the European Convention on International Commercial Arbitration 1961, Art VI(2).

14 Spanish Arbitration Act 2003, Art 9(6), which follows Swiss law verbatim; Algerian Code of Civil Procedure, Art 458 bis 1(3); Swedish Arbitration Act 1999, Art 48.

15 See *eg*, the Indian Supreme Court judgment in *M S Dozo India P Ltd v M/S Doosan Infracore Co* [2010] INSC 839, paras 12–13; *Thyssen Canada Ltd v Mariana Maritima SA* [2000] 3 FC 398, para 22 (Canada, CA); *Comandate Marine Corp v Pan Australia Shipping Pty Ltd* [2006] FCAFC 192 (Australian Fed Ct).

16 Final Award in ICC Case No 6162 in (1992) 17 Ybk Commercial Arbitration 153, 160–162; ICC Case No 8384 in K P Berger, *The Practice of Transnational Law* (The Hague, Kluwer Law International 2002) 228; ICC Case No 8502, 1996, 10(2) ICC Bulletin 72; Final Award in ICC Case No 1507 in S Jarvin and Y Derains (eds), *Collection of ICC Arbitral Awards 1974–1985* (Kluwer Law International 1990) 216.

17 *Enka v Chubb*, paras 125–141. As will be explained later, English courts apply common law rules when determining the law applicable to the arbitration agreement other than under Art V(1)(a) of the New York Convention, which is given effect in English law by s 103(2)(b) of the Arbitration Act 1996. The effect of the common law rules

2.12 However, even if one assumes that the conflict of laws rule in Article V(1)(a) of the New York Convention applies across the board to determine the law governing the arbitration agreement tout court, this quite simply begs the question whether 'the law to which the parties have subjected' the arbitration agreement must be a law expressly chosen in relation to an arbitration clause or can be a law impliedly chosen by the parties, for example, by choosing the law applicable to the main contract or by choosing the seat of the arbitration. The better view is probably that the choice may be implied.[18] So, the problem still arises as to what amounts to an implied choice of the law applicable to the arbitration agreement. Is the choice of the law governing the main contract an implied choice of such a law? And what about the choice of the seat of the arbitration? And could the law to which the parties have subjected the arbitration agreement be a set of transnational rules and principles or should it be a national law?

2.13 Therefore, extending the application of the conflict rule under Article V(1)(a) of the New York Convention to all cases in which the existence, validity or effectiveness of the arbitration agreement is in issue does not answer the questions asked in this article. Nor could Article V(1)(a) of the New York Convention ever achieve full harmonisation, even only at the enforcement stage. Article VII of the Convention allows Contracting States to apply their national law rules if they result in the enforcement of an award the enforcement of which would be refused under the Convention. Therefore, under the Convention, approaches to the law applicable to the arbitration agreement *in favorem validitatis* coexist with the conflict rule under Article V(1)(a) in enforcement proceedings.

The 'main contract' approach

2.14 International commercial contracts usually contain a clause specifying the law governing the substance of the dispute.[19] The question is whether the choice of law of the main contract applies, or should apply, to the arbitration clause. Whereas the main authorities following the coming into force of the Arbitration Act 1996 had initially emphasised the importance of the seat,[20] English law has answered this question in the affirmative.[21]

---

and of s 103(2)(b) of the Arbitration Act 1996, and, therefore, of Art V(1)(a) of the New York Convention, would, however, be the same under the UK Supreme Court majority judgment in *Enka v Chubb*, para 141. A number of national courts have applied the conflict of laws rule under Article V(1)(a) of the Convention at pre-enforcement stages directly: see eg, *Della Sanara Kustvaart – Bevrachting & Overslagbedrijf BV v Fallimento Cap. Giovanni Coppola srl*, in liquidation, Corte di Appello [Court of Appeal], Genoa, Not Indicated, 3 February 1990 (1992) 17 Ybk Commercial Arbitration 542–544 and *Insurance Company v Reinsurance Company*, Tribunal Fédéral [Swiss Supreme Court], Not Indicated, 21 March 1995 (1997) 22 Ybk Commercial Arbitration 800–806.

18 See eg, *Enka v Chubb*, para 129; *Consortium member A v Consortium member B* (Switzerland), Polimeles Protodikio [Court of First Instance, Multi-Judge Panel], Rodopi, Decision no 84 of 2005 (2008) 33 Ybk Commercial Arbitration 552–554.

19 Lord Collins of Mapesbury and J Harris (eds), *Dicey, Morris & Collins on the Conflict of Laws* (15th ed, London, Sweet and Maxwell 2012) Rule 64, para 16R – 001; J Lew, L Mistelis and S Kröll, *Comparative International Arbitration* (The Hague, Kluwer Law International 2003) 106.

20 *Abuja International Hotels Ltd v Meridien SAS* [2012] EWHC 87 (Comm), [2012] 1 Lloyd's Rep 461; *C v D* [2007] EWCA Civ 1282, obiter, applying the closest connection test to a London arbitration clause in a contract that was expressly governed by New York law; and *XL Insurance Ltd v Owens Corning* [2001] 1 All ER (Comm) 530.

21 In line with previous authorities leaning towards the extension of the choice of the law of the matrix contract to the arbitration clause: *Channel Tunnel Group Ltd v Balfour Beatty Construction Ltd* [1993] AC 334, 357–358; *Sumitomo Heavy Industries v Oil and Natural Gas Commission* [1994] 1 Lloyd's Rep 45; *Sonatrach*

2.15 In *Sulamérica Cia Nacional de Seguros v Enesa Engenharia SA*, the Court of Appeal had to decide which law applied to an arbitration clause providing for arbitration under the ARIAS Rules in London. The arbitration clause was part of an insurance policy governed by Brazilian law. The validity of the arbitration clause was a relevant consideration to determining whether an anti-suit injunction should be maintained or discharged. The insured maintained that, under Brazilian law, the arbitration clause could be enforced only with their consent.[22]

2.16 It was common ground before the Court that the proper law of the arbitration agreement was to be determined in accordance with the established common law rules for ascertaining the proper law of any contract. These require the court to recognise and give effect to the parties' choice of proper law, express or implied, failing which it is necessary to identify the system of law with which the contract has the closest and most real connection.[23] There was no express choice of the law governing the arbitration agreement. The question was whether the parties had made an implied choice of such a law by choosing Brazilian law as the law applicable to the main contract or whether English law, as the law of the seat of the arbitration, governed the arbitration agreement, either by having been impliedly chosen by the parties or as the law having the closest connection with the arbitration agreement, in the absence of an implied choice.

2.17 Moore-Bick LJ, with whom Hallett LJ agreed, said:[24]

> In the absence of any indication to the contrary, an express choice of law governing the substantive contract is a strong indication of the parties' intention in relation to the agreement to arbitrate. A search for an implied choice of proper law to govern the arbitration agreement is therefore likely (as the dicta in the earlier cases indicate) to lead to the conclusion that the parties intended the arbitration agreement to be governed by the same system of law as the substantive contract, unless there are other factors present which point to a different conclusion. These may include the terms of the arbitration agreement itself or the consequences for its effectiveness of choosing the proper law of the substantive contract.

However, this was only a *rebuttable* presumption, which, on the facts, was displaced by two factors: (1) the choice of England as the seat of the arbitration and (2) the consequences that would follow if Brazilian law were to apply to the arbitration clause.[25] The second factor was particularly powerful. The arbitration clause was clearly drafted so as to bind both parties whereas, under Brazilian law, the clause would have bound only the insurers.

Petroleum Corp v Ferrell International Ltd [2002] 1 All ER (Comm) 627. English law is by no means alone in adopting this approach, for example see the Indian case of *National Thermal Power Corporation v The Singer Company, and Others*, Supreme Court, 1978, 7 May 1992 (1993) 18 Ybk Commercial Arbitration 403–414; *Eitzen Bulk A/S v Ashapura Minechem Limited* AIR 2011 Guj 13 and *Aastha Broadcasting Network Limited v Thaicom Public Company Ltd* [2011] OMP 528/2011 & IA No. 11308/2011 (Delhi High Court, India); *Enercon India v Enercon GMBH* [Civ. App. 2086/7 of 2014] (India). See also ICC Case No 2626 (1977) in Sigvard Jarvin and Yves Derains (eds), *Collection of ICC Arbitral Awards, Vol I* (1974–1985) (The Hague, Kluwer Law International 1994) 316; ICC Case No. 6379 (1992) 17 Ybk Commercial Arbitration 211–220; ICC Case No 6752 (1993) 18 Ybk Commercial Arbitration 54–57.

22 *Sulamérica Cia Nacional de Seguros SA and others v Enesa Engelharia SA and others* [2013] 1 WLR 102 (*Sulamérica*), paras 1–6, 9 (Moore-Bick LJ).

23 ibid, para 9 (Moore-Bick LJ).

24 ibid, para 26.

25 ibid, paras 29–31.

Moore-Bick LJ said that this suggested that the parties did not intend Brazilian law to apply to the arbitration clause.[26] Having found that the presumption that the law applicable to the matrix contract also applied to the arbitration clause had been rebutted, Moore-Bick LJ did not, however, go on to consider whether the choice of London as the seat of the arbitration was an implied choice of English law as the law governing the arbitration clause. He assumed that there was no implied choice of such a law. As a consequence, he applied the closest connection test and found that the arbitration agreement 'has its closest and most real connection with the law of the place where the arbitration is to be held'.[27]

2.18 Lord Neuberger MR, as he then was, preferred not to decide, as a matter of general principle, the question whether the law of the arbitration clause is the chosen law of the contract or the law of the arbitration seat because, on the facts, under either approach the appeal would be dismissed.[28]

2.19 It has been argued that the decision in *Sulamérica* is correct on the facts of the case. There is no doubt that the ineffectiveness of arbitration clause under Brazilian law was a compelling reason against finding that the parties had, impliedly, chosen Brazilian law to govern their rights and obligations under the arbitration clause.[29] Others, however, are critical of the *Sulamérica* approach because of the unpredictability of the outcome of a full-fledged inquiry into the parties' implied choice of the law governing the arbitration clause.[30] When it comes to construction of contractual clauses, absolute certainty is hardly ever achievable. However, whether the approach in *Sulamérica* is correct or desirable in law or policy, its application is sufficiently clear. There is a presumption that an express choice of the law applicable to the main contract is an implied choice of the law governing the arbitration clause, which can be rebutted on the facts of each individual case.

2.20 This approach was confirmed in the subsequent case of *Arsanovia Limited & others v Cruz City 1 Mauritius Holdings*.[31] In this case, a dispute arose out of a slum clearance programme in India which was subject to considerable delay. There was a suite of contracts in relation to the programme, the relevant shareholders' agreement being governed by Indian law and providing for LCIA arbitration in London. In addition, the arbitration clause in the shareholders' agreement expressly excluded the application of certain provisions of the Indian Arbitration and Conciliation Act of 1996, in particular with respect to the seeking of interim relief in the Indian courts. Two sets of arbitral proceedings were commenced. The same arbitral tribunal was appointed in both sets of proceedings and found against Arsanovia, who challenged the awards under section 67 of the Arbitration Act 1996. Applying *Sulamérica*, Andrew Smith J decided that the arbitration clause was governed by Indian law, that being the law governing the main contract. He even suggested, *obiter*, that the choice of the law of the main contract may be an express, rather than implied, choice of the law of the arbitration clause.[32]

---

26 ibid, para 30.

27 ibid, para 32.

28 ibid, para 59.

29 A Trukhtanov, 'The Proper Law of Arbitration Agreement – a Farewell to Implied Choice?' (2012) 15 Intl Arb L Rev 140.

30 P Charles, 'The Proper Law of the Arbitration Agreement' (2014) 80 Arbitration 55, 59–60.

31 *Arsanovia Limited & others v Cruz City 1 Mauritius Holdings* [2012] EWHC 3702 (Comm), [2013] 2 All ER (Comm) 1 (QB).

32 ibid, paras 21–23.

2.21 The UK Supreme Court upheld this approach in *Enka v Chubb*. The issue arose in an application for an anti-suit injunction. Whether the arbitration clause was governed by English law or Russian law could be material to the exercise of an English court's discretion as to whether to grant an injunction. In the end, the Supreme Court unanimously held that the governing law of the arbitration clause was not a relevant consideration.[33] However, it decided the issue of the governing law and settled English law on this point, at least for the foreseeable future.

2.22 The principles were summarised by Lord Hamblen and Lord Leggatt, with whom Lord Kerr agreed, in the following way:[34]

a Where a contract contains an agreement to resolve disputes arising from it by arbitration, the law applicable to the arbitration agreement may not be the same as the law applicable to the other parts of the contract and is to be determined by applying English common law rules for resolving conflicts of laws rather than the provisions of the Rome I Regulation.

b According to these rules, the law applicable to the arbitration agreement will be (1) the law chosen by the parties to govern it or (2) in the absence of such a choice, the system of law with which the arbitration agreement is most closely connected.

c Whether the parties have agreed on a choice of law to govern the arbitration agreement is ascertained by construing the arbitration agreement and the contract containing it, as a whole, applying the rules of contractual interpretation of English law as the law of the forum.

d Where the law applicable to the arbitration agreement is not specified, a choice of governing law for the contract will generally apply to an arbitration agreement which forms part of the contract.

e The choice of a different country as the seat of the arbitration is not, without more, sufficient to negate an inference that a choice of law to govern the contract was intended to apply to the arbitration agreement.

f Additional factors which may, however, negate such an inference and may in some cases imply that the arbitration agreement was intended to be governed by the law of the seat are: (1) any provision of the law of the seat which indicates that, where an arbitration is subject to that law, the arbitration will also be treated as governed by that country's law; or (2) the existence of a serious risk that, if governed by the same law as the main contract, the arbitration agreement would be ineffective. Either factor may be reinforced by circumstances indicating that the seat was deliberately chosen as a neutral forum for the arbitration.

g Where there is no express choice of law to govern the contract, a clause providing for arbitration in a particular place will not by itself justify an inference that the contract (or the arbitration agreement) is intended to be governed by the law of that place.

h In the absence of any choice of law to govern the arbitration agreement, the arbitration agreement is governed by the law with which it is most closely connected. Where the parties have chosen a seat of arbitration, this will generally

33 *Enka v Chubb,* paras 184, 261, and 293.
34 ibid, para 170.

be the law of the seat, even if this differs from the law applicable to the parties' substantive contractual obligations.

i The fact that the contract requires the parties to attempt to resolve a dispute through good faith negotiation, mediation or any other procedure before referring it to arbitration will not generally provide a reason to displace the law of the seat of arbitration as the law applicable to the arbitration agreement by default in the absence of a choice of law to govern it.

While the majority judgment held that, in the absence of the parties' express or implied choice, the arbitration agreement is governed by the law of the seat, Lord Burrows, with whom Lord Sales agreed, took the 'main contract' approach even further and held that even in the absence of an express or implied choice, the arbitration agreement is governed by the law of the main contract as the law with which it is most closely connected.[35]

2.23 The 'main contract' approach has been adopted in Singapore. In *BCY v BCZ*, Steven Chong J, as he then was, held that the law governing an arbitration clause for arbitration in Singapore in a contract governed by New York law was the law of the main contract. He considered that it is reasonable to assume that the parties intend their entire relationship to be governed by the same law, unless they specifically agree otherwise.[36] Separability does not insulate the arbitration clause from the main contract but serves the more limited purpose of ensuring that the invalidity of the main contract does not affect the arbitration clause.[37] And, finally, neutrality does not require the law governing the arbitration clause to be the same as the procedural law and the law governing the main contract may itself be neutral.[38]

2.24 The Singaporean Court of Appeal in *BNA v BNB* adopted the same approach. The main contract was governed by the law of the People's Republic of China and the seat of the arbitration was Shanghai. In principle, therefore, the 'main contract' approach or the seat approach would have led to the same result. However, Steven Chong JA, delivering the judgment of the Court of Appeal, endorsed the *BCY* framework, which followed closely the *Sulamérica* approach, and noted that both parties in the case accepted that the starting point in determining the implied choice was the law of the main contract.[39] The law governing the arbitration clause was, therefore, the law of the People's Republic of China. This inference could be displaced only if the law of the seat is materially different from the law governing the arbitration clause.[40]

2.25 There is no doubt, therefore, that the 'main contract' approach is now firmly established in English law and followed in other common law jurisdictions. The question is whether the 'main contract' approach gives proper consideration to the expectations of the parties and to the importance that the seat plays in international arbitration. The law of the seat generally governs the arbitral procedure which, according to some, should include the substantive validity of the arbitration agreement given that such an agreement is more

35 *Enka v Chubb*, paras 256 (*per* Lord Burrows) and 281–292 (*per* Lord Sales).
36 *BCY v BCZ* [2017] 3 SLR 357, [2016] Lloyd's Rep 583, para 59.
37 *BCY v BCZ* [2017] 3 SLR 357, [2016] Lloyd's Rep 583, paras 60–61.
38 *BCY v BCZ* [2017] 3 SLR 357, [2016] Lloyd's Rep 583, paras 62–63.
39 *BNA v BNB* [2020] 1 SLR 456, [2020] 1 Lloyd's Rep 55, para 47.
40 *BNA v BNB* [2020] 1 SLR 456, [2020] 1 Lloyd's Rep 55, paras 62–63.

closely connected with the curial law than it is with the law governing the substantive rights and obligations of the parties.[41]

The seat approach

2.26 If the arbitration clause indicates the seat of the arbitration and, according to some commentators, even if the choice of seat is delegated,[42] there are good arguments for holding that the law of the seat applies to the arbitration agreement.[43]

2.27 Indeed, following the implementation of the Arbitration Act 1996, there appeared to have been a trend of placing greater emphasis on the law of the seat.[44] *XL Insurance v Owen Corning* is a prominent example.[45] A US company, XL Insurance Limited ('XL') agreed to insure Owens Corning ('Owens'), incorporated in Bermuda, against property damage, the contract being negotiated on Owens' behalf by a broker at Marsh & McLennan. The policy contained an arbitration clause stating that '[a]ny dispute, controversy or claim arising out of or relating to [the] Policy or the breach, termination or invalidity thereof shall be finally and fully determined in London, England under the provisions of the Arbitration Act 1996'. The governing law clause stated that the policy 'shall be construed in accordance with the internal laws of the State of New York, United States except in so far as such laws are inconsistent with any provision of this Policy'.

2.28 Owens brought an action against XL in Delaware, United States. XL applied to the English court for an order to restrain Owens from pursuing the claim in any forum other than arbitration in London, relying on the arbitration clause. The question was whether the arbitration clause was valid and enforceable. Toulson J, as he then was, noted that it was an established principle that the parties may choose the applicable law and that this may differ from the law governing their substantive obligations.[46] In contrast to the structured approach later adopted in *Sulamérica*, Toulson J directly considered the likely intentions of the parties. He regarded the reference in the arbitration clause to the Arbitration Act 1996 as indicative of the parties' intention to use the law of the seat to govern the arbitration agreement. This was particularly so given the provisions in the Arbitration Act which deal

41 Bernardini, 'Arbitration Clause: Achieving Effectiveness in the Law Applicable to the Arbitration Clause' 200; JF Poudret and S Besson, *Comparative Law of International Arbitration* (London, Sweet & Maxwell 2002) 258.

42 Bernardini, 'Arbitration Clause: Achieving Effectiveness in the Law Applicable to the Arbitration Clause' 201.

43 ibid, 200. See generally K P Berger, 'Re-examining the Arbitration Agreement: Applicable Law – Consensus or Confusion?' 301–334. On the importance on the seat in international arbitration and the problems relating to the determination of the seat, see J Hill, 'Determining the Seat of an International Arbitration: Party Autonomy and the Interpretation of Arbitration Agreements' (2014) 63 ICLQ 517.

44 Prior to the Arbitration Act 1996, it was considered rare for the proper law of arbitration agreement to differ from the express choice of substantive law. See *Channel Tunnel Group Ltd v Balfour Beatty Construction Ltd* [1993] AC 334; *Sumitomo Heavy Industries v Oil and Natural Gas Commission* [1994] 1 Lloyd's Rep 45, 57 (Potter J), *Black Clawson International Ltd v Papierwerke Waldhof-Aschaffenburg AG* [1981] 2 Lloyd's Rep 446, 455. Following the Arbitration Act, see *XL Insurance Ltd v Owens Corning* [2001] 1 All ER (Comm) 530; *C v D* [2007] EWCA Civ 1282; *Shashouaand others v Sharma* [2009] EWHC 957 (Comm); *Abuja Hotels Ltd v Meridien SAS* [2012] EWHC 87 (Comm), [2012] 1 Lloyd's Rep 461.

45 *XL Insurance Ltd v Owens Corning* [2001] 1 All ER (Comm) 530.

46 Citing Lord Mustill in *Channel Tunnel Group Ltd v Balfour Beatty Construction Ltd* [1993] AC 334: *XL Insurance Ltd v Owens Corning* [2001] 1 All ER (Comm) 530, 540–541.

with matters of jurisdiction, such as section 30 and section 5. Thus, it was held that the law of the seat was applicable to the arbitration agreement in this case.

2.29 The English courts have reached similar conclusions in other cases. *C v D*[47] concerned a dispute arising under a Bermuda form contract of insurance, which expressed New York law as the governing law of the contract and London to be the seat of any arbitration. In this case, following an arbitration award in favour of the claimant, the claimant sought to restrain the defendant from appealing the award in New York, on the basis of the US legal doctrine of 'manifest disregard of the law'. Longmore LJ devoted part of his judgment to considering the applicable law of the arbitration agreement. In his view, the question was whether, if there is no express law of the arbitration agreement, the law with which that agreement has its closest and most real connection is the law of the underlying contract or the law of the seat of arbitration.[48] Having reviewed the authorities on this issue, Longmore LJ answered this question in favour of the law of the seat.[49] Notably, the arbitration clause in this case contained strong indications that it would be governed by English law rather than New York law. Specifically, the contract provided that the arbitral decision would be 'a complete defence to any attempted appeal or litigation of such decision in the absence of fraud or collusion'. Longmore LJ considered that this provision would 'be rendered otiose if either party could say in New York that there had been a manifest disregard of New York law'.[50] Thus it was held that the law of the seat was applicable.[51] As a result of these authorities the position in England and Wales has been unclear, although this has been rectified to some extent by the judgment in *Sulamérica.*

2.30 The less controversial case is when there is no choice of the law governing the main contract. The seat approach has been adopted in England even after the decision of the Court of Appeal in *Sulamérica*, which clearly does not extend the rebuttable presumption of the applicability of the law of the main contract to the arbitration clause beyond cases in which there is an express choice of the law of the main contract. In *Habas Sinai Ve v VSC Steel Company Ltd*[52], the claimant, Habas, a Turkish company, entered into a contract (through its agents, Charter Alpha Limited and Steel Park Limited) with the defendant, VSC, a Hong Kong company, for the sale by Habas of 15,000mt of steel. No delivery was made and VSC commenced arbitration proceedings. The contract specified ICC arbitration in London but did not provide for a governing law. Hamblen J held that where the matrix contract does not contain an express governing law clause, the significance of the choice of seat of the arbitration is likely to be 'overwhelming' because the system of law of the country of the seat will usually be that with which the arbitration agreement has its closest and most real connection. On the facts, the arbitration agreement was therefore governed by English law even if the main contract was governed by Turkish law.[53] The Supreme Court majority in *Enka v Chubb* endorsed this approach by holding that, in the absence of

47 *C v D* [2007] EWCA Civ 1282.

48 ibid, para 22.

49 ibid, para 29.

50 ibid, para 28.

51 This approach was cited with approval in *Abuja Hotels v Meridien SAS* [2012] EWHC 87 (Comm), [2012] 1 Lloyd's Rep 461, para 21.

52 *Habas Sinai Ve Tibbi Gazlar Istihsal Endustrisi AS v VSC Steel Company Ltd* [2013] EWHC 4071 (Comm).

53 ibid, paras 101–103.

the parties' express or implied choice, the default rule at common law is that the arbitration agreement is governed by the law of the seat.[54]

2.31 But even when there is an express choice of the law of the main contract, the approach established in the *Sulamérica* case and upheld in *Enka v Chubb* is by no means uncontroversial. In fact, Moore-Bick LJ himself in *Sulamérica* emphasised that the arbitration agreement is much more intimately intertwined with the procedural law than it is with the substantive law,[55] which casts doubt on the very foundation of the main contract approach. Lord Burrows and Lord Sales in *Enka v Chubb* in their dissenting judgments made the same point that it is odd that the application of the implied choice test and the closest connection test should lead to different outcomes.[56] The point of principle is well made. After all, if the arbitration agreement can be governed by a different law from that which governs the main contract and has much more to do with the procedure than with the substance of the dispute, why are the parties presumed to have chosen the law of the substance and not the law of the procedure to govern the arbitration clause?

2.32 Such arguments have persuaded the courts in other jurisdictions to diverge from the approach in *Sulamérica*. In *FirstLink Investments Corp Ltd v GT Payment Pte Ltd and others*, Shaun Leong Li Shiong AR in the High Court of Singapore held that, when there is a choice of the law of the matrix contract and a choice of seat, the arbitration clause is likely to be governed by the law of the seat, even if this law is different from the law of the matrix contract.[57] Singaporean conflict of laws rules are, on this matter, the same as those of English law. Therefore, the Judge applied a three-stage inquiry, exactly as the Court of Appeal in *Sulamérica* and the UK Supreme Court in *Enka v Chubb*. The conclusion was, however, that the choice of seat is an implied choice of the law governing the arbitration agreement.

2.33 It is instructive to look at the reasons given by the Judge in *FirstLink* to support his conclusions. They are the following:

a There cannot be any inference that the parties want their rights and obligations under the arbitration clause to be governed by the same law that applies to the substance of the dispute because the two, potentially different, laws concern different legal relationships, namely the performance of the contract and the resolution of disputes when the substantive relationship breaks down.[58]

b The natural inference would be that, when the substantive relationship breaks down, the parties' desire for neutrality comes to the fore and the law chosen as the procedural law of the arbitration takes precedence over the substantive law.[59]

c '[T]he arbitral seat is the juridical centre of gravity which gives life and effect to an arbitration agreement'.[60]

---

54 *Enka v Chubb*, para 170.

55 *Sulamérica*, paras 29 and 32.

56 *Enka v Chubb*, paras 256 (*per* Lord Burrows) and 281–292 (*per* Lord Sales). Their views were, of course, that consistency in the application of the two tests should mean that the law governing the main contract applies also to the arbitration clause even in the absence of express or implied choice.

57 *FirstLink Investments Corp Ltd v GT Payment Pte Ltd* [2014] SGHCR 12.

58 ibid, para 13.

59 ibid, para 13.

60 ibid, para 14.

d The importance of the seat is recognised internationally, in particular in Article V(1)(a) of the New York Convention and Articles 36(1)(a)(i) and 34(2)(a)(i) of the Model Law.[61]

e The choice of seat determines the choice of remedies against the award, including the power of the courts to determine the jurisdiction of the arbitral tribunal and it would be reasonable for the parties to demand consistency between the substantive law and the procedure of determining the validity of the arbitration agreement.[62]

FirstLink has since been overruled by the Singaporean Court of Appeal in *BNA v BNB* but remains a good example of why courts around the world may consider a choice of seat as an implied choice of the law governing the arbitration clause.[63] The arguments supporting this approach will no doubt continue to influence courts and arbitration tribunals around the world.

2.34 While the bright-line seat test may be advantageous for the reasons given in *FirstLink*, there are many instances where the application of the law of the seat would not be appropriate. The most obvious is when the court may have to consider the validity of an arbitration agreement when the seat has yet to be determined or the seat can be changed in the course of arbitral proceedings even after, for example, the arbitral tribunal has ruled on the validity of the arbitration agreement.

2.35 Furthermore, the argument that the choice of seat is considered to be an implied choice of law governing the arbitration agreement, is certainly much less persuasive where that choice is delegated to an arbitral institution or to the arbitral tribunal. Some argue that a delegated choice of seat is not totally divorced from the will of the parties, as they intended to delegate this choice, so that it can be imputed to the parties.[64] However, as a matter of construction, it becomes difficult to argue that the intention of the parties was that the law of the seat would apply to the arbitration agreement if they did not choose the seat, presumably either because the seat was a matter of indifference or they could not agree on it.[65]

2.36 This argument also posits that the parties would have made an arbitration agreement not subject to any applicable law and, therefore, without being able to ascertain whether they were making a valid agreement. This would be absurd as it assumes that the parties made a conscious choice in favour of absolute uncertainty as to the effectiveness of their chosen method of dispute resolution. This is because, if the seat has not been agreed by the

---

61 ibid.

62 ibid, para 15.

63 See *Matermaco SA v PPM Cranes Inc*, Legris Industries SA, Tribunal de Commerce [Court of First Instance] (2000) 25 Ybk Commercial Arbitration 641–1164 (Belgium); *Owerri Commercial Inc v Dielle Srl, Gerechtshof* [Court of Appeal] The Hague, Not Indicated, 4 August 1993 (1994) 19 Ybk Commercial Arbitration 703–707 and *Petrasol BV v Stolt Spur Inc*, Arrondissementsrechtbank [Court of First Instance] (1997) 22 Ybk Commercial Arbitration 762–765 (Netherlands); *Bulgarian Foreign Trade Bank Ltd v AI Trade Finance Inc*, Swedish Supreme Court, T 1881–99, 27 October 2000 (2001) 26 Ybk Commercial Arbitration 291–298 (Sweden); *Insurance Company v Reinsurance Company, Tribunal Fédéral* [Supreme Court], Not Indicated, 21 March 1995 (1997) 22 Ybk Commercial Arbitration 800–806 (Switzerland).

64 Bernardini, 'Arbitration Clause: Achieving Effectiveness in the Law Applicable to the Arbitration Clause' 200.

65 E Gaillard and J Savage, *Fouchard Gaillard Goldman on International Commercial Arbitration* (Kluwer Law International 1999) 226–227; Berger, 'Re – examining the Arbitration Agreement: Applicable Law – Consensus or Confusion?' 321; F Russel, *Russell on Arbitration* (21st edn, Sweet & Maxwell, 1997) No 2–094.

parties, it will be difficult, if not impossible, to predict with any degree of certainty where the seat will be as the institution or the tribunal can select a seat in almost any jurisdiction. It follows that the seat cannot determine the law applicable to the arbitration agreement if the choice of seat is delegated. In such a case, the law of the underlying contract arguably ought to apply, either because this is the implicit intention of the parties or because it is the one most closely connected to the arbitral agreement.[66]

The transnational approach

2.37 A third way of answering the question of the law governing the arbitration agreement is to disregard the application of a given State legal system determined on the basis of a conflict of laws analysis and to resort to transnational rules directly applicable to the arbitration clause.

2.38 In the context of arbitration, it is now widely accepted that parties may choose transnational principles to govern their substantive dispute.[67] In England and Wales, guidance was provided by the Court of Appeal in *Deutsche Schachtbau-und Tiefbohrgesellschaft v Ras al Khaimal National Oil Co.*[68] Sir John Donaldson MR considered whether the choice was sufficiently certain and concluded that:[69]

> By choosing to arbitrate under the rules of the ICC and, in particular, article 13.3, the parties have left proper law to be decided by the arbitrators and have not in terms confined the choice to national systems of law. I can see no basis for concluding that the arbitrators' choice of proper law – a common denominator of principles underlying the laws of the various nations governing contractual relations – is outwith the scope of the choice, which the parties left to the arbitrators.

It follows that, if the parties can choose transnational principles to apply to the substantive contract, they can also choose such principles to apply to the arbitration agreement, which is indisputably also a contract, albeit one having as its subject matter the choice and regulation of a dispute resolution method rather than substantive rights and obligations. Indeed, the common law makes no distinction in principle between the conflict of laws rules applicable to substantive contracts and to arbitration agreements.[70] What is, however, less clear is whether, in the absence of an express or implied choice by the parties, the court may apply transnational principles to determine the validity of an arbitration agreement.

66 This is the approach adopted in England and Wales: *International Tank and Pipe SAK v Kuwait Aviation Fuelling Co KSC* [1975] QB 224; *Mitsubishi Corporation v Castletown Navigation Ltd, The Castle Alpha* [1989] 2 Lloyd's Rep 383.

67 Indeed, this is now expressly provided for in s 46(1)(b) of the Arbitration Act 1996. See also Art 1496 of French Code of Civil Procedure, Article 187(1) of the Swiss Federal Law on private international law and Art 28 of the UNCITRAL Model Law. The International Law Association (ILA) expressly accepted such a choice in their 1992 Cairo Conference. ICC Case No 8502; Y Derains, *The ICC Arbitral Process Part VIII: Choice of the Law Applicable to the Contract and International Arbitration* (1995) 6 ICC Intl Ct Arb Bull 10, 14.

68 *Deutsche Schachtbau-und Tiefbohrgesellschaft v Ras al Khaimal National Oil Co* [1987] 3 WLR 1023.

69 ibid, 1035. The judgment was subsequently reversed by the House of Lords in *DST v Rakoil* [1988] 3 WLR 230, however the choice of transnational principles to govern the substantive dispute was still accepted.

70 *Sulamérica*, para 9.

2.39 In England and Wales, absent an express or implied choice of the parties, the courts have been particularly resistant to the possibility of applying rules other than those of a national legal system to arbitration agreements. The position was explained by Clarke J sitting in the High Court in *Halpern v Halpern.*[71] In that case, the court had to determine whether an arbitration agreement was governed by Jewish, English or Swiss law. There were strong indications that Jewish law was intended to apply, as it was chosen to govern both the substance of the dispute and the procedure of the arbitration. Clarke J decided that the common law principles 'require selection of the law of a country as the proper law of the agreement',[72] and thus ruled out the applicability of transnational Jewish law. This was considered to be an established rule and was thus not considered in detail, although it was partly justified on the grounds that 'the agreement to arbitrate should, itself, be enforceable under a national system of law'.[73] The English approach is an obstacle to the application of transnational principles only to the extent that transnational principles are not part of a national legal system. In reality, any transnational rule, in order to be fully effective, must be recognised by the legal system which is called upon to determine the validity of the arbitration agreement. English law can, therefore, itself incorporate transnational principles and give effect to transnational principles adopted by other national legal systems.

2.40 That a transnational approach detached from any national legal system does not, currently, exist is demonstrated by the experience of perhaps the most internationalist approach in the field of international commercial arbitration, that of French law. The French courts consider the validity of the arbitration agreement to be governed by *régles matèrielles* independent of any national legal system, even if the parties did not make any express or implied choice in this regard. In the *Dalico* case,[74] the Cour de Cassation ruled:

> according to a substantive rule of international arbitration law, the arbitration clause is legally independent from the main contract in which it is included or which refers to it and, provided that no mandatory provision of French law or international public policy is affected, its existence and its validity depends only on the common intention of the parties, without it being necessary to make reference to a national law.

This approach has consistently been adopted in subsequent French authorities and has not been affected by recent amendments to the French Code of Civil Procedure.[75]

2.41 The international public policy referred to in *Dalico* is intended to reflect the consensus of the international business community, and includes public policy rules

---

71 *Halpern v Halpern* [2006] 2 Lloyd's Rep 83.

72 ibid, para 52. This judgment was appealed successfully, however the Court of Appeal did not address this point in *Halpern v Halpern* [2007] EWCA Civ 291.

73 *Halpern v Halpern* [2006] 2 Lloyd's Rep 83, para 51. This view was restated with approval in *Musawi v RE International (UK) Ltd* [2008] 1 All ER (Comm) 607, para 19.

74 Judgment of 20 December 1993, *Municipalité de Khoms El Mergeb v Société Dalico*, 1994 Rev Arb 116, 117 (French Cour de cassation civ 1e).

75 Judgment of 8 July 2009, *Société d'études et représentations navales et industrielles v Société Air Sea Broker Ltd*, 2009 Rev Arb 529 (French Cour de Cassation civ 1e); Judgment of 30 March 2004, *Société Uni-Kod v Société Ouralkali*, 2005 Rev Arb 959 (French Cour de Cassation civ 1e); Judgment of 21 May 1997, *Renault v* 2000, 1997 Rev Arb 537 (French Cour de Cassation civ 1e); Judgment of 25 November 1999, *SA Burkinabe des ciments et matériaux v Société des ciments d'Abidjan*, 2001 Rev Arb 165 (Paris Cour d'appel); *Société d'études et representations navales et industrielles v Société Air Sea Broker Ltd*, 2009 Rev arb 529 (French Cour de Cassation civ 1e); Judgment of 7 April 2011, 2011 Rev arb 747, 750 (Cour d'appel Paris).

which, 'if not universal, [are] at least common to the various legal systems'.[76] A noteworthy example of this approach can be found in the interim arbitration award in *Dow Chemical Company v ISOVER Saint Gobain.*[77] In that case, the tribunal with its seat in France held that the applicable ICC rules

> establish in particular, the principle of the complete autonomy of the arbitration clause ... and confer on the arbitrator the power to take any decision as to his own jurisdiction upon the Court's determination that the arbitration will take place ... without obliging him to apply any national law whatever in order to do so.

Accordingly, the tribunal referred only to the 'common intent' of the parties, in order to determine their jurisdiction. The tribunal applied the group of companies doctrine and considered Dow Chemical (France) and Dow Chemical (USA) to be party to the arbitration agreement by virtue of their being part of the same group of companies that had signed the agreement. In doing so, the tribunal noted that this was not prohibited by the French legal system or by any rule of international public policy, and took into account the needs of international commerce.[78] This reasoning was expressly accepted by the Paris Court of Appeal.[79]

2.42 This approach is controversial. Some commentators criticise it because, in their view, the results are unpredictable and arbitrary.[80] Others, probably more correctly, point out that the 'transnational' principles of law do not represent an autonomous and stand-alone legal system but depend on their recognition by national law or public international law.[81] Indeed, the French *régles matèrielles* are rules of French law. They may be 'international' or 'transnational' because French law applies them only to international, and not domestic, arbitration and because their origin is, or is thought to be, in the practice and the requirements of the international business community, but this does not turn them into rules applicable across national legal systems regardless of their adoption by each national legal system according to its own rules of legal normativity.

2.43 Facts speak louder than words. If the French 'transnational' rules are not also recognised by the national courts having supportive or supervisory jurisdiction over the arbitration or the award, this may give rise to inconsistent results. In *Peterson Farms*, an ICC tribunal had awarded damages not only to the party to the contract, and, therefore, to the arbitration clause, but also to other companies belonging to the same corporate group. The tribunal proceeded on the basis that, even if the contract was expressly governed by Arkansas law, there was no choice of the law governing the arbitration agreement. Because the arbitration agreement is separate from the matrix contract, the tribunal would therefore

76 P Lalive, 'Transnational (or Truly International) Public Policy and International Arbitration' in P Sanders (ed), *Comparative Arbitration Practice and Public Policy in Arbitration* (Kluwer, 1987) 257, 278.

77 *The Dow Chemical Company v ISOVER Saint Gobain*, Interim Award, ICC Case No 4131, 23 September 1982 (1984) 9 Ybk Commercial Arbitration 131.

78 ibid, 136.

79 *Dow Chemical France v ISOVER Saint Gobain*, 21 October 1983, 110 (Cour d'appel Paris) Journal du droit international (Clunet) 899 (1983).

80 M Blessing, 'Choice of Substantive Law in International Arbitration' (1997) 14 Journal of International Arbitration 39, 40–41.

81 B Wortmann, 'Choice of Law by Arbitrators: The Applicable Conflict of Laws System' (1998) 14 Arbitration International 97, 101–102.

determine its scope in light of the common intention of the parties. Applying the 'group of companies doctrine' adopted in *Dow Chemical*,[82] and subsequently applied in ICC awards[83] and upheld by the French courts,[84] the tribunal found that an arbitration agreement expressed to be made between A and B could be relied upon by companies belonging to the same corporate group as A, provided that the common intention of the parties was to that effect.

2.44 When the case came before the English High Court on an enforcement application, however, Langley J considered that the law governing the main contract, that is, Arkansas law, also applied to the arbitration clause and that there was nothing in Arkansas law, which was in all material respects the same as English law, which justified the approach adopted by the tribunal. The principle of privity of contract meant that, unless there was an agency relationship, the tribunal had jurisdiction only on the signatory parties to the contract. On this ground, an application to set aside the award in part for lack of jurisdiction vis-à-vis non-signatory claimants was upheld under section 67 of the Arbitration Act 1996.[85]

2.45 In a similar vein, the German Federal Supreme Court held that, in order to determine whether an arbitration agreement extended to include a member of a group of companies who was a non-signatory to the agreement, the correct approach was to undertake a detailed conflict of laws analysis to determine the applicable *national* law.[86]

From national rules to transnational convergence

2.46 The current problems surrounding a transnational approach do not mean that such an approach is not desirable as a matter of policy and principle and that, incrementally, it should not become more widely accepted.

2.47 While the French approach may currently be considered extreme and does not find favour in certain jurisdictions, including England, there are different ways of achieving the same result of excluding the unintended application of peculiar national rules invalidating arbitration agreements whereby the parties clearly intended to arbitrate.

The non-discrimination principle

2.48 The first possibility may be defined as a non-discrimination principle. Under such an approach, a national law still applies to the arbitration agreement but with the exclusion of rules reflecting national policy interests that invalidate an arbitration agreement that would otherwise be valid as a matter of contract. Under this approach, an arbitration agreement may be invalidated only on grounds 'that can be applied neutrally on an

---

82 *Dow Chemical* case, 131–137.

83 ICC Case No 3131, award of 26 October 1979 (1984) 9 Ybk Commercial Arbitration 109 and ICC Case No 5103 in S Jarvin, Y Derains and JJ Arnaldez (eds), *Collection of ICC Arbitral Awards, Vol II (1986–1990)* (The Hague, Kluwer Law International, 1995) 361.

84 *KIS France SA v SA Société Générale* 31 October 1989, 1992 Rev Arb 90 (Cour d'appel Paris); *Société Korsnas Marma v Société Durand-Auzias* Nov 30 1988 (Cour d'appel Paris) and *Société Ofer Brothers v The TokyoMarine and Fire Insurance Co Ltd et autres* 14 Feb 1989, 1989 Rev Arb 691 (Cour d'appel Paris).

85 *Peterson Farms Inc v C&M Farming Ltd* [2004] 1 Lloyd's Rep 603.

86 German Federal Supreme Court dated 8 May 2014 (Case Reference No III ZR 371/12).

international scale'.[87] In other words, the courts may not find that an arbitration agreement is not existent, valid or effective based on rules that are applicable solely to arbitration agreements as opposed to contracts in general. A body of decisions in the United States may be interpreted as an application of this principle. For example, in *Ledee v Ceramiche Ragno*, the US courts refused to apply a rule of Puerto Rican law, which specifically invalidated arbitration contracts in automobile dealer contracts.[88]

2.49 The case of *Rhone Mediterrannee v Lauro* is particularly instructive.[89] This case involved an appeal of an order staying litigation in favour of arbitration with its seat in Italy. The claimant, Rhone, argued that the law applicable to the arbitration agreement was the law of the seat, in Italy. An expert on Italian law claimed that an arbitration agreement calling for an even number of arbitrators, as was the case here, was null and void under this law. The US District Court noted there was considerable uncertainty in determining the applicable law in this context. However, what was clear was that

> the meaning of Article II section 3 which is most consistent with the overall purposes of the Convention is that an agreement to arbitrate is "null and void" only (1) when it is subject to an internationally recognized defense such as duress, mistake, fraud, or waiver, ... or (2) when it contravenes fundamental policies of the forum state. The "null and void" language must be read narrowly, for the signatory nations have jointly declared a general policy of enforceability of agreements to arbitrate.[90]

As such, the appeal was dismissed and proceedings were stayed in favour of arbitration. This approach to international agreements mirrors the application of the Federal Arbitration Act (FAA) in the United States, which is said to pre-empt the parochial policy interests of individual federal States. The prevailing view in the United States is that the arbitration agreement is governed by a 'body of federal substantive law of arbitrability, applicable to any arbitration agreement within the coverage of the Act'.[91] This precludes the application of individual State laws, which specifically create higher standards for the validity, existence or effectiveness of arbitration agreements.

2.50 This more conservative, but still transnational approach could be generalised: it is still necessary to determine a national law that governs the validity of the arbitration agreement but this is subject to minimum international standards which negate specific national policies which would invalidate an otherwise clear agreement to arbitrate. *Sulamérica* itself can be seen as an example of this approach. The Court of Appeal, having set out a presumption according to which the arbitration clause is governed by the choice of law of the matrix contract, was quick to rebut it on the ground that the law of the matrix contract would have made the arbitration agreement ineffective. Brazilian law would have applied a parochial, national policy in favour of insureds, who are given a choice not to arbitrate even if they signed otherwise binding arbitration agreements. Therefore, English law applied instead, with its more neutral, international approach. While this framework

87 *Ledee v Ceramiche Ragno* 684 F2d 184 (1st Cir 1982), 187.

88 ibid.

89 *Rhone Mediterranee v Achille Lauro,* 444 F Supp 481 (DVI 1982), 712 F2d 50 (3d Cir 1983).

90 ibid, para 19.

91 *International Paper Co v Schwabedissen Maschinen & Anlagen GmbH*, 206 F 3d 411, 417 n 4 (4th Cir 2000).

yields similar results to the French approach in cases such as *Dalico*, it differs in that it does not purport to require a body of international law directly applicable to the arbitration agreement. It still applies national law, provided that such laws do not create additional hurdles for the arbitration agreement to be valid. Thus, it does not suffer from the current absence of clear and definable international rules in this area.[92]

The estoppel principle

2.51 A second possibility can be described as the estoppel approach. Under this approach, a party to an arbitration agreement may be precluded from arguing that the law applicable to the arbitration agreement is one that would render the agreement non-existent, invalid or ineffective. This can be justified as part of an overriding duty of good faith or as part of the court's inherent powers to prevent an abuse of process. These are principles recognised by virtually every major legal system, even if the precise scope and content of these principles varies across States.[93] Several US cases can be interpreted as applying this reasoning to disapply a law applicable to the arbitration agreement. The first is *Scherk v Alberto-Culver Co*. In that case, the court noted that to invalidate an arbitration agreement made with full knowledge of the facts would 'allow the respondent *to repudiate its solemn promise*'.[94] This supported the court's decision to uphold the validity of the agreement under the United States Federal Arbitration Act. These *dicta* were relied on in the controversial decision in *Chromalloy v Egypt*, where the Columbia district court ordered enforcement of an award that had been annulled at the seat of the arbitration in Egypt. The court found the argument that Egypt should not be able to 'repudiate its solemn promise to abide by the results of the arbitration' to be 'persuasive'.[95]

2.52 Subsequent decisions such as *Termo Rio*[96] and *Baker Marine*[97] have established that the discretion to enforce an award in these circumstances is, in fact, a narrow one, and the test is whether refusing enforcement in these circumstances would violate basic notions of justice and fairness. This may be the case when the conduct of a party is incompatible with the invalidity of the arbitration agreement. In *COMMISA v Pemex*, the courts followed the approach in *Chromalloy* and upheld the validity of an arbitration agreement after the award had been annulled at the seat by the courts of Mexico.[98] A significant factor in the decision was that Pemex's conduct 'showed that it considered itself subject to arbitration' and that none of their initial objections to jurisdiction reflected the domestic law that was eventually applied to invalidate the agreement. The court considered that this helped to give 'COMMISA the "settled expectation" that its dispute could be arbitrated'. To deny the validity of the arbitration agreement at a later stage would therefore violate basic notions of justice and fairness.

---

92 G Born, *International Commercial Arbitration* (2nd ed, Kluwer Law International 2014) 552–559.

93 B M Cremades, 'Good Faith in International Arbitration' (2013) 27 Am U Int'l Rev 761.

94 *Scherk v Alberto – Culver Co*, 417 US 506, 519, 94 S Ct 2449, 2457, 41 L Ed 2d 270 (1974) (emphasis added).

95 *In Re Chromalloy Aeroservices and the Arab Republic of Egypt*, 939 F Supp 906 (DC Cir 1996).

96 *Termo Rio SAESP v Electranta* SP 06–7058, 2007 WL 1515069 (DC Cir May 25, 2007).

97 *Baker Marine Ltd v Chevron Ltd* (1999) 14(8) Mealey's International Arbitration Report D-1 – D-2.

98 *Corporación Mexicana de Mantenimiento Integral, S De RL de CV v Pemex-Exploración y Producción*, No 10 Civ 206 (AKH), 2013 WL 4517225, (SDNY Aug 27, 2013).

2.53 While these cases do not cite the principle of estoppel explicitly, the language used, for example the references to 'fairness', 'promise' and 'expectations', betrays an estoppel-type reasoning. Certain French decisions also reveal hints of this reasoning. For example, in *Ministry of Public Works v Société Bec Frères*, Bec Frères had sought enforcement of an award in France, despite it being annulled at the seat in Tunisia on the basis of a domestic statute prohibiting arbitration clauses in domestic public contracts. As we have seen, the French courts adopt a transnational approach to the arbitration agreement, and therefore it was not strictly necessary to apply the estoppel approach. Nonetheless, the court noted that 'by stipulating an arbitration clause, the Ministry of Public Works, which has subjected itself to the jurisdiction of the arbitrators, has also accepted that their award may be granted leave for enforcement and has waived its immunity from jurisdiction'.[99] It could be argued that the party was effectively estopped from going back and claiming the arbitration agreement was invalid under domestic law, having accepted the jurisdiction of the tribunal by signing the arbitration agreement.

2.54 The effect of these decisions was much the same as the examples of the non-discriminatory principle provided earlier – peculiar domestic laws used to invalidate the arbitration agreement were disapplied by the enforcing court.

The validation principle

2.55 The third option is well known and is generally referred to as the validation principle. Arbitral tribunals and courts around the world, being presented with an agreement clearly evidencing an unequivocal intention of the parties to arbitrate, will be slow in finding that the agreement is invalid based on the technicalities of the applicable law. When one potentially applicable law has this effect, they will look for another applicable law under which the agreement is valid. This validation principle is the reflection of a well-established contract law doctrine whereby a clause in a contract must be construed so as to be given effect instead of being invalidated.[100]

2.56 A statutory example of such an approach is Article 178(2) of the Swiss Federal Private International Law Act, which provides:

> 2 As regards its substance, an arbitration agreement is valid if it conforms either to the law chosen by the parties, to the law governing the subject-matter of the dispute, in particular the law governing the main contract, or to Swiss law.

This approach is increasingly popular with national courts as well as arbitral tribunals. In the Award in ICC case No 11869 it was stated that 'arbitration agreements should be interpreted in a way that leads to their validity in order to give effect to the intention of the parties to submit their disputes to arbitration'.[101] The decisions in the United States courts in this area can also be interpreted as an unstated application of the validation principle.

99 *Ministry of Public Works v Société Bec Frères* (Cour d'Appel de Paris) (1997) 22 Ybk Commercial Arbitration 682, 686.

100 See, extensively, Born, *International Commercial Arbitration* 541–548 and Berger, 'Re-examining the Arbitration Agreement: Applicable Law – Consensus or Confusion?' 312–313.

101 Award in ICC Case No 11869 (2011) 36 Ybk Commercial Arbitration 47, 57; see also J Lew, 'The Law Applicable to the Form and Substance of the Arbitration Clause', in A van den Berg (ed), *Improving the Efficiency*

In *Rhone Mediterranee v Lauro*, it was said that 'the policy of the Convention is best served by an approach which leads to upholding agreements to arbitrate'.[102] In Austria, the courts have expressly relied on the validation principle, stating that 'if the wording of the declaration of intent allows for two equally plausible interpretations, the interpretation which favours the validity of the arbitration agreement ... is to be preferred'.[103]

2.57 In English law, *Sulamérica* could be seen as a straightforward application of this approach.[104] While the Court of Appeal applied an orthodox common law conflicts analysis, one of the key factors it considered in choosing English law was that this gave effect to the arbitration agreement and displaced the law that invalidated it. The Supreme Court in *Enka v Chubb* has now strongly endorsed the validation principle. This is not a change or new development in English law,[105] but it is the strongest restatement of the principle in the field of arbitration in recent times. Lord Hamblen and Lord Leggatt, with whom Lord Kerr agreed, said that, when a putative law would make an arbitration clause ineffective, this may

> support an inference that [the arbitration clause] was intended to be governed by a different law from the other provisions of the contract – or may at least negate an inference that the law generally applicable to the contract was intended to apply to the arbitration clause.[106]

What probably does constitute a development is the wider scope of the validation principle that the majority in *Enka v Chubb* adopted. Their Lordships understood the validation principle as a form of purposive interpretation. Therefore, any impairment of the commercial purpose of an arbitration clause may engage the validation principle. What degree of impairment will be sufficient to displace the inference that a choice of law of the main contract is intended to apply to the arbitration clause as well depends on

> the particular words used in the contract and the surrounding circumstances, as well as the nature and extent of the risk that the purpose of the arbitration agreement would be undermined if its validity and scope were governed by the relevant system of law.[107]

The majority gave, however, one example of a case in which an impairment other than one affecting the validity or effectiveness of an arbitration clause would be sufficient to engage the validation principle: if the law of chosen by the parties to govern the main contract fails to recognise the presumption that arbitration has been chosen as a one stop method of dispute resolution, 'it is inherently less likely that reasonable commercial parties would have intended that law to determine the validity and scope of their agreement to arbitrate (rather than litigate) disputes'.[108]

---

of Arbitration Agreements and Awards: 40 Years of Application of the New York Convention ICCA Congress Series No 9 1999, 114, 139–140.

102 *Rhone Mediterranee v Achille Lauro,* para 21.

103 Judgment of 2 August 2008 (Austrian Oberster Gerichtshof) (2009) 34 Ybk Commercial Arbitration 404, 405.

104 S Pearson, '*Sulamérica v Enesa*: The Hidden Pro-validation Approach Adopted by the English Courts with Respect to the Proper Law of the Arbitration Agreement' (2013) 29 Arbitration International 115.

105 See, already, *Hamlyn & Co v Talisker Distillery* [1894] AC 202.

106 *Enka v Chubb*, para 97.

107 ibid, para 109.

108 ibid, paras 107–108. The minority disagreed on this point and believed that the validation principle applies only when validity, not interpretation or scope, is in issue: ibid, para 198 (*per* Lord Burrows) and para 277 (*per* Lord Sales).

Conclusions

2.58 Leading jurisdictions around the world have grappled with the question of the law governing an arbitration clause and have reached different solutions, either in their case law or jurisprudence or in their statutes. The New York Convention and the UNCITRAL Model Law have their own conflict of laws rules. This chapter suggests that, without embracing extreme approaches that purport to determine the validity of the arbitration clause without reference to any national legal system, a more transnational approach should be encouraged and may emerge based on principles on which international convergence would be desirable.

2.59 First, more convergence could, in theory, be achieved when applying national conflict of laws rules. However, at this level, different jurisdictions choose different approaches. When the parties choose the seat of the arbitration in the arbitration clause, there are strong arguments to hold that the law of the seat should apply to the arbitration clause. Jurisdictions such as Scotland and Sweden placed this principle on a statutory footing. However, the Court of Appeal in *Sulamérica*, first, and, then, the Supreme Court in *Enka v Chubb*, adopted the 'main contract' approach: the choice of law governing the main contract is a strong indication that the same law governs the arbitration clause as well. Only when there is no choice of law of the main contract, express or implied, then the arbitration clause will be governed by the law of the seat as the law with which the clause is most closely connected.

2.60 This English law approach is somewhat paradoxical. Both the Court of Appeal in *Sulamérica* and the Supreme Court in *Enka v Chubb* took the view that the arbitration agreement is more closely connected with the seat of the arbitration rather than with the substantive contract, which begs the question as to why parties who have expressly chosen the seat are instead presumed to have chosen, as the law applicable to the arbitration clause, a law which has a weaker relationship with the arbitration clause.

2.61 However, although the 'main contract' approach in *Sulamérica* and *Enka v Chubb* may give rise to some perplexity, the strong endorsement of the validation principle by the Supreme Court in *Enka v Chubb* mitigates or even eliminates potential problems: if there is a serious risk that the law of the main contract would seriously undermine the commercial purpose of the arbitration clause, then the law of the seat would apply. Therefore, whenever it really matters, even under *Enka v Chubb*, it is the law of the seat that prevails. It can be said, therefore, that a degree of convergence towards the law of the seat has been achieved notwithstanding the 'main contract' approach in *Enka v Chubb* even in English law.

2.62 Second, when the parties have not chosen the seat of the arbitration, the *Enka v Chubb* approach is correct. In the absence of a choice of seat in the agreement, the closest connection factor points to the law applicable to the main contract, whether this is chosen by the parties or determined by the court under other conflict of laws rules.

2.63 Third, national laws should further develop or adopt a non-discrimination principle, whereby courts should refuse to apply those rules of the law applicable to the arbitration clause which specifically invalidate arbitration agreements in a way that goes beyond general principles of contract law that can be applied neutrally on an international scale.

2.64 Fourth, courts should adopt, or apply more robustly, the estoppel principle, whereby a party whose conduct has been incompatible with the invalidity of the arbitration agreement should be precluded from relying on such invalidity at a later stage.

2.65 Fifth, courts should develop, or apply more robustly, the validation principle. There is a presumption that the parties intended their choice of law to uphold the validity of the arbitration agreement. Therefore, among several potentially applicable laws, the arbitration agreement should be governed by a law under which it is valid and most effective rather than by a law under which it is invalidated or rendered less effective. *Enka v Chubb* is a strong restatement of the validation principle in English law and widens its application to, potentially, all cases in which the commercial purpose of an arbitration clause may be impaired.

2.66 The rules described are, and will remain, rules of national law. Their transnational nature depends on them being developed in a dialogue among arbitral tribunals and courts around the world and being shared, over time, by more and more jurisdictions.

2.67 Party autonomy has a fundamental role to play in this process of international convergence. If parties more and more often choose the law applicable to the arbitration agreement itself, this will give rise, incrementally, to a recognisable and well-established body of jurisprudence in the few jurisdictions the laws of which will be most frequently chosen. Other courts may take guidance from this jurisprudence, which will in turn promote harmonisation and convergence of the approach of national courts to this issue.

2.68 This is precisely what happened in the well-known case of *Fiona Trust*, where the House of Lords noted that 'the trend of recent authority has risked isolating the approach that English law takes to the wording of [arbitration] clauses from that which is taken internationally'. It therefore considered that 'it makes sense in the context of international commerce for decision about [arbitration clauses'] effect to be informed by what has been decided elsewhere'.[109] The court went on to look at cases from Germany and the United States in order to provide guidance as to the true intention of the parties in their agreement.

2.69 A comparative methodology adopted by the courts, together with tighter and clearer drafting, will in itself facilitate the emergence of rules and principles that could over time converge and give more meaningful substance and more precise contours to the admittedly still vague and underdeveloped transnational principles applicable to the validity of the arbitration agreements.

109 *Fiona Trust v Privalov* [2007] UKHL 40, paras 29–33.

CHAPTER 3

The Singapore Convention on Mediation

Its impact on international construction disputes

Shouyu Chong

Introduction

3.1 The Singapore Convention on Mediation is set to change the landscape of cross-border alternative dispute resolution. It is the first multilateral treaty that advances a legal mechanism promoting the circulation of international mediated settlement agreements ('**iMSAs**')[1] across territorial borders. An iMSA, which has not been 'transformed' into a consent arbitral award or court order, falling within the scope of the Singapore Convention will enjoy a unique status above and beyond its substance as a contractual agreement between disputing parties to settle conflicts at the mediation table. It may be argued that the Convention elevates iMSAs to the status of a novel form of legal instrument recognised under international law, because it establishes a framework – akin to the New York Convention – for judicial recognition and enforcement of commercial settlement agreements arising from mediation. This chapter examines the key features of the Convention and promotes debate over its potential impact on international construction disputes, which has increasingly favoured mediation in recent years.[2]

3.2 Knowledge about the Convention is important for stakeholders dealing with parties that have assets situated in jurisdictions that have signed on to it, including China, India and the United States. Pending a decision with the European Commission over whether the EU or its individual member States have the competence to sign on to the Convention in 2021,[3] there appears to be a good chance that EU States would do so in the near future,[4] which could complement the Directive 52/2008 on certain aspects of mediation in civil and commercial matters.[5] Post-Brexit, the United Kingdom is also expected to sign on to the Convention.[6]

1 The abbreviation 'iMSA' for international mediated settlement agreements is first coined by Professor Nadja Alexander in Nadja Alexander, Sabine Walsh & Martin Svatos (eds), *EU Mediation law Handbook: Regulatory Robustness Ratings for Mediation Regimes* (Wolters Kluwer 2017).

2 See ARCADIS, *Global Construction Disputes Report 2019*, (2019).

3 Herman Verbist, 'United Nations Convention on International Settlement Agreements Resulting from Mediation' [2019] *Belgian Review of Arbitration* 53, para 68.

4 Michael Fletcher, 'Signed but Not Sealed: The Impact & Reach of the Singapore Convention on Mediation' (2019) *New Law Journal* 20 (20 September 2019), 20.

5 Haris Meidanis, 'Enforcement of Mediation Settlement Agreements in the EU and the Need for Reform' (2020) 16(2) *Journal of Private International Law* 275.

6 Michael Fletcher, 'Signed but Not Sealed: The Impact & Reach of the Singapore Convention on Mediation' (2019) *New Law Journal* 20 (20 September 2019), 20.

Background

3.3 The Convention on International Settlement Agreements Resulting from Mediation[7] (the '**Singapore Convention**') was recommended for submission to the UN General Assembly at the 51st Session of the United Nations (UN) Commission on International Trade Law (UNCITRAL) on 25 June 2018. At that session, the UNCITRAL Model Law on International Commercial Mediation and International Settlement Agreements Resulting from Mediation, 2018[8] (the '**2018 Model Law**') was adopted as well. A resolution to designate the Convention as the 'Singapore Convention on Mediation' was approved.[9] Thereafter, the UN General Assembly adopted the Convention on 20 December 2018.[10] The Singapore Convention has come into force on 12 September 2020.[11] The signing ceremony of the Singapore Convention was organised in Singapore at the Shangri-La Hotel on 7 August 2019, attended by 70 official State delegations.[12] Altogether, 46 States (see Table 3.1) signed the Convention at the signing ceremony.[13]

Table 3.1 States that signed the Singapore Convention on 7 August 2019

1 Afghanistan	17 Iran (Islamic Republic of)*	33 Republic of Korea
2 Belarus*	18 Israel	34 Samoa
3 Benin	19 Jamaica	35 Saudi Arabia*
4 Brunei Darussalam	20 Jordan	36 Serbia
5 Chile	21 Kazakhstan	37 Sierra Leone
6 China	22 Lao People's Democratic Republic	38 Singapore
7 Colombia	23 Malaysia	39 Sri Lanka

7 The United Nations Convention on International Settlement Agreements Resulting from Mediation, GA Res 73/198, adopted at the United Nations General Assembly, 73rd Session (20 December 2018) (hereinafter '**The Singapore Convention**').

8 The UNCITRAL Model Law on International Commercial Mediation and International Settlement Agreements Resulting from Mediation, 2018 (amending the UNCITRAL Model Law on International Commercial Conciliation, 2002) GA Res 73/199, adopted at the United Nations General Assembly, 73rd Session (20 December 2018) (hereinafter the '**2018 Model Law**').

9 Beate Czerwenka, Chairperson of the 51st session of the United Nations Commission on International Trade Law, address to the Sixth Committee of the General Assembly (15 October 2018) p 2.

10 United Nations General Assembly, *Resolution Adopted by the General Assembly on 20 December 2018: Seventy-third Session* (A/RES/73/198) (11 January 2019); 'Press Release: General Assembly Adopts the United Nations Convention on International Settlement Agreements Resulting from Mediation' (UNIS/L/271) (21 December 2018).

11 Nadja Alexander & Shouyu Chong, '12 September 2020: The Singapore Convention on Mediation Comes into Force', *Kluwer Mediation Blog* (12 September 2020).

12 Nadja Alexander & Shouyu Chong, 'UN Treaty on Mediation Signed in Singapore' (2019) 23(2–3) *Nederlands-Vlaams tijdschrisft voor Mediation en conflictmanagement* 71; also see the Singapore Convention, Article 11.

13 An asterisk (*) indicates that the relevant State entered a reservation. At the signing ceremony of the Singapore Convention in August 2019, reservations were made by Belarus (invoking Article 8(1)(a) of the Singapore Convention) and Iran (invoking Article 8(1)(a) and 8(1)(b)). Saudi Arabia made an Article 8(1)(a) reservation when it ratified the Convention on 5 May 2020.

Table 3.1 (Continued)

8 Congo	24 Maldives	40 Timor-Leste
9 Democratic Republic of the Congo	25 Mauritius	41 Turkey
10 Eswatini	26 Montenegro	42 Uganda
11 Fiji	27 Nigeria	43 Ukraine
12 Georgia	28 North Macedonia	44 United States of America
13 Grenada	29 Palau	45 Uruguay
14 Haiti	30 Paraguay	46 Venezuela (Bolivarian Republic of)
15 Honduras	31 The Philippines	
16 India	32 Qatar	

3.4 At the time of writing, 54 States have signed the Convention. Five additional States had signed on in September 2019 – Armenia, Chad, Ecuador, Gabon and Guinea-Bissau. Rwanda signed in January 2020, and Ghana signed in July 2020. In June 2021, Brazil signed the Convention. Singapore began the ratification process in February 2020, passing the Singapore Convention on Mediation Act 2020,[14] becoming (alongside Fiji) the first countries to ratify the Convention. Qatar, Saudi Arabia and Ecuador have also ratified the Convention. Belarus submitted an instrument of Approval of the Convention to the UN Headquarters in July 2020. At the time of writing, there are six State parties to the Convention which have submitted their instruments of ratification or approval.

3.5 Stakeholders of the international mediation community including mediators, lawyers and repeat corporate users have expressed optimism that these UNCITRAL instruments – especially the Singapore Convention – may engender for mediation the advantages the 1958 New York Convention on the Recognition and Enforcement of Arbitral Awards[15] (the '**New York Convention**') is said to have brought for international arbitration.[16] The Convention provides the mediation forum with the regulatory robustness needed for validation as a formidable player in the market for cross-border dispute resolution. This is in line with observations from a 2014 survey conducted by Strong amongst members of the international business and legal communities, where 74% of respondents revealed that they thought a multi-lateral instrument facilitating the international enforcement of settlement agreements resulting from mediation would encourage respondents to mediate

14 Nadja Alexander & Shouyu Chong, 'Singapore Convention Series: Bill to Ratify before Singapore Parliament' *Kluwer Mediation Blog* (4 February 2020); Nadja Alexander & Shouyu Chong, 'Mediation and Appropriate Dispute Resolution' (2019) 20 SAL Ann Rev 614, para 22.1.

15 330 UNTS 3 (10 June 1958; entry into force 7 June 1959).

16 See Khory McCormick & Sharon S.M. Ong, 'Through the Looking Glass: An Insider's Perspective into the Making of the Singapore Convention on Mediation' (2019) 31 *Singapore Academy of Law Journal* 520, paras 68–69.

disputes (or push for mediation).[17] Users also increasingly prefer to proceed to mediation because of the many advantages it offers, especially those flowing from the benefits of preserving existing business relationships.[18] Such benefits are crucial in dispute resolution mechanisms put in place in the construction industry.[19] It follows that the enforceability mechanism under the Singapore Convention is likely to legitimise mediation as an attractive international dispute resolution forum, because the result of mediation (that is, an iMSA) becomes an enforceable instrument, similar to court judgments and international arbitral awards.[20]

The application of the Singapore Convention

3.6 Under ordinary circumstances, parties usually comply with the terms of the iMSA they have concluded.[21] However, in cases of non-compliance, the Singapore Convention provides parties to iMSAs falling within its scope (Article 1) with an avenue to proceed to a relevant court of a State to enforce it (Article 3(1)). The party seeking enforcement must apply to that court and furnish the relevant evidence: for instance, showing that the iMSA bears the parties' signatures and an attestation by the mediator or mediation institution that it was indeed an outcome from mediation[22] (Article 4). Provided none of the grounds for refusal stipulated in Article 5 applies, the iMSA will be directly enforced. Alternatively, discrete issues settled and embodied in the iMSA may be applied as a complete defence to the initiation of litigation or arbitral proceedings, where parties bound by that iMSA seek to contest those issues which have already been resolved and incorporated inside it (Article 3(2)). As iMSAs may be directly enforced under the Singapore Convention, there is no prerequisite for it to be reviewed by judicial authority at the place where it was concluded (*ie*, the State of origin). This is because there is no concept of a 'seat' of mediation, in the same way a 'seat' is understood in the context of arbitration.[23]

17 Stacie Strong, 'Use and Perception of International Commercial Mediation and Conciliation: A Preliminary Report on Issues Relating to the Proposed UNCITRAL Convention on International Commercial Mediation and Conciliation' (2014), University of Missouri School of Law Legal Studies Research Paper No. 2014–28, available at SSRN <https://papers.ssrn.com/sol3/papers.cfm?abstract_id=2526302> (accessed on 25 November 2018) p 45.

18 Dorcas Quek Anderson, 'The Singapore Convention on Mediation: Supplying the Missing Piece of the Puzzle for Dispute Resolution' July [2020] *Journal of the Malaysian Judiciary* 194, para 9.

19 Josephine Hage Chahine, Ettore Lombardi, David Lutran & Catherine Peulve, 'The Acceleration of the Development of International Business Mediation after the Singapore Convention' (*forthcoming*) *European Business Law Review*.

20 Dorcas Quek Anderson, 'The Singapore Convention on Mediation: Supplying the Missing Piece of the Puzzle for Dispute Resolution' July [2020] *Journal of the Malaysian Judiciary* 194.

21 Chang-fa Lo & Janice Lee, 'A New Approach for the Settlement of Regional Disputes to Maintain Dynamic Stability – A Selective Elaboration of the Draft Agreement of the Establishment of the Asia-Pacific Regional Mediation Organization' (2018) 13(1) *Asian Journal of WTO & International Health Law and Policy* 27, 40–41; Shouyu Chong & Felix Steffek, 'Enforcement of International Settlement Agreements Resulting from Mediation under the Singapore Convention: Private International Law Issues in Perspective' (2019) 31 *Singapore Academy of Law Journal* 448, para 5.

22 Article 4 additionally provides that other forms of relevant evidence may be tendered in the absence of the mediator's signature on the iMSA or an attestation by the mediator or mediation institution that the settlement agreement resulted from mediation.

23 Shouyu Chong & Nadja Alexander, 'Singapore Convention Series: Why Is There No Seat of Mediation?' *Kluwer Mediation Blog* (1 February 2019).

3.7 Judicial review of iMSAs under the Singapore Convention *only occurs* at the State of recognition and enforcement – generally, in a jurisdiction where a party to the dispute yields significant assets to satisfy the obligations under that iMSA. Hence, the mediation, which produced the iMSA to be enforced, may be conducted *anywhere* in the world. It is conceivable (and, perhaps, part of the new 'normal' in dispute resolution practice during the COVID-19 pandemic) for parties to agree to mediate their disputes online over a conference call, whilst they are each located in separate territorial jurisdictions: it is *unnecessary* for mediation to be conducted in a jurisdiction that has ratified the Convention.

Key provisions of the Singapore Convention

3.8 This section explores the key provisions of the Singapore Convention.

Forms of mediated settlement agreements falling within the scope of the Convention

3.9 The Singapore Convention provides a mechanism for the expedited court recognition and enforcement of international settlement agreements resulting from mediation,[24] which have been recorded in writing[25] by parties to resolve a commercial dispute.[26]

3.10 Under the Singapore Convention, only mediated settlement agreements with an *international* character may be recognised and enforced. Article 1(1) generally defines what constitutes an international dispute, where:

- a at least two parties to the settlement agreement have their places of business in different States; or
- b the State in which the parties to the settlement agreement have their places of business is different from either:
  - i the State in which a substantial part of the obligations under the settlement agreement is performed; or
  - ii the State with which the subject matter of the settlement agreement is most closely connected.[27]

If parties have more than one place of business, the applicable place of business for the purposes of determining the international character of the iMSA will be benchmarked against the location which bears the closest connection to the dispute resolved by the settlement agreement, having regard to the circumstances known to, or reasonably envisaged by, the parties *at the time of the conclusion of the settlement agreement*.[28] If a party to the iMSA is a natural person, reference will be made to their habitual residence.[29]

24 See the Singapore Convention, Article 1(a) – (b).

25 See the Singapore Convention, Article 1.

26 ibid.

27 The Singapore Convention, Article 1(1).

28 The Singapore Convention, Article 2(1)(a). This caveat is important in instances where parties move their businesses from one State to another, or when parties merge or become acquired by another out-of-state business. For further analysis, see Nadja Alexander & Shouyu Chong, *The Singapore Convention on Mediation: A Commentary* (Wolters Kluwer, 2019) paras 2.03–2.04.

29 The Singapore Convention, Article 2(1)(b).

3.11 The Singapore Convention provides a functional definition of what constitutes an 'international' dispute, as there is no concept of a seat of mediation,[30] in the same way a 'seat' is understood in the context of international commercial arbitration.[31] Whereas the internationality of a *foreign* court judgment or arbitral award enforced under prevailing multi-lateral treaties such as the Hague Convention of 30 June 2005 on Choice of Court Agreements ('**HCCCA**') and the New York Convention respectively is apparent on its face,[32] the internationality of a mediated settlement agreement has to be elucidated, because it is a non-starter to describe it as 'foreign' with no reference point:[33] without an originating 'seat' of mediation, there would be no benchmark against which the settlement agreement may be referred to as 'foreign'.

3.12 The Singapore Convention applies to expedite iMSAs that resolve cross-border commercial disputes. However, the term 'commercial' is not defined in the Convention.[34]

30 Shouyu Chong & Nadja Alexander, 'Singapore Convention Series: Why Is There No Seat of Mediation?' *Kluwer Mediation Blog* (1 February 2019); Shouyu Chong & Felix Steffek, 'Enforcement of International Settlement Agreements Resulting from Mediation under the Singapore Convention: Private International Law Issues in Perspective' (2019) 31 *Singapore Academy of Law Journal* 448, para 15. There is simply no need to discern the seat of mediation as it is not a determinative process as is arbitration: the nature of the natural justice considerations is fundamentally different, because in mediation, parties may not be *compelled* to arrive at their dispute resolution outcome. Accordingly, the power of the competent authority of the State to refuse to enforce an iMSA based on the fairness of the mediation process resulting in an iMSA is strictly confined to cases where mediator misconduct is so egregious that it materially influences parties to enter into it inadvertently (see the Singapore Convention, Article 5(e) – (f)).

31 As an aside, one should note that the relevance of the seat is fundamental in international arbitration because it is crucial in the determination of whether the award sought to be enforced is a foreign or domestic award (see the New York Convention, Article I): *ST Group Co Ltd and others v Sanum Investments Limited and another appeal* [2020] 1 SLR 1, para 96. Secondly, it is generally understood that the courts of the seat of arbitration have been traditionally entrusted with the powers by the drafters of the New York Convention through Article V(1)(e) of the Convention to engage in a principal review of awards made by the tribunal (see Nadia Darwazeh, 'Article V(1)(e)' in Kronke, et al (eds), *Recognition and Enforcement of Foreign Arbitral Awards: A Global Commentary on the New York Convention* (Kluwer Law International 2010) p 327.

32 Take for instance, Art I of the New York Convention provides, 'This Convention shall apply to the recognition and enforcement of arbitral awards made in the territory of a State [*ie*, the 'seat'] *other than the State where the recognition and enforcement of such awards are sought*' (with emphasis added).

33 Shouyu Chong & Nadja Alexander, 'Singapore Convention Series: Why Is There No Seat of Mediation?' *Kluwer Mediation Blog* (1 February 2019); Shouyu Chong & Felix Steffek, 'Enforcement of International Settlement Agreements Resulting from Mediation under the Singapore Convention: Private International Law Issues in Perspective' (2019) 31 *Singapore Academy of Law Journal* 448, para 15; also see United Nations Commission on International Trade Law, Working Group II (Dispute Settlement), *Report of Working Group II (Arbitration and Conciliation) on the Work of Its Sixty-third Session* (Vienna, 7–11 September 2015), (A/CN.9/861) (2015) para 35.

34 For academic purposes, it bears noting that what *commercial law* entails is difficult to define. Baskind, Osborne and Roach have identified it as a set of unifying principles which remains constantly in flux, adapting itself to facilitate new business procedures, new instruments and new demands (Eric Baskind, Greg Osborne & Lee Roach, *Commercial Law* (2nd ed, Oxford University Press 2016) p 3). Sealy and Hooley have described – albeit in a somewhat circular fashion – that '[c]ommercial law is the law of commerce. It is concerned with commercial transactions, *ie*, transactions in which both parties deal with each other in the course of business'. (Len S Sealy & Richard JA Hooley, *Commercial Law: Text, Cases and Material* (4th ed, Oxford University Press 2009) p 4). It may also be noted that in the Alberta Supreme Court, Walsh J in *R v Wah Kee* [1920] 3 WWR 656 (at 656) – when the court had to decide if a laundry shop run by the Defendant may be considered a commercial business – opined:

I read the word 'commercial' in the sense of relating to commerce partly on the *ejusdem generis* principle and partly because that is its ordinary and generally understood meaning. ... The word 'commercial' conveys to the mind the idea of dealing or trading in some article of commerce. ... In a sense, of course, every business which has profit for its object ... is a commercial business.

Yet a definition has been provided in footnote 1 of the 2018 Model Law, which was drafted alongside the Convention – this reference may be helpful to jurisdictions without a discrete body[35] of commercial law:

> The term 'commercial' should be given a wide interpretation so as to cover matters arising from all relationships of a commercial nature, whether contractual or not. Relationships of a commercial nature include, but are not limited to, the following transactions: any trade transaction for the supply or exchange of goods or services; distribution agreement; commercial representation or agency; factoring; leasing; construction of works; consulting; engineering; licensing; investment; financing; banking; insurance; exploitation agreement or concession; joint venture and other forms of industrial or business cooperation; and carriage of goods or passengers by air, sea, rail or road.[36]

This quote illustrates that the commercial dispute resolution outcomes covered by the Singapore Convention may include iMSAs resolving 'construction of works' and 'engineering' enterprises. The UNCITRAL Working Group II's proposal to confine the scope of the Convention to 'commercial agreements between businesses only'[37] was not accepted by the delegates. Thus, States may be parties to iMSAs enforced under the Convention, in the absence of a reservation to the contrary.[38]

3.13 Conversely, consumer disputes 'for personal, family or household purposes' and disputes regarding 'family, inheritance or employment law' are excluded.[39]

3.14 Mediation is defined broadly as:

> a process, irrespective of the expression used or the basis upon which the process is carried out, whereby parties attempt to reach an amicable settlement of their dispute with the assistance of a third person or persons ('the mediator') lacking the authority to impose a solution upon the parties to the dispute.[40]

This definition embraces a range of facilitative and advisory dispute resolution processes but excludes determinative forums, such as arbitration and adjudication.[41]

---

35 For instance, English law does not have a commercial law code; Goode and McKendrick have described English commercial law as a collection of 'ill-assorted statutes bedded down on an amorphous mass of constantly shifting case law' (Roy Goode & Ewan McKendrick, *Goode on Commercial Law* (4th ed, Penguin 2010) p 1347).

36 See UNCITRAL Model Law on International Commercial Mediation and International Settlement Agreements Resulting from Mediation, 2018 (amending the UNCITRAL Model Law on International Commercial Conciliation, 2002) GA Res 73/199, adopted at the United Nations General Assembly, 73rd Session (20 December 2018), footnote 1.

37 Cf United Nations Commission on International Trade Law, Working Group II, *Note by the Secretariat on Comments received from States on the Settlement of commercial disputes: Enforceability of settlement agreements resulting from international commercial conciliation/mediation – Revision of the UNCITRAL Notes on Organizing Arbitral Proceedings* (New York, 2–6 February 2015), (A/CN.9/WG.II/WP.188) (2015) p 3.

38 Khory McCormick & Sharon SM Ong, 'Through the Looking Glass: An Insider's Perspective into the Making of the Singapore Convention on Mediation' (2019) 31 *Singapore Academy of Law Journal* 520, para 31. Note that the relevant reservation may be found in Article 8(1)(a) of the Singapore Convention.

39 The Singapore Convention, Article 1(2).

40 The Singapore Convention, Article 2(3).

41 Shouyu Chong & Felix Steffek, 'Enforcement of International Settlement Agreements Resulting from Mediation under the Singapore Convention: Private International Law Issues in Perspective' (2019) 31 *Singapore Academy of Law Journal* 448, para 17.

3.15 Establishing a broad definition of mediation reflects a recognition of the diversity in cross-border mediation practices across the globe.[42] As Quek Anderson has helpfully observed, mediators are generally said to help 'parties make their own decisions through a range of techniques, including facilitating communication, crystallising the underlying issues [in dispute] and helping the parties to develop options'.[43] The definition of mediation in the Convention is therefore a functional one, emphasising on the *nature* and *substance* of the dispute resolution mechanism rather than its label.[44] Essentially, parties need not pedantically describe what facilitated the conclusion of their iMSAs as a 'mediation', for the Convention to be applicable.[45] Thus, processes such as neutral evaluation and mini-trial may conceivably fall inside the wide definition of mediation. Technically, it is possible for parties to enforce complex cross-border contractual arrangements governing future commercial relations under the Convention: in order to do so, they must prove that the contract was *in substance* a product of *mediation* to *resolve existing commercial disputes*, as opposed to a sham process.

3.16 Whilst the Singapore Convention seeks to fill gaps in the cross-border enforcement regimes of iMSAs, its drafters were mindful to avoid overlaps with the enforcement regimes for foreign judgments,[46] foreign arbitral awards[47] and iMSAs.[48] Hence, the Convention excludes settlement agreements that:

a have been approved by a court or have been concluded in the course of court proceedings; and are enforceable as a judgment in the state of that court; or
b have been recorded and are enforceable as an arbitral award.[49]

These carve out provisions were drafted to deconflict the administration of the Singapore Convention with other prevalent international Conventions, such as the New York

42 Consider Nadja Alexander, 'Ten Trends in International Mediation' (2019) 31 SAcLJ 405, paras 50–54.

43 Dorcas Quek Anderson, 'The Singapore Convention on Mediation: Supplying the Missing Piece of the Puzzle for Dispute Resolution' July [2020] *Journal of the Malaysian Judiciary* 194, para 6.

44 Nadja Alexander & Shouyu Chong, 'An Introduction to the Singapore Convention on Mediation – Perspectives from Singapore' (2018) 22(4) *Nederlands-Vlaams tijdschrisft voor Mediation en conflictmanagement* 37, 41.

45 Shouyu Chong & Felix Steffek, 'Enforcement of International Settlement Agreements Resulting from Mediation under the Singapore Convention: Private International Law Issues in Perspective' (2019) 31 *Singapore Academy of Law Journal* 448, para 17. Take for instance, a mediated settlement agreement which carries the label of a 'Memorandum of Understanding' will still, in substance, be recognised as a settlement agreement which was procured as a result of mediation (see *Ram Niranjan v Navin Jatia and others and another suit* [2019] 3 SLR 1037; and *Navin Jatia and others v Ram Niranjan and another and other appeals* [2020] 1 SLR 1098).

46 Notably, the Hague Convention of 30 June 2005 on Choice of Court Agreements (30 June 2005; entry into force 1 October 2015), as well as the Hague Convention of 2 July 2019 on the Recognition and Enforcement of Foreign Judgments in Civil or Commercial Matters (2 July 2019), which has been adopted by the Hague Conference on Private International Law on 2 July 2019 but has not come into force at the time of writing (Uruguay and Ukraine have since signed on to the Convention, as of September 2020 at the time of writing, but none have deposited an instrument of ratification, accession, acceptance or approval, *per* Article 28 of the Convention).

47 Notably, the New York Convention.

48 Natalie Y Morris-Sharma, 'Constructing the Convention on Mediation – The Chairperson's Perspective' (2019) 31 *Singapore Academy of Law Journal* 487, para 45. See also UNCITRAL, *Report of Working Group II (Disputes Settlement) on the Work of Its Sixty-third Session* (Vienna, 7–11 September 2015) (A/CN.9/861) (17 September 2015) p. 6.

49 The Singapore Convention, Article 1(3).

Convention and the HCCCA, which already provide enforcement mechanisms for some iMSAs.[50]

3.17 The Convention provides a recognition and enforcement remedy to parties in instances where those other Conventions are otherwise inapplicable.[51] It should be noted that Article 7 of the Convention, which serves as a 'more-favourable-right' clause, preserves the right of parties to enforce their iMSAs under enforcement regimes aside from the Singapore Convention, if a more favourable result ensues.[52] The 'more favourable' enforcement regime may be embedded in domestic law or in another treaty.

Enforcement under the Convention

3.18 The Convention provides wide latitude for the contracting State Parties to comply with their Convention obligations by not specifying a precise form for enforcement.[53] Contracting State Parties may, in accordance with their domestic law, administer their rules of procedure to facilitate the recognition and enforcement of iMSAs, on condition that they fulfil the requirements set out in respect to scope (as examined earlier), form and evidence (analysed later).[54] To reiterate, the mediation may have taken place *anywhere* in the world: there is no requirement that the mediation should be conducted in a jurisdiction that has ratified the Convention. For convenience, the recognition and enforcement mechanism of the Convention will be referred to collectively as one of enforcement in this chapter.

3.19 The operation of the Convention's enforcement mechanism may be better understood by applying the metaphors of a 'sword' and 'shield'.[55] Article 3(1) provides that iMSAs may be administered as a 'sword', such that parties may initiate proceedings to compel the performance of another party to that iMSA, enforcing the contractual obligations contained therein, if the requirements laid out by the Convention are satisfied and no defences under Article 5 may be proven. Article 3(2) provides that parties may apply an iMSA as a 'shield' (or a defence against impending litigation), compelling the relevant courts to functionally 'recognise' the discrete issues – which have been reflected in a concluded *written* iMSA[56] – already settled at mediation, and dismiss (or strike out) those issues 'already resolved' to avoid their re-litigation in court.[57]

50 Natalie Y Morris-Sharma, 'Constructing the Convention on Mediation – The Chairperson's Perspective' (2019) 31 *Singapore Academy of Law Journal* 487, para 45. Consider, for instance, the Hague Convention of 30 June 2005 on Choice of Court Agreements, Article 12.

51 For example, where out-of-court settlements are not taken back into the courtroom for judicial approval for enforcement under the HCCCA regime, and consequently do not qualify as a final court 'judgment'.

52 Nadja Alexander & Shouyu Chong, *The Singapore Convention on Mediation: A Commentary* (Wolters Kluwer 2019) para 7.02; and Khory McCormick & Sharon SM Ong, 'Through the Looking Glass: An Insider's Perspective into the Making of the Singapore Convention on Mediation' (2019) 31 *Singapore Academy of Law Journal* 520, para 30.

53 See the Singapore Convention, Article 3.

54 For the applicable conditions, see the Singapore Convention, Articles 1, 2 and 4.

55 The metaphors were helpfully applied by Schnabel in Timothy Schnabel, 'The Singapore Convention on Mediation: A Framework for the Cross-Border Recognition and Enforcement of Mediated Settlements' (2019) 19 *Pepperdine Dispute Resolution Law Journal* 1, 35 *ff.*

56 Cf *Rakna Arakshaka Lanka Ltd v Avant Garde Maritime Services (Pte) Ltd* [2019] 2 SLR 131; and Nadja Alexander & Shouyu Chong, 'Mediation and Appropriate Dispute Resolution' in KS Teo & Yihan Goh (eds), *Singapore Academy of Law Annual Review of Singapore Cases (2019)* (Academy Publishing 2020), para 22.7 *ff.*

57 This also assumes if the conditions established in the Convention are satisfied and no grounds for refusal under Article 5 can be proven.

3.20 Whilst the Singapore Convention does not expressly make reference to the concept of 'recognition' (in the private international law sense) in relation to iMSAs in a similar manner as the New York Convention does to the recognition of foreign arbitral awards, Article 3(2) provides functionally for such recognition. This carefully drafted wording is a reflection of the discourse and compromise achieved within the Working Group as to how the use of the term 'recognition' may muddle civil procedural rules in some jurisdictions (specifically those of non-common law traditions).[58] As conceived by lawyers versed in non-common law traditions, private international law 'recognition' would not embrace dispute resolution outcomes procured outside of litigation and arbitration forums, which engender a '*res judicata* effect'.[59] The conflict between the common law and civilian law traditions was overcome through the integration of a functional description of the effect intended into the phrasing of Article 3(2).[60]

3.21 Parties enforcing an iMSA under the Convention shall:

a produce the *written* iMSA signed by the parties; and
b provide evidence that it was procured as a result of a mediation process.

This means that State Parties to the Convention may simply legislate for iMSAs to be *prima facie* enforceable, in accordance with domestic procedural law.

3.22 Under the Convention, the formal prerequisites for enforceable iMSAs are minimal. The iMSA must be in writing[61] and signed by the parties.[62] There are no additional formalities, such as notarisation.[63] The 'in writing' prerequisite is easily satisfied 'if its content is recorded in any form ... [including] an electronic communication if the information contained therein is accessible so as to be useable for subsequent reference'.[64] Accordingly, disputes resolved through a variety of online dispute resolution **(ODR)** forums administered through numerous channels of electronic communication (including text messaging, email, online conference calls and dedicated ODR platforms)[65] may be

58 Timothy Schnabel, 'The Singapore Convention on Mediation: A Framework for the Cross-Border Recognition and Enforcement of Mediated Settlements' (2019) 19 *Pepperdine Dispute Resolution Law Journal* 1, 35 *ff*; Natalie Y Morris-Sharma, 'Constructing the Convention on Mediation – The Chairperson's Perspective' (2019) 31 *Singapore Academy of Law Journal* 487, para 40.

59 See Natalie Y Morris-Sharma, 'Constructing the Convention on Mediation – The Chairperson's Perspective' (2019) 31 *Singapore Academy of Law Journal* 487, para 39; Clemens Treichl, 'The Singapore Convention: Towards a Universal Standard for the Recognition and Enforcement of International Settlement Agreements?' (2020) 11 *Journal of International Dispute Settlement* 409, 413.

60 Natalie Y Morris-Sharma, 'Constructing the Convention on Mediation – The Chairperson's Perspective' (2019) 31 *Singapore Academy of Law Journal* 487, para 40.

61 The Singapore Convention, Article 1.

62 The Singapore Convention, Article 4(1)(a).

63 In contrast and for instance, in Austria, a mediated settlement agreement needs to be concluded before a competent Austrian court or integrated into a notarial deed before direct enforcement is possible: Günther Horvath, Katherine Khan & Niamh Leinwather, 'Michael Moser's Journey in Mediation: The "Triple-A" Approach' in Neil Kaplan, Michael Pryles & Chiann Bao (eds), *International Arbitration: When East Meets West – Liber Amicorum Michael Moser* (Wolters Kluwer 2020) p 125.

64 The Singapore Convention, Article 2(2).

65 Consider as an example the e-negotiation and e-mediation services available under the recently constituted Singapore Employment Claims Tribunals online filing module; whilst it is acknowledged that employment law claims are excluded under the Singapore Convention's scope, the electronic platform tools may be transferable in the future to resolving small-scale cross-border commercial disputes. See Joanna Seow, 'New Employment Claims Tribunals Portal Allows Users to Have Disputes Mediated Online' *The Straits Times* (4 January 2019),

amenable to enforcement under the Convention, if parties may conclude their iMSA by endorsing it with a recognised electronic signature,[66] and furnish the enforcement authority with proof that it was an outcome of mediation.[67]

3.23 To prove that the iMSA was an outcome of mediation, parties *may* produce a mediation agreement,[68] the mediator's signature on the settlement agreement, a separate document signed by the mediator confirming that mediation was carried out in respect to the settlement agreement concerned or an official attestation by the institution or dispute resolution service provider administering the mediation.[69] Additionally, there is a 'catch-all' clause (Article 4(1)(b)(iv)) which enables the competent authority to decide what other forms of evidence may be produced to show that the iMSA was a result of mediation.[70]

Grounds for refusal to enforce an iMSA

3.24 Article 5 of the Singapore Convention circumscribes exhaustively the exceptions to the enforcement of iMSAs that have otherwise fulfilled the Article 4 prerequisites. The competent authority *may*[71] refuse to enforce an iMSA if one or more of these grounds are proven. The defences falling under Article 5(1) of the Convention require parties to submit evidence to the relevant competent authority proving that one or more grounds for refusal under that provision exists. In contrast, Article 5(2) establishes that the relevant competent authority may by its own volition rule that such grounds for refusal may exist, without – technically – first having parties plead it and furnish the necessary evidence. The Article 5 defences may be examined in four categories: contract-related grounds for refusal, mediator conduct-related grounds for refusal, public policy justifications and where the subject matter is incapable of settlement by mediation.

Contract-related grounds for refusal

3.25 Article 5(1) of the Singapore Convention sets out seven grounds for refusal founded in contract law, if:

---

available at <https://www.straitstimes.com/singapore/new-employment-claims-tribunals-portal-allows-users-to-have-disputes-mediated-online> (accessed on 8 June 2021).

66 The Singapore Convention, Article 4(1)(a) read with Article 4(2).

67 The Singapore Convention, Article 4(1)(b).

68 United Nations Commission on International Trade Law, Working Group II (Dispute Settlement), *Report of Working Group II (Arbitration and Conciliation) on the Work of Its Sixty-third Session* (Vienna, 7–11 September 2015), (A/CN.9/861) (2015) para 68.

69 The Singapore Convention, Article 4(1)(b)(i) – (iii).

70 The Singapore Convention, Article 4(1)(b)(iv).

71 It is theoretically within the prerogative of the competent authority to exercise some discretion and, nonetheless, enforce the iMSA even though one or more of the Article 5 grounds were successfully proved. As to theories behind how such discretion may be yielded, see Jonathan Hill, 'The Exercise of Judicial Discretion in Relation to Applications to Enforce Arbitral Awards under the New York Convention 1958' (2016) 36 *Oxford Journal of Legal Studies* 304. Hill has observed, albeit in the arbitration context, that such a discretion is likely administered within highly circumscribed circumstances: 'As a general rule, if a defence to enforcement ... is established, enforcement will be (and should be) refused. [However, to] this general principle, there is a limited number of exceptions ..., which are based on intelligible legal principles, rather than the court's perception of what would be fair in all the circumstances'. This is an area which should be left for further research in another article, in the cross-border mediation context.

a a party to it was under some form of incapacity at its conclusion;[72]
b it is null and void, inoperative or incapable of being performed according to the applicable law;[73]
c it is not binding, or is not final, according to its terms;[74]
d it has been subsequently modified;[75]
e the obligations in it have been performed;[76]
f the obligations in it are not stated clearly or comprehensibly;[77] or
g granting relief would be contrary its terms.[78]

First, the incapacity defence applies to parties that are natural or legal persons. The term 'incapacity' must be examined with reference to the governing law of the iMSA,[79] which may generally be defined by an express choice of law clause. If no express choice were made, or if the choice were invalid,[80] courts may normally administer the law that is most-closely connected with the dispute.[81] Other legal techniques to derive the governing law, such as the validation principle[82] and *renvoi*, may also be administered.[83] Broadly, the incapacity defence may be relevant when parties involved in the conclusion of iMSAs are minors, natural persons with intellectual deficits or legal persons that are not validly represented at mediation.

3.26 Second, a defence is available to parties when an iMSA is null and void, inoperative or incapable of being performed under the applicable law. iMSAs which are 'null and void' contain defects at the time when the agreements are concluded. With reference

72 The Singapore Convention, Article 5(1)(a).

73 The Singapore Convention, Article 5(1)(b)(i).

74 The Singapore Convention, Article 5(1)(b)(ii).

75 The Singapore Convention, Article 5(1)(b)(iii).

76 The Singapore Convention, Article 5(1)(c)(i).

77 The Singapore Convention, Article 5(1)(c)(ii).

78 The Singapore Convention, Article 5(1)(d).

79 Shouyu Chong & Felix Steffek, 'Enforcement of International Settlement Agreements Resulting from Mediation under the Singapore Convention: Private International Law Issues in Perspective' (2019) 31 *Singapore Academy of Law Journal* 448, para 46.

80 For instance, when conflicting express choices of law were made: see *Dubai Electricity Co and ors v Islamic Republic of Iran Shipping Lines (The Iran Vojdan)* [1984] 2 Lloyd's Rep 380, 385.

81 Take for example, courts in the European Union are bound by the Regulation (EC) No. 593/2008 of the European Parliament and of the Council of 17 June 2008 on the law applicable to contractual obligations (Rome I), which generally provides a framework for the determination of the law of closest connection governing contracts with cross-border elements in the EU.

82 *Enka Insaat Ve Sanayi AS v OOO Insurance Company Chubb* [2020] UKSC 38, para 95 *ff.*

83 Shouyu Chong & Felix Steffek, 'Enforcement of International Settlement Agreements Resulting from Mediation under the Singapore Convention: Private International Law Issues in Perspective' (2019) 31 *Singapore Academy of Law Journal* 448, paras 65–67. At this juncture it should be noted that the administration of the validation principle and *renvoi* have not received overwhelming judicial support at this point in time. The validation principle has recently been rejected by the Singapore High Court as a general statement of the law: *BNA v BNB* [2019] SGHC 142, paras 52–66. Yet it is noteworthy that the majority of the UK Supreme Court has been inclined to apply the validation principle as a choice of law technique to validate, specifically, arbitration agreements which would be valid under one jurisdiction's law but invalid under another (*Enka Insaat Ve Sanayi AS v OOO Insurance Company Chubb* [2020] UKSC 38, para 108); whether the validation principle as a choice of law methodology would be extended to the examination of iMSAs remains a matter up for debate. But it bears note that the 'pro-enforcement bias' underpinning the validation principle may be subject to much criticism in practice and theory, as it could potentially compromise party autonomy. *Renvoi* is a difficult concept to grasp, and also apply: David Alexander Hughes, 'The Insolubility of '*Renvoi*' and Its Consequences' (2010) 6 *Journal of Private International Law* 195.

to the governing law, the competent authority may address the following private law vitiating factors: misrepresentation, fraud, duress, undue influence or unconscionability.[84] Settlement agreements concluded in breach of anti-trust rules may be refused enforcement under this provision, as such agreements are likely to be deemed void by statute.[85] Defects that materialise subsequently should normally not render the iMSA 'null and void'.[86] Rather, the 'inoperative' limb may be relevant, where iMSAs may have become ineffective owing to circumstances transpiring at or following contractual conclusion.[87] This may be a result of poor drafting or careless incorporation of standard forms, producing iMSAs with inherently contradictory clauses that cancel each other out, rendering it sterile of any effect in the first place.[88] Alternatively, an iMSA may be rendered inoperable because of subsequent agreements to waive rights to pursue remedies under it.[89] iMSAs that are 'incapable of being performed' are (or become) impossible to execute, possibly due to supervening events transpiring after its conclusion,[90] or poor drafting.[91] The competent authority would, when applying the relevant governing law, administer contract law defences relating to contractual impossibility, frustration or other related defences.[92]

3.27 Third, iMSAs which are not binding, or are not final, according to their terms may be refused enforcement. These iMSAs may be conditioned by clauses that expressly or implicitly stipulate that they have no final or binding effect.[93] Reference to the appropriate governing law of the iMSA is essential. If Singapore law applies, where the iMSA resolves social and domestic disputes associated with a family business, a legal presumption that

---

84 Shouyu Chong & Felix Steffek, 'Enforcement of International Settlement Agreements Resulting from Mediation under the Singapore Convention: Private International Law Issues in Perspective' (2019) 31 *Singapore Academy of Law Journal* 448, para 69.

85 See, for instance, Competition Act 1998 (UK), s 2(4).

86 Nadja Alexander & Shouyu Chong, 'An Introduction to the Singapore Convention on Mediation – Perspectives from Singapore' (2018) 22(4) *Nederlands-Vlaams tijdschrisft voor Mediation en conflictmanagement* 37, 45.

87 Nadja Alexander & Shouyu Chong, 'An Introduction to the Singapore Convention on Mediation – Perspectives from Singapore' (2018) 22(4) *Nederlands-Vlaams tijdschrisft voor Mediation en conflictmanagement* 37, 45.

88 Shouyu Chong & Felix Steffek, 'Enforcement of International Settlement Agreements Resulting from Mediation under the Singapore Convention: Private International Law Issues in Perspective' (2019) 31 *Singapore Academy of Law Journal* 448, para 71.

89 Consider *Apple & Eve LLC v Yantai N Andre Juice Co* 610 F Supp 2d 226 (ED NY, 2009).

90 Nadja Alexander & Shouyu Chong, 'An Introduction to the Singapore Convention on Mediation – Perspectives from Singapore' (2018) 22(4) *Nederlands-Vlaams tijdschrisft voor Mediation en conflictmanagement* 37, 45.

91 See *Polish Supreme Court (Sqd Najwyzszy) Civil Chamber Division, Case No. V CSK 231/14 of (5 February 2015)* (Reported in English in the *Czech (& Central European) Yearbook of Arbitration* (2015) pp 214–216). Also see Aldo Frignani, 'Interpretation and Application of the New York Convention in Italy' in George A Bermann (ed), *Recognition and Enforcement of Foreign Arbitral Awards – The Interpretation and Application of the New York Convention by National Courts* (Springer 2017) p 568: an interesting example was reported in this publication, where a party from Italy and one from Syria agreed that 'any dispute arising ... shall be settled by a sole arbitrator. ... [T]he arbitrator shall be an expert in Swiss law and in the production of Arabic bread'. However, this agreement was determined by courts to be incapable of being performed for no arbitrator satisfying both conditions may be identified.

92 Shouyu Chong & Felix Steffek, 'Enforcement of International Settlement Agreements Resulting from Mediation under the Singapore Convention: Private International Law Issues in Perspective' (2019) 31 *Singapore Academy of Law Journal* 448, para 70.

93 Shouyu Chong & Felix Steffek, 'Enforcement of International Settlement Agreements Resulting from Mediation under the Singapore Convention: Private International Law Issues in Perspective' (2019) 31 *Singapore Academy of Law Journal* 448, para 48.

parties do not intend to create legal relations may need to be rebutted to prove its binding effect.[94]

3.28 Fourth, if the clauses in an iMSA have been validly modified (under the relevant governing law), the original agreement will be deemed ineffectual to the extent of the agreed variations. Consequently, only the varied iMSA shall be enforced. It follows logically that the iMSA under its original terms must be refused enforcement.

3.29 Fifth, if the obligations under an iMSA have been performed or satisfied (under the relevant governing law), it logically follows that the competent authorities must refuse its enforcement, since those obligations have been discharged. This circumvents the making of doubled claims by parties.

3.30 Sixth, if the iMSA is not drafted clearly or in comprehensible terms, the competent authorities may refuse to enforce it. Meticulous drafting is crucial. Key clauses and obligations (*eg*, price in a specified currency, or consideration owing from one party to another in exchange for specifically defined performances, or instalment payment schemes) must be elucidated with sufficient meticulousness and precision. The drafters of an iMSA should ideally set out the precise steps or measures expected or demanded of parties, particularly when the arrangements flowing from a compromise at mediation do not involve monetary payments. To illustrate, where a party has agreed to apologise to another, the obligations may be encapsulated in the resulting iMSA as such:

> Sara Pte Ltd shall publish the following words, 'We unconditionally and sincerely express our deepest apologies to Ellie AB and their associates for any embarrassment resulting from the words our employees have caused to be published on the *FunTube*, which is a popular video sharing site, and on their behalf offer to rescind those embarrassing statements made.' On the front pages of the relevant local newspapers, *The Fun Times* and *The Cheerful Nightly*, and on their social media platforms (such as *FunBook* and *Fun-Gram*), as a form of apology to Ellie AB, in return for Ellie AB's application to discontinue Suit No. XYZ/2020.

To conclude an iMSA on simplistically worded terms (*eg*, 'Sara Pte Ltd shall apologise to Ellie AB') is not advisable, as it may be deemed too unclear and imprecise for enforcement.

3.31 Seventh, an iMSA may be refused enforcement if enforcing it would be contrary to its terms. For instance, when conditions precedent or conditions subsequent have not been satisfied, the competent authority may refuse to enforce an iMSA, because the obligations may not have accrued at the time when enforcement is sought.[95] This provision accommodates instances where parties contractually opt out of the application of the Singapore Convention entirely.[96] It also gives effect to *force majeure* clauses: where a

94 *Ram Niranjan v Navin Jatia and others and another suit* [2019] 3 SLR 1037, para 84. Readers unfamiliar with Singapore law should note that the presumption is easily rebutted; but the High Court caveats that 'the facts, context and circumstances in each case must be carefully considered'.

95 United Nations Commission on International Trade Law, Working Group II (Dispute Settlement), *Report of Working Group II (Dispute Settlement) on the Work of Its Sixty-eighth Session* (A/CN.9/934) (New York, 5–9 February 2018) para 57.

96 Timothy Schnabel, 'The Singapore Convention on Mediation: A Framework for the Cross-Border Recognition and Enforcement of Mediated Settlements' (2019) 19 *Pepperdine Dispute Resolution Law Journal* 1, 56 *ff*; Hal Abramson, 'New Singapore Convention on Cross-Border Mediated Settlements: Key Choices' in Catherine Titi & Katia Fach-Gomez (eds), *Mediation in International Commercial and Investment Disputes* (Oxford University Press 2019) p 373.

contractually provided supervening event occurs and the iMSA accommodates for a discharge of obligations accordingly, the competent authority may refuse its enforcement under this provision, because it would be contrary to its terms to do so.[97]

Mediator conduct-related grounds for refusal

3.32 Article 5(1) of the Convention sets out two mediator conduct-related grounds for refusal. First, iMSAs may be refused enforcement where there was 'a serious breach by the mediator of standards applicable to the mediator or the mediation *without which breach that party would not have entered into the settlement agreement*' [emphasis added].[98] Parties must demonstrate that not only was there *egregious* conduct contravening mediator standards when the iMSA was concluded – taking reference from the proper standards[99] governing that mediation – the contravention must also be proven to have *caused or influenced* them to agree to that settlement agreement. Proving the element of causation is essential for this defence to succeed.[100]

3.33 The second mediator conduct-related defence is a narrower illustration falling inside the scope of the first ground, where:[101]

> [t]here was a failure by the mediator to disclose to the parties circumstances that raise justifiable doubts as to the mediator's impartiality or independence and *such failure to disclose had a material impact or undue influence on a party* without which failure that party would not have entered into the settlement agreement. [emphasis added]

Similarly, parties must prove that the mediator misconduct here has *caused or influenced* them to agree to the challenged settlement agreement. Specifically, parties must furnish real and credible evidence that the mediator's misconduct was one affecting their ability to be impartial or independent at mediation, leading to justifiable doubts of their aptitude. Consequently, there lies a duty for the affected mediator to reveal and disclose their compromised circumstances to the parties at mediation; where the mediator fails to do so, parties relying on this defence must *additionally* demonstrate that they were subject to undue influence[102] to enter into the iMSA, or that there was some other material influence flowing from the mediator's compromised circumstances – possibly manifesting itself as a misrepresentation as to the terms of the iMSA, a material non-disclosure of facts

97 Nadja Alexander & Shouyu Chong, *The Singapore Convention on Mediation: A Commentary* (Wolters Kluwer 2019) para 5.35.

98 The Singapore Convention on Mediation, Article 5(1)(e). Note that this aligns with Articles 6(4), 6(5) and 7(3) of the 2018 Model Law on International Commercial Mediation.

99 For a closer examination on how the proper standards governing a mediation may be determined, see Nadja Alexander & Shouyu Chong, *The Singapore Convention on Mediation: A Commentary* (Wolters Kluwer 2019) paras 5.99–5.102.

100 Nadja Alexander & Shouyu Chong, *The Singapore Convention on Mediation: A Commentary* (Wolters Kluwer 2019) para 5.88.

101 The Singapore Convention on Mediation, Article 5(1)(f). Note that this aligns with Articles 6(4), 6(5) and 7(3) of the 2018 Model Law on International Commercial Mediation.

102 See generally *Chan Gek Yong v Violet Netto (practising as L F Violet Netto) and another and another matter* [2019] 3 SLR 1218, where a party to a mediated settlement agreement attempted to challenge its validity owing to duress, some of which was allegedly attributed from the mediators; also see, for a case summary, Nadja Alexander & Shouyu Chong, 'Singapore Case Note: What Happens When a Party to an MSA Has a Change of Heart?' *Kluwer Mediation Blog* (17 October 2018).

and circumstances,[103] or an unconscionable[104] action amidst an unfortunate set of circumstances – *swaying its outcome*.

3.34 It bears note that the mediator conduct-related grounds for refusal, discussed in the preceding paragraphs, impose an exceptionally high threshold for the parties to show any mediator misconduct, if they plead these grounds when arguing that an iMSA should not be enforced. Both provisions require parties relying on the defences to show *egregious* breaches of the mediator, which *must raise justifiable doubts* on that mediator's ability to be impartial, all the circumstances of which *must have caused* the parties at the mediation table to have entered into the impugned iMSA.

Public policy

3.35 Under Article 5(2)(a), a competent authority may, by its own initiative,[105] refuse to enforce an iMSA that is 'contrary to the public policy'[106] of the State where enforcement is pursued. The public policy exception must be administered in light of prevailing private international law rules, which contemplates a scrutiny of *both* domestic and international conditions.[107] Whilst the domestic public policy of the State where enforcement is sought may be paid some regard, it has to be administered 'in a manner that is consistent, insofar as possible, with the objectives of the Convention and the public policies and interests of other Contracting States'.[108] Thus, the competent courts should only under *exceptional circumstances* exercise their discretion to refuse to enforce iMSAs by reason of public policy,[109]

103 As to what may constitute a material non-disclosure of facts and circumstances which could sway the outcome of a mediated settlement agreement, see the Singapore case of *Ram Niranjan v Navin Jatia and others and another suit* [2019] 3 SLR 1037, paras 75–79, and the appeal judgment delivered by the Singapore Court of Appeal at *Navin Jatia and others v Ram Niranjan and another and other appeals* [2020] 1 SLR 1098, paras 52–61.

104 The definition of unconscionable action by parties to a contract during the process of contract formation which may result in the avoidance of some contractual obligations has been clarified in the Singapore Court of Appeal recently in *BOM v BOK* [2019] 1 SLR 349: see para 142 *et seq*. An instance of an unconscionable action which may vitiate contractual obligations may be illustrated by the facts in *BOM v BOK* [2019] 1 SLR 349: where a wife takes advantage of the immense grief suffered by her estranged husband, whose mother had passed away suddenly and violently in a murder, to compel him to sign away *the entirety* of his multi-million dollar inheritance and put it on trust in favour of their infant child, this could be viewed by the Singapore courts as an unconscionable action which engenders vitiation of contractual obligations tainted by the wife's conduct.

105 Nadja Alexander & Shouyu Chong, *The Singapore Convention on Mediation: A Commentary* (Wolters Kluwer 2019) para 5.113; Timothy Schnabel, 'The Singapore Convention on Mediation: A Framework for the Cross-Border Recognition and Enforcement of Mediated Settlements' (2019) 19 *Pepperdine Dispute Resolution Law Journal* 1, 42. Of course, parties remain free to plead for the public policy defence to apply and submit evidence into court accordingly.

106 The Singapore Convention on Mediation, Article 5(2)(a).

107 Shouyu Chong & Felix Steffek, 'Enforcement of International Settlement Agreements Resulting from Mediation under the Singapore Convention: Private International Law Issues in Perspective' (2019) 31 *Singapore Academy of Law Journal* 448, para 55.

108 Gary Born, *International Commercial Arbitration* (2nd ed, Wolters Kluwer 2014) p 3655; although taken out of context (*ie*, Born's words refer to the Convention on the Recognition and Enforcement of Foreign Arbitral Awards (330 UNTS 3) (10 June 1958; entry into force 7 June 1959)), the phrasing of the words applies with equal logical force to the Singapore Convention on International Settlement Agreements Resulting from Mediation as well. See *Renusagar Power Co Ltd v General Electric Co* [1994] AIR 860, para 63.

109 Shouyu Chong & Felix Steffek, 'Enforcement of International Settlement Agreements Resulting from Mediation under the Singapore Convention: Private International Law Issues in Perspective' (2019) 31 *Singapore Academy of Law Journal* 448, para 55; see also Tiong Min Yeo, 'Statute and Public Policy in Private International Law: Gambling Contracts and Foreign Judgments' (2005) 9 *Singapore Yearbook of International Law* 133. The Singapore Court of Appeal has described exceptional circumstances as those which would 'shock the conscience'

for it is trite that under private international law rules, the public policy defence functions as an exceptional 'escape mechanism'.[110]

Subject matter of dispute not capable of settlement by mediation

3.36 Under Article 5(2)(b), competent authorities may, by their own initiative,[111] refuse to enforce iMSAs if the 'subject matter of the dispute is not capable of settlement by mediation under the law of that [State]'.[112] Quek Anderson observes that in the context of enforcing iMSAs under the Singapore Convention, it is likely that disputes involving disputants with seriously unequal bargaining power may be considered by the competent authorities to be not capable of settlement by mediation.[113] Although the choice of law defined here appears to point towards the *lex fori* of the competent authority, the court should administer and interpret it with similar private international law considerations as the 'public policy' defence, as discussed in the preceding paragraph. The subject matter defence functions as another exceptional 'escape mechanism' defence.[114] Whilst the enforcing court may decide under its own domestic laws that some subject matter areas are not susceptible to mediation (*eg*, some jurisdictions may consider certain types of intellectual property disputes are not capable of resolution at mediation),[115] they ought to provide due consideration of the extent

or be 'clearly injurious to the public good or ... wholly offensive to the ordinary reasonable and fully informed member of the public', or violate 'the forum's most basic notion of morality and justice' (*PT Asuransi Jasa Indonesia (Persero) v Dexia Bank SA* [2007] 1 SLR(R) 597, para 59).

110 Consider *IPCO Nigeria Ltd v Nigerian National Petroleum Corp* [2005] EWHC 726, para 13, where in the context of refusing to enforce arbitral awards under the New York Convention by reason of the relevant public policy exception, Gross J warned that 'considerations of public policy, if relied upon to resist enforcement of an [arbitral] award, should be approached with extreme caution ... [the public policy exception] was not intended to furnish an open-ended escape route for refusing enforcement of New York Convention awards'. It is also useful to consider a recent example where a dispute resolution outcome was not enforced based on the public policy exception: in *Daiichi Sankyo Company Limited v Malvinder Mohan Singh and ors* (2016) OMP(EFA) (Comm) 6/2016, the High Court of New Delhi exercised its discretion on public policy grounds to refuse to enforce part of an international arbitral award, because it bound young children (who were between the ages of 8 and 12 when the arbitration was conducted) to be jointly and severally liable to pay the equivalent of *more than £400 million* in damages, awarded by an arbitral tribunal seated in Singapore. It does not take a stretch of imagination to consider the rendering of such a whopping sum of damages against minors objectionable on both domestic and international levels of public policy. It is likely that similar considerations would apply when the courts in India – a party to the Singapore Convention – are presented with an iMSA binding young children for enforcement under the Singapore Convention.

111 Nadja Alexander & Shouyu Chong, *The Singapore Convention on Mediation: A Commentary* (Wolters Kluwer 2019) para 5.113; Timothy Schnabel, 'The Singapore Convention on Mediation: A Framework for the Cross-Border Recognition and Enforcement of Mediated Settlements' (2019) 19 *Pepperdine Dispute Resolution Law Journal* 1, 42. Of course, parties remain free to plead for the public policy defence to apply and submit evidence into court accordingly.

112 The Singapore Convention on Mediation, Article 5(2)(b).

113 Dorcas Quek Anderson, 'The Singapore Convention on Mediation: Supplying the Missing Piece of the Puzzle for Dispute Resolution' July [2020] *Journal of the Malaysian Judiciary* 194, para 50.

114 Nadja Alexander & Shouyu Chong, *The Singapore Convention on Mediation: A Commentary* (Wolters Kluwer 2019) para 5.110; Nadja Alexander & Shouyu Chong, 'An Introduction to the Singapore Convention on Mediation – Perspectives from Singapore' (2018) 22(4) *Nederlands-Vlaams tijdschrisft voor Mediation en conflictmanagement* 37, 49; Timothy Schnabel, 'The Singapore Convention on Mediation: A Framework for the Cross-Border Recognition and Enforcement of Mediated Settlements' (2019) 19 *Pepperdine Dispute Resolution Law Journal* 1, 55.

115 For instance, under South Korean law, some intellectual property disputes which touch on validity of intellectual property rights are not capable of settlement at mediation, as it is the orthodox view that such disputes must fall within the exclusive jurisdiction of the Korean Intellectual Property Office: see Gyooho Lee,

to which the said subject matter yields a sufficient nexus to the forum, before categorically applying domestic conditions unto the iMSA.[116] In private international law disputes, Born has convincingly postulated (albeit in the context of international commercial arbitration, but this may justifiably be analogised to the international commercial mediation context) that the courts should avoid parochialism when administering the 'subject matter' defence.[117] Instead, courts may apply the law of closest-connection to the dispute.[118]

How the Singapore Convention may impact international construction disputes

3.37 In recent years, mediation has become an increasingly popular forum for dispute resolution in the construction industry.[119] The *ARCADIS Global Construction Disputes Report 2019* reports that mediation is the overall second-most common method of alternative dispute resolution in ARCADIS's international construction law practice from 2017–2018;[120] in its practices in North America, the UK and Continental Europe, mediation was more commonly used than arbitration in construction disputes. Interestingly, these findings diverge from observations in an empirical study on international dispute resolution mechanisms, suggesting that users of dispute resolution services, for whom expedited enforceability of dispute resolution outcomes is of critical importance, are inclined to proceed to arbitration.[121]

Desirability of mediation

3.38 Yet in the context of international construction disputes, mediation is desirable because of several factors. First, mediation prioritises a preservation of working relationships between disputants, which is crucial in the construction industry as it is always hoped that works would resume either throughout the disputes process or after its conclusion;[122]

Keon-Hyung Ahn & Hacques de Werra, 'Euro-Korean Perspectives on the Use of Arbitration and ADR Mechanisms for Solving Intellectual Property Disputes' (2014) 30 *Arbitration International* 91, 104.

116 Shouyu Chong & Felix Steffek, 'Enforcement of International Settlement Agreements Resulting from Mediation under the Singapore Convention: Private International Law Issues in Perspective' (2019) 31 *Singapore Academy of Law Journal* 448, para 75.

117 Gary Born, *International Commercial Arbitration* (2nd ed., Wolters Kluwer 2014) p 3702.

118 Take the hypothetical scenario where under the laws of Country X, commercial tax disputes are subject matters incapable of settlement at mediation. The forum of Country X is presented with an iMSA that was concluded in Country Y, of which the choice of law for that settlement points to the laws of Country Z (noting that under the rules of Y and Z tax disputes are susceptible to mediation). If the mediated dispute has *no connection* whatsoever to Country X, the courts of Country X should not refuse relief owing to their convention obligations to enforce dispute resolution outcomes – see Gary Born, *International Commercial Arbitration* (2nd ed, Wolters Kluwer 2014) pp 606 & 3700.

119 Josephine Hage Chahine, Ettore Lombardi, David Lutran & Catherine Peulve, 'The Acceleration of the Development of International Business Mediation after the Singapore Convention' (forthcoming) *European Business Law Review*.

120 ARCADIS, *Global Construction Disputes Report 2019*, (2019) p 11.

121 See generally, Nadja Alexander, Janet Checkley, Shouyu Chong, *et al*, 'International Dispute Resolution Survey: Currents of Change (2019 Preliminary Report)', Singapore International Dispute Resolution Academy.

122 In the empirical study conducted by the Singapore International Dispute Resolution Academy in 2019 cited in the preceding note, it was observed that where relationship preservation is also considered critical, there is a marked shift towards the use of multi-tiered dispute resolution procedures *combining both mediation and arbitration*, especially in relation to complex and long-term projects in industries such as energy, construction and investment.

these relationships are likely to be destroyed when parties litigate their claims in court. Second, the mediation forum provides flexibility for parties to work around conflict and keeps disputants in the driver's seat when it comes to compromise solutions. The flexibility of mediation leaves disputants with the prerogative to fashion reasonable compromises with each other, procured along a reasonable case management timeline – keeping in mind that mediation may generally lead to a settlement agreement after one continuous session. Third, mediation is a cost-effective forum to resolve lower dollar-value disputes. Fourth, mediation is a confidential forum where disputants cannot be compelled against their will to disclose evidence, which may consist of sensitive commercial information.

Doubts about mediation

3.39 In another empirical study[123] involving stakeholders[124] in the construction industry in England, it was found that whilst mediation enjoys a high success rate for construction disputes – and that a majority of respondents were satisfied with the mediation process, cost and outcome – parties nevertheless had significant reservations about the forum. Importantly, the perceived lack of enforceability of a settlement agreement was flagged as a major concern.[125] These concerns may discourage them from proceeding to mediation, barring any form of direction from legal advisers and the courts.

3.40 Whilst, for instance, some legal practitioners have argued that parties' concerns may be alleviated by the fact that iMSAs can already be easily enforced under the English common law,[126] users may remain reluctant to proceed to mediation, especially if they are foreign parties unfamiliar with the nuances of English law, assuming that the iMSA is to be enforced in England. Besides, the risk of an English court refusing to enforce the terms of an iMSA is not insubstantial as it is subject to an array of common law and equitable contractual defences, whereas under the Singapore Convention, an iMSA may only be refused enforcement if the circumscribed defences set out in Article 5 are proven.[127]

3.41 Take for instance, the rule against penalty clauses[128] in English law remains a dynamic source of uncertainty in the enforcement of iMSAs, if it were left to be subsumed under ordinary contract law principles. It is not uncommon for commercially minded parties, when negotiating to conclude an iMSA, to insert clauses which provide for circumstances (*ie*, the triggering of secondary obligations, such as payment or transfer of assets) when terms of the main settlement agreement (*ie*, the primary obligations) are not

123 Jacquelyne Ann Gregory-Stevens, *Construction Disputes in England: The Option for Mediation* (2016) (Unpublished Doctoral Thesis, Anglia Ruskin University).

124 Participants in this study include clients (including local authorities), consultants, major/main contractors and sub-contractors/specialists/suppliers.

125 Jacquelyne Ann Gregory-Stevens, *Construction Disputes in England: The Option for Mediation* (2016) (Unpublished Doctoral Thesis, Anglia Ruskin University) pp 7–224, 8-239–8-240.

126 Michael Fletcher, 'Signed but Not Sealed: The Impact & Reach of the Singapore Convention on Mediation' (2019) *New Law Journal* 20 (20 September 2019), 21.

127 See Nadja Alexander & Shouyu Chong, *The Singapore Convention on Mediation: A Commentary* (Wolters Kluwer 2019) para 3.13.

128 *Cavendish Square Holding BV v Makdessi* [2015] UKSC 87; [2015] 3 WLR 1377.

complied with.[129] But since penalty clauses are taken to be *not enforceable*[130] under English law (rather than null and void, inoperative or incapable of being performed),[131] it appears unlikely that parties may successfully impugn an iMSA on the basis of any of the contract-related grounds for refusal set out in Article 5 of the Convention, if a dispute arises in relation to the iMSA over some provisions for secondary obligations which may arguably be construed as penalties.

Mediation of construction disputes and the Singapore Convention

3.42 It is undoubtedly important to disputants that once a settlement agreement has been concluded after mediation, any dispute resolution outcome would be worth its weight in respect to the time, expense and effort invested by the parties to negotiate for an amicable resolution to their dispute, so that disrupted projects may move forward accordingly. This is normally the case, because ordinarily, parties usually comply with the terms of the settlement agreements they have concluded.[132] In the worst-case scenario, where there is non-compliance or breach of the terms of the settlement agreement, additional expense is ordinarily required to commence further legal proceedings against the non-complying party, and it would be necessary to prove the existence of the mediated settlement agreement as an enforceable contract. In so doing, mediation confidentiality may (consequently) be compromised, because the parties are likely to need to submit mediation communications as evidence in court to prove the terms of the mediated settlement agreement.[133]

3.43 Therefore, it is argued that the Singapore Convention could potentially play a role in allaying these stakeholder concerns. As a multi-lateral instrument providing an *expedited* cross-border mechanism for enforcement of iMSAs, not only does the Convention legitimise mediation as a means of dispute resolution, it should also reduce the reluctance of stakeholders in the construction industry to proceed to mediation at the occurrence of a dispute, across jurisdictions which are State Parties to the Convention. The

129 See for instance, *Leiman, Ricardo and another v Noble Resources Ltd and another* [2020] 2 SLR 386: the parties in this case concluded a settlement agreement in relation to the plaintiff's departure from the defendant's employment. The effect of the settlement agreement was to provide for a severance package of share entitlements to the plaintiff. The terms of the settlement agreement contained a provision which purportedly allowed the defendant to disentitle the plaintiff from those shares in the event of non-compliance with the latter's non-competition and confidentiality obligations. The Singapore Court of Appeal found that the purported disentitlement clause, being a secondary obligations clause which comes into effect on the plaintiff's breach of his primary obligations under the settlement agreement to comply with his non-competition and confidentiality obligations, was not enforceable as it was a penalty clause.

130 Andrew Burrows, *A Restatement of the English Law of Contract* (Oxford University Press 2016) p 136; Mindy Chen-Wishart, *Contract Law* (6th ed, Oxford University Press 2018) p 656. The rule against penalty clauses in English law also applies to commercial contracts: see *Cavendish Square Holding BV v Makdessi* [2015] UKSC 87; [2015] 3 WLR 1377.

131 See the Singapore Convention, Article 5(1)(b)(i).

132 Chang-fa Lo & Janice Lee, 'A New Approach for the Settlement of Regional Disputes to Maintain Dynamic Stability – A Selective Elaboration of the Draft Agreement of the Establishment of the Asia-Pacific Regional Mediation Organization' (2018) 13(1) *Asian Journal of WTO & International Health Law and Policy* 27, 40–41; Shouyu Chong & Felix Steffek, 'Enforcement of International Settlement Agreements Resulting from Mediation under the Singapore Convention: Private International Law Issues in Perspective' (2019) 31 *Singapore Academy of Law Journal* 448, para 5.

133 Dorcas Quek Anderson, 'The Singapore Convention on Mediation: Supplying the Missing Piece of the Puzzle for Dispute Resolution' July [2020] *Journal of the Malaysian Judiciary* 194, para 17.

expedited enforcement mechanism lowers the cost of enforcement, as well as preserves the confidentiality of mediation proceedings. The Convention's impact on international dispute resolution in the construction industry is two-fold: not only will existing users enjoy greater confidence in the enforceability of their dispute resolution outcomes across borders, it is likely that more users would be encouraged to proceed to mediation when a dispute arises.[134]

Conclusion

3.44 The Singapore Convention offers to leave a significant impact on international dispute resolution practice. In theory, it will change the way we understand private international law. In practice, the Convention offers stakeholders, especially those in the construction industry, a useful risk management mechanism for disputes which may be best settled out of court, in appropriate[135] dispute resolution forums. As the Convention garners more signatories in the years to come, it is expected that mediation will become a more attractive forum for cross-border dispute resolution, as parties may engage in mediation with the confidence that an outcome flowing from the mediation process does not lead to futility, for it may be enforced under the Singapore Convention. It is hence imperative for stakeholders in the construction industry, especially those heavily involved or reliant on cross-border projects, to take a keen notice of its developments.

134 Stacie Strong, 'Use and Perception of International Commercial Mediation and Conciliation: A Preliminary Report on Issues Relating to the Proposed UNCITRAL Convention on International Commercial Mediation and Conciliation' (2014), University of Missouri School of Law Legal Studies Research Paper No. 2014–28, available at SSRN <https://papers.ssrn.com/sol3/papers.cfm?abstract_id=2526302> (accessed on 25 November 2018) p 45.

135 Sundaresh Menon, Chief Justice at the Supreme Court of Singapore, 'Mediation and the Rule of Law', keynote address at the Law Society Mediation Forum (10 March 2017), para 26.

PART II

ARTIFICIAL INTELLIGENCE
A game changer?

CHAPTER 4

The relevance of artificial intelligence for construction disputes

Erik Schäfer

Introduction

4.1 *LegalTec* has become a buzz-word for in-house lawyers and the providers of legal services. As is often the case one fashionable notion does not come alone. *LegalTec* as topic never comes alone. In public discourse *LegalTec* is related to artificial intelligence (AI), machine learning, and Distributed Ledger Technology (blockchain). A majority of debaters seems to assume that *LegalTec* will simply be a tool for more efficiently carrying out known tasks based on known processes. Thus, the debate focusses on AI aided document/information disclosure and decision making including legal research and semantic analysis of submissions. Another focus is the ethical aspect of legal decisions, which are partially or fully delegated to machines. Not much is to be heard of the question of how AI aided decision making may impact the development of the law, *eg*, may AI implicitly lead to a petrification of the law. Unfortunately, the discussion is not characterized by a solid understanding of how AI or machine learning work, the investment to make it work, and the capabilities of those systems.

4.2 This chapter will not deal with ethical implications. Using construction disputes as an example, it will rather challenge the idea that *LegalTec* will simply *offer old wine in new wineskins* and speculate about the likely uses of AI and other ICT-tools for dealing with issues arising in the course of construction projects that can become legal disputes.

Legal AI in construction disputes

4.3 Major civil and plant engineering projects will rarely end without any dispute having arisen among the various players. Insofar as these disputes concern the work as such and not only related matters, such as project finance alone, there are certain categories of issues that reoccur on a frequent basis, namely defects, variation orders, and delay. Especially, if FIDIC conditions are used for contracting contractual structures and allocations of risk and burden of proof also the basic features of contractual framework may reoccur in various projects. In spite of the unique facts of each dispute this allows us to recognize certain reoccurring patterns. Today, it is common knowledge that AI deploys its potential best whenever such reoccurring elements exist and are recorded in a form that the machine may process, *ie*, in digitized form.

4.4 One may be tempted to leapfrog fact finding and to focus directly on the dispute resolution (DR) process when thinking about a possible role of AI in future construction disputes. Indeed, DR specialists probably tend to analyze the prospects of implementing systems with an AI component within the framework of the professional processes they know and use. Either with certain fears or from the perspective of Tankredi in the famous novel by Giuseppe Tomasi di Lampedusa, *Il Gattopardo*: '*For everything to stay the same, everything must change.*' However, this hope may turn out to be futile. Whilst it is true that AI today offers fairly good levels of translation from one language to another, speech and text recognition, or semantic analysis for retrieving relevant content dispersed over storages devices in a network (*eg*, tools for document production and *privilege* analysis, or legal sources), its heralded reliable use in the decision making process is more uncertain in the middle term or even in the near future.

4.5 Why may this be the case? AI started many decades ago after the Second World War and relied on hierarchical rule modeling. This hit certain obstacles. Today's AI relies predominantly on machine learning that creates models and is based on sophisticated statistical algorithms. AI does not correlate to the real world, does not understand, but simply digests binary data.[1] Even if the output in the form of results that humans can read may look plausible and results produced by a human may look less plausible, there is no simple way to verify or falsify a result which is by its nature normative. Moreover, at this stage the algorithms obtained by machine learning do not 'explain' to humans the way in which they arrived at the results. This would even apply if the machine would use the result to assemble snippets from a repository of underlying reasons taken from a vast stock of data on judicial or arbitration decisions. There are also questions about development of the law by distinguishing cases and deciding cases on the basis of different facts. Another aspect requiring reflection is cultural or other bias of the AI system that result from the data input used for training. In the legal realm this is no trivial issue because a system trained on common law data may not automatically be supposed to have equal reliability in a Chinese or German law context. If one takes other areas of IT and the considerable investment for developing such huge AI systems as a reference point, there is a realistic probability that this kind of AI will be offered by a limited number of software providers with a small geographical spread even in cases where these license out to a much larger number of service providers. This, however, does not mean that such systems will not be rolled out and be trusted by users. If we correctly understand current trends, these will not affect construction disputes but rather the legal mass market in areas like recurring claims for transport fee recovery, traffic accidents, or private landlord-tenant disputes in a foreseeable future.

4.6 The pivotal element will remain the fact finding meaning that the facts of the case have to be established and transformed in a standardized format into binary sets of data which can be correlated to the legal data available to the machine. Presently, one may expect that these data are keyed or spoken in by humans in a required format. Thus, the validation of the accuracy of such input remains an issue and could leave opportunities for manipulation.

4.7 The manifold technical and ethical challenges do, however, not mean that AI will not gather momentum in the legal profession also for complex disputes such

1 A good concise summary of the present (2020) status of AI capabilities and limitations may be found the June 13th 2020 Edition of The Economist at p 36 ff. 'Steeper than expected,' in particular, see p 2 'The future Autumn is coming.'

as the typical construction dispute. For example, AI will play a role for automated translations,[2] transcripts, document retrieval and management, and literature search, where it will reduce the need for employing human resources. AI or *IT based smart solutions* may also play a role for preparing the agreements that underlie construction projects and the disputes which arise. AI or IT based smart solutions may also be used for selecting arbitrators and other decision makers from the increasingly vast pool of candidates by correlating information from the already known data bases and other sources such as published awards, etc. with the goal of identifying such qualified persons who are not only competent but also statistically most likely to rule in one's interest[3]. Interestingly, there is a possibility that this may favor the select group of people who are already very active, since more reliable data will be available on them. This contrasts to the *vending argument* that such systems will produce more diversity and open the path to new talent.

AI and ICT within the construction industry

The state of the art

4.8 Whilst the author does not share the '*AI Hype*' regarding comprehensive AI based decision making systems, he expects a greater impact on the level where the disputes arise, *ie*, on the party level. This will affect the kind of evidentiary means presented to arbitral tribunals or relied upon by the expert witnesses. It may also affect the parties' approach to claims and the disputes that arise.

4.9 As early as during the preparation of a bid and until the conclusion any construction project generates massive data. Until recently such data were recorded in a dispersed manner and – consequently – identifying, extracting, and understanding relevant information can be a daunting resource consuming task. One may assume that a lack of timely adequate information is, in addition to the human factor, at the root of many disputes that pile up during construction projects.

4.10 Any company involved in a construction project will strive to operate according to its financial plan and requirements. This requires stringent and efficient project management that seamlessly adapts to variations of external circumstances and optimizes resource usage. Claim management is only one annexed aspect.

4.11 Provided the cost of deployment and usage of IT Systems for managing construction projects is proportionate, their expected savings will cause any company and other stakeholders in construction projects to use an Integrated Engineering or Construction ERP (Enterprise Resource Planning)[4] system covering all activities related to its project activities. Since these ERPs allow nearly instant access to any new information or report

2 See for example Deeply at <www.deepl.com/translator> (last accessed 11 January 2021).

3 See for example from another legal field ipQuants at <https://ipquants.com/about-us/> (last accessed 11 January 2021).

4 Defined by WIKIPEDIA as 'integrated management of main business processes, often in real time and mediated by software and technology' (<https://en.wikipedia.org/wiki/Enterprise_resource_planning> (last accessed 11 January 2021)). An overview of some of those ERPs can be found for example on the Capterra website at: <www.capterra.com/construction-management-software/user-research-infographic> (last accessed 11 January 2021); <www.capterra.com/construction-management-software/> (last accessed 11 January 2021).

and all other project data, they can extract and relate any relevant information quasi in real time. They include functions such as document control, change orders, requests for information and submittals, project scheduling, transmittals, purchase orders, equipment and resources, bid proposals, job costing, communication and collaboration, safety management, time management, quality management, tailored workflows, and interfaces to other software. They can be connected to external information on databases on the Internet, such as currency exchange rates or weather forecasts/reports. Presently, this is achieved by preconfigured database queries that are displayed onscreen to the project management or whoever else within the company may need the information.

4.12 Another tool that may interface with the internal ERPs is Building Information Modeling Solutions (BIM).[5] ISO 19650:2019 defines BIM as: 'Use of a shared digital representation of a built asset to facilitate design, construction and operation processes to form a reliable basis for decisions.' If properly employed by timely and correctly entering the relevant data at all times during a project, these often Cloud[6] based solutions that are increasingly offered as Software as a Service[7] (SaaS) provide all stakeholders in a construction project the information they need in real time. This fact alone is likely to reduce the number of disputes which may arise from information deficits or delays in information receipt.

The immediate implications for today's arbitration procedures

4.13 Because these systems store all project data in machine readable defined formats they allow a retrospective analysis and digital reconstruction of recorded events, *ie*, the facts underlying any dispute that arises during or after the construction project. Therefore, such data will increasingly be used as means of proof or as evidence with which witnesses of fact or expert witnesses are confronted. To appropriately assess the evidence in such settings any decision maker, such as an arbitrator, will need to understand not only the representation of the system output (human-machine-interface) but also how these systems generally work and what their capacities and limitations are. They should also know the factors that may compromise the veracity and integrity of data that are being displayed.[8] Even if experts are used for 'educating' the decision makers, such knowledge will be needed in the event the experts do not agree. Of course, this type of requirement is as such

5 Defined by WIKIPEDIA as 'process supported by various tools, technologies and contracts involving the generation and management of digital representations of physical and functional characteristics of places.' <https://en.wikipedia.org/wiki/Building_information_modeling> (last accessed 11 January 2021), Some relevant solutions may be found here: <www.capterra.com/construction-management-software/#top-20> (last accessed 11 January 2021) or on the PAT RESEARCH website at <www.predictiveanalyticstoday.com/top-construction-project-management-software/> (last accessed 11 January 2021).

6 For a definition see WIKIPEDIA at <https://en.wikipedia.org/wiki/Cloud_computing> (last accessed 11 January 2021).

7 For a definition see WIKIPEDI at <https://en.wikipedia.org/wiki/Software_as_a_service> (last accessed 11 January 2021).

8 Experienced experts and lawyers in construction disputes realistically point out that all too often data capture on the construction site is and will remain deficient. However, since the stakeholders operate these systems for their immediate economic benefit they will continuously strive to remedy such deficiencies in one way or the other. Nonetheless, this aspect needs to be factored in when assessing the probative value of the presented digital information.

not new, especially in construction disputes, but additional skills are nonetheless becoming relevant.

The immediate implications for the pre-arbitral stages of disputes

4.14 More importantly, however, these Construction ERP and BIM use (virtual) central storage of all project data in databases that can be queried in real time and track all project related activities, which can also be more easily correlated by the operators. This as such is likely to improve project management efficiency and, consequently, also early problem identification and dispute avoidance. This creates massive amounts of data that are stored in machine readable and standardized formats and can be accessed easily by machines. These data are related to recurring activities/processes and multiple construction projects, and accessible to the system owners. This is a particularly good technical environment for machine learning components. Given the quantity of data available at any time, it is very difficult for humans to identify and interpret relevant critical data in the data heap. The weak human factor can be strengthened by using machine learning and AI for alerting to critical events and for planning their avoidance or mitigation. No wonder, therefore, that predictive analytics are about to be offered as functionality for such systems.[9] It is therefore rather likely that machine learning/AI components will be introduced step by step into Construction ERP and BIM on a modular basis where standardization potential is inherent to the concerned processes. Of course, these functionalities will essentially focus on improving project-, financial-, and risk-management as 'looking glasses' into the future. Resources for machine learning AI deployment will also be allocated to processes where the technical and financial risks are great enough for being critical to (financial) success; *ie*, also in the field of claims or disputes and their management. The outcome of past claims originating from comparable contractual agreements and circumstances could also be recorded in the Construction ERP and BIM systems or in interfacing systems, allowing for non-legal outcome prediction with increasing precision.

4.15 Considering that the ERP and BIM systems' reporting and accounting modules and their analytics user interfaces permit financial, project path, and other overviews, these data will narrow the gaps between conflicting interests and – increasing confidence and trust of users in their reliability assumed – will permit much better identification of the deltas in the parties' respective positions and their financial implications as is probably still the case today. This foreshadows that fewer disagreements need to escalate into legal disputes or that their scope will be narrower, unless they are driven by factors which exist outside the data heap in the BIM or ERP.

Windows of opportunity

4.16 As discussed earlier, data analytics' especially predictive methods based on machine learning AI are presently conceived as a forward looking tool for increasing performance

9 *Eg*, see PAT SEARCH at <www.predictiveanalyticstoday.com/category/reviews/construction-project-management-software/> (last accessed 11 January 2021).

on the project management and financial level. But it does not take much to identify their potential for running conflict outcome scenarios by running them backwards also on data coming from other projects and forwards for the project at issue depending on its stage with a view of obtaining a non-legal probability-based outlook on chances for succeeding with claims and their likely quantum. This provides a good ground for principled and more stringent and efficient settlement discussions that may dispose at least of some claims. All it takes is a provider of ERP or BIM solutions, especially among those who provide these as SaaS and host the data heaps to identify this opportunity and convert it into a coding task and find means to monetize the functionality. If such a solution is successfully rolled out, the next possible step could be factoring in past decisions rendered by arbitral tribunals and national courts which increasingly are available – probably in cooperation with another provider from the legal analytics field – with a view of further refining the outcome probability prediction. Given the earlier caveats concerning legal AI as decision producing technology, this is not likely to produce decisions but rather a drastic reduction of the issues that are submitted for a decision by way of adjudication (or expedited) arbitration proceedings.

Conclusion

4.17 If one considers the complexity, duration, and associated cost of most construction disputes, and the often-voiced need in the construction industry for swifter resolution, this kind of reduction of issues and the simplification concerning the establishment of facts seem to indicate that there should be a sufficiently great market for such functionalities. Whether external lawyers and arbitrators will embrace such changes is another matter.

4.18 This, however, does not imply that disputes related to construction projects will disappear because disputes can be triggered by external factors unrelated to project data, such as external (financial/political) interests of parties and/or the human factor.

4.19 Furthermore, the stakeholders of a project may use different Construction ERP or BIM that capture data relating to the same events but these data may not match for technical or other reasons. The construction software platforms may not have interfaces allowing for data exchange in critical fields. Consequently, also the machine learning/AI components may produce diverging results.

4.20 Therefore, due to technical imperfections, which are due to the immense complexity of construction, a project's Construction ERP and BIM may not provide sufficiently reliable and useful results for some time to come.

CHAPTER 5

Administering AI in arbitration

Maud Piers and Christian Aschauer

Introduction

5.1 In 2018, we published a series of contributions by eminent colleagues on the subject of new technologies and their impact on arbitration[1]. Since then, our profession has undergone much faster changes than we could reasonably foresee. In the wake of serious climate emergencies, there has been a growing awareness of environmental issues related to the conduct of arbitral proceedings such as the issue as to whether it is sustainable to promote in-person meetings even though there are more environmentally friendly alternatives in the form of virtual meetings.[2] As from January 2020, moreover, the COVID-19 emergency has been transforming our working lives, leading to a spectacular acceleration of the digitisation process and a proliferation of virtual hearings.[3] Against this background, the issue if and how artificial intelligence ('AI') might be used to assist or even replace arbitrators received less attention. From a broader perspective, commentators even speak about the advent of a new 'AI winter', mimicking the period from the early 1970s to the mid-1980s, when earlier excitement about the potential to build human-level intelligence had gone lost.[4]

5.2 However, since we are now able to see the limitations of AI more clearly, this may also be the ideal point in time to assess if and to what extent AI might be useful to conduct arbitral proceedings and decide controversies. In this vein, we will provide a definition of the term AI in a first step and refer to selected applications where AI is presently used in a legal context. Thereafter, we will deal with legal and non-legal barriers related to the use of AI, focusing in particular on the *intuitu personae* character of the arbitrator's work; the hidden biases built in AI as well as the lack of proper reasoning in decisions generated by AI and two issues related to the reasoning of the decision, *ie*, the *iura novit arbiter* discussion

1 M Piers and C Aschauer (eds), *Arbitration in the Digital Age – The Brave New World of Arbitration* (CUP 2018); with more contributions from MS Abdel Wahab, E Katsh, P Schaumann, M Burger-Scheidlin, E Schaefer, A Van Hooft, J Kroes-Lastochkina, S Nappert, P Cohen, R Wolff, A J Schmitz, P Cortés, T Cole, N Bassiri and M D Veit.

2 See a similar remark by S Nappert and P Cohen on 'ethical choices' in 'Robots redux: blockchain, AR and quantum computing explained to lawyers, their impact on the arbitral process, and why the time to act is now', p 22, at <www.researchgate.net/publication/335776761_ROBOTS_REDUX_Blockchain_AR_and_Quantum_Computing_Explained_to_Lawyers_Their_Impact_on_the_Arbitral_Process_and_Why_The_Time_To_Act_Is_Now> (last accessed 23 July 2020).

3 G Flecke-Giammarco, G Bücheler & L Zahner, *Arbitrating in Uncertain Times – Institutional Responses to COVID-19* (SchiedsVZ 2020) p 133.

4 *The Economist*, 11 July 2020 edition.

and equitable elements of decision-making. We have reserved a special subsection for the critical issues that may arise if we use AI in the arbitrator selection process. Lastly, we will draw tentative conclusions.

Definition of artificial intelligence and examples where AI is presently used in a legal context

5.3 AI is a term that was devised in 1956 by a computer scientist named John McCarthy to describe the science and engineering of computer systems that behave in a way that seems to require brains.[5] Throughout the history of AI, various definitions have been offered and they all reflect on the question of what makes a machine 'intelligent'.[6] In an effort to detect when a machine is intelligent, researches have consistently drawn comparisons with human intelligence and intelligent tasks that we intuitively associate with the human mind.[7] However, the understanding of intelligence which is based on the Binet-Simon Scale – also known as the IQ test – has also been challenged. Human intelligence is now understood to be a much broader concept that is not exclusively measured by the standard of linguistic and logical-mathematical skills but also includes a diverse range of components including creative, spatial, kinaesthetic and emotional intelligence.[8] This broader concept of intelligence, in fact, allows us better to distinguish between artificial intelligence and human intelligence where it is now accepted that there are a number of intelligences that are unique to humans.

5.4 A more recent definition of AI, which avoids the circular reference to human intelligence, is proposed in a European Commission Communication from the Commission to the European Parliament, the European Council, the Council, the European Economic and Social Committee and the Committee of the Regions on Artificial Intelligence for Europe.[9] According to this definition, AI refers to '*systems that display intelligent behaviour by analysing their environment and taking actions – with some degree of autonomy – to achieve specific goals. AI-based systems can be purely software-based, acting in the virtual world (eg voice assistants, image analysis software, search engines, speech and face recognition systems) or AI can be embedded in hardware devices (eg advanced robots, autonomous cars, drones or Internet of Things applications)*'. Under

5 J McCarthy, 'What Is Artificial Intelligence?' (2007) at <http://jmc.stanford.edu/articles/whatisai/whatisai.pdf> (last accessed 23 July 2020) at p 2.

6 S Russell & P Norvig, *Artificial Intelligence: A Modern Approach* (Pearson Education Limited 2016) 1020.

7 Think of the Turing test where the intelligence of a machine is measured based on whether its actions can be distinguished from a human's. This was then later challenged by John Searle who, on the basis of his Chinese room argument, argued against the idea that machines could have intelligent minds like humans. JR Searle, 'Minds, Brains and Programs' (1980) 3(3) *Behavioral and Brain Sciences* 417–457. On the latter argument, see also: <www.youtube.com/watch?v=18SXA-G2peY> (last accessed 23 July 2020).

8 K Davis, J Christodoulou, S Seider & H Garner, 'The Theory of Multiple Intelligences' in Robert J Sternberg & Scott Barry Kaufman (eds), *The Cambridge Handbook of Intelligence* (Cambridge University Press 2011) 485–503, see also at: <https://howardgardner01.files.wordpress.com/2012/06/443-davis-christodoulou-seider-mi-article.pdf> (last accessed 23 July 2020).

9 Communication from the Commission to the European Parliament, the European Council, the Council, the European Economic and Social Committee and the Committee of the Regions on Artificial Intelligence for Europe, Brussels, 25.4.2018 COM(2018) 237 final.

this definition, rationality or '*the ability to choose the best action to take in order to achieve a certain goal, given certain criteria to be optimized and the available resources*' is a primary indicator of intelligence.[10]

5.5 Building onto this definition, the High-Level Expert Group on Artificial Intelligence, set up by the European Commission in 2018,[11] proposed that

> *Artificial intelligence (AI) systems are software (and possibly also hardware) systems designed by humans that, given a complex goal, act in the physical or digital dimension by perceiving their environment through data acquisition, interpreting the collected structured or unstructured data, reasoning on the knowledge, or processing the information, derived from this data and deciding the best action(s) to take to achieve the given goal. AI systems can either use symbolic rules or learn a numeric model, and they can also adapt their behaviour by analysing how the environment is affected by their previous actions.*

Thus, an essential feature of AI is machine-learning and the fact that AI systems are able to improve their own performance by modifying and creating new algorithms in response to new data with limited human intervention.[12]

5.6 Computers that mimic human intelligence have caught on in various white-collar sectors. One of the most notable examples is the field of medicine where machines have proficient knowledge on particular diseases and have been seen to outperform human medical professionals in diagnostics regarding their very specific clinical expertise. Unsurprisingly, the whole idea of having an AI reading and analysing thousands of pages has also been explored and made operational in the legal sector.[13] Various commercial AI tools are promoted as being quicker[14] and more thorough than counsel in performing

10 AI HLEG, A Definition of AI: Main Capabilities and Disciplines, 8 April 2019, p 1, at <https://ec.europa.eu/futurium/en/ai-alliance-consultation/guidelines> (last accessed 23 July 2020).

11 This AI HLEG was set up to support the European Union's Strategy on Artificial Intelligence. See also: <https://ec.europa.eu/digital-single-market/en/high-level-expert-group-artificial-intelligence> (last accessed 23 July 2020).

12 The AI HLEG makes clear that AI includes several approaches and techniques, 'such as machine learning (of which deep learning and reinforcement learning are specific examples), machine reasoning (which includes planning, scheduling, knowledge representation and reasoning, search, and optimization), and robotics (which includes control, perception, sensors and actuators, as well as the integration of all other techniques into cyber-physical systems)'. Artificial intelligence is indeed mentioned alongside various terms such as algorithms, machine learning, neural networks, robotics, etc. Also, there are various types of AIs, such as narrow or weak and general or strong AI, etc. For an explanation of all these definitions, we would refer to the relevant literature (See references in, for instance: M Scherer, 'Chapter V: The Vienna Innovation Propositions, International Arbitration 3.0 – How Artificial Intelligence Will Change Dispute Resolution' in C Klausegger, P Klein, et al (eds), *Austrian Yearbook on International Arbitration 2019*, Austrian Yearbook on International Arbitration (Manz'sche Verlags- und Universitätsbuchhandlung 2019), 503–514; J Hope, 'Chapter 7: Can a Robot Be an Arbitrator?' in A Calissendorff & P Schöldstrom (eds), *Stockholm Arbitration Yearbook 2019*, Stockholm Arbitration Yearbook Series, Volume 1 (Kluwer Law International 2019) pp 103–120 as well as to the document defining AI and these related terms (AI HLEG, A Definition of AI: Main Capabilities and Disciplines, 8 April 2019, p 2–5, at <https://ec.europa.eu/futurium/en/ai-alliance-consultation/guidelines> (last accessed 23 July 2020)).

13 For a recent overview of the top ten applications of AI in law, see: KC Cheung, 'Top 10 Applications of AI in Law', at <https://algorithmxlab.com/blog/top-10-applications-artificial-intelligence-in-law/#The_Automation_of_Basic_Tasks> (last accessed 23 July 2020).

14 Which may also have the perhaps undesirable effect of leading to fewer billable hours?

legal research (eg, ROSS Intelligence,[15] CARA AI[16]) and drafting legal documents (eg, Compose,[17] Leverton[18]).

5.7 AI has also proven to be relevant in the context of adjudication, and in particular for the purpose of predictive justice, where pattern recognition comes into play (eg, Ravel Law[19] or Premonition[20]). In 2016, an AI was developed that predicted verdicts of the European Court of Human Rights with 79% accuracy.[21] In 2002 and again in 2014, AI specialists designed a computer that predicted the outcome of proceedings before the U.S. Supreme Court and, more specifically, forecasted whether the U.S. Supreme Court would quash or confirm a specific decision of a lower court. It did so with a 70.9% accuracy rate.[22] When the same task was assigned to a group of legal experts, they did so with a mere 59% accuracy.[23] To properly assess these results, however, it is necessary to be aware of the different methods applied by human legal experts as opposed to the computer: While the human legal experts studied the law and applied it to the facts of the case (and presumably used also a bit of their legal 'instinct'), the computer was provided only with five categories of information: the circuit of the lower court; the field of law (such as criminal law or labour law); the characterisation of the parties (such as banks, consumers); the possible political bias in the decision of the lower court (such as conservative or liberal); and the question of whether the matter related to the constitutionality of a legal norm. Importantly, and contrary to what lawyers have been trained to do, the computer did not consider the facts of the case or the applicable law.[24]

5.8 As impressive as the accuracy of predictive justice algorithms may seem, we do not wish to embark on a tentative assessment of what surprises or horrors await us if we actually begin working with AI. In what follows, we will rather focus on specific legal and non-legal barriers which would appear to directly prohibit the use of AI in the arbitrator's decision-making process and pose questions (rather than provide answers) on the issues that may arise when we reflect on introducing AI.

---

15 <https://rossintelligence.com/> (last accessed 23 July 2020).

16 <https://casetext.com/cara-ai> (last accessed 23 July 2020).

17 <https://compose.law> (last accessed 23 July 2020).

18 <https://leverton.ai> (last accessed 23 July 2020).

19 <https://home.ravellaw.com> (last accessed 23 July 2020).

20 <https://premonition.ai/tag/artificial-intelligence> (last accessed 23 July 2020).

21 N Aletras, D Tsarapatsanis, D Preoţiuc-Pietro & V Lampos, 'Predicting Judicial Decisions of the European Court of Human Rights: A Natural Language Processing Perspective' (2016) 2 *PeerJ Computer Science* 93, at <https://peerj.com/articles/cs-93> (last accessed 23 July 2020).

22 DM Katz, MJ Bommarito & J Blackman, 'A General Approach for Predicting the Behavior of the Supreme Court of the United States' (2017), at <https://doi.org/10.1371/journal.pone.0174698> (last accessed 23 July 2020).

23 DM Katz, MJ Bommarito & J Blackman, 'A General Approach for Predicting the Behavior of the Supreme Court of the United States' (2017), at <https://doi.org/10.1371/journal.pone.0174698> (last accessed 23 July 2020).

24 L Bull & F Steffek, *Die Entschlüsselung rechtlicher Konflikte* (ZKM 2018) 166.

Legal and non-legal barriers related to the use of AI

AI as decision-maker

Intuitu personae character of the arbitrator's work

5.9 In many jurisdictions, the law requires arbitrators to have full legal capacity. Sometimes, the law or the applicable rules of arbitration refer to qualities only humans possess, such as gender or nationality. To give an example, one might think of section 26(1) of the English Arbitration Act 1996, which states that (emphasis added) '*[t]he authority of the arbitrator is personal and ceases on* his death'. Similarly, section 812(1) of the Italian Civil Procedure Code[25] or to Section 606(1) of the Austrian Civil Procedure Code[26] refer to the legal capacity of the arbitrator or his or her signature, respectively. Death, legal capacity and the command of a signature are characteristic of human beings.

5.10 Furthermore, the default solution under many arbitration laws is a panel of three arbitrators, with each side selecting one arbitrator.[27] However, the concept of a three-member arbitral tribunal is moot if we use AI. It is difficult to establish the role one AI might have within a panel of three AIs. In addition, we find barriers to non-human arbitrators present in arbitration rules, such as Article 6.1 of the LCIA Rules 2020 or Art. 15(5) of the 2020 Rules of the Milan Chamber of Arbitration, which refer to the nationality of arbitrators.

5.11 This being said, the question remains whether the human decision-maker is allowed to rely on an AI as an 'assistant', 'helper' or 'administrative secretary'. A number of legal issues come to mind here, which will require resolution. To what extent may a tribunal employ AI in writing an award? May a tribunal 'outsource' the assessment of the credibility of testimonies to an AI which could then help notice inconsistencies between a witness's statements and the file presented by the parties, or spot lies through the assessment of a witness's body language? To what extent can arbitrators be said to retain their decision-making function if AI systems weigh up the data pertaining to the case and lead arbitrators by the hand, so-to-speak, to a conclusion? Must tribunals obtain the parties' consent to use AI or is AI a regular legal research tool unless parties opt out? Will parties and courts dealing with annulment/enforcement be entitled to see the advice of the AI? If yes, could an award rendered in breach of this unwritten rule be annulled or not enforced? It is evident that, here, some inspiration might be drawn from the rules concerning administrative secretaries and tribunal-appointed experts,[28] such as the ICC Notes to parties and arbitral tribunals on the conduct of arbitration.[29]

---

25 'Non può essere arbitro chi è privo, in tutto o in parte, della capacità legale di agire.' / 'Those who are lacking legal capacity to act, in part or entirely, cannot act as arbitrators'.

26 'Der Schiedsspruch ist schriftlich zu erlassen und durch den Schiedsrichter oder die Schiedsrichter zu unterschreiben' / 'The award shall be made in writing and shall be signed by the arbitrator or arbitrators'.

27 Article 11(3) UNCITRAL Model Law.

28 It will also be interesting to draw the parallel with the courts' reliance on technological tools to help them come to a decision. See also, in this regard, the reference in footnote 33 to the US courts' reliance on COMPAS. On this point, see also: F Uribarri Soares, 'New Technologies and Arbitration', *Indian Journal of Arbitration Law*, 2018/VII, 97.

29 Marg nos. 184–185.

Hidden biases of the AI

5.12 It will also be important to consider the requirement of independence and impartiality that applies in the context of non-human decision-makers. The avoidance of an appearance of bias on the part of an arbitrator is the cornerstone of arbitration. The IBA Guidelines on Conflict of Interest ('Guidelines') are often consulted to assess the impartiality and independence of an arbitrator. There are numerous examples of instances where the AI-arbitrator would appear to be biased and thus needed to be challenged.

5.13 To give but one example, a scenario that always objectively raises doubt as to independence and impartiality is where an arbitrator and a party or counsel share the same 'identity' (Guidelines, Part II (1)). Lawyers in the same law firm are considered to have the same 'identity' (Guidelines, General Standard (6)). One could wonder whether an AI shares the same 'identity' as the software company that built it or whether the identity of an AI is the result not of its creator, but rather of the data fed into it?

5.14 Another example that might cast doubt over an arbitrator's impartiality or independence is where there are more than two previous appointments of an arbitrator by the same party or its affiliates within the past three years (Guidelines, Part II (3.1)). Since one AI-arbitrator could replace multiple human arbitrators, the occurrence of multiple re-appointments or use of an AI-arbitrator by a party or its affiliates would not be unlikely. Would multiple re-appointments or multiple use of the same AI-arbitrator be permitted under the Guidelines (or any other laws on this subject, for that matter)?

5.15 These legal issues are related to questions that may arise if we consider the possible bias inherent in AI as such, but at the same time they are of a fundamentally different nature. As explained earlier, AI systems are self-learning. Depending on the learning approaches and the learning tasks associated with those,[30] they enhance their output through a feedback system.[31] The feedback system that improves AI may, at the same time, also turn out to be its Achilles' heel, since it is prone to reinforcing the unconscious bias of its developers. Algorithmic bias is a direct result of the 'human element' that influences either the design of the algorithm or the data that are used to train the algorithm, or both.[32] For example, there was considerable criticism on the AI powered risk assessment system known as COMPAS[33] which was used by a number of U.S. courts in the context of parole decisions to help predict criminal recidivism.[34] This self-learning algorithm was said to

30 On the different approaches to machine learning and on the different feedback systems, see: TO Ayodele, 'Types of Machine Learning Algorithms' in Y Zhang (ed), *New advances in Machine Learning* (IntechOpen 2010), available at <www.intechopen.com/books/new-advances-in-machine-learning/types-of-machine-learning-algorithms> (last accessed 23 July 2020).

31 With Ross, for instance, lawyers can give the response a thumbs-up or thumbs-down so that the system can learn and perfect future responses.

32 On algorithmic bias and the role of the human element in this, see: W Byrne, 'Now Is the Time to Act to End Bias in AI' 2 August 2018, available at <www.fastcompany.com/40536485/now-is-the-time-to-act-to-stop-bias-in-ai> (last accessed 8 July 2020); B Dickson, 'What Is Algorithmic Bias?' 26 March 2018, available at <https://bdtechtalks.com/2018/03/26/racist-sexist-ai-deep-learning-algorithms/> (last accessed 23 July 2020); M McElaney, 'Cognitive Bias in Machine Learning' 17 August 2018, available at <https://medium.com/codait/cognitive-bias-in-machine-learning-d287838eeb4b> (last accessed 23 July 2020).

33 COMPAS stands for Correctional Offender Management Profiling for Alternative Sanctions. On this tool, see: <https://en.wikipedia.org/wiki/COMPAS_(software)> (last accessed 23 July 2020).

34 C Sim, 'Will Artificial Intelligence Take Over Arbitration' in L Boo and GB Born (eds) (2018) 14(1*) Asian International Arbitration Journal*, 3; A Liptak, 'Sent to Prison by a Software Program's Secret Algorithms', *New York Times*, at <https://nyti.ms/2qoe8FC> (last accessed 23 July 2020); I Ng and V Benedetti del Rio,

reflect and even exacerbate the bias of its programmers and thus the data with which it was trained. Another criticism was that it was impossible for these robots to 'unlearn' their biases unless their algorithms could be corrected and were thus transparent – which they were not. This black box problem[35] – also known as the replication problem – as well as the potential algorithmic bias of an AI are important considerations in favour of having a *human* tribunal carefully overlook the predictions made by an AI.[36]

AI and 'reasoning'

5.16 The black box or replication problem that we touched upon is also a cause for reflection when it comes to the obligation to have a reasoned decision. AI does not produce reasons within the current definition of that concept, *ie*, an account of the facts which the tribunal found to be true, the evaluation of the evidence adduced by the parties, the discussion of the relevant legal norms, the parties' comments on the relevant legal norms and the final legal assessment of the tribunal. If we work with AI, the reasons underlying its decision or prediction are to be found in the way its algorithm is devised and in the data that are used to train the algorithm. Hence, the precise reasons for the AI's decision may be inscrutable.

5.17 What does this mean for a society where the duty to give reasons for legal decisions is part of the rule of law? When an AI proposes a certain decision for the tribunal's review, one might wonder whether an AI-award should not be subjected to more thorough human oversight prior to adoption of the award by a tribunal, for instance, through some form of judicial scrutiny as is now performed by some arbitration institutions.[37]

5.18 A question also arises as to what happens when a tribunal is later called upon to correct or supplement the award made by an AI or in which an AI assisted. 'Flawed' algorithms can produce flawed or at least unintended outputs. Presumably, in order for an AI to correct such an error one must first correct its algorithm. Could the human operating the AI directly intervene to quickly correct a computational error or would that usurp the AI or the arbitrator's decision-making power?

5.19 Moreover, to supervise or at least understand the work of AI, specialised knowledge and experience is required. Will the courts need technical schooling to understand how an arbitration procedure came about and to assess whether it complies with the standard of due and equitable process? Should courts be supplied with knowledge as to how the AI weighs factors in delivering its decisions?

'Chapter 8: When the Tribunal Is an Algorithm: Complexities of Enforcing Orders Determined by a Software under the New York Convention' in Katia Fach Gomez and Ana M. Lopez-Rodriguez (eds), *60 Years of the New York Convention: Key Issues and Future Challenges* (Kluwer Law International 2019) 122.

35 P Hocquet, 'Trust, and Don't Verify: The AI Black Box Problem', *medium.com*, 2 October 2017, at <https://medium.com/@PhilippeHocquet/trust-and-dont-verify-the-ai-black-blox-problem-442c2b15e79e> (last accessed 23 July 2020).

36 The European Commission also seems to suggest that the 'black-box effect' of AI-based products that are used in what the Commission calls 'critical domains' may require some form of human oversight. Report from the Commission to the European Parliament, the Council and the European Economic and Social Committee on the safety and liability implications of Artificial Intelligence, the Internet of Things and Robotics, Brussels 19 February 2020, COM(2020) 64 final, p 9. The Commission indicates that it would be particularly important for human enforcers to be able to trace the responsibility of AI systems behaviours and choices, and to do so without having to understand how the system reached the algorithmic decisions it reached. Even though the Commission does not specify what it means by critical domains, we believe it is relevant to ponder on this recommendation in the context of arbitration, as well.

37 With as a foremost example the ICC International Court of Arbitration.

5.20 We all know the maxim that arbitration is only as good as its arbitrators. Perhaps we will have to get used to the new aphorism that arbitration is only as good as the algorithm that drives it and the data-set on which it relies. In other words, AI arbitration, if permitted, will not completely rule out human intervention, but it may change the emphasis and nature of human intervention.

Iura novit arbiter

5.21 Another question that alludes to the role of arbitrators concerns the way in which arbitrators ascertain the contents of the applicable law. With only rare and modest exceptions, arbitration laws and rules do not specify how arbitrators should acquire information about the contents of the applicable law. There are only instruments of soft law to rely on for guidance.[38] If arbitrators' sole function is to resolve the dispute presented by the parties, then arbitrators presumably may (or perhaps *must*) determine the law based solely on what the parties tell them it is. However, arbitrators may be said to have further obligations, deriving from professionalism, from a pledge to the parties or an institution that they will decide a dispute according to law, or from public policy considerations. In light of those further duties, it may be imperative for arbitrators to retain the ability to probe beyond what the parties say about the applicable laws and rules.[39]

5.22 Building on this '*iura novit curia*' discussion, one must consider whether an AI(-assisted) arbitrator ought to have the freedom to investigate beyond the parties' arguments and pleadings as to the contents of the applicable law. But which sources of law should such an AI rely on to determine the contents of the applicable law? Besides statutes and regulations, should weight be given to judicial decisions, scholarly articles, legislative history or even non-national sources, such as the *lex mercatoria*, or customary law usages/course of dealing/contractual provisions? What is the relative weight to be given to each such source of law and importantly, who will identify the relevant legal sources and determine their priorities? Another issue concerns the question whether AI(-assisted) arbitrators should and could accept (or invoke) novel interpretations of the law in the event that the contents of the applicable rules cannot be sufficiently ascertained (as may be the case where the applicable law is undergoing rapid, radical and comprehensive legal transformations).

Equitable element of arbitral decision-making

5.23 These issues also raise more technical questions on the data fed into an AI-arbitrator and the weight that an AI algorithm should give to all these different data. In order to create a high-performance, legitimate AI(-assisted) arbitrator, from a merely legal point of view,[40] it will be important to clearly establish the various considerations that underlie an arbitral tribunal's decision on the merits. This will require a decision as to whether arbitrators

38 Recommendations 9 et seq of the ILA Resolution No. 6/2008 on Ascertaining the Contents of the Applicable Law in International Commercial Arbitration.

39 ILA Resolution No. 6/2008 on Ascertaining the Contents of the Applicable Law in International Commercial Arbitration.

40 We are not even talking about whether it will be possible to gather sufficient relevant data, given the confidential nature of arbitration and the limited number of cases that are produced through arbitration as opposed to litigation. Again, on this question of the potential of AI for arbitration, see: K Ongenae, 'AI and Arbitrators ... Does Not Compute' in J De Bruyne en C Van Leenhove, *Robots, AI and the Law in Belgium*, (Intersentia 2021).

should merely apply (positive) law, or may also consider equitable factors even when they are not specifically empowered to act as *amiable compositeurs*.

5.24 Research indicates that when reaching a decision on the merits, arbitrators take account of equitable factors in addition to the application of the law and, in effect, sometimes act – at least to a certain extent – as hidden *amiable compositeurs*.[41] This reliance on what some might call the 'intuitive sense of justice'[42] may disappear where the decision is made or inspired by AI, since its algorithm will need to factor in whether or not the AI should also consider equitable factors.

5.25 This raises a number of legal questions. For instance, if we take as our starting point the principle that arbitrators make decisions in accordance with the applicable law, would an AI that considers non-legal factors then contravene the parties' mandate that the dispute be decided in accordance with the applicable law? The concept of an AI arbitration thus unavoidably revives the age-old jurisprudential debate between natural law and legal positivism theorists[43] and will need to be discussed. This is also where some commentators flag a few essential limits to the AI's ability to adjudicate and call for a human arbitrator to have the last word if we do not want a mere sterile application of the law in arbitration.[44]

5.26 Presumably, data mining of past awards will be used to determine to which (legal and non-legal) factors arbitrators should attach weight. Using a text-based predictive model to build an AI-assistant or AI-arbitrator is in essence a direct application of the third key theory of law, namely legal realism, which prescribes that law should be understood and determined by the actual practices of courts.[45] This leads to a more fundamental question: Is it desirable that the output of past cases should chiefly dictate the model by which AI-assistants and arbitrators make predictions? If yes, do we have to fear that future changes of societal views and values that affect such decisions are not reflected proportionately in an AI-award?[46]

5.27 These and many other questions will be governed by the *lex arbitri* that governs the arbitration procedure. However, one could wonder whether the *lex arbitri* will have the same impact when parties agree on an arbitration that is supported or conducted by an AI. Could an AI-arbitrator and the algorithm underlying its functioning be considered a 'law' or an 'institutional set of rules' that the parties have chosen? Also, would the AI and the algorithm be governed by the *lex arbitri* or rather by one or the other substantive law? This also begs the question of where these rules must be situated in the hierarchy of norms.

---

41 See eg. E Sussman, 'Arbitrator Deliberations: The Impact of the Unconscious on Decision Making' (2014) 7(2) *New York Dispute Resolution Lawyer* 8; S Farnck, A van Aaken, et al, 'Inside the Arbitrator's Mind' (2017) 16 *Emory Law Journal* 1115; MH Malin and M Biernat, 'Do Cognitive Biases Infect Adjudication? A Study of Labor Arbitrators' (2008) 11(1) *U of Pennsylvania Journal of Business Law* 175.

42 F Uribarri Soares, 'New Technologies and Arbitration' (2018) VII *Indian Journal of Arbitration Law* 97.

43 HLA Hart, *The Concept of Law* (Oxford University Press 1961) 261.

44 E Montoya Zorrilla, 'Towards a Credible Future: Uses of Technology in International Commercial Arbitration' (2018) 6 *SchiedsVZ* 112; G Van Nieuwenhuyse, 'Arbitration and New Technologies: Mutual Benefits' (2018) 35(1) *Journal of International Arbitration* 126.

45 C Wells, 'Holmes on Legal Method: The Predictive Theory of Law as an Instance of Scientific Method' *Boston College School Faculty Papers*, 1994, 329; OW Holmes, Jr, Book Notices, (1880) 14 AM L REV 233–34.

46 Or is AI not at all suitable for decision-making, assessment and prediction in areas of great societal change (such as the law), and would it need frequent human curating or modification to update its performance?

AI, outcome prediction and arbitrator selection

5.28 Algorithmic bias and the replication problem also lead to a number of challenging practical and legal questions with regard to the selection process. The selection of arbitrators is often said to be the most critical step in the proceedings. Parties aim to nominate an arbitrator with a minimum appearance of bias, but who is nevertheless positively predisposed towards their case. Parties learn about a human arbitrator's legal disposition by considering publications or prior legal engagements as arbitrator or counsel.

5.29 This brings us back to the example of outcome prediction discussed earlier, where a computer had forecast the outcome of U.S. Supreme Court decisions with a higher accuracy rate than human legal experts. If we consider the nature of cases which reach the highest courts of any given jurisdiction, we will note that they involve very complex legal and factual patterns and that they are highly contentious. Otherwise, they would not find their way through the lower courts. In deciding these cases, the highest courts actually exercise a broad margin of interpretation and can apply all kinds of legal craftmanship. We submit that in these situations, non-legal factors are much more relevant than in other cases – the huge majority of cases – where everything revolves around settled law.

5.30 Now, if we consider the nature of cases that are submitted to (international) arbitral tribunals in B2B disputes, we find that a huge majority are not cases where one party is simply unwilling (or unable) to pay. To the contrary, most cases in international arbitration are 'genuine disputes', where the facts and the law are highly controversial and/or where the law is not settled, so that a neutral third party has to step in.[47] And, as we have seen, this is the type of case where predicting outcome on the basis of non-legal factors can be hugely promising, similar to predicting the outcome of cases submitted to the U.S. Supreme Court.

5.31 There are already a number of AI tools specifically designed to assist counsel with the selection of arbitrators (eg, Jus Mundi[48]; ArbitratorIntelligence).[49] We see a huge potential for outcome prediction if we link basic case information of the kind that was used in the experiment with the U.S. Supreme Court to non-legal data on individual arbitrators, whether from Jus Mundi or ArbitratorIntelligence, or from regular social media. To give a simple example, one might be tempted to link preferences a certain person has shown on social media (eg, for animal protection, skiing, Amalfi as a holiday destination) with the outcome of a given arbitration. The use of AI might bring this process to as-yet untold levels of accuracy. Hence, it might one day be possible for us to predict that arbitrators who like skiing or gardening (which might be inferred from their internet activity) are more (or less) likely to take a more restrictive (or more open) approach when it comes to

47 Many of the decisions that have to be made by arbitrators require people skills and sometimes even psychological insight. J Hope, 'Chapter 7: Can a Robot Be an Arbitrator?' in A Calissendorff and P Schölstrom (eds), *Stockholm Arbitration Yearbook 2019* (Kluwer Law International 2019) 115; F Kreis and M Kaulartz, 'Smart Contracts and Dispute Resolution – A Chance to Raise Efficiency?' (2019) ASA Bulletin 351; C Sim, 'Will Artificial Intelligence take over Arbitration' in L Boo and GB Born (eds) (2018) 14(1) *Asian International Arbitration Journal* 8–9; G Van Nieuwenhuyse, 'Arbitration and New Technologies: Mutual Benefits' (2018) 35(1) *Journal of International Arbitration* 124.

48 <https://jusmundi.com/en/> (last accessed 23 July 2020).

49 <https://arbitratorintelligence.com/> (last accessed 23 July 2020).

written form clauses in a contract. We leave it to our readers to speculate what this will mean (or may already mean) for our work as arbitrators and counsel. For good reason, the French legislature recently prohibited the use of data regarding the identity of French judges to evaluate, analyse, compare or predict their decision-making.[50] It is worthwhile to discuss whether similar prohibitions should be put in place with regard to the identity of arbitrators.

Liability for the use (or non-use) of AI

5.32 Several questions may arise concerning liability when an arbitration is supported or decided by an AI. An interesting issue arises in the event that AI is found, for instance, to produce systematically discriminatory outputs as a result of poorly selected, incorrect, incomplete or outdated data.[51] Since law does not recognise the computer as a legal entity,[52] would the software company that built the AI be afforded with the same liability/immunity from liability that an arbitrator would be afforded?[53] Conversely, does the arbitrator, who is bound by a duty to conduct the arbitration efficiently, have an obligation to use AI if this could effectively contribute to a more accurate, faster and more user-friendly arbitration? Another example of a relevant case is where an outside agent is able to penetrate the security of the AI software and influence the final award. Who should then be held liable for the lapse in security?

Conclusion: AI as acronym for 'Augmented Intelligence'

5.33 At the present stage, where everything is still evolving, it is a difficult exercise to draw conclusions. The advent of AI alongside a human arbitrator will most definitely impact the mission of an arbitral tribunal and change the expectations placed on the arbitrator. But if one considers what AI can achieve, or is most likely to be able to achieve in the near future, we do not believe that AI will replace human decision-makers any time soon. The deciding of complex B2B disputes will remain a human prerogative. This notwithstanding, there is still plenty of scope for the use of AI within the meaning of 'Augmented Intelligence' in many stages of a predominantly human arbitration. While this will not automatically make arbitration less costly, arbitration will presumably benefit in terms of the time necessary to

50 LOIn°2019–222du23mars2019deprogrammation2018–2022etderéformepourlajustice(1).

51 On this matter, see: 'Big Data: A Report on Algorithmic Systems, Opportunity, and Civil Rights' (2016) p 7–9, available at <https://obamawhitehouse.archives.gov/sites/default/files/microsites/ostp/2016_0504_data_discrimination.pdf> (last accessed 23 July 2020).

52 The EU also seems to reject the idea that an AI should be granted legal personality. T Burri, 'The EU Is Right to Refuse Legal Personality for Artificial Intelligence', *EURACTIV.com*, available at <www.euractiv.com/section/digital/opinion/the-eu-is-right-to-refuse-legal-personality-for-artificial-intelligence/> (last accessed 23 July 2020).

53 There is quite some discussion on the liability of robots and for instance self-driving cars in the academic literature. See eg. J De Bruyne and C Vanleenhove, 'Law 2.0 – Robots, Social Media and the Traditional Legal Framework' in V Vebraite, K Mickute and I M Ragaisyte (eds), *Law 2.0. – New Methods, New Laws: 7th International Conference of PhD Students and Young Researchers* (Vilnius: Vilnius University Press 2019) 78–92. It is, however, quite doubtful that one could apply the same reasoning of liability of self-driving cars to that of an AI-arbitrator. A first and foremost question would probably be whether the AI's liability concerns an arbitrator's liability or a contractual liability.

issue the award as well as the quality of the legal work. It seems beyond doubt that arbitral institutions have an important role to play in promoting, supervising and limiting where necessary the use of 'Augmented Intelligence'. Arbitrators and administrative secretaries will need even more training and experience, not only in order to work with modern technologies but even more so in order to be able to monitor the work done by counsel. There are challenging times ahead of us, but this can probably be said about every period in human history.

PART III

GOOD FAITH AND COLLABORATIVE DISPUTE RESOLUTION

CHAPTER 6

The relevance of good faith in transnational construction contracts

A civil law perspective

Olivier Caprasse and Maxime Tecqmenne

Introduction

6.1 The importance of the principle of good faith in international arbitration has been emphasised in many awards. Bernardo Cremades observes, in that regard, that 'it is difficult to find any international arbitration award not based on, or that does not at least mention, good faith'.[1] Yet, despite acceptance that it plays a prominent role in arbitration, the concept of good faith is a thorny one, whose meaning and functions remain nebulous.[2] In particular, the scope and content of the principle of good faith vary across states and its manifestations in national laws and case law are varied and manifold. In some jurisdictions, it is not even accepted that the principle of good faith indeed constitutes – or should constitute – a self-standing principle underpinning the law of contract. In most civil law systems, the law of obligations recognises the existence of an overarching principle of good faith. In contrast, in common law, concerns about legal certainty stand as an obstacle to the recognition of a general principle of good faith.[3]

6.2 From the outset, the contrasting approaches of civil and common law jurisdictions as regards the recognition of a general principle of good faith may give rise to difficulties in the resolution of construction disputes. Major construction projects often feature a transnational element and typically involve parties originating from different jurisdictions with different cultural and legal backgrounds.[4] In the event of a dispute, these parties have particular expectations as regards the way in which their claims will be handled.[5] In this regard, international arbitration appears to constitute the most suitable method for the resolution of construction disputes insofar as it embodies a transnational approach towards the resolution of disputes.[6] More specifically, the international character of arbitration

1 Bernardo M Cremades, 'Good Faith in International Arbitration' (2012) 27(4) *American University International Law Review* 761.

2 ibid, 761ff.

3 Elizabeth MacDonald and Ruth Atkins, *Koffman and MacDonald's Law of Contract*, (9th edn, Oxford University Press 2018) ch 16, 401–402.

4 Renato Nazzini, 'Introduction' in Renato Nazzini (ed), *Transnational Construction Arbitration. Key Themes in the Resolution of Construction Disputes* (Informa Law 2018) ch 1, 3.

5 Jane Jenkins, *International Construction Arbitration Law*, vol 1 (2nd edn, Kluwer Law International 2013) 2.

6 Jane Jenkins and Kim Rosenberg, 'Engineering and Construction Arbitration' in Julian DM Lew and others (eds), *Arbitration in England, with Chapters on Scotland and Ireland* (Kluwer Law International 2013) ch 9, 159; David Kiefer and Adrian Cole, 'Suitability of Arbitration Rules for Construction Disputes' in Stavros Brekoulakis

enables arbitrators to decide disputes 'in a way that is consistent with parties' expectations that duly takes into account the transnational nature of the dispute'.[7] Therefore, it is hardly surprising that international construction disputes account for a significant portion of commercial disputes submitted to arbitral institutions.[8]

6.3 The disparate approaches of civil and common law jurisdictions as regards the recognition of a general principle of good faith would appear to render any attempt to adopt a transnational approach towards this concept nugatory. In particular, the arbitrators' understanding of the concept of good faith might be influenced by their legal culture, which might in turn exacerbate the divide between the civil and the common law traditions. It is plain, however, that 'an experienced arbitrator in a globalised economy knows how to interpret and apply legal concepts from other systems although they may seem unusual to him'.[9] In addition, in recent years, the divisiveness between common and civil law over good faith has progressively been attenuated.[10] More specifically, despite common law's traditional reluctance to recognise a general principle of good faith, there appears to be growing acceptance that the concept of good faith requires a certain degree of cooperation as between the parties to a long-term commercial contract. Hence, it seems that, even in common law systems, good faith may play some role in the performance of long-lasting commercial contractual relationships.[11]

6.4 Against that backdrop, this chapter revolves around an assessment, from a civil lawyer's perspective, of the practical implications of good faith in the resolution of transnational construction disputes submitted to international commercial arbitration. After discussing the potential sources of good faith, with a particular focus on civil law systems such as Belgium and France, we will delve into an analysis of the different ways in which that principle may help shape alternative dispute resolution mechanisms and contractual arrangements in the construction industry.

Sources of good faith in international construction arbitration

Law applicable to the contractual obligations of the parties

6.5 The parties to a construction contract may select a substantive governing law that explicitly recognises that the principle of good faith is binding upon the parties in the

---

and David Brynmor-Thomas QC (eds), *The Guide to Construction Arbitration* (2nd edn, Law Business Research Ltd 2018) ch 10, 129.

7 Renato Nazzini, note 4, 4.

8 David Kiefer and Adrian Cole, note 6, 135.

9 Bernardo M Cremades, note 1, 776.

10 Severine Saintier, 'The Elusive Notion of Good Faith in the Performance of a Contract, Why Still a Bete Noire for the Civil and the Common Law ?' (2017) 6 *Journal of Business Law* 441ff.

11 David Campbell, 'Good Faith and the Ubiquity of the "Relational" Contract' (2014) 77(3) *The Modern Law Review* 475–492; Klaus Peter Berger and Thomas Arntz, 'Good Faith as a "General Organising Principle" of the Common Law', (2016) 32 *Arbitration International* 167, 167–178; Rupert Jackson, 'The Role of Good Faith in Construction Contracts' (11th International Conference on Construction Law and Alternative Dispute Resolution, Mauritius, May 2018); Shy Jackson, 'Of Chocolate Mousse and Good Faith' in Julian Bailey (ed), *Construction Law, Costs and Contemporary Development: Drawing the Threads Together. A Festschrijft for Lord Justice Jackson* (Hart Publishing 2018) ch 10, 165–187; Pieter Goodrich, 'The Wrecking Ball: Good Faith, Preemption and US Exceptionalism' in Pier Giuseppe Monateri (ed), *Comparative Contract Law* (Edward Elgar Publishing 2018) ch 16, 385–407.

negotiation and/or performance of the contract. When the law governing the dispute includes good faith requirements, the difficulty lies in ascertaining the meaning of these requirements. In most civil law countries, the requirement to behave in good faith informs and shapes the content of the parties' contractual obligations during the life of the contract. The principle of good faith is enshrined in various contemporary civil codes, such as in Italy,[12] Germany,[13] the Netherlands[14] and Spain.[15] It is also explicitly recognised in France and Belgium.

6.6 Although most continental systems recognise the principle of good faith, the meaning and scope of that principle may vary across national jurisdictions. In particular, considerable differences remain as regards the ways in which that principle manifests itself in national laws and jurisprudence.[16] In civil law jurisdictions such as France and Belgium, we will see that the contractual rights and duties flowing from the principle of good faith may indeed differ depending on national laws, as well as the judicial interpretation of this principle adopted by national courts and tribunals.[17]

6.7 The difficulty is further compounded by the vagueness inherent in the very idea of good faith. In particular, the conceptual boundaries of good faith are inherently blurred because, as an open-ended tool designed to assess the behaviour of the parties,[18] good faith is 'heavily dependent on context'[19] and ultimately hinges upon the circumstances of each case.[20] In other words, the concept of good faith 'cannot be considered in a vacuum'.[21] The determination of the specific rules and principles flowing from that concept warrants a contextual assessment of the behaviour of both parties in the negotiation or the performance of their contractual obligations. As a result, the concept of good faith is multifaceted and cannot be defined with precision. In order to fully grasp the way in which it operates, it is necessary to make reference to the way in which it is applied in practice. For this reason, even amongst countries in which good faith constitutes a general principle underpinning the law of contracts, one should be cautious not to oversimplify and adopt too broad an approach towards the requirements of good faith.

12 See Art. 1337, 1366 and 1375 of the Italian Civil Code. See also Alberto M Musy, 'The Good Faith Principle in Contract Law and the Precontractual Duty to Disclose: Comparative Analysis of New Differences in Legal Cultures' (2001) 1 *Global Jurist Advances* 1, 7–10; Tommaso Febbrajo, 'Good Faith and Pre-Contractual Liability in Italy: Recent Developments in the Interpretation of Article 1337 of the Italian Civil Code' (2016) 2(2) *The Italian Law Journal* 291–312.

13 See §242 of the German Civil Code (BGB). See also Werner F Ebke and Bettina M Steinhauer, 'The Doctrine of Good Faith in German Contract Law' in Jack Beatson and Daniel Friedman (eds), *Good Faith and Fault in Contract Law* (Oxford University Press 1997) ch 7, 171–190.

14 See Art. 6:2 and 248 of the Dutch Civil Code (BW).

15 See Art. 7 and 1258 of the Spanish Civil Code.

16 Giuditta C Moss, 'International Contracts between Common Law and Civil Law: Is Non-state Law to be Preferred? The Difficulty of Interpreting Legal Standards Such as Good Faith' (2007) 7(1) *Global Jurist Advances* 1, 25–26.

17 See section III.B.

18 Gaël Chantepie and Mathias Latina, *La réforme du droit des obligations. Commentaire théorique et pratique dans l'ordre du Code civil* (Dalloz 2016) 99.

19 Severine Saintier, note 10, 448.

20 Jean-François Romain, 'Le devoir et l'Obligation de Bonne Foi dans les Droits de Créance et les Droits Réels', in Rafaël Jafferali (ed), *Le Droit Commun des Contrats, Questions Choisies* (Bruylant 2016), 249.

21 Shy Jackson, ibid, 183.

Contractual provisions agreed upon by the parties

6.8 Irrespective of whether the law applicable to the contract recognises a general principle of good faith, the parties to an international construction project may be willing to commit themselves to comply with contractual requirements inspired by the idea of good faith. For instance, the contract may include a provision which stipulates that each party must act in a manner compatible with the requirements of 'mutual trust' or 'good faith' or that the parties must behave in a 'spirit of close cooperation' in the making and/or carrying out of their contractual obligations. In recent years, there has been a trend for construction contracts to include duties of collaboration.[22] In particular, many of the standard forms of contract used in relation to international construction projects include good faith clauses of the kind.[23] In addition, the existence of good faith requirements may also be implied from the terms and context of the contract. For that purpose, regard must be had to criteria such as the nature and duration of the contractual relationship between the parties. In particular, the parties are likely to be subject to increased duties of cooperation in the context of long-lasting commercial relationships such as those involving major construction projects.

6.9 When they interpret good faith contractual requirements, the arbitrators must construe the terms of the parties' contract in accordance with the law applicable to this contract. At this stage, the divergences existing in national laws and jurisprudence as regards the interpretation of good faith clauses may resurface, but these differences should not be overestimated. Ultimately, the arbitral tribunal is not 'an organ of a national legal system', which means that it enjoys a certain leeway in order to 'give effect to the reasonable expectations of the parties'.[24] In this perspective, it falls upon arbitrators to adopt an approach that duly takes into account the international character of the contract.[25] As we will see, certain transnational principles flowing from the general principles of law and what some call *lex mercatoria* may help arbitrators to adopt an interpretation of the relevant contractual good faith clause that is consistent with the reasonable expectations of the parties at the time of contracting and reflect the transnational nature of construction disputes.

Existence of an international general principle?

6.10 The notion of good faith may also constitute a source of law as a general principle of (international) law under Article 38(1)(c) of the Statute of the International Court of Justice.[26] Pursuant to the principle of party autonomy, the parties may specify that general principles of law will govern the merits of the dispute. They may, for that purpose,

22 Shy Jackson, note 11, 173.

23 See eg the NEC3 Suite of Contracts, clause 10.1; the Joint Contract Tribunal (JCT) Standard Building Contract 2011, optional Appendix 8; PPC2000 Standard Form of Contract for Project Partnering, Amended 2013, clause 1.3.

24 Mert Elcin, 'Lex Mercatoria in International Arbitration, Theory and Practice, vol 1' (DPhil thesis, European University Institute 2012) 110–111.

25 Lucy Greenwood, 'Principles of Interpretation of Contracts under English Law and Their Application in International Arbitration' (2019) 35(1) *Arbitration International* 21, 24–25.

26 This provision states that 'the general principles of law recognised by civilised nations' constitute one of the sources of international law.

supplement their choice of a national law by making express reference to general principles of law.[27] Under some arbitration laws, such as France and Belgium, the tribunal may also consider any 'rules of law' which it deems appropriate to settle the dispute in the absence of an express choice of substantive law by the parties. When the parties remain silent as to the substantive law governing the dispute, the arbitrators may therefore draw from transnational rules and principles deriving from non-state sources such as general principles of law in order to meet the requirements of transnational disputes.[28]

6.11 The position of the International Court of Justice (ICJ) itself is not that clear in this regard. It seems reluctant to consider that the principle of good faith constitutes a self-standing obligation of international law.[29] In the *Nuclear Tests Case*, the ICJ initially held that 'one of the basic principles governing the creation and performance of legal obligations, whatever their source, is the principle of good faith'.[30] However, this statement stands in stark contrast to the *Border and Transborder Armed Actions Case*, in which the ICJ stressed that good faith, as a concept, 'is not in itself a source of obligations'.[31]

6.12 In spite of the somewhat cautious approach adopted by the ICJ towards the principle of good faith, some commentators consider that 'there is little doubt that the principle of good faith can be considered both a general principle of law ... and a general principle of international law'.[32] Against that backdrop, good faith is mentioned in a wide array of international legal instruments, which has helped 'solidify the general principle of good faith in international arbitration'.[33]

6.13 More specifically, the principle of good faith may be used as a useful tool in the interpretation of international conventions and treaties.[34] For instance, Article 31, paragraph 1 of the Vienna Convention on the Law of Treatise (VCLT) states that 'a treaty shall be interpreted in good faith in accordance with the ordinary meaning to be given to the terms of the treaty in their context and in the light of its object and purpose'. In addition, Article 7.1 of the UN Convention on Contracts for the International Sales of Goods (CISG) requires that, in the interpretation of that convention, 'regard must be had to ... the observance of good faith in international trade'.

6.14 The principle of good faith may also be used to shape the contractual relationship between the parties in the context of international commercial transactions. That is made clear under Article 1.7 of the Unidroit Principles of International Commercial Contracts (UPICC), according to which 'each party must act in accordance with good faith and fair

27 'General Principles of Law in International Commercial Arbitration' (1988) 101(8) *Harvard Law Review* 1816, 1819.

28 Emmanuel Gaillard, 'General Principles of Law in International Commercial Arbitration – Challenging the Myths' (2011) 5(2) *World Arbitration & Mediation Review* 161, 165.

29 Emily Sipiorski, *Good Faith in International Investment Arbitration* (Oxford University Press 2019) 10–11.

30 *Nuclear Tests Case (Australia v France)*, Interim Protection, 1974 ICJ Rep 253, 268 (December 20).

31 *Border and Transborder Armed Actions Case (Nicaragua v Honduras)*, Judgment, 1988 ICJ Rep 69, 105 (December 20).

32 Andreas R Ziegler and Jorun Baumgartner, 'Good Faith as a General Principle of (International) Law' in Andrew D Mitchell, M Sornarajah and Tania Voon (eds), *Good Faith and International Economic Law* (Oxford University Press 2015) ch 2, 10.

33 Bernardo M Cremades, note 1, 780. See also Jan Klabbers, *International Law* (Cambridge University Press 2013) 34.

34 Eric De Brabandere and Isabelle Van Damme, 'Good Faith in Treaty Interpretation' in Andrew D Mitchell, M Sornarajah and Tania Voon (eds), note 32, ch 5, 37ff.

dealing in international trade'. In other words, the parties' behaviour during the life of the contract must conform with good faith.[35]

6.15 The position of good faith as a general principle of international law is further cemented by its use in international investment arbitration. In practice, the notion of good faith often appears to help shape the outcome of investment protection disputes. In particular, good faith 'has governed the arbitrator's conduct in investment matters since its inception'.[36] By virtue of Article 42(2) of the Convention on the Settlement of Investment Disputes between States and Nationals of other States (ICSID Convention), in the absence of a choice of law clause, the tribunal 'shall apply ... such rules of international law as may be applicable'. This provision empowers the arbitral tribunals constituted under the auspices of the International Centre for the Settlement of Investment Disputes to have recourse to the principle of good faith in the settlement of investment disputes. For instance, in the *Abaclat* award, the tribunal stated that 'the principle of good faith is a fundamental principle of international law, as well as investment law'.[37] This arbitral practice, which establishes the 'universal applicability of the principle ... of good faith',[38] suggests that good faith constitutes a general principle of law applicable in investment arbitration.[39]

Lex mercatoria?

6.16 Another important source from which some arbitrators seem to draw inspiration in the resolution of international construction disputes can be found in what is called *lex mercatoria*.

6.17 The content and legal nature of the *lex mercatoria* have stirred up a lot controversy in academic literature.[40] In particular, the issue of whether it should be considered as an autonomous and independent legal system remains contentious. The present contribution, however, does not touch upon these issues. Instead, this contribution relies on the premise that the *lex mercatoria* may be particularly well-suited to accommodate the peculiarities of international commercial disputes and, more specifically, international construction disputes.[41] Indeed, the emergence of the *lex mercatoria* results from the need to adapt national laws in order to better reflect the transnational nature of commercial disputes and constitutes, as such, one of the 'most conspicuous manifestations of globalization in the field of law'.[42] Most importantly, though, there seems to be a consensus in literature that its

35 On the specific manifestations of the principle of good faith within the framework of the Unidroit principles, see I Rueda, *Incidence des Règles d'Unidroit sur le Droit des Contrats en Europe* (LGDJ 2015).

36 Bernardo M Cremades, note 1, 785.

37 *Abaclat and Others v The Argentine Republic*, ICSID Case No ARB/07/5, Decision on jurisdiction and admissibility, 4 August 2011, para 646.

38 Mert Elcin, 'Lex Mercatoria in International Arbitration, Theory and Practice, vol 1' (DPhil thesis, European University Institute 2012) 26.

39 Emily Sipiorski, note 29, 2.

40 Emmanuel Gaillard and John Savage (eds), *Fouchard Gaillard Goldman on International Commercial Arbitration* (Kluwer Law International 1999) 813ff.

41 Andreas F Lowenfeld, 'Lex Mercatoria: An Arbitrator's View' (1990) 6(2) *Arbitration International* 133, 145.

42 Lorena Carvajal Arenas, 'Good Faith in the Lex Mercatoria: An Analysis of Arbitral Practice and Major Western Legal Systems' (DPhil thesis, University of Portsmouth 2011) 26 <https://researchportal.port.ac.uk/portal/files/5877259/GOOD_FAITH_IN_THE_LEX_MERCATORIA.pdf> (last accessed 28 February 2020);

content, which is determined by reference to comparative law, international instruments, arbitral case law and general usages of international trade,[43] would include the principle of good faith.[44]

6.18 In the context of construction disputes, the transnational principle of good faith that forms part of the *lex mercatoria* may be used in different ways by arbitrators.

6.19 In the first place, this principle may determine the rules applicable to the substance of the dispute submitted to the arbitral tribunal. The application of the transnational rules and principles flowing from good faith may occur if the parties agree to designate these principles as applying to their contractual dispute. However controversial it may seem at a first glance, given the inherent unpredictability resulting from the use of good faith in the name of *lex mercatoria*,[45] this option is endorsed by the UNCITRAL Model Law on International Commercial Arbitration[46] and is explicitly recognised in some countries, especially civil law countries such as France[47] and Belgium.[48,49] In addition, this may also occur in circumstances where, absent a choice of law provision, the arbitrators decide on their own motion that the *lex mercatoria* may have a bearing on the outcome of the dispute.[50]

6.20 In the second place, the *lex mercatoria* may be used as an interpretative tool intended to help arbitrators in applying and interpreting international conventions, as well as the law applicable to the merits of the dispute in a way that reflects the transnational

---

Klaus Peter Berger, 'The Lex Mercatoria (Old and New) and the TransLex-Principles' para 55 <www.trans-lex.org/the-lex-mercatoria-and-the-translex-principles_ID8> (last accessed 28 February 2020).

43 Charles Molineaux, 'Moving Toward a Construction Lex Mercatoria – A Lex Constructionis' (1997) 11(1) *Journal of International Arbitration* 55; Emmanuel Gaillard and John Savage (eds), note 40, 816; Ali Bennani, 'Les Contrats FIDIC, Fondement d'une Lex Constructionis en Devenir' (2018) *Cahiers de l'Arbitrage* 41ff.

44 Michael Mustill, 'The New Lex Mercatoria: The First Twenty-Five Years' (1988) 4(2) *Arbitration International* 86, 110; Andreas F Lowenfeld, note 41, 145; Pierre Mayer, *Le Principe de Bonne foi devant les arbitres du commerce international – Etudes de Droit International en l'honneur de P. Lalive* (Hebing & Lichtenhalm 1993) 548; Charles Molineaux, ibid, 64; Duarte G Henriques, 'The Role of Good Faith in Arbitration: Are Arbitrators and Arbitral Institutions Bound to Act in Good Faith?' (2015) 33(3) *ASA Bulletin* 514, 519.

45 Pierre Mayer, ibid, 556; Mert Elcin, note 38, 57.

46 Article 28(1) of the UNCITRAL Model Law states: '(1) The arbitral tribunal shall decide the dispute in accordance with such rules of law as are chosen by the parties as applicable to the substance of the dispute'. According to the explanatory note by the UNCITRAL secretariat on the 1985 Model Law on International Commercial Arbitration as amended in 2006, para 39: 'by referring to the choice of 'rules of law' instead of 'law', the Model Law broadens the range of options available to the parties as regards the designation of the law applicable to the substance of the dispute. For example, parties may agree on rules of law that have been elaborated by an international forum but have not yet been incorporated into any national legal system'. See also Maren Heidemann, *Does International Trade Need a Doctrine of Transnational Law? Some Thoughts at the Launch of a European Contract Law* (Springer 2012) 22.

47 Article 1511 of the French Code of Civil Procedure: 'The arbitral tribunal settles the dispute in accordance with the rules of law chosen by the parties or, in the absence of a choice of law, in accordance with the rules of law it considers appropriate. In any event, it takes account of trade usages'.

48 Article 1710 of the Belgian judiciary code: '1. The arbitral tribunal settles the dispute in accordance with the rules of law chosen by the parties to govern the substance of the dispute ...; 2. Failing any designation by the parties, the arbitral tribunal applies the rules of law which it considers most appropriate'.

49 This possibility also appears to be implicitly recognised by section 46 of the UK Arbitration Act 1996, which states: '(1) The arbitral tribunal shall decide the dispute- (a) in accordance with the law chosen by the parties as applicable to the substance of the dispute, or; (b) if the parties so agree, in accordance with such other considerations as are agreed by them or determined by the tribunal'. Further details can be found in: Anthony Connerty, 'Lex Mercatoria: Reflections from an English Lawyer' (2014) 30(4) *Arbitration International* 701, 710–714.

50 Pierre Mayer, note 44, 548.

nature of construction disputes and is 'consistent with generally accepted international understanding and usage'.[51] More specifically, it can be used 'to clarify or fill gaps, and to reduce the impact of peculiarities of individual countries' laws'.[52] By enabling arbitrators to adopt an internationally useful interpretation of national laws and case law, the *lex mercatoria* may also help foster a valuable consistency in the interpretation of disputed legal terms such as, *inter alia*, 'hardship'.[53]

Effects of good faith

6.21 In the first section, this chapter sketched out the potential sources of good faith that may be used by arbitral tribunals in the resolution of transnational construction disputes. It was essentially submitted that the principle of good faith may be enshrined in various instruments such as national laws, express contractual provisions, as well as transnational rules and principles deriving from non-state sources. The question remains, however, as to what the principle of good faith actually entails in the resolution of international construction disputes by arbitral institutions. In this section, we will therefore seek to ascertain, from the standpoint of civil law, the practical implications of good faith in relation to the resolution of transnational construction disputes submitted to international commercial arbitration and the shaping of alternative approaches to contracting in the construction industry.

On the resolution of disputes

6.22 At a first glance, good faith may be seen as lacking any concrete and workable content in the resolution of transnational construction disputes. As an open-ended tool designed to assess the behaviour of the parties, the content of good faith ultimately hinges upon the circumstances of each case. Hence, it cannot be defined with precision. The fact remains, however, that the notion of good faith may play an important role in the resolution of transnational disputes such as those involving major construction projects. More specifically, the principle of good faith 'is particularly useful when understood as providing the basis for more specific rules' that may be used in that context.[54]

6.23 The practical implications of good faith in relation to the resolution of transnational construction disputes will vary depending on the source(s) used. When it is called upon to construe the meaning of good faith in a specific set of circumstances, the arbitral tribunal must therefore ascertain the relevant rules and principles deriving from good faith in the light of the national laws applicable to the merits of the dispute. This conclusion is hardly surprising given that, even amongst countries which recognise that good faith constitutes a general principle underpinning the law of contracts, differences remain as to the specific rules and principles deriving from good faith. France and Belgium will serve as illustrations.

51 Andreas F Lowenfeld, note 41, 147.
52 ibid, 149. See also Mert Elcin, note 38, 243–255.
53 Klaus Peter Berger, note 42, para 75.
54 Emmanuel Gaillard and John Savage (eds), note 40, 820.

6.24 In France, following the reform of the law of contracts, introduced by means of order n°2016–13,[55] the meaning and the scope of the concept of good faith have been clarified.[56] As a result of the reform, the provisions of the French Civil Code pertaining to the principle of good faith have been amended substantially and now read as follows.

Article 1103: 'Contracts which are lawfully formed have the binding force of legislation for those who have made them.'

Article 1104: 'Contracts must be negotiated, formed and performed in good faith. This provision is a matter of public policy.'

Article 1112: 'The commencement, continuation and breaking-off of precontractual negotiations are free from control. They must mandatorily satisfy the requirements of good faith.'

Article 1194: 'Contracts create obligations not merely in relation to what they expressly provide, but also to all the consequences which are given to them by equity, usage or legislation.'

Article 1195: 'If a change of circumstances that was unforeseeable at the time of the conclusion of the contracts renders performance excessively onerous for a party who had not accepted the risk of such a change, that party may ask the other contracting party to renegotiate the contract. The first party must continue to perform his or her obligations during renegotiation.

In the case of refusal or failure to renegotiate, the parties may agree to terminate the contract from the date and on the conditions which they determine, or by a common agreement ask the court to set about its adaptation. In the absence of an agreement within a reasonable time, the court may, on the request of a party, revise the contract or put an end to it, as from a date and subject to such conditions as it shall determine'.

6.25 The reform clarifies the scope of the duties flowing from the principle of good faith. Prior to the adoption of the reform, this principle was deemed to apply only after the contract had been entered into. Now, it results from a combined reading of Articles 1104 and 1112 of the French Civil Code that the scope of the obligations imposed upon the parties by virtue of the principle of good faith covers the entire life of the agreement. Each party is therefore bound to comply with that principle during the negotiation and the formation, as well as the performance of the contract.[57]

6.26 In addition, the reform makes clear that the principle of good faith is mandatory, which means that its application cannot be excluded by the parties. The mandatory character of good faith justifies the curtailment of the scope of good faith in a way that does not affect excessively the principle of party autonomy. For instance, the inclusion of the obligation to mitigate one's damage within the principle of good faith is no longer warranted since the

55 Ordonnance n° 2016–131 du 10 février 2016 portant réforme du droit des contrats, du régime général et de la preuve des obligations.

56 Philippe Malaurie, Laurent Aynès and Philippe Stoffel-Munck (eds), *Droit des Obligations* (8th edn, LGDJ 2016) 254.

57 Olivier Deshayes, Thomas Genicon and Yves-Marie Laithier, *Réforme du Droit des Contrats, du Régime Général et de la Preuve des Obligations. Commentaire Article par Article* (LexisNexis 2016) 48.

mandatory character attached to good faith would preclude the parties from dismissing this obligation, thereby impinging excessively upon the principle of party autonomy.[58]

6.27 In spite of the clarifications brought about by the reform, the meaning of the concept of good faith remains essentially disputed.[59] The French Civil Code itself does not define that concept. In practice, the concept of good faith is often defined by reference to bad faith. Accordingly, the parties are required not to abuse their contractual rights. Hence, good faith is understood negatively as prohibiting unfair or dishonest behaviours on the part of the parties. Nevertheless, this approach does not help to grasp the positive meaning of good faith.[60]

6.28 Against that backdrop, the content of good faith is predicated upon the context in which it comes into play. In particular, it constitutes a multifaceted concept which gives rise to a spectrum of situationally-specific obligations rather than a single, overarching duty.[61] During the pre-contractual stage, each party must abstain from behaving in a manner that could deceive the other party as regards their genuine intention or the object of the contract.[62] Subsequently, during the execution of the contract, the duty of good faith obliges each party to behave consistently. In other words, each party is precluded from contradicting themselves to the detriment of the other party.[63] In this perspective, the principle of good faith entails the existence of a specific duty to cooperate and facilitate the efficient performance of the contract by the other party.

6.29 Another major innovation resulting from the reform is the recognition of the 'hardship theory' contained in Article 1195 of the French Civil Code. This provision enables arbitrators to modify the contractual rights and obligations of the parties or, alternatively, to put an end to the contract in the event of an unforeseeable change of circumstances which meets a series of conditions laid down in that provision. This entails a significant redefinition of the relationship between the principle of party autonomy and the very idea of contractual justice. On the one hand, although the doctrine of hardship constitutes an independent and autonomous source of obligations for the parties, this doctrine is a manifestation of the duty to collaborate in the performance of contracts.[64] In this regard, it is intrinsically related to the very idea of good faith.[65] On the other hand, however, the principle of party autonomy is preserved insofar as the parties may also exclude the hardship theory through the inclusion of an express contractual provision whereby they agree to accept the risks arising out of an unforeseeable change of circumstances.[66]

6.30 In Belgium, the Belgian Civil Code reads as follows.

> **Article 1134**: 'Contracts which are lawfully formed have the binding force of legislation for those who have made them. Contracts must be performed in good faith.'

---

58 ibid, 50.

59 Gael Chantepie and Mathias Latina, note 18, 92.

60 ibid, 94.

61 Severine Saintier, note 10, 444–445.

62 Philippe Malaurie, Laurent Aynès and Philippe Stoffel-Munck (eds), note 56, 258.

63 ibid, 256.

64 Isabelle Rueda, note 35, 39.

65 Pierre Mayer, note 44, 550.

66 Olivier Deshayes, Thomas Genicon and Yves-Marie Laithier, note 57, 47; Ludovic Marignol, 'La Prévisibilité en Droit des Contrats' (DPhil thesis, Université de Toulouse 2017) 370–377.

Article 1135: 'Contracts create obligations not solely in relation to what they expressly provide, but also to all the consequences which are given to them by equity, usage or legislation.'

6.31 Under Belgian law, the principle of good faith also applies in relation to the 'entire life of the contract'.[67] This period includes the negotiation and the performance of the contract, but also several duties of collaboration and loyalty applicable after the contract has expired such as, *inter alia*, obligations of non-compete.[68]

6.32 In this context, the principle of good faith fulfils three main functions.

6.33 First, the concept of good faith may be used as an interpretative tool in the determination of the common intention of the parties to the contract. According to Article 1156 of the Belgian Civil Code, the terms contained in a contract must be interpreted in accordance with the intention of the parties. In the ascertainment of the common intention of the parties, regard must be had to the meaning that a reasonable and honest person would give to it in the same circumstances.[69]

6.34 Second, the concept of good faith constitutes a behavioural standard binding upon the parties which can be used to carve out specific duties and obligations beyond the duties expressly included in the contract.[70] More specifically, the principle of good faith manifests itself in several fact-specific duties such as the duty to give information, the duty to mitigate one's damage and the duty for the creditor to take all measures necessary to facilitate the repayment of its debt by the debtor.[71]

6.35 Third, the concept of good faith may also constrain each party's ability to rely on their contractual rights in order to act in a manner that is such as to create a disproportionate detriment to the other party. Thus, the prohibition of abuse of rights mandates each party to refrain from exercising their contractual rights in a manner that goes manifestly beyond the limits of the exercise of such rights by a reasonable and honest person in the same circumstances.[72] In practice, the concept of abuse of rights encompasses several situationally-specific duties. For instance, it precludes each party from acting with the exclusive intent of harming the other party. It can also be used to sanction the exercise of a right which inflicts damages to the other party in the absence of any legitimate interest on the part of the right bearer. In addition, when a party must choose between two equally advantageous ways of exercising a right, the prohibition of abuse of rights obliges that party to choose the option that is the least restrictive towards the other party's interests.

6.36 Some commentators also consider that good faith may fulfil a fourth function, which would entitle arbitrators to modify or even put an end to the contractual agreement

---

67 Patrick Wéry, *Droit des Obligations. Volume 1: Théorie Générale du Contrat* (2nd edn, Larcier 2011) 141. Since the first drafting of this section, different draft laws have been and are discussed to review and develop the principles governing the conclusion and performance of contracts in Belgium. See Doc. 55-1806/001, 24 February 2021, proposition de loi Livre 5 'Les Obligations'.

68 ibid, 142.

69 Pierre Van Ommeslaghe, *Traité de Droit Civil Belge – Tome II. Les obligations. Volume I: Introduction: Source des obligations* (Bruylant 2013) 193.

70 Jean Van Zuylen, 'Fautes, Bonne Foi et Abus de Droit: Convergences et Divergences' (2011) 71(3) *Annales de droit de Louvain* 265, 272ff.

71 Patrick Wéry, note 67, 136.

72 ibid, 138.

of the parties if, as a result of unforeseeable circumstances, the rights and duties of the parties become imbalanced.[73] However, contrary to what the French Civil Code holds, the Belgian Civil Code does not recognise the theory of hardship. To this day, the Belgian Cour de Cassation has never explicitly accepted this possibility,[74] but things could soon change given that a recent draft law, which has not yet been passed into law, intends to enact the theory of hardship.[75]

6.37 As is clear from the foregoing, the meaning and scope of good faith differ across civil law jurisdictions. In the context of transnational construction disputes, the somewhat contrasted approaches adopted by national laws and case law towards good faith may give rise to difficulties.

6.38 Take, for instance, the theory of hardship. Most construction projects are likely to be affected by changing natural and economic conditions that may alter the contractual bargain struck by the parties. As a result, international construction contracts typically include hardship clauses. Yet, it is unclear how arbitrators should construe the meaning of such clauses in the light of the applicable law, given that the theory of hardship is not recognised in all countries.[76] Although French law empowers arbitrators to adapt the contract in order to alleviate the consequences of an unforeseeable change of circumstances, such possibility does not seem to exist in Belgium at the time this paper has been drafted. The differing domestic approaches of hardship may also render any attempt to adopt an internationally useful interpretation of this concept unsuccessful.

6.39 In order to construe national laws and contractual clauses in a way that reflects the transnational nature of major construction disputes, some arbitrators tend to draw inspiration from transnational principles such as the general principles of law and the *lex mercatoria*.[77] In this regard, some commentators have identified a list of principles that would, in their view, pertain to the *lex mercatoria*. Most notably, the Centre for Transnational Law (CENTRAL) codified a non-exhaustive, open list of principles and rules that would allegedly pertain to *lex mercatoria*. The result of the impressive work carried out by Prof. Peter Klaus Berger and his team can be found in the TransLex-Principles,[78] an online database containing a list of more than 130 transnational principles and rules of commercial law. This list contains many transnational rules and principles which constitute concrete manifestations of the general principle of good faith. Therefore, it provides an invaluable tool for the application and interpretation of good faith in a transnational setting.

---

73 Pierre Van Ommeslaghe, note 69, 196.

74 Patrick Wéry, note 67, 136.

75 Proposition de loi portant insertion du Livre 5 'Les obligations' dans le nouveau Code civil, Doc Parl, Ch Rep, 2018–2019, n° 3709/001 du 3 avril 2019, 79. See also the more recent Doc. 55-1806/001, 24 February 2021, proposition de loi Livre 5 'Les Obligations'.

76 Further details can be found in Norbert Horn, 'Procedures of Contract Adaptation and Renegotiation in International Commerce' in Horn (ed) *Adaptation and Renegotiation of Contracts in International Trade and Finance* (Kluwer 1985) 181–182.

77 Larry A DiMatteo, 'Soft Law and the Principle of Fait and Equitable Decision Making in International Contract Arbitration' (2013) *The Chinese Journal of Comparative Law* 1–35; Giuditta Cordero-Moss, 'Limits on Party Autonomy in International Commercial Arbitration' (2015) 4(1) *Penn State Journal of Law & International Affairs* 186–212.

78 The TransLex Principle are available at: <www.trans-lex.org/principles/of-transnational-law-(lex-mercatoria)> (last accessed 28 February 2020).

6.40 In the TransLex-Principles, the principle of good faith is defined as follows:

No. I.1.1 – Good faith and fair dealing in international trade:

(a) Parties to international business transactions must act in accordance with good faith and fair dealing in international trade. This standard applies to the negotiation, formation, performance and interpretation of international contracts.
(b) The standards and requirements imposed on the parties by this principle vary depending on the individual circumstances involved such as trade sector in which the parties are operating, their size and degree of professional sophistication, and the nature and duration of the contract.
(c) The parties may not exclude or limit the application of this principle to their legal relationship.

6.41 The standard of good faith described in subsection (a) entails that, during the entire life of the contract, each party has the 'obligation to display a behaviour towards the other party which cannot harm the latter and which takes into account the reasonable expectations of businessmen in the shoes of the other side'.[79] Ultimately, the concept of good faith appears to mandate each party to act in a manner compatible with the objective behavioural norm of an honest and reasonable man. In particular, the standard of reasonableness is the source of a duty 'not to act in a way which has a potential to unduly surprise or inflict damages on the other party'.[80]

6.42 In addition, the principle of good faith manifests itself in many other general but more specific and concrete obligations and duties vested in the parties in the making and carrying out of contracts, such as:

No. I.2.1 – Standard of reasonableness: 'The parties always have to act according to what is reasonable in view of the particular nature of the transaction and the circumstances involved, in particular the economic interests and expectations of the parties.'

No. I.1.4 – Abuse of rights: 'A party may not exercise a right merely to damage the other party or to achieve a result which is disproportionate to the result intended by the legal principle out of which the right arises.'

No. I.1.2 – Prohibition of inconsistent behaviour: '(a) A party cannot set itself in contradiction to its previous conduct vis-à-vis another party if that latter party has acted in reasonable reliance on such conduct.

(b) Violation of this principle may result in the loss, suspension, or modification of rights otherwise available to the other party violating this principle or in the creation of rights otherwise not available to the aggrieved party.'

No. IV.6.9 – Duty to notify and cooperate with the other side: '(a) Each party is under an obligation to notify in a timely fashion the other party of any problems that occur in the performance of the contract and of any other facts or

79 <www.trans-lex.org/901000/_/good-faith-and-fair-dealing-in-international-trade/> (last accessed 28 February 2020).

80 ibid.

circumstances on whose knowledge the other party is discernibly dependent, provided that such information can reasonably be expected from that party.

(b) Each party is under a good faith obligation to cooperate with the other party when such cooperation can reasonably be expected for the performance of that party's obligations.'

No. IV.6.7 – Duty to renegotiate: 'Each party has a good faith obligation to renegotiate the contract if there is a need to adapt the contract to changed circumstances and the continuation of performance can reasonably be expected from the parties.'

6.43 As was seen in the introduction, the concept of good faith is often relied upon by arbitral institutions in the settlement of international disputes. This suggests that the principle of good faith plays an important role in international commercial arbitration. Be that as it may, there is no denying that the extent to which good faith may help shape the outcome of transnational disputes and, in particular, those involving international construction projects remains difficult to appreciate. In practice, it would appear that, except in situations involving obvious instances of abuse of rights, the concept of good faith will seldom provide the parties with the smoking gun they need to succeed in the claims and obtain recovery. For the most part, good faith acts as an interpretative device which arbitrators may use in order to explore the broader contextual nexus of the case, including the behaviour of the parties, contract usages, the terms of the contract and the national legal framework applicable to the merits of the dispute.[81]

On the shaping of alternative approaches to contracting

6.44 The principle of good faith may also have practical implications as regards some of the contractual tools and arrangements developed and used in the construction industry. Major construction contracts often involve many project participants that are involved at different stages of the carrying out of the construction project. As a consequence, it is not uncommon to find that an international construction project relies on a very complex and intricate network of contracts. More specifically, construction contracts usually consist of 'many documents of different origins, authorship and development'.[82] In practice, the complexity that may result from the implementation of this bundle of contracts requires close cooperation between the parties involved.

6.45 It is no surprise, then, that in recent years the peculiarities of the construction industry set the stage for the emergence of contract practices designed to foster the effective management of construction projects. Even if these developments are primarily motivated by the search for efficiency in the development of major construction projects,[83] they also seem to be inspired to a certain extent by the very idea of good faith.

81 Emily Sipiorski, note 29, 13–14.

82 Jane Jenkins, *International Construction Arbitration Law*, vol 1 (2nd edn, Kluwer Law International 2013) 15.

83 Mohammad Suprapto, 'Collaborative Contracting in Projects' (DPhil thesis, Technische Universiteit Delft 2016) ch 3, 49–50.

6.46 In this context, the recent move towards collaborative forms of contracting such as partnering and alliancing illustrates the practical impact of good faith on the shaping of certain forms of contracting in construction.[84] Indeed, these contractual arrangements aim to foster the creation of a certain degree of cooperation and joint-working between the parties involved in a construction project.[85] Partnering, in particular, includes varying forms of contracts and documents according to the intention of the participants: it may be intended to have 'enforceable legal consequences or it may comprise a non-binding ... charter'.[86] In this respect, it appears that the very idea of good faith permeates the 2011 Joint Contracts Tribunal (JCT) Partnering Charter which includes non-binding commitments on the part of the signatories to act: 'in good faith; in an open and trusting manner; in a co-operative way; in a way to avoid disputes by adopting a 'no blame culture'; fairly towards each other; and valuing the skills and respecting the responsibilities of each other'. It remains to be seen, however, how these commitments will effectively help frame the legal and management aspects of the construction industry. In particular, the non-binding nature of these commitments makes it difficult to envision how exactly they might be translated into concrete and specific project processes.[87]

6.47 Another important development inspired by the idea of good faith is the creation of modelling softwares such as Building Information Modelling (BIM). In particular, the development of collaborative BIM systems supported by contractual provisions whereby the parties agree to act in a collaborative manner is intended to increase the degree of coordination between contract participants.[88] By enabling all participants to access and share relevant information pertaining to the construction project, this process goes a long way towards facilitating and encouraging 'collaborative working between professional consultants and contractors involved in the design and construction' of the project.[89]

6.48 The technical complexity inherent in the resolution of construction disputes also accounts for the inclusion, within construction contracts, of mechanisms designed to better manage the day-to-day operation of the project and to encourage the early resolution of construction disputes. For that purpose, construction contracts usually contain multi-stage or sequential dispute resolution clauses.[90] For instance, the FIDIC 2017 contracts' approach towards dispute resolution is sequential insofar as it requires the parties to follow a multi-stage procedure intended to avoid or prevent disputes from going all the way through to arbitration.[91] The multi-stage procedure entails that, if a dispute arises during the project, the parties must follow a number of dispute resolution mechanisms such as dispute boards

84 Shy Jackson, note 11, 185.

85 Jane Jenkins, note 81, 21; Gustavo Scheffer da Silveira, *Les Modes de Règlement des Différends dans les Contrats Internationaux de Construction* (Bruylant 2019) 35.

86 John Uff, *Construction Law* (12th edn, Sweet & Maxwell 2017) 367.

87 King's College Centre of Construction Law and Dispute Resolution, 'Enabling BIM through Procurement and Contracts' (2016) 13; John Uff, ibid, 367.

88 FIDIC Conditions of Contract for Construction for Building and Engineering Works Designed by the Employer Second Edition, 2017 (Fidic Red Book) 53.

89 Jane Jenkins, note 81, 92.

90 Phillip Capper and Anthony Bunch, 'Construction Industry Arbitrations' in Ronald Bernstein and others (eds), *Handbook of Arbitration Practice* (3rd edn, Sweet & Maxwell 1998) pt 5, 346–347.

91 Stavros Brekoulakis, 'Change and Continuity: The FIDIC 2017 Red and Yellow Book Amendments' in Stavros Brekoulakis and David Brynmor Thomas QC (eds), note 6, ch 4, 58.

and amicable settlements before 'culminating ... in a final and binding decision-making process'.[92]

6.49 In practice, the interaction between the 'escalating steps' followed by the parties raises fundamental questions as regards the timeframe allocated to each of these steps, as well as the extent to which the parties are required to respect them.[93] This contribution, however, does not touch upon these issues. Rather, it only purports to discuss the good faith implications of the multi-stage procedure followed in the construction industry.

6.50 In this perspective, it appears that the multi-stage approach towards the resolution of disputes is driven to a certain extent by good faith considerations. Of course, the main objective behind the development of these tools is to facilitate the early settlement of disputes[94] by professionals who 'are, by their training, better able to accomplish substantial justice among themselves'.[95] Nevertheless, two elements support the view that these contractual tools also involve certain aspects pertaining to good faith. First, the escalating steps followed by the parties 'commonly include one or more good faith discussions'.[96] Second, the notion of good faith is also relevant in circumstances where the parties submit the dispute to the Dispute Avoidance/Adjudicatory Board (DAAB) set up within the framework of the FIDIC contracts. The FIDIC 2017 Red Book provides, in Article 6.3 of the model contract, that '(i)n connection with the DAAB's activities, each party shall: (a) cooperate in good faith with the DAAB'. These considerations suggest that, during the multi-stage procedure, each party should respect the objective norm of a reasonable man in the same circumstances, which goes to show that the process of early resolution of disputes is driven and framed by good faith requirements.

92 Jane Jenkins and Kim Rosenberg, 'Engineering and Construction Arbitration' in Julian D. M. Lew and others (eds), note 6, 176.

93 Suffice it to say, for present purposes, that these questions are addressed in many ICC awards. See, for instance, ICC Case No 14431 (2015) ICC Dispute Resolution Bulletin 1; ICC Case No 16155 (2015) ICC Dispute Resolution Bulletin 37; ICC Case No 16262 (2015) ICC Dispute Resolution Bulletin 41; ICC Case No 16765 (2015) ICC Dispute Resolution Bulletin 67. Further details can be found in: Christopher R Seppala, 'International Construction Contract Disputes: Commentary on ICC Awards Dealing with The FIDIC International Conditions of Contract' (1998) 9(2) *The ICC International Court of Arbitration Bulletin* 32–45; Christopher R Seppala, 'Commentary on Recent ICC Arbitral Awards Dealing with Dispute Adjudication Boards under FIDIC Contracts' (2015) *The ICC International Court of Arbitration Bulletin* 1, 8–9; Nicholas Gould and Christina Lockwood, 'Dispute Boards' in Renato Nazzini (ed), note 4, 193–219.

94 Axel-Volkmar Jaeger and Götz-Sebastian Hök, *Fidic – A Guide for Practitioners* (Springer 2010) 400.

95 *Ernst, Inc. v Manhattan Construction Co. of Texas*, 387 F. sup. 1001 (1974), 1005–1006.

96 Jane Jenkins and Kim Rosenberg, note 92, 176.

CHAPTER 7

Searching for convergence between the common law and civil law traditions on good faith through international arbitration

David Arias and James Doe

Introduction

7.1 An undoubtedly positive and interesting aspect of international commercial arbitration practice is that it frequently brings together legal practitioners from different legal systems as co-counsels, opposing counsel or as members of tribunals. This in turn results in the sharing of different perspectives and thinking about common commercial legal problems.

7.2 From the authors' experience, it can still be surprising, positively so, that whilst different legal systems have approached these problems from different starting points very often the outcomes (tribunal decisions) turn out the same. There appears to be an internationally recognised commonality as to what the right outcome should be. Whether that is due to a convergence over centuries of international trade between nations, or an independent but distinctly human appreciation of similar moral and ethical standards required to maintain successful commercial life, the trend is quite clear.

7.3 This sharing and exchanging of ideas on how commercial legal problems should be dealt with can result in developments in substantive law. Canivet observes:

> *The two great legal cultures are certainly not monolithic and closed; they mutually define and influence themselves; they assert themselves in confrontation and comparison much more than in withdrawal and the illusory protection of legal 'sovereignism'.*[1]
>
> *Globalization is so powerful that, by now, all lawyers have the feeling of living a sort of generalized legal acculturation due to the competition legal systems engage in.*[2]

Furthermore, Pejović notes:[3]

> *The examination of common law and civil law reveals that there are more similarities than differences between these two legal systems. Despite very different legal cultures, processes, and institutions, common law and civil law have displayed a remarkable convergence in their treatment of most legal issues.*

However, in some aspects of commercial law, there remain clearly distinct approaches which can and do result, from time to time, in differing outcomes to certain problems between

1 G Canivet, 'The Interrelationship between Common Law and Civil Law' (2003) 63(4) *La L Rev* 937, 938.

2 ibid, 937–938.

3 Č Pejović, 'Civil Law and Common Law: Two Different Paths Leading to the Same Goal' (2001) PPP god 7–32, 31.

common and civil law. Indeed, such distinctions frequently act as a driver for decisions about the governing law of commercial agreements and in the choice of arbitrators. The concept of good faith may be one such aspect of commercial law.

7.4 Some believe there to be a fundamental difference between common law and civil law when it comes to implied duties of good faith as well as what such a duty means in terms of the rights and obligations of the parties.

7.5 However, relatively recently this consensus has started to be questioned, both from civil law scholars and the highest levels of the English judiciary. One of the most ardent proponents of a duty of good faith in English law is Lord Leggatt, a recent appointee to the English Supreme Court:[4]

> *I respectfully suggest that the traditional English hostility towards a doctrine of good faith in the performance of contracts, to the extent it still persists, is misplaced.*[5]

While a member of the Commercial Court bench, Lord Leggatt gave a number of judgments which may be considered as potentially opening the door to further judicial development in this area, particularly when it comes to what are commonly referred to as 'relational contracts'. In respect of the construction and infrastructure sector, there is the potential for change in long-term build and operate type contracts, such as those used for PFI and PPP procured projects.

7.6 The purpose of this chapter is to consider, as far as the authors are able, whether the increase in the use of international arbitration as a means to determine commercial disputes provides some insight into the convergence of common and civil law concepts of good faith.

7.7 Before considering how international arbitration might be a source of convergence between common law and civil law systems, it is worth reflecting on the differing approaches taken by common law and civil law systems when it comes to the concept of good faith.

Common law: orthodox English law position

7.8 The concept of 'good faith' has had, certainly historically, very different treatment as between civil law jurisdictions and common law jurisdictions. The English judges of the 19th century took the view that the world of commerce was an unforgiving place which a person should not step into unless they understood the risks. However, that had not always been the English law position.

7.9 Early on in the development of English law, 'good faith' had been recognised as a fundamental governing principle of contracts. In *Carter v Boehm*, Lord Mansfield commented that:[6]

---

4 Lord Leggatt took up his appointment to the Supreme Court of the United Kingdom on 21 April 2020.

5 *Yam Seng Pte Ltd v ITC* [2013] EWHC 111, [153].

6 *Carter v Boehm* [1766] 3 Burr 1905, 1910.

> *Good faith forbids either party by concealing what he privately knows, to draw the other into a bargain, from his ignorance of that fact, and his believing the contrary.*

It has been suggested that the importance of good faith in these early cases derived from the mercantile customs of the period. Customs which, even then, were international in nature.

7.10 Before the development of sophisticated systems of contract law, the practice of international trade between merchants of different countries was governed by mercantile customary law administered by merchant courts. In these courts, commercial disputes were resolved in a business-like fashion. One of those customs was good faith.[7] In this sense, in the days before the development of sophisticated legal systems, when it came to good faith, the commercial laws of the future civil and common law countries treated good faith in a similar way.

7.11 However, from these beginnings, the development of English contract law did not follow the path taken by civil law jurisdictions which maintained good faith at the centre of commercial law. To the English courts, the predictability of legal outcomes became more important. As a result, the concept of good faith, which had previously formed an important part of the old merchant law, appeared to have no place in the emerging common law system of England and Wales.

7.12 In contrast, across continental Europe a different approach to commercial contracts was taking shape. The French Code Napoleon and German law systems, consistent in keeping with the previous international merchant customs and practices, placed good faith at the centre of their commercial law.

7.13 Instead, the common law addressed unconscionable unfairness on a piecemeal basis, adopting solutions when specific problems arose, for example, by placing restrictions on pre-contract misstatements and penalty clauses, the use of implied terms where necessary and development of concepts such as estoppel. As stated by Bingham LJ in *Interfoto Picture Library*:[8]

> *English law has, characteristically, committed itself to no such overriding principle but has developed piecemeal solutions in response to demonstrated problems of unfairness.*

As a result of this approach, there was no apparent role for an implied duty of good faith. Even with express duties of good faith, English law has historically struggled to reconcile such a duty with other express obligations. In particular those obligations which might objectively appear unfair or suggest an inequality of bargaining power between the parties.

7.14 Confronted with the entirely rational argument that the inclusion of an express duty of good faith must mean something (otherwise why include it), English courts have historically tended to have interpreted such clauses as simply putting a gloss of 'reasonableness' over the enforcement of other contractual rights, rather than altering the fundamental nature of those rights.

---

7 R Goode, 'The Concept of "Good Faith" in English Law', Saggi, Conferenze e Seminari, no 2, Centro di Studi e recerche di dirito comparator e straniero, diretto da KJ Bonell (Rome 1992).

8 *Interfoto Picture Library Ltd v Stiletto Visual Programmes Ltd* [1989] QB 433, 439.

7.15 In terms of implied duties of good faith, the orthodox position is that there can only be such an implied duty in a limited category of transactions, for example insurance contracts (utmost good faith/uberrimae fidei) and 'relational' contracts.

7.16 This orthodoxy was clearly expressed by Andrews J in *Greenclose Ltd v National Westminster Bank*:[9]

> *[T]here is no general doctrine of good faith in English contract law and such a term is unlikely to arise by way of necessary implication in a contract between two sophisticated commercial parties negotiating at arms' length.*

However, there are suggestions by some that good faith and fair dealing may be more significant in the English legal system than this orthodoxy suggests. This is discussed next. However, it is first necessary to better understand the civil law position on good faith.

Civil law approach to 'good faith'

7.17 Many civil law countries have taken inspiration from the French Civil Code and the German Civil Code. Both contain a general obligation of good faith which applies to every contract. As observed by Blanke:[10]

> *the principle of good faith is one of the bedrocks of civilian contract law and as such constitutes a cause of action in its own right in the civil law. It even extends to the performance of arbitration agreements, imposing a requirement to arbitrate in good faith.*

Article 1134(3) of the French Civil Code requires contracts to be performed in good faith. Since the contractual law reforms which came into effect in 2016, pursuant to new Article 1104 of the French Civil Code, contracts must not only be performed, but also negotiated and formed, in good faith. This provision is a public policy provision and cannot be contracted out of.

7.18 The French Civil Code does not precisely define what is meant by good faith, and what the effect of this obligation actually is in practical terms. However, it is generally accepted that good faith is the expression of a duty of loyalty by each party consistent with the purpose of the contract and not to act with fraud or malice.

7.19 Professor Le Tourneau has stated that '*this disposition, by its form, seems to be a general maxim of law, of ethical inspiration, long dormant but rich in potential*'.[11] Whilst Professor Cadiet specifies that '*from the legal demand of good faith, jurisprudence has inferred a duty of loyalty in execution of contracts*'.[12]

---

9 [2014] EWHC 1156 (Ch), [150].

10 G Blanke, 'Document Production in International Arbitration: From Civil and Common Law Dichotomy to Operational Synergies' (2017) 83(4) *The International Journal of Arbitration, Mediation and Dispute Management* 423, 430.

11 Guy Robin, 'The Notion of Contractual Good Faith: Perspectives from Comparative Law' (*la Revue*, 31 Mai 2006) <https://larevue.squirepattonboggs.com/the-notion-of-contractual-good-faith-perspectives-from-comparative-law_a1010.html> (last accessed on 8 January 2021).

12 Guy Robin, 'The Notion of Contractual Good Faith: Perspectives from Comparative Law' (*la Revue*, 31 Mai 2006) <https://larevue.squirepattonboggs.com/the-notion-of-contractual-good-faith-perspectives-from-comparative-law_a1010.html> (last accessed on 8 January 2021).

7.20 Some authors consider that, besides the duty to cooperate to facilitate the execution of the contract, a duty of transparency and of contractual honesty also exists in those agreements where the '*affectio contractus*' is strong.

7.21 Ideally, a contract motivated by the ideal of good faith ought to be just, an equilibrium where each of the parties obtains a comparable advantage. In this way the duty of good faith acts in certain situations as a moderating element, a valve of commutative justice or of '*contractual solidarity*.'[13]

7.22 However, under French law the obligatory force of agreements (*Pacta sunt servanda*) is certainly a cornerstone of French contract law. By definition, this makes the extensive application of the express terms of the contract on the one hand, and contractual equilibrium on the other, difficult to achieve.

7.23 There is evidence that judges, confronted with flagrant abuses, may take more creative interpretations or apply other parts of the Civil Code to reach the desired result. For example, recent decisions of the Cour de Cassation (Commercial Chamber on 3 November 1992 and 24 November 1998 and the Second Civil Chamber from 17 March 2004) seem to impose a duty to renegotiate contracts that have become profoundly imbalanced in the course of their execution due to a change in circumstances.[14]

7.24 Whilst it is undisputed that a breach of the duty of good faith is a separate cause of action under French law, it would appear that there remains a considerable amount of uncertainty, and therefore flexibility, in its meaning and application in any particular circumstance.

7.25 Turning to the German Civil Code, German contract law is highly influenced by certain undefined legal terms ('*unbestimmte Rechtsbegriffe*') which are used as a vehicle to transport legal values and standards into practice. The principle of good faith probably comprises the most important of these undetermined legal concepts.

7.26 The German law concept of good faith is referred to as '*treu und glauben*' (sincerity and faith). This principle applies both to the execution and to the formation of the contract. Paragraph § 242 of the German Civil Code (BGB) establishes the obligation to execute contracts in good faith, whereas, paragraph § 157 provides that contract interpretation should be made in light of good faith. Furthermore, paragraph § 138 considers null

> *any legal act contrary to accepted standards of good behaviour. Also null is any legal act by which a person exploits the neediness, the weakness or the inexperience of another to get that person to promise or agree to confer upon him or a third person, in exchange for what is given, proprietary interests that exceed the value of what is given to such a degree these proprietary interests are shockingly disproportionate to what is given.*

7.27 German judges have a tendency to apply the fundamental paragraphs of § 242 directly. However, in theory, this paragraph does not constitute a cause of action nor does it have direct legal effect. For almost a century now, German jurisprudence has attempted to define the function of paragraph § 242.

13 Guy Robin, 'The Notion of Contractual Good Faith: Perspectives from Comparative Law' (*la Revue*, 31 Mai 2006) <https://larevue.squirepattonboggs.com/the-notion-of-contractual-good-faith-perspectives-from-comparative-law_a1010.html> (last accessed on 8 January 2021).

14 Cour de Cassation, 03/11/92; Cour de Cassation, 24/11/98; Cour de Cassation, 16/03/04; and Cour de Cassation, 29/06/10.

7.28 Under Spanish law good faith is introduced as one of the overarching principles of civil law. Article 7 of the Spanish Civil Code establishes the obligation to exercise the rights in good faith. Therefore, the duty to act in good faith is a standard recognised at a fundamental level, applicable to all legal obligations. The Spanish Civil Code does not provide a specific definition of what 'good faith' means, but legal scholars have described it as '*honesty, fidelity, loyalty, consideration or compliance with the trust generated in the other party*'.[15] The principle of good faith is closely linked to the prohibition against the abuse of right, also laid down in Article 7 of the Spanish Civil Code. The Spanish courts have connected that prohibition with unfair delay (*Verwikug*) and the estoppel and waiver principle (*contra factum propium venire non potest*).[16]

7.29 In the context of contract law, Article 1258 of the Spanish Civil Code states that contracts are binding on the parties to the extent of the content agreed between them, but also their effects according to the interpretation of that content in good faith given the nature of the contract in question. Therefore, good faith is used to construe contracts and to determine their content and scope; however, a contract's essence, customary practice and the law must at all times be respected. The latest legal doctrine in Spain holds that good faith is a way to supplement existing express terms but not contradict them. Spanish courts also appear to be seeking to establish certain limits on what a party can legitimately require of the other party in the name of good faith.[17]

International arbitration as a conduit for the convergence of common and civil law principles

7.30 It is important to acknowledge the challenges in seeking to identify any sort of trend in the development in substantive law through international arbitration awards.

7.31 Crucially, as international arbitration awards are almost always kept private and confidential how any particular tribunal has decided a particular legal issue is often impossible to determine, other than through personal experience and the anecdotal views of colleagues.

7.32 The one exception to this is investment treaty arbitrations, where the governing principles are often defined by international treaty (such as ICSID), and the parties to the disputes often come from different legal traditions. Not infrequently, these awards are published and available for review by third parties. The use of these awards as a quasi-authority has become more common (even though the principle of stare decisis does not technically apply) in investment arbitration, not only by legal counsel in support of their submissions but also by tribunals to justify decisions.[18] As a result, they can be a useful place to start for the purposes of seeking evidence of convergence between common law and civil principles.

15 JM Miquel Gonzalez, 'Buena fe', *Enciclopedia Jurídica Básica* (1995).

16 *Tribunal Supremo* 22 June 2010; 3 December 2010; 19 July 2013.

17 *Tribunal Supremo* 14 March 2011; 12 November 2013.

18 B Le Bars, 'Investment Arbitration Tribunals: Beyond the Civil-Common Law Dichotomy', (2017) 83(4) *The International Journal of Arbitration, Mediation and Dispute Management* 459, 467–468.

Is there any evidence of convergence of principles of good faith in international treaty arbitration?

7.33 We have sought to identify any trends identifiable from a number of published awards.

7.34 As a general observation, there does not appear to be a tendency for arbitral tribunals in investment treaty arbitration to take into account both the civil-common law principles when determining procedure, and when assessing the application of certain substantive law issues such as good faith, particularly when parties come from different legal traditions. As le Bars observes:[19]

> *Where diverging civil and common law cultures are most apparent, i.e. with respect to procedural or evidentiary matters, tribunals as well as international instruments strive to find common ground between both systems. ... The civil-common law dichotomy is thus becoming less relevant to decision-making by investment tribunals, and investment arbitration itself is moving towards convergence rather than divergence.*

In *Crystallex v Venezuela*, the tribunal recognised that it was '*operating as an international arbitral body established under the framework of an international treaty*'.[20] In that context, the tribunal sought to apply an approach to the quantification of damages which would be '*prone to satisfy common law and civil law minds*'.[21]

7.35 In *Noble Ventures v Romania*,[22] the tribunal was asked to adopt an American style of document disclosure. The tribunal refused on the basis that the ICSID Convention and the ICSID Arbitration Rules did not authorise any particular type of discovery process. Accordingly, the tribunal encouraged the parties to agree on the procedure for the disclosure of documents, taking into account that Romania was a civil law country where a more limited style of disclosure was used in court processes.

7.36 The issue of good faith has been considered on numerous occasions by tribunals considering investment treaty obligations.

7.37 In the case of *Europe Cement v Turkey*[23] (CIVIL) (Award), the tribunal noted that it is '*well accepted in investment arbitrations*' that the principle of good faith is a principle of international law applicable to the interpretation and application of obligations under international investment agreements (including the Energy Charter Treaty).

7.38 In *HOCHTIEF v Argentina* a tribunal determined that it was certainly arguable that there is a duty on both parties to the dispute to act in good faith during the pursuit of a settlement of the dispute. The tribunal opined:[24]

> *It is no doubt arguable that there is a duty on both parties to the dispute to act in good faith during the pursuit of a settlement of the dispute.*

---

19 B Le Bars, 'Investment Arbitration Tribunals: Beyond the Civil-Common Law Dichotomy' (2017) 83(4) *The International Journal of Arbitration, Mediation and Dispute Management* 459, 468.

20 *Crystallex International Corp v Venezuela*, ICSID Case No ARB(AF)/11/2, Award, 4 April 2016, at [866].

21 *Crystallex International Corp v Venezuela*, ICSID Case No ARB(AF)/11/2, Award, 4 April 2016, at [869].

22 ICSID Case No ARB/01/11, Award, 12 October 2005, at [20].

23 *Europe Cement Investment & Trade SA v Republic of Turkey* ICSID Case No ARB(AF)/07/2, 13 August 2009, at [171] – [174].

24 *HOCHTIEF Aktiengesellschaft v Argentine Republic*, ICSID Case No ARB/07/31, Decision on Jurisdiction, 24 October 2011, at [50].

In *Quiborax v Bolivia*[25] the tribunal determined that there was a duty on parties to arbitrate in good faith; the respondent's obligation to arbitrate implies the duty not to act in a manner that will undermine or frustrate the arbitral process; this includes, for instance, the duty to refrain from harming the procedural integrity of the arbitration or aggravating the dispute; actions directed against the efficient conduct of the arbitral proceedings may breach this duty even if such action is not prohibited by the express terms of the BIT or the ICSID Convention.

7.39 However, it has also been said (in *Mobil Investments Canada Inc v Government of Canada*) that good faith in respect of international investment arbitration is not a stand-alone basis of claim:[26]

> *In the context of the law of treaties ... the principle of good faith is not called upon to be 'a source of obligation where none would otherwise exist'. A party to a treaty is under a specific obligation to perform its obligations under the treaty, derived from the principle pacta sunt servanda, which can reasonably be described as one of the cornerstones of international law. Good faith is pertinent to the manner in which that obligation is to be performed; it is not put forward as a free-standing obligation.*[27]

In contrast, a more expansive approach to good faith has been taken by other tribunals:[28]

> *Good faith is a supreme principle, which governs legal relations in all of their aspects and content. Concerning the scope and content of the principle of good faith, it is necessary to take into account the following comments: 'The Latin expression bona FIDE is used in the original or translated into various languages, in Spanish "buena fe," to indicate the spirit of loyalty, respect for the law and fidelity, in other words, absence of dissimulation or fraud in relations between two or several parties in a legal act.'*

Similarly:

> *In the contractual field, good faith means absence of deceit and artifice during the negotiation and execution of instruments that gave rise to the investment, as well as loyalty, truth and intent to maintain the equilibrium between the reciprocal performance of the parties.*[29]

And:

> *As we know, good faith is a standard of conduct regulated by the ethical imperatives required under prevailing social conscience.*[30]

---

25 *Quiborax SA and Non Metallic Minerals SA v Plurinational State of Bolivia*, ICSID Case No ARB/06/2, Award, 16 September 2015.

26 *Mobil Investments Canada Inc v Government of Canada* ICSID Case No ARB/15/6, 13 July 2018, referring to Article 26 of the Vienna Convention on the Law of Treaties, 1969.

27 *Mobil Investments Canada Inc v Government of Canada* ICSID Case No ARB/15/6, 13 July 2018, referring to Article 26 of the Vienna Convention on the Law of Treaties, 1969.

28 Diccionario Jurídico Mexicano, Universidad Nacional Autónoma de México, Editorial Porrúa, Mexico, 1991, p 362.

29 *Inceysa Vallisoletana, SL v Republic of El Salvador* ICSID Case No ARB/03/26, 2 August 2006, at [231].

30 L Díez Picazo, *Fundamentos del Derecho Civil Patrimonial* (5th edn, Madrid, Editorial Civitas 1996) 398.

In *Methanex v United States*,[31] it was held that disputing parties have a duty to each other and to the tribunal to conduct themselves in good faith:[32]

> *In the Tribunal's view, the Disputing Parties each owed in this arbitration a general legal duty to the other and to the Tribunal to conduct themselves in good faith during these arbitration proceedings and to respect the equality of arms between them, the principles of 'equal treatment' and procedural fairness being also required by Article 15(1) of the UNCITRAL Rules. As a general principle, therefore, just as it would be wrong for the USA ex hypothesi to misuse its intelligence assets to spy on Methanex (and its witnesses) and to introduce into evidence the resulting materials into this arbitration, so too would it be wrong for Methanex to introduce evidential materials obtained by Methanex unlawfully.*

Therefore, there appears to be a general willingness by tribunals to try and find common ground between common law and civil law traditions when the parties to the arbitration come from different legal traditions.

Is there any evidence of convergence in international commercial arbitration?

7.40 For the reasons stated earlier, there is a fundamental difficulty in seeking to use commercial arbitration as a means of identifying trends in the development of substantive as well as procedural law – privacy of proceedings and confidentiality of awards being the principal ones. However, it is still possible to consider indirect sources and anecdotal evidence to identify how and why commercial arbitration might well be a driver of convergence between the common law and civil law traditions of good faith.

7.41 Professor Birke Hacker[33] has sought to identify, by reference to both civil and common law legal systems, the main factors that tend to promote a convergence or divergence of those systems:

a political and economic factors;
b institutional and procedural factors;
c factors relating to the sources of substantive law; and
d jurisprudential factors.[34]

In respect of institutional and procedural factors, Professor Hacker identifies these as legal training, court setup and everyday judicial practice. Whilst her analysis only makes reference to court systems, she comments that different countries sharing the same forensic traditions tend to follow each other more closely when it comes to developing concepts

31 *Methanex Corporation v United States of America*, UNCITRAL, Final Award, 3 August 2005. Methanex was cited with approval in *Cementownia "Nowa Huta" SA v Republic of Turkey*, ICSID Case No ARB(AF)/06/2, Award, 17 September 2009.

32 *Methanex Corporation v United States of America, UNCITRAL*, Final Award, 3 August 2005. Methanex was cited with approval in *Cementownia "Nowa Huta" SA v Republic of Turkey*, ICSID Case No. ARB(AF)/06/2, Award, 17 September 2009, at [153].

33 Professor of Comparative Law at the University of Oxford and a Professorial Fellow of Brasenose College, Oxford.

34 B Hacker, 'Divergence and Convergence in the Common Law – Lessons from the Ius Commune' (2015) *The Law Quarterly Review* 131.

such as good faith. It is submitted that, based on the authors' experience, this is also the case with arbitrators from countries with similar legal systems.

7.42 Guy Canivet is also of the view that common law and civil law systems are converging, partly due to globalisation:[35]

> *The two great legal cultures are certainly not monolithic and closed; they mutually define and influence themselves; they assert themselves in confrontation and comparison much more than in withdrawal and the illusory protection of legal 'sovereignism'…*
>
> *… Globalization is so powerful that, by now, all lawyers have the feeling of living a sort of generalized legal acculturation due to the competition legal systems engage in.*[36]

Legrand cites Basil Markesinis, as follows,

> *There is thus a convergence of solutions in the area of private law as the problems faced by courts and legislators acquire a common and international flavour; there is a convergence in the sources of our law since nowadays case law de facto if not de jure forms a major source of law in both common and civil law countries … there is a growing rapprochement in judicial views.*[37]

Pejović is also of the view that globally private law, particularly in Europe, is converging:[38]

> *Whether courts are bound or not by precedents, judges in all legal systems are aware that the need of reasonable certainty and predictability requires that like cases be treated alike. Hence, in contemporary civil law the role of judges in the creation of law is increasingly important, while the difference between civil law and common law courts shows a tendency of disappearing, or at least looking less significant. The presence or absence of a formal doctrine of stare decisis does not have crucial importance and it may be expected that differences between the common law and civil law systems in this area will diminish over time.*

Likewise:[39]

> *If a foreign legal system has some advantages, why not incorporate them in the domestic legal system? In that way the resulting convergence of the two legal systems can only contribute to their common goal of creating a fair and just legal system which can provide legal certainty and protection to all citizens and legal persons.*

Globalisation, and resultant interconnectivity, between countries, companies and legal jurisdictions is also promoting convergence.

---

35 G Canivet, 'The Interrelationship between Common Law and Civil Law' (2003) 63(4) La L Rev 937, 938.

36 ibid.

37 P Legrand, 'European Legal Systems Are Not Converging' (1996) 45(1) *ICLQ* 52, 54–55, citing B S Markesinis, 'Learning from Europe and Learning in Europe' in B S Markesinis (ed), *The Gradual Convergence, Foreign Ideas, Foreign Influences and English Law on the Eve of the 21st Century* (Clarendon Press, Oxford 1994) 30.

38 Č Pejović, 'Civil Law and Common Law: Two Different Paths Leading to the Same Goal' (2001) PPP god 7–32, p 837.

39 Č Pejović, 'Civil Law and Common Law: Two Different Paths Leading to the Same Goal' (2001) PPP god 7–32, p 840.

> *One trend that is promoting convergence between civil law traditions and the English tradition at present is that Courts, and jurists are increasingly aware that a developing relatively globalised economy and society is throwing up new challenges and it is seen as appropriate for the law to respond to these either in the same way in different jurisdictions, or, if that cannot be achieved, at least in the light of consideration of the same factors.*[40]

Furthermore:

> *Both systems of law tend to reach the same results, although by different routes. ... The common law recognises restrictions on the exercise of contractual discretion. A party must not exercise such discretion in a manner which is arbitrary, capricious or irrational. There is also the implied obligation to co-operate as noted above. These rules usually lead to the same outcome as the 'good faith' provision in a civil law jurisdiction.*[41]

However, complete convergence of legal traditions is not a universally held view.

> *While a certain rapprochement between civil law and common law systems is evident and this tendency will continue, there are still important differences which will continue to exist for an indefinite period.*[42]

Care needs to be taken in mistaking interest in different legal systems and actual convergence:

> *one should not assume always that because there is an interest in material from another legal tradition, and, indeed, direct reference to it that that is evidence of genuine convergence.*[43]

There is even a question whether convergence will ever be possible:

> *to integrate a group of 'legal cultures' does not appear any more feasible than would the integration of the different worldviews privileged by a wide range of societies. Once one moves away from rules and concepts, it is no longer at all clear that the civil law and common law worlds are converging.*[44]

Furthermore:

> *such convergence, even if it were thought desirable (which, in my view, it is not), is impossible on account of the fact that the differences arising between the common law and civil law mentalités at the epistemological level are irreducible.*[45]

---

40 J Blackie, 'Convergence of the Common Law and the Civil Law – The Scottish Experience' (2003) 3 *Hanse Law School Cahier*, 7–8.

41 Lecture by Sir Rupert Jackson on 'The Role of Good Faith in Construction Contracts', 24 May 2018, para 4.2.

42 Č Pejović, 'Civil Law and Common Law: Two Different Paths Leading to the Same Goal' (2001) PPP god 7–32, p 840.

43 J Blackie, 'Convergence of the Common Law and the Civil Law – The Scottish Experience' (2003) 3 *Hanse Law School Cahier*, 11–12.

44 P Legrand, 'European Legal Systems Are Not Converging' (1996) 45(1) ICLQ 52, 60.

45 P Legrand, 'European Legal Systems Are Not Converging' (1996) 45(1) ICLQ 52, 61–62.

Any evidence of convergence between civil and common law?

Is there evidence of movement by English law towards a civil law approach to good faith?

7.43 Earlier, we described the so-called orthodoxy of English law when it comes to the concept of good faith and that there were signs that the orthodoxy may now be being challenged in the courts.

7.44 The judgment of Leggatt J (as he was then) in *Yam Seng Pte Ltd v ITC*[46] is often cited as the most comprehensive articulation of this challenge to the orthodoxy. In his judgment, Leggatt J cited three historical reasons for English law's hostility towards the doctrine of good faith: (1) preference for use of piecemeal, incremental solutions; (2) an ethos of individualism; and (3) the uncertainty this would cause.[47]

7.45 However, Leggatt J challenged the orthodox idea that common law and civil law systems took a fundamentally different approach to good faith:[48]

> *It would be a mistake, moreover, to suppose that willingness to recognise a doctrine of good faith in the performance of contracts reflects a divide between civil law and common law systems or between continental paternalism and Anglo-Saxon individualism. Any such notion is gainsaid by that fact that such a doctrine has long been recognised in the United States.*

He went on to contend that an implied duty of good faith was entirely consistent with English law. Specifically, he said that it was entirely consistent with the English law approach to the interpretation of contracts, and implication of terms:[49]

> *This follows from the fact that the content of the duty of good faith is established by a process of construction which in English law is based on an objective principle. The court is concerned not with the subjective intentions of the parties but with their presumed intention, which is ascertained by attributing to them the purposes and values which reasonable people in their situation would have had.*

Understood this way, Leggatt J explained that there is, in his view, nothing novel or foreign to English law in recognising an implied duty of good faith in the performance of commercial contracts. He gave six reasons for this:[50]

> *147. First, because the content of the duty is heavily dependent on context and is established through a process of construction of the contract, its recognition is entirely consistent with the case by case approach favoured by the common law. There is therefore no need for common lawyers to abandon their characteristic methods and adopt those of civil law systems in order to accommodate the principle.*
>
> *148. Second, as the basis of the duty of good faith is the presumed intention of the parties and meaning of their contract, its recognition is not an illegitimate restriction on the freedom of the parties to pursue their own interests. The essence of contracting is that the parties bind themselves in order to co-operate to their mutual benefit. The obligations which they*

46 *Yam Seng Pte Ltd v ITC* [2013] EWHC 111.
47 *Yam Seng Pte Ltd v ITC* [2013] EWHC 111, [123].
48 *Yam Seng Pte Ltd v ITC* [2013] EWHC 111, [125].
49 *Yam Seng Pte Ltd v ITC* [2013] EWHC 111, [144].
50 *Yam Seng Pte Ltd v ITC* [2013] EWHC 111, [147] – [152].

undertake include those which are implicit in their agreement as well as those which they have made explicit.

149. Third, a further consequence of the fact that the duty is based on the parties' presumed intention is that it is open to the parties to modify the scope of the duty by the express terms of their contract and, in principle at least, to exclude it altogether. I say 'in principle at least' because in practice it is hardly conceivable that contracting parties would attempt expressly to exclude the core requirement to act honestly.

150. Fourth, I see no objection, and some advantage, in describing the duty as one of good faith 'and fair dealing'. I see no objection, as the duty does not involve the court in imposing its view of what is substantively fair on the parties. What constitutes fair dealing is defined by the contract and by those standards of conduct to which, objectively, the parties must reasonably have assumed compliance without the need to state them. The advantage of including reference to fair dealing is that it draws attention to the fact that the standard is objective and distinguishes the relevant concept of good faith from other senses in which the expression 'good faith' is used.

151. Fifth, in so far as English law may be less willing than some other legal systems to interpret the duty of good faith as requiring openness of the kind described by Bingham LJ in the Interfoto case as 'playing fair' 'coming clean' or 'putting one's cards face upwards on the table', this should be seen as a difference of opinion, which may reflect different cultural norms, about what constitutes good faith and fair dealing in some contractual contexts rather than a refusal to recognise that good faith and fair dealing are required.

152. Sixth, the fear that recognising a duty of good faith would generate excessive uncertainty is unjustified. There is nothing unduly vague or unworkable about the concept. Its application involves no more uncertainty than is inherent in the process of contractual interpretation.

In terms of context, the fact that a particular contract creates a longer term relationship between the parties is particularly relevant:[51]

English law has traditionally drawn a sharp distinction between certain relationships – such as partnership, trusteeship and other fiduciary relationships – on the one hand, in which the parties owe onerous obligations of disclosure to each other, and other contractual relationships in which no duty of disclosure is supposed to operate. Arguably at least, that dichotomy is too simplistic. While it seems unlikely that any duty to disclose information in performance of the contract would be implied where the contract involves a simple exchange, many contracts do not fit this model and involve a longer term relationship between the parties which they make a substantial commitment. Such 'relational' contracts, as they are sometimes called, may require a high degree of communication, cooperation and predictable performance based on mutual trust and confidence and involve expectations of loyalty which are not legislated for in the express terms of the contract but are implicit in the parties' understanding and necessary to give business efficacy to the arrangements. Examples of such relational contracts might include some joint venture agreements, franchise agreements and long term distributorship agreements.

A number of judgments appear to have recognised the legitimacy of this challenge to the good faith orthodoxy of English law.

7.46 In *Emirates Trading Agency LLC v Prime Mineral Exports Private Ltd*, Leggatt J's analysis was described by Teare J as '*masterly*'.[52] It was also stated that '*the obligation*

51 *Yam Seng Pte Ltd v ITC* [2013] EWHC 111, [142].

52 [2014] EWHC 2104 (Comm), [51].

to seek to resolve disputes by friendly discussions must import an obligation to seek to do so in good faith'[53] and, '*In traditional terms such an obligation goes without saying and is necessary to give business efficacy to the contract. In modern terms that is what the contract would be reasonably understood to mean*'.[54]

7.47 In *Mid Essex Hospital Services NHS Trust v Compass Group UK and Ireland Ltd*,[55] the agreement in dispute contained an express duty to '*co-operate ... in good faith*' and it was held that this was subject to the same consideration Leggatt J placed on context in *Yam Seng* when determining whether an implied duty of good faith exists. Context was also relevant when considering the extent of an express duty of good faith:[56]

> *Leggatt J gave extensive consideration to the question of implying a duty of good faith into a contract. His discussion emphasised that 'what good faith requires is sensitive to context', that the test of good faith is objective in the sense that it depends on whether, in the particular context, the conduct would be regarded as commercially unacceptable by reasonable and honest people, and that its content 'is established through a process of construction of the contract'. ... Those considerations are also relevant to the interpretation of an express obligation to act in good faith.*

Furthermore:[57]

> *The scope of the obligation to co-operate in good faith in clause 3.5 must be assessed in the light of the provisions of that clause, the other provisions of the contract, and its overall context.*

In *Sheikh Tahnoon Bin Saeed Bin Shakhboot Al Nehayan v Ioannis Kent*,[58] Leggatt LJ commented that:[59]

> *In the circumstances the contract made between these parties seems to me to be a classic instance of a relational contract. In my view, the implication of a duty of good faith in the contract is essential to give effect to the parties' reasonable expectations and satisfies the business necessity test which Lord Neuberger in Marks & Spencer Plc v BNP Paribas Securities Services Trust Co (Jersey) Ltd [2016] AC 742, [2015] UKSC 72 at paras 16 to 31 reiterated as the relevant standard for the implication of a term into a contract.*

Furthermore:[60]

> *I do not consider that, on the authorities I have identified, English law rejects a legal requirement of good faith. What the cases make clear is that such a duty will not be routinely applied to all commercial contracts.*

---

53 *Emirates Trading Agency LLC v Prime Mineral Exports Private Ltd* [2014] EWHC 2104 (Comm), [38].

54 *Emirates Trading Agency LLC v Prime Mineral Exports Private Ltd* [2014] EWHC 2104 (Comm), [51].

55 [2013] EWCA Civ 200.

56 *Mid Essex Hospital Services NHS Trust v Compass Group UK and Ireland Ltd* [2013] EWCA Civ 200, [150].

57 *Mid Essex Hospital Services NHS Trust v Compass Group UK and Ireland Ltd* [2013] EWCA Civ 200, [151].

58 *Sheikh Tahnoon Bin Saeed Bin Shakhboot Al Nehayan v Ioannis Kent* [2018] EWHC 333 (Comm).

59 *Sheikh Tahnoon Bin Saeed Bin Shakhboot Al Nehayan v Ioannis Kent* [2018] EWHC 333 (Comm), [174].

60 *Bates & Ors v Post Office* [2019] EWHC 606 (QB), [710].

However, this challenge to the orthodoxy has not been universally welcomed.

7.48 In *Hamsard 3147 Ltd v Boots UK Ltd*, Norris J stated,

> *I do not regard the decision in Yam Seng Pte Ltd v International Trade Corporation as authority for the proposition that in commercial contracts it may be taken to be the presumed intention of the parties that there is a general obligation of 'good faith'.*[61]

7.49 In *Greenclose Ltd v National Westminster Bank*, Andrews J stated that '*Leggatt J's judgment in Yam Seng Pte Ltd v International Trade Corporation Ltd ... is not to be regarded as laying down any general principle applicable to all commercial contracts*'.[62]

7.50 In *Globe Motors Inc v TRW Lucas Variety Electric Steering Ltd*, the Court of Appeal confirmed that, in the context of relational contracts, the '*implication of a duty of good faith will only be possible where the language of the contract, viewed against its context, permits it. It is thus not a reflection of a special rule of interpretation for this category of contract*'.[63]

7.51 Furthermore:[64]

> *There is no general doctrine of 'good faith' in English contract law. ... If the parties wish to impose such a duty they must do so expressly. ... The obligation to co-operate in good faith is not a general one which qualifies or reinforces all of the obligations on the parties in all situations where they interact. The obligation to co-operate in good faith is specifically focused upon the two purposes stated* [in the agreement in dispute].

In respect of these reactions, Leggatt LJ acknowledged that the observations he made in '*the Yam Seng case about the scope for implying duties of good faith in English contract law have provoked divergent reactions, [though] there appears to be growing recognition that such a duty may readily be implied in a relational contract*'.[65]

7.52 However, it is certainly arguable that the door is now more open than it was, for courts and tribunals applying English law to look more broadly at the interpretation of contractual terms and identify whether in respect of a particular contract, when read in its particular context, the implication for a duty of good faith might be appropriate.

7.53 However, as stated by Mr Justice Jackson,[66] whether such a duty is in fact necessary is debatable:[67]

> *Both systems of law tend to reach the same results, although by different routes. ... The common law recognises restrictions on the exercise of contractual discretion. A party must not exercise such discretion in a manner which is arbitrary, capricious or irrational. There is also the implied obligation to co-operate as noted above. These rules usually lead to the same outcome as the 'good faith' provision in a civil law jurisdiction.*

---

61 [2013] EWHC 3251 (Pat), [86].

62 [2014] EWHC 1156 (Ch), [150].

63 [2016] EWCA Civ 396, [68].

64 *Mid Essex Hospital Services NHS Trust v Compass Group UK and Ireland Ltd* [2013] EWCA Civ 200, [105] – [106].

65 *Sheikh Tahnoon Bin Saeed Bin Shakhboot Al Nehayan v Ioannis Kent* [2018] EWHC 333 (Comm), [168].

66 Former Head of the Technology and Construction Court and former Lord Justice of Appeal.

67 Lecture by Sir Rupert Jackson on 'The Role of Good Faith in Construction Contracts', 24 May 2018, para 4.2.

Have other common law systems moved towards a general principle of good faith?

7.54 In the United States, where the common law system regarding contracts has been codified, a principle of good faith has formed part of US Federal commercial law for some time.

7.55 The Uniform Commercial Code states at §1–304: '*Every contract ... imposes an obligation of good faith in its performance or enforcement*'. Furthermore, US Restatement (Second) of Contracts states at §205: '*Every contract imposes upon each party a duty of good faith and fair dealing in its performance and its enforcement*'.

7.56 This has been confirmed in a number of cases. For example, in *Wigand v Bachmann-Bechtel Brewing Co*:[68]

> *Every contract implies good faith and fair dealing between the parties to it.*

Similarly in Canada, the courts have, at least in some situations, been willing to imply such duties with a view to securing the performance and enforcement of the contract.

7.57 In *Bhasin v Hrynew*, the Supreme Court of Canada stated:[69]

> *The first step is to recognize that there is an organizing principle of good faith that underlies and manifests itself in various more specific doctrines governing contractual performance. That organizing principle is simply that parties generally must perform their contractual duties honestly and reasonably and not capriciously or arbitrarily.*
>
> *... a contracting party should have appropriate regard to the legitimate contractual interests of the contracting partner. While 'appropriate regard' for the other party's interests will vary depending on the context of the contractual relationship, it does not require acting to serve those interests in all cases. It merely requires that a party not seek to undermine those interests in bad faith.*

In Singapore, whilst there is no implied duty of good faith, the court has '*lef[t] open the possibility that such a duty could be implied by way of the narrower category of "terms implied in fact"*'.[70]

7.58 In Australia, whilst an implied contractual duty of good already exists, the precise juridical basis of the doctrine has still not been settled. The leading judgment is the New South Wales Court of Appeal in *Renard Constructions (ME) Pty v Minister for Public Works*, where Priestley JA said that:[71]

> *people generally, including judges and other lawyers, from all strands of the community, have grown used to the courts applying standards of fairness to contract which are wholly consistent with the existence in all contracts of a duty upon the parties of good faith and fair dealing in its performance. In my view this is in these days the expected standard, and anything less is contrary to prevailing community expectations.*

---

68 222 NY 272, [277].

69 2014, SCC 71, [63] – [65].

70 *The One Suits Pte Ltd v Pacific Motor Credit (Pte) Ltd* [2015] 3 SLR 695 (Singapore Court of Appeal), [44].

71 (1992) 44 NSWLR 349, [95].

In *Paciocco v ANZ Banking Group Federal Court of Australia* it was held that:

> *(G)ood faith ... is a conception that has been recognised (though not by all courts in Australia) as an implication or feature of Australian contract law attending the performance of the bargain and its construction and implied content. ...*[72]
>
> *The usual content of the obligation of good faith is ... an obligation to act honestly and with a fidelity to the bargain; an obligation not to act dishonestly and not to undermine the bargain entered or the substance of the contractual benefit bargained for; and an obligation to act reasonably and with fair dealing having regard to the interests of the parties (which will, inevitably, at times conflict) and to the provisions, aims and purposes of the contract, objectively ascertained.*[73]
>
> *None of these obligations requires the interests of a contracting party to be subordinated to those of the other. It is good faith or fair dealing between the parties by reference to the bargain and its terms that is called for, be they both commercial parties or business dealing with consumers.*[74]

Has there been any movement in civil law jurisdictions towards more limited good faith obligations akin to the common law approach?

7.59 In terms of developments of French law, there has been no legislative limitation placed on the duty of good faith. On the contrary, as referred to earlier, the application of good faith has recently been expanded to cover pre-contractual behaviour.[75]

7.60 However, some French commentators have considered whether, in reality, English and French laws are really that different when it comes to good faith and judicial outcomes.

7.61 Severine Saintier[76] is of the view that although good faith has been codified in the French Civil Code, the concept of good faith has not been defined and thus operates flexibly, which is not too dissimilar from the contextualist approach of Leggatt J in *Yam Seng*.

> *The French civil code does not define good faith and the French courts have used the notion as a tool to impose a certain standard of behaviour on the parties when performing their obligations. It is therefore a comportmental norm, a rule of conduct.*[77]

7.62 Saintier draws comparisons between the flexibility of the two systems in the context of good faith, highlighting the similarities between French and English laws and that good faith is not as divisive a notion as is perceived. In this respect, Saintier praises Leggatt J's approach in *Yam Seng*, in linking good faith to existing norms.

7.63 Commenting on Leggatt J's approach in *Yam Seng*:

> *Such a contextual approach is pragmatic and flexible, and, interestingly, bears similarities with the French approach ...*[78]

---

72 [2015] FCAFC 50 (April 2015), [287].

73 [2015] FCAFC 50 (April 2015), [288].

74 [2015] FCAFC 50 (April 2015), [289].

75 See earlier, two paragraphs after the section, '**Civil law approach to "Good Faith"**'.

76 Dr Saintier is Associate Professor in commercial law (Education and Research) at Exeter University.

77 S Saintier, 'The Elusive Notion of Good Faith in the Performance of a Contract, Why Still a Bête Noire for the Civil and the Common Law?' (2017) 6 JBL 441, 444.

78 ibid.

> ... *as a rule of conduct, good faith in France is traditionally seen as requiring duties of loyalty, co-operation and coherence of the parties* ...[79]
>
> ... *The continuation of Leggatt J 'shared values and norms of behaviour' is clear. Good faith, in this context, is therefore used by the judiciary, in a manner similar to its French judicial counterpart, as a standard, as a social (contractual) norm* ...[80]
>
> ... *Leggatt J affirms the importance of the context, hereby, adopting a 'contextualist bent'.*[81]

Moreover:[82]

> *there seems to be a broad consensus in France and in the UK that good faith includes honesty at a minimum, that honesty is broader than merely avoiding fraud and deception and that only a serious breach will amount to bad faith. ... This commonality between the two big legal families represents an important step in highlighting that good faith should indeed not separate them.*

Jan van Duneé also agrees that the French and English approaches to good faith are similar in reality:[83]

> *Civil law countries, e.g. France, over the last century have known a discussion strikingly similar to the one carried on in the UK, which at times has a replay in our time.*
>
> ... *The common approach of French courts is that good faith is not taken for the vague, ambiguous general rule as often presumed, but on the contrary as the source for a specific rule of conduct or obligation for contracting parties. The resulting duties, such as to provide safety to persons or goods carried in transport, to co-operate with the other party or to disclose information, are not unlike what the English courts have decided in comparable contract disputes, over the years.*

Promoting good faith, whether under civil or common law, must be a feature of sophisticated legal systems.

> *The aim of any mature system of contract law must be to promote the observance of good faith and fair dealing in the conclusion and performance of contracts. The first imperative of good faith and fair dealing is that contracts ought to be upheld. But there is another theme of good faith and fair dealing: the reasonable expectations of honest men must be protected. It occasionally requires that the law should treat contractual obligations as defeasible or that a discretionary remedy should be denied. In these broad terms the common law and the civil law have a shared view of the aim of the law of contract.*[84]

79 S Saintier, 'The Elusive Notion of Good Faith in the Performance of a Contract, Why Still a Bête Noire for the Civil and the Common Law?' (2017) 6 JBL 441, 447.

80 S Saintier, 'The Elusive Notion of Good Faith in the Performance of a Contract, Why Still a Bête Noire for the Civil and the Common Law?' (2017) 6 JBL 441, 453.

81 S Saintier, 'The Elusive Notion of Good Faith in the Performance of a Contract, Why Still a Bête Noire for the Civil and the Common Law?' (2017) 6 JBL 441, 444.

82 S Saintier, 'The Elusive Notion of Good Faith in the Performance of a Contract, Why Still a Bête Noire for the Civil and the Common Law?' (2017) 6 JBL 441, 453.

83 J van Duneé, 'On a Clear Day, You Can See the Continent – The Shrouded Acceptance of Good Faith as a General Rule of Contract Law on the British Isles' (2015) 31(1) Const LJ 3.

84 The Hon Mr Justice Steyn, 'The Role of Good Faith and Fair Dealing in Contract Law: A Hair-Shirt Philosophy?' (1991) 6(1) *The Denning Law Journal* 131, 131.

However, it has been suggested that good faith is not appropriate in every contract.

> *There are so many varieties of contract. In some contexts good faith and fair dealing have no significant role to play. Such is the case, for example, in many commercial contracts where one is not concerned with fault but simply with an allocation of the risks of a particular undertaking or enterprise.*[85]

Conclusions

7.64 By its very nature, international arbitration acts as a conduit for the exchange of legal concepts between civil law and common law. Published awards in investment treaty arbitrations suggest that where the parties are from differing legal traditions tribunals will try, where possible, to find a compromise between the two. There is evidence that this approach has been taken in respect of principles of good faith when applied in the context of international treaties.

7.65 It is much harder to draw conclusions from international commercial arbitration applying the contract law of specific jurisdictions, given that relatively few awards are ever published. However, from the personal experience of the authors and anecdotal evidence of colleagues there remain differences between common law and civil law approaches to good faith and these are almost always respected and enforced according to the governing law of the contract, regardless of the legal traditions of the individual arbitrators. That being said, in the context of commercial disputes, different governing laws often reach similar practical end results albeit through differing routes.

7.66 As to evidence of actual convergence of the substantive law, relatively recent developments in English law suggest that there may be a movement towards a more consistent approach between civil law and common law and that such convergence may accelerate in the future. The appointment of Lord Leggatt to the UK Supreme Court may be a catalyst for that acceleration. Indeed, some academic commentators on comparative law have suggested that the English and French law approaches to good faith have already reached convergence, particularly after Lord Leggatt's judgment in *Yam Seng* and following cases.

85 The Hon Mr Justice Steyn, 'The Role of Good Faith and Fair Dealing in Contract Law: A Hair-Shirt Philosophy?' (1991) 6(1) *The Denning Law Journal* 131, 140.

CHAPTER 8

Collaborative dispute resolution

Shy Jackson

Introduction

8.1 Over recent years, there has been a growing recognition that collaborative contracts can help deliver better outcomes, and this trend is reflected in the publication and use of collaborative contracts such as the New Engineering Contract (NEC), the Project Partnering Contract (PPC2000) and the JCT's Constructing Excellence contract as well as the more recent alliancing forms of contract such as FAC-1 and the NEC Alliance Contract. From a legal perspective, such contracts often set out and rely on obligations akin to good faith, even where the term good faith is not expressly used. In that context, the courts have begun to accept that some contracts, referred to as 'relational' contracts, are a type of contract where it may be appropriate to imply a good faith obligation where one is not already included.

8.2 Disputes, or differences, are a natural part of construction and to some degree are a feature of every project. Quite often, the approach has been to have any disputes managed as a separate part of the construction project, which takes place following completion when both parties try to justify their view of the correct contractual entitlement. This will be through arbitration or court proceedings, which will take place over several years at a very great expense to the parties. The difficulty with that approach is that by the time the matter comes to trial, there is little direct knowledge of what happened and much of the expense involves lawyers and expert witnesses trying to piece together what happened several years earlier. This requires an extensive review of the contemporaneous project documents, which are seen as more reliable than witness evidence, but adds to the cost and duration of such proceedings. The parties themselves soon realise that even if the majority of the dispute related work is done by lawyers and other consultants, being involved in such a dispute results in a diversion of management time and significant opportunity cost, as well as having a detrimental impact on the parties' long-term relationship. The resolution of the dispute is based on the contractual rights and obligations, not the wider relationship between the parties.

8.3 This raises the question as to whether collaborative techniques can also be used in order to prevent and resolve disputes more efficiently, in the same way that they can improve project delivery. Applying good faith or collaboration to a dispute resolution process seems counter-intuitive, but this is consistent with one of the over-arching principles of collaborative contracts, namely the desire to create a strong and long-lasting working relationship which results in better delivery to ensure projects are completed on time, on budget and to the required quality. This also reflects the thinking behind relational contracts, which are based on the idea that in certain commercial relationships it is necessary, and beneficial to the parties, to look at the wider relationship and beyond the four corners of the contract. That, however, goes against the traditional approach to contract law and is far from straightforward.

8.4 This chapter will therefore look at how the approach to good faith and relational contracting has developed over recent years, recognising a contract cannot be seen as just a set of rights and obligations, before looking at some of the recent trends in dispute resolution and the various processes which have been developed to resolve disputes collaboratively and in a way that avoids the hostile and adversarial environment that is usually associated with dispute resolution and the costs and other downsides of a lengthy formal dispute resolution process.

Good faith under English law: the traditional view

8.5 Before looking at collaborative dispute resolution, it is useful to consider how good faith has been regarded by traditional English lawyers. This is because the emphasis on certainty and contractual freedom, relied on to reject a concept of good faith, is also relevant when lawyers come to consider different ways of resolving disputes and how such methods would operate in practice.

8.6 It is not necessary or possible to set out in this chapter the full background to the application of good faith under English law. The traditional position has been that, save for specific areas of law, there is no general principle of good faith that applies to commercial dealings and it is not part of the law of contract. On one view, this is not due to any objections in principle, as English law does apply good faith in certain areas of law, but because, as Bingham LJ noted in *Interfoto Picture Library Ltd v Stiletto Visual Programs Ltd*,[1] English law has not committed itself to an overriding principle of good faith but has instead developed piecemeal solutions in response to demonstrated problems of unfairness.

8.7 A different view, however, was expressed in the House of Lords' decision in *Walford v Miles*[2] where Lord Ackner stated that

> *the concept of a duty to carry on negotiations in good faith is inherently repugnant to the adversarial position of the parties when involved in negotiations. Each party to the negotiations is entitled to pursue his (or her) own interest, so long as he avoids making misrepresentations. ... A duty to negotiate in good faith is unworkable in practice as it is inherently inconsistent with the position of a negotiating party.*[3]

8.8 This decision addressed the position during pre-contractual negotiations, but the clear message is that negotiations are an adversarial process where a party can do anything it wants in order to gain a commercial advantage, short of misrepresentation. In other

1 [1989] QB 433.

2 [1992] 2 AC 128. The same approach was followed in *Ultraframe (UK) Limited v Tailored Roofing Systems* [2004] EWCA Civ 585, para 17, where Waller LJ agreed with Bingham MR's observation in *Philips Electronique Grand Public SA v British Sky Broadcasting Ltd* [1995] EMLR 472, 484, that the implication of terms is so potentially intrusive that the law enforces strict constraints on the exercise of this extraordinary power, all the more so when parties enter into lengthy and carefully drafted contracts.

3 [1992] 2 AC 128, 138.

words, caveat emptor is the basis for commercial dealings and, for example, a party may remain silent if it serves its purpose and it has not been asked a direct question. There are no obligations, or rights, other than what is expressly included in the contract.

8.9 Some lawyers hold the view that, in modern commerce, a party is therefore entitled to take any steps it wishes unless there is an express prohibition against such conduct. In a decision concerning the construction of the new Wembley stadium, Jackson J (as he then was) described a party's conduct, based on a deliberate strategy of issuing certificates for the lowest values it believed it could defend, as being ruthless but lawful.[4] A similar sentiment was expressed by Lord Rodger in a case concerning the disclosure of information in *Hamilton v Allied Domecq PLC* when he stated that '*a failure on the part of Mr Beatty to speak might be regarded as morally questionable. But that is different from saying that he was under a legal duty to speak*'.[5]

8.10 The same approach can be taken to dispute resolution, a situation where quite often procedural issues will come up and parties will raise arguments which are aimed at affecting the other side's ability to present an argument, rather than addressing the underlying substantive issues or seeking to assist the tribunal to reach the correct decision.

8.11 Another objection to recognising, and enforcing, good faith is the difficulty in applying what is seen as a subjective term that cannot be addressed with certainty. This was the sentiment expressed more recently in *Costain Ltd v Tarmac Holdings Ltd*[6] where in considering an argument for good faith under an NEC form of contract the judge stated that:[7]

> *it is a form of contractual duty which requires the obliger to have regard to the interests of the obligee, while also being entitled to have regard to its own self-interest when acting ... I respectfully agree with that summary ... although I am a little uneasy about a more general obligation to act 'fairly'; that is a difficult obligation to police because it is so subjective.*

This uneasiness with a subjective good faith concept is similar to the difficulty some courts have faced with seeking to identify what makes commercial sense in the content of contract interpretation[8] and as noted in *S&T (UK) v Grove Developments*,[9] where Lord Justice Jackson observed that '*Judges should not generally impose their notions of commercial common sense upon the parties to business disputes*'.

8.12 The other uncertainty created by recognising good faith as an enforceable obligation is the issue of how such a general concept interacts with other express contractual provisions. This uncertainty was highlighted in *Mid Essex Hospital Services NHS Trust v Compass Group UK and Ireland Ltd*[10] where the Court of Appeal reversed the High

4 *Multiplex Constructions (UK) Ltd v Cleveland Bridge UK Ltd* [2006] EWHC 1341 (TCC), para 628.

5 *Hamilton and others v Allied Domecq Plc* [2007] UKHL 33, 2007 SC (HL) 142, 2007 SLT 697, para 20. See also S Jackson, 'The Duty to Disclose: A Clash of Laws and Morality' (2008) 24 Const LJ 675.

6 [2017] EWHC 319 (TCC).

7 ibid, paras 122–123.

8 *Skanska Rashleigh Weatherfoil Ltd v Somerfield Stored Ltd* [2006] EWCA Civ 1732 and *BMA Special Opportunity Hub Fund Ltd v African Minerals Ltd* [2006] EWCA Civ 1732, para 22.

9 [2018] EWCA Civ 2448, para 121.

10 [2013] EWCA Civ 200. See also S Jackson, 'Of Chocolate Mousse and Good faith' in Julian Bailey (ed), *Construction Law, Costs and Contemporary Developments: Drawing the Threads Together – A Festschrift for Lord Justice Jackson* (Hart Publishing 2018).

Court's finding that there was a breach of the express good faith clause included in the contract. Beatson LJ pointed out that the scope of the obligation to cooperate in good faith had to be considered in light of the rest of the contract and its overall context and warned against construing a good faith clause in a general and open-ended manner. The same point was made by Lord Justice Moore-Bick in *MSC Mediterranean Shipping Company SA v Cottonex Anstalt* when he warned of the danger that a general principle of good faith would often be invoked to undermine the terms on which the parties have reached agreement.[11]

8.13 Indeed, even where good faith has been recognised, the courts have made it clear it would not require a party to act against its own interest. In *Sainsbury's Supermarkets Ltd v Bristol Rovers (1883) Ltd*[12] the court confirmed the principle that an obligation of good faith in relation to the fulfilment of a specific obligation contained in a contract cannot be used to require the parties to do things not specified by the agreement. Similarly, in *Mears Ltd v Shoreline Housing Partnership Ltd*, which concerned the NEC3 Term Service Contract with reference to clause 10.1, the judge stated that:[13]

> *however, I am, further, not satisfied that there would be any such implied term or that the obligation to act in a spirit of mutual trust and cooperation or even in a 'partnering way' would prevent either party from relying on any express terms of the contract freely entered into by each party.*

The traditional resistance to recognising good faith is therefore driven by a desire for certainty and a reluctance to rely on what is seen as a subjective and nebulous concept, but also by a belief that commercial dealings are an adversarial process where each party can act in its own interest and is under no obligation to 'play fair' or assist the other party. If that is the position in relation to the performance of contractual obligations during the life of a contract, it is not surprising that even less is expected of the parties when they are in a dispute and engaged in a process that is adversarial by definition. But if the parties have taken the decision to enter into a collaborative contract and are also behaving collaboratively (the latter does not always follow the former), it is difficult to see why they would not use the same approach to resolve any differences that may arise.

Managing disputes in good faith

8.14 In commercial contracts that concern the sale and purchase of standard or off the shelf goods, where the main consideration is price and there is no long-term relationship between the parties, one can see why collaboration or good faith would have a limited role. That is not however the case in construction projects, where parties will have to work together, often over a number of years, so that over the course of a project it is likely that both parties will need the assistance of the other party in managing the impact of risks they are responsible for.

8.15 This gave rise to the use of partnering contracts in construction, something that came up before the courts over 20 years ago in *Birse Construction Limited v St. David*

11 [2016] EWCA Civ 789, para 45.

12 [2016] EWCA Civ 160.

13 *Mears Ltd v Shoreline Housing Partnership Ltd* [2015] EWHC 1396 (TCC), para 70.

Limited.[14] The case revolved around whether there was a binding contract between the parties, but it was clear that the parties had intended to enter into an alliancing arrangement based on the JCT 1980 form of contract. In a decision a few years after *Walford v Miles* Lloyd J observed as follows about the expected conduct from parties during the negotiation stage:[15]

> *The terms of that [partnership charter], though clearly not legally binding, are important for they were clearly intended to provide the standards by which the parties were to conduct themselves and against which their conduct and attitudes were to be measured. If Mr Heath had thought that Mr Goff had agreed to something that he ought not to have accepted Mr Heath would have said so, for that would be consistent with an expression of 'mutual cooperation and trust' and a relationship which was intended 'to promote an environment of trust, integrity, honesty and openness' and 'to promote clear and effective communication'.*

The idea that if one party appreciates that the other has made a mistake in understanding what was intended, it should say so should not be controversial, but it does not reflect the views of those who see commercial dealings as opportunistic as opposed to collaborative.

8.16 More recently, a similar issue was considered in *Willmott Dixon Housing Ltd v Newlon Housing Trust*[16] where the issue was the parties' conduct during the dispute resolution process. The contract was the ACA Standard Form of Contract for Project Partnering (PPC 2000) and the issue before the court was the enforcement of an adjudication decision. In an attempt to resist enforcement, one party raised arguments as to whether the referral to adjudication had been served properly and on time, as two adjudications were being run in parallel and there was some initial confusion about the documents being served.

8.17 The Technology and Construction Court (TCC) rarely entertains such arguments, and it is not surprising that the attempt to resist enforcement failed. Ramsey J however did go on to address the relevance of the parties having entered into a partnering contract and observed as follows:[17]

> *This was a Contract where the parties had agreed to use the standard form of project partnering contract. They had agreed to work in mutual cooperation, as reflected in clause 3.1 by 'transparent and cooperative exchange of information in all matters relating to the project' which, in my judgment, also includes performing the problem solving and dispute avoidance or resolution provisions in clause 27, including adjudication in clause 27.5. In such circumstances, I would have expected Newlon to have contacted Willmott Dixon to confirm that the Referral document of 27 July 2012 was really intended to be Willmott Dixon's Referral document for the current dispute. It is quite evident that, had that been done, Newlon would have received the Referral document at that time, consistent with rule 14. Any failure to serve the Referral document at that time would therefore not have occurred had Newlon not been in breach of their obligations and Newlon cannot rely on its own breach.*

14 [1999] BLR 194.
15 *Birse Construction Limited v St David Limited* [1999] BLR 194.
16 [2013] EWHC 798 (TCC).
17 ibid, para 55.

In other words, it was held that in a partnering contract the obligation to work in mutual cooperation applied to the parties' obligations under the contractual dispute resolution provision. In practice, that meant that in an adjudication a party that identifies that the other side had made a mistake, cannot keep quiet and try to rely on that matter at a later stage, as it will be in breach of its contractual obligations. That decision reflects the fact that the dispute avoidance and resolution provisions were part of the contract and, as adjudication is a contractual process, any general contractual obligation would also apply to it. A different approach may however be taken when the dispute is more formal and heading towards litigation or arbitration.

8.18 This was considered in *Costain Ltd v Tarmac Holdings Ltd*[18] where the issue was whether the dispute was subject to the jurisdiction of the courts or whether there was a binding arbitration clause. One party's solicitors sought to reach agreement on this point before commencing proceedings in court, but the other side's lawyers refused to confirm their agreement and once proceedings had been issued in the High Court they argued the dispute should have been referred to arbitration and that the court proceedings should be stayed. The dispute concerned the NEC Supply Contract standard form and it was argued that clause 10.1, which requires the parties to act in a spirit of mutual trust and cooperation, meant that, when a dispute arose, the parties were required to liaise between themselves and agree which possible dispute resolution route should be adopted for that particular dispute.

8.19 Mr Justice Coulson (as he then was) rejected this argument because, on the facts, he thought it was unworkable in practice. In his view, dispute resolution provisions require certainty and as it was possible no agreement could be reached, it was a recipe for uncertainty and confusion. He also observed that even if clause 10.1 meant that the parties had to co-operate before commencing proceedings, that would in no way lessen the uncertainty, or the scope for disagreement.[19]

8.20 This decision highlights the tension between the need for certainty and the reliance on the parties reaching agreement. The judge questioned in that case how the applicable dispute resolution route would be determined if no agreement was reached and one possible answer is to ensure that there is a clear contractual mechanism to unlock any situations where there is no agreement. Collaboration does not mean that the contract does not need to provide clear mechanisms to resolve issues and instead simply rely on agreement being reached. Providing a mechanism to ensure agreement is reached or is more likely is the approach taken in alliancing contracts as further discussed later.

8.21 Another example of the way the requirement under the NEC form of contract to act in a spirit of mutual trust and cooperation has been applied in an adversarial situation is the decision in *Northern Ireland Housing Executive v Healthy Buildings (Ireland) Ltd*[20] which concerned an application for disclosure of cost records. The Court's view was that the refusal to provide these records was '*entirely antipathetic to a spirit of mutual trust and cooperation. Further clauses in the contract such as Clause 15 reinforce that spirit*'. In

18 [2017] EWHC 319 (TCC).

19 ibid, paras 41–42.

20 *Northern Ireland Housing Executive v Healthy Buildings (Ireland) Limited* [2017] NIQB 43, para 43. See the first decision in that matter (*Northern Ireland Housing Executive v Healthy Buildings (Ireland) Ltd* [2014] NICA 27, para 29) for an example of clause 10.1 being used in aid of interpretation.

the specific circumstances of this case, the Court relied on the obligation in clause 10.1 to act in a spirit of mutual trust and cooperation in support of a decision that documents were relevant and should be disclosed as part of the court proceedings.

8.22 The aforementioned decisions demonstrate that while it will be difficult to apply a good faith obligation where that can create uncertainty and undermine the operation of the contract or any express terms, in the right context the courts are willing to find that the parties are bound by and should act in accordance with a good faith obligation even in an adversarial dispute situation.

Relational contracts

8.23 The aforementioned cases demonstrate a willingness to consider when good faith may be relevant, and in recent years this has been addressed by the willingness of some judges to recognise the concept of relational contracts, as a specific type of contract where it would be appropriate to imply good faith obligations.

8.24 In *Yam Seng Pte Ltd v International Trade Corp Ltd*[21] Leggatt J (as he then was) put forward a comprehensive and detailed argument for recognising good faith in English law. In his view it was unlikely that a wider good faith duty would be implied where the contract involved a simple exchange but it could be relevant to contracts which involve longer term relationships between the parties in which they make a substantial commitment. He described such contracts as 'relational contracts', requiring a high degree of communication, cooperation and predictable performance based on mutual trust and confidence and involving expectations of loyalty which are not provided for in the express terms of the contract, but are implicit in the parties' understanding and necessary to give business efficacy to their arrangement.

8.25 The concept of relational contracts was recognised in a number of later cases[22] but most recently was considered in detail by the court in *Bates v Post Office Ltd (No 3)*[23] where Fraser J began by making it clear that the concept of relational contracts was well established in English law and listed a number of recent cases that supported that proposition.[24] He then went on to consider good faith and held that

> *there is a specie of contracts, which are most usefully termed 'relational contracts', in which there is implied an obligation of good faith (which is also termed 'fair dealing' in some of the cases). This means that the parties must refrain from conduct which in the relevant context would be regarded as commercially unacceptable by reasonable and honest people.*

8.26 It was found in that case that the contracts between the parties amounted to relational contracts and that

> *this means the contracts included an implied obligation of good faith. This means that both the parties must refrain from conduct which in the relevant context would be regarded as*

21 [2013] EWHC 111 (QB).

22 See for example *Bristol Groundschool Ltd v Intelligent Data Capture Ltd* [2014] EWHC 2145 (Ch) and *D&G Cars v Essex Police Authority* [2015] EWHC 226 (QB).

23 [2019] EWHC 606 (QB).

24 ibid, para 705.

commercially unacceptable by reasonable and honest people. Transparency, cooperation, and trust and confidence are, in my judgment, implicit within the implied obligation of good faith.[25]

8.27 The way the courts have applied the concept of relational contracts is not free from uncertainty and a number of recent decisions have questioned the practical impact of recognising a relational contract.[26] It is however important to note that this concept was introduced as a way to deal with some of the problems experienced with traditional contractual models which attempt to provide complete certainty even where parties recognise that situations may change over a number of years and where it is difficult, if not impossible, to address in advance within the contract the full range of circumstances that may arise. In addition, there is the issue as to how parties are to conduct themselves and are they bound by the express terms alone or are they entitled to assume that the other party will '*refrain from conduct which in the relevant context would be regarded as commercially unacceptable by reasonable and honest people*' as suggested in the *Bates* decision.

8.28 Some of the decisions concerning relational contracts were considered in Professor Hugh Collins' paper '*Is a relational contract a legal concept?*'[27] in which he suggested that the building blocks for relational contracts as a legal concept were in place, allowing for what he described as a loose legal concept as opposed to particular rules. This would mean that courts take a more contextual approach towards interpretation, giving equal weight to the express wording and the need to support the long-term payoffs for the business or preserve the necessary trust in the relationship. He thought that this would usually be achieved by implying terms but these would not necessarily include a requirement of good faith in performance.

8.29 Ian MacNeill, who introduced the term relational contracts in the 1970s, saw it as a way to create the flexibility for complex and long-term contracts that traditional contracts are unable to provide, by looking beyond the contract itself and relying on what can be achieved by using the wider context of the overall relationship between the parties. When looking at dispute resolution, he contrasted traditional litigation, which he saw as a bipolar process which is retrospective and based on the remedy being directly related to a party's contractual right, to a different form of dispute resolution for relational contracts, where the dispute is defined in the context of the full relationship and can look at the future, not just the past, and the remedy is not imposed but negotiated and mediated. He also suggested that for relational contracts the award does not terminate the dispute resolver's role and the dispute resolver continues to actively administer matters and helps organise and share the dispute process.[28] This is of course similar to the role that standing dispute boards are intended to play when they are appointed as part of a construction project.

25 ibid, para 738.

26 See for example *UTB LLC v Sheffield United Ltd* [2019] EWHC 2322 (Ch), para 202, and *TAQA Bratani v RockRose UKCS8 LLC* [2020] EWHC 58 (Comm), para 44–56.

27 S Degeling, J Edelman and J Goudkamp (eds), *Contracts in Commercial Law* (Thomson Reuters 2016).

28 I MacNeil, 'Contracts Adjustment of Long-Term Economic Relations Under Classical, Neoclassical, and Relational Contract Law' (1977–1978) 72 Nw U L Rev 854.

8.30 The same issues were addressed more recently by Professor David Mosey[29] who considered relational contracts in the context of what he described as 'classical contracts' such as a contract for the purchase of building materials and a 'neo-classical contract' which involves a more complex transaction where it is not possible to provide for all future contingencies, such as a contract for complex construction works. He identified the risk of uncertainty which makes contractual structures vulnerable but has proposed that where the parties agree to utilise machinery set out in the contract itself in order to arrive at more complete information, then their collaborative contract (and looser obligations such as good faith) should not be open to challenge as unenforceable.

8.31 This would lead to the use of techniques resulting in what he describes as an enterprise contract. This is a contract that includes machinery for a joint activity that governs the collection and development of information and limits negotiation, to deal with the evolving scope of works. The intention is to go beyond the reactive adaptations of a neo-classical contract and by providing for a brief and a timetable of actions, which would be more precise than the open-ended goals and objectives of a relational contract. This will also provide more certainty and address any concerns that such looser arrangements have limited value and carry risks as they may be unenforceable.

8.32 The Courts' acceptance of relational contracts as a specific type of contract, where good faith duties may apply, should encourage parties to accept that relational contracts are different and that disputes under such contracts can be dealt with in a way that reflects the different nature of such contracts, as opposed to traditional and adversarial dispute resolution methods. Ideally, however, such disputes should be dealt with before reaching formal proceedings in court or arbitration and that is an area which is currently developing.

Collaborative dispute resolution methods

8.33 The dispute resolution process is different from works on a project and it may seem counter-intuitive to suggest that dispute resolution can be undertaken on a collaborative basis. Disputes, or disagreements, are however to some extent part of any major project. The presence of disagreement does not mean there is no collaboration and there are instances where parties genuinely cannot reach agreement, for example as to the actual cause of a defect that has been identified, the correct interpretation and operation of a contractual clause or the correct valuation of an item of works instructed as a variation and its impact on the critical path.

8.34 Where such a dispute arises in the context of an existing collaborative contract, the parties have two options. They can allow the dispute to escalate and affect the wider working relationship, leading to distrust and loss of the benefits of collaboration, or they can seek to agree a process that is aimed at resolving the dispute in a way both parties will find acceptable, without it affecting the wider working relationship. It is common to speak about alignment of interests when discussing collaboration and it is important to remember that even where there is a dispute, it is in both parties' interests to have that dispute resolved

29 See D Mosey, *Collaborative Construction Procurement and Improved Value* (Wiley, 2019) and D Mosey and S Jackson, 'Good Faith and Relational Contracting – Do Enterprise Contracts Offer a Way Through the Woods?' SCL Paper 228, March 2020.

quickly and efficiently, in a way that limits legal and other costs and preserves the ongoing working relationship.

8.35 As will be demonstrated later, there are different ways of achieving such aims but the common features appear to be a focus on the substantive matter in dispute itself and avoiding incidental or satellite disputes, an acceptance by both parties that any process needs to be flexible so that each party feels it had a fair opportunity to present its case and an independent party facilitating resolution which has the necessary knowledge and experience so that both parties accept any recommendation or decision even where it is unfavourable. Such a process can also be undertaken on a without prejudice basis or be limited to a recommendation, where that is seen as more conducive to resolution and less likely to result in escalation.

8.36 In the construction sector, adjudication as provided for under the Housing Grants, Construction and Regeneration Act 1996 has become the common way of resolving disputes. Its popularity is due to the fact that it results in an enforceable decision which is given within a matter of weeks, or at most a few months, at a cost which is significantly lower than High Court litigation or arbitration.

8.37 Adjudication however has its disadvantages. The speed of the process means that sometimes parties do not have a full opportunity to present their case and the need to rely on the Adjudicator Nominating Body can result in an adjudicator being appointed who may not have the necessary skills or experience to provide a decision that both parties accept. There is also a tendency to raise arguments about jurisdictional issues and to seek further opportunities for additional rounds of submissions, which increase the costs and duration of adjudication. Adjudication can be a hostile and intensive process which once started may well pit parties against each other and make it much more difficult to maintain a collaborative working environment. In addition, the speed of the process makes it difficult to explore settlement while it is ongoing, unlike other forms of dispute resolution.

8.38 That has resulted in parties being reluctant to use adjudication to resolve disputes, despite the clear advantages of the process. Instead, other methods have been put forward by various construction industry bodies.

8.39 As part of such efforts, the RICS, the ICE, RIBA, the CIArb and the DRBF published a Guide to Conflict Avoidance & Dispute Resolution for the Construction and Engineering Industry. This guide highlighted the financial costs of disputes and the causes of disputes in construction in order to set out the benefits of conflict avoidance and early intervention techniques. As a starting point, the guide notes the importance of contractual provisions which must have clarity, applicability, effective contract management, early warning and workable procedures for dealing with compensation events. This is said to help to avoid and resolve conflict but where further steps are needed, the guide also outlines the options open to parties identified as conflict avoidance panels, early neutral evaluation, project-based dispute boards and evaluative mediation.

8.40 The publication of this guide led to the introduction in 2018 of the Conflict Avoidance Pledge by the Conflict Avoidance Coalition Steering Group, aimed at driving behavioural change by encouraging all organisations to consider their working practices and the way they deal with disputes. The pledge was promoted by industry professional bodies (the RICS, ICE, RIBA, CIArb, DRBF and CICES) as well as two of the largest employers in the UK, Transport for London (TfL) and Network Rail (NR). The pledge is supported by a toolkit which is based on pre-contract preparation, followed by dispute avoidance and early intervention, leading to amicable resolution or dispute resolution. This campaign needs to be considered in the context of two specific procedures introduced by TfL and NR to deal with disputes on their projects.

8.41 TfL looked to introduce that process as a result of commencing a substantial station upgrade programme where it sought to avoid the commercial tensions and disputes that can lead to uncertainty as to outcomes as well as a negative impact on team relationships and ultimately delivery. A Conflict Avoidance Panel (CAP) process was therefore developed with the RICS in order to resolve existing claims and reduce future disputes, but also with the aim of providing a fair and reasonable outcome that would maintain relationships and provide certainty of outcome. This works on the basis of a without prejudice process that results in a recommendation by an independent third party.

8.42 The RICS CAP process has been run for several years and by March 2019 has led to the resolution of over 25 disputes between TfL and its supply chain. Where the process has been used at an early stage, it addressed disputes with an average value of £3.9m and cost as a percentage of the value in dispute was 0.06%. Where the process was used at a later stage, in lieu of adjudication, the average dispute value was £11.7m and cost as a percentage of the value in dispute was 0.11%.[30]

8.43 Similarly, in 2016 NR introduced an Industry Guidance Note on Dispute Avoidance Panels (DAP) described as being '*on 'fire watch' looking for the smouldering embers of dispute in the dry grass and putting them out before the fire can begin*'. The process seeks to prevent disputes from arising in the first place and is based on appointing a panel of two to four members, from legal, quantum, planning/construction and behavioural sciences to identify and report observations on possible sources and warning signs of potential disputes through the review of live projects reports, programmes and commercial data but also on the basis of interviews and an assessment of current behaviours. It is not intended that the DAP would give advice, mediate or make decisions, but instead it would offer its observations to the parties in the hope that these will be considered and acted upon.

8.44 The use of the CAP and DAP process has been considered in detail by Jonathan Cope,[31] who reviewed the basis for introducing them and how they have operated in practice since then. He has noted their growing popularity but has also proposed their introduction in the subcontracts with the supply chain and has made three suggestions for improving the process, based on educating key stakeholders about the importance of collaborative working (as compared to an unnecessary aggressive approach being taken), the importance of early-stage dispute avoidance and the various options that are available to resolve disputes such as mediation and without prejudice negotiation. As noted by Cope, the CAP and DAP processes are now being incorporated into the standard forms of contract used by TfL and NR.

8.45 This trend has also been reflected in the 4th edition of the New Engineering Contract (NEC4) when it was published in 2017. The dispute resolution process in clauses W1 and W2 has been amended to include a process for senior representatives discussions, and W3, a new dispute resolution option, introduced the ability to set up a Dispute Avoidance

30 M Burns, 'Conflict Avoidance and Early Intervention', presentation given at the RICS Legal Issues in Construction Conference, 5 November 2019.

31 J Cope, 'Recent Development in Conflict Avoidance Processes in use in the UK Infrastructure Sector', November 2018, SCL Paper D215.

Board of one to three members, which is appointed at the start of the works and reviews potential disputes and helps their settlement without a formal referral, but can provide a recommendation. Where option W3 is chosen, a referral to the Dispute Avoidance Board is required before it can be referred to the tribunal. This option was aimed at international projects, but in 2019 NEC acknowledged that the DAB should also be provided as an option for projects governed by the Housing Grants, Construction and Regeneration Act 1996, so it can apply in addition to adjudication.[32] In May 2021, JCT published a Dispute Adjudication Board agreement, to be used with its Design & Build and Major Project forms of contract.

8.46 The use of dispute boards is also a feature of the FIDIC forms of contract, and the 2017 suite of contracts has introduced the Dispute Avoidance/Adjudication Board (DAAB). In addition to asking the DAAB to resolve disputes, by agreement they can assist the parties to resolve disputes through informal discussions. This is an improvement from the Dispute Adjudication Board used in earlier editions, and there is more clarity on the requirement to make payment without delay and the binding nature of a decision, which must be complied with even where a Notice of Dissatisfaction is issued.

8.47 The growing use of dispute boards in the UK and internationally provides a welcome alternative to arbitration and a process which makes experts available to assist in an early resolution of disputes. To be effective, however, dispute boards need to try to avoid the tendency to treat them as very formal processes which are dominated by issues related to procedure and delaying tactics as opposed to focusing on providing an efficient answer to the underlying substantive dispute. Whether or not that is the case is likely to depend on the relationship the parties had and their behaviours in managing the works. Where parties have behaved collaboratively, they should be able to continue such behaviours during the dispute resolution process and recognise the need to preserve the long-term relationship. Where the conduct has been adversarial throughout, this is unlikely to change when disputes are referred to the Dispute Adjudication Board.

8.48 In 2017 a new Framework Alliancing Contract (FAC-1) was also published, described by Professor Mosey as providing collaborative machinery and governance that goes beyond a relational contract, aimed at delivering efficiencies and cost savings.[33] In relation to disputes, this is managed using a system based on a shared risk register and early warnings but disputes are then dealt with by a core group of agreed individuals who represent the Alliance members and have the option of using an independent adviser and alternative dispute resolution.

8.49 NEC published its Alliance Contract in 2018, a form of contract designed for use on major projects or programmes of work where longer term collaborative ways of working are to be created. Clause 94.1 provides that the parties to the Alliance agree that any failure by a member of the Alliance to comply with their obligations stated in these conditions of contract does not give rise to any enforceable right or obligation at law except for limited exceptions and that any disputes between the members of the Alliance arising out of or in connection with the contract are only resolved in accordance with these conditions of

32 NEC4 ECC – Practice Note 5 (April 2019): Using a Dispute Avoidance Board for contracts covered by the HGCRA.

33 Professor David Mosey, 'Improving Value Through the FAC-1 Framework Alliance Contract', SCL paper D209, November 2017.

contract. Clause 95 provides for the Alliance Board to refer the dispute to an independent expert for an opinion or to the senior representatives of each member of the Alliance in dispute.

8.50 The aforementioned reflect a growing recognition within the construction industry that it is crucial to explore alternatives to traditional formal dispute resolution methods which are not only costly and lengthy but focus on specific issues but cannot address the wider relationship between parties. If parties choose to collaborate and achieve a collaborative environment, it makes no sense to use adversarial processes to resolve differences.

Formal dispute resolution

8.51 Formal dispute resolution methods also recognise that they must become more efficient and focused on what the parties need to achieve. In that respect, litigation in the Technology and Construction Court is governed by the detailed Civil Procedure Rules and may not therefore be seen as an example of collaborative dispute resolution. Over the last 20 years, however, litigation in the High Court has gone through a number of changes with the aim of making the process more efficient and to a large extent that has been done by putting an emphasis on reducing costs and creating a process that seeks to avoid unnecessary satellite litigation.

8.52 This process began in 1999, with the introduction of the Woolf civil procedure reforms, which put in place '*the overriding objective of enabling the court to deal with cases justly and at proportionate cost*'. Further detail is then provided to make it clear that this is done by '*dealing with a case justly and at proportionate cost*' which includes ensuring that the parties are on an equal footing but also saving expense and dealing with the case in ways which are proportionate (having regard to the amount at stake, the importance and complexity of the case, the financial position of each party and ensuring that it is dealt with expeditiously and fairly).[34] The aim is reinforced in the Technology and Construction Court Guide which repeats the overriding objective and adds that the court will also endeavour to ensure expedition, and to allot to each case an appropriate share of the court's resources.[35]

8.53 On a practical level, this has generally resulted in a more pro-active court where judges expect parties to behave reasonably and to avoid unnecessary applications and other procedural steps that are not necessary and may result in unnecessary or disproportionate costs and delay. In *Three Rivers District Council v Governor and the Company of the Bank of England*[36] the court observed, '*Civil litigation conducted pursuant to the current Civil Procedure Rules is in many respects no longer adversarial*'.

8.54 This change in approach has been reinforced by other initiatives, which included the introduction of a Pre-Action Protocol for certain types of claims, including construction and engineering disputes. The aim of the Protocol is to enable an exchange of information which would lead to a meeting where the parties would discuss on a without prejudice basis whether ADR can be used and court proceedings avoided. In 2016 the second edition was

34 Para 1.1 of Part 1 of the Civil Procedure Rules.

35 Para 1.1.4 of the Technology and Construction Court Guide 2nd edition.

36 [2004] UKHL 48.

published which introduced the role of the referee as an independent third party, which was aimed at ensuring the effectiveness of the Protocol.

8.55 Generally, the English courts recognise and encourage the early resolution of disputes. This can be seen from the approach to the enforcement of multi-tiered dispute resolution clauses. In *Emirates Trading Agency LLC v Prime Mineral Exports Private Ltd*[37] the dispute resolution clause provided that the parties shall first seek to '*resolve the dispute or claim by friendly discussion*' for a continuous period of four weeks, failing which it would be referred to arbitration. The issue before the court was whether such an obligation was enforceable or was it merely an agreement to agree.

8.56 Teare J held that where commercial parties have agreed a dispute resolution clause aimed at preventing them from launching into an expensive arbitration without first seeking to resolve their dispute by friendly discussions the courts should seek to give effect to the parties' bargain. In his view there was a public interest in giving effect to dispute resolution clauses which require the parties to seek to resolve disputes before engaging in arbitration or litigation. Such a clause raises issues similar to good faith and it is noteworthy that he distinguished *Walford v Miles* but approved of the approach in *Yam Seng* and held that the obligation to seek to resolve disputes by friendly discussions must import an obligation to seek to do so in good faith. In his view a time limited obligation to seek to resolve a dispute in good faith was enforceable, although he recognised that it may be difficult to establish that a party has not sought to resolve a dispute in good faith but suggested that there will be cases where that can be shown, for example, where a party asserts his claim, refuses to negotiate and seeks to commence arbitration.[38]

8.57 As highlighted by Teare J, this issue is not unique to English law and in support of his approach he referred to a decision of the Singapore High Court[39] which held as enforceable a clause requiring mediation before arbitration and he also noted that at least some ICSID tribunals also regarded obligations to seek to resolve disputes by negotiation in good faith as binding and enforceable obligations.[40]

8.58 More recently, in *Telecom Centre (UK) Ltd v Thomas Sanderson Ltd (Early Neutral Evaluation)*[41] the Master considered that the case was appropriate for judicial early neutral evaluation (ENE) pursuant to CPR rule 3.1(2)(m) and provided guidance on how such a procedure would operate in the Queen's Bench division. That followed an earlier Court of Appeal decision in *Lomax v Lomax*[42] where it was held that the court can order ENE even where one party does not agree. This is due to the benefits of requiring parties to focus on whether a case might be capable of settlement and hear a judge's neutral evaluation, which will often result in a saving of costs.

8.59 Arbitral institutions have placed a similar emphasis on alternative dispute resolution and providing parties with alternative options to arbitration. Traditional ADR methods such as mediation and conciliation are not the same as the collaborative techniques discussed

37 [2014] EWHC 2104 (Comm).

38 ibid, paras 50–52.

39 *International Research Corp PLC v Lufthansa Systems Asia Pacific Pte Ltd* [2012] SGHC 226, [2013] 1 SLR 973.

40 He referred to *Tulip Real Estate Investment and development Netherlands BV v Republic of Turkey* (ICSID Case No. ARB/11/28), paras 56–72.

41 [2020] EWHC 368 (QB).

42 [2019] EWCA Civ 1467.

earlier, but they are similar in that they seek an efficient resolution which is often based on preserving the long-term relationship. An arbitral tribunal however is unlikely to have the powers to force parties to undertake such a process albeit it may feel it is able to suggest such an option.

8.60 Arbitration can provide much more flexibility as can be seen from the use of med-arb (or arb-med) which while presenting its own challenges, can also be seen as an innovative and collaborative form of ADR. It is necessary to understand how med-arb is intended to work in the context of traditional litigation and the potential conflicts for the arbitrator but it is common in Asia, especially in China where it is estimated that around a quarter of disputes referred to the China International Economic and Trade Arbitration Commission (CIETAC) are resolved through med-arb. In Australia, the use of med-arb is addressed by the relevant Commercial Arbitration Acts, based on written consent, and its use has also been considered by the courts.[43]

8.61 The aforementioned show that while more formal dispute resolution methods have less scope for using collaborative techniques as they take place at a later stage, often after the project has been completed, they recognise that in resolving a dispute it may be beneficial to consider not just the contractual rights and obligations but also the wider commercial relationship and environment. As noted earlier, it is usually the case that both parties would want a swift and efficient resolution of a dispute that provides certainty, as opposed to a costly dispute that continues for years.

Conclusions

8.62 Traditional dispute resolution methods have their place and will not disappear any time soon. But it is legitimate to question whether they satisfy the commercial needs of parties or whether they should be seen as a last resort choice only when all other routes to resolution have failed, with the parties incorporating and implementing other forms of dispute resolution into their contracts. It goes without saying, but the costs of traditional dispute resolution methods and the length of time they take can be disproportionate to the value they bring.

8.63 The growing acceptance of good faith obligations and the recognition of relational contracts show that even the courts and traditional lawyers recognise that commercial relationships cannot be viewed narrowly as limited to the four corners of the contract. This is especially the case in complex construction projects, as demonstrated by the trend to explore the use of collaborative contracts. This is not meant to prevent disputes or differences from arising, but it recognises that they need to be dealt with within the same collaborative framework and not be seen as a stand-alone process that happens in parallel or after the works phase.

8.64 As shown earlier, there are a variety of ways in which that can be done, either through a contractual structure based on discussions between the parties or the use of external third parties but in a non-adversarial environment. There are different ways of structuring these processes and parties should make the effort to consider such processes

43 See *Ku-ring-gai Council v Ichor Constructions Pty Ltd* [2018] NSWSC 610 for an example of the issues that med-arb can raise in terms of the need for consent and the process.

when setting up the contract rather than wait until a difference arises and consider what works best for them as the key is to create a process which the parties will trust. The real test will be whether a party will be willing to accept and not challenge a decision which goes against its position in the dispute.

8.65 It is however possible to identify some underlying themes to consider when looking to resolve a dispute collaboratively.

- **Flexibility** – The process should have a framework in terms of its procedure, but it should not be applied rigidly and it should contain provisions that allow for flexibility so that it can be adapted by the parties or the dispute resolver as may be necessary.
- **Third party involvement** – An independent third party, or a panel, can be involved from the beginning or be appointed at a later stage. This has the benefit of providing a neutral position and can assist the parties, but parties also need to recognise that this should not be seen as an alternative to direct discussions in the first place and that they must still remain responsible for acting collaboratively. Where the third party provides its views, it is important to consider whether that should be a non-binding recommendation or an enforceable decision. The latter provides certainty and is more effective, but can lead to escalation and there are benefits to having a non-binding view which is nonetheless seen as authoritative.
- **Timing** – Differences are easier to resolve, or prevent, the sooner they are addressed and before they are escalated, especially if there are steps that can still be taken to limit the impact of the events in dispute. Parties need to ensure that any process is used promptly and avoid the inclination to delay matters and avoid dealing with what may be seen as difficult questions to be addressed. Ignoring a problem which is known to exist is likely to make matters worse.
- **Involving the right people** – Dispute resolution clauses often have an escalation mechanism which is based on the seniority of the people involved increasing at each stage. This is sensible and recognises that while disputes start at site level, they are easier to resolve by people who are not directly involved (and may therefore not feel as personally committed to a position) and who can take account of the wider position and the importance of the long-term relationship.

Such methods will not be suitable for all contracts in the same way that good faith duties are not implied into every contract and not all commercial contracts will be regarded as relational contracts. Where parties however seek to engage in collaborative contracting and see it as a way to improve delivery, they need to recognise that differences are inevitable and that unless they are also managed collaboratively, they could undermine the benefits of collaboration and result in an adversarial environment, which is the direct opposite of what collaboration seeks to achieve.

8.66 When it comes to more formal dispute resolution, such as arbitration, there is less scope for collaborative behaviour and the emphasis will be more on having an efficient and cost-effective process and the use of ADR. Nonetheless, a lesson from collaborative dispute resolution is that the parties' efforts and focus should be on the substance of the dispute and less on procedural issues that are often used tactically but are unlikely to affect the overall outcome. Indeed, a complex dispute which spans a number of years is similar to a construction project in that at different times each party may need the assistance of the other party, whether it is in agreeing to a longer period to comply with directions or accepting the need for proportionality and reasonableness.

8.67 Experienced parties learn soon enough that it is unhelpful to object as a matter of course to anything the other side requests and, to some extent, that is collaboration. Whether or not parties who collaborate on a contract will be more collaborative if they engage in formal dispute resolution remains to be seen but hopefully they will recognise that their interests are still aligned in the sense they both should wish to avoid unnecessary costs and delay. Once this is recognised, there are a number of ways that disputes can be resolved in a way which is more efficient and collaborative.

PART IV

CONTRACTUAL ADJUDICATION

Dispute boards in international construction disputes

CHAPTER 9

Dispute boards

Trends, observations, developments and procedures

Nicholas Gould and Robbie McCrea

Introduction

9.1 Dispute boards (DBs) originated in North America as a pre-arbitral procedure designed to avoid formal proceedings by having an independent expert (or board of experts) issue non-binding recommendations to the parties. They first entered international usage in the late 1980s and early 1990s where they were successfully used in mega-projects such as the Channel Tunnel[1] and Hong Kong International Airport.[2]

9.2 Since then, DBs have proliferated in popularity and are now included by default in most international construction contracts. They were included in the World Bank's Standard Bidding Documents for projects with an estimated cost over US$50 million from 1995,[3] and were adopted by FIDIC[4] in its Orange Book (for design, build and turnkey) the same year. FIDIC's 1999 Rainbow Suite[5] provided for DBs empowered to make binding decisions, becoming the benchmark for DBs in international projects, and this mechanism has been developed in each subsequent iteration of FIDIC's contracts.

9.3 In the last decade the role of DBs has expanded into claims management with a greater focus on dispute avoidance. This is largely a response to the increasing costs, time, and disruption to projects when disputes are referred to court or arbitration, as well as the success of statutory adjudication regimes in places like the United Kingdom,[6] which has seen a renewed emphasis on contract administration, claim management, and dispute avoidance. Most of the main forms of international construction contracts and dispute resolution institutions have now developed DB mechanisms that explicitly target claim management and dispute avoidance.

1 *The Channel Tunnel Group Ltd v Balfour Beatty Construction Ltd* [1993] AC 334, [1993] 2 WLR 262. The project used a panel of three independent experts charged with making decisions that became immediately binding on the parties until revised in arbitration. The House of Lords legitimised this mechanism as a matter of English law, finding that dispute resolution mechanisms chosen by competent parties should not be interfered with.

2 The construction of the Hong Kong International Airport at Chek Lap Kok used a seven-member disputes review group, from which a panel of one or three members were selected to make determinations of any particular dispute, which would be binding until finally determined in arbitration. This is not dissimilar to the panel dispute board now in place at CERN, and discussed at the end of this chapter.

3 Ellis Baker, et al, *FIDIC Contracts: Law and Practice* (Informa 2009) para 9.9.

4 FIDIC is the acronym for its French name Fédération Internationale Des Ingénieurs-Conseils. The International Federation of Consulting Engineers was founded in 1915 by Belgium, France and Switzerland.

5 The 1999 Red, Yellow, and Silver Books.

6 Under the Housing Grants, Construction and Regeneration Act 1996.

9.4 The evolution of the DB mechanism is exemplified in FIDIC's 2017 Red, Yellow and Silver Books[7] (FIDIC's 2017 Contracts), which is the first update of FIDIC's most popular contracts in nearly 20 years. FIDIC's 2017 Contracts provide for a substantially expanded claims and dispute resolution procedure. At the core of this procedure is the latest iteration of the dispute board: the Dispute Adjudication Avoidance Board (DAAB). Sir Vivian Ramsey commented as follows:[8]

> *The world of international contracting is changing. The management of contracts has become increasingly important in order to effectively avoid and deal with disputes before they escalate. ... The change in FIDIC forms from DABs to DAABs, by adding a dispute avoidance role to the dispute board reflects a major shift in the way disputes are handled. Experience, including that of the Independent Dispute Avoidance Panel for the London 2012 Olympics, has shown that disputes can be avoided if the issues are properly dealt with at an early stage.*

This chapter considers the role of dispute boards in international contracting today, in light of the latest FIDIC Contracts and expected developments, the use of DBs by development banks, recent case law, and current trends in DB usage around the world.

Dispute boards

What is a dispute board?

9.5 A dispute board is an independent and impartial person or panel of three or more persons appointed by the parties to a contract to avoid and resolve disagreements that may arise in the course of the contract. The overarching purpose of DBs is to resolve disagreements as quickly and sensibly as possible, and in doing so, hopefully avoid them escalating to formal proceedings (arbitration and/or court).

9.6 Ideally, DBs should be set up at the commencement of a project and remain in existence for its duration. In contrast to other forms of dispute resolution (such as arbitration, adjudication under a statutory scheme,[9] or litigation in court) DBs are intended to become part of the project team and act in real time, rather than dealing with events that happened in the distant past. DBs are different from the other forms of dispute resolution because they provide, or are intended to provide, a continuing forum for discussion of any issues that might become contentious, and thus avoid disputes or resolve them as soon as they arise.

Legal basis for dispute boards

9.7 DBs are created by contract. This means that a DB will only have such powers as are expressly given to it by the contracting parties, and the basis for a DB's powers

7 That is, the Rainbow Suite.

8 Vivian Ramsey, in the Foreword to: J Glover and S Hughes QC, *Understanding the FIDIC Red and Yellow Books* (3rd edn, Sweet & Maxwell 2018).

9 For instance, the Housing Grants, Construction and Regeneration Act 1996 in the United Kingdom, and the Construction Contracts Act 2002 in New Zealand.

and decisions will be grounded in the contractual force provided under the law of the country in which the contract is executed (or the country agreed on by the parties in the contract).[10]

9.8 However, whereas every country or jurisdiction has its own laws relevant to its domestic courts, almost every country has its own laws and/or has adopted international standards[11] relating to arbitration, and some countries have adopted laws relating to adjudication schemes;[12] DBs are purely creations of contract. Consequently, the jurisdiction of a DB and execution of any resulting decisions are wholly dependent on how they are viewed by the applicable law, and their treatment varies widely between jurisdictions.

9.9 It should be noted that DBs do not supplant formal dispute mechanisms such as arbitration and litigation (except in limited circumstances).[13] Rather, DBs serve as a first, often mandatory, step aimed at encouraging the parties not to pursue formal proceedings.

Demand for amicable dispute resolution

9.10 DBs have deep roots in arbitration. However, these two forms of alternative dispute resolution (ADR) have many fundamental differences. For instance:

- a Whereas arbitration has been largely standardised across the world and arbitral awards (including foreign awards)[14] are readily enforceable in most countries, DBs come in many different forms according to the contract under which they are established, and their decisions are enforceable as a contractual obligation.
- b Arbitration is effectively privatised litigation, with similar procedures and often comparable timeframes and costs. DBs are customisable; focussed on dispute avoidance; and where decisions are required, have significantly reduced procedural steps, timeframes, and costs.
- c DB members are not arbitrators. Arbitrators listen to the evidence presented to them, whereas DB members have a broader-based function: that of inquisitor and dispute avoider. DB members do listen to evidence presented to them and may be required to make decisions, but they also work with the parties in order to avoid disputes and to find out the relevant facts about an emerging dispute.

In the last 25 years there has been an increasing demand for less adversarial dispute resolution methods such as mediation and DBs. In this period DBs have become an internationally recognised concept, and they are frequently included by default in international construction contracts, for example, by the use of standard FIDIC Contracts, or by imposition of the development banks by virtue of their procurement procedure.

---

10 For example, the FIDIC Contracts state: '*The Contract shall be governed by the law of the country (or other jurisdiction) stated in the Contract Data*' (Sub-clause 1.4).

11 Most particularly the United Nations Convention on the Recognition and Enforcement of Foreign Arbitral Awards (New York, 10 June 1958), which as at September 2019 had 163 contracting states.

12 For instance, the Housing Grants, Construction and Regeneration Act 1996 in the United Kingdom, and the Construction Contracts Act 2002 in New Zealand.

13 For instance, in the FIDIC 1999 and 2017 Contracts, where a DB decision becomes 'final and binding' because neither party issued a 'notice of dissatisfaction' within 28 days of receiving a decision from the DB.

14 Under the United Nations Convention on the Recognition and Enforcement of Foreign Arbitral Awards (New York, 10 June 1958), which as at September 2019 had 163 contracting states.

9.11 The last few years have seen the continued evolution of the DB away from its arbitration origins, to an increasingly diverse mechanism oriented to dispute avoidance.

Types of dispute boards

9.12 There are several established types of DBs and sets of institutional DB rules, and within these the types of powers granted to the DB can vary widely. The main types of DBs are dispute review boards (DRBs) and dispute adjudication boards (DABs). These traditional types of DBs and recent developments are discussed next.

DRBs

9.13 Dispute review boards originated in the construction industry in the USA and are still predominantly found there. DRBs make non-binding recommendations about disputes arising during a project. The board takes in all the facts of a dispute and makes recommendations on the basis of those facts and its own expertise. A DRB could also be considered a flexible and informal advisory panel, who might be asked for general (albeit expert) advice on any particular matter before issuing a recommendation.[15]

9.14 Sometimes called dispute resolution boards, the most common iteration of a DRB is by the American Arbitration Association (AAA). The AAA Dispute Resolution Board Guide Specification provides for an independent DRB that '*will assist in and facilitate the timely resolution of disputes*' by issuing written non-binding recommendations.[16] It will not make a binding decision.

DABs

9.15 As adjudication developed in the 1990s, the World Bank and FIDIC opted for a binding dispute resolution process, so the dispute adjudication board was born. DABs were first used, and continue to be most widely used, in FIDIC's 1999 Conditions of Contract (the '1999 FIDIC Contracts').[17] They are also used by the World Bank and a number of other multilateral development banks (MDBs) in particular in the special MDB harmonised edition of the FIDIC 1999 Conditions of Contract for Construction (the 'Pink Book'), which was first released in May 2005.[18]

9.16 However, the release of 2017 FIDIC Contracts appears to have resulted in a move away from the harmonised MDB contract, in respect of which the World Bank and some

15 A typical set of DRB procedural rules is provided by the Florida Department of Transportation, and can be accessed on their website: <www.fdot.gov/construction/constadm/drb/guideline.shtm> (last accessed 16 June 2020). These rules define the purpose of a DRB as to '*provide specialized expertise in technical areas and in administration of construction contracts to assist the Department and the Contractor in resolving disputes or claims in a timely and equitable manner*', and make clear that '*although both parties should place weight upon the recommendations of the RDRB, they are not binding*'.

16 The AAA Dispute Resolution Board Guide Specification, effective 1 December 2000, is available on the AAA website: <>www.adr.org/sites/default/files/AAA_Dispute_Resolution_Board_Operating_Procedures.pdf>, (last accessed 26 June 2020).

17 These encompass the FIDIC Red Book (building and engineering works designed by the Employer) the Yellow Book (building and engineering works designed by the Contractor), and the Silver Book (EPC/Turnkey Contract), which are often referred to as FIDIC's 'Rainbow Suite'.

18 As discussed further under the heading 'multilateral development banks', this harmonisation of the MDB contracts has been disrupted by the release of FIDIC's 2017 Contracts.

MDBs have adopted the 2017 Contracts,[19] while other MDBs continue to endorse the Pink Book and other 1999 Contracts.[20]

CDBs

9.17 The International Chamber of Commerce (the ICC) gives parties a choice between three alternative types of dispute board, each distinguished by the type of conclusion it issues upon a formal referral: DRBs, DABs, and Combined Dispute Boards (CDBs).[21] The CDB procedure is a hybrid between the DRB and DAB. CDBs may prove useful for those parties who cannot decide if they need a DRB or a DAB, but the combination could make the dispute board procedure somewhat cumbersome.

9.18 CDBs issue recommendations with respect to disputes, but they may instead issue a (temporarily binding) decision if one party requests this and the other party does not object. Such a decision must be implemented immediately. However, if one party objects to the CDB issuing a binding decision, the CDB shall decide whether to issue a recommendation or decision. This leads to a period of uncertainty as to what type of determination (binding decision or non-binding recommendation) the CDB will issue.

DAABs

9.19 FIDIC introduced the dispute avoidance/adjudication board as its flagship dispute mechanism, and successor to the DAB, in the 2017 FIDIC Contracts.[22] The DAAB seeks to offer an 'all-inclusive' DB mechanism. It remains at its core a DAB, with beefed up and corrected enforcement provisions. However, it also includes a new provision for 'Avoidance of Disputes',[23] which permits the parties to jointly ask the DAAB to informally discuss and/or provide assistance with any issue or disagreement.[24]

9.20 This has been mirrored in the latest New Engineering Contract (NEC) edition also launched in 2017,[25] NEC4, which offers a similar 'dispute avoidance board' for construction projects that are not based in the United Kingdom and/or subject to the statutory adjudication scheme under the Housing Grants, Construction and Regeneration Act 1996 (HGCRA).

---

19 Refer for instance, to the World Bank's SPD Request for Bids, Section IX, Part B, Sub-Clause 1.17 and Part C – Fraud and Corruption.

20 For instance, the European Bank for Reconstruction and Development's standard procurement documents include the FIDIC 1999 editions and the Pink Book, as well as several of the World Bank's standard forms, ICE, NEC3, IChemE, and JCT standard forms; <www.ebrd.com/work-with-us/procurement/project-procurement/standard-procurement-documents.html> (last accessed 26 June 2020).

21 Dispute Board Rules of the International Chamber of Commerce in force as from 1 October 2015 (the ICC Rules). Article 6 of the ICC Rules defines a combination of DRBs and DABs as Combined Dispute Boards (CDBs).

22 FIDIC in fact first introduced the DAAB within its 2008 Conditions of Contract for Design, Build and Operate Projects (the Gold Book), however, the Gold Book is not as widely used as the Rainbow Suite (the Red, Yellow, and Silver Books).

23 Sub-clause 21.3 (Sub-clause 20.4 of the Gold Book).

24 The power to provide 'informal assistance' is also offered under the ICC Rules, and is discussed further later.

25 NEC4 was launched in June 2017, whereas the 2017 FIDIC Contracts were launched in December 2017 (although the FIDIC Contracts were issued as a 'pre-release' for discussion in substantially the same form in December 2016).

Fundamental procedures and development

9.21 In the last few years each of the main construction contract and dispute resolution institutions[26] have launched updated or entirely new DB rules. Although the procedures within these rules and the powers given to the DBs vary, there is a large degree of consistency in terms of how the fundamental procedures and functions of the DB have developed.

9.22 Each set of DB rules shares the following fundamental elements:[27]

a The parties must agree to use the rules, and if applicable, specify the type of DB to be used.

b The DB should be appointed early and remain in place for the contract duration (*ie*, a standing DB)[28]; with very few exceptions ad hoc DBs are no longer provided for.[29]

c The DB members are to be appointed by the parties, and/or a specified nominating entity in the event of disagreement or failure to appoint by a specified time.

d The DB will be constituted by the execution of a tripartite agreement(s) between both parties and the DB member(s).

e The parties will be jointly responsible for paying the fees and reasonable costs of the DB members.

f The parties may refer a dispute to the DB following which the DB will have a specified period of time to give a recommendation or decision (whichever applies).

g Upon receipt of a decision or recommendation, the parties will have a limited period of time to notify the other party of their dissatisfaction with it,[30] failing which they will be deemed to have accepted it.[31]

h Obtaining a DAB decision or recommendation is a condition precedent to referring a dispute to arbitration, except in limited circumstances.[32]

Furthermore, all of these rules share an expanded emphasis on the DB's role in 'dispute avoidance'. Each of the rules now expressly states that the DB has a dispute avoidance role (the word 'avoidance' appears 48 times in the 2017 FIDIC Contracts), and this intent is most clearly given effect to in the use of standing DBs over ad hoc, expressly encouraging (and requiring)[33] routine visits and dialogue with the parties, and the adoption of 'informal advice' provisions.[34]

---

26 With the notable exception of the AAA, which continues to use its DRB Rules effective 1 December 2000.

27 FIDIC, ICC, CIArb, Institute of Chartered Engineers.

28 For instance, 14 days for the AAA rules, and 28 days in the 2017 FIDIC Contracts.

29 For instance, if the parties fail to appoint the DB before a dispute arises, or if the parties amend the rules. Whereas for instance the 1999 FIDIC Silver Book provided for an ad hoc DB, the 2017 edition calls for a standing DB.

30 Between 14 days for the AAA rules and up to 30 days under the ICC Rules.

31 Although in the case of a recommendation, failure to issue a notice of dissatisfaction does not have any substantive effect.

32 For instance, if a DB is not in existence at the time a dispute arises (pursuant to Sub-clause 21.8 of the 2017 FIDIC Contracts).

33 For instance, the CIArb Rules require the DB members to hold an initial meeting with the parties 'as soon as practicable' after the commencement of the contract, and conduct periodic meetings thereafter.

34 The ICC DB Rules first provided for the giving of informal advice in their 2004 Rules, followed by the FIDIC Gold Book in 2008.

9.23 For instance, the dispute board rules of the Chartered Institute of Arbitrators (the CIArb Rules)[35] spell out the importance of dispute avoidance and informal advice in Article 12:

Article 12: Informal advice

(1) *The true mission of a Dispute Board is not judicial; rather it is to prevent formal Disputes. The Parties may at any time jointly refer a matter or Dispute to the DB for it to give an informal advisory opinion as a means of Dispute avoidance and/ or informally discuss and attempt to resolve any disagreement that may have arisen between the Parties during the performance of the Contract. The DB may provide the requested advisory opinion during a conversation with the Parties, during any meeting or site visit in the presence of both Parties or in a written note to the Parties, or, with the prior agreement of the Parties, provide informal assistance to resolve a disagreement in any other form. The Parties are not bound to act upon any advice given during the informal assistance process.*

(2) *The DB may on its own initiative raise an issue with the Parties in order to establish a dialogue between them and to clarify matters in the presence of the DB. The Parties have the right to stop the DB's initiative if they regard it as unnecessary, provided that they notify the DB promptly, jointly and in writing.*

(3) *If the DB is later called upon to make a Determination concerning a matter with respect to which it has provided an informal advisory opinion, the DB shall not be bound by any views expressed in such verbal or written advisory opinion.*

The rationale is that parties are less likely to adopt extreme positions in order to keep credibility with the DB members, in view of the DBs power to issue decisions and the possibility that the DB's decision will be admissible as evidence in formal proceedings. This will be more effective if the DB is proactively involved throughout the project.[36]

9.24 An engaged, standing DB provides the parties with a forum to discuss project issues as they arise with an impartial expert. Furthermore, the parties will understand that if any disagreements become disputes, they can readily refer them to the DB for decisions. The DB will have the advantage of starting from a position of knowledge about the project, and the resolution of disputes in 'real time' allows the DB to see the project work as it progresses and hear from those involved in the works while matters are fresh in their memory. This should lead to better decisions.

9.25 It also saves goodwill: the early resolution of disagreements or disputes by a readily available DB can help the parties resolve their differences before they become polarised in their views, and it is much more cost-effective and less acrimonious than arbitration or litigation. Another benefit is the resolution of disputes in manageable packages. It is

35 Under the CIArb Rules, the parties are able to choose either a DRB or DAB. It is up to the parties to elect which alternative they favour and incorporate the corresponding dispute board clause into their contract. The only difference arising from the parties' choice of a DRB or a DAB under the CIArb Rules is that DRBs issue non-binding recommendations, whereas DABs issue binding decisions.

36 For instance, the Introduction in the ICE Rules provides: '*The ICE considers that the earlier the DB becomes involved in contractual issues the more effective the process becomes. It is suggested that DBs are used as soon as project level negotiations reach an impasse and with the minimum of intermediate, pre-referral procedural steps*'.

unlikely (albeit not impossible) that a referral to a dispute board contains the entirety of the issues arising between the parties during a project. The ongoing dispute resolution by a DB usually minimises the aggregation of claims.

9.26 These benefits may well be lost if the DB is only established because a dispute has arisen after the work has commenced or has even been completed. Once the work is completed, the DB will be no more familiar with the project or the individuals involved than an arbitration tribunal. It might then be more appropriate to refer the dispute to a final dispute resolution process such as arbitration.

9.27 The main argument against the early appointment of a DB is cost. DB members are remunerated throughout the project, usually by way of a monthly retainer, which is supplemented with a daily fee covering the time spent for activities such as travel, attending hearings, meetings and site visits, and producing written recommendations or decisions. An effective DB, which reduces conflict (and lost productive time) and/or avoids disputes being referred to arbitration or court, will provide far greater cost savings than the maintenance costs of the DB. However, maintaining a standing DB is nonetheless an appreciable cost, and is likely only to be cost-effective in mid-sized to large projects.[37]

Use of DBs

9.28 It is not surprising that disputes arise in the construction and engineering industry. The size and complexity of projects, the number of participants, environmental regulations, lower profit margins, the use of detailed standard and non-standard contracts, and a confrontational approach of parties with different objectives all contribute to generate disagreements. The use of DBs in the construction industry has over many years significantly contributed to the avoidance and early resolution of disputes.[38]

9.29 The need for prompt, cost-effective, and impartial dispute resolution exists in many contractual relationships in several industries and on a wide range of commercial projects. DBs have their origins in the construction industry, but the scope for DBs is far wider. DBs have been used in the following industries:

a The financial services industry (and project finance)
b Concession contracts[39]
c Operational and maintenance contracts
d Information technology (IT) projects

37 For instance, the World Bank's Standard Bidding Documents updated in December 2019 established a scale based on project value for when standing DBs are to be used, as follows: '*For a Contract estimated to cost above USD 50 million, the DAAB shall comprise of three members. For a Contract estimated to cost between USD 20 million and USD 50 million, the DAAB may comprise of three members or a sole member. For a Contract estimated to cost less than USD 20 million, a sole member is recommended*'.

38 The Dispute Resolution Board Foundation states that studies and analysis of the DRBF database show 85–98% of recommendations/decisions have not gone on to further arbitration or litigation, <https://www.drb.org/db-faqs> (last accessed 26 June 2020).

39 Awarded for a limited but potentially renewable period, during which the concessionaire (private partner) enjoys the exclusive right to use the (public) asset. The concessionaire is responsible for all investments in the asset and developing new facilities, under supervision of the state or regulator. The concessionaire is remunerated in accordance with agreed tariffs collected directly from users.

e Manufacturing: clothing
f Intellectual property agreements
g Process plant: brewing
h PPP projects: roads, hospitals, and rail projects
i Aerospace procurement
j Insurance contracts
k The maritime industry (particularly shipbuilding)
l Telecommunications
m Film and TV production

The ICC Rules and the CIArb Rules are not industry specific and can be adapted for any type of project. They each provide a set of stand-alone DB rules that can be used in any commercial or construction contract by the incorporation of a short precedent DB clause. If the parties incorporate one clause into their contract, then, by reference, the entire DB conditions, procedure, and DB members are incorporated.

9.30 The Institution of Civil Engineers (ICE)[40] also offers a stand-alone set of DB rules, albeit designed specifically for construction projects. Being UK-based, the ICE Rules consist of two alternatives: 'Procedure One' for use on international projects, and 'Procedure Two' which is HGCRA compliant.

9.31 NEC, the commercial arm of ICE, has also now adopted DB rules for the first time. The NEC4 Contract offers an option for international projects (*ie*, that are not bound by the HGRCA) to incorporate DB rules. This latest iteration has a stronger focus on dispute avoidance,[41] and provides for a standing 'Dispute Avoidance Board' which is required to visit the site at specified intervals and can proactively offer informal advice. The parties can refer 'potential disputes' to the DAB (and this is a condition precedent to formal proceedings), who must then issue a non-binding recommendation.

9.32 Finally, the FIDIC dispute board rules are included in the FIDIC Conditions of Contract. The FIDIC Contracts provide for a three-tiered dispute mechanism that has the DAB/DAAB[42] at its core.

DAABs under FIDIC 2017: procedures and issues in practice

9.33 The 1999 FIDIC Contracts (inclusive of the MDB Harmonised edition) are the most widely known contracts for international construction projects in the world. Since their release in 1999 FIDIC have championed the use of DBs. FIDIC's 2017 Contracts are intended to address nearly 20 years of evolution in the international construction industry, and the now infamous claims procedure from the 1999 Conditions[43] has been expanded in almost every sense.

40 The United Kingdom's leading organisation for civil engineers.

41 NECs intention is clearly displayed, with the relevant section renamed from 'Dispute Resolution' to 'Resolving and Avoiding Dispute'.

42 1999/2017.

43 See for instance, R McCrea, 'The Court of Appeal in Persero II: How to Enforce "Binding but Non-Final" Dispute Board Decisions under the FIDIC form of Contract' <www.fenwickelliott.com/research-insight/annual-review/2015/persero-II-dispute-board-decisions> (last accessed 26 June 2020).

9.34 The claims procedure in the 2017 Contracts can be broken down into six constituent parts:

a Making a claim
b Obtaining the Engineer's determination (or the other Party, in the Silver Book)
c Avoidance of Disputes (new)
d Obtaining the DAAB's decision
e Amicable settlement
f Arbitration (or court)

The preceding steps 1–5 (but excepting 3) are mandatory pre-conditions to commencing formal proceedings. The process is designed to address claims and disagreements quickly, to de-escalate disputes, and avoid the need for formal proceedings. Together, they create a pathway to resolving claims. This pathway is procedurally driven, running to 11 pages of the contract, and it includes strict deadlines that need to be observed. Some of the key developments and issues are discussed later.

Making a claim

9.35 'Claims' and 'disputes' are now dealt with in separate clauses that apply equally to both the Contractor and Employer.[44] Notifying the other party of a claim is the first step in FIDIC's claims procedure, in respect of which FIDIC has included more prescriptive requirements and additional time-bars.[45] This reflects a global trend of increasingly strict requirements for how and when claims are to be brought.[46]

9.36 The 1999 Contracts provide a time-bar that applies only to Contractors, under which Contractors must make a claim within 28 days of becoming aware of the event or circumstance giving rise to the claim or they will lose all entitlement to it.[47] No such time-bar applies to the Employer, who need only provide notice of a claim '*as soon as reasonably practicable*'.[48]

9.37 In the 2017 Contracts both the Contractor and Employer are bound by the same requirements in respect of making a claim, including the same 28-day time-bar,[49] and a further time-bar will now apply if the party does not set out the contractual and/or other legal basis of the claim within 84 days of the event giving rise to it.[50]

9.38 Furthermore, the 1999 Conditions do not specify any particular form that a notice of claim is to take, other than it be in writing[51] and '*describe the event or circumstance giving rise to it*'.[52] This has allowed a broad interpretation of 'notice' to be applied, under

44 Clauses 20 and 21, respectively.

45 Time-bars are where a contract provides a time limit to fulfil a mandatory requirement (for instance to issue a notice), failing which a certain right (for instance to make a claim) will be lost.

46 See for instance, R McCrea, 'Notices of Claim and Time Bars: Don't Be Another "Sympathy" Statistic' <www.fenwickelliott.com/research-insight/newsletters/international-quarterly/notices-claim-time-bars> (last accessed 26 June 2020).

47 Sub-clause 20.1.

48 Sub-clause 2.5.

49 Sub-clause 20.2.

50 Sub-clause 20.2.4.

51 Sub-clause 1.3.

52 Sub-clause 20.1.

which it is generally recognised that progress reports, project correspondence, meeting minutes, and informal agreements (or a combination) may satisfy the requirement provided they are '*recognisable as a claim*'.[53]

9.39 The 2017 Contracts have removed this ambiguity, and leniency. 'Notices' are now strictly defined and must be expressly identified as a Notice of claim,[54] and furthermore, nothing stated in any progress report, programme, or supporting report shall constitute a Notice.[55] The NEC4 contract has taken a similar direction and now requires notices of claim to be '*communicated separately from other communications*'.[56]

9.40 Recent case law suggests that these requirements will be strictly applied, with cases in Hong Kong[57] and the United Kingdom[58] involving judges concluding that while they had sympathy for the claimant, they had no choice but to find against them where clear contract terms (relating to a time-bar provision) had not been complied with.

Obtaining the Engineer's determination

9.41 Once a claim has been submitted it falls to the Engineer (or the other Party in the Silver Book) to take responsibility for determining the claim. This procedure has been enlarged from requiring the Engineer to consult with the parties and make a fair determination within 42 days, to now requiring the Engineer to:

- a State whether it considers a Notice has been issued late, and if so, it may decide whether circumstances exist that excuse the late submission[59]
- b Consult with the parties to attempt to reach agreement on the claim,[60] and if no agreement is reached within 42 days[61]
- c Make a 'fair determination' within a further 42 days[62]

The Engineer's determination will be binding on the parties unless or until revised by the DAAB or in arbitration (this is the same under both the 1999 and 2017 Contracts), however, the 2017 Contracts add that unless either party issues a notice of dissatisfaction (NOD) within 28 days of receipt of the determination it will become final and conclusive, and immediately enforceable in arbitration.[63]

53 Mr Justice Akenhead in *Obrascon Huarte Lain SA v Her Majesty's Attorney General for Gibraltar* [2015] EWCA Civ 712 found that given its serious effect, Sub-clause 20.1 should 'be construed reasonably broadly', and although no particular form of notice is required, '*it must [nonetheless] be recognisable as a "claim"*' under the contract.

54 Sub-clause 1.3, and Notices must also be signed by the authorised representative of the party named in the contract, identified as a Notice, and delivered to the address stated in the Contract Data (formerly the Particular Conditions).

55 Sub-clauses 4.20 and 8.3.

56 Sub-clause 13.7.

57 *Maeda Corporation & China State v Bauer Hong Kong* [2019] HKCFI 918.

58 In the Northern Irish case, *Glen Water Ltd v Northern Ireland Water Ltd* [2017] NIQB 20.

59 Sub-clauses 20.2.2 and 20.2.4.

60 After receiving the 'fully detailed claim' required from the claiming party within 84 days of event or circumstance giving rise to the claim.

61 Sub-clauses 20.2.5 and 3.7.

62 Sub-clauses 20.2.5 and 3.7.

63 Sub-clause 3.7.5.

9.42 The Engineer is employed by the Employer and some Contractors will no doubt be concerned about the expansion of the Engineer's role in the 2017 Contracts. FIDIC have at least attempted to address this concern by now requiring that the Engineer act 'neutrally' in discharging the aforementioned duties.[64] This extends the Engineer's existing obligation to issue a 'fair' determination,[65] although in practice there is often little a Contractor can do to enforce this obligation.

9.43 The 2017 Contracts have therefore extended the Engineer's role in claim resolution from a minimum 42 days to 84 days, with the prospect of its determination becoming final if neither party issues a valid NOD. Parties will need to be conscious of the new time limits.

Avoidance of Disputes

9.44 A new 'Avoidance of Disputes' provision has been added which permits the parties to jointly ask the DAB to informally discuss and/or provide assistance with any issue or disagreement.[66] The parties will not be bound to act on any advice given in this process. This provision has its origins in the 2008 Gold Book,[67] and it reflects similar 'Informal Advice' provisions in the ICC, ICArb, ICE, and NEC4 dispute board rules.

9.45 This type of provision is arguably better suited to the role of a DRB than a DAB, and one might question whether FIDIC has gone too far in providing a 'one-stop-shop' DAAB. The issue is that the DAB is being asked to act as a quasi-mediator in this clause, whereas in the following clause it must act as adjudicator, and these functions are not usually compatible. A mediator will often become privy to confidential and commercially sensitive information from the parties, and is there to facilitate settlement, and this is plainly not compatible with the role of adjudicator who must decide the parties' legal rights and obligations.

9.46 This type of dual role scenario has been met with some concern in the UK,[68] and there is a real risk that having an adjudicator present during informal discussions could make any subsequent decision or the DAAB itself prone to challenge on the grounds of impartiality. Care will be needed. Sub-clause 21.3 makes it clear that both parties must be present in any such meetings with the DAB and this should certainly be respected.

Obtaining the DAAB's decision

9.47 Once the mandatory steps in parts 1 and 2 have been complied with, if a party is dissatisfied with the Engineer's determination (and has issued an NOD within 15 days

64 Sub-clause 3.7.

65 Although this obligation was arguably already included in the existing obligation, and this was found to be the case as a matter of English law by the Court of Appeal in *Amec Civil Engineering Limited v Secretary of State for Transport* [2005] CILL 2288.

66 Sub-clause 21.3.

67 The FIDIC Guide to the Gold Book states: 'Prevention is better than cure, and the DAB is entrusted also with the role of providing informal assistance to the Parties at any time in an attempt to resolve any agreement'.

68 For instance, in *Glencot Development and Design Co Ltd v Ben Barrett & Son (Contractors) Ltd* [2001] EWHC Technology 15 (TCC), HHJ Lloyd QC commented that the conduct of the adjudicator meant that this was a case of 'apparent bias' in that he appeared to lack impartiality, having been privy to a number of without prejudice offers and some rather heated discussions in his capacity as mediator.

of receipt of the determination) or the other party fails or refuses to comply with it, the claiming party may say that a 'Dispute' has arisen and refer it to the DAAB for a decision.

9.48 The DAAB is the centrepiece of the FIDIC claims mechanism. The FIDIC Contracts are accompanied by five non-binding 'Golden Principles', which is FIDIC's attempt at protecting what it deems to be the fundamental and inviolable features of the FIDIC Contract from party amendments.[69] The fifth Golden Principle provides:

> *Unless there is a conflict with the governing law of the Contract, all formal disputes must be referred to a Dispute Avoidance/Adjudication Board (or a Dispute Adjudication Board, if applicable) for a provisionally binding decision as a condition precedent to arbitration.*

Obtaining a DAAB decision is a contractual condition precedent to commencing formal proceedings in respect of a dispute, and this will be upheld in most jurisdictions. The key features of this procedure are discussed next.

Setting up the DAAB

9.49 In keeping with the stronger dispute avoidance function of the DAAB, FIDIC now provides for standing DAABs to be set up at the start of the project in all the 2017 Contracts.[70] Sub-clause 21.1 requires the DAAB to be appointed by the time stated in the Contract Data, or if none is stated, 28 days after the Contractor receives the Letter of Acceptance. By contrast, the 1999 Yellow and Silver Books provide for the DAB to be appointed within 28 days of either party giving notice to the other of its intention to refer a dispute to a DAB.[71]

9.50 The procedure for appointing the DAAB remains materially the same as under the 1999 Contracts, and is as follows:

- *(a)* If the DAAB is to comprise:[72]
  - *(1)* One member: they shall be jointly appointed by the parties from a list of candidates included in the Contract Data.
  - *(2)* Three members: each party shall select one member for the agreement of the other Party. The parties shall then consult with both those members and agree the third member, to act as chairperson.
- *(b)* If the parties are unable to agree on any of the members, or either party fails to select a member, by the date stated in the Contract Data, then either party may request the appointing entity or official named in the Contract Data to make the appointment(s) (after due consultation with both parties).[73]

Appointing a standing DAAB early facilitates the new and broader role of dispute avoidance provided in the updated mechanism, making the DAAB more than solely an adjudicator.

---

69 Although the Golden Principles themselves do not have contractual standing and the parties can agree to amend the contracts in contravention of the principles.

70 Previously only the Red Book provided for a standing DAB, although this was followed in the MDB Harmonised Edition in 2005 (the Pink Book) and the Gold Book in 2008.

71 Sub-clause 20.2. The 1999 Red Book provided for a standing DAB.

72 Sub-clause 21.1.

73 Sub-clause 21.2.

It also ensures that when disputes do arise they can be heard promptly as intended. One of the major problems encountered under the 1999 Contracts is severe delay to setting up the DAB, once a dispute has arisen, if one of the parties does not cooperate.

9.51 Further to this issue, the 2017 Contracts also provide that if a dispute arises and no DAAB has been constituted, the claiming party may refer the dispute directly to arbitration.[74] This is a significant revision. The 1999 Contracts contain a similar provision, Sub-clause 20.8 '*Expiry of Dispute Adjudication Board's appointment*',[75] which has been found to refer only to the exceptional situation where the mission of a standing DAB has expired before a dispute arises between the parties, and not to the situation where a DAB has not yet been constituted.[76]

9.52 Although the new Sub-clause 21.8 is a welcome revision, it should be noted that once the parties begin the process of setting up a DAAB, the DAAB will become mandatory and the process will not be able to be abandoned other than in exceptional circumstances (if at all). Two issues arise from this:

a First, what is necessary to validly appoint the DAAB when one party is not cooperating?

b Second, once the process to appoint the DAAB has commenced, can it be bypassed in any circumstances?

Appointing the DAAB when one party is not cooperating

9.53 In the event that one party does not comply with their obligations to appoint the DAAB, or to replace a member in the event of their resignation or termination, the reality under both the 1999 and 2017 FIDIC Contracts is that the appointment process can be delayed by many months.

9.54 The contractual procedure provides for this scenario by requiring the parties to name an appointing entity (such as FIDIC) who can make an appointment on behalf of the parties. However, the procedure also requires the parties to consult with one another and the two appointed DAB members, and for the appointing entity to appoint after 'due consultation' with the parties. There is debate as to exactly what is needed to fulfil this obligation where one party is not cooperating.[77]

9.55 FIDIC's nominating service states that it will discharge the obligation of due consultation by notifying the parties who FIDIC proposes to appoint, and providing a period of 48 hours for either party to provide any specific reasons as to why the named person is unsuitable, in the absence of which that person will be appointed.[78] Some commentators have raised concerns that FIDIC's stated procedure does not satisfy the contractual requirement for 'due consultation',[79] and on its face, it is difficult to reconcile a 48-hour objection period with an obligation to consult.

74 Sub-clause 20.8.

75 ibid.

76 The Swiss Supreme Court in Decision 4A_124/2014, and UK Technology and Construction Court *in Peterborough City Council v Enterprise Managed Services Limited* [2014] EWHC 3193 (TCC).

77 Sub-clauses 21.1 and 21.2.

78 FIDIC Guidelines for DAB Appointments, <https://fidic.org/node/816> (last accessed 26 June 2020).

79 See for instance: <www.corbett.co.uk/fidics-procedures-for-the-appointment-of-a-dab-need-improvement/> (last accessed 26 June 2020).

9.56 However, it is suggested that the word '*due*' applies an important caveat to the obligation, namely to require such consultation as is proportionate/appropriate in the circumstances.[80] Viewed in all the circumstances, it should be noted for instance that the appointing entity will only be asked to make an appointment after a 28-day and/or 42-day period resulted in no agreement being reached, FIDIC asks to be provided with any requirements or preferences stated by the parties in the contract or subsequent correspondence, and FIDIC (and most other nominating entities) will only appoint from its own public list of pre-approved adjudicators which the parties should be deemed to be familiar with when naming the appointing entity.

9.57 In context then FIDIC's procedure may well satisfy the 'due consultation' obligation. This was the view of the arbitral tribunal in ICC Case 16262, who accepted that the obligation had been satisfied under the 1999 FIDIC Yellow Book notwithstanding that the appointing authority had not informed the parties of the person it was considering appointing or invited comments before deciding whether or not to confirm the appointment. Specifically, the arbitral tribunal noted:

> *the Arbitral Tribunal does not read Sub-Clause 20.3*[81] *as indicating an express expectation that the 'appointing entity' will discuss with the parties the identity of the possible appointees. ... In the opinion of this Tribunal and notwithstanding the practice adopted by FIDIC, it would be wrong to limit the discretion of the appointing entity by requiring the identification of possible candidates in the absence of express language. To do so would provide yet another opportunity for a party to engage in tactical manoeuvres.*

Whether or not the preceding conclusion is correct in a specific jurisdiction, failing to fulfil the obligation could be disastrous to a claim. In practice, FIDIC (and most other nominating entities) spend far longer attempting to satisfy the 'due consultation' obligation than their published procedure states, particularly if the recalcitrant party belatedly decides to engage.

9.58 A claiming party should proactively seek to engage with the recalcitrant party through every stage to avoid arguments that the contractual procedure was not followed and/or natural justice has been breached. The parties may also wish to delete the contractual requirement of consultation by the appointing entity, or specify the precise periods, to reduce the scope for the types of '*tactical manoeuvres*' referred to by the Tribunal in ICC Case 16262.

Bypassing the DAAB

9.59 Despite the best efforts of one party to appoint the DAAB, exceptional circumstances can arise which frustrate the process or rob the mechanism of its intended benefit. There are differing views as to what circumstances will qualify to allow a DB to be bypassed once the process to set it up has started (under the 2017 Contracts), or at all (under the 1999 Contracts). The two leading cases on this issue come down on different sides:

80 For instance, see Dr Nael Bunni, *The FIDIC Forms of Contract* (3rd edn, Blackwell Publishing 2005) 616–617.

81 Sub-clause 21.3 in the 2017 Contracts.

a In the English case *Peterborough*,[82] the court refused to allow the litigation to proceed until the DAB procedure was completed. Although the Judge had sympathy with the claimant's argument that the other party's position meant the DAB procedure would inevitably have to be followed by court proceedings anyway, it stopped the proceedings on the basis the DAB was a mandatory pre-condition that had to be completed first.[83]

b By contrast, the Swiss Supreme Court in Decision 4A_124/2014 also found that completing the DAB procedure was a mandatory pre-condition to commencing arbitration. However, it found that in the circumstances before it, in which the claiming party had spent over 18 months attempting to have the DAB constituted without success, the DAB procedure could be bypassed.

In reaching its decision the Swiss Supreme Court relied on the civil law principle of good faith, finding both that the claiming party could not be blamed for skipping the DAB in the circumstances, and that given the other party's 'passivity' in appointing the DAB during the preceding 15 months, it could not then insist on the mandatory nature of the DAB. No general obligation of good faith exists in common law jurisdictions such as England, and if faced with the same set of facts it is unclear whether an English court would reach the same result as its Swiss counterpart.

9.60 There must however be circumstances in any jurisdiction when obtaining a DB decision can be bypassed. The most commonly cited example is where one party fails to sign the tripartite Dispute Adjudication Agreement (DAA) constituting the DB. In this scenario it is difficult to see how it can be said that the DB is validly constituted, and subject to the applicable law, it is likely that the DB procedure will be deemed to be waived and the claiming party may proceed directly to formal proceedings.[84] This was the view of the arbitral tribunals in ICC cases 16155[85] and 18505.[86]

9.61 Nonetheless, some commentators suggest that the claiming party should, or at least could, choose to proceed to obtain a DB decision notwithstanding the other party's refusal to sign the DAA Agreement.[87] This view has been supported by the arbitral tribunal in ICC Case 15956, and endorsed (although no decision was required on the point) in ICC Case 165705.

9.62 Given the serious consequences of a premature referral to arbitration[88] and if there is ambiguity under the applicable law, it is suggested that a claiming party could seek to enter into the DAA with the DB member(s) notwithstanding the other party's refusal

---

82 *Peterborough City Council v Enterprise Managed Services Limited* [2014] EWHC 3193 (TCC).

83 Similarly in the United Arab Emirates, *Commercial Case 757 of 2016,* the Court ordered the annulment of an arbitral award on the basis that the claiming party had not first obtained an Engineer's decision as required under the 1987 FIDIC Red Book.

84 The non-complying party's failure in setting up the DB could then be dealt with as a breach of contractual obligation when considering costs.

85 In that case, relating to the 1999 FIDIC Red Book, the arbitral tribunal held that the Employer had foregone its right to insist on the appointment of the DAB because it had ignored the contractor's attempt to appoint a DAB during the performance of the contract.

86 In a contract relating to the 1999 FIDIC Yellow Book.

87 Cyril Chern, *Chern on Dispute Boards: Practice and Procedure* (4th edn, Informa Law Routledge 2019) 211.

88 In the UK and Switzerland, and many other countries, failure to follow the pre-arbitration procedure might result in the claim being dismissed for lack of jurisdiction and any resulting award could be void.

to sign, in order to obtain a DB decision, and then commence arbitration based on both the DB's decision and, in the alternative, the exceptional circumstances justifying the DB being bypassed.

9.63 Considering the preceding scenarios, it is sensible to ensure the DB is set up early and not to wait until a dispute has arisen. To that end, it is important that financiers such as MDBs play a role in ensuring this is complied with. In a welcome addition, the 2017 Contracts also expressly permit an arbitral tribunal to take account of any non-cooperation in constituting the DAAB in its awarding of costs.[89]

Obtaining the DAAB's decision

9.64 The DAAB procedure under the 2017 Contracts retains its core aspects, as follows:[90]

- a When any dispute arises in relation to a contract either party may refer it to the DAAB for a decision.
- b The DAAB must issue a decision within 84 days of the dispute being referred to it.[91]
- c The decision '*shall be binding on both Parties, who shall promptly give effect to it*'.
- d Obtaining a DAAB decision is a condition precedent to referring that dispute to arbitration.[92]

Either party may issue a NOD with a DAAB decision within 28 days of receiving it, which will preserve the parties' ability to refer the underlying dispute to be finally determined in arbitration.[93] If neither party issues a valid NOD then the decision will become final, and the decision itself will be enforceable in arbitration without the merits of the underlying dispute being looked at any further.

9.65 The 2017 Contracts also include a number of revisions that clarify and assist in enforcing these obligations. Because a DAB procedure is purely a contractual mechanism, any ambiguity will be vulnerable to '*tactical manoeuvres*'[94] by a party seeking to avoid a decision. In its new DAAB procedure FIDIC has taken care to address some of the vulnerabilities exposed in its 1999 Contracts. The key amendments are:

- a 'Dispute' is now a defined term,[95] and helpfully, it can include the situation where the other party has failed to oppose or respond to the claim.[96]

---

89 Sub-clause 21.6.

90 Sub-clause 21.4 of the 2017 Contracts, Sub-clause 20.4 of the 1999 Contracts, and Sub-clause 20.6 of the 2008 Gold Book.

91 Unless the parties agree to extend the period.

92 With limited exceptions, Sub-clause 21.4.4: Except as stated in the last paragraph of Sub-Clause 3.7.5 [Dissatisfaction with Engineer's determination], in Sub-Clause 21.7 [Failure to Comply with DAAB's Decision] and in Sub-Clause 21.8 [No DAAB In Place].

93 Although in another useful addition, the 2017 Contracts provide that a party issuing an NOD must clearly identify the parts of the DAB decision they are dissatisfied with, and the remainder of the decision shall become final and binding as if the NOD had not been given (Sub-clause 21.4).

94 So described by the arbitral tribunal in ICC Case 16262.

95 Sub-clause 1.1.29.

96 Recalcitrant parties frequently seek to delay or prevent a claim crystallising into a dispute (and therefore being able to be referred to a DAB), by not responding or not expressly rejecting the claim.

b If the DAAB awards payment of a sum of money, that amount shall be immediately due and payable after the claiming party issues an invoice for that amount, without any requirement for certification or notice.[97]

c The parties *and Engineer* must comply with the DAAB's decision '*whether or not a Party gives a NOD*'.[98]

d If either party fails to comply with a DAAB decision, whether final or not-final,[99] the other party may refer the failure itself directly to arbitration pursuant to Sub-clause 21.6.[100]

The latter two points in particular were intended by FIDIC to have already been provided for in the DAB mechanism in its 1999 Contracts.[101] However, as many Contractors have painfully found out, the 1999 wording contains ambiguity that has been the subject of fervent debate and legal gymnastics[102] since those contracts were released. This debate is most famously captured in the *Persero v PGN* series of cases in Singapore,[103] in which the claimant Contractor was eventually able to enforce a not-final DAB decision, albeit after going through two sets of arbitration, High Court, and Court of Appeal proceedings, over a period of six years.[104]

9.66 The 2017 Contracts now make it clear that DAAB decisions can be summarily enforced (*ie*, without the merits of the dispute being determined) irrespective of whether they have become final or not. However, even with clear contract wording, the enforceability of DB decisions will depend on the applicable law, as discussed later under '*Jurisdiction and enforcement*'.

Amicable settlement

9.67 The FIDIC procedure includes a mandatory stand-down period before a DAB/DAAB decision can be referred to arbitration, as a final period to encourage amicable settlement and avoid formal proceedings.[105] This has been reduced from 56 days to 28 days. Both the

97 Sub-clause 21.4.

98 ibid.

99 If no NOD is issued by either party within 28 days of receipt of the DAAB's decision, the decision becomes 'final' and cannot be appealed to formal proceedings (arbitration or court). Where a valid NOD has been issued for a decision, it will be a 'not-final' decision, and the either party may seek to have it overturned in formal proceedings.

100 Sub-clause 21.7.

101 This was expressly clarified by FIDIC in its Guidance Memorandum of April 2013, which provides an optional addition to the 1999 Contracts that makes it clear non-final DAB decisions can be summarily enforced.

102 For instance, much of the debate split into two camps of legal thought, in which proponents of the 'two-dispute' approach suggested that non-compliance with a not-final DAB decision created a new 'dispute' itself and that discrete dispute needed to be referred back to the DAB, whereas proponents of the 'one dispute' approach suggested that non-compliance did not create a new dispute and could simply be summarily enforced in arbitration (as FIDIC intended, and has now expressly drafted into the 2017 Contracts). Other contributors, such as the dissenting voice in *Persero II*, Senior Judge Chan Sek Keong, held that non-compliance with a DAB decision could not qualify as a 'dispute' under the contract at all and would need to be dealt with separately in the courts.

103 Culminating in *PT Perusahaan Gas Negara (Persero) TBK v CRW Joint Operation* [2015] 4 SLR 364, [2015] SGCA 30.

104 For a detailed review of these cases see R McCrea, 'The Court of Appeal in Persero II: how to enforce "binding but non-final" Dispute Board decisions under the FIDIC form of contract': <www.fenwickelliott.com/research-insight/annual-review/2015/persero-II-dispute-board-decisions> (last accessed 26 June 2020).

105 Sub-clause 21.5.

1999 and 2017 Contracts confirm that a dispute can be referred to arbitration at the end of this period '*even if no attempt at amicable settlement has been made*'.

9.68 Furthermore, if a party fails to comply with a DAAB decision, the other party can refer that failure directly to arbitration and the amicable settlement period will not apply.[106] This clarifies that the parties' obligation to '*promptly*' comply with a DAB decision[107] means in less than 28 days.

Arbitration

9.69 Once the preceding steps have been completed and complied with, either party may refer a dispute to arbitration.[108] The arbitration provisions for resolving the merits of DAAB decisions that have not become 'final and binding' (*ie*, where an NOD has been issued) are effectively the same under the 1999 and 2017 Contracts; namely that either party may refer the dispute (or parts of the dispute)[109] to be finally settled in arbitration.[110]

9.70 However, the 2017 Contracts expand the circumstances where DAAB decisions can be summarily enforced. As noted under '*Obtaining the DAAB's decision*', the expanded Sub-clause 21.7 permits any failure to comply with a DAAB decision, whether final or not-final, to be referred directly to arbitration for summary enforcement. In relation to not-final DAAB decisions, the right to enforcement by interim relief or award is subject to the fact that the merits of the dispute are reserved until resolved in a final arbitral award. Although this revised contractual clarification/position[111] will be welcomed by Contractors, there are still likely to be challenges in many jurisdictions as to whether the enforcement of not-final DAAB decisions via an arbitral award is supported by the applicable law.

Other FIDIC Contracts

FIDIC's Red Book (2010) and Yellow Book (2019) Subcontracts

9.71 FIDIC released its Conditions of Subcontract for Construction (the Red Book Subcontract) in 2011,[112] designed to be used with FIDIC's 1999 Red Book.[113] The Red Book Subcontract provides for an ad hoc DAB to be set up once a dispute arises, and the claims and DAB procedure follow the same structure as the 1999 Red Book provisions, albeit designed to work within and assist the Contractor to comply with it.[114]

9.72 For instance, notification of claims under the Subcontract are required to come before they will be due under the main contract. The Subcontractor must notify the

---

106 Sub-clause 21.7.

107 Sub-clause 21.4.

108 Or to court if the parties agree on litigation instead of arbitration.

109 The 2017 Contracts now provide that if only parts of the dispute are identified in the NOD, the remaining parts will not be subject to it and shall become final and binding as if no NOD had been given. This is helpful narrowing the focus of any dispute to be taken forward. However, in practice it may cause difficulties where parts of a dispute are not easily severable and should be heard together.

110 Sub-clause 20.6 of the 1999 Yellow Book and Sub-clause 21.6 of the 2017 Yellow Book.

111 Depending on your interpretation of the wording in Sub-clauses 20.4 and 20.6 of the 1999 Contracts.

112 Updating its first edition Subcontract of 1994.

113 It can also be used with the multilateral development bank's 'Pink Book'.

114 Clause 20 of the Red Book Subcontract, and Clause 20 of the 1999 Red Book.

Contractor of any claim within 21 days or the event or circumstances giving rise to it[115] (whereas the Contractor's claims must be notified to the Employer within 28 days under the 1999 Red Book),[116] and provides its fully detailed claim within 35 days (compared to the Contractor's 42 days in the 1999 Red Book).[117] If the Subcontractor fails to comply with these obligations, and it prevents the Contractor from recovering a corresponding sum from the Contractor under the main contract, this lost amount may be deducted from the Subcontract price.[118]

9.73 Decisions under the Subcontract, on the other hand, are scheduled to come *after* corresponding decisions by the Engineer and the DAB in the main contract:

a The Contractor is required to issue a binding decision within 49 days of receiving the Subcontractor's detailed claim in the Red Book Subcontract, which is seven days after the Engineer is required to determine the Contractor's claim under the 1999 Red Book.

b More pertinently, if either party notifies the other of its intention to refer a dispute to the DAB, the Contractor may within 14 days of receipt notify the Subcontractor that the dispute involves an issue or issues which are involved in a dispute between the Contractor and the Employer under the main contract. The effect of that will be to defer any referral to the Subcontract DAB until a date that is no earlier than 112 days later,[119] in order to allow the Contractor to resolve the dispute under the main contract first.

In 2019 FIDIC released its Conditions of Contract for Plant & Design Build contract (the Yellow Book Subcontract). However, the Yellow Book Subcontract was drafted to be used with the 1999 Yellow Book, and not the 2017 Yellow Book. This means that the dispute board process is modelled after the 1999 DAB process rather than the new DAAB process. The Yellow Book Subcontract claims and DAB procedures are substantially the same as those provided in the Red Book Subcontract, with perhaps the most notable difference being an extension of the deferment period for the Subcontract DAB process from 112 days to 140 days.

Other recent FIDIC Contracts approach to dispute boards

9.74 In 2016 FIDIC issued a new Form of Contract for Dredging and Reclamation Works (the Blue-Green Book) updating the 2006 First Edition. The Blue-Green Book provides for a truncated and consolidated claims and DAB procedure, whereby a 'dispute or difference' can be referred at any time to a DAB, who must issue its decision within 56 days of a dispute being referred to it.[120] The procedure is materially the same in both the 2006 and 2016 editions.

115 Failing which the claim will be time-barred.
116 Sub-clause 20.2.
117 Sub-clause 20.2. of the Red Book Subcontract and 1999 Red Book.
118 Sub-clause 20.3.
119 Sub-clause 20.4 of the Red Book Subcontract.
120 Or the DAB Agreement coming into effect, whichever is later.

9.75 In 2019 FIDIC issued a new contract in collaboration with the International Tunnelling and Underground Space Association (ITA-AITES); the Conditions of Contract for Underground Works (the Emerald Book). The Emerald Book is designed to cater for the unique features of underground works but is otherwise intended to form part of the Rainbow Suite,[121] and it accordingly adopts the DAAB procedure in the 2017 Contracts.

Multilateral development banks

9.76 The World Bank and a number of other MDBs have insisted on the use of DBs since their inclusion in the 1999 FIDIC Contracts.[122]

Originally, MDBs would adopt FIDIC's 1999 Red Book[123] as part of their standard bidding documents, that their borrowers or aid recipients had to follow, but they included additional clauses that were specific to and varied between the MDBs. This created inefficiencies and uncertainties amongst the users of the documents.

9.77 In 2005, a collaboration between the FIDIC Contracts Committee and a group of participating MDBs[124] resulted in the first standardised contract specifically designed for use in projects funded by MDBs; the MDBs Harmonised Edition of the 1999 Red Book. Referred to as the Pink Book, its third edition, published in June 2010, was until very recently the standard set of contract conditions adopted by the leading development banks.[125]

9.78 The Pink Book consolidates the special conditions incorporated by MDBs to comply with their procurement guidelines, for instance in relation to corruption and social issues, and provides for the MDB to inspect the site and audit the Contractor's project accounts.[126] It also includes a slightly updated DAB mechanism, with particular requirements as to who can be appointed to the DAB,[127] and requiring that any notice of dissatisfaction with a DAB decision include a statement that the issuing party has the '*intention to commence arbitration*'.[128]

9.79 The 2017 FIDIC Contracts signal an end to the harmonisation achieved through the Pink Book. There has been no suggestion of a new Pink Book, and instead, MDBs are encouraged (once more) to use the new Red Book amended with their own special requirements. The 2017 Red Book has been drafted to assist this usage, including specific

---

121 The Red, Yellow, and Silver Books.

122 See for instance World Bank Standard Bidding Documents (Procurement of Works), <https://documents1.worldbank.org/curated/en/458841468739545677/pdf/multi-page.pdf> (last accessed 14 June 2021), May 2000.

123 Several MDBs still use the 1999 Red Book, including the European Bank for Reconstruction and Developments, and the Caribbean Development Bank.

124 African Development Bank, Asian Development Bank, Black Sea Trade and Development Bank, Caribbean Development Bank, European Bank for Reconstruction and Development, InterAmerican Development Bank, International Bank for Reconstruction and Development (the World Bank), Islamic Bank for Development, and Nordic Development Fund.

125 <https://fidic.org/MDB_Harmonised_Construction_Contract> (last accessed 16 June 2020).

126 FIDIC Pink Book 1.15. As the MDB remains a third party to the contract, legally it is unable to enforce these obligations within the contract itself. However, practically MDBs can encourage compliance through their separate contractual arrangements with the Employer, or via sanctions in their procurement and anticorruption mechanisms. The Pink Book also includes the same claims and DAB mechanism as the 1999 Red Book, albeit with some minor improvements.

127 Sub-clause 20.2.

128 Sub-clause 20.4.

guidance for development banks[129] to incorporate their special requirements into the Particular Conditions of Contract,[130] and template clauses often required by MDBs.[131]

9.80 The World Bank has already endorsed this change, and now includes the 2017 Red Book in its Standard Procurement Documents,[132] incorporating the DAAB mechanism. The World Bank's own special conditions[133] restore some of the features of the Pink Book, including the right to conduct inspections and audits,[134] and placing more prescriptive requirements on who can be appointed to the DAAB.

9.81 Several other MDBs have followed suit, and FIDIC has entered into a number of non-exclusive licence agreements with leading MDBs to use the 2017 Contracts, and in some instances the 1999 Contracts as well, *but not the Pink Book.*[135] Uptake of the 2017 Contracts has not however been universal. The European Bank for Reconstruction and Developments, for instance, has not adopted the 2017 Contracts and continues to use the 1999 Red Book and the Pink Book.[136]

9.82 The endorsement of the latest DAAB mechanism by a number of MDBs is a helpful addition to the continued evolution of the DB. However, the pathway to and through the DAAB is procedurally driven and complex, and buy-in from the parties is essential for it to work. Both the 1999 Red Book and the Pink Book require standing-DBs to set up when the project commences, yet this frequently does not happen until a dispute has arisen.

9.83 If MDBs are serious about using and seeing the benefits of this mechanism in their projects, they will need to do more to ensure their partners set up the DAAB early, and implement (and maintain) sufficient contract administration resources to use it. There are promising signs that this will be the case on World Bank projects going forward, as its Standard Procurement Documents now include strong new provisions bolstering the procedure.[137]

Jurisdiction and enforcement

9.84 Most DB rules now specify that the law governing the DB procedure is the same as the law governing the main contract.[138] Arbitration agreements on the other hand

129 As well as aid agencies and international financing institutions.

130 Page 42 of the Guidance for the Preparation of Particular Conditions, to the FIDIC Red Book 2017.

131 Dealing with, for instance, child and forced labour, non-discrimination, and equal opportunity.

132 World Bank Standard Bidding Documents, Procurement of Works, updated in July 2019.

133 Its Conditions of Particular Application (COPA).

134 Refer, for instance, to the World Bank's SPD Request for Bids, Section IX, Part B, Sub-Clause 1.17 and Part C – Fraud and Corruption.

135 For instance, the African Development Bank, the Caribbean Development Bank, the European Bank for Reconstruction and Development, the InterAmerican Development Bank, and the Asian Infrastructure Investment Bank.

136 See for instance the tender documents for a Single Stage Open Tendering Procedure <www.ebrd.com/work-with-us/procurement/project-procurement/standard-procurement-documents.html> (last accessed 1 July 2020).

137 For instance, the World Bank's Standard Procurement Document for Design and Build Works, updated December 2019, includes provisions that: the bidder and Employer shall furnish the names of three potential DAAB members at the. The Notice of Commencement shall not be issued until the DAAB has been appointed (Sub-clause 8.1), the Contractor must include a Provisional Sum that shall be used to cover the Employer's share of the DAAB members' fees and expenses, and no prior instruction of the Engineer shall be required with respect to the work of the DAAB (Sub-clause 13.4).

138 For instance, the 2017 FIDIC Yellow Book (Sub-clause 21.2), ICArb Rules (Article 1, Definitions).

are usually treated as separate contracts and may have a different applicable law.[139] When considering adopting a DB mechanism, it is important to identify the law that will be applicable to it and to formal proceedings, and how DBs are treated in those jurisdictions.

Determining the applicable law

9.85 If only one law is referred to in the contract, it is likely that this law would primarily govern everything. However, it is possible for one legal system to govern the merits of the dispute (in other words, the contractual relations) between the parties, whilst a different legal system could govern the arbitration agreement (and therefore, potentially, the enforceability of any DB decision). This was the position in the *Persero v PGN*[140] series of cases, which involved a project in Indonesia governed by Indonesian law, yet the DB procedure was enforced in Singapore under Singaporean law, because Singapore was chosen for the seat of the arbitration.

9.86 As a matter of English law, the Court of Appeal in *Sulamérica Cia Nacional de Seguros SA v Enesa Engenharia SA*[141] sought to clarify what had, for some time, been an uncertain area of jurisprudence as to which law should apply to the arbitration agreement where none is expressly stated.

9.87 The Court of Appeal formulated a three-stage test to determine the law of an arbitration agreement: (1) is there an express choice of law governing the arbitration agreement? (2) if not, can a choice be implied? and (3) in the absence of a choice, with which law does the arbitration agreement have the 'closest and most real connection'? Three stages should be undertaken separately and in this particular order: express choice; implied choice; and closest and most real connection. In reality, the second and third stages often merge because in order to decide whether the parties had made an implied choice of proper law it is necessary to consider the system of law with which the agreement had its closest and most real connection.

9.88 In that case the governing law of the contract was Brazilian law and the seat of the arbitration was London. The Court of Appeal stated that the starting point, absent any indication to the contrary, was that the parties intended their relationship to be governed by the same system of law.[142] However, two factors pointed away from Brazilian law being implied as also governing the arbitration agreement: (1) the choice of London as the seat, and (2) the fact that the effect of Brazilian law would mean that the arbitration agreement was only enforceable with both parties' consent.[143] Applying the third stage of its test, the Court concluded that English law was the applicable law of the arbitration, because the parties could not have intended to choose a law that could significantly undermine their agreement.

139 The principle of separability, which is provided in Article 16(1) of the UNCITRAL Model Law on International Commercial Arbitration, and for instance, section 7 of the Arbitration Act 1996 (England).

140 Culminating in *PT Perusahaan Gas Negara (Persero) TBK v CRW Joint Operation* [2015] 4 SLR 364, [2015] SGCA 30.

141 *Sulamérica Cia Nacional de Seguros SA v Enesa Engenharia SA* [2012] EWCA Civ 638.

142 ibid, para 11.

143 ibid, paras 29 and 30.

9.89 The outcome of the application of the *Sulamérica* three-stage test, however, remained unpredictable in practice.

9.90 On 29 April 2020 the English Court of Appeal in *Enka Insaat ve Sanayi AS v OOO Insurance Co Chubb* released a decision that, once again, sought to '*impose some order and clarity on this area of the law*'.[144] The Court of Appeal held that the starting point was to apply the three-stage test articulated in *Sulamérica*. However, in applying this test, the Court held:

a The first stage, '*is there an express choice of law governing the arbitration agreement*', may be satisfied either by words in the arbitration agreement itself, or alternatively, in the minority of cases where the choice of law governing the main contract (properly construed in the circumstances) informs an express choice of law for the arbitration agreement.[145]

b In all other cases, the general rule is that the parties' implied choice is that the law of the arbitration agreement will be the same as the law of the seat of the arbitration, unless there are '*particular features of the case demonstrating powerful reasons to the contrary*'.[146]

The case involved a subcontract relating to the construction of a power plant in Russia, with an arbitration agreement seated in London. When a fire damaged the power plant, OOO 'Insurance Company Chubb' (Chubb Russia) commenced court proceedings against Enka Insaat Ve Sanayi AS (Enka) in Moscow. Enka then commenced proceedings in London seeking to enforce the arbitration agreement[147] and to confirm the applicable law. In applying the aforementioned principles, the court held that the proper law of the arbitration was English. It reasoned that although the governing law of the subcontract was Russian, that was not by the express choice of the parties, and even if it was, it was '*not one of those rare cases where it is or informs an express choice of the AA [arbitration agreement] law*'.[148] Consequently, and in the absence of any compelling countervailing factors, the Court applied the presumption that the law of the arbitration agreement was the law of the seat of the arbitration.

9.91 The position under English law therefore is that the seat of the arbitration will be the applicable law of the dispute resolution provision, unless the parties have expressly chosen otherwise or there are compelling reasons otherwise.[149] This has cast out the position that was still commonly held prior to *Sulamérica* that it would be 'exceptional' for the law of the arbitration agreement to differ from law of the main contract.[150] It must however be noted that, at the time of writing, the decision in *Enka v Chubb* has been appealed to the Supreme Court of England and may soon be clarified even further.

---

144 *Enka Insaat ve Sanayi AS v OOO Insurance Co Chubb* [2020] EWCA Civ 574, para 89.

145 ibid, paras 90 and 108.

146 ibid, para 91.

147 Via an anti-suit injunction restraining Chubb Russia from continuing the Russian proceedings.

148 *Enka Insaat ve Sanayi AS v OOO Insurance Co Chubb* [2020] EWCA Civ 574, para 108.

149 This is in contrast to the position as it stood following the *Channel Tunnel Group Ltd v Balfour Beatty Construction Ltd* [1993] AC 334, where it was regarded as being 'exceptional' for the law of the arbitration agreement to differ from that governing the interpretation of the agreement.

150 See for instance the view of Lord Mustill in *Channel Tunnel Group Ltd v Balfour Beatty Construction Ltd* [1993] AC 334, 357–578.

9.92 The position in Singapore has also been unsettled. In *FirstLink Investments Corp Ltd v GT Payment Pte Ltd*[151] the High Court welcomed the three-stage test applied in *Sulamérica*, however, it disagreed that the starting point for the second-stage of the test should be a presumption that the main contract law would apply to the arbitration agreement. The Court stated that[152]

> *it cannot always be assumed that commercial parties want the same system of law to govern their relationship of performing the substantive obligations under the contract, and the quite separate (and often unhappy) relationship of resolving disputes when problems arise.*

The court went on:

> *In fact, the more commercially sensible viewpoint would be that the latter relationship often only comes into play when the former relationship has already broken down irretrievably. There can therefore be no natural inference that commercial parties would want the same system of law to govern these two distinct relationships. The natural inference would instead be to the contrary. When commercial relationships break down and parties descend into the realm of dispute resolution, parties' desire for neutrality comes to the fore; the law governing the performance of substantive contractual obligations prior to the breakdown of the relationship takes a backseat at this moment (it would take the main role subsequently when the time comes to determine the merits of the dispute), and primacy is accorded to the neutral law selected by parties to govern the proceedings of dispute resolution.*

This presumption was reversed in 2016 in *BCY v BCZ*.[153] The High Court there confirmed that the correct position under Singapore law is to apply the three-stage test in *Sulamérica*, in respect of which it emphasised that the governing law of the main contract is a 'strong indicator' of the governing law of the arbitration agreement, unless there are indications to the contrary.[154] The Court therefore held that the applicable law of the arbitration agreement was that of the governing law of the contract (New York) and not the arbitration seat (Singapore).

Enforcement of DB decisions

9.93 It is important that parties consider the applicable law for the contractual dispute procedure when negotiating its terms, because some jurisdictions do not acknowledge the binding nature of DB decisions and will therefore make such a mechanism inappropriate. Typical issues with the enforcement of not-final DB decisions (*ie*, where a NOD has been issued in respect of the decision) are as follows:

a whether an arbitral award enforcing a not-final DB decision will comply with the definition of an enforceable arbitral award in a jurisdiction's arbitration legislation, given that such an award (1) will not review the underlying merit of the dispute and (2) will be followed by a final substantive arbitral award on the underlying merits

151 *FirstLink Investments Corp Ltd v GT Payment Pte Ltd* [2014] SGHCR 12.

152 ibid, para 13.

153 *BCY v BCZ* [2017] 3 SLR 357, [2016] SGHC 249.

154 ibid, para 65.

b whether such an award will be prevented by the principle of *res judicata* (that a matter which has already been decided cannot be decided again), because the final substantive arbitral award will need to decide the same matters that are subject to the enforced DAB decision

A summary of how some jurisdictions have dealt with these issues is next:

Singapore

9.94 Following the *Persero v PGN*[155] series of cases the position in Singapore is that not-final DAB decisions can be summarily enforced in arbitration, notwithstanding that either party may also choose to have the underlying merits of the dispute finally decided as well. This will be the case whether FIDIC's 1999 DAB mechanism is used or the 2017 DAAB mechanism.[156]

Romania and Bulgaria

9.95 As of January 2017, the position in Romania appears to be that not-final DAB decisions cannot be enforced, and this is likely to apply to both FIDIC's 1999 and 2017 Contracts. The position has been unsettled for a number of years during which time there have been cases allowing not-final DB decisions to be enforced as well as cases barring enforcement.[157] However, in the most definitive statement to date a High Court decision in January 2017 found that not-final DB decisions cannot be enforced under Romanian law. The reasons for barring the enforcement of not-final DB decisions in Romania is generally as summarised at the start of this section, namely that any arbitral award enforcing a not-final DAB decision will not comply with Romanian legislation,[158] and *res judicata.*

9.96 Interestingly, just one month later in February 2017, the highest court in Bulgaria decided that although obtaining an Engineer's decision (under the 1992 FIDIC Red Book) was a condition precedent to arbitration, not-final decisions by the Engineer were not enforceable.[159]

South Africa and Namibia

9.97 By contrast to the preceding positions, in South Africa the courts have had no problems giving effect to the intention of the contract. The position is set out in the case of *Tubular Holdings v DBT Technologies*[160] which considered the standard DAB mechanism in the 1999 FIDIC Contracts. The court focussed only on the question of the intention of

155 Which culminated in subsequently the Singapore Court of Appeal *in PT Perusahaan Gas Negara (Persero) TBK v CRW Joint Operation* [2015] 4 SLR 364, [2015] SGCA 30.

156 Although, in relation to the 1999 mechanism, it remains open to the Court of Appeal to renege on its decision in *Persero II* and adopt instead the reasoning of the dissenting judgment that non-compliance with a DAB decision cannot be a 'dispute' within the meaning of the 1999 FIDIC Contracts, and must therefore be referred to the courts.

157 C Leaua and FA Baias (eds), *Arbitration in Romania: A Practitioner's Guide* (Kluwer Law International 2016).

158 Article 1.121(3) of the Romanian New Civil Procedure Code requires arbitral awards to be 'final' in order to be enforceable.

159 Court Ruling No. 59 of 03.02.2017 under case No. 788/2016 of the Supreme Court of Cassation, I Commercial Division.

160 *Tubular Holdings (Pty) Ltd v DBT Technologies (Pty) Ltd (06757/2013)* [2013] ZAGPJHC 155; 2014 (1) SA 244 (GSJ) (3 May 2013).

the contract, from which basis it had no difficulty in giving effect to what it described as the '*perfectly clear*' intention that the parties are '*obliged to promptly give effect to a decision by the DAB ... [and] that the issue of a notice of dissatisfaction does not in any way detract from this obligation*'.

9.98 The position in Namibia is the same, and in a judgment issued in April 2019 the Namibian Supreme Court confirmed that a DB decision under the FIDIC Contracts had to be complied with '*irrespective of the fact that a party aggrieved by such decision could take the decision on arbitration*'.[161]

United Arab Emirates

9.99 The position in the UAE, and which is representative of the Middle East and North Africa region generally, is untested but is very unlikely to permit not-final DAB decisions to be enforced. While UAE law does recognise arbitral awards, the UAE Civil Procedures Law only recognises final awards and therefore any bifurcation would likely jeopardise the entire arbitration agreement,[162] whereas not-final awards would also likely be disputed on grounds of *res judicata*. It is worth noting however that UAE courts do enforce pre-arbitral procedures (provided they are clearly stated and do not offend public policy),[163] and the Dubai Court of Appeal has recently upheld FIDIC's 1999 DAB as a condition precedent to arbitration.[164]

The embracing of DBs

CERN's LHC project and the use of dispute board

9.100 The European Organisation for Nuclear Research, known as CERN, comprises the world's largest particle physics laboratory. The Large Hadron Collider (LHC) at CERN sits underneath the Franco Swiss border with entry points in Switzerland at Meyrin Geneva and Cessy in France. CERN houses the largest and most sophisticated scientific instrument ever constructed for research purposes. The research focuses on the basic constituents of matter, which really is an exploration at the very frontier of high-energy. Subatomic particles are accelerated and forced to collide together close to the speed of light. Collisions cause the particles to break apart allowing researchers to examine what those particles are made of.

9.101 The data collected from these collisions are then used to analyse the understanding of energy and help to increase our understanding of what has built the world that we live in and unravel some of the mysteries of the origin of the universe. There is a global community of more than 7,000 scientists across 60 countries receiving and analysing the data. CERN has also led to other notable advances in science. In 1989 Tim Berners-Lee

---

161 *Zillion Investment Holding (Pty) Ltd v Salz-Gossow (Pty) Ltd* (SA 17/2017) [2019] NASC 10 (17 April 2019); (Case No. SA 17/2017), para 1.

162 There is at least one case that has endorsed the right of arbitral tribunals to issue partial awards where this is provided in the parties' arbitration agreement; Dubai Court of Cassation, Petition No. 274 of 2013, dated 19 January 2014. However, as the UAE does not have a system of binding precedent, it is questionable whether this can be relied upon in light of the body of law against it.

163 A Ibrahim, *Multi-tiered Dispute Resolution Clauses in the UAE* (Fenwick Elliott LLP 2020): <www.fenwickelliott.com/research-insight/annual-review/2019/multi-tiered-dispute-resolution-clauses-uae> (last accessed 1 July 2020).

164 Court of Appeal Case 795/2018.

proposed the creation of a distribution information system that later became the World Wide Web. The world's first web page was CERN's. Previous famous developments of the CERN innovations include MRI and PET scanners for unobtrusive detailed 3D human body scanning, as well as many other substantial medical applications.

9.102 The LHC comprises a 27 km ring of superconducting magnets that accelerates the particles to near the speed of light. Inside the accelerator the high-energy particle beams travel in opposite directions so that they collide. An ultrahigh vacuum is maintained in the tunnel. The magnets are built from coils of special electric cable operating in a superconducting state without resistance or loss of energy. However, to be effective this requires cooling the magnets to −271.3°C. This is a temperature just above absolute zero and colder than outer space. To achieve this the accelerator is connected to a distribution system of liquid helium in order to cool the magnets and supply services for the magnets. The power requirements are substantial as indeed are the connectivity and control systems required in order to run the accelerator at CERN.

9.103 In order to increase the potential for further discoveries CERN have embarked on a project to install a more powerful LHC with more accurate measurements of the particles providing a greater level of sensitive data gathering. As a result, the High Luminosity LHC project (HiLumi or HL-LHC Project) was developed. CERN hope to push beyond their understanding of the Higgs boson and investigate mysterious dark matter (energy and matter that makes up the universe).

9.104 The existing CERN facility comprises a 27 km tunnel spanning across the Swiss Franco border at a depth of around 80 m at the entry points down to around 175 m. In order to facilitate the new project two new shafts have been sunk, one in France and one in Switzerland, together with all of the facilities above and below ground to house, maintain, and operate the new ground breaking scientific apparatus.

9.105 The new HiLumi Project pushes at and exceeds the design and construction of known scientific apparatus. This unique project has a funding of almost Euros 1 billion and will take around six years to complete. The work commenced in 2015 is due for completion at the end of 2021 with operation taking it into 2022.

9.106 The first phase of the work involves innovative design and procurement by work package. The next phase involves the civil engineering works comprising shafts, tunnels, caverns, and the construction of surface buildings. The work takes place both in Geneva and Cessy, and therefore within the Swiss jurisdiction and French jurisdiction. This has necessitated dedicated procurement teams on each side of the border making use of common standards and documentation where possible, but of course complying with local legislation and local building requirements.

9.107 CERN has used DABs on past projects. They are aware of the benefits, and so included the DAB process in the FIDIC based documentation for the HiLumi Project. The dispute board comprises five members, one of which is a chair person.[165] This five-member dispute board is referred to as the Panel of Adjudicators (POA). The POA covers four fundamental work packages of the project: the civil engineering contracts in each jurisdiction and the related appointment of the Engineer with CERN in each jurisdiction. The aim was to facilitate commonality of approach as well as understanding, and the

165 Nicholas Gould is the Chair of the Panel of Adjudicators at CERN for the HiLumi Project.

development of avoidance techniques in relation to any potential disputes across the project. An important point about this project has been CERN's recognition of the dispute avoidance function of the POA, with the dispute resolution mechanism a secondary fall back should it be required.

9.108 All members of the POA attend three site visits per year, so approximately every four months. A timetable was established at the outset providing one day in France and the other day in Switzerland at each visit. This means that there is sufficient time to meet and discuss general aspects of the project sites with the parties before carrying out a site visit underground. The rest of the day can be dedicated to presentations and discussions about the project focusing also on any outstanding issues relating to technical challenges, potential delay, and the financial implication of change or delay.

9.109 One of the benefits of the five-member POA is the spread of expertise. The chair is dual qualified (in construction and as a lawyer) whilst other members of the team comprise a lawyer, an architects and varying underground engineering and tunnelling expertise. This means that the POA should have sufficient expertise to cover the breadth of the project to completion. It does not mean that all five members of the POA would make a decision in relation to any dispute. If a dispute arises then the chair of the POA selects three members from the POA to deal with the dispute. The DAB of three may include the POA chair, or the POA chair can if required identify a chair of the three-member DAB.

9.110 All of the POA follow the project to ensure familiarity with the progress and therefore can assist in avoidance. However, the more economic approach of identifying three who are most suitably qualified to deal with the particular aspects of a dispute is cost efficient. This approach also takes into account how busy certain POA members might be on other projects unrelated to CERN, a factor often completely ignored by many engaging DABs. Further, if several disputes on different contracts arise at a similar time the resources of the POA could be divided across the claims. Given also that the project spans two jurisdictions and comprises four contracts over a six-year period a panel of five was felt to be useful and necessary.

9.111 Good information flow, clear presentations by the parties during site visits, and open discussions have helped to make the process a successful one. The impact of lockdown arising from the outbreak of COVID-19 early in 2020 resulted in a change from a planned site visit to a virtual meeting in the spring of 2020 rather than any delay to the POA presence. The POA already had expertise with the project and had gained knowledge of the individuals involved. Virtual meetings comprising videoconferences together with slide presentations, photos, progress reports, reviews of the programme, and resource information comparing as built to as planned proved to be extremely effective and cost efficient. It may well be that future dispute boards could after an initial visit or perhaps a restriction of one site visit per year hold update meetings virtually in order to save on the cost and time of travel resulting in a reduced carbon footprint, but while still retaining the benefits of the dispute board function.

Caltrans and the use of dispute resolution boards

9.112 In line with the North American preference for DBs that issue non-binding recommendations rather than binding decisions, the California Department of

Transportation (Caltrans) has developed a scalable dispute resolution system focussed on dispute avoidance. Broadly, this entails:

a There is Partnering in all projects, where an independent facilitator meets with key people from both parties to evaluate goals and discuss issues and risks.
b One-person Dispute Resolution Advisors are used for projects valued between US$3 million and $10 million.
c Three-member dispute resolution boards are used for projects larger than US$10 million.

From 1979 to 1999 Caltrans projects became increasingly involved in litigation. In 2000, Caltrans began using DRBs and Partnering by default on its projects and since then it has seen a steady decrease in litigation proceedings each year back to 1979 levels.[166]

9.113 While it may seem surprising, non-binding DRBs have a very good success rate at resolving disputes. Between 1994 and 2015 Caltrans used DRBs on 623 projects. Of those projects, 310 referred disputes to the DRB, totalling 891 dispute referrals. Caltrans accepted 65% of the DRB recommendations issued against it, and Contractors accepted 45% of unfavourable recommendations.[167]

Conclusion

9.114 In the last decade the main dispute resolution institutions have developed DB mechanisms to have a broader role focussed on claims management and dispute avoidance.

9.115 The extraordinary circumstances brought about by COVID-19 highlight the importance of this more responsive and flexible dispute mechanism. Construction projects in many parts of the world have been stopped altogether, and those that can reopen face continuing disruption to working conditions on site, supply chains, and cash flow. This is a disruption in respect of which there is no precedent, no certainty as to its conclusion, varying contractual entitlements to relief, and widely varying (and often confused) responses from governments.[168]

9.116 A Contractor may be entitled to relief via contractual provisions for force majeure/ exceptional events, change of law, or (possibly) frustration, or in the minority of countries, via emergency government action. However, many Contractors have no contractual remedy or statutory relief and remain fully responsible for completing the project on schedule. Even where relief from performance is available it will very rarely cover the costs incurred in the delayed period or the increased costs to complete. Employers similarly are having to bear enormous financial burdens and delay to their projects, and face the prospect of losing their Contractor(s).

166 Statistics provided by Caltrans, at the DRBF Annual Meeting and Conference, October 2015.

167 ibid.

168 For instance, in Singapore the COVID-19 (Temporary Measures) Act 2020 includes what is effectively a *force majeure* provision implied into contracts for the duration of the Act, along with limitations on pulling performance bonds and certain debt recovery and insolvency proceedings. By comparison, in England, the private sector has largely been left alone albeit encouraged to use ADR and act 'responsibly and fairly' (per the Cabinet Office, Guidance on responsible contractual behaviour in the performance and enforcement of contracts impacted by the COVID-19 emergency (published 7 May 2020).

9.117 These novel circumstances call for a rapid response and collaboration. A DB mechanism will require the parties to notify each other of the effects of the claim event immediately, to keep each other notified and provide (and maintain) proper records,[169] and to meet to resolve or mitigate the effects,[170] and it will entitle them to receive fast, interim recommendations or relief pending the option of a final decision following in the future. The option of informal advice offered in almost all DB rules now, or Partnering as used by Caltrans, should also encourage the parties to maintain effective rather than litigious dialogue.

9.118 While COVID-19 is an extraordinary event, construction projects frequently face unforeseen issues and whatever the specific situation, it is unlikely that either party's interests will be served by proceeding directly to arbitration or court. The development of a broader function for the DB, exemplified by FIDIC's DAAB, should be encouraged. However, the administrative burden and delay to formal proceedings will not suit all parties and projects, and the type of DB (if any at all), along with any amendments to suit the parties, project, and applicable law, should always be carefully considered.

169 Although of course good records should always be maintained.

170 In person, or possibly now virtually. At the time of writing, guidelines are being developed to cater for virtual meetings and hearings.

CHAPTER 10

Enforcement of DAB decisions under the FIDIC forms of contract

Taner Dedezade

Introduction

10.1 At the heart of the multi-tiered dispute resolution mechanism of the FIDIC 1999 forms of contract (as amended in 2017) is the Dispute Board ('DAB' or 'DAAB' as it is now known). Fundamental to its successful operation is for the parties to have not only an obligation to comply with the DAB decision pending arbitration, but a working and effective mechanism to enforce that obligation should the DAB's decision be disregarded. Absent such a mechanism, a party, usually an Employer, can wantonly disregard the DAB's decision and there will be no incentive for the parties to settle in the amicable settlement period. The Employer is in a much stronger negotiating position if it can withhold payment until the final award due to inevitable cash-flow considerations that all contractors have.

10.2 The shortcomings of the FIDIC 1999 forms, rehearsed in detail in the previous edition of this book, were that whilst there is express wording included in the contract at Sub-Clause 20.4[4] that the parties '*shall promptly give effect to [the DAB decision]*', there was no corresponding clear enforcement mechanism should that obligation be disregarded after one party issued a Notice of Dissatisfaction ('NOD').

10.3 On 1 April 2013, FIDIC finally acknowledged the shortcomings of the FIDIC 1999 forms and issued a Guidance Memorandum that recommended alternative and more robust wording for Sub-Clause 20.7, which followed the wording of the 2008 Gold Book. This wording provided a clearer contractual enforcement mechanism to ensure enforceability of 'non-final' DAB decisions, but questions still arose as to what sort of award should be issued by an arbitrator seeking to enforce.

10.4 This chapter will focus on whether the innovations in the FIDIC 2017 Conditions of Contract for Construction have further improved the Gold Book or Memorandum wording.

FIDIC 2017

10.5 One of the key changes in 2017 is that the Dispute Adjudication Board ('DAB') has now become the Dispute Avoidance/Adjudication Board ('DAAB') and a new provision – Sub-Clause 21.3 – has been added to reflect the emphasis that the 2017 form has put on dispute avoidance. Another welcome and significant improvement is the introduction of a deemed signature of the DAAB Agreement if one of the parties fails to sign the DAAB Agreement. Most significantly, the 2017 form provides a new ground of termination that can be exercised either by the Employer, under Sub-Clause 15.2(a), or by the Contractor, under Sub-Clause 16.2.1(d)(ii), if there is a failure by a Party to comply with a DAAB decision.

10.6 The key points dealing with enforcement can be found in Sub-Clauses 21.4.3 and 21.7 as follows:

- a It is now clear that a DAB decision shall be binding regardless of whether a party gives a NOD[1].
- b The obligation to comply with the DAB decision is the same as before: The parties '*shall promptly comply with it*'. As before, there is no guidance on what 'promptly' means. In South Africa, 'promptly' was considered to mean within 28 days of the decision being given[2].
- c The words: '*The Employer shall be responsible for the Engineer's compliance with the DAAB's decision*' are new. As the Engineer is the Employer's agent, the Engineer's non-compliance would amount to a breach of contract on the Employer's part in any event. The effect of this wording perhaps reminds the Employer of that obligation and its requirement to comply with the DAAB decision.
- d It has now been clarified that a sum adjudicated to be due by the DAB is immediately due without certification or notice being required.
- e Another new innovation is the ability for the DAAB to require one party to provide security in circumstances where it is reasonable to do so after a decision has been made for one party to pay the other a sum of money.
- f The DAB process is an intermediate step prior to arbitration, and it has been clarified that the DAAB proceedings do not constitute arbitration proceedings and hence cannot be enforced using the New York Convention, as DAB decisions do not constitute awards.

As before, the DAAB shall give a decision within 84 days[3] (unless the parties agree to revise that period).

- a The decision is binding (all DAB decisions are binding).
- b The parties have 28 days from the date they receive the decision to give a NOD. If no DAB decision is given within 84 days, the parties have 28 days from the expiry of the 84 days to give a NOD in relation to the failure by the DAB to give a decision.
- c The decision becomes final if no NOD is given with 28 days of receipt of the decision (in such circumstances the DAB's final decision can be enforced via Sub-Clause 21.7).
- d It is still not clear what happens if a DAB fails to give a decision within 84 days and neither party gives a NOD in relation to the failure by the DAB to give its

1 Fourth paragraph of Sub-Clause 21.4.3.

2 *Tubular Holdings (Pty) Ltd v DBT Technologies (Pty) Ltd* (06757/2013 ZAGPJHC 155; 2014 SA 244 (GSJ) (3 May 2013). Under the FIDIC 1999 wording, the judge held 'given that a dissatisfied party has 28 days within which to give his notice of dissatisfaction, it follows that the requirement to give prompt effect will precede any notice of dissatisfaction'.

3 Sub-Clause 21.4.3.

decision. In these circumstances, does the referral fall into a black hole which cannot then be taken to arbitration?

e If a timely NOD is given, the DAB's decision remains binding but is not final. In these circumstances, the underlying dispute ('primary dispute') can be referred to arbitration under Sub-Clause 21.6 after expiry of the 28-day amicable settlement period.[4]

The 'secondary dispute' arises if a DAB adjudges that a sum should be paid ('the Adjudicated Sum'), a NOD is issued (hence the DAB decision does not become final) and one of the parties fails to pay that Adjudicated Sum.

10.7 In FIDIC 1999, Sub-Clause 20.7 gave express wording enabling the enforcement of a 'final' DAB decision but gave no express wording allowing for the enforcement of a DAB decision which has not become final as a result of one or other party issuing a NOD. This lack of express wording became known as 'the gap' and was first highlighted by Professor Nael Bunni in an article he wrote in 2005.[5] The 2017 form has rectified this in Sub-Clause 21.7 which now expressly states that if a party fails to comply with any decision of the DAAB, whether binding or final and binding, then the party may, without prejudice to any other rights it may have, refer the failure itself directly to arbitration.

10.8 Has FIDIC 2017 therefore fixed the problem with the 'gap'?

The issues

10.9 In the first edition of this book, I subdivided the issues arising on the enforcement of DAB decisions under FIDIC 1999 Contracts into six parts. I will follow the same approach in this chapter setting out which issues are still alive, and which have been resolved by the new FIDIC 2017 forms:

a What is the contractual obligation of a party in relation to compliance with a DAB's decision?

b Does the 'failure to pay' amount to a dispute that can be referred to arbitration under Sub-Clause 20.6?

c What effect, if any, does a NOD have on the contractual obligation on a party to give prompt effect to the DAB's decision? It has been argued that the giving of a NOD absolves the paying party from complying with the DAB's decision.

d Is it necessary for the parties to refer both the primary (the merits of the underlying dispute) and secondary (dispute concerning non-payment of the DABs decision) disputes in a single arbitration?

e What sort of award? Partial? Interim? Final? Provisional?

4 The time-limit has been reduced from 56 days (1999) to 28 days (2017).

5 Nael Bunni 'The Gap in Sub-Clause 20.7 of the 1999 FIDIC Contracts for Major Work' [2005] ICLR 272.

What is the contractual obligation of a party in relation to compliance with a DAB's decision?

10.10 The wording has been changed from this: 20.4[4] FIDIC 1999:

> *The decision shall be binding on both Parties, who shall promptly give effect to it unless and until it shall be revised in an amicable settlement or an arbitral award as described below*

to this, 21.4.3[4] in 2017:

> *The decision shall be binding on both Parties, who shall promptly comply with it whether or not a Party gives a NOD with respect to such decision under this Sub-Clause. The Employer shall be responsible for the Engineer's compliance with the DAAB's decision*

As before, therefore, there is a contractual obligation on a party to comply with the DAB's decision and if the DAAB orders the payment of money, a contractual obligation arises to pay that money promptly[6]. As noted earlier, there is still not clarification of what 'promptly' means. In South Africa, 'promptly' was considered to mean within 28 days of the decision being given[7]. There is helpful clarity that the contractual obligation remains whether or not a NOD has been issued.

10.11 FIDIC 2017 goes further and states:

> *If the decision of the DAAB requires a payment of an amount by one Party to the other Party*
>
> *i* *subject to sub-paragraph (ii) below, this amount shall be immediately due and payable without any certification or Notice; and*
>
> *ii* *the DAAB may (as part of the decision), at the request of a Party but only if there are reasonable grounds for the DAAB to believe that the payee will be unable to repay such amount in the event that the decision is reversed under Sub-Clause 21.6 [Arbitration], require the payee to provide an appropriate security (at the DAAB's sole discretion) in respect of such amount.*

Does the 'failure to pay' amount to a 'dispute' that can be referred to arbitration?

10.12 Under the 1999 forms, because of the gap, this was an issue. The question was whether a failure to pay could amount to a dispute referable under Sub-Clause 20.6 (as there was no express wording allowing it to be referred under Sub-Clause 20.7). Under the FIDIC 2017 forms, as the wording in Sub-Clause 21.7 has been amended to include both binding and final and binding decisions, the issue does not arise as it is not necessary to shoe horn the dispute into Sub-Clause 21.6 where there is an express contractual right to refer the dispute under Sub-Clause 21.7.

---

6 CA Dissenting judgment in *Persero 2* at paras 120 and 124 he records that 'there could be no dispute whatsoever on this proposition of law referring to the contractual obligation to pay and the failure to pay being a breach of contract'.

7 *Tubular Holdings (Pty) Ltd v DBT Technologies (Pty) Ltd* (06757/2013 ZAGPJHC 155; 2014 SA 244 (GSJ) (3 May 2013), the judge held 'given that a dissatisfied party has 28 days within which to give his notice of dissatisfaction, it follows that the requirement to give prompt effect will precede any notice of dissatisfaction'.

10.13 As an aside, it is pertinent to note that the opening words of Sub-Clause 20.4 in 1999[8] which allow a dispute to be referred to the DAB have been updated in the 2017 form in Sub-Clause 21.4 as follows:

> *If a Dispute arises between the Parties then either Party may refer the Dispute to the DAAB for its decision.*

Dispute is now defined in Sub-Clause 1.1.29 and provides that a Dispute arises when one party makes a claim, the other party or the Engineer rejects it and the first party does not acquiesce with the rejection. At that point, a dispute arises which is capable of referral to the DAB. It is not understood why the 2017 form dispensed with the words '*of any kind whatsoever*' and '*in connection with or arising out of the Contract*'. These appeared, to the author at least, to be useful to explain the mandatory nature of all disputes being referable to the DAAB.

What effect, if any, does a NOD have on the contractual obligation on a party to give prompt effect to the DAB's decision?

10.14 In FIDIC 1999 the effect of a NOD on the contractual obligation to comply with the DAB decision was unclear. This lack of clarity has been resolved in the 2017 form as there are now express words in Sub-Clause 21.4.3 which provide that the DAB's decision is binding and that the parties shall promptly comply with it '*whether or not a Party gives a NOD*'.

Is it necessary for the parties to refer both the primary and secondary disputes in a single arbitration?

10.15 In the 1999 form, as discussed in detail in the previous edition of this chapter, there was no express wording to deal with this issue and a lot of debate in both the judgments and articles on how this issue should be resolved.

10.16 The 2017 form stipulates that:[9]

> *In the case of a binding but not final decision of the DAAB, such interim or provisional measure or awards shall be subject to the express reservation that the rights of the Parties as to the merits of the Dispute are reserved until they are resolved by an award.*

It would appear that this wording is intended to provide that any interim or provisional measure or award issued enforcing a binding but not final DAAB decision has to make it clear on its face that it can be revised following a consideration of the merits. It is not specified whether such merits would need to be resolved in the same arbitration or whether another arbitration is required.

8 *'if a dispute (of any kind whatsoever) arises between the parties in connection with or arising out of, the Contract ... either Party may refer the dispute in writing to the DAB for its decision'.*

9 Sub-Clause 21.7.

10.17 In the circumstances, the questions that arose and were dealt with at length in the previous edition are still relevant and have not been resolved in the FIDIC 2017 form. It is not intended to rehearse all those arguments again. Should the reader be interested in those arguments, they are encouraged to refer to the previous edition. The conclusion I reached following a consideration of the issues was as follows:

> *Accordingly, in conclusion, both the High Court and the Court of Appeal in Persero 1 reached the clear conclusion that it was necessary to refer both the 'primary' and 'secondary' disputes to an arbitral tribunal and not just the 'secondary' dispute. The CA Majority in Persero 2 reverses that ideology.*

What sort of award?

10.18 In the previous edition of this book regarding the 1999 form I stated as follows: '*Perhaps the most difficult issue conceptually to resolve is whether an arbitral tribunal should make an interim, partial or final award in relation to the enforcement of the DAB's decision.*'

The FIDIC 2017 form states that:

> *the arbitral tribunal (constituted under Sub-Clause 21.6 [Arbitration]) shall have the power, by way of summary or other expedited procedure, to order, whether by an interim or provisional measure or an award (as may be appropriate under applicable law or otherwise) the enforcement of that decision.*

The clause foresees that the final award on the merits will reverse the 'interim or provisional' nature of whatever award is made to enforce the DAB's decision and the same difficulties that were not addressed at all in the FIDIC 1999 forms still exist, namely that the award now expressly sanctioned by the 2017 form as being 'interim or provisional' may not in itself be enforceable. Accordingly, this remains the most difficult issue under the FIDIC 2017 forms.

10.19 Again, I will not repeat all the arguments set out in the previous chapter of this book which are still very much alive. I will simply recap that the following arguments are still possible under the FIDIC 2017 forms:

- a A DAAB decision amounts to interim relief.
- b A final award cannot and/or should not be given to enforce a non-final decision.
- c A provisional award is not enforceable under the New York Convention in any event.

Should these arguments succeed, the mechanism envisaged to enforce the award (a provisional award) will fail to achieve its apparent purpose.

Conclusion

10.20 Ultimately, a winning party at DAB-level wants to be paid the money adjudged as due by the DAB following the issuance of a NOD pending final resolution of the dispute. If the winning party is the contractor, then this will alleviate essential cash-flow issues. The 1999 FIDIC forms provide a clear obligation for payment in the fourth paragraph of

Sub-Clause 20.4 – prompt effect should be given to the DAB's decision – but unfortunately fails to provide a correspondingly clear enforcement mechanism should the obligation be ignored. The revised wording in the FIDIC 2017 form is vastly improved and clearly provides a contractual mechanism in 21.7 (as did the Gold Book and Memorandum before it) but still does not resolve all the problems.

10.21 The following issues have been resolved in FIDIC 2017:

a There is express wording that enables a party to refer to arbitration a failure to comply with any DAB decision, whether it be *binding* or *final and binding*. FIDIC 2017 states in terms in Sub-Clause 21.7 '*whether binding or final and binding*'.

b FIDIC 2017 makes it clear that the parties do not have to pursue a claim based on damages for breach of contract. A clear contractual right has been given to enforce the DAB's decision (akin to a power of specific enforcement) in Sub-Clause 21.7.

c In Sub-Clause 21.7 of the 2017 form [equivalent of 20.7 in the 1999 forms], Sub-Clause 21.4 [equivalent of 20.4 in the 1999 forms] is expressly dis-applied. Accordingly, the dispute does not have to be referred back to the DAB first.

d The failure to comply with a DAAB decision itself can be referred to arbitration in FIDIC 2017. Accordingly, it is not necessary for the merits to be considered when seeking to enforce a binding but not final DAB decision.

FIDIC 2017 wording does not conclusively resolve:

a the question of whether the enforcement issue and the merits must be referred in a single arbitration

b whether 'summary relief' will be considered as a provisional measure only, which will not be enforceable as a final award under the New York Convention

Obviously, FIDIC does not have the power to change either the New York Convention or local laws. This is recognised by FIDIC 2017: '*as may be appropriate under applicable law or otherwise*'. It will be necessary for whatever arbitrator or court is appointed to be willing to read the contract and the New York Convention in such a way as to give effect to the expressly stated intentions and wishes of the parties. In the circumstances, the best that the draughtsman of an international standard form of contract can do is to spell out its intentions and wishes as clearly as possible, so as to encourage the local court/arbitrator to give effect to them.

10.22 I concluded in the previous edition of this book that:

a *One has to question whether the DAB can, or should, survive in its present form when uncertainty and argument is bound to remain even with the new wording.*

b *FIDIC may wish to revise its approach and focus on dispute avoidance in the next edition of the FIDIC forms. Opinions and recommendations from Dispute Boards can be powerful pointers for parties to settle.*

FIDIC certainly did enhance the dispute avoidance function of the DAB in the 2017 forms and made standing boards mandatory across the rainbow, hence dispensing with the ad-hoc DAB. This was a big step forward. It is unfortunate, however, that despite numerous arbitral awards, judgments and academic contributions on a gap that has been present for over a decade, that FIDIC has persisted in the 2017 forms to maintain a system in which uncertainty still exists and arguments are likely to continue. The additional termination ground that has been provided in the FIDIC 2017 form, which enables the Parties to terminate in the event of non-compliance with the DAAB decision, may be the saving grace for the FIDIC 2017 form and may prevent the enforcement provisions being put under pressure, as the threat of termination may well be sufficient to lead to the Party wishing to ignore the DAB decision to comply with the DAAB decision. Only time will tell.

CHAPTER 11

Emergency arbitration and the interplay with other pre-arbitral mechanisms

Patricia Shaughnessy

Introduction

11.1 Emergency arbitration (EA) has developed across the globe to provide expedited urgent arbitral interim relief[1] to parties who have agreed to arbitrate their dispute pursuant to an arbitral institution's rules that include this procedure. Arbitral institutions have provided for emergency arbitration in their rules to fill the gap between the time when urgent relief may be needed and when the 'regular' arbitral tribunal will be constituted. This allows parties to avoid seeking urgently needed relief from a national court, which may provide a less attractive venue for parties who have agreed to arbitrate. The development of emergency arbitration has contributed to the autonomy and effectiveness of arbitration.

11.2 The chapter considers the applicability and effectiveness of emergency arbitration and explores issues that may arise when the parties have agreed to other pre-arbitral dispute resolution mechanisms. This can be particularly relevant in the context of construction and infrastructure projects where contractual dispute resolution clauses often contain pre-arbitral dispute mechanisms. Disruptions and disputes can occur in long-term contracts and construction projects that may necessitate quickly seeking provisional remedies to secure evidence, prevent deterioration of the status quo, ensure continued work, protect assets, etc. When the dispute resolution agreement contains provisions for cooling-off periods, negotiations, mediation, or dispute boards to precede arbitration, these pre-arbitral mechanisms may affect the right to proceed to arbitrate. It remains unclear to what extent, if at all, such pre-arbitral mechanisms may affect emergency arbitration procedures in many jurisdictions.

11.3 The procedures for seeking interim relief pose issues of the relationships between emergency arbitrators, the regular arbitral tribunal, national courts, and other pre-arbitral mechanisms such as mediation and dispute boards. As courts and arbitral tribunals confront these issues, greater clarity is emerging. This is a relatively new and evolving area of practice, which has been the subject of limited study. More and more attention has been given to these issues in national courts, arbitral institution reports, practice notes, and commentary in the past few years. For example, the ICC recently published a report on Emergency Arbitration.[2] This chapter refers to some recent developments, including

1 The term 'interim relief' is used in this chapter interchangeably with the terms 'provisional measures', 'conservatory measures', and 'interim measures of protection'.

2 Report of the ICC Commission on Arbitration and ADR Task Force on Emergency Arbitration Proceedings, (ICC Publication 895–0 ENG, 2019). The report is available at: <https://iccwbo.org/publication/emergency-arbitrator-proceedings-icc-arbitration-and-adr-commission-report/> (last accessed November 20, 2020).

revisions to some arbitral rules relating to emergency arbitration procedures, as well as some recent cases, practices, and commentary.

11.4 The background and development of emergency arbitration, together with an overview of the procedure, will first be noted to provide the foundation for identifying and analyzing the issues relating to pre-arbitral relief. The nature and legal basis of emergency arbitration remains a controversial topic despite the general acceptance of the procedure in practice. The legal effects and enforceability of an emergency arbitration decision generate uncertainties and divergent practice in national courts. These issues play into the analysis of the interplay between various pre-arbitral mechanisms. As the practice of emergency arbitration grows, its relationship to other pre-arbitral relief will raise issues in the developing practice and theory.

The development of emergency arbitration

11.5 Prior to the arrival of emergency arbitration, the arbitration community sought to enhance arbitration's autonomy, effectiveness, and attractiveness by equipping arbitral tribunals with the ability to render interim measures and to facilitate court recognition and enforcement of such measures. The 2006 amendments to the UNCITRAL Model Law on International Commercial Arbitration (Model Law) focused primarily on strengthening arbitral interim measures.[3] The work to revise the 1985 Model Law general provision for interim measures began in 2000 and finally after six years of contentious debates, the UNCITRAL Working Group arrived at a highly detailed revised provision, Article 17, which was approved by the Commission.[4] The new Article 17 provides for the types of interim measures, the conditions for granting such measures, other relevant provisions, and importantly provides for court recognition and enforcement of interim orders made by arbitral tribunals.[5] The Model Law has had significant impact on the development of arbitral interim measures, including in countries that have traditionally not recognized the power of tribunals to order interim measures.

11.6 However, before the commencement of arbitration and during the time needed to constitute the arbitral tribunal – which typically can take between two and four months following the commencement of arbitral proceedings – there exists a risk that the arbitration may be frustrated as the situation for an allegedly aggrieved party may significantly deteriorate. In most jurisdictions, during this period, parties could seek interim relief from an appropriate court.[6] However, in some cases, national courts may not provide an attractive alternative for a number of factors. A party may not want to use the court that will have jurisdiction when the party perceives this court as an 'unfriendly' forum. Even

3 Article 17, UNCITRAL Model Law.

4 James E Castello, 'Generalizing about the Virtues of Specificity: The Surprising Evolution of the Longest Article in the UNCITRAL Model Law' *World Arbitration and Mediation Review*, pp 7–33, Vol 6, nr 1, (2012). *See also,* Patricia Shaughnessy, 'The New SCC Emergency Arbitrator Rules' in K Hobér, A Magnusson, et al (eds), *Between East and West: Essays in Honor of Ulf Franke* (Juris Publishing 2010) pp 460–463, Chapter 37.

5 Article 17(H), UNCITRAL Model Law.

6 Article 17(J), UNCITRAL Model Law provides: 'A court shall have the same power of issuing an interim measure in relation to arbitration proceedings, irrespective of whether their place is in the territory of this State, as it has in relation to proceedings in courts. The court shall exercise such power in accordance with its own procedures in consideration of the specific features of international arbitration.'

if this is not the case, the courts will use national language and national civil procedures, which may require using local counsel.[7] The national judges may not have the specialized legal or technical knowledge that is relevant to the dispute. The national court forum may have limited opportunities to ensure the privacy of the proceedings. In some jurisdictions, the national courts may not offer a sufficiently expedited process for obtaining urgent measures. While courts offer compulsory powers within their jurisdiction, court orders and judgments may not be enforceable across borders without an enforcement instrument such as the Brussels Regulation.

11.7 Arbitral institutions responded to the needs of users by providing new procedures to obtain needed early interim relief. Prior to the development of 'emergency arbitration' as it is known today, there were some procedures developed to offer arbitration users early provisional relief without needing to resort to national courts. Already in 1990, the International Court of Arbitration (ICC) introduced an innovative 'Pre-Arbitral Referee Procedure' to provide early interim relief prior to the constitution of an arbitral tribunal.[8] However, this procedure has seldom been used, probably due to its 'opt-in' nature. In an early decision under this procedure, the Paris Court of Appeals held that a decision made by a pre-arbitral referee in the ICC procedure was not an enforceable arbitral award, finding that the procedure was merely contractual and the referee was consequently not an arbitrator.[9] The Pre-Arbitral Referee remains an option for parties to agree to in advance of a dispute or after a dispute may arise.[10] The referee is contractually empowered to issue provisional orders prior to the 'competent authority' – an arbitral tribunal or a national court – is seized with the case.[11] The powers of the referee to make provisional orders are similar to an emergency arbitrator, however the orders of the referee are only contractually enforceable.[12] There is a significant difference in their respective legal status as the referee procedures are not an integrated part of the arbitral rules and process, but in practice this distinction may be of less importance. While the referee's order may not be enforced as an arbitrator's order and is not binding on the competent authority,[13] the competent authority who is seized with the dispute may decide to find liability for loss or damage caused by the failure of a party to comply with the order,[14] or for requesting the order.[15] The Pre-Arbitral

7 Many jurisdictions may not grant foreign counsel the right to appear in national courts for interim measure proceedings. But even if it is possible, it may not be practical given local procedural rules and language.

8 See eg, Jean-Yves Garaud and Charles-Henri de Taffin, *The ICC Rules for Pre-Arbitral Referee Procedure,* ICC Bulletin, Vol 16, no 1 Spring 2005, pp 33–70; and Mark Kantor, *The ICC Pre-Arbitral Referee Procedure: Momentum for Expanded Use,* Mealy's International Arbitration Report, Vol 20, nr 9, September 2005.

9 16 ICC Bulletin, pp 53–55, (No 1, 2005). See also, Michael W Bühler, *ICC Pre-Arbitral Referee and Emergency Arbitrator Proceedings Compared,* ICC International Arbitration Bulletin, Vol 22, Special Supplement, pp 93–98 (2011).

10 ICC Pre-Arbitral Referee Rules, <https://iccwbo.org/content/uploads/sites/3/2012/03/1990-Rules-for-a-Pre-Arbitral-Referee-Procedure-ENGLISH-1.pdf> (last accessed November 16, 2020).

11 Article 1.1, ICC Pre-Arbitral Referee Rules. The referee will have some limited residual power following the case being subject to a competent authority pursuant to Article 2.2, which provides: 'If the Competent Authority becomes seized of the case after the appointment of the Referee, the Referee shall nevertheless retain the power to make an Order within the time provided by Article 6.2, unless the parties otherwise agree or the Competent Authority orders otherwise.'

12 Article 6.6, ICC Pre-Arbitral Referee Rules.

13 Article 6.2, ICC Pre-Arbitral Referee Rules.

14 Article 6.8.1, ICC Pre-Arbitral Referee Rules.

15 Article 6.8.2, ICC Pre-Arbitral Referee Rules.

Referee procedure may be particularly suited for provisional relief in long-term contracts, whether the final adjudication of the dispute will be made in litigation or arbitration.[16]

11.8 In 1998, the Netherlands Arbitration Institute (NAI) introduced 'Summary Arbitral Proceedings', a precursor to emergency arbitration, which provides for an independent (stand-alone) procedure to obtain provisional relief.[17] Although the procedure has been subject to revisions, the fundamentals of the procedure remain based on the original 1998 procedures.[18] Unlike the ICC Pre-Arbitral Referee procedures, which are a stand-alone procedure requiring specific agreement to use, the NAI Summary Arbitral Proceedings are available to parties who agree to submit their disputes to NAI arbitration seated in the Netherlands, unless the parties opt-out of the procedures. The summary proceedings may result in an enforceable award, unlike the ICC Pre-Arbitral Referee procedure. In the 20 years since the procedure was introduced, 275 proceedings have been brought resulting in 145 awards.[19] In 70% of the summary proceedings, an award was reached within two months.[20] This time period is significantly shorter than for regular arbitration and even shorter than expedited arbitration procedures, although it is longer than the time period for emergency arbitration, as is discussed in more detail in this chapter.

11.9 Since 1998, the London Court of International Arbitration (LCIA) Rules have provided for expedited formation of the arbitral tribunal in urgent situations, which allows the tribunal to order interim relief. This provision has been retained in subsequent revisions to the LCIA Rules, including in the latest revision which became effective on October 1, 2020.[21] This is a procedure which allows a party to request the LCIA Court to allow the rapid formation of the regular arbitral tribunal in cases of exceptional urgency. Although the LCIA Rules introduced emergency arbitration in its 2014 Rules,[22] it retained the alternative procedure of expedited formation of the arbitral tribunal.[23] Some parties prefer to seek interim relief from the regular tribunal which has been constituted on an expedited basis although this will take significantly longer than seeking such relief from an emergency arbitrator. In some situations, parties may prefer to refer an interim request to a three-person tribunal of arbitrators that they have selected to adjudicate the entire dispute, rather than to a sole arbitrator appointed by the institution for the interim measure request.

11.10 The earliest procedures for emergency arbitration were introduced by the International Centre for Dispute Resolution (ICDR),[24] which introduced 'Emergency

16 Introduction, ICC Pre-Arbitral Referee Rules.

17 Articles 35 and 36, NAI Rules. For commentary on the NAI Rules, see Bommel van der Bend, Marnix Leijten, et al (eds), *A Guide to the NAI Arbitration Rules Including a Commentary on Dutch Arbitration Law* (Kluwer Law International 2009) pp 189–216.

18 *NAI Summary Proceedings Report (December 2019), available at:* <www.nai-nl.org/downloads/NAI%20 Summary%20Proceedings%202019.pdf> (last accessed October 26, 2020) p 2.

19 *Rogier Schellaars and Martje Verhoeven-de Vries Lentsch, 20 Years of Dutch Emergency Arbitration Proceedings, Global Arbitration Reports, October 5, 2020.*

20 *NAI Summary Proceedings Report, supra at n 18, p 2.*

21 Article 9 A, LCIA Arbitration Rules, (2020).

22 Article 9 B, LCIA Arbitration Rules, (2014, 2020).

23 See LCIA Notes on Emergency Procedures, available at: <www.lcia.org/adr-services/lcia-notes-on-emergency-procedures.aspx> (last accessed October 26, 2020).

24 ICDR is affiliated with the American Arbitration Association, a non-profit organization that administers arbitral proceedings.

Measures of Protection' in 2006.[25] In 2007, the International Institute for Conflict Prevention & Resolution (CPR) created a new procedure for the appointment of a 'special arbitrator' to issue early relief.[26] These procedures were available to parties who agreed to arbitrate under the rules of the institution, and the emergency arbitrator could be requested after the commencement of arbitration but prior to the constitution of the arbitral tribunal, unless the parties opted-out. The emergency arbitrator was empowered to make a decision in the form of an order or an award.

11.11 In 2010, the Arbitration Institute of the Stockholm Chamber of Commerce (SCC) introduced an 'emergency arbitration' procedure as an integrated part of its rules, offering parties who had subjected their dispute to the SCC Rules an opportunity to seek interim measures from a specially appointed arbitrator prior to the constitution of the regular arbitral tribunal.[27] The SCC emergency arbitration provisions introduced some significant new features; in particular the rules provided for seeking the appointment of an emergency arbitrator prior to the commencement of arbitration and applied retroactively to any agreement to arbitrate under the SCC Rules, unless the parties agreed to opt-out of the EA Rules. Six months later, the Singapore International Arbitration Center (SIAC) introduced a largely identical emergency arbitration provision to its rules.[28] In 2012 the ICC introduced emergency arbitration provisions into their rules.[29] In June 2012, the Swiss Rules of International Arbitration (Swiss Rules) introduced new provisions on emergency arbitration.[30] As noted earlier, the 2014 edition of the LCIA Rules included a provision on emergency arbitration,[31] which was slightly revised in the new LCIA Rules revisions which came into effect on October 1, 2020.[32] SIAC introduced revised rules in the fall of 2016, which somewhat revised its emergency arbitration provisions, and recently began

25 ICDR, International Dispute Resolution Procedures, Article 37 (2006 Rules). See, Mark Appel, 'Instant Relief When You Need It', Cahiers de l' Arbitrage, (April 23, 2007); and Guillaume Lemenez and Paul Quigley, *The ICDR Emergency Procedure in Action, parts I and II*, Dispute Resolution Journal (Aug-Oct, 2008 and Nov 2008 – Jan 2009). In the current edition of the International Commercial Arbitration Rules, (effective June 1, 2014), the emergency arbitration procedure is contained in Article 6.

26 Rule 14, CPR Rules for Non-Administered Arbitration, (effective November 1, 2007), providing for the appointment of a special arbitrator to grant interim measures of protection. <www.cpradr.org/resource-center/rules/international-other/arbitration/2007-international-non-administered-rules> (last accessed October 26, 2020).

27 Article 32(4), SCC Rules, (effective January 1, 2010). See, Patricia Shaughnessy, 'Pre-arbitral Urgent Relief: The New SCC Emergency Arbitrator Rule' (2010) 27(4) Journal of International Arbitration 337–360.

28 Article 26.2, SIAC Rules, (effective July 1, 2010). SIAC somewhat revised the Emergency Arbitration provision in its rules that entered into force on August 1, 2016: pursuant to the 2016 Rule the provisions are contained in Article 30.2 and Appendix I.

29 Article 29, ICC Rules (effective January 1, 2012); the ICC introduced new rules in March 2017, however the emergency arbitrator rules were not revised from the 2012 Rules. The emergency arbitrator provisions are contained in Article 29 of the ICC Rules and in Appendix V. See: Jason Fry, Simon Greenberg, and Francesca Mazza, *The Secretariat's Guide to ICC Arbitration* (International Chamber of Commerce 2012), pp 302–305; Nathalie Voser and Christopher Boog, *ICC Emergency Arbitrator Proceedings: An Overview*, ICC International Court of Arbitration Bulletin, Vol 22, Special Supplement, pp 85–86 (2011).

30 Article 43, Swiss Rules (effective June 1, 2012). The Swiss Rules will soon begin a revision process.

31 For a discussion of the LCIA emergency arbitration provisions in the 2020 Rules, see, Maxi Scherer, Lisa M Richman and Remy Gerbay, *Arbitrating Under the 2020 LCIA Rules, A User's Guide* (Wolters Kluwer 2021), Chapter 10.

32 Article 9.12 became 9.13 in the 2020 LCIA Rules, which relates to the right of a party to seek interim measures from a court (as discussed *infra*).

work on a new revision of its rules.[33] In January 2017, the SCC introduced Arbitration Rules but did not revise the emergency arbitration provisions other than adding a provision relating to costs and their allocation.[34] The ICC emergency arbitration provision was revised in the new ICC Rules that entered into force on January 1, 2021, as is discussed in more detail in this chapter.[35]

11.12 Emergency arbitration procedures have now spread around the globe, appearing as part of the regulatory framework of most arbitral institutions, although there is some variance in the provisions of different rules. Emergency arbitration allows parties to quickly seek interim measures within the privacy of the arbitral process, thus enhancing the autonomy and effectiveness of arbitration and enabling arbitration to provide a 'one-stop' dispute process. Emergency arbitration builds upon the evolution of interim measures to provide parties with quick relief that ensures the efficacy and hence autonomy of the arbitral process. Today arbitral interim measures are largely integrated into the procedural and tactical landscape of arbitration.

11.13 A distinction should be made between expedited arbitration procedures and emergency arbitration. Expedited procedures provide for a more efficient, simpler arbitration by a sole arbitrator, which may be well-suited for less complex and lower-value cases where saving time and money may be an important consideration. The time periods for the expedited arbitration are significantly shorter, written submissions may be limited, and under many expedited arbitration rules, the case may be decided on documents only. However, basic procedural rights of the parties – the right to be heard and equal treatment – must be observed. Expedited arbitration procedures have been introduced at many arbitration institutions in the past several years, and the UNCITRAL Working Group II is currently working on developing such procedures as part of the UNCITRAL Arbitration Rules.[36]

11.14 Some institutions incorporate the expedited arbitration procedures into the main arbitration rules, while others offer expedited arbitration as a stand-alone, separate set of rules.[37] For example the SCC, which has had expedited rules for several years and which

33 SIAC announced the revision work on July 7, 2020. The SIAC Rule revision committee include a sub-committee on revising the rules relating to expedited arbitration and emergency arbitration. <https://siac.org.sg/ysiac/about-us/69-siac-news/669-siac-announces-commencement-of-revisions-for-siac-arbitration-rules> (last accessed October 27, 2020).

34 Article 10, Appendix II, SCC Rules, (2017).

35 Article 29, ICC Rules (entering into force January 1, 2021). The new Rules were approved by the ICC Commission on October 6, 2020, and may be subject to some minor editorial revisions prior to their effective dates of January 1, 2021, and may be accessed at: <https://iccwbo.org/dispute-resolution-services/arbitration/rules-of-arbitration/rules-of-arbitration-2021/> (last accessed October 27, 2020).

36 A/CN.9/1082, Draft UNCITRAL Expedited Rules, <https://undocs.org/A/CN.9/1082> (last accessed June 28, 2021), and Draft Explanatory Note to the UNCITRAL Expedited Rules, <https://undocs.org/A/CN.9/1082/Add.1> (last accessed June 28, 2021), which will be presented to the UNCITRAL Commission 54th Session, Vienna, 28 June to 16 July, 2021. *See also,* Report of Working Group II (Dispute Settlement) on the work of its seventy-third session (New York online, 22–26 March 2021), A/CN.9/1049, March 31, 2021, <https://undocs.org/A/CN.9/1049> (last accessed June 28, 2021).

37 Patricia Shaughnessy, *UNCITRAL Working Group II: Expedited Arbitration Provisions as Stand-Alone-Rules or Appendix and When they Should Apply*, Kluwer Arbitration Blog (September 16, 2020). <http://arbitrationblog.kluwerarbitration.com/2020/09/16/uncitral-working-group-ii-expedited-arbitration-provisions-as-stand-alone-rules-or-appendix-and-when-should-they-apply/> (last accessed November 14, 2020).

are frequently used, provides for a stand-alone set of rules for the expedited procedure.[38] The ICC has incorporated the expedited procedures into the regular rules, with procedural details contained in a special appendix.[39] Under most rules, the expedited procedures will apply upon the agreement of the parties, however under some rules, the expedited procedures will be applied to cases with a value under a certain amount unless the parties agree to opt-out.[40] For example, the ICC introduced expedited procedures in 2017, which applied to cases with a value less than 2,000,000 USD, unless the parties agree to opt-out of the expedited procedures.[41] In the ICC Rules revisions coming into effect in 2021, this amount has been increased to 3,000,000 USD.[42]

11.15 Emergency arbitration may be available to parties arbitrating under expedited arbitration rules, if the applicable rules provide for this. For example, the SCC expedited rules provide for emergency arbitration which replicates the same emergency arbitration procedures as are contained in the regular arbitration rules.[43] Emergency arbitration provides for the appointment of a special arbitrator to decide upon a party's request for interim measures prior to the constitution of the arbitration tribunal. Expedited arbitration procedures provide for the entire arbitral proceeding pursuant to a simplified and quick procedure.

An overview of emergency arbitration procedures

11.16 In the past few years, nearly every arbitral institution that has revised its rules has included provisions for emergency arbitration.[44] While the scope, time periods, and other details of emergency arbitration procedures vary between institutional rules, the procedures all provide a highly expedited process for obtaining urgent interim measures prior to the constitution of the regular arbitral tribunal. The most common approach of rules is to provide for emergency arbitration as a part of the agreement to use the institutional rules, unless the parties have specifically opted-out of the application of emergency arbitration procedures.

11.17 In most emergency arbitration regimes, the emergency arbitrator is a sole arbitrator appointed by the administering arbitral institution pursuant to its emergency arbitration

38 SCC Expedited Arbitration Rules, <https://sccinstitute.com/media/1407445/expeditedarbitrationrules_eng_2020.pdf> (last accessed November 14, 2020).

39 Article 30, and Appendix IV ('Expedited Procedure Provisions'), ICC Rules, (effective March 1, 2017).

40 For a summary of 23 arbitral institutions' approaches to expedited procedures see, Responses to UNCITRAL Questionnaire on Expedited Arbitration Procedures, (2019), <https://uncitral.un.org/sites/uncitral.un.org/files/media-documents/uncitral/en/responses_to_questionnaire_27_september.pdf> (last accessed November 16, 2020).

41 Article 30, Appendix IV ('Expedited Procedure Provisions'), ICC Rules, (effective March 1, 2017)

42 Appendix IV, Article 1(2), ICC Rules, (effective January 1, 2020).

43 Article 38, and Appendix II, SCC Rules for Expedited Arbitration Rules.

44 In 2011, prominent arbitration practitioners James Hosking, Erin Valentine, and David M Lindsey presented a paper to the American Bar Association Section of International Law comparing the emergency arbitration procedures of four arbitral institutions, and provocatively questioning whether these procedures represented 'creeping consensus or a passing fancy'. Now about a decade later we can conclude that emergency arbitration represents creeping consensus with some significant differences in the details of the procedure, but with broad acceptance within the arbitration community. James Hosking, Erin Valentine, and David M Lindsey, *Emergency Measures of Protection: Creeping Consensus or a Passing Fancy?* Available at: <www.chaffetzlindsey.com/wp-content/uploads/2011/04/00070460.PDF> (last accessed November 21, 2020).

rules. A sole arbitrator will be appointed for an emergency arbitration request although the parties' arbitration agreement provides for a tribunal composed of three arbitrators. The emergency arbitrator has a limited mandate and, unless the parties agree otherwise, may not be appointed as a member of the tribunal in the subsequent arbitration. Any decision made by an emergency arbitrator will be limited in time and will have no binding effect on any issue or determination of the arbitral tribunal constituted in the subsequent arbitration. Pursuant to most rules, the regular arbitral tribunal may modify, continue, or terminate any interim measure ordered by the emergency arbitrator.[45] The limitation on the legal effect and enforceability of the emergency decision will be discussed in more detail later.

11.18 Some of the variance between the various emergency arbitration rules may be significant for parties – for example, whether a request may be made prior to commencing arbitration. Under some rules, such as the SCC[46] and the ICC,[47] the emergency arbitration procedure may be obtained prior to filing a request for arbitration, but not after the arbitration file has been transmitted to the regular arbitral tribunal, as any request for interim relief may be made to the regular arbitral tribunal after it is constituted. However, a request for arbitration must be filed within a set period of time following thereafter or the emergency arbitration may be discontinued or any decision made by an emergency arbitrator may lose its legal effect.[48] Some institutions' emergency arbitrator provisions require that a party files the request for arbitration concurrently or before the request for an emergency arbitrator to be appointed.[49]

11.19 Other varying factors include the period for appointing the emergency arbitrator and time allowed for making the decision, the form of the decision, and the fees and cost allocations. The SCC Rules provide for a highly expedited procedure with the Board seeking to appoint the emergency arbitrator within one day of the request and the decision to be rendered within five days of the appointment, unless the Board extends the period based on a reasoned request from the emergency arbitrator.[50] The practice of the SCC demonstrates that these time limits are usually met.[51] The ICC, LCIA, and SIAC procedures provide for 14 to 15 days for the emergency arbitrator to render the decision, unless an extension is granted.[52] All of the emergency arbitrator regimes have expedited

45 See eg, Article 29(3) ICC Rules (2017), this provision has not been changed in the 2021 revisions of the ICC Rules; Article 9, Appendix II, SCC Rules (2017); Para 10, Schedule I, SIAC Rules (2016); and 9.11, Article 9B, LCIA Rules (2020).

46 Article 37(4) and Article 1(1), Appendix II, SCC Rules.

47 Article 29(1) and Article 2(2), Appendix V, ICC Rules.

48 See eg, Article 1(6), Appendix V, ICC Rules, which provides that the President may terminate the emergency arbitration if a Request for Arbitration has not been received within ten days of the application for emergency relief, unless the emergency arbitrator determines that a longer period of time is necessary. See also, Article 9(4)(iii), Appendix II, SCC Rules which provides that an emergency decision will cease to be binding if arbitration has not been commenced with 30 days of the emergency arbitrator's decision.

49 For example, Schedule 1(1), SIAC Rules, (2016); and Article 6(1), ICDR International Arbitration Rules (2014).

50 Article 8(1) of Appendix II, SCC Rules.

51 A summary of the EA case statistics for 2010 to 2019 can be found here: <https://sccinstitute.com/about-the-scc/news/2020/emergency-arbitration-at-the-scc-a-decade-in-review/> (last accessed November 20, 2020). See also, Lotta Knapp, 'Emergency Arbitrator Decisions Rendered' (2014) <www.sccinstitute.com/media/62020/scc-practice-emergency-arbitrators-2014_final.pdf> (last accessed November 20, 2020).

52 Article 2(1), Appendix V, ICC Rules provide that the 'President shall appoint an emergency arbitrator within as short a time as possible, normally within two days from the Secretariat's receipt of the Application'. Article 6(4), Appendix V, ICC Rules provides that the emergency arbitrator shall render the decision with 15 days, unless

time frames for challenging an emergency arbitrator for a lack of the requisite impartiality and independence.

11.20 There are some differences in the scope and applicability of the emergency provisions. For example, the scope of application of the ICC emergency arbitrator procedure is more restrictive than the SCC procedure.[53] The ICC procedure is only available when the arbitration agreement was entered into after the effective date for the new rules, while the SCC procedure applies retroactively.[54] The retroactive application of emergency arbitration procedures has become less significant as time has passed since such procedures have been made part of the applicable rules.[55] Additionally, the ICC procedure is only available for parties that are signatories or successors to parties to the arbitration agreement, thus excluding non-signatories who are not successors.[56] The ICC Rules also exclude the procedure in treaty-based investment arbitration; this practice under the 2017 ICC Rules has been codified as an exemption in the recent revision of the ICC Rules, which became effective on January 1, 2021.[57] The SCC Rules may be and indeed have been used in investment cases, resulting in some emergency arbitration orders and awards.[58]

11.21 As will be further discussed later, the 2012 and 2017 ICC Rules specifically exclude the applicability of the emergency arbitration procedure when the parties have agreed to other pre-arbitral procedures that provide for conservatory, interim, or similar measures.[59] Notably, the 2021 ICC Rules will remove this restriction to the applicability of the emergency arbitration procedures. This is a key issue which this chapter addresses next. It should also be noted that the ICC Rules, unlike other approaches such as the SCC and

the President extends the time. Article 9b, 9.8, LCIA Rules, provides that the emergency arbitrator shall make the decision 'as soon as possible, but no later than 14 days following the Emergency Arbitrator's appointment', with the possibility for an extension in exceptional circumstances. Schedule I(3), SIAC Rules provides for appointment of the emergency arbitrator within one day, Schedule I(9) and for the decision to be made within 14 days.

53 For a discussion of the SCC Emergency Arbitrator Rules, see, Patricia Shaughnessy, *supra* at n 27, pp 337–360. For a discussion of the ICC Emergency Arbitration Rules, see, *ICC Commission Report, Emergency Arbitration Proceedings* (2019); <https://iccwbo.org/content/uploads/sites/3/2019/03/icc-arbitration-adr-commission-report-on-emergency-arbitrator-proceedings.pdf> (last accessed November 17, 2020).

54 Shaughnessy, *supra* at n 27, pp 350–55. As regards the Swiss Rules approach to retroactive application of the emergency arbitration procedures, see, Phillip Habegger, 'Article 43 Swiss Rules' in Manuel Arroyo (ed), *Arbitration in Switzerland, the Practitioner's Guide* (2nd ed Vol 1, Wolters Kluwer 2018) p 881.

55 Global Arbitration Review recently reported a September 14, 2020, decision of the Kyiv Court of Appeal, *Vnesheconombank v Ukraine*, denying enforcement of an SCC emergency arbitration award in part on the grounds that Ukraine did not consent to the emergency procedures because the arbitration agreement contained in the bi-lateral treaty was implemented by Ukraine in 1999 and preceded the emergency arbitration procedures becoming part of the SCC Rules. <https://globalarbitrationreview.com/emergency-arbitration/russian-banks-emergency-award-rebuffed-in-ukraine> (last accessed November 11, 2010). The Court decision in Ukrainian can be accessed at: <https://s3.eu-west-2.amazonaws.com/files.lbr.cloud/secure/gar/assets/articles/embedded_files/VEB-v-Ukraine_KAC_07092020.pdf> (last accessed November 20, 2020).

56 Article 29(5), ICC Rules (2017), this provision is unchanged in the 2021 edition of the ICC Rules.

57 Article 29(6)(c), ICC Rules (2021) 'codifies the ICC Court's established practice that emergency arbitration is not available in investor-State disputes'. *ICC Unveils revised rules of arbitration,* (October 8, 2020) quoting ICC Court President Alexis Mourre, <https://iccwbo.org/media-wall/news-speeches/icc-unveils-revised-rules-of-arbitration/> (last accessed November 20, 2020).

58 Alexey Pirozhkin, *Emergency arbitrator's decisions in Investment Treaty Disputes at the SCC (2017–2019)* (May 2020) <https://sccinstitute.se/media/1718853/emergency-arbitrators-decisions-in-investment-treaty-disputes-at-the-scc-2014-201.pdf > (last accessed June 28, 2021).

59 Article 29(6)(c).

SIAC, do not provide for an emergency arbitrator decision to take the form of an award, but only allow for it to be an order.[60]

11.22 Emergency arbitration provisions have become a common feature of institutional arbitration rules, although such procedures will not be applicable to ad hoc arbitration, including arbitration conducted pursuant to the UNCITRAL Rules. Emergency arbitration provisions rely upon an institution to process the application, appoint the emergency arbitrator, handle the fees, and generally administer the proceedings. An interesting question, which will not be pursued here, is whether parties who chose to use the UNCITRAL Rules with the administration of an Arbitration Institute could also agree in their arbitration agreement to use the emergency arbitration procedures of the administering arbitral institute.

The legal nature and effects of emergency arbitration

11.23 The legal nature of emergency arbitration presents an unsettled issue, as does the status of the emergency arbitrator, as well as the legal nature and effects of any decision. It is unclear whether emergency arbitration constitutes a separate, autonomous proceeding or if it is part of the 'regular' arbitration proceeding. When arbitral institution rules provide for emergency arbitration procedures, the parties have agreed to the procedure by agreeing to arbitrate pursuant to the rules, unless they specifically 'opt-out' of the emergency arbitration procedures.[61] The agreement to use the selected rules has a contractual basis. Generally, an agreement to arbitrate is a contract with procedural and jurisdictional effects, namely the agreement to arbitrate and the agreement not to bring the claims to court litigation – the so-called positive and negative effects of the arbitration agreement.[62] But the agreement to use particular rules in the arbitration may be seen as purely contractual, or as a procedural agreement by the parties, or as a hybrid agreement that has both contractual and procedural elements. The characterization of the agreement to use the arbitral rules will affect the analysis of the legal effects of the agreement.

11.24 The emergency arbitrator derives its power from the parties' agreement to arbitrate under arbitral rules that provide for emergency arbitration, as does the 'regular' arbitral tribunal. Parties delegate their party autonomy to the arbitral institution whose rules they have chosen. If these rules provide for emergency arbitration, then by choosing to arbitrate under these rules, parties are deemed to have agreed to these provisions, unless they have opted-out.[63] Arbitrators may also derive authority from the applicable national arbitration law (*lex arbitri*). There have been discussions on whether an emergency arbitrator is an arbitrator at all and if the power of the emergency arbitrator exists only in the contractual

60 Article 29(2) ICC Rules. This may be a pragmatic approach as an ICC Award requires scrutiny which would take additional time. However, the ICC will provide an informal review if time permits and also has designed a drafting check-list to guide the emergency arbitrator when making an order. See, Fry, Greenberg, and Mazza, *supra* at n 29, Section 3–1081.

61 Most parties, unless highly familiar with dispute resolution or advised by counsel who is, will not consider whether to opt-out of emergency arbitration provisions contained in the chosen arbitral rules. Patricia Shaughnessy, *supra* at n 4, pp 466–471.

62 Gary B Born, *International Commercial Arbitration* (2nd ed, Wolters Kluwer 2014) §8.01, pp 1252–53.

63 Some rules, such as the ICC, do not apply retroactively to arbitration agreements entered into prior to the adoption of emergency arbitration provisions, while others such as the SCC do apply retroactively. See, Shaughnessy, *supra* at n 27, at p 347.

obligations between the parties. Webster and Buhler argue that despite the limited role of the emergency arbitrator, it 'has all of the attributes of an arbitrator and for all purposes should be treated as such'.[64] They note that despite the provisional nature of the emergency decision and the limited mandate of the emergency arbitrator – which does not empower the emergency arbitrator to make decisions on the merits of the dispute – the decision of the emergency arbitrator qualifies as a judicial decision.[65] They conclude that the emergency arbitrator order should be assimilated with an interim relief order issued by a regular arbitral tribunal.[66]

11.25 Regular arbitral tribunals may benefit from national arbitration laws that recognize and empower the arbitrators. Recently, legislation in Singapore, Hong Kong, and South Korea has recognized emergency arbitration, and more jurisdictions may follow in the future.[67] However, the lack of specific legislation leaves the matter to courts and there remains great variance in the approaches of national courts in recognizing and enforcing emergency arbitration decisions.[68] Given the broad acceptance of emergency arbitration by the arbitration community, the controversy about the status of the emergency arbitrator may become increasingly less relevant in practice. Nonetheless, the underlying theoretical and analytical issues remain and enforcement of decisions continues to be relatively unpredictable in many jurisdictions. The ICC report on emergency arbitration noted that:[69]

> From the analysis of 45 National Reports, a wide range of interpretations emerge, from expressing an unequivocal view that the EA is an arbitrator and that provisions applicable to the arbitral tribunal should apply to EAs, to others that consider that EA proceedings cannot be equated to proceedings before an arbitral tribunal.

The legal nature of emergency arbitration may be determined by the enforceability of decisions made by emergency arbitrators – in other words, whether national courts will enforce emergency arbitrator decisions as an arbitral interim measure order or as an arbitral award. Most emergency arbitration rules provide that the decision may be made in the form of an order or an award, as is similarly provided for interim measures decided by the regular 'arbitral tribunal'. It is controversial if an interim measure in the form of an award

64 Thomas H Webster and Michael W Buhler, *Handbook of ICC Arbitration, Commentary, Precedents, Materials* (3rd ed, Sweet and Maxwell 2014) p 448.

65 ibid at p 465.

66 ibid.

67 Singapore legislatively recognized emergency arbitration in 2012 through an amendment to its International Arbitration Act (Cap 143A) expanding the definition of 'arbitral tribunal' to include 'an emergency arbitrator appointed pursuant to the rules of arbitration agreed to or adopted by the parties'. In July 2013, Hong Kong amended its Arbitration Ordinance (Cap 609) to add Part 3A, which expressly permits the recognition and enforcement of emergency relief granted by an emergency arbitrator, regardless of whether the seat of arbitration is in Hong Kong or overseas. In July 2016, Korea passed amendments to its Arbitration Act to permit the enforcement of interim measures ordered by an arbitral tribunal seated in Korea, which is understood to apply to orders rendered by emergency arbitrators. See, Eun Young Park and Joel Richardson, *Rush to Judgment: Speed v Fairness in International Arbitration*, Asian Dispute Review, (Hong Kong International Arbitration Centre (HKIAC) 2016, Volume 2016 Issue 4) pp 174–180.

68 Report of the ICC Commission on Arbitration and ADR Task Force on Emergency Arbitration Proceedings, *supra* at n 2, pp 30–31.

69 ibid at p 30.

has the necessary finality to be enforced under the New York Convention.[70] It is far more controversial if an emergency arbitration decision could be enforced as an award under the New York Convention. The New York Convention does not define an award and the label 'Award' on the decision is not decisive; national courts may determine what constitutes an award when determining whether to recognize and enforce the alleged award.[71]

11.26 There have been some reported cases where an emergency arbitrator decision has been enforced by a court.[72] Given the increased use of emergency arbitration, more courts will address the issue. In a case which gained significant attention, *JKX v Ukraine*, a Ukrainian court of appeal ordered the recognition and enforcement of an SCC emergency arbitration award in an investment case.[73] This was particularly noteworthy because the SCC emergency arbitration rules, similar to some of the other regimes, provide that while the emergency arbitrator's decision is binding upon the parties, it does not have any binding effect on the subsequent tribunal.[74] Upon the reasoned request of a party, the emergency arbitrator may amend or revoke the decision.[75] Notably, a decision of an emergency arbitrator will cease to have any legal effect upon certain events occurring, namely when the emergency arbitrator or the regular arbitral tribunal so decides, when the regular arbitral tribunal makes a final award, when the main arbitration is not commenced within 30 days from the date of the emergency decision, or when the case is not referred to a regular arbitral tribunal within 90 days of the date of the emergency decision.[76] Furthermore, the relevant treaty contained a three-month cooling-off period prior to commencing arbitration, which had not expired.

11.27 However, on appeal, the Ukrainian Supreme Court refused the enforcement of the emergency award on a number of grounds, including that the cooling-off period provided for in Article 26(2) of Energy Charter Treaty had not been complied with, the notice of the dispute had not been properly served upon the Ministry of Justice, and that enforcement would be contrary to public policy as it would result in application of different tax rates to a particular person without amendment of relevant tax laws.[77] The Supreme Court did not

70 Gary B Born, *supra* at n 62, p 2513, noting that: 'There was (and remains) a substantial body of commentary also concluding that provisional measures are not recognizable or enforceable as "final" arbitral "awards" under either the New York Convention or national arbitration legislation.'

71 Born suggests that 'the better view is that provisional measures should be and are enforceable as arbitral awards under generally-applicable provisions for the recognition and enforcement of awards in the Convention and most national arbitration regimes. Provisional measures are "final" in the sense that they dispose of a request for relief pending the conclusion of the arbitration' (ibid at p 2515).

72 An early case enforcing an emergency arbitration award is *Yahoo v Microsoft*, 983 F. Supp. 2d 310 (S.D.N.Y. 2013) (enforcing an ICDR emergency arbitrator award). See, Report of the ICC Commission on Arbitration and ADR Task Force on Emergency Arbitration Proceedings, *supra* at n 2, pp 30–34. See also, Grant Hanessian and E Alexandra Dosman, *Songs of Innocence and Experience: Ten Years of Emergency Arbitration* (2016) 27 Am Rev Int'l Arb 215.

73 See, Yaroslav Petrov, *JKX vs. Ukraine: An Update on the Enforcement of Emergency Arbitrator's Award,* Kluwer Arbitration Blog (August 12, 2016) <http://arbitrationblog.kluwerarbitration.com/2016/08/12/jkx-vs-ukraine-an-update-on-the-enforcement-of-emergency-arbitrators-award/> (last accessed June 28, 2021).

74 Article 9, Appendix II, SCC Rules.

75 ibid.

76 Article 9(4), Appendix II, SCC Rules.

77 Olexander Martinenko et al, *Ukraine's Supreme Court pulls the plug on JKX emergency award enforcement,* Lexology, November 22, 2018, available at: <www.lexology.com/library/detail.aspx?g=07954e15-1426-465a-9b12-fde7945827c3> (last accessed November 21, 2020).

generally rule out enforcing emergency arbitration awards under the New York Convention, leaving this an open issue.[78]

11.28 In a recent Ukrainian case, *Vnesheconombank v Ukraine*, the Kyiv Court of Appeal refused enforcement of an SCC emergency arbitration award.[79] Enforcement was refused on three grounds. First, the Court found that the Respondent Ukraine did not consent to the retroactive application of the SCC emergency arbitration procedures, which were introduced in 2010 while the investment treaty containing the arbitration agreement was implemented in 1999.[80] Second, the Court noted that the five-day period in which the emergency arbitrator was required to make his decision overlapped a national holiday weekend, leaving just three working days for Ukraine to respond and thereby Ukraine was deprived of fully presenting its case. Third, the Court found enforcement of the emergency award incompatible with Ukrainian public policy as it would undermine the rule of law and legal certainty because enforcement would require suspending pending enforcement proceedings relating to an award in another case, the 'Everest estate creditors'.[81]

11.29 While some courts have enforced the decisions of emergency arbitrators, the nature and enforceability of emergency arbitrator decisions remains controversial.[82] A distinction may be made if the decision is made in the form of an order or an award. In the 2006 amendments to the interim measure provisions of the UNCITRAL Model Law, a new provision was introduced which provides for the recognition and enforcement of arbitral interim orders.[83] Those jurisdictions that have adopted this approach may enforce an emergency arbitrator order if the jurisdiction considers such an emergency arbitrator decision to constitute such an interim measure order. If an emergency arbitrator decision falls within the categorization of an arbitral interim measure, then it may be enforceable as such an order. However, the limited time period for the existence of an emergency arbitrator order may affect the enforceability.

11.30 Even if the enforcement of an emergency arbitrator decision may be uncertain, the procedure may nonetheless have benefits. The regular tribunal may extend the emergency decision, turning it into a tribunal order or an interim award. An example of an emergency arbitration order becoming an interim award issued by the regular tribunal is the 'Sauber case' involving an emergency arbitration under the Swiss rules, seated in Geneva.[84] In this case, a Formula One driver, Mr van der Garde, successfully obtained an emergency arbitrator order prohibiting Sauber from taking any action that would deprive the driver from participating in the 2015 Formula One season. Three days after the regular tribunal rendered the partial award, the driver brought enforcement proceedings in Australia, just shortly before the start of a race. While the expedited appeal of the enforcement was

---

78 ibid.

79 *Vnesheconombank v Ukraine*, (September 14, 2020), *supra* at n 55.

80 ibid.

81 ibid.

82 Ank Santens and Jaroslav Kudrna, 'The State of Play of Enforcement of Emergency Arbitrator Decisions' (2017) 34(1) *Journal of International Arbitration* 1–16.

83 UNCITRAL Model Law on International Commercial Arbitration, with amendments as adopted in 2006, Article 17 (H) and (I).

84 Christoph Muller and Sabrina Pearson, 'Waving the Green Flag to Emergency Arbitration under the Swiss Rules: The Sauber Saga' (2015) 33(4) ASA Bulletin.

pending, just a day before the start of the Melbourne Grand Prix, the parties reached a settlement.[85]

11.31 Reportedly, parties often follow the decisions of the emergency arbitrators without court enforcement in order to avoid additional costs and to show their good faith cooperation with the arbitral process. Indeed, most emergency arbitration rules provide that the decision of the emergency arbitrator is binding upon the parties. There may also be increased incentives to settle a case once the parties have received a preliminary assessment of the case by an emergency arbitrator and have had an opportunity to better consider the opposing party's position. Anecdotally, there are reports of parties settling the dispute following an emergency arbitrator decision which has contained detailed and convincing reasoning indicating that one of the parties is likely to prevail on the merits of the case.[86] However, it should be noted the decision of the emergency arbitrator is based on a limited evidentiary record and has been reached after a highly expedited procedure. Furthermore, the conditions for granting emergency relief are not settled and some emergency arbitrators may not require a high standard of the likelihood of success on the merits when considering a request for emergency relief.[87] This interesting and important topic is beyond the focus of this chapter. Finally, and importantly, the decision of the emergency arbitrator is not binding on the subsequent regular arbitral tribunal. Nonetheless, an emergency arbitration procedure may provide important interim protection, help to identify contentious issues, and create procedural postures and settlement discussions.

Emergency arbitration and other pre-arbitral relief

11.32 Unsettled issues may arise relating to obtaining emergency arbitration relief when the parties have agreed to other pre-arbitral steps such as cooling-off periods, mediation, dispute boards, and other proceedings that may provide interim relief. Increasingly, parties enter into dispute resolution clauses that provide for more than one dispute resolution method. For example, the clauses may provide that the parties will first attempt to resolve the dispute through mediation and if this is unsuccessful, then by arbitration; these clauses are often referred to as 'med-arb' clauses. Clauses may provide for amicable settlement discussions, more or less structured negotiations, expert evaluations, dispute boards or other dispute resolution procedures that will be used prior to final and binding arbitration. These clauses are often referred to as 'multi-step clauses', 'multi-tier clauses', or 'escalation clauses'. Some agreements to arbitrate, notably in treaty-based investment arbitration, provide for cooling-off periods before arbitration may commence.

---

85 ibid at p 822.

86 The connection between settlement rates and use of emergency arbitration has not been well studied or verified, but has been discussed. See, Report of the ICC Commission on Arbitration and ADR Task Force on Emergency Arbitration Proceedings, *supra* at n 2, p 9. See also, SCC Statistics 2019, where the SCC notes in its experience parties sometimes use the emergency arbitration procedure to assist in facilitating settlement negotiations. <https://sccinstitute.com/statistics/> (last accessed November 21, 2020).

87 The UNCITRAL Model Law, Article 17(a) provides conditions for granting interim relief, which have been replicated in the UNCITRAL Rules, and which may be considered in the context of emergency arbitration, although there may be a heightened element of urgency in emergency arbitration. For anecdotal reports on the conditions required, see, Shaughnessy, *Emergency Arbitration, Justice on the Run,* pp 326–328, Arbitration, Scandinavian Studies in Law, Vol 63, (2017). See also, Report of the ICC Commission on Arbitration and ADR Task Force on Emergency Arbitration Proceedings, *supra* at n 2, p 6 and 22–28.

11.33 Particularly in the construction industry, pre-arbitral mechanisms are often included in dispute resolution agreements.[88] There has been considerable commentary and case law relating to whether contractually agreed pre-arbitration dispute resolution mechanisms are enforceable and if so whether they constitute a condition precedent to arbitration.[89] If such mechanisms constitute an enforceable condition precedent, the pre-condition could be characterized either as a jurisdictional or an admissibility issue. There appears to be a developing modern view that such contractual provisions are usually considered as procedural requirements that should be viewed as an issue of the admissibility of the claim rather than jurisdictional.[90] This characterization, which has significant legal and practical effects, requires interpreting the parties' contractual agreement and considering the procedural nature of the alleged pre-conditions to arbitration. If the objection to arbitration is based on jurisdiction, then while competence-competence will allow the arbitral tribunal to make a determination on its jurisdiction, this decision will be reviewable by a court in challenge or enforcement proceedings. If the objection is viewed as an admissibility issue, then it is a matter of the merits for the arbitral tribunal to finally decide with limited later court review on the decision.[91] These issues in the context of the regular arbitration will not be further discussed here, as the focus of this article is on how such mechanisms may interact with emergency arbitration proceedings.

11.34 However, the theoretical and analytical approach to conditions precedent to arbitration might (or might not) be transferrable to analyzing pre-arbitral procedures' impact on emergency arbitration proceedings. If emergency arbitration constitutes a part of the regular arbitration, rather than an independent proceeding, then theoretically the analysis of the character and effects of conditions precedent to arbitration could be applied to emergency arbitration. If, however, emergency arbitration should be characterized as an independent, autonomous proceeding, then the conditions precedent analysis relating to regular arbitration arguably should not be applied to emergency arbitration. If emergency arbitration is viewed as a form of arbitral interim measures and thus integrated into the regular arbitration process, should it be treated analytically different than interim measures requested from the regular arbitral tribunal? The legal status of an emergency arbitrator and the legal status of the decisions made by the emergency arbitrator could also affect

88 Jurgita Petkute-Guriene, 'Access to Justice in Construction Disputes' in Baltag and Vasile (eds), *Construction Arbitration in Central and Eastern Europe* (Wolters Kluwer 2020) 2; and Scherer, Ehle, and Moss, 'Construction Arbitration in Switzerland' in Manuel Arroyo (ed), *Arbitration in Switzerland, the Practitioner's Guide* (2nd ed Vol 1, Wolters Kluwer 2018) 1020–1021.

89 For a discussion on pre-conditions to arbitrate, see Gary B Born, supra at n 62, §5.08, pp 915–941.

90 The UK High Court recently provided clarity to this issue and held that pre-conditions to arbitration, such as negotiation periods, are matters of admissibility and not jurisdiction and thus not subject to judicial review under Article 67 of the English Arbitration Act of 1996. Republic of Sierra Leone v. SL Mining Ltd [2021] EWHC 286 (Comm). The Hong Kong High Court recently reached the same conclusion finding that pre-arbitral conditions were admissibility issues rather than jurisdictional (unless the parties have specifically provided that failure to comply will exclude arbitral jurisdiction). *C v D [2021] HKCFI 1474*. Similar decisions have been reached by the Court of Appeal in Singapore in *BBA v. BAZ* [2020] SLR 453 and *BTN v. BTP* [2020] SGCA 105, and by the United States Supreme Court in BG Group v Republic of Argentina 134 S.Ct.1198 (2013). See generally, Jan Paulsson, 'Jurisdiction and Admissibility' in G Askens, et al (eds), *Global Reflections on International Law, Commerce and Dispute Resolution: Liber Amicorum in Honor of Robert Briner* (ICC Publishing 2005) 601, 617.

91 Jan Paulsson, *The Idea of Arbitration* (Oxford University Press 2013) 82–90. If applicable national law provides the admissibility of claims in arbitration are reviewable by a court, then a court could make such a review. But such a national law 'is emphatically not the modern trend' (ibid at p 84).

the analysis of the impact of conditions-precedent to arbitration on the availability of emergency arbitration. To make matters more complex, choice-of-law issues should also be considered. A full analysis of these issues is beyond the scope of this chapter, but the issues should be borne in mind.[92]

Dispute boards

11.35 In construction and large infrastructure projects, it is common to provide for the use of dispute boards, either 'standing' or 'ad hoc', the former are set up at the outset of the project and the latter created when a dispute arises. The dispute adjudication boards (DABs) are empowered to make a provisional or a 'binding' decision on a dispute. However, the DAB decision, is not 'final' as the dispute may be subsequently referred to arbitration, following serving a timely Notice of Dissatisfaction (NOD).

11.36 Both the 1999 and the 2017 editions of the International Federation of Consulting Engineers (FIDIC) Suite of Contracts contain dispute resolution clauses that provide for pre-arbitral relief. The 2017 provisions strengthen the role of dispute boards, as the boards are now 'Dispute Avoidance/Adjudication Boards' (DAABs). The new Clause 21.3 provides for avoiding disputes through the DAAB's assistance and informal facilitated discussions, prior to formal adjudication. The DAABs underscore FIDIC's core 'Golden Principles' to avoid lengthy contentious adjudication through early dispute management and resolution by requiring that all formal disputes may first be referred to a dispute board for a provisionally binding decision as a condition precedent to arbitration.[93] An engineer is given an important role in dispute resolution and the procedure involves a sequence of steps that must be followed prior to commencing arbitration.[94]

11.37 The 1999 FIDIC suite of contracts contain 'clause 20', which provides for dispute boards as part of the dispute resolution process.[95] Under the FIDIC 'Red Book', which is commonly used in construction projects, once a dispute is referred to a DAB, a binding decision must be made within 84 days. A dissatisfied party may file a formal notice of dissatisfaction, which triggers amicable settlement negotiations for up to 56 days. Following this process, if the dispute has not been settled, the dissatisfied party may commence ICC arbitration.[96] This pre-arbitral process must be complied with before referring a dispute to arbitration for a final decision.[97] The 2017 FIDIC contracts' changes to the DAABs

92 For discussion of these issues in the context of the SCC Rules, see, Patricia Shaughnessy, *The New SCC Emergency Arbitrator Rules, supra* at n 4, pp 471–73.

93 Aisha Nadar, 'The Dispute Settlement Provisions of the 2017 FIDIC Forms of Contract and Their Potential on Construction Arbitration' in Baltag and Vasile (eds), *Construction Arbitration in Central and Eastern Europe* (Wolters Kluwer 2020) pp 26–27, Chapter 2.

94 ibid.

95 Mark Goodrich, *Dispute Adjudication Boards: Are They the Future of Dispute Resolution?* (White and Case publication, September 2, 2016), at: <www.whitecase.com/publications/article/dispute-adjudication-boards-are-they-future-dispute-resolution> (last accessed October 16, 2020); Bernardo M. Cremades, *Multi-tiered Dispute Resolution Clauses* (2004), available FIDIC publications at: <http://fidic.org/sites/default/files/36%20 cremades_2004.pdf> (last accessed October 16, 2020).

96 Webster and Buhler, *supra* at n 64, p 473.

97 See, *A. SA v B. SA,* 4A_124/2014 (7 July 2014). An unofficial translation of the Court judgment can be accessed here: <www.swissarbitrationdecisions.com/sites/default/files/7%20juillet%202014%204A%20124%20 2014.pdf> (last accessed November 22, 2020).

emphasize both the dispute avoidance measures and also the prescriptive nature of the procedural multi-tier steps that precede arbitration.[98] The FIDIC 2017 Red Book, Clause 21, envisions a standing DAAB that can be used for informal dispute resolution prior to moving to a formal decision process.[99]

11.38 There are other similar dispute board rules that parties may agree to use. The Chartered Institute of Arbitrator introduced dispute board rules in August 2014 providing for non-binding dispute review boards (DRBs)[100] and binding dispute adjudication boards (DABs).[101] The ICC introduced new rules for dispute board procedures on October 1, 2015,[102] providing for dispute review boards (DRBs),[103] dispute adjudication boards (DABs),[104] and combined dispute boards (CDBs).[105]

11.39 In a Swiss case from 2014, the Supreme Court was faced with determining whether the contractor could bring arbitration proceedings to recover payment against the employer although the DAB procedure had not been completed.[106] The parties' contract contained a FIDIC clause that provided for a DAB, followed by amiable settlement should a party be dissatisfied, and subsequent arbitration. The contractor approached the employer to constitute the DAB, but following lengthy delays in the appointment process, the contractor commenced ICC arbitration. The employer objected to the jurisdiction of the arbitrators because the pre-arbitral DAB process had not been completed. The arbitrators rejected the jurisdictional objection and issued a majority partial award.[107] The Court found that the DAB process was a contractual mandatory procedure that must be completed before commencing arbitration.[108] However, the Court found that under Swiss law, the parties had a duty to cooperate in good faith in the DAB process and the employer had delayed the constitution of the DAB. The Court found that the employer could not undermine the DAB process and then rely upon the failure to constitute the DAB to object to jurisdiction in the arbitration. Consequently, the arbitrators had jurisdiction to issue the partial award.[109]

11.40 The Swiss case can be compared with a recent English case, where the Court found that the DAB procedures were mandatory.[110] In the English case, the dispute clause

98 Aisha Nadar, *supra* at n 93, pp 26–31. Nadar notes at p 31: The Rainbow Suite is multi-tiered and mandatory. For a dispute to be heard in arbitration, it must first have been referred to the Engineer for a determination that has been subject to an in-time notice of satisfaction, have been referred to the DAAB for a decision and the resultant DAAB decision must have been the subject of an in-time notice of dissatisfaction, and the period set aside for amicable settlement under Sub-Clause 20.5 must have elapsed. Alternatively, the dispute must relate to the enforcement of DAAB decision under Sub-Clause 21.7.

99 See, Petkute-Guriene, *supra* at n 88 for a discussion on the mandatory and non-mandatory aspects of FIDIC dispute clauses.

100 Article 3, Chartered Institute of Arbitrators Dispute Board Rules (CIArb Dispute Board Rules).

101 Article 4, CIArb Dispute Board Rules.

102 The 2015 Rules followed the earlier dispute board rules from September 2005. See Carroll S Dorgan, 'The ICC's New Dispute Board Rules' (2005) 22 International Construction Law Review 142–150.

103 Article 4, ICC Dispute Board Rules.

104 Article 5, ICC Dispute Board Rules.

105 Article 6, ICC Dispute Board Rules.

106 *A. SA v B. SA*, 4A_124/2014 (7 July 2014).

107 ibid at p 5.

108 The arbitral tribunal had found the DAB procedure was not mandatory, but the court in extensive reasoning found that it was mandatory.

109 See Scherer, Ehle and Moss, *supra* at n 88, pp 1024–1027, for a discussion of enforceability of pre-arbitral mechanisms in FIDIC Clause 20 under Swiss law.

110 *Peterborough City Council v Enterprise Managed Services, Ltd* [2014] EWHC 3193 (TCC).

provided for a DAB process followed by court litigation. A party brought court action without first attempting the DAB process. The Court found that the contractual pre-litigation DAB process must be complied with prior to initiating the court action. While pre-conditions to arbitration may deemed an issue of admissibility rather than jurisdiction and thus subject to the arbitrators' determination, they may remain enforceable contractual obligations.

11.41 Article 29(6)(c) of the ICC emergency arbitration rules (2017) specifically excluded the applicability of the emergency procedures when the parties had agreed to other pre-arbitral procedures that provide for the granting of conservatory, interim, or similar measures.[111] As noted herein, the newly revised 2021 ICC Rules have removed this exclusion. The ICC Secretariat's Guide (2012) notes that agreeing to such other pre-arbitral procedures 'amounts to an implied opt-out' of the emergency arbitration procedure.[112] It further notes that this exclusion will apply when the parties have agreed 'to use a dispute board that may issue interim measures'.[113] Dispute adjudication boards (DABs) would fit within this exclusion as these boards make binding decisions on the parties that have the effects of interim measures. The 2017 FIDIC contracts dispute clause clearly requires that the procedural steps preceding arbitration must be complied with prior to commencing arbitration. It is not clear if this would apply to the emergency arbitration, which does not provide a final adjudication of a dispute, but rather only interim measures of protection. However, the background to Article 29(6) seems to suggest that FIDIC pre-arbitral mechanisms were intended to prevent the admissibility of applications for emergency arbitration, at least when such pre-arbitral measures had not yet been fully complied with.

11.42 Notably, the new revisions to the ICC Rules have modified Article 29 to remove the exception for the application of emergency arbitration procedures when there are other agreed pre-arbitral procedures. The revised rules came into effect on January 1, 2021. The new rules apply to arbitrations initiated from January 1, 2021. However, it remains relevant to consider the background to the 2012 ICC Rules, which introduced emergency arbitration procedures, and which remained unchanged in the 2017 Rules.

11.43 The exception in Article 29(6)(c) 'other agreed pre-arbitral procedures' (which was removed in the 2021 rules) has been attributed to accommodating FIDIC concerns that the emergency arbitration procedures would undermine the Clause 20 provisions for dispute boards to first deal with disputes and then followed by arbitration.[114] However, the language of the ICC exception was not limited to FIDIC dispute boards and could be applied to any dispute board that could provide interim relief, which would be most, if not all, DABs. Voser and Boog comment that this exception should be applied restrictively in order to not deprive contracting parties the benefit of emergency arbitration.[115] Webster and Buhler note that the former ICC exception should be limited to DABS that are already in place at the time of filing an application for emergency arbitration.[116] They note that although the parties may have agreed to a standing DAB in their contract, the parties may

111 ICC Rules, Article 29(6)(c) (2017).
112 Fry, Greenberg, and Mazza, *supra* at n 29, Section 3–1102.
113 ibid.
114 Nathalie Voser and Christopher Boog, *supra* at n 29, Section 3.8, p 88.
115 ibid.
116 Webster and Buhler, *supra* at n 64, p 474.

have failed to appoint the DAB and the mere contract reference to a DAB should not be deemed an exclusion under the ICC Rule.[117]

11.44 The appointment process to establish a DAB can take time. Often in a dispute arising in the context of a construction or infrastructure project, one party will seek payment and the other will want to prevent it. A party may want to quickly prevent the calling of an 'on-demand bond' or a performance bank guarantee. Under the SIAC emergency arbitration rules there have been several cases where a party has successfully obtained an emergency arbitration order to prevent the calling of the on-demand bond or performance bank guarantee.[118] Importantly, SIAC and other rules such as the SCC and LCIA do not have an exception and thus have not limited the availability of emergency arbitration when the parties have agreed to other pre-arbitral relief.

11.45 Dispute boards have the power to make orders to prevent the payment of a demand bond or performance guarantee,[119] but the dispute board process may not be sufficiently nimble to address the issue in a timely manner, particularly if the dispute board is not yet constituted when the issue arises. When parties have agreed to a pre-arbitral dispute board procedure prior to arbitration, there may be an issue as to whether the failure to initiate or complete the DAB process may be a jurisdictional or admissibility objection to the emergency arbitration procedure. The analysis of this issue will implicate the characterization of the objection and will require interpreting the dispute resolution agreement. It may also depend on the type of relief sought in the emergency arbitration.

11.46 Generally, if the parties have agreed to emergency arbitration by agreeing to arbitral rules and these rules do not limit access to emergency arbitration if the parties have agreed to other pre-arbitral procedures, the parties should be able to apply for emergency arbitration in urgent situations where relief is needed to maintain the status quo or to prevent imminent serious harm that cannot later be compensated. This however raises the issue of whether the party seeking the emergency relief will be able to commence the regular arbitration concurrently or within the time period as prescribed by the applicable emergency arbitration rules. This is an issue that was raised in the first ICC emergency arbitration application where the parties had agreed to a 'med-arb' clause, which will be discussed next.

Contractually agreed negotiations, mediation, and cooling-off periods

11.47 The first ICC emergency arbitrator application presented the issue of the contractual obligation to mediate before going to arbitration. The parties had agreed to a 'med-arb' clause that provided that arbitration could be commenced if the dispute was not resolved 60 days after the Request for ADR pursuant to the ICC Arbitration Rules. The Claimant filed a Request for ADR and at the same time it filed the Request for an Emergency Arbitrator, requesting an asset-freeze order against the Respondent. The Respondent

117 ibid.

118 N Vivekananda, *The SIAC Emergency Arbitration Experience,* available on the SIAC website: <www.siac.org.sg/2013-09-18-01-57-20/2013-09-22-00-27-02/articles/338-the-siac-emergency-arbitrator-experience> (last accessed October 27, 2020).

119 Webster and Buhler, *supra* at n 64, p 473.

raised jurisdictional objections to the emergency proceedings. The ICC reports the case as follows:[120]

> The responding party argued that as the 60-day interval had not elapsed, the parties could not yet be considered to have committed themselves to arbitration. Hence the emergency arbitrator was not entitled to take jurisdiction. The responding party also pointed out that the Application was premature as a Request for Arbitration could not be filed within the mandatory ten days without breaching the 60-day interval set by the multi-tiered clause. The emergency arbitrator dismissed the objection and upheld his jurisdiction. He observed, inter alia, that to hold otherwise would deprive the parties of the possibility of obtaining interim relief when it was most needed (after the dispute had arisen but before the arbitral tribunal was constituted). He also noted that the emergency arbitrator proceedings constitute a largely separate process which should be able to take place notwithstanding the requirement to wait 60 days before commencing arbitration proceedings. However, he added that no Request for Arbitration could be filed during those 60 days, which led him to point out the tension between the waiting period of 60 days between the Request for ADR and the Request for Arbitration laid down in the parties' contract and the need to submit a Request for Arbitration within ten days of the Application laid down in the Rules. In the end, the emergency arbitrator concluded that the tension could be resolved pursuant to Article 1(6) of the Emergency Arbitrator Rules, which enables the emergency arbitrator to extend the 10-day time limit for filing a Request for Arbitration. Ultimately, the emergency arbitrator left the question of the timing of the Request for Arbitration for the arbitral tribunal to determine in the ensuing arbitration proceedings.

As this author understands, the Respondent shortly thereafter became insolvent and the claim did not proceed to mediation or arbitration. There are reports of other cases where emergency arbitration has been allowed despite pre-arbitral negotiation and mediation requirements. Since emergency arbitration proceedings are private and usually do not become enforced in courts in part due to the short lifespan of the order or award, it is difficult to gain access to actual practice.

11.48 There have been a few reported cases where the emergency arbitrator has ordered emergency relief despite cooling-off periods which should expire prior to commencing arbitration.[121] In the *JKX v Ukraine* case the emergency arbitrator found that the six-month cooling-off period set forth in the Treaty did not prevent the Claimant from requesting emergency relief. The emergency arbitrator noted:[122]

> that it would be procedurally unfair to Claimant and contrary to the purpose of the Emergency Arbitrator procedure to apply the Cooling-Off Period to the appointment of an Emergency Arbitrator or to an emergency decision on interim measures to be made by the Emergency Arbitrator, not least since Claimant seems to be facing a serious risk of suffering irreparable harm before the expiry of the Cooling-Off Period if interim measures are not granted.

120 Andrea Carlevaris and José Ricardo Ferris, 'Running in the ICC Emergency Arbitrator Rules: The First Ten Cases' (2014) 25(1) *ICC International Court of Arbitration Bulletin* 25.

121 See, Joel Dahlquist, *Emergency Arbitrators in Investment Disputes,* Kluwer Arbitration Blog (March 10, 2015) <http://arbitrationblog.kluwerarbitration.com/2015/03/10/emergency-arbitrators-in-investment-treaty-disputes/> (last accessed June 28, 2021).

122 *Emergency Decision on Interim Measures, Made on 29 April 2014,* in Emergency Arbitration No. EA(2014/053) para 66, p 16.

However, as discussed earlier, in the action to enforce the emergency award, the Ukrainian Supreme Court found that the failure to comply with the cooling-off period was a ground for refusing enforcement of the award.[123] If emergency arbitration is considered to be part of arbitration, rather than an independent interim procedure, then the contractual obligation to comply with a pre-arbitral procedure may make a stronger argument against admissibility than if emergency arbitration is characterized as a separate pre-arbitral provisional measure. In the latter case, emergency arbitration may be treated differently and deemed compatible with contractual obligation to comply with pre-arbitral conditions.

11.49 When parties have agreed to pre-arbitral dispute mechanisms such as cooling-off periods, amicable negotiations, and mediation, they usually do so in order to first attempt to reach a settlement efficiently, before launching into a lengthy adjudicated resolution to their dispute. Arguably, interim measures to maintain the status quo and thereby avoid further escalation of the dispute, will enhance the possibility for the parties to reach an agreed resolution and the likelihood of preserving the business relationship. However, launching into adversarial emergency arbitration proceedings could also escalate the dispute and aggravate the discord between the parties. Emergency arbitration will require legal representation and bring added expenses, which may cause the situation between the parties to further deteriorate. The emergency arbitration procedures will not necessarily prevent compliance with other pre-arbitral measures and will be conducted rather quickly. However, if any relief is granted and enforcement is sought, there may be prolonged litigation, as the *JKX v Ukraine* case demonstrates.

11.50 In a widely noted case, the Swiss Supreme Court considered the consequences of the failure to comply with agreed mediation proceedings prior to arbitration in an action to set aside an interim jurisdictional award.[124] There have been persistent discussions and conflicting case law regarding whether the failure to comply with pre-arbitral procedures constitutes an issue of jurisdiction or admissibility. The Swiss court found that the agreed ICC mediation procedure had been initiated but not completed pursuant to the rules. The Court held that the failure to comply with this mandatory condition to arbitration required the arbitrators to stay the arbitration until the contractually required procedures were met. The Court declined to characterize the pre-arbitral condition as an issue of jurisdiction or admissibility, and declined finding damages resulting from the failure to comply with the mediation requirement, as such consequences would be impracticable.[125] While this case has provided a persuasive approach to enforcing pre-arbitral procedures prior to arbitrating, it remains an open issue as to whether the same approach would be applied by most courts in various jurisdictions in the context of seeking emergency arbitration interim measures prior to completing other agreed pre-arbitral procedures. Perhaps the pre-arbitral procedures could be considered compatible in the pre-arbitration stage. But

123 *Supra* at text accompanied in n 77.

124 *4A_628/2015, Supreme Court of Switzerland,* (March 16, 2016). An unofficial translation can be accessed at the Swiss Arbitration Decisions website: <www.swissarbitrationdecisions.com/sites/default/files/16%20 mars%202016%204A%20628%202015.pdf> (last accessed November 22, 2020).

125 ibid, at pp 18–20, unofficial translation. See also, Christopher Boog and James Menz, *Landmark Swiss Decision on Failure to Comply with Mandatory Pre-arbitral-tier,* Kluwer Arbitration Blog (May 4, 2016) <http://arbitrationblog.kluwerarbitration.com/2016/05/04/landmark-swiss-decision-failure-comply-mandatory-pre-arbitral-tier/> (last accessed November 22, 2020).

as noted earlier, there may be an issue when the arbitration must be commenced within a short period of time.

11.51 In most jurisdictions and under most rules, courts have concurrent jurisdiction to order interim measures and a party seeking interim relief could approach a court. Consequently, seeking interim measures from a court would not be incompatible with an arbitration agreement. However, seeking measures at a national court would also result in an adversarial proceeding, conducted pursuant to national procedural law and in the language of the court, and potentially would be public. The purpose of emergency arbitration is to allow parties to seek urgent relief when needed in the arbitral forum rather than at a court, as in some instances a court would be less desirable. In some jurisdictions, a court may not order interim measures in a dispute which is subject to arbitration unless there is not an effective remedy available in arbitration; this is sometimes termed the 'court-subsidiary model', such as in the UK and Singapore.[126] Some arbitration rules also indicate a preference for seeking interim measures from the arbitral tribunal rather than from a court, unless relief is needed from a court, for example when the requested measure is directed to a person or entity not subject to the arbitrator's authority.

11.52 For example, the ICC Rules provide: 'Before the file is transmitted to the arbitral tribunal, *and in appropriate circumstances even thereafter*, the parties may apply to any competent judicial authority for interim or conservatory measures.'[127] The ICC Secretariat's Guide to the ICC Rules (2012) provides that resort to a court rather than the constituted tribunal should only occur when there are reasons that justify the party approaching a court rather than a tribunal.[128] The LCIA Rules provide that the interim measures may be sought from a court after the formation of the arbitral tribunal only in exceptional cases and with the arbitral tribunal's authorization.[129] The LCIA approach, which is relatively unique, imposes two relatively strict requirements: that there are exceptional reasons for seeking relief from a court rather than the tribunal and that the tribunal authorizes seeking the measures from the court.[130] This approach allows the tribunal to retain control over the proceedings and to ensure that the arbitration is not obstructed by court proceedings that are not exceptionally needed.[131] Issues can arise if a party wishes to seek *ex parte* interim

---

126 Joseph Lee, 'Court – Subsidiarity and Interim Measures in Commercial Arbitration: A Comparative Study of U.K., Singapore & Taiwan' (2013) 6 Contemp Asia Arb J 227.

127 Article 28(2), ICC Rules (2017) (emphasis added). The ICC Rules entering into force on January 1, 2021, have not revised this provision; it retains the same text as the 2012 and 2017 Rules.

128 Jason Fry, Simon Greenberg, and Francesca Mazza, *supra* at n 29, Section 3–1048 and 3–1049 note: 'After the case file has been transmitted to the arbitral tribunal pursuant to Article 16, the Rules require there to be circumstances making it "appropriate" for parties to resort to state courts for such relief. Therefore, once the arbitral proceedings are under the control of a fully constituted arbitral tribunal (see paragraph 3–655), a party must carefully consider whether resorting to a judicial authority is consistent with the arbitration agreement.

The Rules do not state what circumstances are "appropriate", leaving this for the arbitral tribunal to determine in the event that the appropriateness of an application for interim or conservatory measures is contested in the arbitration by the other side. The circumstances are generally considered appropriate if the arbitral tribunal is not in a position to provide suitable interim relief to the requesting party. Such may be the case, for instance, where third parties are involved, where the measures will be effective only if granted *ex parte*, or where court enforcement is required and is more easily obtained directly from the relevant court. An arbitral tribunal may even lack the authority to grant the requested relief under the rules of law governing the merits.'

129 Article 25(3), LCIA Rules (2020). The same approach was contained in the 2014 LCIA Rules.

130 Maxi Scherer, Lisa Richman, et al, *Arbitrating under the 2014 LCIA Rules: A User's Guide* (Kluwer Law International 2015) pp 280–81.

131 ibid, at p 281.

measures from a court but would need to inform the arbitrators and thus the opposing party.[132] When the arbitral tribunal is not yet constituted, parties to LCIA Arbitration may seek interim measures from an emergency arbitrator.[133]

11.53 In a recent case, *Gerald Metals SA v Timis*, a party sought interim measures (for a freezing injunction) at the English Court following the LCIA Secretariat rejecting its request for the appointment of an emergency arbitrator.[134] The English High Court, in an opinion of Mr Justice Leggatt, found that the applicant could obtain effective relief through the expedited formation of the arbitration tribunal or through the appointment of an emergency arbitrator. Consequently, the Court found that pursuant to 44(3) and 44(5) of the Arbitration Act 1996 it lacked the authority to order the requested relief, which could be obtained through the arbitration procedures. Section 44(3) of the Arbitration Act allows the Court to make such orders as are necessary to protect evidence or assets.[135] Section 44(5) provides that such power shall only be exercised when the arbitral procedure is not available or not effective.[136] This approach seems to limit the options of parties to the LCIA Rules, which purport to offer parties the option of either seeking interim measures at a court or through emergency arbitration or the regular arbitral tribunal. The LCIA Rules provided in Article 9.12 that the emergency arbitration provision 'shall not prejudice any party's right to apply to a state court ... for any interim or conservatory measures before the formation of the Arbitration Tribunal'.[137] The 2020 revisions to the LCIA Rules made a slight amendment to this provision, which now is contained in Article 9.13, which may clarify to some extent the intended approach of providing parties with alternative options of seeking urgent relief from either a court or an emergency arbitrator.[138] In any case, the Court will determine the interpretation and application of the English Arbitration Act provisions relating to the court-requested interim relief in cases subject to arbitration.

11.54 Finally, it can be noted that pre-arbitral relief procedures appear to be growing in use across the globe, and procedures are revised to facilitate efficient and effective dispute resolution methods that offer flexibility and to accommodate the needs of particular cases

132 ibid.

133 Article 9B, LCIA Rules (2020).

134 '845 [2016] EWHC 2327 (Ch). The LCIA rejected the application as it was deemed not urgently needed.

135 Section 44(3), English Arbitration Act provides: 'If the case is one of urgency, the court may, on the application of a party or proposed party to the arbitral proceedings, make such orders as it thinks necessary for the purpose of preserving evidence or assets.'

136 Section 44(5), English Arbitration Act provides: 'In any case the court shall act only if or to the extent that the arbitral tribunal, and any arbitral or other institution or person vested by the parties with power in that regard, has no power or is unable for the time being to act effectively.'

137 Article 9.12, LCIA Rules (2014) provides: 'Article 9B shall not prejudice any party's right to apply to a state court or other legal authority for any interim or conservatory measures before the formation of the Arbitration Tribunal; and it shall not be treated as an alternative to or substitute for the exercise of such right. During the emergency proceedings, any application to and any order by such court or authority shall be communicated promptly in writing to the Emergency Arbitrator, the Registrar and all other parties.' Article 25.3, LCIA Rules (2014) contains a similar provision relating to interim measures from the regular tribunal.

138 Article 9.13, LCIA Rules (2020) provides: 'Notwithstanding Article 9B, a party may apply to a competent state court or other legal authority for any interim or conservatory measures before the formation of the Arbitral Tribunal; and Article 9B shall not be treated as an alternative to or substitute for the exercise of such right. During the emergency proceedings, any application to and any order by such court or authority shall be communicated promptly in writing to the Emergency Arbitrator, the Registrar and all other parties.' A similar slight amendment was made to Article 25.3, LCIA Rules (2020) relating to concurrent interim relief at the court and the arbitral tribunal.

and circumstances. For example, the SCC recently launched a new tool, 'SCC Express', which provides for the parties to agree to have an independent expert appointed to conduct a neutral legal evaluation of the parties' case within a three-week period for a fixed fee.[139] The evaluation is non-binding, unless the parties agree to make it binding. Neutral evaluations, expert determinations, facilitated negotiations, dispute boards, and other dispute resolutions methods will likely continue to be part of the dispute resolution landscape and grow in variety and use.

Conclusions

11.55 Emergency arbitration offers an important mechanism that helps ensure the effectiveness and autonomy of the arbitral system. The procedure has become a standard feature of arbitral institutions' rules and a useful tool for parties seeking urgent interim relief. While emergency arbitration practice is developing, a number of issues regarding its legal status remain. One of these issues is the interplay between emergency arbitration and other pre-arbitral procedures such as mediation and dispute boards, as well as court concurrent jurisdiction and enforcement of emergency orders and awards. As the practice of emergency arbitration develops, these issues need to be addressed to enhance predictability and avoid procedural battles. When parties have agreed to pre-arbitral procedures, their contractual undertaking should be respected. When they have also agreed to emergency arbitration, this contractual undertaking should also be respected. One process does not need to exclude the other. Pragmatic solutions that also promote a coherent theoretical and analytical approach need to be developed. These solutions can be legislated, addressed in rules, forged through case law, guided by 'soft-law', and set-out through careful dispute clause drafting. Party autonomy and flexibility must be the core principles of the solutions to the issues, as well as recognition that arbitration seeks to provide efficient and effective dispute resolution.

139 <https://sccinstitute.com/our-services/scc-express/> (last accessed June 28, 2021).

PART V

STATUTORY CONSTRUCTION ADJUDICATION

A global perspective

CHAPTER 12

Statutory adjudication in the United Kingdom

Recent developments

James Pickavance

Introduction

The United Kingdom's regime

12.1 Adjudication is an interim dispute resolution procedure by which the parties to a construction contract are provided with a unilateral right to refer a dispute to an independent determiner who, having received a submission from each party, will make a final binding decision. It provides an interim dispute resolution process by which, for statutory adjudication at least, cannot be contracted out of. The adjudicator's decision is binding on the parties, unless or until the dispute is determined by litigation, arbitration or by agreement.[1]

12.2 This statutory right was enacted by the Housing Grants, Construction and Regeneration Act 1996 (the '**1996 Act**')[2] and came into effect on 1 May 1998. The 1996 Act was amended by the Local Democracy, Economic Development and Construction Act 2009 (the '**2009 Act**').[3] The amendments apply to contracts entered into on or after 1 October 2011. The 1996 Act as amended by the 2009 Act shall be referred to in this chapter as the Act.

12.3 The Act provides a more efficient and cost-effective means of resolving (mainly) low to medium value construction disputes, producing a cash-flow remedy during the progress of a construction project while avoiding the chronic issue of time-consuming and expensive final resolution forums or interim forums that produce a result which has no binding effect. Parties may avail themselves of the statutory adjudication process where:

- a there is a construction contract within the meaning of the Act;[4]
- b there is a single dispute (there is no limit or qualification on the type of dispute, or the number of sub-issues that comprise that dispute) arising out of one contract; and[5]
- c the dispute is not the same or similar to an issue previously decided between the parties.[6]

1 Section 108(3) of the Act.
2 <www.legislation.gov.uk/ukpga/1996/53/contents> (last accessed 10 March 2021).
3 <www.legislation.gov.uk/uksi/2011/1582/made> (last accessed 10 March 2021).
4 Section 104 and 105 of the Act.
5 Section 108(1) of the Act.
6 Section 108(1) of the Act.

Statutory adjudication is also an accessible, flexible process. For example, the dispute may be referred to adjudication at any time and parties are free to determine their own rules for adjudication provided that those rules comply with the few mandatory provisions set out in section 108(2) to (4) of the Act. These features, and others, are the reasons why adjudication has become the number one method of dispute resolution in the construction industry in the UK, and why a number of other countries have enacted a statutory adjudication regime.

12.4 Statutory adjudication is confined to those construction contracts that fall within the scope of or are excluded by the Act. However, adjudication can and does take place for other construction contracts. These adjudications are referred to as contractual or ad hoc adjudications. Contractual adjudication sits outside of the scope of the Act, yet remains enforceable by way of a contractual mechanism agreed between the parties that outlines a process for adjudication. Ad hoc adjudication refers to a form of adjudication where the parties have agreed to submit their dispute to adjudication in the absence of any statutory right or pre-existing contractual agreement.

12.5 A statutory adjudication is commenced by the service of a notice of adjudication. The adjudicator must be appointed and the claim (known as the referral) must be served seven days following receipt of the notice. On receipt of the referral, the adjudicator has 28 days to provide a decision on the dispute referred, unless the timetable for adjudication is extended pursuant to the provisions in the Act. During the 28-day period, the adjudicator issues directions and will receive further submissions from both parties. The adjudicator will issue the award, which typically must be complied with under seven days.

12.6 If the losing party does not comply with the adjudicator's decision, the winning party will typically either commence an action in the Technology and Construction Court or make a summary judgment application to enforce the adjudicator's decision. In limited circumstances, the unsuccessful party may mount a successful defence to the application by demonstrating that the adjudicator has exceeded his jurisdiction or breached the rules of natural justice.

This chapter

12.7 The purpose of this chapter is to examine the recent developments in adjudication law. The next section will provide an analysis of some areas of adjudication law that have been developed in the past few years pursuant to court judgments. This is not intended to be a definitive review of all cases decided in recent years, not least because there are between 20 and 30 cases published each year. However, it does examine the cases that have led to a shift or a development in the law. The following section examines the introduction of law value adjudication schemes. The final section considers the responses received to the UK government's consultation on changes brought about by the 2009 Act and 2011 Scheme for Construction Contracts.

Recent developments in the law

Construction contracts and exclusions

12.8 The Act applies to construction contracts, as defined by the Act. The scheme presented by the Act is that sections 104 and 105(1) define what is meant by a construction contract and sections 105(2) and 106 exclude industries or activities which would otherwise fall within scope.

12.9 Recent case law has provided further guidance on the way in which these sections are intended to interact and whether certain scenarios are caught by the provisions. Section 104(5) was at the centre of the dispute in *C Spencer Ltd v MW High Tech Projects UK Ltd.*[7] This section provides that:

> *where an agreement relates to construction operations and other matters, this Part applies to it only so far as it relates to construction operations ... the contract is to be treated as severable between those parts ... and the provisions for adjudication are to apply to the contract only in as far as the contract relates to construction operations.*

Most consider this subsection difficult to navigate, interpret or apply in practice because often the subject matter of a contract may be so intertwined that the part within and the part outside the Act cannot be separated.

12.10 In *Spencer*, the court determined that section 104(5) does not create a requirement for a hybrid contract to contain a term requiring the separate notification and breakdown of sums due in respect of construction operations only. This restricts the need for parties to use two separate mechanisms for payment, which should allow a more efficient approach to be taken in future contracts. It is also an indication to commercial parties that overly complex payment provisions within hybrid construction contracts are not necessary.

12.11 The exception at section 105(2)(c) is triggered where the '*primary activity*' covered by a contract is, among other things, power generation. Determining what the primary activity is at such a site will likely require consideration of a number of factors, and can, dependent on the case, throw up a host of issues for an adjudicator.[8]

12.12 In *Engie Fabricom UK Ltd v MW High Tech Projects UK Ltd,*[9] the issue of what the primary activity at a site was came under examination. The site in question was a gasification power plant, which used certain forms of waste to generate power. A dispute arose over whether the site's primary activity was power generation or waste disposal, and an application for summary judgment was made. As the decision in this case made clear:

> *It is common ground that if the primary activity of the site is power generation, the works are not 'construction operations' under the Act and there is no legal right or entitlement to adjudicate so that the decision is without jurisdiction and unenforceable.*

The court determined that the facts of the matter were too complex to be assessed in a summary judgment application and so the claimant's application was refused and the matter proceeded to trial. In making this decision, the court stressed the fact that '*the wording of the* [Main] *EPC contract and Sub-contract is consistent only with power generation*' had played a role in their thinking. Further, it was not sufficient for the claimant to rely on the investor materials produced by the site owner, which clearly stated the use as the treatment of waste. This case highlighted the difficulties adjudicators and courts can face when forced

7 [2019] EWHC 1876 (TCC).

8 For an example of this, see *Laker Vent Engineering Ltd v Jacobs E&C Ltd* [2014] EWHC 1058 (TCC), *per* Ramsey J at [66] – [71].

9 [2019] EWHC 1876 (TCC).

to deal with multi-faceted sites, and the need to bear in mind the wording of the contract in question when dealing with dual-purpose sites.

12.13 The challenges involved in identifying exceptions under section 105(2) were again highlighted in the case of *Universal Sealants (UK) Ltd v Sanders Plant and Waste Management Ltd.*[10] This case concerned a sub-contractor contracted to deliver concrete. Upon delivery, the driver of the delivery wagon, at the claimant's request, poured the concrete into where it would ultimately be used. The question was whether this delivery was caught by section 105(2)(d)(ii) of the Act, which excludes contracts for delivery except where such a contract '*also provides for their installation*'. In this case, it was ruled that the pouring of the concrete did not, in and of itself, amount to installation, and so the adjudicator had no jurisdiction.

12.14 Finally, the decision in *Howsons Ltd v Redfearn*[11] has introduced a new element to the '*dwelling house*' exemption under section 106 of the Act. This section creates an exemption which excludes an adjudicator's jurisdiction where the contract being considered relates to a dwelling house. *Howsons* saw the occupant of a building attempt to rely on this exemption, where their occupancy was in breach of planning permission. The court refused to allow this argument on the basis that unlawful use of a property logically precluded any reliance on section 106. Again, this clearly underlines the willingness of the courts to take a practical view in their approach to statute, and adjudicators will now need to bear in mind that illegal occupancy bars reliance on the section 106 exemption.

Adjudication and insolvency

12.15 Until recently, adjudicating a monetary dispute where one of the parties was insolvent was certainly a fraught, and likely a doomed exercise. Even if the referring party managed to commence the adjudication without objection, enforcement was out of the question. These challenges are created by two pieces of legislation where little thought was given by the drafters as to how the two rules could coexist. These regimes of insolvency and adjudication have been described as '*fundamentally incompatible*'.[12]

12.16 Statutory insolvency is defined as a company's inability '*to pay its debts as they fall due*'.[13] Liquidators,[14] administrators and administrative receivers[15] are empowered by the Insolvency Act 1986 to bring any legal action, including adjudication, on behalf of the company. Section 108 of the Act entitles the parties to a construction contract to adjudicate '*at any time*'. The Insolvency (England and Wales) Rules 2016, however, impose a mandatory and automatic insolvency set-off, when a company enters administration[16] or liquidation.[17] This balancing of all mutual[18] claims and cross-claims between the parties[19]

10 [2019] EWHC 2360 (TCC).
11 [2019] EWHC 2540 (TCC).
12 *Bresco Electrical Services Ltd v Michael J Lonsdale (Electrical) Ltd* (2019) EWCA Civ 27.
13 Insolvency Act 1986 ('**IA 1986**'), section 123(1).
14 IA 1986, Sch. 4, Part II, Para 4.
15 IA 1986, Sch.1, Para 5.
16 Rule 14.24 Insolvency Act 2016.
17 Rule 14.25 Insolvency Act 2016.
18 *BCCI v Prince Fahd Abdul Asis Al-Soud* [1997] BCC 63.
19 Rule 4.90 Insolvency Act 1986.

overrides any other statutory set-offs or contract terms, including adjudication. In *Wilson and Sharp Investments Ltd v Harbour View Developments Ltd*,[20] Gloster LJ commented that '*the HGCRA did not expressly set out what was to occur on the insolvency of a party to a construction contract*', arguing that the '*interrelation between the HGCRA and insolvency law has to date largely been a matter of case law*'.[21] In *Enterprise Managed Services Ltd v Tony McFadden Utilities Ltd*,[22] Coulson J as he then was, argued there was a '*fundamental clash*' between the certainty and conclusiveness '*envisaged by the full rule 4.90*'[23] and the ephemerality, or '*temporary, quick-fix solution offered by construction adjudication under the Act*'.[24]

12.17 The key issues that have arisen in the body of case law, brought to the fore and resolved in the second only Supreme Court decision in adjudication law of *Bresco Electrical Services Ltd (in liquidation) v Michael J Lonsdale*,[25] are (i) is there jurisdiction for an insolvent party to refer a dispute to adjudication; and (ii) is an adjudicator's award in favour of or against an insolvent party enforceable.

12.18 Bresco entered into a sub-sub-contract in August 2014 with Lonsdale for electrical installation works at a site in London. In December 2014, Bresco stopped attending site, alleging acceptance of a repudiatory breach of the contract by Lonsdale. In 2015, Bresco went into liquidation. There were a number of claims and cross-claims and Bresco served a notice of intention to refer a dispute to adjudication. Lonsdale responded asserting that the adjudicator had no jurisdiction as Bresco was insolvent. Lonsdale also issued proceedings in the TCC for a declaration that the adjudicator lacked jurisdiction and for an injunction restraining the further conduct of the adjudication.

12.19 In the first instance decision, the judge granted the injunction to prevent Bresco from commencing an adjudication. The judge leant heavily on the decision in *Stein v Blake*[26] to determine that because of the triggering of mandatory insolvency set-off arising from Lonsdale's cross-claim, the effect of merging the claims and cross-claims thereby extinguishes the claims under the contract. Therefore, there would only be a single claim and a balance of the account between the parties. Since that merged claim did not arise from the construction contract, Lonsdale argued and the court held, the adjudicator would have no jurisdiction.

12.20 The Court of Appeal overturned that decision. In contrast to the previous court's finding, it held that adjudications *could* still be validly commenced by companies in liquidation. However, Coulson LJ stated clearly that there was an incompatibility between adjudication and the insolvency rules. It made clear that the court will not, save in exceptional circumstances, enforce adjudication decisions in favour of companies in

---

20 [2015] EWCA Civ 1030.

21 Ibid at [37].

22 [2009] EWHC 3222 (TCC).

23 Rule 4.90 of the Insolvency Rules 1986 is substantially replicated by Rule 14.25 of the Insolvency Act 2016, providing that '(1) where, before the company goes into liquidation there have been mutual credits, mutual debts or other mutual dealings between the company and any creditor of the company proving or claiming to prove for a debt in the liquidation, (2) [a]n account shall be taken of what is due from each party to the other in respect of the mutual dealings, and the sums due from one party shall be set off against the sums due from the other'.

24 [2009] EWHC 3222 at [70].

25 [2020] UKSC 25.

26 [1995] UKHL 11.

liquidation where the responding party has a cross-claim. To do otherwise would force the responding party to pay the amount of the adjudication decision, while being left to prove its cross-claim in the liquidation and most likely receive only a fraction of its claimed amount as part of the divvying up of funds between other unsecured creditors. This would deprive the paying party of the benefit it was intended to have through the set-off under the Insolvency Rules. Thus, the court determined that an adjudication by a company in liquidation would be liable to be stopped at enforcement stage as an '*exercise in futility*' where the other party has a cross-claim.[27]

12.21 What amounted to exceptional circumstances was very quickly tested in *Meadowside Building Developments Ltd v 12–18 Hill Street Management Company Ltd.*[28] The court held that enforcement of an adjudicator's decision in favour of an insolvent company *could* be permitted provided that the following four criteria are met:

- a The adjudication deals with a final net position between the parties under the relevant contract.
- b '*Satisfactory security*' is given in respect of both the amount awarded and any costs in relation to any subsequent proceedings to enforce/challenge the adjudication decision.
- c Such satisfactory security may involve the liquidator ring-fencing the award sum so that it cannot be distributed.
- d Any security given or underlying funding agreement cannot be an abuse of process.

Ultimately this test was not met by the claimant in *Meadowside*, but it does provide clarity that what was missing from the judge in the *Bresco* Court of Appeal decision as to what is needed in order for an insolvent party to commence an adjudication.

12.22 That case was followed by *Balfour Beatty Civil Engineering Ltd v Astec Projects Ltd (In Liquidation)*,[29] which concerned an injunction to prevent adjudication, not an enforcement of an award. Notwithstanding, Waksman J referred to *Meadowside* and held that the conditions had (unusually) been met and so an injunction was refused. In *Meadowside*, the dispute referred to adjudication was only part of the mutual dealings between the parties. However, in *Balfour Beatty* there were three separate contracts between the parties encompassing their mutual dealings. In the absence of an agreement otherwise, a single adjudication could not settle the final net position between the parties. However, the court observed that three adjudications could resolve all disputes arising under the separate contracts, therefore they refused to grant an injunction. Taking a pragmatic approach, the court imposed other conditions, including that the parties must appoint the same adjudicator for each adjudication, the level of security and the terms of the insurance policy required. This decision demonstrates what the courts can put in place to enable insolvent parties to adjudicate without imposing unfair risk on the respondents.

27 See *Straw Realisations (No 1) Ltd v Shaftsbury House Developments Ltd* [2010] EWHC 2597. It was held that if at the time of the application hearing for enforcing an adjudicator's decision the winning party is formally insolvent, a summary judgment will not be entered by the courts. See also *Twintec Ltd v Volkerfitzpatrick Limited* [2014] EWHC 10.

28 [2019] EWHC 2651 (TCC).

29 [2020] EWHC 796 (TCC).

12.23 The Supreme Court decision in *Bresco* overturned the Court of Appeal decision. Lord Briggs agreed that the application of the insolvency regime did not deprive an adjudicator of jurisdiction. He described the analysis of *Stein* in the court of first instance as an '*over-literal reading*' of the language of Lord Hoffmann's speech, noting that Lord Hoffmann himself acknowledged this in stating '*the cross-claims must obviously be considered separately for the purpose of ascertaining the balance*'. Therefore, the dispute under contract remained intact, and the existence of a cross-claim operating by way of insolvency set-off did not '*melt away*'.

12.24 The court did not agree with the Court of Appeal's view that the adjudication was an exercise in futility. It held that whether or not an adjudication decision obtained by a party in liquidation would need to be assessed on a case-by-case basis and at the point of enforcement depends on the financial position of the receiving party and the nature of any cross-claims. That said, enforcement may still risk depriving the paying party of the benefit of the insolvency set-off on the basis that any claim to overturn the adjudication decision and for the return of money paid would rank alongside other unsecured creditors in the liquidation. In such circumstances, Lord Briggs commented that '*the court will be astute to refuse summary judgment*'[30] unless the arrangements, as set out in *Meadowside*, can be made to protect the paying party's interests.

12.25 The decision in *John Doyle Construction Ltd (in liquidatation) v Erith Contractors Ltd*[31] was the first decision after the Supreme Court decision to test the water. Given the high hurdle to meet, perhaps unsurprisingly, enforcement was refused due to the claimant providing insufficient security in respect of the cross-claim. The Court provided guidance on what level of security would be sufficient to allow enforcement. The claimant had made no offer to ring-fence the sums awarded in escrow. Fraser J said that it is unusual for an insolvent party to be able to provide the required financial assurance thus decisions will rarely be enforced. Third-party funder agreements and ATE insurance, the court said, were inadequate to pass the court's test for providing adequate security.

12.26 The most recent and less well-known decision in this area is *Styles & Wood Ltd (in administration) v GE CIF Trustees Ltd.*[32] In that case, Styles successfully enforced an adjudication decision using the principles in *Bresco*. The adjudication related to the final account for a project in Manchester. GECIF refused to comply with the adjudicator's decision on the ground of futility and sought a stay of execution. Styles brought enforcement proceedings which sought to satisfy the conditions of enforcement as laid down in *Meadowside*. The Court accepted the type and level of security offered and gave judgment in favour of Styles.

12.27 The Supreme Court decision in *Bresco* made it very clear statutory adjudication and insolvency are compatible:

> *I do not regard construction adjudication as in any way incompatible with the operation of the insolvency code in general, or with insolvency set-off in particular.*[33]

30 *Bresco Electrical Services Ltd (In Liquidation) v Michael J Lonsdale (Ltd)* [2020] UKSC 25.

31 [2020] EWHC 2451 (TCC).

32 (unreported), 4 September 2020 (County Court at Central London).

33 *Bresco Electrical Services Ltd (In Liquidation) v Michael J Lonsdale (Ltd)* [2020] UKSC 25.

Nevertheless, given that the two regimes were developed independently, many years apart and to serve very different purposes, without seemingly any consideration as to their comparability by the draftsman, there is still an awkwardness between the two regimes. However, the Supreme Court decision, coupled with the important first instance decisions in *Meadowside* and *John Doyle* that provide definition to the Supreme Court's determination, appear to have provided much-needed clarity and offer solutions (available through the courts' discretion) to ensure that the two regimes co-exist and provide appropriate outcomes to litigants. Thus, claims and cross-claims brought by an insolvent party in adjudication are not extinguished by the insolvency rules but instead can form part of the insolvency accounting process, provided a final net position between the parties can be established and suitable security put in place.

12.28 The requirements that have to be met in order to get an enforced adjudication decision will not mean a flood of adjudications by insolvent parties, though the gongoozler will observe a steady flow of water from the lock's sluice gate. Where the conditions are met, insolvency practitioners may view the cost savings that attach to adjudication favourably and prefer a quicker resolution of disputes, claims and cross-claims. There will, therefore, be some increase in adjudication proceedings by insolvent parties to construction contracts and in turn, an increase in enforcement cases. Considering the economic impact from the COVID-19 pandemic (which at the time of writing is unpredicted and is unlikely to fully recover for a decade), this newfound communion between adjudication and insolvency is particularly relevant. The recently passed Corporate Insolvency and Governance Act 2020, which adds a new moratorium to the protection available under the Insolvency Act 1986, will have an impact on adjudications against parties in financial difficulties, but it is yet to be determined how the impact of this legislation will mesh with the statutory right to adjudicate.

Crystallisation of a dispute

12.29 Section 108(1) of the Act grants a party '*the right to refer a <u>dispute</u> arising under the contract for adjudication under a procedure complying with this section*' (*emphasis added*).

12.30 A dispute arises where one party makes a claim to the other party and the responding party either denies all or part of the claim, either expressly or by its conduct. The court's approach to determining whether there is a dispute has, to date, been characterised by the need to '*adopt a rigorous and common sense approach*',[34] whilst avoiding '*an over legalistic analysis of what the dispute between the parties are; instead it will determine in broad terms what the disputed claim, assertion or position is*'.[35] It is within the context of this paradigm that recent case law has developed.

12.31 The court in the Scottish case of *Dickie & Moore Ltd v Mcleish*[36] held that the adjudicator did not have jurisdiction to decide a large part of the claim because the contractor's claims for an extension of time, prolongation and loss and expense had increased by an order of magnitude in the period from the dispute arising to the notice of adjudication being filed. More recently in the English court, the judge refused to be bogged

34 *All in One Building and Refurbishments Ltd v Makers UK Ltd* [2005] EWHC 2943 (TCC), *per* Wilcox J at [21] – [22].

35 *Allied P&L Ltd v Paradigm Housing Group Ltd* [2009] EWHC 2890 (TCC), *per* Akenhead J at [30].

36 [2019] CSOH 71.

down by technocratic arguments that concerned the validity of a claim in *LJH Paving Ltd v Meeres Civil Engineering Ltd.*[37] Here, the court refused to consider in detail the merits of each side's stated position, relying instead on the fact there was a clear dispute between the parties. In doing so, they refused to engage with an argument that since part of the dispute in question concerned the validity of a contractual claim, there could not be a separate dispute which had not yet crystallised regarding the true value of the final payment claim. This case also addressed the principle that a dispute cannot be said to have arisen where the claim in question was '*so nebulous and ill-defined that the respondent cannot sensibly respond to it*'.[38] The court again took a practical approach in agreeing that it was unlikely to be appropriate to look at the requests for information following the presentation of the claim and draw an inference about crystallisation from the reasonableness (or lack thereof) in both these requests and a response to them.

12.32 The court also exercised its pragmatism in *MW High Tech Projects UK Ltd v Balfour Beatty Kilpatrick Ltd.*[39] In this case, five notices of delay were served on the defendant by the claimant, each of which led to the alleged crystallisation of a dispute when the defendant failed to respond within 16 weeks, which was the contractual response period. The referring party then served an expert's report that included a critical path analysis and sought a response to its claim within seven days. As none was forthcoming, the dispute was referred to adjudication. The question was whether the expert report was a new notification that triggered a new 16-week notification period, or whether the referring party could rely on the initial expired period. The court held that the report was not a fresh notification. It was not materially different to the claim advanced previously; it was expert analysis to support that claim. The contention argued for by the defendant in the enforcement application required thinking that could be quite fairly characterised as an '*over legalistic*' rather than '*common sense*' approach.

Smash and grab adjudications

12.33 Regular payments form an integral part of the machinery that is construction contracts, and yet it is their non-payment, partial or otherwise, that forms the basis of one of the more controversial issues arising out of the Act. Should a paying party dispute a payment sum and decide to pay less than the amount due to a payee party without issuing a necessary pay less notice within the time required, the payee party is entitled to commence adjudication to recover the sums due to it. The term 'smash and grab' is given because, theoretically, it is a sure-fire way for the payee party to obtain an award in its favour based on the simple fact that the paying party has failed to issue a pay less notice, and not based on the merit of any claim that the contractor was entitled to the sums that were applied for.

12.34 The tactical use of such adjudication to circumvent a merits based dispute as to the correct entitlement was considered in a string of cases culminating in *S&T (UK) Ltd v Grove Developments Ltd.*[40] The court held that the payee party can commence a *consequential*

37 [2019] EWHC 2601 (TCC).

38 *AMEC Civil Engineering Ltd v Secretary of State for Transport* [2004] EWHC 2339 (TCC), [2004] 10 WLUK 256.

39 [2020] EWHC 1413 (TCC).

40 [2018] EWCA Civ 2448.

adjudication following payment of a smash and grab award, in order to ascertain the '*true value*' of a payment and recover and excess payment. *M Davenport Builders Ltd v Greer and another*[41] elucidated the process of resultant true value adjudications, confirming that the paying party generally must first pay the balance of the initial smash and grab adjudication before it can commence a true value adjudication (rather than attempt to set-off any excess owed to them with any payment due to the contractor). This principle applied to both interim and final applications for payment.

12.35 *Broseley London Ltd v Prime Asset Management Ltd*[42] brings *M Davenport* into focus in the current climate for contractors; the court again emphasised the need for the defendant to have paid the sum awarded in the first smash and grab adjudication before embarking on a true value adjudication. It noted that the defendant had waited some six months to bring the second adjudication and drew attention to the concept that '*a failure by the defendant to pursue its cross-claim or challenge with diligence may itself be a bar to a successful application for a stay of execution*'.[43] Rather unfortunately for the defendant, the COVID-19 pandemic took hold during this period which only underlined the damaging economic changes that can befall an industry in six months of dithering. This significantly compromised the defendant's ability to ascertain whether the claimant would have been able to repay the judgment sum at the conclusion of its dispute (due to the economic impact of COVID-19 measures on the claimant's projected turnover), the burden of which fell on the claimant to do so.

12.36 As to the resolution of a true value adjudication, the court tends to resolve disputes by taking a literal approach to contract interpretation, as demonstrated in *Amey LG Ltd v Aggregate Industries UK Ltd*,[44] a case in which the defendant sub-contractor undertook additional work which incurred additional fees and a dispute subsequently arose as to the amount payable. The court maintained that it would not '*rewrite the parties' bargain*', underscoring the need for unambiguous contractual drafting. While this case does not give credence to reading between the lines, it did clarify that parties have a statutory right to adjudicate on interim applications '*at any time*', rather than a first and last chance saloon which would unduly fetter adjudication. A recent case served as an overarching reminder that there are very few instances in which the court will choose to overrule an adjudicator's decision in an initial smash and grab adjudication. In *J Tomlinson Ltd v Balfour Beatty Group Ltd*,[45] the defendant as paying party attempted to dispute an obligation to fulfil a payment (which became due and payable in the absence of any pay less notice) on the basis that wording in the sub-contract rendered the hand delivery of a default payment notice invalid. It did not escape the court that the sub-contract wording was not mandatory, nor was the defendant's argument accompanied with a Part 8 application; thus, the court granted a summary judgment and enforced the initial smash and grab adjudication.

12.37 This recent line of cases only reiterates that smash and grab adjudications are particularly unforgiving for defendants who find themselves on the receiving end of such

---

41 [2019] EWHC 318 (TCC).

42 [2020] EWHC 944 (TCC).

43 Sir Peter Coulson, *Coulson on Construction Adjudication* (4th ed, Oxford University Press 2018) para 17.28.

44 [2019] EWHC 3488 (TCC).

45 [2020] EWHC 1483 (TCC).

proceedings. Whilst there is scope for the defendant to rebut the value of the payment owed by way of a subsequent true value adjudication, it must be minded to act promptly, and in all circumstances, discharge its payment obligations under the initial adjudication before seeking recourse in the second, for fear of invoking the disparagement of the court and further prejudicing its position in what some may describe a 'stick up' rather than an avenue of justified recourse for the claimant.

Reserving the position

12.38 If a party seeks to challenge the jurisdiction of the adjudicator as a defence to adjudication, it is required to reserve its position to do so in submissions and correspondence accordingly, even if done as a matter of course. If a party reserves its position and maintains it throughout the adjudication (generally or specifically), it may be able to refuse to comply with the decision. The other party may then commence proceedings to enforce the adjudicator's decision and the jurisdictional issue can be raised in defence. However, if the challenger fails to reserve the position at the appropriate time or at all, it will be precluded from contesting the adjudicator's decision.

12.39 The case of *Fern and another v West and others*[46] rather disparagingly discounted the defendants' attempt to resist enforcement of an adjudication award based on mere technicalities, that the defendants' names were allegedly not listed correctly in the proceedings. The argument was deemed '*wholly unmeritorious*', not least because the issue was raised before the adjudicator without a proper reservation, but leaving the defendants' argument without '*any prospect of life whatsoever*'. *ICCT Ltd v Sylvein Pinto*[47] serves as the ultimate warning that ignorance is no defence and the failure to suitably reserve one's own position when there are reasonable grounds for doing so equates to a submission to the adjudication process by waiver. The adjudicator is in no way obliged to inform a party of the rights they should otherwise be privy to, but is entitled to accept the appointment and continue with the adjudication, even if one party is exempt from engaging.

12.40 *Ove Arup and Partners International Ltd v Coleman Bennett International Consultancy plc*[48] went one step further by establishing the need for the reliant party to make specific jurisdictional reservations at the appropriate juncture, rather than relying on general catch-alls. The court cautioned against using general reservations that are ultimately insufficient to direct an adjudicator to deal with specific points. A party must give details as to the basis of its assertion before relying on it to dispute an adjudication rather than trying to keep open the '*lines of jurisdictional challenge*' with ambiguous wording. The court referred to the Court of Appeal judgment in *Bresco* when concluding that the purpose of adjudication would be defeated if a party could merely use blanket reservations on jurisdiction, rather than challenging it succinctly.

46 [2019] EWHC 141 (TCC).
47 [2019] EWHC 2134 (TCC).
48 [2019] EWHC 413 (TCC).

Failing to exhaust jurisdiction

12.41 Possibly the most common jurisdictional challenge raised in enforcement proceedings concerns the scope of the decision. The principal rule on this topic is this: the adjudicator must deliver a decision that is responsive to the dispute and the questions referred to him to decide. Provided he does this, even if he makes a mistake that decision will be enforceable. In other words, the scope of his decision must marry with the scope of the dispute. This accords with section 108 of the Act and subparagraphs 9(2) and 23 of the Scheme. The failure of the adjudicator to exhaust his jurisdiction is considered hand in hand with a claim that the adjudicator breached the rules of natural justice by failing to consider an issue, part or all of a submission, or evidence put before him.

12.42 Whilst cases usually concern circumstances where it is alleged that the adjudicator has acted outside of the jurisdiction given to him, recently there has been a quartet of Scottish cases that have considered allegations that the adjudicator failed to exhaust his jurisdiction.

12.43 The first case is *Babcock Marine (Clyde) Ltd v HS Barrier Coatings Ltd*[49] which concerned a dispute arising out of works carried out by HS Barrier Coatings (HSBC) at HM naval base in Scotland. The parties had contracted on the NEC3 Engineering and Construction Short Contract (June 2005), with bespoke Z clause amendments. There were a number of disagreements between the parties, culminating in Babcock terminating the contract. Consequently, HSBC prepared a termination application seeking a payment of just under £1 million. There was further disagreement concerning whether HSBC's termination application was a valid payment notice, and whether a valid pay less notice had been issued in return. An adjudication followed, with the adjudicator finding in HSBC's favour. Babcock paid the sum the adjudicator had awarded and issued a notice of dissatisfaction, as required by the contract. HSBC also issued a notice of dissatisfaction. A second 'valuation' adjudication followed in which Babcock referred the value of the works at the date of termination to adjudication. HSBC had to pay back Babcock £600,000. HSBC did not pay and Babcock commenced enforcement proceedings.

12.44 As an aside, Babcock tried to enforce the adjudicator's decision in England but the Court found that while the courts in Scotland, England and Wales all had jurisdiction, Scotland was the more appropriate forum and granted a stay of the English enforcement proceedings. HSBC resisted enforcement on two grounds: that there had been a material breach of the rules of natural justice in the way the adjudication had been conducted and the adjudicator had failed to exhaust his jurisdiction. The circumstances of the first ground provide an interesting analysis of when an adjudicator can use help and if he should tell the parties. The jurisdiction point arose because while it was clear that the adjudicator had preferred the Babcock's valuation to that put forward by HSBC, he had not explained why he had preferred it. HSBC, it said, was entitled to know why the adjudicator had decided the matter the way that he had.

12.45 The court held that this was an instance of an issue where the acceptance by an adjudicator of one position is sufficient to indicate the reasons for rejecting the other position. This, perhaps, is a frustrating position for HSBC and indeed not a ringing endorsement

49 [2019] CSOH 110.

for the adjudication regime where an adjudicator's bald rejection of a party's position is sufficient reason. HSBC also argued that the adjudicator refused to consider a report setting out HSBC's position on base scope works because, he said, it was not competent for HSBC to advance a valuation that was higher than the termination application. On the evidence the court found that the adjudicator did consider the report. Therefore, whilst adjudication has grown into a sophisticated tool for resolving disputes, it seems that no reasons will suffice as a reason for rejecting a party's position.

12.46 The case of *Field Systems Designs Ltd v MW High Tech Projects UK Ltd*,[50] decided about six weeks later, followed a similar fact pattern. An adjudicator's decision did not refer to a particular issue, or the parties' submissions on it, but he arguably did decide the overarching issue, he listed the documents presented to him and stated that he had given careful consideration to all of them. The case turned on issues 6 and 7 in relation to which it was determined that the parties were £12,000 apart. Had the adjudicator failed to consider the issue so that the decision was unenforceable? The judge noted the distinction between a deliberate and an inadvertent failure to consider an issue. There appeared to the judge to be no example from the English cases cited of a challenge (whether based on a failure to exhaust jurisdiction or a breach of natural justice) succeeding on the ground of an inadvertent, rather than deliberate, failure to consider an issue.

12.47 The court said that it will determine that there will be a failure to exhaust jurisdiction in only the plainest of cases (*DC Community Partnerships Ltd v Renfrewshire Council*[51]), and the failure must be material, in the sense of having had a potentially significant effect on the overall result of the adjudication. The burden of showing this materiality must rest on the party asserting it. In this case, the court considered that the question of whether the adjudicator had exhausted his jurisdiction, by considering the issue, was very finely balanced, but, overall, the judge concluded that consideration of the issue was, at least to some extent, implicit in the findings that the adjudicator made and that the defender has not established that the adjudicator failed to address the point. It was clear, however, that the adjudicator had failed to give reasons, or adequate reasons, for any view reached on the issue, but the inadvertent failure was not material as it had no potentially significant effect on the outcome of the adjudication.

12.48 The third case in this quartet is *Barhale Ltd v SP Transmission plc*.[52] Barhale brought an action to enforce an adjudicator's decision in its favour and SP Transmissions applied to set aside the decision on the grounds that the adjudicator had amongst other things failed to exhaust his jurisdiction by not considering a critical issue raised in their defence. SP Transmission had entered into a contract with Barhale to carry out and construct certain civil works at an electricity sub-station under an NEC3 form of contract, Main Option B, Third Edition, April 2013. There was a dispute about the basis on which payment was entitled for excavation works. Barhale said that it was entitled to BoQ (undefined) rates at actual quantities, whereas SP Transmission argued the entitlement was only for the net volume. The adjudicator accepted Barhale's case and made an award accordingly.

50 [2020] CSOH 17.

51 [2017] CSOH 143, [2018] C.I.L.L. 4073, [2017] 11 WLUK 525.

52 [2021] CSOH 2.

12.49 On the question of failure to exhaust jurisdiction, the court was asked whether such failure had to be deliberate. Lord Tyre reviewed both English and Scottish authorities and determined that he preferred the view expressed by Stuart Smith J in *KNNCoburn LLP v GDHoldings Ltd*[53] to the narrower view of Jefford J in *RGBP&C Ltd v Victory House*.[54] He decided that not every failure amounting to a reason not to enforce a decision has to be deliberate as opposed to inadvertent. There was no clear distinction between deliberate and inadvertent failure to address critical issues in Scottish law. Rather the touchstone was whether the adjudicator has effectively addressed the major issues raised on either side. The dispute before the adjudicator raised four major issues, the second of which was how were the works to be measured, which was not addressed at all. It was clear it was a critical issue raised in both the Response and Rejoinder and it amounted to a failure to exhaust jurisdiction and the decision could not be enforced. It was not necessary to characterise the failure as deliberate though if he was wrong about that Lord Tyre would have said it could fairly be so characterised.

12.50 The most recent case in the quartet, and the only appeal court decision, is that of *Hochtief Solutions AG v Maspero Elevatori S.p.A.*[55] In this case, the Hochtief were an unincorporated joint venture which had designed and constructed a bridge. They engaged Maspero to design, manufacture and install a lift in each tower of the bridge. Progress was slow, so the parties met in Como, Italy to try and resolve matters and recorded a revised arrangement (the '**Como Agreement**') in signed meeting minutes. However, that did not solve matters and Hochtief served a notice of termination, claiming payment of the cost of redoing the lift works. Maspero refused to pay and so Hochtief commenced adjudication. The adjudicator found for Hochtief and in doing so found the Como Agreement fell within the scope of the adjudication and that it constituted a variation of the sub-contract. Maspero did not agree with the decision and declined to make payment and Hochtief made an application to enforce, contending that the adjudicator had exceeded his jurisdiction by wrongly taking into account the Como Agreement. The judge held that: (1) the Como Agreement fell within the scope of the adjudication; (2) the Agreement varied the sub-contract; (3) Maspero had not validly challenged jurisdiction; (4) in any event, if there was a valid challenge, it had come too late.

12.51 Maspero's appeal to the Inner House also failed. First, Lord Woolman considered the wording of the parties' sub-contract and held that the phrase '*a dispute or difference arises under this subcontract*' (clause 19.2.1) was wide enough to allow the adjudicator to decide whether the sub-contract was varied or a separate agreement was entered into. In this regard, the judge relied on the Supreme Court decision in *Bresco Electrical Services Ltd (In Liquidation) v Michael J Lonsdale (Electrical) Ltd*,[56] which held that the statutory words should receive a broad construction. Further, the sub-contract provided for variations (clause 9.3.3) and the parties, as '*reasonable commercial parties*', would have wished variation disputes to be included in any adjudication. Conversely, it was also clear the adjudicator could not have reached a meaningful decision by looking only at the sub-contract. Had he not determined the variation issue, he would have failed to exhaust his

53 [2013] EWHC 2879.
54 [2019] EWHC 1188.
55 [2021] CSIH 19.
56 [2020] UKSC 25, [2021] 1 All E.R. 697, [2020] 6 WLUK 202.

jurisdiction. The parties were therefore bound by his decision that the Como Agreement constituted a variation of the sub-contract, whether it was right or wrong.[57]

Stay of execution

12.52 Where both parties are solvent but the evidence shows that the enforcing party is unlikely to be able to repay the sums awarded, the defendant may make a cross-application to the court for a stay of execution in the event judgment is granted, or to put it another way, a suspension of the consequences of the decision. Stays tend to be limited to situations of near insolvency or financial hardship on the part of the payer, although there are other circumstances in which a stay has exceptionally been granted.

12.53 Evidence is required to demonstrate that the risk of the claimant being unable to repay the sum awarded by the adjudicator is sufficiently great to warrant a stay of execution. Unless the evidence is compelling, the court is unlikely to grant a stay because it would '*cut across* [the principles of enforcement] *if a losing party could avoid enforcement of the decision simply by pleading poverty*'.[58] Further, '*this is an area which is particularly fact sensitive, and each case must be considered in the light of its own particular facts and all the surrounding circumstances*'.[59]

12.54 Recently, a new ground for a stay of execution has been developed. In *Gosvenor London Ltd v Aygun Aluminium UK Ltd*[60] the court declined to lift the stay of execution imposed in *Gosvenor London Ltd v Aygun Aluminium UK Ltd*.[61] The stay was imposed because

> *the evidence demonstrates that there is a real risk that any judgment would go unsatisfied by reason of the Claimant organizing its financial affairs with the purpose of dissipating or disposing of the adjudication sum so that it would not be available to be repaid, then this would also justify the grant of a stay.*

12.55 The court ruled that this ground allows the court to grant a stay even where allegations of fraud were not included in the defence during the adjudication. It has been made clear that the test for this new ground is in essence the same as that for a freezing injunction – that there must be a real risk that assets will be dissipated before the substantive dispute is determined.

12.56 In *Noble Construction Ltd v Wilson*,[62] the defendant (1) offered security prior to issuing court proceedings and (2) relied on the reason highlighted in *Gosvenor* to grant a stay. The court made clear that the offer of security carried little weight; given the statutory scheme was aimed at enforcing the adjudicator's decision, there seemed little point in undermining this decision while a defendant sought an alternative opinion. The court also

57 *Supablast (Nationwide) Ltd v Story Rail Ltd* [2010] EWHC 56 (TCC), [2010] B.L.R. 211, [2010] 1 WLUK 386, considered (paras 39–42).

58 *Volker Stevin Ltd v Holystone Contracts Ltd* [2010] EWHC 2344 (TCC), *per* Coulson J at [27].

59 *Partner Projects Limited v Corinthian Nominees Limited* [2011] EWHC 2989 (TCC), *per* Edwards-Stuart J at [51].

60 [2019] EWHC 3619 (TCC).

61 [2018] EWHC 227 (TCC).

62 [2019] EWHC 1907 (TCC).

rejected the attempt to rely on the principles found in this ground, making clear the need to demonstrate both a probable inability on the claimant's part to repay the judgment sum and a likelihood that they would seek to dissipate or dispose of its assets. Neither criteria came close to being met in this case.

Fraud

12.57 A more uncommon ground that may be relied upon to render an adjudication invalid is the defence of fraud. As expected, the reliance on fraud as a defence comes with lofty thresholds to meet; clear and unambiguous evidence of fraud showing a '*real prospect of success*' is paramount, and it must be raised at the earliest reasonable opportunity, rather than used as a shield at enforcement despite knowledge of the fraud predating enforcement, otherwise it will fail. Whilst it is unclear as to whether fraud can be used as the basis for a claim under adjudication as such a claim would not arise under a contract, but as a tort, it can be used as a defence to a claim in adjudication and if successful, would overturn an adjudication decision.

12.58 As established in several cases such as *SG South v King's Head Cirencester*,[63] the defence of fraud is treated differently in accordance to *when* it is raised, *ie*, during an adjudication or the enforcement process. In *BM Services Inc Ltd v Greyline Builders Ltd*,[64] the defendant stated that the adjudicator ignored the allegations of fraud that it raised against the claimant during adjudication, but the adjudicator rebuffed the allegations due to the abject lack of evidence from the defendant to support its case. Whilst the adjudicator referred to the allegations in his decision as a collusion which led to an overvaluation, it could not have constituted an independent defence without the defendant adducing further evidence. Again, in *Grandlane Developments Ltd v Skymist Holdings Ltd*,[65] a summary judgment was granted in favour of the claimant as the defendant failed to substantiate its defence of fraud with clear and unambiguous evidence. The defendant's further applications for adjournment and a stay of execution were refused for the same reasons – none of the evidence that was submitted by the defendant went remotely far enough to justify an adjournment or a stay of execution.

12.59 However, pursuing fraud as a defence is not an entirely thankless endeavour, as shown in *PBS Energo AS v Bester Generacion UK Ltd*.[66] The defendant resisted a summary judgment on the basis that it was procured by fraud, which was upheld as a '*properly arguable*' case by the court, as the evidence made clear that false representations were made to the defendant and there was good evidence that the claimant knew the representations were false when they made them. It was also held that the allegations of fraud could not reasonably have been brought at the initial adjudication, as disclosure of the key documents forming the evidence for fraud had not been given in time for the fraud to be identified during the course of the litigation. As a result, the adjudicator's decision as a whole was deemed invalid and unenforceable against the defendant, as it was held to have

63 [2009] EWHC 2645 (TCC).
64 [2018] EWHC 3884 (TCC).
65 [2019] EWHC 747 (TCC).
66 [2019] EWHC 996 (TCC).

been procured by fraud. The claimant attempted to appeal the decision[67] on two grounds: the defendant had not filed a defence alleging fraud, so it should not have been able to rely on such a defence, and the judge failed to distinguish between granting a summary judgment and enforcing the judgment, and instead ought to have granted the summary judgment and then stayed the judgment. The appeal was dismissed, and it was noted by the judge that, '*in a case where substantial allegations of fraud are found to be arguable, the right course will usually be ... to refuse summary judgment ... no question of a stay of execution then arises*'.

12.60 The defence of fraud, while the ideal defence to the enforcement of an adjudication as it essentially nullifies the cause of action, proves to be a high bar to clear. Parties seeking such a defence must be sure to have collated clear and unambiguous evidence as to the fraud so as to present a '*properly arguable*' case, and present such a defence at the earliest reasonable opportunity, rather than waiting until enforcement to deal the hammer blow.

The introduction of low value adjudication schemes

12.61 Although adjudication as a dispute resolution process is less costly than litigation or arbitration, the debate surrounding the affordability of adjudication was fuelled in 2014 when in *Walker Construction (UK) Ltd v Quayside Homes Ltd*,[68] the defendant accumulated £345,000 of legal costs on a claim worth £23,400, leading many to question the affordability of adjudication. *Walker* is an extreme example, but it became even more apparent that smaller and medium sized companies were deterred from using adjudication as a form of dispute resolution due to spiralling costs outweighing the value of the claim.

12.62 As part of the Consultation, the Business, Energy & Industrial Strategy (the '**BEIS**') sought input on the affordability of adjudication, to which 23% of responses believed that the costs of adjudication had prevented them from using it as a dispute resolution procedure on more than 20% of cases. Further, the average cost of adjudication over the last five years was £28,000,[69] and it was suggested that adjudication no longer provides a cost-effective remedy where the value of the claim is less than £30,000.[70]

12.63 Such complaints prompted industry bodies to react by launching low value adjudication procedures, with the TeCSA being the first past the post with its Low Value Disputes Adjudication Service pilot on 21 June 2019 (the '**LVD AS**'). Following its successful pilot, the LVD AS came into effect on 1 January 2020.

12.64 The LVD AS provides certainty as to the costs of the adjudicator for claims up to £100,000, and limits the fees an adjudicator can charge with their fee directly linked to the amount claimed. In the event that during the course of the adjudication it becomes apparent that the claim has been undervalued, the adjudicator is permitted to (1) resign and claim their fees up to the date of resignation; (2) charge up to the relevant fee cap; or (3)

67 *PBS Energo AS v Bester Generacion UK Ltd* [2020] EWCA Civ 404.
68 [2014] EWCA Civ 93.
69 BEIS Summary of Responses, page 22.
70 BEIS Summary of Responses, page 21.

if the claim exceeds £100,000, continue with the adjudication but charge their normal fees subject to a daily cap.[71]

12.65 On 1 May 2020, the Construction Industry Council ('**CIC**') followed suit and published the Low Value Disputes Model Adjudication Procedure ('**LVD MAP**'), which aims to encourage the use of adjudication where the value of the claim is even lower than the threshold set for the LVD AS, typically £50,000 or less, and the issues in dispute are relatively straightforward. The LVD MAP is a separate set of adjudication rules whereby the LVD AS applies when TeCSA makes the relevant adjudicator appointment. As the LVD AS is not a separate set of rules, unlike the LVD MAP, the parties do not need to agree to use the procedure, and absent any explicit terms in the contract, a party can unilaterally apply to the TeCSA to use the LVD AS without the consent of the opposing party.[72]

12.66 For claim values of less than £50,000, the adjudicator's fee under the LVD MAP is fixed between £2,000 and £6,000. Where the value of the claim exceeds £50,000, the parties may elect to negotiate the adjudicator's fees or the adjudicator is permitted to write to the parties setting out the basis of their proposed fees.[73] The LVD AS caps the adjudicators fees between £2,000 to £5,000 for claims worth between £10,000 and £100,000.

12.67 Whilst there is no restriction on the type of financial claims that can be submitted to the LVD AS, it will only apply to claims for the payment of money of a specified amount, and a party will be prohibited from using the LVD AS if the amount sought is not yet quantified.[74] The LVD AS is therefore not suitable for claims for declarations as to the meaning of contractual terms, but most relevant for parties seeking unpaid fees. Theoretically speaking, a party may submit any type of dispute to the LVD MAP which sets out a simplified adjudication procedure whereby the dispute is decided on a documents only basis.[75] There are, however, a number of rules set to limit the complexity and size of disputes referred to it, and although the LVD MAP contains a helpful boilerplate adjudication clause for inclusion in construction contracts,[76] it is for the appointed adjudicator to decide whether the dispute is suitable for the LVD MAP (absent any reasonable objection from the respondent).[77] The adjudicator may deem the dispute unsuitable in the event that, amongst other things, (1) the value of the claim is in excess of £50,000, (2) a non-financial remedy is sought, (3) the documents in the submission exceed one A4 lever arch file, and/or (4) the dispute in hand is prima facie not suitable for the adjudicator to make its decision on a documents only basis.[78]

12.68 In the interests of reducing costs and streamlining the adjudication process, the LVD MAP confers additional powers on the adjudicator than the LVD AS, namely to (1)

71 TeCSA Low Value Disputes Adjudication Service: Guidance for Users of the TeCSA LVD Adjudication Service, 1 January 2020, [13] ('**LVD AS Guidance**'). <https://tecsa.org.uk/download/summary-of-tecsa-lvd-service//> (Last accessed 10 March 2021).

72 [4] LVD AS Guidance.

73 Section 45, CIC Low Value Disputes Model Adjudication Procedure, 1st Edition, May 2020: <http://cic.org.uk/admin/resources/cic-low-value-disputes-model-adjudication-procedure-first-edition.pdf> (Last accessed 10 March 2021) ('**LVD MAP**').

74 [8] LVD AS Guidance.

75 Sections 23 and 1, LVD MAP.

76 Section 7, LVD MAP.

77 There are currently ten participating adjudication nomination bodies who have agreed to maintain a panel of qualified adjudication fully compliant with the LVD MAP.

78 Section 48, LVD MAP.

request only the key documents reasonably required to decide the dispute; (2) obtain only particular submissions they require, including written responses; and (3) give directions as to deadlines, time limits and the length of written documents.[79] If, without sufficient cause, a party fails to comply with any direction of the adjudicator, the adjudicator may continue in the absence of that party.[80] Although the TeCSA explains that parties can expect the adjudicators to limit the number and length of submissions made, there are currently no restrictions on the size of submissions.[81]

12.69 Both the LVD AS and LVD MAP have effectively provided a simplified adjudication process which contains explicit measures to keep a cap on costs, and has been welcomed in a system where the successful party is generally not entitled to recover its costs subject to an award. An added bonus of the LVD MAP is that it aims to provide a platform on which newly qualified adjudicators can gain experience – a helpful and progressive tool for the adjudication regime. Notwithstanding this, neither of these low value adjudication procedures prescribe any mechanism to limit the costs of the parties' legal representatives, which as we have learned from *Walker*, may be the source of the problem. Whilst the LVD MAP and LVD AS may be a step in the right direction, it may not be the cost-effective solution SMEs have been looking for, not at least until we see mechanisms to limit the involvement of, or keep a cap on the costs of, legal representatives.

A consultation on the 2009 Act

12.70 Five years following the enactment of the 2009 Act and 2011 Scheme, the BEIS undertook a post-implementation review to determine whether the amendments had secured their objectives (the '**Consultation**'). The BEIS pulled responses from a range of stakeholders including construction and civil engineering businesses, business representative organisations and trade bodies, legal representatives, consultants, arbitrators and adjudicators, in addition to formal submissions from representative associations and individuals. The Consultation sought to determine a more general review on the existing adjudication and payment framework, including (1) the effectiveness of the 2011 amendments, (2) general questions on the adjudication regime and its misuse, and (3) the affordability of adjudication.[82] The results of the Consultation were belatedly published on 26 February 2020. There was input from only 54 respondees in addition to '*wider stakeholder engagement*' including trade associations and organisations.[83] The responses are as a result heavily contractor focused and the BEIS forewarns that the results of the Consultation are only '*indicative*'.[84]

79 Section 23, LVD MAP.

80 Section 23, LVD MAP.

81 [16] LVD AS Guidance.

82 BEIS, 2011 *Changes to Part 2 of the Housing Grants, Construction and Regeneration Act 1996: A consultation to support a Post-Implementation Review: Summary of responses*, page 2, <https://assets.publishing.service.gov.uk/government/uploads/system/uploads/attachment_data/file/868629/2011-changes-to-part-2-of-the-housing-grants-construction-and-regeneration-act-1996-summary-responses.pdf> ('**BEIS Summary of Responses**') (Last accessed 10 March 2021).

83 BEIS Summary of Responses, page 4.

84 BEIS Summary of Responses, page 5.

Costs

12.71 The 2009 Act introduced a prohibition on parties agreeing to who will be liable for the costs of the adjudication until the notice of adjudication has been issued, with any such agreement prior to service deemed ineffective.[85] The parties are still permitted to confer jurisdiction on the adjudicator to allocate his expenses between them, provided he does so in writing pursuant to the contract or following the notice of adjudication. The intention of the amendment was to promote adjudication as a cost-effective remedy; however, the Consultation revealed that 76% of the responses believed that there had been no change in the average cost of an adjudication.[86] Further, the majority of respondents claim to have been a party to contracts which included contractual agreements on the allocation of party costs.

In writing

12.72 The 2009 Act repealed section 107 of the 1996 Act, abolishing the requirement for a construction contract to be in writing for a right to adjudicate to arise. Many acclaimed the amendment in light of the fact that construction contracts were frequently oral or subject to oral variations; however, it was also sharply criticised for the uncertainty it created, as explained by Mr Justice Fraser in *RSC Contracts v Conway*:[87]

> *Section 107 was, in my view, unthinkingly repealed, meaning that (as here) adjudicators have now to grapple with entirely oral contracts, with all the uncertainty and contention that such a situation can engender ... in this case, the result of the repeal of section 107 has been a process lasting 16 months and the incurring of large sums by way of costs. That is the opposite of the quick, cheap dispute resolution service that adjudication was intended to provide.*

The responses to the Consultation reported that the respondents were largely divided on how the lifting of the restriction had affected the costs of adjudication, with the majority asserting that it had created no change. Some respondents believed that the repeal had extinguished the most common challenges to the jurisdiction of the adjudicator.[88] Some suggested that the amendment had reduced adjudication costs by removing a source of legal argument, whereas others argued oral contracts had increased costs by importing an intermediary exercise of establishing the agreed terms into the adjudication process.[89]

Payment

12.73 It is generally acknowledged that the 2009 Act did not revise the underlying defective payment culture of the industry, but did address some poor practices. A surprising statistic of the Consultation revealed that only 57% of responses reported that over 75%

85 Section 108A of the 1996 Act.
86 BEIS Summary of Responses, page 6.
87 [2017] EWHC 715 (TCC).
88 BEIS Summary of Responses, page 10.
89 BEIS Summary of Responses, page 10.

of contracts they had come across in the past year were compliant with the Act.[90] The most common examples of non-compliance included (1) pay-when-paid clauses, (2) lack of clarity of content and timing of payment notices and (3) the allocation of costs to the sub-contractor.[91] Although perhaps uncommon in main construction contracts, such disobedience is perhaps more prevalent in smaller construction contracts or sub-contracts. Wider stakeholders reported that the payer often looks to '*push the* [Act] *to its limit*' by linking payment provisions to an event which the payer controls.[92] It is, however, important to bear in mind that the court will not hesitate to strike out a clause incompatible with the Act.[93]

12.74 The amendments removed the restriction on who could serve a payment notice and introduced a fallback provision where in the absence of a payment notice, the payee is permitted to submit its own notice. Of those who had relied on the payee notice provision, 66% believed that it had been effective in establishing the amount due to be paid.[94] Criticisms included its inefficiency in establishing the amount due with those contending that it simply prompted the payer to re-value the amount.

12.75 The amendments prohibited the use of any contractual term that makes payment conditional on the performance of obligations under an alternative contract ('pay-when-paid' clauses). However, the majority of respondents had come across payment clauses in contracts that were dependent on the performance of obligations under other contracts, the most common of which were for retentions and cross-contract set-off.[95]

12.76 The amendments introduced the ability for the payer to suspend performance of some of its obligations under the contract in the event of non-payment, whilst also requiring the party in default to meet their reasonable costs and expenses of doing so. The respondents indicated that it is not common to suspend performance, with 67% of the responses from contractors and contractors' trade associations indicating that they had either not suspended work, or had suspended on less than 5% of their contracts over the last five years.[96] Other respondents commented that the threat of suspension can be an effective means of focusing the attention on the payer, and is often used in discussions as leverage.[97] The right of suspension therefore appears to have been well received by the industry – even if only to be used as a bargaining chip.

Access to adjudication

12.77 The overriding objective of the 2009 Act was to expand the accessibility of the adjudication regime. The Consultation sought information on the frequency of adjudications over the last five years, with 49% of responses reporting as having been involved in more adjudications.[98] Of those who suggested that the frequency of adjudications was decreasing,

90 BEIS Summary of Responses, page 10.
91 BEIS Summary of Responses, page 10.
92 BEIS Summary of Responses, page 11.
93 *Manor Asset Limited v Demolition Services Limited* [2016] EWHC 222 (TCC).
94 BEIS Summary of Responses, page 13.
95 BEIS Summary of Responses, pages 11 and 14.
96 BEIS Summary of Responses, page 15.
97 BEIS Summary of Responses, page 16.
98 BEIS Summary of Responses, page 7.

this was attributed to the fact that more disputes were being settled prior to adjudication in order to avoid rising costs and preserve commercial relationships.[99] Those who felt that the number of adjudications had increased attributed this partly to the extension to oral contracts, and expressed that in general, confidence had increased in adjudication as a dispute resolution procedure.[100] The Adjudication Society in its Report No 18, December 2019,[101] reported a 13% increase in the number of referrals to adjudicator nominating bodies from May 2017 to April 2018 and May 2018 to April 2019. The Adjudication Society reported that the latest results indicate a continuing trend of year-on-year growth in the number of referrals, although the general trend line indicates a continuous fluctuation of rising and falling referral numbers.[102] The statistics therefore do not clearly testify to an increase in the number of adjudications.

Clarity of the adjudication process

12.78 With regard to the clarity of the adjudication regime, just over half of legal representatives considered that the amendments had increased clarity, a similar proportion of adjudicators reported that clarity had been reduced, whilst contractor organisations reported no change.[103] Criticisms of the amendments included that the framework itself had layers of complexity, and that whilst the framework improved clarity on timing and the amount of payment, amendments coupled with the sheer size of some construction contracts can introduce conflicting provisions and confusion.[104]

Conclusion

12.79 The Consultation revealed mostly positive change in the adjudication regime, although the absence of uniform agreement by the respondents on certain issues suggests that there is still scope for improvement. Issues remain with the 1996 Act that were not addressed by the 2011 amendments, for example, the complexity and uncertainty in what constitutes and falls outside of the scope of '*construction operations*' in section 105(2) and excluding many industries or types of operation that many consider should be included. The BEIS has ambiguously explained that it will '*now take forward the Post-Implementation Review*'[105] and so it can be expected that at some point in the future a proposal for further amendments to the Act will be published, although it is unclear from the Consultation what amendments will foment. Those who recall the long drawn out and painful process that attached to the 2009 Act amendments will not be filled with optimism that the process for implementing further changes will be any more effective.

99 BEIS Summary of Responses, page 8.
100 BEIS Summary of Responses, page 8.
101 Adjudication Society, Report No 18, December 2019 <www.adjudication.org/sites/default/files/Adjudication%20Report%2018%20-%20December%202019%20Rev%20A.pdf> ('**Report No 18**') (Last accessed 10 March 2021).
102 Report No 18, page 5.
103 BEIS Summary of Responses, page 12.
104 BEIS Summary of Responses, page 12.
105 BEIS Summary of Responses, page 29.

CHAPTER 13

Statistory adjudication in Canada

Duncan W Glaholt

Overview

13.1 Almost a quarter century after the introduction of statutory construction adjudication in the United Kingdom, and about 20 years after that concept was first adopted in Australia and New Zealand, Ontario became the first Canadian jurisdiction to adopt adjudication as part of its *Construction Act* on October 1, 2019. This chapter will present the adjudication model as introduced in Ontario and will attempt to situate that scheme internationally.

13.2 In Ontario, adjudication was introduced together with a new prompt payment regime. Under this statutory regime, once a contractor delivers a 'proper invoice' to an owner, that owner is obliged to pay that proper invoice within 28 days of receipt, unless the owner has issued a notice of non-payment to the contractor within 14 days of receiving the proper invoice. A contractor receiving payment of a proper invoice must then forward that payment down to its responsible subcontractors within seven days of receiving payment, unless the contractor has issued a notice of non-payment to a particular subcontractor. Similarly, a subcontractor receiving payment must pay a sub-subcontractor within seven days of receiving payment unless the subcontractor has issued a notice for non-payment, and so on down the construction pyramid.

13.3 This prompt payment regime is buttressed by a mandatory statutory adjudication process on all projects, with the exception of limited AFP project issues. Statutory adjudication in Ontario is administered by a single provincially authorized nominating authority, called Ontario Dispute Adjudication for Construction, or 'ODACC'. ODACC registered adjudicators provide parties with interim binding decisions within compressed timeframes based on a single payment cycle. Statutory adjudication in Ontario is described as 'targeted', in the sense that it applies only to the subject matters of dispute listed in the *Construction Act*, namely:

- **a** The valuation of services or materials provided under the contract.
- **b** Payment under the contract, including in respect of a change order, whether approved or not, or a proposed change order.
- **c** Disputes that are the subject of a notice of non-payment under Part I.1.
- **d** Amounts retained under section 12 (set-off by trustee) or under subsection 17 (3) (lien set-off).
- **e** Payment of a holdback under section 26.1 or 26.2.
- **f** Non-payment of holdback under section 27.1.
- **g** Any other matter that the parties to the adjudication agree to, or that may be prescribed.

If a duly appointed adjudicator issues a determination under the *Construction Act* that an amount should be paid to a party, that payment must be made promptly, failing which the party entitled to payment may suspend work and receive reasonable costs incurred as a result of the resumption of work in addition to the amount of the determination.

13.4 The adjudicator's determination remains binding upon the parties until displaced by an order of a court, or an arbitrator's award under the *Arbitration Act, 1991*, or by written agreement between the parties.

13.5 An adjudicator's decision can be judicially reviewed by Ontario's Divisional Court, but only with leave sought within 30 days of the determination at issue, and leave applications may be dismissed without reasons. It is notable that seeking leave does not stay a party's payment obligations unless the Divisional Court orders otherwise. The grounds for setting aside an adjudicator's determination under s. 13.18 (5), should leave be granted, are more related to issues of natural justice than correction of error:

- a The applicant participated in the adjudication while under a legal incapacity.
- b The contract or subcontract is invalid or has ceased to exist.
- c The determination was of a matter that may not be the subject of adjudication under this Part, or of a matter entirely unrelated to the subject of the adjudication.
- d The adjudication was conducted by someone other than an adjudicator.
- e The procedures followed in the adjudication did not accord with the procedures to which the adjudication was subject under this Part, and the failure to accord prejudiced the applicant's right to a fair adjudication.
- f There is a reasonable apprehension of bias on the part of the adjudicator.
- g The determination was made as a result of fraud.

The remedial aim of statutory adjudication

13.6 While statutory adjudication has its skeptics and critics, it is welcomed by the construction industry itself. The legislative amendments bringing prompt payment and statutory adjudication to Ontario were passed without a single vote to the contrary. Prior to the enactment of these amendments, it had been well-established by research and investigation in Ontario and in other jurisdictions that without a prompt payment and statutory adjudication regime, construction project disputes impaired cash flow and magnified issues that burdened all stakeholders, many of them innocent, for years leading in turn to unnecessary bankruptcies, artificial restriction on entry into the construction industry marketplace, and massive financial inefficiencies. Without such a regime, construction industry disputes remove working capital and human resources from the economy unnecessarily and on a significant scale.[1]

13.7 The need for legislative intervention was confirmed by an Ipsos Reid survey commissioned by Prompt Payment Ontario, an unincorporated association of Ontario trade contractors interested in payment security and late payment issues. The Ipsos Reid report claimed that the average age of current construction industry receivables was 61.3 days,

1 Bruce Reynolds, Sharon Vogel, *Striking the Balance: Expert Review of Ontario's Construction Lien Act* (Toronto: Publications Ontario April 30, 2016) p 202.

that approximately 84.7% of the participants reported receivables aged more than 30 days, with 18% carrying receivables 90 days or more. Over the previous three years, 67.6% or two thirds of overdue invoices that were outstanding for 30 days were outstanding for over 45 days.[2] Between 2002 and 2013, the average collection period in the Ontario construction industry increased from 57.3 days to 71.1 days, while all the other industries remained stable at about 47 days[3].

13.8 Traditional lien and trust remedies continue to serve an important purpose in regulating construction industry credit, but until recently no traditional lien legislation or other legislation has addressed the core issue of *timing* of payment and *timing* of dispute resolution. Provincial lien and trust remedies are designed to provide remedies and procedures after-the-fact; prompt payment and statutory adjudication are intended to provide remedies during the course of construction.[4]

13.9 Similarly, insurance and bonds also do not provide a satisfactory answer to concerns over timing. Insurance indemnifies for insured losses and does not resolve performance disputes. While the surety is effective in redistributing construction industry losses, including injection of new capital in some cases even during the period of construction, there are often associated delays, defences, legal challenges, and transaction costs, all of which are ultimately resolved in judicial or arbitral process after-the-fact.

13.10 The enactment of statutory prompt payment obligations along with a companion adjudication regime now fill this gap. Prompt payment obligations buttressed by summary adjudication processes now allows a quick determination of entitlement issues associated with payment, binding on an interim basis and enforceable as if by order of the court, facilitating orderly cash flow and striking a balance among competing interests.[5]

The authorized nominating authority

13.11 Like other international models, Ontario chose to provide for an authority in charge of qualifying and nominating adjudicators, the Authorized Nominating Authority. Unlike other models such as the United Kingdom one, however, Ontario chose to limit the number of such authorities to a single one, with a view to ensuring quality control.[6]

13.12 Ontario's authorized nominating authority, ODACC, plays a central role in the adjudication process. It is responsible for administering construction-related adjudications and for training and qualifying adjudicators. On July 18, 2019, the Attorney General designated ADR Chambers Inc. as Authorized Nominating Authority. The role of ODACC in administering adjudications and certifying adjudicators is set out in s. 13.3 of the *Construction Act*, set out next, and will be discussed following:

---

2 ibid, p 178.

3 Prompt Payment Ontario, *Trade Contractor Survey Results,* Ipsos Reid, November 2015, cited *ibid.*

4 Duncan W Glaholt, 'The Adjudication Option: The Case for Uniform Payment & Performance Legislation in Canada' (2006) 53 CLR (3d) 8.

5 Bruce Reynolds, Sharon Vogel, *Striking the Balance: Expert Review of Ontario's Construction Lien Act* (Toronto: Publications Ontario April 30, 2016) p 202.

6 Bruce Reynolds, Sharon Vogel, *Striking the Balance: Expert Review of Ontario's Construction Lien Act* (Toronto: Publications Ontario April 30, 2016) p 234.

13.3 Duties and powers of Authority

Duties

(1) The Authority shall,

(a) develop and oversee programs for the training of persons as adjudicators;
(b) qualify persons who meet the prescribed requirements as adjudicators;
(c) establish and maintain a publicly available registry of adjudicators;
(d) appoint adjudicators for the purposes of subsection 13.9 (5); and
(e) perform any other duties of the Authority set out in this Part or that may be prescribed for the purposes of this Part.

Powers

(2) The Authority may,

(a) subject to the regulations, set fees, costs or other charges related to the administration of adjudication under this Part, including fees, costs or charges for the training and qualification of persons as adjudicators or for the appointment of adjudicators, and require their payment; and
(b) exercise any other power of the Authority set out in this Part or that may be prescribed for the purposes of this Part.

Setting fees

(3) In setting the fees, costs and charges referred to in clause (2) (a), the Authority may, subject to the regulations, specify their amounts or the method for determining the amounts.

Fee retention

(4) Money collected by the Authority under clause (2) (a),

(a) is revenue belonging to the Authority and not public money within the meaning of the *Financial Administration Act*; and
(b) may be retained and used by the Authority for its own account.

Basic concepts

Statutory minimums

13.13 Section 108 of the UK *Construction Act* sets out minimum procedural requirements governing adjudications. If those minimums are not met in the contract, a statutory default scheme called the Scheme for Construction Contracts will apply.

13.14 Similarly, section 13.6 of the Ontario Act provides that an adjudication must be conducted in accordance with the adjudication procedures set out in the Act and the regulations, and in accordance with any additional adjudication procedures that may be set out in the contract or subcontract. Adjudication procedures set out in a contract or subcontract apply only to the extent that they do not conflict with the Act and the regulations, and their application is subject to the exercise of the adjudicator's powers under section 13.12.

13.15 In other words, the Act also sets out minimums for adjudication. The parties may agree to more, but the statutory minimums must be met.

Targeted adjudication

13.16 The various jurisdictions in which adjudication has been adopted have taken different approaches with respect to the scope of disputes that can be adjudicated. Those scopes range from all disputes with a few enumerated exceptions, such as in the UK and New Zealand, to Singapore and Australia, where only payment matters can be referred to adjudication.[7]

13.17 Ontario has adopted a middle ground. As outlined earlier, only disputes with respect to the following matters may be referred to adjudication in Ontario:

- a The valuation of services or materials provided under the contract.
- b Payment under the contract, including in respect of a change order, whether approved or not, or a proposed change order.
- c Disputes that are the subject of a notice of non-payment under Part I.1.
- d Amounts retained under section 12 (set-off by trustee) or under subsection 17 (3) (lien set-off).
- e Payment of a holdback under section 26.1 or 26.2.
- f Non-payment of holdback under section 27.1.
- g Any other matter that the parties to the adjudication agree to, or that may be prescribed.[8]

Section 13.5(4) of the Act stipulates that an adjudication may only address a single matter, unless the parties and the adjudicator agree otherwise.[9] Parties may also agree to consolidate multiple adjudications.[10] If the same matter or related matters in respect of an improvement[11] are the subject of disputes to be adjudicated in separate adjudications under subsections 13.5(1) and (2), the contractor may, in accordance with the regulations, nevertheless require the consolidation of the adjudications over the objections of the other party.[12]

13.18 Case law from the UK gives the word 'dispute' in adjudication legislation its ordinary meaning. UK courts have said that they 'should not adopt an over legalistic analysis of what the dispute between the parties are; instead [they] will determine in broad terms what the disputed claim, assertion or position is'.[13]

7 Bruce Reynolds, Sharon Vogel, *Striking the Balance: Expert Review of Ontario's Construction Lien Act* (Toronto: Publications Ontario April 30, 2016) p 213.

8 *Construction Act*, s 13.5(1) and (2).

9 *Construction Act*, RSO 1990, c C.30, s 13.5(4).

10 *Construction Act*, RSO 1990, c C.30, s 13.8.

11 *Construction Act*, RSO 1990, c C.30, s 1.

12 *Construction Act*, RSO 1990, c C.30, s 13.8(2).

13 James Pickavance, *A Practical Guide to Construction Adjudication* (Chichester: Wiley Blackwell 2016) at 100, citing *Allied P & L Limited v Paradigm Housing Group Limited* [2009] EWHC 2890 (TCC).

13.19 In Canada, 'dispute' has been defined simply to mean a 'conflict or controversy, especially one that has given rise to a particular lawsuit'.[14] If an issue has arisen in the context of an attempt to avoid dispute, the situation is not yet ripe for arbitration, for example.[15] In other words, it is not enough that the parties' interests are opposed on a matter. There must be some 'formulated dispute',[16] subject to party agreement to the contrary.[17]

13.20 It remains to be seen how adjudicators and courts will interpret the added words 'under the contract' in s. 13.5(1). In the United Kingdom, where parties can refer 'any dispute arising under the contract' to adjudication, it has been held that while adjudication is not available for non-contractual claims such as a negligence claim against a contractor, claims for rectification, restitution, and specific performance have been allowed to proceed to adjudication under the specific wording of the contract.[18]

Proper invoice

13.21 The trigger for the obligation to pay under the new prompt payment regime is delivery of a 'proper invoice'. Parties may refer a dispute to adjudication that flows from a proper invoice under a contract or subcontract. 'Proper invoice', as discussed earlier, is defined in the Act.

Binding until and unless overturned

13.22 Just like in all other jurisdictions with statutory construction adjudication, an Ontario adjudicator's determination is binding on an *interim* basis. Under s. 13.15(1), the determination is binding on the parties to the adjudication until a determination of the matter by a court, a determination of the matter by way of an arbitration conducted under the *Arbitration Act, 1991*, or a written agreement between the parties respecting the matter. Nothing in the Act prevents a party from commencing proceedings in court or before an arbitrator to finally determine the matter at any time. All the Act does is to keep the money flowing while that process takes place.

Enforcement of adjudicator's determination

13.23 Under most international adjudication schemes, an adjudicator's decisions can be enforced through court proceedings. In the UK, for example, they are enforced through enforcement proceedings in the Technology and Construction Court, which has fashioned

14 *Sport Hawk USA Inc v New York Islanders Hockey Club* [2008] OJ No 1732 at para 8 (Ont SCJ), supp. reasons [2008] OJ No 2294 (Ont SCJ).

15 *Sport Maska Inc v Zittrer* [1988] SCJ No 19, [1988] 1 SCR 564 (SCC).

16 *Cummings v Solutia SDO Ltd* [2008] OJ No 3259, 49 BLR (4th) 307 (Ont SCJ), aff'd [2009] OJ No 2618, 59 BLR (4th) 23 (Ont CA); *Sport* Maska Inc v Zittrer [1988] SCJ No 19, [1988] 1 SCR 564 (SCC).

17 *Huras v Primerica Financial Services Ltd* [2001] OJ No 3318, 55 OR (3d) 449 (Ont CA). This paragraph is cited from DW Glaholt and M Rotterdam, *The Law of ADR in Canada* (2nd ed, Markham: LexisNexis 2018) 70–71.

18 James Pickavance, *A Practical Guide to Construction Adjudication* (Chichester: Wiley Blackwell 2016) 115–116.

a procedure whereby enforcement applications are dealt with promptly.[19] In Ontario, adjudicators' determinations are enforceable as orders of the court. In other words, there is no need to go to court to obtain judgment on a determination; the determination is akin to a judgment, albeit an *interim* one. While an application to set aside a determination will only rarely succeed based on the very strict test stipulated by s. 13.18, nothing in the Act prevents a party from commencing proceedings in court or before an arbitrator to finally determine the matter. All the Act does is to keep the money flowing while that process takes place.

Adjudication timelines in Ontario

13.24 With respect to statutory timelines within which the whole process, from notice of adjudication to determination, must take place, Ontario sits somewhere near the middle when compared to other jurisdictions. Generally speaking, in Ontario, a determination will be made within 45 days of the notice of adjudication. The process is therefore longer than the extremely short 10 days in the Australian West Coast model or the 14 days on the Australian East Coast and in Singapore, but significantly shorter than the 133 allowed in Malaysia.

13.25 Readers are referred to the ODACC website, https://odacc.ca, for current information as to adjudication processes and suggested timelines. Consistent with its mandate, ODACC has provided a complaints procedure, an adjudicator registry, fee schedules, a custom ODACC online dispute resolution system, and more.

ODACC predetermined processes

13.26 Statutory adjudication applies province wide. Thus, the expectations of parties with relatively low dollar value claims must by met and managed. Low dollar value disputes required low cost solutions. The issue of course is one of proportionality. In order to address this issue in a province-wide scheme, ODACC has created four predetermined adjudication processes which may be summarized as follows:

- a **Two-Page Written Adjudication:** Adjudication in writing only, with parties' submissions and photographs limited to two pages each (not including the contract, and disputed invoice, which may be required by the adjudicator), and the adjudicator's reasons are expected to be approximately one to two pages.
- b **Five-Page Written Adjudication:** Adjudication in writing only, with the parties' submissions and photographs limited to five pages each (not including the contract, and disputed invoice which may be required by the adjudicator), and the adjudicator's reasons are expected to be approximately one to two pages.
- c **Five-Page Written Adjudication plus Ten Pages of Documents:** Adjudication in writing only, with the parties' submissions and photographs limited to

19 *The Technology and Construction Court guide* (2nd ed, London: HM Courts & Tribunals Service, 2005), s. 9.2; accessible at: <>www.gov.uk/government/publications/technology-and-construction-court-guide>.

five pages each (not including the contract and disputed invoice, which are mandatory), plus additional documents, excerpts, and/or witness statements limited to ten pages. The adjudicator's reasons are expected to be approximately five pages.

d **Oral Webcast Adjudication, Ten Page Submissions and Documents:** Adjudication in writing only, with submissions and photographs limited to ten pages each (not including the contract and disputed invoice, which are mandatory), plus additional documents, excerpts, and/or witness statements limited to 25 pages. The oral presentation will not be in person and will be conducted by videoconference or teleconference. Reasons are expected to be approximately five pages.

e The fifth option is that the adjudication process will be determined during a teleconference with the adjudicator.

While certain processes restrict the page limit of submissions and/or supporting documentation, all of the processes allow for submission of the disputed contract and invoice. All four predetermined processes share the same four suggested first steps, all triggered by the appointment of an adjudicator on the first day. Step-by-step, the ODACC process would proceed as follows:

a **Day 1:** The adjudicator is selected by the parties or appointed by ODACC.

b **Day 5:** The claimant submits a copy of the disputed invoice and construction contract. The claimant also submits its submissions, depending on the value of the claim, the types of documents allowed in the predetermined process, and the page limit of those supporting documents.

c **Day 7:** The adjudicator determines the balance of the adjudication process and communicates that to the parties, including the respondent's deadline to respond to the claimant's submission.

d **Day 12:** The respondent submits a response, the length and content of which depends on the value of the claim, the types of documents allowed in the predetermined process, and the page limit of those supporting documents.

Following these initial four steps, the remaining steps are suggested as follows:

- Predetermined processes one through three all contemplate adjudicators' draft decisions being released to ODACC on Day 20.
- Predetermined process four contemplates an oral hearing on Day 18 followed by submission of the draft decision to ODACC on Day 25.
- Where no predetermined process is chosen, the adjudicator may suggest a site visit on Day 17, an oral hearing on Day 20, the appointment of an assistant on Day 22, and a draft determination to ODACC on Day 28.

All of the predetermined processes state that a decision will be released by ODACC 35 days after an adjudicator is appointed pursuant to the requirements in the Act. Parties can suggest a process to the adjudicator and the adjudicator can suggest a process, and it will be a rare case in which the adjudicator will not follow the process agreed by the parties.

13.27 This statute contemplates exceptionally short timeframes for certain stages of an adjudication. Among the shortest timelines is a four-day deadline for a claimant to provide its complete submission package after the appointment of an adjudicator.

Statutory timelines

13.28 A party giving the other party written notice of adjudication must include in that notice the name of a proposed adjudicator.[20] If the parties cannot agree on the proposed adjudicator within four days, or if the proposed adjudicator does not consent to conducting the adjudication within four days, the party who gave the notice of adjudication must request that an Adjudicator Nominating Authority ('ANA') make the appointment.[21] The ANA has seven days from receiving that request to nominate the adjudicator.[22]

13.29 No later than five days after an adjudicator is agreed upon or nominated, the party giving notice of adjudication must provide the adjudicator with a copy of the originating notice, a copy of the relevant contract or subcontract, and any documents it intends to rely on during the adjudication.[23]

13.30 The adjudicator must make a 'determination' of the referred issues no later than 30 days after receiving these documents. This period may be extended by 14 days to a total of 44 days at the adjudicator's request, but only if the parties agree.[24] The parties may agree on further extensions.[25] A party who is required by an adjudicator's determination to pay an amount to another person must pay that amount no later than ten days after the determination has been communicated to the parties.[26]

13.31 Any motion for leave to bring an application for judicial review of the determination must be filed with the Divisional Court within 30 days of the determination.[27]

Choosing an adjudicator

13.32 An adjudication may only be conducted by an adjudicator listed in a registry to be established and maintained by ODACC.[28] A party wishing to initiate adjudication must name an adjudicator in the notice of adjudication.[29] If no agreement can be reached on an adjudicator, the parties may request that ODACC nominate an ODACC registered adjudicator for them.[30] Importantly, and unlike their counterparts in the UK or New Zealand, for example, the parties' choice of an adjudicator cannot be made part of the underlying contract or subcontract.[31]

20 *Construction Act*, RSO 1990, c C.30, s 13.7(1)(d).
21 *Construction Act*, RSO 1990, c C.30, s 13.9(2) and (4).
22 *Construction Act*, RSO 1990, c C.30, s 13.9(5).
23 *Construction Act*, RSO 1990, c C.30, s 13.11.
24 *Construction Act*, RSO 1990, c C.30, s 13.13(1) and (2)(a).
25 *Construction Act*, RSO 1990, c C.30, s 13.13(2)(b).
26 *Construction Act*, RSO 1990, c C.30, s 13.19(2).
27 *Construction Act*, RSO 1990, c C.30, s 13.18(2).
28 *Construction Act*, RSO 1990, c C.30, ss 13.9(1); 13.3(1)(c).
29 *Construction Act*, RSO 1990, c C.30, s 13.7(1)(d).
30 *Construction Act*, RSO 1990, c C.30, s 13.9(2).
31 *Construction Act*, RSO 1990, c C.30, s 13.9(3).

Minimum qualifications

13.33 An adjudicator's minimum qualifications are set out in ss. 3 to 5 of O. Reg. 306/18. Aside from having at least ten years of relevant experience in the construction industry,[32] adjudicators must complete a training program designed by ODACC called *Construction Adjudication and ODACC Orientation Program* and, upon completion, may apply to ODACC for certification.[33]

13.34 The Ontario Act is in line with other jurisdictions, almost all of which require a minimum number of years of experience in the construction industry, but it does not go as far as Ireland, for example, where the *Construction Contracts Act* provides that an adjudicator must be qualified as a barrister or solicitor; a fellow of the Chartered Institute of Arbitrators; a chartered member of the Institution of Engineers of Ireland; a registered professional as defined in section 2 of the *Building Control Act 2007*; or a person with equivalent qualifications obtained in any other Member State of the European Union.[34]

13.35 Matters such as conflicts of interest and related procedural issues are governed by the ODACC Adjudicator's Code of Conduct.[35]

13.36 As for adjudicator qualifications, it has been suggested that a capable adjudicator should possess excellent technical ability (*ie*, knowledge of construction industry and legal issues, experience and awareness of current developments), procedural competence (*ie*, awareness of procedural requirements common in adjudications), and case management skills (*ie*, the ability to steer the adjudication through its very dense timelines).[36] They should possess strong writing skills (*ie*, the ability to write clearly and concisely). Obviously, they should have sufficient time to devote to the adjudication.

Preparing a claim for adjudication

13.37 No more than five days after the appointment of the adjudicator, the notice of adjudication must be provided to the adjudicator, and a copy of the contract and all documents the party intends to rely on during the adjudication must be provided to the adjudicator and to the other party.[37]

The notice of adjudication

13.38 The notice of adjudication is a crucial document that requires careful attention. In the United Kingdom, the purpose of the notice has been described as follows:

> The purposes of such a notice are first, to inform the other party of what the dispute is; secondly, to inform those who may be responsible for making the appointment of an adjudicator, so that the correct adjudicator can be selected; and finally, of course, to define

32 Which may include experience working in the industry as an accountant, architect, engineer, quantity surveyor, project manager, arbitrator, or lawyer: O Reg 306/198, s 3(3).

33 <https://odacc.ca/en/adjudicators/certification-process/> (accessed 10 January 2021).

34 *Construction Contracts Act 2013*, s 8(6).

35 O Reg 306/18, s 7.

36 James Pickavance, *A Practical Guide to Construction Adjudication* (Chichester: Wiley Blackwell 2016) 165–166.

37 *Construction Act*, RSO 1990, c C.30, s 13.11.

> the dispute of which the party is informed, to specify precisely the redress sought, and the party exercising the statutory right and the party against whom a decision may be made so that the adjudicator knows the ambit of his jurisdiction.[38]

It has further been held that it is the notice of adjudication, not the subsequent and more detailed referral notice served in UK adjudications, that defines the scope of the adjudication.[39]

Detailed submissions

13.39 In the UK, the notice of adjudication is followed by a referral notice, a more detailed statement of the party's case that has been described as the equivalent of a statement of case in an arbitration.[40] Pickavance suggests the following contents for the referral notice:

> The referral notice should set out the referring party's case in full. Often this will include an overview of the case and the redress sought, the relevant contractual provisions relied on, the factual background to the dispute and claims, and the legal basis for making the claim and a detailed statement of the redress sought.
>
> A focused chronology of events is appropriate more often than not, although if it is a long chronology, it may be better to consign it to the supporting documents and cherry-pick events to insert into the submission.[41]

While such a document is not mandated by the Ontario *Construction Act*, it is likely that in all but the most straightforward disputes, similar documents will be submitted to the adjudicator here as well. For the predetermined processes discussed earlier, this will all be part of what the parties submit.

Documents relied upon

13.40 Documents relied upon must be submitted to the adjudicator no later than five days after the notice of adjudication. The Act does not prescribe what types of document may be admissible. The scope of production should be informed by the type of dispute referred. Voluminous documentation might be necessary where the valuation of services is concerned, while in straightforward cases of non-payment of holdback in the absence of a **s. 27.1** notice, for example, a few documents (or even no documents) might suffice. Evidence of fact or expert witnesses may be made without formality.

13.41 Adjudicators are expected to issue practical, efficient, and effective directions respecting disclosure of reliance documents while ensuring in the extremely tight timeframes available that each party has an opportunity to review the documents produced.[42]

---

38 *Ken Griffin & John Tomlinson, T/A K & D Contractors v Midas Homes Limited*, 2000 WL 1544681 (TCC).

39 *J G Walker Groundworks Ltd v Priory Homes (East) Ltd* [2013] EWHC 3723 (TCC).

40 James Pickavance, *A Practical Guide to Construction Adjudication* (Chichester: Wiley Blackwell 2016) 174. See generally Sir Peter Coulson, *Coulson on Construction Adjudication* (3rd ed, Oxford: Oxford University Press 2015) at 18.25 et seq.

41 James Pickavance, *A Practical Guide to Construction Adjudication* (Chichester: Wiley Blackwell 2016) 177.

42 O Reg 306/18, s 20.

Serving the claim

13.42 Both the notice of arbitration and the documents a party intends to rely upon must be 'given' to the other party. Under s. 87 of the Act, 'giving' documents means serving them in any manner permitted under the Rules of Civil Procedure or by certified or registered mail addressed to the intended recipient at the recipient's last known mailing address. ODACC is developing a platform that will facilitate service of documents as well as communications between the parties and adjudicators.

Responding to a claim

13.43 Under s. 13.11.1, a party has a right to respond to a notice of arbitration. Section 17 of O. Reg. 306/18 states that the right of a party to respond to a notice of adjudication is subject to the directions of the adjudicator as to the time and manner of the delivery of the response. Section 13 of the Act gives the adjudicator the general power to conduct the adjudication in the manner he or she considers appropriate and to issue directions respecting the conduct of the adjudication. At a minimum, the responding party will be entitled to bring any defence within the scope of the dispute.[43] It has been held in the UK, however, that a defence that the amount claimed is exaggerated, or that there are amounts to be deducted from the amount claimed, should only be admitted where the respondent has served a valid withholding notice or pay less notice in respect of the disputed claim.[44] Of course, the parties can expressly make provision for a response in their contract or subcontract.[45]

Rebuttals, replies, sur-rebuttals, and sur-replies

13.44 The Act does not provide for replies or further submissions. In lien actions, replies require leave, as the Rules of Civil Procedure regarding replies are inconsistent with the Act, which does not otherwise provide for such a pleading. Given the wide powers given to an adjudicator to conduct the adjudication, it is likely entirely within the adjudicator's discretion to allow or disallow replies and sur-replies in appropriate circumstances, although given the extremely tight timelines, it would seem unlikely that such material would be allowed except in rare circumstances.

In-person hearings will be the exception, not the rule

13.45 Subject to party agreement, it is up to the adjudicator whether or not an in-person hearing takes place. Section 13.12(1) of the Act allows the adjudicator to issue directions regarding the conduct of the adjudication; to take the initiative in ascertaining the relevant facts or law; to obtain the assistance of an expert to determine a matter of fact in question; and to conduct an on-site inspection of the improvement.

43 James Pickavance, *A Practical Guide to Construction Adjudication* (Chichester: Wiley Blackwell 2016) 181.

44 *ibid*, at 181–182.

45 *Construction Act*, RSO 1990, c C.30, s 13.6(2).

13.46 Presumably, all of these details will be the subject of party submissions and an early procedural order. The adjudicator may convene meetings to discuss such matters. Given the very tight time frames mandated by the Act, however, it is likely that most adjudications will be decided on a documents-only basis. That is the experience after more than 20 years in the United Kingdom.[46]

13.47 Should the adjudicator find it necessary to request an in-person hearing, it is important that the adjudicator identify the issues the parties must address to allow the parties to focus their limited time available on those issues.[47] While oral submissions at hearings will not be the norm, there will be scenarios in which they may be useful or even necessary. As explained in *Coulson on Construction Adjudication*:[48]

> It is rare for an adjudicator to require oral evidence to be given in an adjudication. However, this is principally because of the time constraints, rather than the existence of any sort of rule that outlaws the reception of such oral evidence in adjudication. Indeed, there will be some disputes in respect of which the adjudicator may have no alternative but to hear oral evidence and make decisions on the basis of which evidence or oral explanation he accepts, if he is going to resolve the dispute properly. Take again the example of the dispute as to what was said at a particular site meeting. If the adjudicator is faced with two entirely conflicting statements as to the contents of the discussions on a particular occasion, he would probably have to arrange for a hearing at which this evidence can be tested orally. It is almost inevitable that he is going to have to conclude that one or other of the parties is mistaken as to what was said at the meeting and it is unlikely, in the absence of any other relevant contemporaneous documentation, that he could reach such a conclusion without hearing oral evidence. Likewise, if extensive experts' reports have been attached by both parties to the referral notice and/or the response, the adjudicator may feel it necessary to arrange a short hearing at which the principal points advocated by each expert can be tested by way of cross-examination.

The adjudicator's determination

Form and timing

13.48 The adjudicator must make a determination no later than 30 days after receiving the copy of the contract or subcontract and supporting documentation from the party that gave the notice of adjudication. That deadline can be extended at any time before its expiry, either on the adjudicator's request and the written consent of the parties, for a period of no more than 14 days; or upon the written agreement of the parties and the adjudicator's consent, for the period specified in the agreement.[49] A determination made by an adjudicator after the date so determined is of no force or effect.[50]

---

46 Sir Peter Coulson, *Coulson on Construction Adjudication* (3rd ed, Oxford: Oxford University Press 2015) at 19.12; James Pickavance, *A Practical Guide to Construction Adjudication* (Chichester: Wiley Blackwell 2016) 186. According to a survey cited by the author, only about 30% of adjudications in the UK involve some kind of interview, meeting, or conference call.

47 James Pickavance, *A Practical Guide to Construction Adjudication* (Chichester: Wiley Blackwell 2016) 492.

48 Sir Peter Coulson, *Coulson on Construction Adjudication* (3rd ed, Oxford: Oxford University Press 2015) at 19.12.

49 *Construction Act*, RSO 1990, c C.30, s 13.13(1) and (2).

50 *Construction Act*, RSO 1990, c C.30, s 13.13(5).

13.49 The adjudicator's determination must be reasoned and written. In Ontario, the determination of an adjudicator is admissible as evidence in court.[51] As the adjudication is summary in the extreme and likely conducted on a very preliminary record, it is unlikely in most cases that determinations will carry much weight. The adjudicator must provide the parties with an electronic copy of the determination on the day it is made and further provide them with a certified copy of the determination no later than five days following the making of a determination.[52]

Interim binding nature of determination

13.50 Determinations are binding on an interim basis and enforceable as if orders of the court.[53] There is no need to go to court to obtain judgment on a determination; the determination is akin to a judgment, albeit an interim one.

13.51 An application to set aside a determination will only rarely succeed based on the very strict test stipulated by s. 13.18. Nothing in the Act prevents a party from commencing proceedings in court or before an arbitrator to finally determine the matter. This is a substantial improvement on the entirely unsatisfactory situation that prevailed prior to these reforms.

Costs

13.52 Generally, the parties to an adjudication will bear their own costs. If, however, the adjudicator determines that a party to the adjudication has acted in a manner that is frivolous, vexatious, an abuse of process, or other than in good faith, the adjudicator may require that party to pay some or all of the other party's costs, any part of the adjudicator's fee that would otherwise be payable by the other party, or both.[54]

13.53 The parties and the adjudicator may try and negotiate an agreed upon fee. ODACC will list suggested hourly rates and will state whether adjudicators are willing to adjudicate on a flat fee basis. If the parties and the adjudicator cannot agree, they may turn to ODACC, in which case set fees approved by the Minister will apply.

Compliance with determination

13.54 Within ten days of receiving the determination, the party ordered to make payment in the determination must pay the amount it is ordered to pay.[55] That requirement is made subject only to any requirement that the payor retain holdback.[56]

13.55 If such payment is not made to a contractor or subcontractor, the contractor or subcontractor may suspend further work under the contract or subcontract until the party ordered to pay pays the amount required to be paid under the determination, together with

---

51 *Construction Act*, RSO 1990, c C.30, s 13.13(6) and (7).

52 O Reg 306/18, s 22.

53 *Construction Act*, RSO 1990, c C.30, s 13.20(1).

54 *Construction Act*, RSO 1990, c C.30, ss 13.16 and 13.17.

55 *Construction Act*, RSO 1990, c C.30, s 13.19(2).

56 *Construction Act*, RSO 1990, c C.30, s 13.19(1).

any interest accrued on that amount and the reasonable costs incurred by the contractor or subcontractor as a result of the suspension of work.[57]

Application to set aside adjudicator's determination

Statutory grounds

13.56 There are very limited grounds on which a court may set aside an adjudicator's determination. These grounds mirror the grounds on which arbitral awards may be set aside:[58]

- a A party participated in the adjudication while under a legal incapacity.
- b The contract or subcontract is invalid or has ceased to exist.
- c The determination was of a matter that may not be the subject of adjudication under this Part, or of a matter entirely unrelated to the subject of the adjudication.
- d The adjudication was conducted by someone other than an adjudicator.
- e The procedures followed in the adjudication did not comply with the procedures to which the adjudication was subject under this Part, and the failure to comply prejudiced the applicant's right to a fair adjudication.
- f There is a reasonable apprehension of bias on the part of the adjudicator.
- g The determination was made as a result of fraud.

An application to set aside an adjudicator's determination must be made no later than 30 days after the determination is communicated to the parties. Such application does not stay the enforcement of the determination unless a court orders otherwise.

Natural justice

13.57 In virtually all jurisdictions in which adjudication has been enacted, an adjudicator's determination can be set aside if there has been a denial of natural justice. While it is true that the Ontario Act does not mention natural justice by name, there is little doubt that natural justice is a fundamental requirement of adjudication in Ontario. Section 13.18.(5) requires that the procedures followed must provide the parties with a 'fair' adjudication. The Expert Review held as follows:

> A summary of each jurisdiction's enforcement procedures is found in Appendix C. To oversimplify, these jurisdictions generally provide that an adjudicator's decision will be enforced barring a breach of natural justice or want of jurisdiction. These fundamentals should carry forward into adjudication in Ontario.

In a different context, it has been held that the adjudication of a dispute is quasi-judicial in character and the rules of natural justice must be strictly observed.[59]

---

57 *Construction Act*, RSO 1990, c C.30, s 13.19(5).
58 *Construction Act*, RSO 1990, c C.30, s 13.18.
59 *Greenhut v Scott* [1975] 4 WWR 645 (BC SC).

13.58 Similarly, domestic arbitration legislation also does not expressly mention natural justice, but requires that the parties be treated equally and fairly. It is clear that arbitrations are subject to natural justice.[60] In *Kane v University of British Columbia*,[61] the Supreme Court of Canada enumerated the following fundamental principles a quasi-judicial tribunal must adhere to:

13.59 The following propositions, in my view, govern the outcome of this appeal:

1. It is the duty of the courts to attribute a large measure of autonomy of decision to a tribunal, such as a board of governors of a university, sitting in appeal, pursuant to legislative mandate. The board need not assume the trappings of a court. There is no *lis inter partes*, no prosecutor and no accused. The board is free, within reason, to determine its own procedures, which will vary with the nature of the inquiry and the circumstances of the case. Members of the board are drawn from all constituencies of the community. They normally serve without remuneration in the discharge of what is frequently an arduous and thankless form of public service. Few, if any, of the members of the board will be legally trained. It would be wrong, therefore, to ask of them, in the discharge of their quasi-judicial duties, the high standard of technical performance which one may properly expect of a court. They are not fettered by the strict evidential and other rules applicable to proceedings before courts of law. It is sufficient that the case has been heard in a judicial spirit and in accordance with the principles of substantial justice: per Lord Parmoor in *Loc. Govt. Bd. v Arlidge*, [1915] A.C. 120 at 140 (H.L.). Let me make it clear that in this appeal nothing has been said which in any way impugns the integrity or bona fides of any member of the Board of Governors of the University of British Columbia.
2. As a constituent of the autonomy it enjoys, the tribunal must observe natural justice which, as Harman L.J. said (*Ridge v Baldwin*, [1963] 1 Q.B. 539, [1962] 1 All E.R. 834 at 850, reversed on other grounds [1964] A.C. 40, [1963] 2 All E.R. 66 (H.L.)) is only 'fair play in action'. In any particular case, the requirements of natural justice will depend on 'the circumstances of the case, the nature of the inquiry, the rules under which the tribunal is acting, the subject-matter that is being dealt with, and so forth': per Tucker L.J. in *Russell v Norfolk (Duke)*, [1949] 1 All E.R. 109 at 118. To abrogate the rules of natural justice, express language or necessary implication must be found in the statutory instrument.
3. A high standard of justice is required when the right to continue in one's profession or employment is at stake: *Abbott v Sullivan*, [1952] 1 K.B. 189 at 198, [1952] 1 All E.R. 226; *Russell v Norfolk (Duke)*, supra, at p. 119. A disciplinary suspension can have grave and permanent consequences upon a professional career.
4. The tribunal must listen fairly to both sides, giving the parties to the controversy a fair opportunity 'for correcting or contradicting any relevant statement prejudicial to their views': *Bd. of Education v Rice*, [1911] A.C. 179 at 182 (H.L.); *Loc. Govt. Bd. v Arlidge*, supra, at pp. 133 and 141.

60 DW Glaholt and M Rotterdam, *The Law of ADR in Canada* (2nd ed, Markham: LexisNexis 2018) 91.
61 [1980] 1 SCR 1105.

5. It is a cardinal principle of our law that, unless expressly or by necessary implication empowered to act *ex parte*, an appellate authority must not hold private interviews with witnesses (de Smith, Judicial Review of Administrative Action, 3rd ed. (1973), p. 179) or, a fortiori, hear evidence in the absence of a party whose conduct is impugned and under scrutiny. Such party must, in the words of Lord Denning in *Kanda v Govt. of Malaya*, [1962] A.C. 322 at 337 (P.C.), 'know the case which is made against him. He must know what evidence has been given and what statements have been made affecting him: and then he must be given a fair opportunity to correct or contradict them ... whoever is to adjudicate must not hear evidence or receive representations from one side behind the back of the other'. In *Errington v Minister of Health*, [1935] 1 K.B. 249 (C.A.), Greer L.J. held that a quasi-judicial officer must exercise powers in accordance with the rules of natural justice, and must not hear one side in the absence of the other (p. 268):

> ... if ... he takes into consideration evidence which might have been, but was not, given at the public inquiry, but was given *ex parte* afterwards without the owners having any opportunity whatsoever to deal with that evidence, then it seems to me that the confirming Order was not within the powers of the Act.

Since adjudicators fulfil a quasi-judicial role, there is no reason why they should not be held to these principles.

13.60 It has been held, however, that the principles of natural justice must be weighed against the time constraints inherent in the adjudication model, as well as the provisional nature of the decision.[62] A leading UK text interprets this as follows:

In effect, this means that the goalposts of what might amount to a breach of natural justice in other circumstances are shifted in adjudication. Only in instances where it is clear that there is actual or apparent bias, or a party's right to a fair hearing has been impinged, such that it is likely to have had a significant effect on the outcome of the adjudication, will there be a breach of natural justice.[63]

Other Canadian jurisdictions

Federal

13.61 In 2017, Public Services and Procurement Canada retained the authors of the Ontario Report to conduct a review of the federal statutory scheme and make recommendations to accelerate payment within the construction industry on federal government projects. On August 2, 2018, their report, titled *Building a Federal Framework for Prompt Payment and Adjudication in Canada*,[64] was released. The main recommendations contained in

62 *Try Construction Ltd v Eton House Group Ltd* [2003] EWHC 60 (TCC); cited in James Pickavance, *A Practical Guide to Construction Adjudication* (Chichester: Wiley Blackwell 2016) 363.

63 James Pickavance, *A Practical Guide to Construction Adjudication* (Chichester: Wiley Blackwell 2016) 363.

64 B Reynolds, S Vogel, *Building a Federal Framework for Prompt Payment and Adjudication in Canada*; accessible at <www.cca-acc.com/wp-content/uploads/.../Building-a-Federal-Framework-Report.pdf> (last accessed 10 January 2021).

the Federal Report include the following, as summarized by the Manitoba Law Reform Commission:[65]

- The Government of Canada should enact legislation introducing prompt payment and adjudication on federal construction projects.
- The preferred model for prompt payment legislation is that adopted by Ontario as opposed to the model which to date has found its way into various stand-alone Bills, including Bill S-224 previously introduced in the Senate.
- The consequences of a failure to pay should be modelled after Ontario's legislation. Specifically, where a party fails to pay, the following consequences should be legislatively available: the right to commence an adjudication, mandatory interest accrued, the right to suspend work without breach of the claimant's contract where the adjudicator's determination isn't paid within a period of time, and resumption of work contingent on payment of the determination amount, interest, and costs incurred as a result of the suspension.
- Prompt payment and adjudication legislation should apply to all federal departments and federal Crown corporations that do federal construction work under their own contracting authority.
- The federal government should consider adding a trust regime to the current legislation to provide additional protection or, in the alternative, mandatory bonding requirements.

Bill C-97, the *Budget Implementation Act, 2019 No. 1* was introduced on April 8, 2019, and received Royal Assent on June 21, 2019. Division 26 of that Act enacts the *Federal Prompt Payment for Construction Work Act*, which adopts aspects of the Ontario prompt payment and adjudication model.

British Columbia

13.62 In May, 2019, Bill M223, the *Prompt Payment (Builders Lien) Act*, was introduced in British Columbia. The Bill provides for a prompt payment regime loosely based on the Ontario *Construction Act*, but without reference to adjudication beyond an undertaking to conduct an adjudication that forms part of the notice of non-payment requirements.[66]

Manitoba

13.63 In November 2018, the Manitoba Law Reform Commission published *The Builders' Liens Act: A Modernized Approach*.[67] The Commission recommends the

65 Manitoba Law Reform Commission, *The Builders' Liens Act of Manitoba: A Modernized Approach* (Winnipeg: MLRC 2016); accessible at <www.manitobalawreform.ca/pubs/pdf/136-full_report.pdf> (last accessed 10 January 2021).

66 See B Reynolds, J Little, 'British Columbia Introduces Prompt Payment Legislation', <www.singleton.com/2019/06/british-columbia-introduces-prompt-payment-legislation/> (last accessed 10 January 2021).

67 Manitoba Law Reform Commission, *The Builders' Liens Act of Manitoba: A Modernized Approach* (Winnipeg: MLRC 2016); accessible at <www.manitobalawreform.ca/pubs/pdf/136-full_report.pdf> (last accessed 10 January 2021).

implementation of a prompt payment regime as well as a private adjudication system akin to the adjudication system established by Part II.1 of Ontario's *Construction Act*, with such modifications as are necessary to synchronize its contents with other remedies in the Act.

13.64 Also in 2018, a private member's bill, Bill 218, *The Prompt Payments in the Construction Industry Act*, passed Second Reading on April 24, 2018, but was not proceeded with. However, the Law Reform Commission held that, based on the reliance in Bill 218 upon certain definitions and other provisions found in the Act which illustrates the close connection of prompt payment with the remedial schemes already in place, any new prompt payment process ought to be incorporated within *The Builders' Liens Act* and not legislated as a stand-alone statute.

New Brunswick

13.65 The Legislative Services Branch of the New Brunswick Office of the Attorney General intends to implement changes based on those in Ontario. In its Law Reform Notes #41, the Branch states as follows:[68]

> In our view, a prompt payment scheme similar to that in Ontario should be adopted in New Brunswick. As in Ontario, it should apply to both the public and private sector, to all construction projects (from small home renovations to P3s), at all levels of the construction pyramid (with the exception of wages).

Nova Scotia

13.66 Nova Scotia introduced a prompt payment and adjudication regime in Bill 119, which went through all readings and received Royal Assent in less than a month. The Bill went through first reading on March 15, 2019, and received Royal Assent on April 12, 2019, but has not yet been proclaimed.

Saskatchewan

13.67 On November 20, 2018, the Saskatchewan government introduced Bill 152, *The Builders' Lien (Prompt Payment) Amendment Act, 2018*. The Act received Royal Assent on May 15, 2019. The 'in force' date has not yet been announced, but it is anticipated that proclamation will occur sometime in July of 2021. The Ministry of Justice for the Province of Saskatchewan is now inviting comments before introducing regulations to accompany the Act.

68 Legislative Services Branch, Office of the Attorney General, Government of New Brunswick, 'Law Reform Notes (#41)' issued May 2018, available online at: <http://www2.gnb.ca/content/dam/gnb/Departments/ag-pg/PDF/en/LawReform/Notes41.pdf> (last accessed 10 January 2021).

CHAPTER 14

Statutory adjudication in Singapore

Toh Chen Han[1]

Introduction

14.1 Statutory adjudication remains an unusual form of alternative dispute resolution. It became available in Singapore in 2005, following the enactment of enabling legislation the year before. Singapore was only the fourth country to adopt this form of dispute resolution, after the United Kingdom, Australia and New Zealand. Statutory adjudication has since been adopted by (at least parts of) three other countries, namely Malaysia, the Republic of Ireland and Canada. As things stand, therefore, only seven countries in the world today have adopted statutory adjudication, fewer than half of the common law jurisdictions, and not a single civil law country amongst them.

14.2 As with its territorial reach, there are limits to statutory adjudication's utility as an adjective due to the distinct lack of uniformity in approach between jurisdictions. Significant differences exist as regards the kinds of disputes covered, overall timeframes and the degree of party autonomy over procedure and adjudicator appointments.

14.3 Singapore's statutory adjudication scheme is based on the New South Wales model, and is underpinned by two key pieces of legislation, both of which are publicly accessible on Singapore Statutes Online, a website maintained by the Attorney-General's Chambers.[2]

14.4 The first is the Building and Construction Industry Security of Payment Act (Chapter 30B), widely referred to in Singapore's construction industry as the '***Security of Payment Act***', the '***SOP Act***' or simply '***SOPA***'. This legislation was passed in November 2004, and came into force on 1 April 2005. It underwent its first major amendment following the passing of the Building and Construction Industry Security of Payment (Amendment) Act in 2018, which came into effect on 15 December 2019.

14.5 Most of the reforms apply even in respect of contracts made before 15 December 2019. There are broadly two exceptions to this:[3]

a The pre-amendment Section 10 (which deals with how and when payment claims may be made) continues to apply in respect of contracts made before 15 December 2019; and

1 The author acknowledges with immense gratitude the invaluable input and time contributed by Melissa Heng Li Ya, Tom Heading and Chan Yong Neng. The law is stated as at 29 October 2020.

2 <https://sso.agc.gov.sg/Index> (last accessed 29 October 2020).

3 Section 25 of Building and Construction Industry Security of Payment (Amendment) Act.

b The pre-amendment provisions will continue to apply in respect of payment claims served before 15 December 2019, and the various subsequent procedural steps taken pursuant to such payment claims.

14.6 In other words, all of the 2019 amendments (apart from those relating to Section 10) apply to payment claims made from 15 December 2019, and subsequent steps taken pursuant to such claims, even in respect of underlying contracts made before that date.

14.7 The SOP Act is supplemented by a subordinate legislation in the form of the Building and Construction Industry Security of Payment Regulations ('**SOP Regulations**'), which has seen a number of updates, most recently on 15 December 2019.

14.8 The primary motivation behind the introduction of statutory adjudication in Singapore was to address serious cash flow problems that plagued its construction industry. The SOP Act was conceived of in around 2002, in the context of a prevalence of poor payment behaviour on the part of some employers, which would be replicated down the contractual chain, creating severe cash flow issues for many at various levels.

14.9 The principal object of the SOP Act was to tackle such issues, by helping to unlock cash flow for contractors, sub-contractors and suppliers through the introduction of a quick and inexpensive process for securing payment. As the then Minister of State of National Development explained in Parliament, in the context of the recent statutory reforms:[4]

> *The [SOP Act] was introduced in 2005 to facilitate cash flow in the construction industry. The SOP Act introduced a fast and low-cost adjudication mechanism to deal with payment disputes. For a typical construction project, the developer pays the main contractor, who in turn pays its sub-contractors or suppliers. As a construction project can take several years to complete, progress payments are made periodically throughout the project duration. Parties along the value chain often fund their own work first, and collect payment thereafter. So, it is critical that parties are paid in a timely manner for work done or goods supplied.*

14.10 Despite these laudable aims, the initial response to statutory adjudication in Singapore was decidedly cool. In its inaugural year (2005), there was a grand total of one statutory adjudication. The number of cases however gradually rose over subsequent years, to about 130–170 cases per year in the period from 2009 to 2012, and significantly greater numbers in the years since, indicating a growing level of confidence and acceptance of statutory adjudication as a means of alternative dispute resolution in Singapore.[5] There have been over 400 adjudication applications each year since 2014.[6]

4 Mr Zaqy Mohamad (Minister of State for National Development), 'Building and Construction Industry Security of Payment (Amendment Bill)', 2nd reading, *Singapore Parliamentary Debates, Official Report*, 13th Parl, 2nd Sess, Vol 94, No 84 (2 October 2018).

5 Figures that follow are based on data from adjudication cases handled by the Singapore Mediation Centre from 1995 to 2014, taken from Singapore Academy of Law Reform Committee, 'Proposals for Amending the Building and Construction Industry Security of Payment Act' (September 2015).

6 *Supra* note 4.

Figure 14.1 Adjudication applications by year (2005–2014)

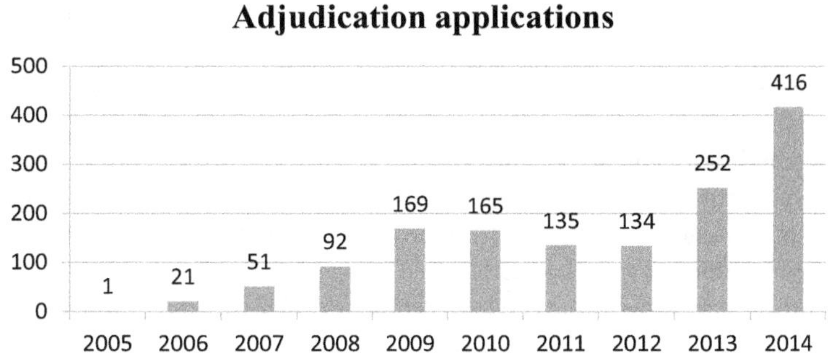

14.11 Unlike jurisdictions such as the United Kingdom and New Zealand, which have cast the scope of their statutory adjudication regimes to cover a broader range of disputes, Singapore has followed the New South Wales model in confining statutory adjudication to disputes over monetary entitlements, under the terms of specified contracts, for work done or for goods or services supplied.

14.12 This excludes claims for damages (whether in contract or in tort) and time extensions. Only claims 'up the contractual chain' can be pursued, *eg*, claims by contractors against employers, or sub-contractors against main contractors, but not *vice versa*.

14.13 In this regard, Singapore's statutory adjudication regime bears similarity with those of Ireland, Malaysia and the Australian states that have followed the New South Wales model, *eg*, Queensland, Victoria, South Australia, the Australian Capital Territory, Tasmania and most recently Western Australia.

14.14 By contrast, statutory adjudication in the United Kingdom and New Zealand covers a wider range of payment-related and, in some cases, non-payment-related disputes, for example claims for time extensions and for damages in contract and in tort.

Confidentiality

14.15 Statutory adjudication proceedings under the SOP Act are confidential.

14.16 This precludes disclosure of any statement made or document created for the purposes of an adjudication and any information that is, in the course of the adjudication, disclosed for the purposes of the adjudication.[7]

14.17 There are of course exceptions, for example where there is consent in respect of the disclosure, where the relevant information is already in the public domain, and where disclosure is necessary for the purposes of enforcement or any proceeding before a court or tribunal or any other dispute resolution proceeding.[8]

7 Section 33 of SOP Act.
8 Section 33(2) of SOP Act.

General scope and applicability: 'construction' and 'supply' contracts

14.18 Singapore's statutory adjudication regime generally applies only in respect of construction work undertaken in Singapore, or goods or services supplied in relation to such construction work, and even then, only in the context of two prescribed categories of contract, namely '*construction*' and '*supply*' contracts.

14.19 The distinction between these two categories is quite technical, possibly even abstruse, but nevertheless highly significant in that different procedures apply to each, and severe consequences can result from invoking the wrong procedure. The accurate characterisation of contracts is thus critical.

14.20 A '*construction contract*' is an agreement under which a party either undertakes to perform '*construction work*' or '*services*'.[9]

14.21 For these purposes, '*construction work*' means:[10]

- a the construction, alteration, repair, restoration, maintenance, extension, demolition or dismantling of permanent or temporary buildings or structures or any works that form, or are to form, part of the land;
- b the installation in any building, structure or works of fittings that form, or are to form, part of the land;
- c any operation which forms an integral part of, is preparatory to, or is for rendering complete, works of the kinds described;
- d the cleaning of buildings, structures or works, in the course of their construction, alteration, repair, restoration, maintenance or extension; or
- e the painting or decorating of the external or internal surfaces of any building, structure or works.

14.22 Construction contracts include contracts for the fabrication, supply and installation of furniture intended to be permanently attached to a building,[11] and contracts for the supply of prefabricated components.[12] This includes the prefabrication of components overseas for works in Singapore.[13] It also includes the prefabrication in Singapore of components for construction works overseas, but only if all contracting parties are Singaporean (*ie*, either corporations, partnerships or businesses registered in Singapore).[14]

14.23 '*Services*' refers to the following activities provided they relate to construction work:[15]

- a feasibility studies, planning services, submissions to relevant authorities, site supervision services, professional engineering services or architectural, design, surveying or quantity surveying services;
- b project management services;

9 Section 2 of SOP Act.
10 Section 3(1) of SOP Act.
11 *JFC Builders v Permasteelisa* [2016] SGHC 247.
12 *Eng Seng Precast v SLF Construction* [2015] 3 SLR 252.
13 Section 4(2A)(a) of SOP Act.
14 Section 4(2)(c) of SOP Act.
15 Section 3(1) of SOP Act.

c building, engineering, exterior or interior decoration or landscape advisory services; or
d the provision of labour.

14.24 A '*supply contract*' on the other hand is an agreement under which a party undertakes to supply '*goods*' to anyone in the business of construction work, or who causes construction work to be performed. In this regard, '*goods*' are materials or components that are to form part of any building, structure or works; or plant or materials for use in connection with the carrying out of construction work.[16]

14.25 The supply must be for the purpose of construction work, and it must be a pure supply arrangement in the sense that there is no element of assembly, construction or installation having to be performed at the construction site.[17] Any such assembly, construction or installation would come within the definition of '*construction work*' and thus result in the contract being characterised as a '*construction contract*', despite the goods supply element.[18]

14.26 A supply contract must also specify or identify the construction site or project for which the goods are to be supplied.[19] This requirement is linked to the territorial limits of the SOP Act, which will be explained next.

Contracts made in writing

14.27 The SOP Act only applies to contracts which are '*made in writing*',[20] but adopts a fairly expansive approach for these purposes, in that:[21]

a Signatures are unnecessary;
b Contracts made by exchange of written communications qualify;
c Unwritten contracts recorded by a party or an authorised person also qualify; and
d Unwritten agreements which refer to written terms also qualify.

14.28 Section 4(4) of the SOP Act provides interestingly that '*[w]here a contract is not wholly made in writing, the contract shall be treated as made in writing ... if ... the matter in dispute between the parties thereto is in writing*'.

14.29 This has been applied where the '*matter in dispute*', *ie*, the subject matter of the adjudication application, was the claimant's works which could be found in an exchange of communications in writing which included bills of quantities, drawings, payment claims, payment responses and tax invoices.[22]

---

16 Section 3(1) of SOP Act.
17 Section 2 of SOP Act.
18 Per definition of 'construction contract' at Section 2 of SOP Act.
19 Regulation 3 of SOP Regulations.
20 Section 4(1) of SOP Act.
21 Section 4(2A) of SOP Act.
22 *Qingjian International (South Pacific) Group Development Co Pte Ltd v Capstone Engineering Pte Ltd* [2014] SGHCR 5.

Exclusions

14.30 There are four important exclusions from the scope of the SOP Act.

14.31 First, it does not *generally* apply in respect of construction work outside Singapore, or goods or services supplied in relation to such overseas work.[23] There are however some limited exceptions to this territorial constraint in the context of component prefabrication.[24]

14.32 Second, it does not apply in respect of relatively minor residential property projects which do not require the approval of the Commissioner of Building Control under Building Construction Act.[25]

14.33 Third, it does not apply in respect of any contract to the extent that it contains provisions under which one party undertakes to perform construction work, or to supply goods or services, as employee of the other.[26] The legislation is not aimed at employee-employer claims.

14.34 Fourth, whilst the SOP Act will apply in respect of accrued entitlements under contracts which have been terminated,[27] it does not apply in respect of any construction work done, or goods or services supplied, post-termination.[28]

14.35 There is no exclusion in respect of government contracts. The legislation in fact provides explicitly that it binds the Singapore government.[29] This is important because government-procured public infrastructure accounts for a major proportion of construction work done in Singapore, and so the aims of the SOP Act would have been severely undermined if the Singapore government were not bound.

Anti-avoidance

14.36 The SOP Act cannot be circumvented by subjecting the contract to a foreign governing law. Section 4(1) provides that the Act applies to the specified types of contract '*whether or not the contract is expressed to be governed by the law of Singapore*'.

14.37 Similarly, other attempts to exclude, avoid or contract out of the SOP Act will be ineffective because of the anti-avoidance measures at Section 36, which provides that:

- a The provisions of the SOP Act will have effect notwithstanding any contractual provision to the contrary;
- b Any agreement or contractual provision will be void if it aims at, or has the effect of, excluding, modifying, restricting or prejudicing the operation of any part of the SOP Act; and
- c Any provision reasonably construed as an attempt to deter the taking of action under the SOP Act will also be void.

---

23 Per Section 4(2)(b)(ii) of SOP Act.

24 See Sections 4(2)(d) and 4(2A)(a) of SOP Act.

25 Section 4(2)(a) of SOP Act.

26 Section 4(2)(b)(i) of SOP Act.

27 *Stargood Construction Pte Ltd v Shimizu Corp* [2019] SGHC 261; definition of 'contract' at Section 2 of SOP Act.

28 Section 4(2A)(b) of SOP Act.

29 Section 35 of SOP Act. 'Government' is defined at Section 2(1) of the Interpretation Act (Chapter 1) to mean the Government of Singapore.

14.38 Conversely, there is no provision for contracting or opting into the statutory adjudication regime where the relevant contract falls outside its ambit.

Invalidation of 'pay when paid' provisions

14.39 One of the principal means by which the SOP Act seeks to resolve cash flow problems has been to confront the use of '*pay when paid*' provisions. Such provisions were prevalent in the construction industry when the legislation was introduced, and were a particular source of difficulty for suppliers and sub-contractors lower down the contractual chain, who often had to contract on a '*pay when paid*' basis and thus effectively assume a disproportionate burden in respect of the financing of construction projects. Such parties were in the invidious position of having to advance the cost of labour, goods, equipment, materials, *et cetera* in discharging their contractual obligations, then often suffer delays in receiving payment, whilst one or more of the parties up the contractual chain awaited payment from above.

14.40 Although these '*pay when paid*' arrangements are, at least conceptually, freely assumed contractual schemes, the bargaining position of those lower down the contracting chain is often such that they have limited (if any) prospects of rejecting such arrangements.

14.41 In the context of such practical realities, the SOP Act makes an exceptional inroad into freedom of contract, by making '*pay when paid*' provisions unenforceable and ineffective in contracts which are the subject of the statute.[30]

14.42 For these purposes, '*pay when paid provision*' is broadly defined[31] to mean any contractual provision, however named, that:

a makes the liability of one party (A) to pay money owing to another (B) contingent or conditional on payment to A by anyone else (C);

b makes the due date for payment of money owing by A to B contingent or conditional on when A is paid by C; or

c otherwise makes the liability or due date for payment of any money owing contingent or conditional on the operation of any other contract or agreement.

Claims covered by SOP Act: 'progress payments'

14.43 As foreshadowed, Singapore's statutory adjudication regime is confined to claims '*up the contractual chain*' for monetary entitlements under the terms of specified contracts.

14.44 Claims for damages (whether for breach of contract, or in tort, liquidated or otherwise) and time extensions are not covered.[32]

14.45 Delay-related loss and expense and prolongation claims were previously capable of being pursued through the statutory adjudication regime, at least insofar as they

---

30 Section 9(1) of SOP Act.

31 Section 9(2) of SOP Act.

32 Issues of entitlement to damages and time extensions do however arise in the context of set-offs and cross-claims asserted by a respondent defensively. However, the scope for such issues has been considerably curtailed by the introduction in 2019 of the new Sections 17(2A) and 19(5A), as explained later.

could be cast as entitlements under the terms of the contract[33] (*cf*, damages for breach of those terms). The scope for such claims is however now circumscribed by the 2019 amendments,[34] which exclude from consideration any claim[35] relating to damage, loss or expense that is not supported by either:

a a documented agreement between the parties as to the quantum; or
b a certificate or other documents required to be issued under contract.

14.46 The Building and Construction Authority has explained that the policy underpinning these new limitations is to ensure that statutory adjudication remains a speedy and low cost process by removing the need for adjudicators to consider complex loss and expense claims.

14.47 The SOP Act uses the expression '*progress payment*' to refer to the kinds of payment that can be pursued.[36] This terminology is not particularly helpful and is apt to confuse. The ambit of '*progress payment*' is somewhat broader than suggested by the ordinary meaning of that expression, in that it is not confined to the periodic payments often provided for in construction contracts but also:

a single or one-off payments and payments based on specified events or dates[37] where contractually provided for, for example where a building contract provides for a single payment upon the date of handover of the completed works; and
b final payments.[38]

14.48 Progress payments pursued under the SOP Act are valued according to the terms of the underlying contract.[39]

14.49 However, where the contract does not deal with the valuation, the claimant's entitlements are assessed based on the value of work done and the goods and/or services provided.[40] A range of factors are relevant here,[41] for example the contract price for the work, goods or services; other rates or prices in the contract or prevailing in the construction industry; and the cost of rectifying any defects.

Stage 1: payment claim

14.50 The adjudication mechanism under the SOP Act begins with the service of a '*payment claim*'. This is a pre-adjudication step, in that it does not start the adjudication proper. It is nevertheless vital not only in defining the scope of the claims which may

33 *Eg*, under Clause 22 of the Public Sector Standard Conditions of Contract for Construction Works, which provides for an entitlement to 'Loss and Expense' sustained or incurred as a result of progress or completion being disrupted, prolonged or materially affected by various specified delay events.

34 Specifically, the new Sections 17(2A) and 19(5A) introduced by those amendments.

35 Whether asserted by a claimant, or relied on by a respondent defensively in response to the claimant.

36 Section 5 of SOP Act.

37 *Per* definition of 'progress payment' at Section 2 of SOP Act.

38 *Per* Court of Appeal in *Lee Wee Lick Terence v Chua Say Eng* [2012] SGCA 63, and now explicitly stipulated in the updated (2019) definition of '*progress payment*' at Section 2 of SOP Act.

39 *Per* Section 7(1)(a) of SOP Act.

40 *Per* Section 7(1)(b) of SOP Act.

41 At Section 7(2) of SOP Act.

later be referred to adjudication, but also in precipitating an obligation on the part of the recipient (respondent) to promptly and appropriately respond to the claim.

14.51 Whereas claims for payment were often neglected with relative impunity prior to the SOP Act, it is now quite imprudent not to promptly and properly respond because, as will be seen, there are potentially significant and expensive consequences for failing to do so. The SOP Act thus motivates respondents to properly engage on claims.

Timing

14.52 The law on when payment claims can and should be served has, at least until recently, been highly complex and technical due to a significant number of decisions that emanated from the courts over the years. Not all of these have been easy to reconcile.

14.53 Those decisions reflect evolving judicial attitudes as to when payment claims could be served, as to the degree of strictness with which such timelines would be enforced, and as to the often dire consequences of even trivial infractions.[42]

14.54 It was obviously unhelpful for such complexity to bear upon an issue as basic as when payment claims can be served, particularly in the context of a scheme intended to be quick, inexpensive and operable without legal representation. Efforts were thus made in the 2019 reforms to streamline and simplify the rules in this area.

14.55 The position post-amendment, which applies in respect of payment claims served pursuant to contracts made from 15 December 2019 onwards, is set out later in this chapter. The pre-amendment rules on timing (an account of which is outside the remit of this chapter) continue to apply to payment claims made under earlier contracts, but their relevance will obviously diminish over time.

14.56 As before, the timing of payment claims depends significantly, but not entirely, on what the relevant contract provides.

14.57 If the contract does not prescribe when payment claims may be served, then the claimant may serve one payment claim by the last day of each calendar month, starting from the month after the contract is made.[43] A payment claim is deemed to be served on the last day of the calendar month in which it is served, even if it was actually served earlier that month.[44] Whilst a claimant in this situation may submit payment claim at monthly intervals, it is not compelled to do so. The claimant is free to decide not to submit a payment claim in any given month and will not be penalised for opting not to.[45]

14.58 However, if the contract prescribes the dates on which, or periods within which, payment claims may be served,[46] then payment claims may be served by the prescribed

42 See the strict approach taken in *UES Holdings Pte Ltd v Grouteam Pte Ltd* [2016] 1 SLR 312 (High Court); *Grouteam Pte Ltd v UES Holdings Pte Ltd* [2016] SGCA 59 (Court of Appeal); *Audi Construction Pte Ltd v Kian Hiap Construction Pte Ltd* [2017] SGHC 165 (High Court); as contrasted with the more sympathetic and flexible approach in *Audi Construction Pte Ltd v Kian Hiap Construction Pte Ltd* [2018] 1 SLR 317 (Court of Appeal), which was almost immediately distinguished in *Benlen Pte Ltd v Authentic Builder Pte Ltd* [2018] SGHC 61 (High Court).

43 *Per* Section 10(2)(a)(ii) of SOP Act, read with Regulations 5(1), (1A) and (3) of SOP Regulations.

44 *Per* Section 10(2A)(b) of SOP Act.

45 *Per* Court of Appeal in *Lee Wee Lick Terence v Chua Say Eng* [2012] SGCA 63 at [90].

46 Contractually prescribed timelines will survive the termination of the contract, and will therefore continue to govern service of payment claims post-termination: *CHL Construction Pte Ltd v Yangguang Group Pte Ltd* [2019] 4 SLR 1382.

dates or by the end of the prescribed periods (as the case may be). Payment claims served before a prescribed date or before the last day of a prescribed period are deemed to be served on that date or day (as the case may be).[47]

14.59 The Building and Construction Authority of Singapore has explained that these amendments are designed to provide claimants with more flexibility in respect of the service of payment claims, and to avoid situations (which were fairly prevalent prior to the reforms) of payment claims being invalidated as a result of having been served before or after the specified periods or dates. Payment claims will now be valid whether served on, before or after contractually specified dates or periods. Those served 'late', *ie*, after such specified dates or periods, are not invalid, but merely deemed to be served in the next claim cycle.

14.60 There is a long stop date to serve payment claims. This used to be six years after the relevant construction work was last performed, or goods or services last supplied,[48] but has been shortened considerably to just 30 months after:[49]

a the last supply of the relevant goods/services; or
b the latest of the dates when the:

 1 relevant construction work was last performed;
 2 last completion certificate was issued; or
 3 last temporary occupation permit was issued.

Formal and substantive requirements

14.61 A payment claim must:[50]

a be in writing;
b identify the contract to which it relates;
c state amount claimed, calculated by reference to period to which payment claim relates; and
d provide details of the claimed amount, including a breakdown of the items constituting the claimed amount, a description of these items, the quantity or quantum of each item, and calculations showing how the claimed amount is derived.

14.62 A payment claim need not identify itself as such, even if the contract purports to impose such a requirement.[51] It will be valid if the stipulated requirements are satisfied. The test is not whether the claimant subjectively intended it to be a payment claim under the SOP Act, but whether the requirements set out in the SOP Act and Regulations are satisfied. However, a claimant who represents to a respondent that a document served is not a payment claim may be estopped from subsequently asserting otherwise.[52]

47 *Per* Section 10(2)(a) and 10(2A) of SOP Act.
48 Old Section 10(4) of SOP Act.
49 Section 10(2)(b) of SOP Act.
50 Section 10(3) of SOP Act and Regulation 5(2) of SOP Regulations.
51 *Audi Construction Pte Ltd v Kian Hiap Construction Pte Ltd* [2017] SGHC 165.
52 *Per* Court of Appeal in *Lee Wee Lick Terence v Chua Say Eng* [2012] SGCA 63, overruling *Sungdo Engineering & Construction (S) Pte Ltd v Italcor Pte Ltd* [2010] 3 SLR 459 in this regard.

Other rules

14.63 There are a number of other rules relating to payment claims which have been developed by the Singapore courts over the years, and which are worth mentioning, particularly since many remain uncodified despite the 2019 statutory reforms.

14.64 First, claimants may serve only one payment claim in each 'claim period' (*ie*, claim interval).

14.65 For example, if a contract provides for payment claims to be made at monthly intervals, then the claimant may serve no more than one payment claim each month. If it provides for payment claims to be made weekly, then only one payment claim may be served each week. This rule can be traced to a 2015 decision of the High Court, which was concerned to avoid the risk of claimants being able to ambush respondents by accumulating and then flooding the respondent with multiple claims in quick succession over a short period.[53]

14.66 Second, each payment claim may only relate to claims arising under one contract.[54] The rationale for this constraint is to avoid over-burdening statutory adjudications with claims and responses based on multiple contracts with potentially different terms. The process is short and fast-paced, and there are clearly limits to how much a respondent can sensibly and fairly be expected to deal with within the constraints of such proceedings.

14.67 Third, claimants are permitted to make 'repeat claims', *ie*, claims which have been the subject of earlier payment claims, provided they have not been adjudicated upon on their merits.[55] A dismissal of a claim for want of evidence is an adjudication on the merits.[56]

14.68 The rule on repeat claims has now been codified following the 2019 amendments to the SOP Act, which also clarify that payment claims may include claims previously referred to adjudication but later withdrawn for any reason or rejected on certain specified technical grounds.[57]

Stage 2: response to payment claim

14.69 The appropriate response to a payment claim turns on the distinction described earlier between '*construction*' and '*supply*' contracts.

14.70 In the case of a supply contract, the respondent should:[58]

a pay the claimant so much of the claimed amount as the respondent agrees to pay (if any); and/or

b raise in writing any objection of any nature that it may have in respect of the payment claim

---

53 *Libra Building Construction Pte Ltd v Emergent Engineering Pte Ltd* [2016] 1 SLR 481.

54 *Rong Shun Engineering & Construction Pte Ltd v CP Ong Construction Pte Ltd* [2017] 4 SLR 359.

55 *LH Aluminium Industries Pte Ltd v Newcon Builders Pte Ltd* [2015] 1 SLR 648; *Lee Wee Lick Terence v Chua Say Eng* [2012] SGCA 63.

56 *Asplenium Land Pte Ltd v CKR Contract Services Pte Ltd* [2016] 3 SLR 1061.

57 See Section 10(4) of SOP Act.

58 See Sections 11(2) and 15(3) of SOP Act.

within the contractually specified due date for progress payments (capped at 60 days after service of the payment claim), or if not contractually specified, within a default period of 30 days after service of the payment claim.[59]

14.71 In the case of a construction contract, the respondent needs to respond more formally by serving a '*payment response*' within the contractually specified period for payment responses (capped at 21 days after service of the payment claim) or if not contractually specified, within a default period of 14 days after service of the payment claim.[60]

14.72 Payment responses must, *inter alia*:[61]

a be in writing, be addressed to the claimant and identify the payment claim to which it relates;
b state the '*response amount*', *ie*, what the respondent proposes to pay (if any), and the reasons for any difference between the response and claimed amounts and the reasons for any amount withheld; and
c include any objection of any nature that the respondent may have in respect of the payment claim.

14.73 Any cross-claim, counter-claim or set-off relied on by the respondent must arise out of the same contract as the payment claim.[62]

Implications of a failure to properly respond

14.74 As foreshadowed, the SOP Act motivates respondents to properly engage on payment claims, or face potentially serious and expensive consequences.

14.75 The Singapore courts have held that a respondent must set out all jurisdictional and substantive objections in its payment response, because having been served with a payment claim, the respondent has a '*duty to speak*', and a failure do so would estop the respondent from later raising the objections before the adjudicator or in court.[63]

14.76 This '*duty to speak*' would not, however, arise in respect of a '*payment claim*' that is outside the ambit of the SOP Act from the outset (*cf*, a payment claim that is merely invalid as a result of breaches of the SOP Act).[64] A respondent who fails to discharge its duty to speak may only plead '*patent errors*' in the material properly before the adjudicator.[65]

59 Section 8(3) – (4) of the SOP Act.

60 Section 11(1) of SOP Act. The default period was increased from seven days to 14 days following the 2019 amendments due to industry feedback that seven days (weekends inclusive) was too short.

61 See Sections 11(3) and 15(3) of SOP Act. See also the other requirements under Regulation 6(1) of SOP Regulations.

62 *Civil Tech Pte Ltd v Hua Rong Engineering Pte Ltd* [2018] 1 SLR 584.

63 *Per* Court of Appeal in *Audi Construction Pte Ltd v Kian Hiap Construction Pte Ltd* [2018] 1 SLR 317.

64 See *Far East Square Pte Ltd v Yau Lee Construction (Singapore) Pte Ltd* [2019] 2 SLR 189 where the Court of Appeal provided examples of the narrow scenarios where a payment claims would fall outside the ambit of the SOP Act, namely where they are made pursuant to contracts falling outside the ambit of the SOP Act, or where they are submitted beyond the limitation period prescribed in the SOP Act. It is however difficult to see how the latter example would qualify as a payment claim falling outside the ambit of the statute 'from the outset', or how it is different from any other payment claim which is invalid simply by virtue of having been made in breach of some requirement under the statute.

65 *Per* Court of Appeal in *Comfort Management Pte Ltd v OGSP Engineering Pte Ltd* [2018] 1 SLR 979.

14.77 Following the 2019 amendments, the SOP Act provides that a respondent will be barred from raising any objection of any nature which is not included in a proper response (in the manner explained earlier), unless:[66]

- a the circumstances of the objection arose after service of the relevant payment response, or could not reasonably have been known to the respondent when it served the payment response; or
- b the objection relates to a '*patent error*'.

'*Patent errors*' are an exceptional and extremely narrow category of errors which are obvious, manifest or otherwise easily recognisable on the face of the claim.[67] It has been said that it is difficult to conceive of errors that may properly be regarded as patent outside situations where:[68]

- a The claimant and/or respondent are not party to the contract on which the payment claim is based;
- b The claimed amount is plainly contradicted by the documentary evidence provided; or
- c No supporting material or explanation whatsoever is adduced in support of the claim.

14.78 Patent errors can be raised even in the absence of a proper response because an adjudicator is under a general duty to adjudicate claims. This requires that he be satisfied that the claimant has established a *prima facie* case that the relevant construction work was completed (or goods or services supplied, as the case may be) and, if so, what its value is. He cannot simply rubber-stamp claims in the absence of a response, but '*must have at least some positive basis for his determination, and not simply lack a reason not to allow the claim*'.[69]

Stage 3: other pre-adjudication requirements

14.79 A claimant may proceed to adjudication proceedings if it does not receive a satisfactory response to the payment claim, or where the payment contemplated in a response is not forthcoming.[70]

14.80 Two pre-conditions may however need to be satisfied before commencing proceedings.

66 Sections 15(3), 15(3A), 17(4A) and 19(6A) of SOP Act. The 2 October 2018 Parliamentary Report on the second reading of the Building and Construction Industry Security of Payment (Amendment) Bill records that these amended provisions 'will make clear that any belated objections by respondents will be disregarded by adjudicators or the Courts, unless respondents can prove that their objections could not have been made known earlier. This is in line with comments made by the Courts in recent decisions, and will also advance the intent of the Act to facilitate speedy dispute resolution.'

67 *Comfort Management Pte Ltd v OGSP Engineering Pte Ltd* [2018] 1 SLR 979. This definition has been codified through the 2019 amendments to Section 2 of SOP Act.

68 *Per* Court of Appeal in *Comfort Management Pte Ltd v OGSP Engineering Pte Ltd* [2018] 1 SLR 979.

69 *Comfort Management Pte Ltd v OGSP Engineering Pte Ltd* [2018] 1 SLR 979.

70 Section 12(3) of SOP Act.

Expiry of 'dispute settlement period'

14.81 First, in circumstances involving a construction contract, and either no payment response or a disputed payment response, the '*dispute settlement period*' must expire before adjudication can commence.[71]

14.82 An adjudication application made in breach of this requirement is premature and would render any associated adjudication determination liable to be set aside, whether or not the respondent is prejudiced.[72]

14.83 This requirement does not apply in the context of supply contracts, or construction contracts where there is simply a failure to pay on an undisputed payment response.[73]

14.84 The '*dispute settlement period*' is the period of seven days following the payment response due date.[74] The significance of the dispute settlement period is that it serves as a moratorium during which:[75]

a Parties may seek clarifications from each other and attempt to resolve the dispute; and

b The respondent may serve a payment response (if it had failed to do so earlier), or vary any payment response previously served.

Notice of intention to apply for adjudication

14.85 The second precondition is that the claimant must give the respondent written notice of its intention to apply for adjudication,[76] containing certain prescribed particulars.[77]

14.86 The late service of such a notice renders any associated adjudication determination liable to be set aside.[78]

14.87 In practice, such notices are often served very shortly before (on the very day on which) the claimant lodges its adjudication application.

Stage 4: adjudication application

Application deadline

14.88 Once the applicable preconditions have been satisfied, the claimant may proceed to make an adjudication application, but must do so within seven days after the right to do

71 Section 12(2) of SOP Act.

72 *Newcon Builders Pte Ltd v Sino New Steel Pte Ltd* [2015] SGHC 226; *Tienrui Design & Construction Pte Ltd v G & Y Trading and Manufacturing Pte Ltd* [2015] 5 SLR 852.

73 Section 12(1) of SOP Act.

74 Section 12(5) of SOP Act.

75 Sections 11(4) and 12(4) of SOP Act.

76 Section 13(2) of SOP Act.

77 Prescribed at Regulation 7(1) of the SOP Regulations. A failure to comply with the prescribed particulars is not necessarily fatal unless the breach impedes the adjudication process. See *eg, UES Holdings Pte Ltd v KH Foges Pte Ltd* [2018] 3 SLR 648.

78 *UES Holdings Pte Ltd v KH Foges Pte Ltd* [2018] 3 SLR 648.

so first arises under Section 12.[79] This translates to different deadlines depending on the circumstances, as depicted in the following:

Table 14.1 Adjudication application deadlines

	Scenario	Adjudication application deadline
	Construction contract	
a	No payment on undisputed payment response	7 days after due date for payment as defined at Sections 8(1) – (2)
b	Disputed payment response/no payment response	7 days after dispute settlement period
	Supply contract	
c	Disputed response amount (less than claimed)	7 days after receiving payment of response amount
d	No payment	7 days after due date for payment as defined at Sections 8(3) – (4)

14.89 A late application will render any associated adjudication determination liable to be set aside.[80]

14.90 It is important in this regard to note that the Singapore Mediation Centre's Adjudication Procedure Rules require that documents be lodged during its opening hours, and that documents submitted after those hours are treated as having been lodged the next working day.[81] This has controversially resulted in documents lodged at 4:32 pm (just 2 minutes past opening hours) being deemed late and thus disregarded.[82]

Application requirements

14.91 The requirements for adjudication applications are found at Section 13(3) of the SOP Act and include having to submit the prescribed information and documents[83] and payment of an application fee.

14.92 The applicant may also include information or documents it considers relevant to the application (*eg*, expert reports, photographs correspondence, submissions).[84]

79 Section 13(3)(a) of SOP Act.

80 *UES Holdings Pte Ltd v KH Foges Pte Ltd* [2018] 3 SLR 648; *Eng Seng Precast Pte Ltd v SLF Construction Pte Ltd* [2015] 5 SLR 948.

81 See Rule 3.2 which provides that the opening hours are 9:00 am–4:30 pm on Mondays–Fridays (excluding Public Holidays); and 9:00 am–12:00 pm on the eves of Christmas, the New Year and the Chinese New Year.

82 *Citiwall Safety Glass Pte Ltd v Mansource Interior Pte Ltd* [2015] 1 SLR 797.

83 See Regulation 7(2) of the SOP Regulations.

84 Section 13(3)(e) of SOP Act.

14.93 Application forms, fee information, adjudication rules and other practical resources can be accessed without charge at the authorised nominating body's (the Singapore Mediation Centre) website.[85]

14.94 Service of the adjudication application on the respondent is not the claimant's responsibility, but the authorised nominating body's. Once it receives the application, the authorised nominating body must serve a copy on the respondent,[86] and usually does this within a day or two. It will also notify the following parties of the application:[87]

a the '*principal*' (if known), *ie*, the person liable to pay respondent for the relevant construction work, goods or services; and

b the '*owner*', *ie*, the person at the top of the contractual chain who is the ultimate procurer of the relevant construction work, goods or services, or if there is no such person, the owner of the relevant construction site.

14.95 Such parties are notified because, as will be seen, a successful claimant who remains unpaid may potentially suspend performance. There is recognition that such a course of action will often impact not only the respondent but other project stakeholders up the contractual chain. Principals are thus given the option of making direct payment to the claimant, if the respondent fails to pay on an adjudication determination.

Stage 5: appointment of adjudicator and adjudication response

14.96 The lodging of an adjudication application triggers two approximately parallel streams of activity, *ie*, the appointment of an adjudicator, and the preparation and lodging of an adjudication response by the respondent.

Appointment of adjudicator by authorised nominating body

14.97 Parties have no autonomy or control over the choice of adjudicator. The sole authorised nominating body (the Singapore Mediation Centre) appoints an adjudicator from its panel of registered adjudicators.[88]

14.98 The authorised nominating body must do this and notify the claimant, respondent, principal (if known) and owner of the appointment within seven days of receiving the application.[89]

Adjudication response by respondent

14.99 The respondent must, in parallel with the appointment process, proceed with the preparation of its adjudication response, as it is due within seven days of its receipt

85 <www.mediation.com.sg/our-services/for-lawyers/adjudication/#contents> (last accessed 29 October 2020).
86 Section 13(4)(a) of SOP Act.
87 Section 13(4)(b) read with Section 2 of SOP Act.
88 Sections 14(1) – (2) of SOP Act.
89 Section 14(3) read with Section 2 of SOP Act.

of the application,[90] *ie*, roughly by when the adjudicator needs to be appointed.[91] It is critical to meet the adjudication response deadline because a late response must be rejected.[92]

14.100 The requirements for adjudication responses are found at Section 15(2) of the SOP Act and include having to be accompanied by such information and documents as may be prescribed.[93] The respondent may also include other information or documents (*eg*, expert reports, photographs, correspondence and submissions) that it considers relevant to the response.

14.101 A respondent will however be barred from including (and the adjudicator therefore barred from considering) any objection of any nature which had not been the subject of an appropriate response to the underlying payment claim unless, as already explained:[94]

a The circumstances of the objection only arose after service of the relevant payment response, or could not reasonably have been known to the respondent when it served the payment response; or
b The objection relates to a '*patent error*'.

Stage 6: the adjudication proper

Timelines for determination

14.102 The adjudication proper commences immediately after the adjudication response deadline (which is seven days after the respondent's receipt of the adjudication application).[95]

14.103 The adjudicator must generally decide within 14 days after commencement. This timeframe is however reduced to seven days in two scenarios, *ie*, when the dispute arises out of a construction contract (*cf*, supply contract) and the respondent has either:[96]

a failed to provide a payment response <u>and</u> adjudication response; or
b failed to pay an undisputed response amount.

14.104 The determination deadline can be extended if more time is sought by the adjudicator and agreed to by both parties.[97]

14.105 An adjudicator who fails to meet the deadline may lose his entitlement to fees.[98] It is presently unclear whether such delay will invalidate the determination,

90 Section 15(1) of SOP Act.

91 The timelines are not however identical. The adjudicator must be appointed within seven days of the authorised nominating body's receipt of the application, whereas the adjudication response is due within seven days of the respondent's receipt of the application (usually a day or two later).

92 Section 16(2)(b) of SOP Act. In *Citiwall Safety Glass Pte Ltd v Mansource Interior Pte Ltd* [2015] 1 SLR 797, the adjudication response was rejected because it was served at 4:32 pm, *ie*, merely two minutes past the Singapore Mediation Centre's opening hours.

93 See Regulation 8(1) of SOP Regulations.

94 Sections 15(3), 15(3A) and 17(4A) of SOP Act.

95 Section 16(1) of SOP Act.

96 Section 17(1) of SOP Act.

97 Section 17(1) of SOP Act.

98 Section 31(2)-(3) of SOP Act.

although there is unreasoned dicta, in a case where the point was not argued, suggesting that it will.[99]

Adjudicator's powers and duties

14.106 Adjudicators enjoy a wide range of powers,[100] including the broad prerogative to conduct the adjudication as he deems fit, and to require submissions from the parties, appoint independent experts, convene conferences, perform inspections, and issue directions as necessary or expedient.

14.107 Adjudicators are subject to an overarching duty to act independently, impartially and in a timely manner; to avoid incurring unnecessary expense; and to comply with the principles of natural justice.[101] See also the discussion on the adjudicator's duty to adjudicate, in the context of '*patent error*' earlier.

The determination

14.108 The adjudicator is required to determine, with reasons:[102]

a any amount payable by the respondent (*ie*, the 'adjudicated amount');
b the date on which that amount is payable;
c the interest payable on the adjudicated amount; and
d the proportion of adjudication costs to be borne by each party.

14.109 An adjudicator may only award 'adjudication costs', which are limited to the application fee payable to the authorised nominating body and the adjudicator's fees and expenses.[103] He has no power to order other kinds of costs (*eg*, the cost of legal representatives and experts).[104]

14.110 Once the determination is released, copies are served by the authorised nominating body on the parties. The principal (if known) and owner are notified that the determination has been made.[105]

14.111 The respondent is obliged to pay the adjudicated amount within seven days of being served with the determination, or by any later date determined by the adjudicator.[106]

99 *CMC Ravenna Singapore Branch v CGW Construction & Engineering (S) Pte Ltd* [2018] 3 SLR 503 at [35(c)].

100 Section 16(4) of SOP Act.

101 Section 16(3) of SOP Act. The principles of natural justice comprise two broad rules, *ie*, that the adjudicator must be disinterested and unbiased; and that parties must be given adequate notice and opportunity to be heard.

102 Section 17(2) of SOP Act.

103 Section 30(2) – (3) read with definition of 'costs' at Section 2 of SOP Act.

104 Section 30(4) of SOP Act.

105 Section 17(8) of SOP Act.

106 Section 22(1) of SOP Act.

Adjudication review

14.112 Dissatisfied parties may invoke the adjudication review process under Sections 18 and 19 of the SOP Act. This is essentially an avenue for appeal. Most of the duties and constraints applicable to adjudicators also apply to review adjudicators, and will not be repeated here.

14.113 The review process is now available to both the claimant and respondent,[107] provided there is a difference of at least S$100,000 between the adjudicated amount and:[108]

- a what was claimed in the payment claim; or
- b what the respondent paid or proposed to pay in response to the payment claim.

14.114 The dissatisfied party must lodge any review application with the authorised nominating body within seven days of being served with the determination.[109]

14.115 Prior to the 2019 reforms, respondents had to pay claimants the adjudicated amount before commencing review proceedings. This created concerns around recoverability from the claimant upon a successful review. To allay such concerns, the respondent must now pay the adjudicated amount to the authorised nominating body instead.[110] This should be resolved in a timely manner to avoid delays in review applications which would warrant rejection.[111]

14.116 Review applications must comply with Section 18(4), include information and documents prescribed at Regulation 10(2), and be accompanied by an application fee. Applications which do not comply with these requirements (apart from those relating to the application fee) must be rejected.[112]

14.117 The authorised nominating body, having received a review application from one party, will serve a copy on the other party and notify the principal (if known) and owner of the application.[113]

14.118 It will also proceed to appoint either a sole review adjudicator (where the amount in dispute does not exceed S$1 million), or a panel of three review adjudicators[114] (if the disputed amount exceeds S$1 million).[115] It must notify the parties, the principal (if known) and owner of the appointment within seven days of receiving the review application.[116]

14.119 The adjudication review process commences the day after confirmation of the appointment. The review adjudicator(s) then have 14 days to make a determination, unless both parties agree to a request for additional time.[117]

---

107 Prior to the 2019 reforms, only the respondent could initiate a review, but once initiated the claimant was also able to challenge the determination.

108 Section 18(1) read with Section 2 of SOP Act; Regulation 10(1) of SOP Regulations.

109 Section 18(2) of SOP Act.

110 Section 18(3) of SOP Act.

111 Sections 19(2) of SOP Act.

112 Section 19(2) of SOP Act.

113 Section 18(5)(a) of SOP Act.

114 Who would decide by majority under Section 19(7) of the SOP Act.

115 Section 18(5)(b) of SOP Act and Regulation 10(3) of SOP Regulations.

116 Section 18(6) of SOP Act.

117 Sections 19(1) and 19(3) of SOP Act.

14.120 The review adjudicator(s) may either reject the review application or allow it by issuing a reasoned determination which deals, *inter alia*, with:[118]

a any amount payable by the respondent to the claimant;
b any amount to be returned by the authorised nominating body to the respondent;
c interest; and
d the allocation of the costs of the adjudication review between the parties.

Determinations binding but not final

14.121 Singapore's rough and ready statutory adjudication process does not aspire to produce accurate outcomes but rather to achieve some form of 'rough justice' between the parties pending an opportunity to have disputes more fully ventilated at an appropriate forum. It will come as no surprise that the outcome of such a process is merely temporarily binding, and not final.

14.122 The SOP Act recognises parties' rights to challenge adjudication determinations (and adjudication review determinations) and to have their dispute finally determined by a court, tribunal or other dispute resolution proceeding.[119]

14.123 Adjudication determinations (and adjudication review determinations) will cease to bind parties if:

a the dispute is finally determined by a court, or tribunal or other dispute resolution proceeding, or is settled by agreement between the parties;[120] or
b a court sets aside the determination[121] or refuses to enforce it[122] (which would indicate that it is seriously flawed in some way).

Setting aside by the courts

14.124 As alluded to earlier, apart from being challenged by way of review under the SOP Act, or by having the underlying dispute referred for final determination by a court, tribunal or other dispute resolution proceeding, adjudication (and adjudication review) determinations may also be set aside by the courts.

14.125 A respondent seeking a setting-aside must pay into court as security any portion of the adjudicated amount that has not been paid, pending determination of those proceedings.[123]

14.126 A court hearing a setting-aside application does not engage in a review of the merits of the adjudicator's determination. It may however set aside a determination on the ground that:[124]

118 Section 19(4) – (5).
119 Sections 21(3) and 34(1)(a) of SOP Act.
120 Section 21(1) – (2) of SOP Act.
121 Section 27(5) of SOP Act.
122 Section 21(1)(a) of SOP Act.
123 Section 27(5) of SOP Act.
124 *CMC Ravenna Singapore Branch v CGW Construction & Engineering (S) Pte Ltd* [2018] 3 SLR 503.

a the adjudicator breached principles of natural justice;
b there was no payment claim;
c the claimant had breached a requirement under the SOP Act that is so important that it is the legislative purpose that an act done in breach of the requirement should be invalid. Examples of such requirements include:

1 the existence of a contract to which the SOP Act applies (Section 4);
2 the fulfilment of the formal requirements of service of a payment claim (Section 10);
3 the making of an adjudication application by the claimant to an authorised nominating body (Section 13);
4 the reference of the application to an eligible adjudicator who agrees to determine the adjudication application (Section 14); and
5 the determination by the adjudicator of the application within the specified period by determining the adjudicated amount (if any) to be paid by the respondent to the claimant; the date on which the adjudicated amount is payable; the interest payable on the adjudicated amount and the proportion of the costs payable by each party to the adjudication (Section 17(1) – (2)); or

d the adjudicator commits a patent error on the face of the record.

14.127 The SOP Act provides further examples of situations warranting setting aside *ie*:[125]

a the payment claim not being served in accordance with Section 10;
b the payment claim being served in respect of claims already adjudicated upon on their merits;
c the adjudication application or the adjudication review application not being made in accordance with the SOP Act;
d the adjudicator failing to comply with the provisions of the SOP Act;
e the determination requiring the claimant to pay an adjudicated amount to the respondent;
f the determination being affected by fraud or corruption.

14.128 The respondent cannot however seek a setting-aside on any ground not included in its adjudication response, unless the relevant circumstances arose subsequently or could not reasonably have been known to the respondent when the adjudication response was lodged.[126] This would, for the most part, limit the respondent to objections which have been the subject of an appropriate response to the underlying payment claim, given the restrictions explained earlier.

14.129 The grounds for setting-aside must be established on a balance of probabilities.[127]

125 Section 27(6) of SOP Act.
126 Section 27(7) of SOP Act.
127 *Per* Court of Appeal in *Glaziers Engineering Pte Ltd v WCS Engineering Construction Pte Ltd* [2018] 2 SLR 1311.

14.130 The Court has the power to set aside the relevant determination in whole or in part; or remit the whole of any part of the determination to the adjudicator; or to correct clerical mistakes, accidental slips or omissions, or defects in form, and award costs.[128]

Enforcement of determinations

14.131 There are a number of relatively quick and effective ways through which determinations can be enforced. Each is subject to certain procedural requirements which are not the focus of this chapter. Instead, what follows is an outline of the substance of the enforcement methods.

Enforcement as judgment debt

14.132 A determination can be converted into a judgment, which can then be against the respondent in the same way as any other judgment.[129]

14.133 This allows an unpaid claimant (as judgment creditor) to:

a commence winding up proceedings against the respondent on the basis of a failure to satisfy a judgment debt;[130]

b examine the respondent (as judgment debtor) to identify assets to execute against;

c seize and sell property in satisfaction of the judgment debt; and/or

d commence garnishee proceedings against the respondent's debtors.

Suspension

14.134 It is usually risky for a contractor to suspend work because it has not been paid, since this can amount to a repudiation which would allow the employer to terminate the contract and hold the contractor accountable for damages. A contractor has no general right at common law to suspend work unless this is expressly agreed upon, even if payment is wrongly withheld.[131]

14.135 The SOP Act however augments this position by giving an unpaid determination creditor the right to suspend.[132] It protects a claimant exercising this right by providing, *inter alia*, that:

a The claimant will not be liable to the respondent, principal or owner for any loss or damage occasioned by the suspension;[133]

b The respondent is liable to pay the claimant for any loss or expense resulting from the removal by the respondent of any part of the work or supply from its contract with the claimant;[134] and

128 Section 27(8) of SOP Act.

129 Sections 23(2) and 27(1) – (2) of SOP Act.

130 *Lim Poh Yeoh (alias Lim Aster) v TS Ong Construction Pte Ltd* [2016] 5 SLR 272.

131 *Jia Min Building Construction Pte Ltd v Ann Lee Pte Ltd* [2004] 3 SLR(R) 288.

132 Section 26(1) of SOP Act.

133 Section 26(2) of SOP Act.

134 Section 26(3) of SOP Act.

c For purposes of contractual time limits, the period of suspension will be disregarded in computing the time taken by claimant to complete the construction work or supply.[135] Any contractual time limit set by reference to a date must be adjusted accordingly.[136] These measures are designed to protect the claimant against liability delay-related damages over the period of suspension.

14.136 The claimant must however resume work within three days of being paid. It may otherwise be liable to the respondent or principal for any resulting loss or damage.[137]

Direct payment from principal

14.137 An unpaid determination creditor may also obtain payment from the respondent's principal,[138] *ie*, the person liable to pay respondent for the construction work, goods or services, which is the subject of the contract between claimant and respondent.[139]

14.138 This remedy is however only available at the principal's option.[140] It is provided for because of the recognition that an unpaid claimant may otherwise suspend performance, and that this may impact not only the respondent but other project stakeholders higher up the contractual chain.

14.139 Any payment made by the principal in this context may be treated as payment to the respondent and reduce any amount that the principal owes, or may in future owe, the respondent. Alternatively, such payment may be recovered by principal as a debt due from the respondent.[141]

Lien on unpaid and unfixed goods

14.140 Finally, the unpaid determination creditor has a lien[142] on goods supplied to the respondent under the relevant contract, provided they are unfixed.[143] Needless to say, such a lien subsists only for so long as claimant has not been paid the adjudicated amount.[144]

135 Section 26(7) of SOP Act.
136 Section 26(8) of SOP Act.
137 Sections 26(4) and 26(6) of SOP Act.
138 Section 24 of SOP Act.
139 Section 2 of SOP Act.
140 See Section 24(1) of SOP Act.
141 Section 24(4) of SOP Act.
142 A lien is essentially a right to retain possession of property until a debt is paid.
143 Section 25 of SOP Act.
144 Section 25(2)(d) of SOP Act.

CHAPTER 15

Statutory adjudication in Australia

Sean Kelly, Julian Bailey and Matthew Bell

Introduction

15.1 The states and territories of the Commonwealth of Australia (prior to 1901, as British colonies) have had various forms of construction industry payment legislation in place since the nineteenth century.[1] The modern history of these schemes began in 1999 when the state of New South Wales passed the Building and Construction Industry Security of Payment Act 1999 (NSW),[2] the template for which was Part II of the UK Housing Grants, Construction and Regeneration Act 1996.[3] Since then, legislation has been enacted across each of Australia's eight states and territories.[4]

15.2 This chapter commences with an overview of the adjudication schemes in Australia and their emergence, and divergence, from the UK Act. It then examines the following aspects of the Australian adjudication schemes:

- a The scope of the dispute that may be the subject of an adjudication
- b The time period within which an adjudication must be commenced
- c The methods of nominating adjudicators
- d The mechanisms that allow a party to enforce an adjudicator's determination
- e Errors and other grounds on which an adjudicator's determination can be challenged

15.3 Following that, this chapter charts the course of reform of the various Australian Acts over the past two decades and considers the prospects for harmonisation. A summary is provided by way of conclusion in the final part.

1 These earlier forms of legislation largely related to imposition of liens for construction work. Some are still in force, notably the Worker's Liens Act 1893 (SA).

2 Referred to in this chapter as the **NSW Act**.

3 Here, **UK Act**.

4 In addition to NSW, the states and territories and their primary respective Acts are as follows. Australian Capital Territory: Building and Construction Industry (Security of Payment) Act 2009 (ACT) (**ACT Act**); Northern Territory: Construction Contracts (Security of Payment) Act 2004 (NT) (**NT Act**); Queensland: Building Industry Fairness (Security of Payment) Act 2017 (Qld) (**Queensland Act**), replacing the earlier Building and Construction Industry Payments Act 2004 (Qld); South Australia: Building and Construction Industry Security of Payment Act 2009 (SA) (**SA Act**); Tasmania: Building and Construction Industry Security of Payment Act 2009 (Tas) (**Tasmanian Act**); Victoria: Building and Construction Industry Security of Payment Act 2002 (Vic) (**Victorian Act**); Western Australia: Construction Contracts Act 2004 (WA) (**WA Act**), to be progressively replaced upon the coming into force of various parts of the Building and Construction Industry (Security of Payment) Act 2021 (**WA 2021 Act**) – see s 9(1) of that Act.

An overview of adjudication in Australia

Eight 'laboratories' with divergent approaches

15.4 Australia is a federation, and regulation of payment in the construction industry falls primarily within the constitutional powers of the states and territories rather than that of the federal (Commonwealth) government. This has resulted in each state and territory having its own legislative scheme.

15.5 As will be seen from the discussion that follows, this means that parties which undertake construction work across Australia need to navigate hundreds of pages of legislation which diverges – in some ways subtly, in other ways fundamentally – across state borders. And, even within states and territories, reviews of the legislation mean that the schemes change significantly and frequently. This divergence has long been recognised as 'absurd' in the context of efficient national operation of Australia's construction industry.[5]

15.6 On the other hand, the 'motley patchwork' of the various Australian Acts, and their reviews, offers something of a 'laboratory' for testing out different approaches which may be of benefit to other jurisdictions around the world which are considering the implementation of similar schemes.[6] That said, there remains little consensus on which of the approaches is the most effective at addressing the underlying rationale of the legislation.[7]

15.7 To a large extent, this lack of consensus may be ascribed to that underlying rationale never having been the subject of precise articulation, let alone consensus as to such a precise statement of principle. There seems broad support for the notion that it is 'unAustralian' that vulnerable subcontractors are not paid for their work, causing severe consequences for their business, themselves and their families (as was stated by the NSW Minister in introducing the state's Bill in 1999).[8]

15.8 However, the 'holy grail' of a legislative scheme which provides an appropriate balance of such protection of the vulnerable against the need not to unnecessarily interfere with the commerce of the industry has proven elusive. Instead, entrenched industry interests, parochial bureaucracies and the two-party system which prevails across Australia's parliaments have combined to make the legislation a 'political football' (or, rather, eight footballs across the states and territories).

15.9 One example of continual amendments, first one way and then the other, relates to the need to endorse a claim for progress payments as a payment claim made under the Act in order to opt-in to the legislative entitlements. The endorsement was required when the NSW Act was first enacted. However, a review of the NSW Act in 2012 accepted evidence that subcontractors were routinely threatened into not including the endorsement

5 Australian Senate (Economic References Committee), '"I Just Want to be Paid": Insolvency in the Australian Construction Industry' (December 2015), [9.105].

6 Matthew Bell and Donna Vella, 'From Motley Patchwork to Security Blanket: The Challenge of National Uniformity in Australian "Security of Payment" Legislation' (2010) 84 *Australian Law Journal* 565.

7 Matthew Bell, Christopher Ennis, Anand Juddoo, Sundra Rajoo, Bruce Reynolds and Sharon Vogel, 'Security of Payment in the Construction Industry: Does International Experience Provide a Crystal Ball for North America?' (2018) 34 *Construction Law Journal* 601, 616.

8 Morris Iemma, NSW Parliamentary Debates, Legislative Assembly, 29 June 1999.

on their claims for progress payments.[9] Accordingly, this requirement was removed from an amended version of the NSW Act.

15.10 This removal was itself soon the subject of criticism on the grounds that it would cause uncertainty as to which documents provided by a claimant to a respondent in the course of business might be deemed as payment claims under the Act.[10] It was also judicially described as 'unwise'.[11] A subsequent review for the Commonwealth Government recommended that the opt-in requirement be reinstated in the NSW Act, primarily on the basis that it avoids confusion as to the formal legal status and consequences of a claim.[12] As a result of this convoluted history, the current iteration of the NSW Act includes the opt-in process whereby a claim for progress payments must contain an express statement that it is made under the NSW Act in order to be a 'payment claim'.[13] In the meantime, however, the requirement had been removed from the Queensland Act.[14]

15.11 This is but one example of the frequent tinkering with the Australian Acts which causes difficulties for all industry participants, including claimants, respondents, legal advisers and even the adjudicators empowered to determine adjudication applications.

Cash flow and protection of vulnerable parties

15.12 Having said that, the broad acceptance that the legislative intervention represented by the Australian Acts is directed at protection of apparently vulnerable parties does explain much of their divergence with the approach taken under the UK. While the UK Act provides an adjudication scheme designed to be 'the key to settling disputes [on construction contracts] in the construction industry',[15] the Australian adjudication schemes were designed as 'more of an independent progress payment certification mechanism than a dispute resolution process'.[16] To promote support for vulnerable parties, the adjudication schemes generally sacrifice procedural and substantive justice for the expediency of cash flow.[17]

15.13 This divergence from the UK Act is especially true of the Australian Acts subscribing to the 'East coast' model, namely those of the ACT, NSW, Queensland, SA,

9 Bruce Collins QC, *Final Report: Independent Inquiry into Construction Industry Insolvency* (2012) 369: https://www.finance.nsw.gov.au/sites/default/files/IICII-final-report.pdf

10 Jeremy Coggins and Matthew Bell, 'Australia's Security of Payment Experience: A Crystal Ball for Malaysia and Hong Kong?' (2015) 32 *International Construction Law Review* 420, 434.

11 *Kitchen Xchange v Formacon Building Services* [2014] NSWSC 1602 (McDougall J).

12 John Murray, *Review of Security of Payment Laws: Building Trust and Harmony* (2018) (**Murray Report**), 144–7 (recommendation 23).

13 NSW Act s 13(2)(c).

14 See Queensland Act s 68.

15 Michael Latham, *Constructing the Team: Final Report of the Government / Industry Review of Procurement and Contractual Arrangements in the UK Construction Industry* (HMSO 1994) 87: <https://constructingexcellence.org.uk/wp-content/uploads/2014/10/Constructing-the-team-The-Latham-Report.pdf>. The UK Act may, to a significant extent, be regarded as having achieved this objective: see *Bresco Electrical Services Ltd (in liq) v Michael J Lonsdale (Electrical) Ltd* [2020] UKSC 25 at [10] – [15].

16 Coggins and Bell (n 10), 420.

17 ibid, 441.

Tasmania and Victoria. Until recently, it was plausible to speak of the NT and WA Acts as forming a contrasting 'West coast' model which was more closely aligned with the UK Act because it was less interventionist into parties' contractual payment regimes.[18] However, in mid-2020, WA signalled its intention – which had been foreshadowed in the Fiocco report[19] – to adopt a new scheme, via a Building and Construction Industry (Security of Payment) Bill; the WA 2021 Act ultimately passed shares many features with other 'East coast' Acts.[20] Thus, the NT Act is now somewhat an outlier.[21] This, along with the lack of harmony across the East coast Acts, means that the utility of the 'East-/West-coast' dichotomy as a useful framework for analysis is diminishing. However, we continue to use it in this chapter to describe the situation as it existed in mid-2021.

15.14 The conceptual and material divergences between the UK Act and the Australian Acts have resulted in UK case law rarely, and only then in small measure, being referred to in Australian judgments regarding adjudication. When UK judgments are referred to, the references are often accompanied with a qualifier that care must be taken when considering in the Australian context judgments in respect of UK adjudications.[22] The following issues (which are discussed in greater detail later in this chapter) are examples of matters in which little regard was had by the Australian courts to the relevant UK case law:

- the impact of claimant insolvency on adjudications and their enforcement;[23]
- failure of an adjudicator to produce a decision within the time limits, and whether it renders the decision a nullity for denial of natural justice;[24]
- impact of errors on law upon adjudication determinations;[25] and
- whether the adjudication scheme is analogous to an expert determination.[26]

18 See, *eg*, Matthew Bell and Jeremy Coggins, 'Beyond the Nutcracker Suite: International Harmonisation of Construction Industry Payment Legislation' (2015) 32 *International Construction Law Review* 186, 200.

19 John Fiocco, 'Final Report to the Minister for Commerce Security of Payment Reform in the WA Building and Construction Industry' (September 2018).

20 Early commentary on the WA 2021 Act, emphasising the features shared with the 'East coast' Acts, includes Clayton Utz, 'WA Passes its Security of Payment Legislation' (www.claytonutz.com, 8 July 2021).

21 And, in any case, the WA (Construction Contracts) Act had already been amended to be more interventionist, such as by its s 10 which placed an upper limit of 42 days between claiming and making progress payments.

22 See, *eg*: *Musico v Davenport* [2003] NSWSC 977 at [52]; *Transgrid v Siemens Ltd* [2004] NSWSC 87 at [58]; *Thiess Pty Ltd v MCC Mining (Western Australia) Pty Ltd* [2011] WASC 80.

23 *Herschel Engineering Ltd v Breen Property Ltd* [2000] BLR 272; *Baldwins Industrial Services PLC v Barr Limited* [2003] BLR 176 at 182; and *Rainford House Ltd v Cadogan Ltd* [2001] BLR 416. These cases were cited in *Grosvenor Constructions (NSW) Pty Ltd (in admin) v Musico* [2004] NSWSC 344; *Straw Realisations (No 1) Ltd v Shaftsbury House (Developments) Ltd* [2011] BLR 47. *Herschel Engineering* and *Bouygues UK Ltd v Dahl-Jensen UK Ltd* [2000] BLR 522 were cited in *Façade Treatment Engineering Pty Ltd (in liq) v Brookfield Multiplex Constructions Pty Ltd* [2016] VSCA 247. However, no UK judgments were discussed in *Seymour Whyte v Ostwald* [2019] NSWCA 11 which addressed the same issue.

24 *St Andrews Bay Development Ltd v HBG Management Ltd* [2003] ScotCS 103 citing (at [21]) *Ballast plc v The Burrell Co (Construction Management)* [2001] SCLR 837; [2001] ScotCS 159. These cases were cited in *MPM Constructions Pty Ltd v Trepcha Constructions Pty Ltd* [2004] NSWSC 103 at [33].

25 *Bouygues* (n 23), cited in *Brodyn Pty Ltd v Davenport* [2004] NSWCA 394.

26 *Bouygues* (n 23), cited in *Musico v Davenport* [2003] NSWSC 977.

Payment claim disputes

Scope of disputes depends on what can be claimed

15.15 A precondition to a claiming party's ability to pursue an interim remedy via statutory adjudication schemes is that there exists a dispute capable of being adjudicated. Arguably, no difference more acutely reflects the underlying philosophical differences between the UK Act and the Australian Acts than the scope of the dispute that may be the subject of the relevant adjudication schemes.

15.16 In the UK, a party to a construction contract can bring an adjudication for any dispute arising under the contract. Section 108(2) of the UK Act states:

> A party to a construction contract has the right to refer a dispute arising under the contract for adjudication under a procedure complying with this section.
>
> For this purpose 'dispute' includes any difference.

This broad gateway allows the adjudication scheme to operate more as a general, albeit interim, form of dispute resolution.[27] On the other hand, in Australia, the adjudication schemes do not operate as a general form of dispute resolution; rather, they are more akin to an independent payment claim certification process which can be enforced on an interim basis.[28]

15.17 Each piece of Australian security of payment legislation creates a legislative framework in relation to claiming progress payments and responding to payment claims. This framework can create what can be described as a 'payment dispute', which then may be the subject of an adjudication application. As with most facets of the Australian legislation, this outcome is achieved by divergent methods.

15.18 Acts that implement the 'East coast' model give a claimant a statutory right to progress payments.[29] Acts that implement the 'West coast model' imply such a right into construction contracts that do not 'have a written provision about whether or not the contractor is able to make a claim to the principal for a progress payment for the obligations the contractor has performed'.[30] By way of examples of each approach, the following discusses the relevant aspects of the NSW Act (with commentary on a Victorian variant to it) and the (2004) WA Act.

Statutory payment process: NSW Act

15.19 Under the NSW Act, a claimant who is or claims to be entitled to a progress payment may serve a payment claim on the principal.[31] Such a payment claim may be served:

- on and from the last day of the month during which the construction work was first carried out or related goods and services were first supplied (unless an earlier date is prescribed by the construction contract);[32] and

27 Dominic Helps and Julian Bailey, 'Construction Act Review' (2013) 29 *Construction Law Journal* 41, 46–47.
28 Coggins and Bell (n 10), 420.
29 See, *eg*, NSW Act s 8, Victorian Act s 9, Queensland Act s 70 and WA 2021 Act s 17.
30 WA Act s 15 and sch 1 div 3.
31 NSW Act s 13(1).
32 NSW Act ss 13(1A) and (1B).

- only within 12 months of when the construction work was last carried out or related goods and services were last supplied (unless a later date is prescribed by the construction contract).[33]

The recipient of a payment claim may respond with a 'payment schedule'.[34] This is a critical stage in the process that can have far-reaching adverse consequences for an unwary respondent. Under the NSW Act:

- if a payment schedule is not served in response within (at most) 10 'business days' (as defined) of the payment claim, the recipient of the payment claim becomes liable to pay the full claimed amount;[35]
- if the full amount is not paid, the claimant may seek payment as a debt due in any court of competent jurisdiction, commence an adjudication or suspend works, and the respondent cannot raise any defences or cross-claims in debt recovery proceedings;[36] and
- the respondent cannot lodge an adjudication response as part of an adjudication process if it has not already issued a payment schedule and may not raise any new reasons for non-payment in an adjudication response not already set out in a payment schedule.[37]

The claimant has a legislative entitlement, independent of the construction contract, to apply for adjudication of that payment claim in any of the following circumstances:[38]

- the respondent submits a payment schedule indicating an amount less than the amount in the payment claim;
- the respondent fails to pay some or all of the amount indicated in a payment schedule by the due date for payment;[39] and
- the respondent fails to provide a payment schedule at all and also fails to pay all or any amount of the amount in the payment claim by the due date for payment.[40]

It can be deduced from the confined circumstances giving rise to an entitlement to apply for adjudication that the scope of the adjudication is narrow, particularly when compared with the scope of an adjudication under the UK Act. The limits of what an adjudicator can determine are prescribed by legislation. For example, s 22(1) of the NSW Act provides that an adjudicator can determine the following three matters:

33 NSW Act s 13(4).
34 NSW Act s 14(1).
35 NSW Act s 14(4).
36 NSW Act ss 15(2), 15(4)(b).
37 NSW Act ss 20(2A), (2B).
38 NSW Act s 17(1).
39 NSW Act ss 11(1A), (1B). The due date for payment depends upon whether the payment schedule is issued to a head contractor (15 business days from the payment claim, or earlier if stated in the head contract) or a subcontractor (20 business days from the payment claim, or earlier if stated in the subcontract).
40 In this scenario, the NSW Act provides the respondent with a second chance to submit a payment schedule, by preventing the claimant from making an adjudication application unless it serves notice of its intention to do so and, within five business days of receiving that notice, the respondent still has not filed a payment schedule (s 17(2)).

- the amount of the progress payment (if any) to be paid by the respondent to the claimant;
- the date on which any such amount became or becomes payable; and
- the rate of interest payable on any such amount.

The matters are confined to payment disputes, which differs substantially from the 'dispute [or] any difference' that may be the subject of an adjudication under the UK Act. The confined compass of an adjudication under the NSW Act reflects the fact that adjudication under Australian security of payment legislation is designed to be a payment claim certification process, which lacks the credentials of a holistic alternative dispute resolution procedure.[41]

15.20 However, this does not mean that adjudicable disputes are limited to mere accounting exercises. While an adjudicator empowered by the NSW Act cannot determine liability for extra-contractual damages,[42] they can determine contractually based claims for delay costs (often incorporating complex and hotly disputed extension of time claims).[43] This has resulted in adjudications grappling with difficult issues such as the prevention principle[44] as part of a 'quick and dirty'[45] adjudication process where submissions are limited[46] and time is generally in short supply.[47]

Victoria's 'excluded amounts' regime

15.21 The scope of an adjudicable dispute under the Victorian Act is yet more confined. Similar provisions to those in the NSW Act apply in respect of payment claims,[48] payment schedules,[49] the consequences of not issuing a payment schedule,[50] the short timeframes for the determination,[51] the permitted subject matter of a determination[52] and limited material that an adjudicator may take into account.[53] The material difference, when compared with the NSW Act, for the purposes of the scope of the 'payment dispute' is the treatment of 'excluded amounts' under the Victorian Act.[54]

---

41 Coggins and Bell (n 10), 447.

42 Bell and Vella (n 6), 573.

43 *Co-ordinated Construction Co Pty Ltd v JM Hargreaves (NSW) Pty Ltd* (2005) 63 NSWLR 385.

44 *Probuild Constructions (Aust) Pty Ltd v DDI Group Pty Ltd* [2017] NSWCA 151.

45 Coggins and Bell (n 10), 447.

46 An adjudicator may only consider the provisions of the NSW Act and the relevant construction contract, the payment claim, the payment schedule (if any), submissions supporting the payment claim and payment schedule (if any), and the results of any inspection carried out by the adjudicator (s 22(2)).

47 An adjudicator must 'determine an adjudication application as expeditiously as possible' and, absent further time being agreed by the claimant and respondent, within no more than 10 business days of the expiry of the period in which the respondent is entitled to lodge an adjudication response (s 21(3)).

48 Victorian Act s 18.

49 Victorian Act s 15.

50 Victorian Act ss 16 and 21(2B).

51 Victorian Act s 22(4).

52 Victorian Act s 23(1).

53 Victorian Act s 23(2).

54 Other apparently minor differences in wording between the NSW and Victorian Acts may have significant impact in practice. Notably, under the Victorian Act (like the UK Act), time does not stop running (via the definition of 'business day') during the traditional Christmas-New Year shutdown period, whereas it does in NSW (and in the ACT, Queensland, SA, Tasmania and WA (under both the 2004 and 2021 Acts)).

15.22 Under s 23(2A) of the Victorian Act 'the adjudicator must not take into account – (a) any part of the claimed amount that is an excluded amount; or (b) any other matter that is prohibited by this Act from being take into account'.[55] These matters are addressed in ss 10(2) and (3), 10A and 10B which relate to 'claimable variations'[56] and 'excluded amounts'. 'Excluded amounts' cannot be included in a payment claim,[57] though a failure by the respondent to submit a payment schedule within the prescribed timeframe makes the respondent liable for full claimed amount.[58] However, as noted earlier, if a payment dispute proceeds to adjudication, the 'excluded amounts' cannot be included within the adjudicator's determination.

15.23 The 'excluded amounts' are listed in s 10B(2) of the Victorian Act. They include amounts:

- relating to a variation that is not a 'claimable variation';
- (other than a claimable variation) due to a latent conditions, time-related costs and changes to regulatory requirements;
- for breach of contract; and
- arising at law other than under a construction contract (for example, a civil penalty under trade practices legislation).

The exclusion of time-related costs operates to the benefit (and detriment) of both the claimant and the respondent: it excludes delay costs based upon extensions of time claims in addition to set-offs of liquidated damages for delay.[59]

15.24 The 'excluded amounts' regime was incorporated into the Victorian Act by amendments made in 2006.[60] Its apparent purpose is to restrict use of the Act's scheme for enforcing payment claims, including via adjudication, to matters which are relatively small value or otherwise lacking in complexity. However, such limitations themselves run contrary to the broad intent of the various Australian legislatures, harking back to their genesis in the Latham Report in the UK,[61] that security of payment legislation have far-reaching goals to reform behaviour across the industry.[62]

15.25 The adjudication scheme in the Victorian Act remains comparatively little used, particularly when compared with the NSW and Queensland Acts, and it has been recognised by Victorian practitioners that this may be a result of the complexity inherent in the 'excluded

---

55 To the extent that an adjudication determination takes these matters into account, the determination is void (s 23(2B)). The regime was considered in detail by the Victorian Court of Appeal in *Yuanda Vic Pty Ltd v Façade Designs International Pty Ltd* [2021] VSCA 44.

56 The first class of 'claimable variations' involves variations on the subject of substantial agreement between the parties (s 10A(2)). The second class involves non-agreed variations where the original contract sum exceeds A$5 million, or is less than A$5 million but the contract does not include a method for resolving disputes under the contract (s 10A(3) and (4)). The finding that a non-binding mediation does not constitute a 'method for resolving disputes' for the purposes of s 10A(3)(d) has, however, created an anomaly whereby non-agreed variations can be included in payment claims under the Act where the contract value substantially exceeded A$5 million: see, *eg*, *SSC Plenty Road Pty Ltd v Construction Engineering (Aust) Pty Ltd* [2016] VSCA 119.

57 Victorian Act s 14(3)(b).

58 Victorian Act s 15(4).

59 *Seabay Properties Pty Ltd v Galvin Constructions* [2011] VSC 183 and *Shape Australia Pty Ltd v The Nuance Group (Australia) Pty Ltd* [2018] VSC 808.

60 Building and Construction Industry Security of Payment (Amendment) Act 2006 (Vic).

61 See n 15.

62 Bell and Vella (n 6), 569.

amounts' regime.[63] Thus, if a central purpose of enacting adjudication schemes is to increase cash flow down the contracting chain, then a salient lesson from the Victorian Act is that the achievement of this purpose is undermined by overly complex legislation.

'West coast' approach

15.26 The final point of comparison in this section is the (2004) WA Act[64] which, along with the NT Act, comprises the only Australian legislation to use a contract-based 'payment dispute' as a defined legislative term.[65]

15.27 The other Australian Acts create a parallel payment claim and response process which creates the legislative framework in which a dispute about payment can arise under the legislation. The WA Act, on the other hand, seeks to do as little damage to the parties' contractual arrangements as possible.[66] The legislation includes a defined concept – a 'payment dispute' – that operates to bring a contractual dispute within the scope of the legislative framework in order to trigger an entitlement to commence an adjudication under the WA Act.

15.28 The definition in s 6 of the WA Act is based upon a 'payment claim' which itself is defined to mean a claim made under a construction contract (and, therefore, not a claim made under a parallel legislative process). The key part of the definition is in sub-s (1):

> 1 For the purposes of this Act, a payment dispute arises if –
> aa a payment claim is rejected or wholly or partly disputed; or
> a the time when the amount claimed in a payment claim is due to be paid under the contract, the amount has not been paid in full; or
> b the time when any money retained by a party under the contract is due to be paid under the contract, the money has not been paid; or
> c the time when any security held by a party under the contract is due to be returned under the contract, the security has not been returned.

If such a 'payment dispute' arises, then any party to the construction contract may apply to have the dispute adjudicated under part 3 of the WA Act.[67] As there is no legislative requirement governing the existence, content and service of a payment schedule as a precondition to a 'payment dispute', the complexities discussed earlier in respect of late or incomplete payment schedules under the NSW and Victorian Acts do not arise.[68]

---

63 Ibid, 574–575.

64 References in [15.26]–[15.28] are to the (2004) WA Act. As was noted earlier (see n 29), WA has adopted, via its 2021 Act, an 'East coast'-style approach; however, its 2004 Act will continue to apply to contracts entered into prior to the relevant commencement date/s of provisions of the 2021 Act (s 9(1) of the 2021 Act).

65 Section 35 of the Queensland Act defines 'payment dispute' in the context of the implementation of project bank accounts to hold funds on trust (ch 2 pt 3). Even in this context, the definitions are by reference to two scenarios, both of which are the product of the parallel legislative payment claim and payment schedule framework, so the scheme is independent of the payment provisions in the parties' construction contract. The statutory entitlement to progress claims and the adjudication schemes are contained in ch 3 of the Queensland Act.

66 The WA Minister for Planning and Infrastructure said in 2004 that the 'West coast' Acts seek to 'enforce the contract between the parties' whereas the 'East coast' Acts 'introduce a separate, and possibly conflicting, statutory right to payment': MacTiernan, Second Reading Speech, Construction Contracts Bill 2004 (WA), 3 March 2004.

67 WA Act s 25.

68 WA Act s 27(2) provides a list of what an adjudication response must contain, but does not exclude from an adjudication response any reasons for non-payment not also raised in the contractual response to the payment claim.

Lessons for other jurisdictions?

15.29 The scope of an adjudicable dispute under Australian security of payment legislation is confined to disputed payment amounts, however the approach to (and complexity of) creating the confined scope differs across the jurisdictions. Therefore, the Australian approach, conceptually, directly focusses on a central reason for the legislative intervention into matters that would otherwise be subject to the parties' right to contract freely: improving cash flow down the contracting chain on construction projects.[69] In this respect, it can be said that the Australian approach promotes the achievement of a goal that is central to all forms of security of payment legislation.

15.30 However, it comes at a cost in other respects. It limits the practical application of the relevant adjudication schemes to the role of an independent payment claim certification procedure. Such a procedure is largely incapable of operating to resolve broader disputes or differences on construction projects, and is therefore unlikely to proffer a compelling basis of a final resolution between the parties, based upon their agreed acceptance of the outcome of the adjudication process. This is reflected in what sometimes appears to be a form-over-substance approach to complicated administrative yet swift processes which, if not followed closely, can result in draconian (albeit, interim) consequences. Aside from the yet more complicated 'excluded amounts' regime in the Victorian Act, discussed earlier in this chapter, the other Australian Acts continue to apply widely to large value and highly technical claims, which can result in prompt but inadequately considered adjudicators' determinations that leave some parties feeling aggrieved and no closer to a final resolution.

15.31 Weighing against such a conclusion, however, are practical considerations based upon the experience of adjudication to date. Although hard data are scarce, there is an appreciable body of information to the effect that adjudications often represent the first and last port of call for parties seeking to resolve disputes under their construction contract.[70] There may be no legal requirement for parties to do so, but the lack of any common propensity for adjudicating parties to re-argue their disputes in final proceedings, whether they be arbitration or court proceedings, suggests that there is a certain acceptance of adjudication providing something which is needed: a decision to break a deadlock. As the Supreme Court of the UK has recently observed:

> There is a chorus of observations, from experienced TCC judges and textbook writers to the effect that adjudication does, in most cases, achieve a resolution of the underlying dispute which becomes final because it is not thereafter challenged ...
>
> Confirmation from leading textbooks may be found in *Glover and Elliott, Building Contract Disputes: Practice and Precedents* ..., and *Keating on Construction Contracts* 10th ed (2016). ... In a 2014 article in *Building*, there is attributed to David Adamson (former Deputy Chair of the Construction Clients' Forum) the suggestion that 'only around 2% of adjudication decisions have since been challenged in the courts'. ... Statistics do not

69 Coggins and Bell (n 10), 446.

70 Observations to this effect include: Frances Kirkham, 'Tomorrow and Tomorrow and Tomorrow: Keynote Address to the Adjudication Society Conference' (2004) 20(4) *Construction Law Journal* 189, 191; Toby Shnookal, 'Security of Payments in Victoria – Its Use as an Effective Payment Tool' *Building Dispute Practitioners' Society Newsletter*, May 2010, at 18.

appear available to confirm this figure, but the overall picture of most adjudication decisions achieving de facto final resolution of the underlying dispute appears clear.[71]

Time for commencing an adjudication

15.32 This section discusses two sets of issues that flow from the timing requirements for commencing an adjudication. The first relates to the time periods themselves: when they commence and expire, and whether they permit 'recycled' claims. The second flows from a consideration of the generally short time periods under the Australian Acts, which can allow what industry participants describe as 'ambush claims'.

15.33 Under the UK Act, an adjudication can be commenced 'at any time'. This is effected by its s 108(2)(a), which states that a construction contract 'shall include a provision in writing so as to (a) enable a party to give notice at any time of his intention to refer a dispute to adjudication'. The effect of this is that a party can commence an adjudication many months, even years, after a project has concluded.[72] Coupled with the very wide scope of an adjudicable dispute, as discussed in the preceding section, it is easily understood how the UK Act focusses more on the resolution of disputes, and less on the facilitation of cash flow during the currency of a project.[73]

15.34 This differs markedly from the temporal constraints implemented by the Australian Acts, which impose time limits on the commencement of an adjudication in respect of a payment dispute. Under the 'East coast' Acts (which, for the purpose of the analysis that follows, includes the WA 2021 Act),[74] the time period within which an adjudication application must be made depends upon the nature of the event that triggers the payment dispute:[75]

- if the dispute relates to a scheduled amount in a payment schedule being less than the claimed amount, the adjudication application must be made within 10 business days (ACT, NSW, Tasmania, Victoria; 30 business days (Queensland); 15 business days (SA); 20 business days (WA 2021 Act)) of the claimant receiving the payment schedule;
- if the dispute relates to a failure by the respondent to pay the full scheduled amount by the due date for payment, the adjudication application must be made within 20 business days (ACT, NSW, SA, Queensland, Tasmania, WA 2021 Act); 10 business days (Victoria) of the due date for payment;[76] and
- if no payment schedule was submitted by the respondent and the claimant provided notice and a further five business days (ACT, NSW, SA, Tasmania, WA 2021 Act; two business days (Victoria)) have elapsed for the submission of a payment schedule,[77] the adjudication application must be made within 10 business

71 *Bresco Electrical* [2020] UKSC 25 at [14] – [15] (references omitted).

72 Helps and Bailey (n 27), 46.

73 This may be contrary to the intent of the UK Act, as Latham recommended that the UK scheme should be limited to the currency of the project: n 15, [9.14]; see also Helps and Bailey (n 27).

74 See the main text accompanying n 20.

75 ACT Act s 19(3)(b) – (d); NSW Act s 17(3)(c) – (e); Queensland Act s 79(2); SA Act s 17(3)(c) – (e); Victorian Act s 18(3)(c) – (e); Tasmanian Act s 21(3) – (4); WA 2021 Act s 28(4).

76 For discussion on the 'due date for payment', see n 39.

77 For discussion on the second chance to issue a payment schedule, see n 40.

> days (ACT, NSW, Tasmania; 15 business days (SA); five business days (Victoria); 20 business days (WA 2021 Act)) of the expiry of the further period.[78]

Under the 'West coast' Acts (NT and (2004) WA), the situation is simpler. As they create a defined legislative concept for a '(payment) dispute' under a contract, the date for commencing an adjudicating is measured from the date the 'payment dispute' arises. The claimant must serve an adjudication application within 90 business days (WA; 65 'working days' (NT)) of the dispute arising.[79]

15.35 The varying time periods, even within Acts subscribing to the 'East coast' model, demonstrate another salient lesson derived from the Australian experience. Constant tinkering with legislation that already contains complex administrative processes often results in yet more layers of complexity instead of refinement and increased efficiency. This is particularly serious in the context presently under discussion, as the time periods operate to limit claimants' rights to access the adjudication schemes. If an adjudication scheme cannot be accessed or used efficiently, the achievement of its underlying rationale, being the facilitation of cash flow down to vulnerable subcontractors, will be undermined.

15.36 Nevertheless, the Australian approach of imposing temporal limits that operate to restrict access does provide benefits. It encourages disputed claims to be adjudicated promptly, which promotes cash flow when it is needed most: promptly and during the currency of a project. Similarly, it discourages claims hoarding until well after a project ends. This improves commercial certainty of participants seeking to move on to new opportunities without needing to make provisions for potential post-project payment claims pursued via expedited adjudication procedures.[80]

15.37 These limitations on post-project payment claims are subject to an important qualifier regarding payment claims during the currency of a project. The Australian Acts permit claims to be 'recycled' by the claimant including them in a subsequent payment claim.[81] Although the legislation does not preserve an entitlement to pursue such claims by adjudication in perpetuity, the legislation does allow for 'claims hoarding' while a project remains on foot. In practice, this can encourage 'ambush claims', especially in the latter stages of projects. An 'ambush claim' is where the claimant develops over time substantial factual, technical and legal submissions and then commences a single adjudication in respect of many months' worth of unpaid claims. This issue emerged soon after the NSW Act became the first Australian security of payment legislation to come into force,[82] and has been legitimately described – at least, from the respondent's point of view – as 'clearly a procedurally unfair practice'.[83]

15.38 However, the permissive approach to ambush claims arguably accurately reflects the intention of the legislatures responsible for enacting the security of payment legislation

78 The corresponding Queensland Act provision refers to disputes relating to a failure to issue a payment schedule and to pay the full amount in the payment claim: the adjudication application must be made within 30 business days of the later of the due date for payment or the last day on which a payment schedule could have been given.

79 NT Act s 28(1); WA Act s 26(1).

80 Helps and Bailey (n 27), 46–7.

81 For example, see paragraph (b) of the definition of 'payment claim' in s 3 of the WA Act, s 13(6) of the NSW Act; s 14(9) of the Victorian Act, and s 75(5) of the Queensland Act.

82 Coggins and Bell (n 10), 432.

83 Ibid, 443. The UK experience has been similar to the Australian one, in this regard.

around Australia. The result has been to effectively swap the burden of proof, from the claimant to the respondent, by requiring that the respondent must always be ready and able to fully defend any decision to not pay a full payment claim on short notice.[84] The legal consequences play out 'on the ground' by shifting the bargaining power towards those further down the contracting chain.

Adjudicator nomination

Qualifications and conflicts of interest

15.39 Once a payment dispute has crystallised and an adjudication application has been submitted by the claimant, the next important consideration is the adjudicator themselves. Adjudicators' qualifications and the manner in which they are selected and appointed is a matter that has generated much controversy in Australia, due mainly to the tension arising from the ability of private companies to be registered to appoint adjudicators. This tension came to a head in Queensland in 2013 when a review by Andrew Wallace heard extensive reports of perceived conflicts of interest, leading him to conclude that

> a fair-minded lay observer might reasonably apprehend that an adjudicator under the current appointment process might not bring an impartial and unprejudiced mind to the resolution of the questions that he or she is called upon to decide.[85]

In grappling with these issues, a disparate array of procedures and oversight mechanisms have been enacted, amended, repealed and replaced across Australia. This picture is very different from that which emerges from the UK experience. Section 108(2)(b) of the UK Act permits the parties to a construction contract latitude in agreeing the process for appointing an adjudicator, or nominating an adjudicator in the contract. This arises from the fact the UK Act is non-prescriptive as to how an adjudicator is appointed, or who an adjudicator can be.

'West coast' approach

15.40 The closest analogue to the UK Act in the Australian context is the NT and (2004) WA Acts. However, even though these Acts permit the parties certain freedom when drafting their construction contract in respect of the nomination of an adjudicator, they do not have carte blanche to select any adjudicator or nominating authority. Instead, they must either nominate a 'registered adjudicator' or select a 'prescribed appointor' to nominate an adjudicator for them. The WA Act permits the following three channels for the selection of an adjudicator:[86]

- The parties may agree in the construction contract to appoint a registered adjudicator, and that registered adjudicator consents to the appointment;

84 Bell and Vella (n 6), 569.

85 Andrew Wallace, *Discussion Paper – Payment Dispute Resolution in the Queensland Building and Construction Industry: Final Report* (May 2013), 160.

86 WA Act s 26(1)(c).

- The parties may instead agree in the construction contract that the adjudicator will be nominated by a prescribed appointor (in this scenario, the appointor must appoint a registered adjudicator within five business days of receiving notice from the claimant; failing such appointment the Building Commissioner may appoint a registered adjudicator);[87] or
- In the absence of agreement between the parties in their construction contract, the claimant may choose a prescribed appointor which will nominate the adjudicator.

There is much to be said for the approach implemented by the (2004) WA Act (and, it essentially remains intact under the WA 2021 Act).[88] It balances the parties' freedom to negotiate their construction contract as they see fit, while ensuring that there is a degree of public oversight of the quality of adjudicators and nominating authorities. In addition, by maintaining as a fallback option the unilateral discretion of the claimant to select its own prescribed appointor at the time the payment dispute arises,[89] the WA Act limits the scope for imbalanced commercial bargaining power during pre-contract negotiations to influence the nomination of adjudicators.[90]

15.41 This balancing of often competing principles – freedom of contract and public oversight of adjudication processes – is supplemented by provisions disqualifying an adjudicator from adjudicating a payment dispute where the adjudicator 'has a material personal interest in the payment dispute concerned or in the construction contract under which the dispute has arisen or in any party to the contract'.[91] Moreover, a registered adjudicator must hold prescribed qualifications,[92] and the Building Commissioner may cancel the registration of an adjudicator if the individual 'has mismanaged, or is incompetent or unsuitable to conduct, adjudications'.[93]

15.42 A prescribed appointor is a person prescribed as such under the regulations, and as of July 2021, includes seven appointing institutions.[94] Finally, the public oversight of adjudicator operating under the WA Act is completed by the availability for public inspection of the result, or a report, of adjudicators' determinations.[95]

87 WA Act s 28(1) and (2).

88 WA 2021 Act s 29(1).

89 Which, as discussed next, is a facet of many of the 'East coast' Acts.

90 Coggins and Bell (n 10), 438.

91 WA Act s 29(1). This provision has been carried through, and expanded, in the WA 2021 Act (s 33).

92 WA Act s 48(1). Reg 9 of the Construction Contracts Regulations 2004 (WA) (**WA Regulations**) provides that a registered adjudicator must have a degree from a university or other tertiary institution in a course in architecture, engineering, quantity surveying, building surveying, building, construction, law or project management, or be eligible for membership in various associated professional institutions, or be a registered builder. The individual must have at least five years' experience in administering construction contracts or resolving disputes under construction contracts, and have completed an appropriate training course which qualifies them for performance of the functions of an adjudicator.

93 WA Act s 48(5)(b).

94 WA Regulations r 11.

95 WA Act s 50. The 'Report of the Building Commissioner for the Financial Year to 30 June 2019' states that no requests for publication of individual adjudicator's determinations were received and therefore no determinations were published in the year to 30 June 2019. In that year 115 adjudication applications were reported in respect of a gross claims value of A$60,524,242.18 (with a mean value of payment dispute of AU$526,297.76). These metrics were lower than has been experienced under the WA Act since the 2008–2009 financial year, which likely reflects the recent abatement of construction activity on mining and resources projects in WA.

'East coast' approach

15.43 The balanced picture that emerges from the WA Act and Regulations is very different from the approach to the nomination of adjudicators under the NSW and Victorian Acts.

15.44 Under the NSW Act, the claimant retains unilateral power to select an 'Authorised Nominating Authority' (**ANA**) at the time the payment dispute arises, and that ANA must refer the adjudication application to a person eligible to be an adjudicator as soon as possible.[96] The NSW Act allows ANAs to operate for profit, and the claimant and respondent are jointly and severally liable for the fees charged by an ANA or in such proportions as determined by an adjudicator.[97]

15.45 Only natural persons are eligible to be an adjudicator, and they must have the qualifications, expertise and experience prescribed by the regulations under the NSW Act. These requirements, in effect from 1 September 2020, incorporate qualifications requirements for adjudicators, including at least 10 years' experience in management of construction contracts or resolution of construction disputes.[98] A person is not eligible to adjudicate a payment dispute if they are a party to the construction contract or in circumstances prescribed by the NSW Regulations.[99] The Victorian Act implements a similar framework, though presently without the level of detail around adjudicator qualifications which was introduced in NSW in 2020–21.[100]

15.46 The approach to the nomination of adjudicators that is currently implemented by the NSW and Victorian Acts has been criticised on the grounds of unfairness and perceived bias. These grounds were examined in Wallace's review; his Report ventilated the following concerns:[101]

- that for-profit ANAs are biased towards claimants, as they stand to gain financially from future referrals from claimants;
- 'adjudicator shopping' was inadvertently encouraged, whereby a claimant could request that an ANA either appoint (or not appoint) a particular adjudicator, failing which another ANA will be selected by the claimant; and
- that some ANAs maintain unhealthy relationships with claims preparers, whereby preparers are recommended by ANAs to claimants under the expectation that the preparers will recommend to the claimants that a referral be made to that ANA.

In response to the Wallace Report a comprehensive set of reforms was implemented in Queensland, including the enactment of an entirely new principal Act.[102] These reforms included a movement away from permitting the claimant to unilaterally nominate its

96 NSW Act ss 17(3)(b) and (6).

97 NSW Act ss 28(3) and (4).

98 Building and Construction Industry Security of Payment Regulation 2020 (**NSW Regulations**) r 19.

99 The NSW Regulations lists the following disqualifying factors: the adjudicator has not completed mandatory continuing professional development or a reasonable person would conclude that the adjudicator has an actual or perceived conflict or would not adjudicate impartially (r 19(2); however, the CPD requirement does not apply until 1 September 2021).

100 Victorian Act ss 18(3)(b), (4) and (7), 19, 42 and 43C.

101 Wallace (n 85), 131–150.

102 See n 4.

preferred ANA. Instead, a claimant may only apply for an adjudication to an Adjudication Registrar appointed by the Governor in Council.[103] The registrar then refers the payment dispute to an eligible adjudicator. A person is ineligible to adjudicate a payment dispute if the person is a party to the construction contract or has a conflict of interest as prescribed by the regulations under the Queensland Act. In keeping with a commitment to increased public oversight of the adjudication process, the Queensland Building and Construction Commission publishes adjudication determinations on its publicly accessible website.[104]

Adjudicator bias: case law

15.47 Actual and apprehended bias, together with obtaining a fair hearing, are core elements of natural justice that the courts in the UK and around Australia apply when asked to consider the validity of adjudicators' determinations. The full scope of Australian courts' approaches to upholding or quashing determinations is discussed in detail later in this chapter (under the section titled 'Errors and other grounds for challenging adjudication determinations'). However, some discussion of this topic is warranted in this part, as it relates to the important question of adjudicator independence which has influenced the divergent approaches to adjudicator nomination implemented by the Australian Acts.

15.48 The intersection of the principles of natural justice and adjudication schemes in the UK[105] gives rise to broadly the same issues when considered in the Australian context. The issue of adjudicator bias falls within the rubric of natural justice, of which there are two main components. The first is that the parties have a fair opportunity to be heard,[106] and the second is that there be no actual or apprehended adjudicator bias.[107] A survey of recent judicial decisions in the UK and Australia reveals that there may be no legislative framework for the nomination of adjudicators that provides a perfect solution.

103 Queensland Act s 150. As at July 2021, the registrar is a representative of the Queensland Building and Construction Commission.

104 This is included within the registrar's functions: Queensland Act s 154(2)(e). As at July 2021, determinations could be accessed here: http://xweb.bcipa.qld.gov.au/ars_xweb/Pages/.

105 For a summary of the key principles, see Julian Bailey, 'Tribunal Bias – Familiarity Breeds Concern' (2016) *International Construction Law Review* 233.

106 For example, in *JKC Australia LNG Pty Ltd v Inpex Operations Australia Pty Ltd* [2018] NTCA 6, it was held that there was no denial of natural justice despite the fact that the adjudicator's determination turned upon a point of law not argued by either party. This was because the adjudicator had identified the issue in his preliminary view of the matter and therefore both parties had the opportunity to respond and ought reasonably to have anticipated that the issue might form part of the adjudicator's determination. On the other hand, there are many cases in which an adjudicator has based a determination on an issue in respect of which the parties were not given an opportunity to be heard, and that provided grounds for quashing the determination. In *Ausenco Operations Pty Ltd & Anor v Ferretti International Ottoway Pty Ltd & Anor* [2020] SASC 46, for example, the Court held that the adjudicator ought to have requested further submissions under s 21(4) of the SA Act from the parties with respect to a particular interpretation. Also, a failure to take into account a payment schedule, as is required by s 22(2)(d) of the NSW Act, can also amount to a denial of natural justice: *TWT Property Group Pty Limited v Cenric Group Pty Limited* [2020] NSWSC 72.

107 Cases involving findings of apprehended bias often involve a party having earlier disputed the adjudicator's fees in a previous unrelated determination and the same adjudicator being appointed for a subsequent adjudication involving the same party. See, *eg*, *Quickway Constructions v Paul J Hick* [2017] NSWSC 830; *Reiby Street Apartments Pty Ltd v Winterton Constructions Pty Ltd* [2005] NSWSC 545; and *Allpro Building Services Pty Ltd v Micos Architectural Division Pty Ltd* [2010] NSWSC 474.

15.49 First, it is apparent that the complex nature of the Australian Acts can cause confusion for adjudicators, which in some instances can lead to an inadvertent denial of natural justice. An example occurred in *National Management Group Pty Ltd v Biriel Industries Pty Ltd*,[108] where a respondent failed to provide a payment schedule and therefore had no legislative right to submit an adjudication response.[109] The respondent still sought to make submissions on the jurisdiction of the adjudicator to determine the dispute, but the adjudicator refused to take those submissions on jurisdiction into consideration. The respondent then sought to have the subsequent adjudicator's determination quashed for being denied a fair opportunity to be heard. This criticism was accepted by the Court, as the absence of a legislative entitlement to submit an adjudication response addressing the merits of the claim did not also mean that the respondent was barred from making submissions on the adjudicator's jurisdiction. Ultimately, however, the adjudicator's determination was not quashed, as Wilson J was not convinced that the submissions, if considered, would have resulted in a different outcome.

15.50 Second, even if someone is nominated by a 'neutral body', this can still give rise to independence issues and questions of actual or apprehended bias. For example, in *Eurocom Ltd v Siemens plc*,[110] which concerned an adjudication under the UK Act, an adjudicator appointed by the (independent) Royal Institution of Chartered Surveyors was found to be without jurisdiction because of fraudulent steps taken by the respondent to secure the appointment of their chosen adjudicator (Mr Bingham). The adjudication resulted in a determination in favour of Eurocom, represented by Mr Knowles. Knowles had successfully manipulated the process for appointing an adjudicator to secure the nomination of Bingham to that role. It was held by Ramsey J that the manipulation provided sufficient justification for not summarily enforcing the adjudicator's determination. This was on the basis that the adjudicator

> was not properly appointed because there was a fraudulent misrepresentation by those acting on behalf of Eurocom in making the application for the appointment of an adjudicator. On that basis the adjudicator would not have jurisdiction.[111]

Finally, as was noted earlier,[112] the for-profit nature of many of the ANAs operating in Australia can also give rise to independence issues and questions of actual or apprehended bias. An example of court consideration of the issue was *Built Environs Pty Ltd v Tali Engineering Pty Ltd*.[113] The manager of an ANA (Mr Sain) was also the CEO of a construction consultant company that had been advising Tali on its disputes with Built Environs. When Tali applied to Mr Sain's ANA for the appointment of an adjudicator, Mr Sain attempted to preclude a perception of bias by recusing himself from the nomination process and leaving it in the hands of his colleague.

15.51 The Court found that there was apprehended bias, noting that the adjudicator must be seen as independent of both parties, and therefore it is equally important for the ANA to

108 *National Management Group Pty Ltd v Biriel Industries Pty Ltd trading as Master Steel* [2019] QSC 219.
109 See the discussion in [15.19]–[15.20] above.
110 *Eurocom Ltd v Siemens plc* [2014] EWHC 3710 (TCC).
111 *Eurocom* [2014] EWHC 3710 (TCC), [83].
112 See the discussion in [15.39] above.
113 *Built Environs Pty Ltd v Tali Engineering Pty Ltd & Ors* [2013] SASC 84.

also be seen as being independent of both parties. In the circumstances of this appointment, an objective bystander could not know what internal communications might take place within the ANA between personnel aligned with one party and other personnel tasked with nominating an adjudicator, leading to the nomination of an adjudicator favourable to the respondent. This gave rise to a reasonable apprehension of bias.[114]

15.52 It is difficult to conceive a legislative framework that will remove all possibility of a deprivation of natural justice in an adjudication under security of payment legislation. Indeed, the NSW Supreme Court has recognised that an element of 'rough justice' is inherent in the adjudication procedure and does not necessarily equate to a denial of procedural fairness.[115] Nevertheless, the pursuit of a perfect adjudication process often appears to drive legislative amendments, even where the added layers of complexity may tend to confuse adjudicators and result in further errors.

Enforcement mechanisms

15.53 Obtaining an adjudication determination in one's favour is not the end of the process for a claimant. An adjudicator is empowered to determine a payment dispute, but an adjudicator does not have the judicial powers of compulsion necessary to enforce payment by the respondent. Therefore, a critical final (or penultimate, should the determination be challenged in a manner discussed in the section titled 'Errors and other grounds for challenging adjudication determinations') phase is to implement the enforcement mechanisms contained in security of payment legislation.

15.54 As with the other elements of statutory adjudication discussed earlier, the position in the UK is markedly different to that in Australia. Under the UK Act, an adjudicator's determination needs to be enforced through the courts or through arbitration if the contract provides for arbitration as the final form of dispute resolution.[116] This is a result of a curious omission from the UK Act. It is wholly silent as to how one enforces an adjudicator's decision. In the absence of any such provision, an adjudicator's decision is treated by the UK courts as if it were a binding contractual determination, in the nature of an expert determination or an arbitral award, which requires homologation through the courts – requiring the attention of a judge – in order to give rise to the desired outcome: a judgment debt.

15.55 By contrast, the Australian approach to enforcement has considerable attractions. It allows a claimant to enforce a favourable adjudication determination through a largely paper-driven exercise, and result in a judicial decision without arguments on the merits of the claim. It is in effect a fast-track enforcement process, which is in keeping with the expedited nature of the statutory adjudication schemes giving rise to the determinations being enforced. The Australian approach is consonant with the 'pay now, argue later' intent of ensuring prompt cash flow down the contracting chain on an interim, but enforceable, basis.

114 *Built Environs* [2013] SASC 84, [194]; this was one of the grounds on which the Court quashed the adjudication: [218].

115 *CC Builders (Aust) Pty Ltd v Milestone Civil Pty Ltd* [2019] NSWSC 1251 [9], [33].

116 Helps and Bailey (n 27), 48.

15.56 The fast-tracked enforcement processes available in the Australian Acts do not prevent a respondent from commencing court proceedings to restrain a claimant from invoking the enforcement procedure, if there are sufficient grounds for challenging the adjudicator's jurisdiction or the validity of the adjudication process (see [15.61]ff below).

15.57 The following is a summary, by way of example of the Australian approach, of the process implemented under the NSW Act. Upon receiving a favourable adjudicator's determination, the claimant may take the following steps to enforce that determination:

- A respondent is under a statutory obligation to pay an adjudicated amount within five business days of service of the adjudicator's determination (or any later date set by the adjudicator).[117]
- Upon a failure to pay the adjudicated amount by the respondent in accordance with the Act, the claimant may request that the ANA to whom the adjudication application was made provide an adjudication certificate, and may also serve notice on the respondent that the claimant intends to suspend carrying-out of the work.[118]
- The adjudication certificate may be filed as a judgment for debt in any court of competent jurisdiction and is enforceable as a debt by virtue of the Act. In filing, the certificate must be accompanied by an affidavit evidencing that the whole or any part of the adjudicated amount has not been paid.[119]
- Any proceedings commenced by the respondent to have the debt set aside cannot involve any cross-claims, defences arising under the construction contract or challenges to the adjudicator's determination, and the respondent must pay into court as security the value of the unpaid adjudicated amount as a condition of commencing any such proceedings.[120]

There are similar statutory enforcement mechanisms under all other Australian Acts.[121]

15.58 In addition, the Victorian Act contains a self-help remedy that is designed to promote cash flow from the principal to a claimant-subcontractor, bypassing a respondent-contractor.[122] The mechanism only applies if the claimant has pursued the Victorian equivalent of the process summarised earlier, and has obtained judgment for the adjudicated amount as a debt from the respondent.[123] Therefore, this process is principally designed to operate where the respondent is experiencing financial difficulties such that debt recovery is impracticable. In these circumstances, the project can successfully continue with funds paid by the principal direct to claimant-subcontractor.[124] The legal entitlement is created by a statutory assignment of debt by which the principal's obligation to pay the respondent under

117 NSW Act s 23.
118 NSW Act s 24(1).
119 NSW Act s 25(1) and (2).
120 NSW Act s 25(4).
121 ACT Act ss 26–27; NT Act s 45; Queensland Act ss 90–93; SA Act ss 24–25; Tasmanian Act ss 26–27; Victorian Act ss 28M – 28R; WA Act ss 42 and 43 (and WA 2021 Act ss 52–54).
122 Victorian Act Pt 3 Div 4.
123 Victorian Act s 30.
124 Victorian Act s 31.

their construction contract is assigned to the claimant (subcontractor),[125] which extinguishes the respondent (contractor)'s entitlement to claim equivalent payments from the principal.

15.59 The enforcement mechanisms in the Australian Acts reduce the likelihood of speculative or weak challenges to adjudicators' determinations, which might occur in circumstances where the only avenue to enforcement of an adjudicator's determination is to commence full court proceedings. Consequently, the mechanisms in the Australian Acts may save time and the cost of enforcement. Both of these savings contribute to achieving the purpose of security of payment legislation: by improving access to funds in a timely and less costly manner, the statutory enforcement mechanisms in and of themselves operate to improve cash flow in the construction industry. They also, in theory, free up the court's time to deal with other matters. In practice, however, aggrieved respondents continue to seek to avoid adjudicators' determinations by raising points of jurisdiction or procedures during summary judgment proceedings.[126]

15.60 This is particularly the case where the respondent feels as though it has received 'rough justice' at the hands of an adjudicator, or where through clerical oversight the respondent failed to respond with a payment schedule and therefore was unable to fully defend its decisions during an adjudication. Even though most challenges to adjudications ultimately fail, the fact that they are attempted has the serious potential to thwart a claimant's desire for rapid access to cash flow. Thus, early success for claimants gained through the legislative adjudication schemes may only be the first step on a long road to recovery against a respondent intent on evading payment.[127]

Errors and other grounds for challenging adjudication determinations

Limited to jurisdictional error?

15.61 The judicial approaches to challenges on the basis of errors made in adjudicators' determinations illustrate interesting conceptual difference between the application of the UK Act and its Australian counterparts.

15.62 The root causes of this difference are not the specific provisions of the legislation, although of course the provisions influence each matter on a case-by-case basis, but how Australian courts have come to characterise the role and powers of an adjudicator. Although an adjudicator holds no public office and is often privately appointed, Australian jurisprudence that has developed since 2010 treats adjudicators as though they exercise public powers and therefore adjudicators' determinations are susceptible to review on public law grounds.

---

125 Effected by s 34 of the Victorian Act.

126 See *John Beever (Aust) Pty Ltd v Roads Corporation* [2018] VSC 635, where summary judgment under the Victorian Act was refused. Digby J held that the Victorian Act had to be applied alongside the local civil procedure legislation regulating the granting of summary judgment. Under the procedural legislation, in order to obtain summary judgment, the claimant had to demonstrate that the respondent's defensive arguments [regarding jurisdiction and the potential inclusion of 'excluded amounts' (see [15.21]–[15.25] above)] had no real prospect of success. This hurdle could not be met, and summary judgment was refused, forcing the claimant to seek enforcement of a favourable adjudicator's determination via full proceeding (albeit, a full proceeding restricted to the limited grounds upon which a respondent can challenge an adjudicator's determination).

127 Bell and Vella (n 6), 572.

15.63 There has been some variation in how adjudicators' functions have been described, but the general position is clear and harmonious across jurisdictions. In Queensland and Western Australia, it has been recognised that adjudicators are 'anomalous tribunals' that are not to be regarded as administrative tribunals, but as being more akin to inferior courts.[128] In respect of the Victorian Act it has been held that, despite the adjudicator's functions being analogous to that of an inferior court, the adjudicator is not part of the court hierarchy and more closely reflects a statutory tribunal exercising governmental power by performing a public function in a quasi-judicial capacity.[129] The rationale for the application of public law concepts is tolerably clear: adjudicators are appointed as a result of statutes being enacted, and they are required to carry out the functions prescribed by statute. Their role may therefore, in broad terms, be seen as having a statutory nature, thus bringing adjudicators within the purview of rules of public law for controlling the administrative action.

15.64 This characterisation and approach are not taken in the UK, where an error in the determination does not provide a basis for vitiating the determination.[130] The English courts have likened the position of the adjudicator to that of a contractually appointed expert and, accordingly, view adjudication as a private dispute resolution process. Although created and made compulsory by statute, adjudication in the UK has been characterised as, in essence, a contractual dispute resolution process which either forms part of the construction contract as express terms or as implied terms by virtue of the UK Act. As such, even though the reason for the adjudicator's involvement is to achieve statutory compliance, the adjudicator is not a statutory decision-maker and the adjudicator's role is not an aspect of public law.

15.65 As a consequence, the merits of an adjudicator's decision are not reviewable if the adjudicator applied the law erroneously, for example by misconstruing the application of the UK legislation.[131] Instead, English courts apply a straightforward test for the validity of an adjudicator's determination: has the adjudicator answered the right question in the wrong way, or the wrong question?[132] If it is the case that the right question was answered the wrong way, the adjudicator will not have exceeded their jurisdiction and the adjudicator's determination will be binding. If, on the other hand, the wrong question was answered, the adjudicator's determination will be a nullity.[133]

15.66 The Australian approach is therefore considerably broader, and gives rise to far greater complexities, than that taken in the UK to dealing with 'errors'. The complexity arises under Australian law primarily because when it comes to 'errors' in adjudicators'

128 Regarding the Queensland Act, see: *Acciona Agua Australia Pty Ltd v Monadelphous Engineering Pty Ltd* [2020] QSC 133, [31]; *Heavy Plant Leasing Pty Ltd v McConnell Dowell Constructors (Aust) Pty Ltd* [2013] QCA 386, [52] – [63]; and *Annie Street JV Pty Ltd v MCC Pty Ltd* [2016] QSC 268 at [22]. Regarding the WA Act, see: *O'Donnell Griffin Pty Ltd v John Holland Pty Ltd* [2009] WASC 19, [98] – [103]; *Thiess Pty Ltd v MCC Mining (Western Australia) Pty Ltd* [2011] WASC 80, [56] – [59]; *Qube Port of Dampier v Philip Loots of Kahlia Nominees Ltd* [2014] WASC 331, [28].

129 *Grocon Constructors Pty Ltd v Planit Cocciardi Joint Venture (No 2)* (2009) 26 VR 172, 182. Even this description of an adjudicator's role focuses on the public function being performed, as opposed to a private dispute resolution role pursuant to that implied by the UK Act. In respect of the NSW Act it has been held that it was not necessary to categorise an adjudicator's role as being akin to an inferior court or an administrative tribunal: *Chase Oyster Bar v Hamo Industries* [2010] NSWCA 190 (*Chase Oyster Bar*).

130 Helps and Bailey (n 27), 49.

131 *Diamond v PJW Enterprises Ltd* [2004] BLR 131, [140] – [141].

132 *Bouygues* (n 23).

133 *Bouygues* (n 23), [12] – [13].

determinations, a distinction (sometimes a difficult one) is made between 'jurisdictional' errors that may vitiate an adjudicator's determination and 'non-jurisdictional errors' that are benign from an enforceability perspective.

15.67 The path of Australian jurisprudence to this position was not a straight one, but the High Court of Australia has now provided guidance on this issue.[134] Prior to 2010, the commonly accepted position in NSW was that the NSW Act precluded judicial review except where an adjudication determination failed to comply with certain 'basic and essential requirements' of the Act.[135] That position changed in 2010 when the decision in *Chase Oyster Bar*[136] removed any doubt that the Supreme Court could at least quash a determination which was infected with jurisdictional error (that is, an error which goes to the authority or power of the adjudicator to make his or her decision). However, *Chase Oyster Bar* did not finally settle whether review might be available for non-jurisdictional errors of law on the face of the record.

15.68 In the first High Court case on the security of payment legislation, *Southern Han*,[137] the Court held that the existence of a statutory 'reference date' was a necessary precondition for a valid payment claim under the NSW Act.[138] The absence of a valid payment claim rendered void any subsequent adjudicator's determination in respect of that payment claim. The High Court revisited the NSW Act in *Probuild Constructions* in the context of the potential to review an adjudicator's determination for non-jurisdictional error of law, and also considered the South Australian Act in the same context and at the same time in *Maxcon Constructions*.

15.69 It is now the case that NSW courts' power under the local judicial legislation[139] to quash a determination for a non-jurisdictional error of law on the face of the record is excluded by the NSW Act. As a result, the mere fact that an adjudicator's determination is wrong (often, plainly wrong) provides no grounds to have the determination quashed. This has empowered the courts to resist challenges to adjudicators' determinations even where the determinations are characterised as 'rough justice'.

Jurisdictional error examples

15.70 Following *Chase Oyster Bar*, adjudicators' determinations have been set aside on numerous jurisdictional grounds (which, because of the complex legislative frameworks

134 *Probuild Constructions (Aust) Pty Ltd v Shade Systems Pty Ltd* [2018] HCA 4 (*Probuild Constructions*) in respect of the NSW Act, and *Maxcon Constructions Pty Ltd v Vadasz* [2018] HCA 5 (*Maxcon Constructions*) in respect of the SA Act.

135 *Brodyn Pty Ltd v Davenport* (2004) 61 NSWLR 421. An even earlier view on this issue was that adjudicators were akin to administrative tribunals and, therefore, adjudicator's determinations were susceptible to review for jurisdictional error of law: *Musico* [2003] NSWSC 977.

136 *Chase Oyster Bar v Hamo Industries* [2010] NSWCA 190.

137 *Southern Han Breakfast Point Pty Ltd (in Liq) v Lewence Construction Pty Ltd* [2016] HCA 52 (*Southern Han*).

138 Because of similarities between the Australian Acts in respect of 'reference dates', including that only one payment claim may be made per 'reference date', the decision in *Southern Han* is widely applicable in other Australian jurisdictions. That said, the concept of 'reference dates' was removed from the NSW Act in 2019 in response to recommendation 14 of the Murray Report (n 12, xviii), essentially made on the basis that – as the *Southern Han* case itself demonstrates – the concept is productive of confusion in practice.

139 Supreme Court Act 1970 (NSW).

which create an adjudicator's jurisdiction, can sometimes be difficult to distinguish from non-jurisdictional grounds). These grounds include where:

- the adjudicator failed to perform the statutory function under s 22(3) of the NSW Act of giving a sufficient statement of reasons;[140]
- the adjudicator had erred in deciding that a payment claim had been properly made in accordance with the NSW Act;[141]
- the adjudicator identified the wrong document as the payment schedule and therefore failed to take into account a matter or circumstance that the Queensland Act required be taken into account;[142]
- there was no applicable 'reference date', including where earlier termination of the construction contract meant that no new 'reference date' was created;[143]
- the payment claim was not sufficiently detailed to comply with the 'relatively undemanding' requirements of the Queensland Act,[144] or an email was not sufficient to constitute a payment claim under the NSW Act;[145]
- the claimant gave notice of an adjudication prior to being permitted to do so;[146]
- payment claims included amounts to recover the cost of obtaining bank guarantees and compensation on a *quantum meruit* basis, which were held not to be claims for compensation under a construction contract for construction work performed or the supply of related goods and services;[147]
- the adjudicator's determination excluded consideration of the underlying contract and took no account of the contract whatsoever;[148] and
- where the claimant was insolvent and no longer able to perform construction works and supply related goods and services.[149]

Many of these decisions emanate from NSW and, therefore, concern the NSW Act. In response to the relatively high number of challenges to adjudicators' determinations under the NSW Act, the legislation was amended in 2018 to include s 32A, by which part of a determination that was made outside the adjudicator's jurisdiction can be severed. This allows the other parts of the determination to remain enforceable under the NSW Act,

---

140 *Bauen Constructions Pty Ltd v Westwood Interiors Pty Ltd* [2010] NSWSC 1359.

141 *Steel Building Systems Pty Ltd v Beks Constructions (NSW) Pty Ltd* [2010] NSWSC 1404.

142 *Heavy Plant Leasing Pty Ltd v McConnell Dowell Constructors (Aust) Pty Ltd* [2013] QCA 386.

143 *Green Suburban Pty Ltd v Vita Built Ltd* [2018] VSC 330; *Vanguard Development Group Pty Ltd v Promax Building Developments Pty Ltd* [2018] VSC 386; and *Impero Pacific Group Pty Ltd v Bonheur Holdings Pty Ltd* [2019] NSWSC 286.

144 *KDV Sport Pty Ltd v Muggeridge Constructions Pty Ltd & Ors* [2019] QSC 178.

145 *Style Timber Floor Pty Ltd v Krivosudsky* [2019] NSWCA 171.

146 *Jantom Construction* [2011] NSWSC 670.

147 *Grocon (Belgrave St) Developer Pty Ltd v Construction Profile Pty Ltd* [2020] NSWSC 409 and *TFM Epping Land Pty Ltd v Decon Australia Pty Ltd* [2020] NSWCA 93.

148 *Laing O'Rourke Australia Construction Pty Ltd v Samsung C&T Corporation* [2016] WASCA 130. The trial decision raised the prospect of an adjudicator's determination being so unreasonable as to be without jurisdiction, but the WA Court of Appeal did not go so far in the appeal decision.

149 *Façade Treatment Engineering Pty Ltd (in liq) v Brookfield Multiplex Constructions Pty Ltd* [2016] VSCA 247. This decision was rejected as 'plainly wrong' in respect of the NSW Act in *Seymour Whyte Constructions Pty Ltd v Ostwald Bros Pty Ltd* [2019] NSWCA 11. However, in line with recommendation 10 of the Murray Report (n 12, xvii)) the NSW Act was amended to exclude insolvent claimants (NSW Act s 32B). See, generally, Helen Anderson and Matthew Bell, 'Timing Is Everything: Security of Payment, Set-off and (In)solvency' (2020) 35 *Building and Construction Law* 453 and, for the English position, *Bresco Electrical Services* [2020] UKSC 25.

which outcome was designed to enhance cash flow to smaller subcontractors who would otherwise be deprived of an interim payment where a severable part of a determination was quashed.[150]

Review adjudications

15.71 This relatively high incidence of challenges to adjudicators' determinations under the NSW Act may be partly caused by the absence of express statutory avenues for review of adjudicators' determinations under the NSW Act, which leaves the courts to consider and set the limits of appeal rights. As with the other aspects of statutory adjudication schemes in the Australian Acts discussed in this chapter, this approach is not consistent around Australia.

15.72 The Victorian and WA (2004 and 2021) Acts contain statutory review processes, allowing an aggrieved participant in an adjudication to have the adjudicator's determination reviewed. By way of broad summary, those review mechanisms are as follows:[151]

- A statutory right of review under the Victorian Act only arises if the adjudicated amount exceeds A$100,000 (or a higher amount prescribed by regulation) and is limited to reviews arising from the application of the 'excluded amounts' regime (see [15.21]–[15.25] above). As with the addition of s 32A to the NSW Act discussed earlier, these strict limits on statutory review under the Victorian Act were expressly enacted to protect small subcontractors which rely upon enforcing favourable adjudicators' determinations to obtain interim payments and maintain cash flow.[152] The respondent may only seek a review if it has submitted a valid payment schedule in accordance with the Victorian Act, and the respondent has paid to the claimant all non-'excluded amounts' of the adjudicated amount and paid the alleged 'excluded amounts' into a trust account. An adjudication review application must be made to the same ANA that regulated the initial adjudication, and the procedures are broadly similar to the procedures of an initial adjudication.[153]
- Where an adjudicator's determination dismisses an adjudication application without making a determination of its merits,[154] the WA Act (but, this has not been carried through into the 2021 Act) permits the aggrieved party to apply to the State Administrative Tribunal for a review of that determination.[155] If the original determination is set aside, then the original adjudicator is provided with an

150 See S MacDonald, Second Reading Speech, Building and Construction Industry Security of Payment Amendment Bill 2018, 24 October 2018. The effect of stemming cash flow to small subcontractors was described as 'unfair' and 'unnecessary'.

151 See, *eg*, Samer Skaik, 'Taking Statutory Adjudication to the Next Level: A Proposal for Legislative Review Mechanism of Erroneous Determinations' (2016) 33 *International Construction Law Review* 287.

152 R Hulls, Second Reading Speech, Building and Construction Industry Security of Payment (Amendment) Bill 2006 (Vic), 9 February 2006, 4: 'these limits ensure this Act does not disadvantage small contractors who rely on prompt payment to stay in business'.

153 Victorian Act ss 28A – 28L.

154 Such a determination is made under s 31(2)(a) of the WA Act.

155 WA Act s 46.

> additional 10 business days to determine on the balance of probabilities whether any party to the payment dispute is liable to make a payment.[156]

Both of these statutory avenues of appeal are limited. The review process under the Victorian Act is confined to the complex issue of 'excluded amounts', and therefore would not be necessary in legislation that does not include an 'excluded amounts' regime.[157] In practice, the right of appeal under the WA Act is also likely to be confined. It may be assumed that it is relatively rare for a claimant's adjudication application to be dismissed without the adjudicator considering the merits, and therefore this review process will also be accessed sparingly.

Towards harmonisation?

15.73 The modern Australian security of payment legislation containing an adjudication scheme was first enacted in NSW more than 20 years ago. In that time there have been three federal reviews and at least nine state and territory reviews. There have also been numerous amendments to the Australian Acts, which in some cases have involved repealing and then reinstating the same content.[158]

15.74 The frequent amendments to the Australian Acts have almost invariably resulted in greater complexity and increasing degrees of divergence between the legislation in force in the various Australian states and territories.[159] This in turn is likely to have reduced the accessibility of the adjudication schemes to industry participants, including the small and vulnerable contractors who are intended to be the schemes' primary beneficiaries. Therefore, it can be reasonably argued that law reform in this area has become a hindrance and not a help. So: why is further reform needed, and what would beneficial reform look like?

15.75 First, the fact that reform has already taken place is not a reason to forego future reform. With appropriate research and analysis, the effects of previous reforms can and should be assessed to determine whether they helped or hindered the purpose of the schemes: to promote cash flow to those who perform construction work and provide related goods and services.

15.76 Second, the specific Australian context provides a powerful reason for reform and guidance on at least one key characteristic of any reform. The federal system in Australia has resulted in eight pieces of legislation, each containing distinct adjudication schemes. This in a country with less than half the population of the UK.

15.77 The differences between the construction sectors in the different Australian states and territories are not sufficiently significant[160] to justify the inefficiencies caused to

---

156 Such a determination is made under s 31(2)(b) of the WA Act. The WA 2021 Act sets out a modified review adjudication regime in its Pt 3 Div 3.

157 Which likely explains the absence of such a regime in other 'East coast' legislation, such as the NSW Act and the Queensland Act.

158 For example, see the discussion in [15.9] above of the requirement for payment claims to be endorsed under the NSW Act.

159 Murray Report (n 12), 69.

160 One example of cross-border economic differences which manifest in the scope of adjudication schemes is the exclusion of work related to mining and resources projects from the scope of 'construction work' in Western

industry participants, who routinely are involved in projects around Australia or which, at least, involve the cross-border supply of materials. Therefore, it is unsurprising that the most consistent characteristic of reform called for is the creation of a nationally uniform adjudication scheme.[161] The constitutional basis of Commonwealth and state/territory legislative powers creates numerous, though not insurmountable, hurdles to national unification.[162] Perhaps the greatest obstacle to national unification is demonstrated by the divergent (and diverging) content of each of the Australian Acts. Obtaining national consensus about each of the numerous facets of an adjudication scheme has proven to be a very difficult exercise.

15.78 In proposing a nationally unified adjudication scheme, the Murray Review in 2017 recommended that the 'East coast' model be adopted nationally, largely based upon the NSW Act. This was on the basis that the prescribed period for submitting a payment schedule and the consequences of non-compliances, being a deemed debt capable of enforcement by court order, meant it was more likely to achieve the primary policy goal of promoting cash flow down the contracting chain.[163] Other reforms proposed in the Murray Review relating to the matters discussed in this chapter include:

- Claims for progress payments should be endorsed to make it clear that they are made under the legislation and are thereby payment claims capable of triggering an adjudication process.[164]
- While statutory adjudications should be quick and efficient, the schemes should provide an appropriate balance regarding the timing of the process so as not to deny procedural fairness. For example, in appropriate circumstances, a respondent ought to be able to apply for additional time to submit an adjudication response (however, it should remain the case that the adjudication response should not include reasons for withholding payment not included in a payment schedule).[165]
- ANAs should be retained to nominate an adjudicator from a prescribed list of registered adjudicators, with regulators responsible for the registration of adjudicators.[166]
- A party aggrieved by an adjudicator's determination should be permitted a limited right of review, which should ensure not only a more transparent process but one that produces superior decisions and enhances industry confidence in the adjudication scheme.[167]

As the preceding sections of this chapter have shown, many of the recommendations in the Murray Review are already characteristics of the adjudication schemes in some, but

Australia (2004 Act s 5(3) and 2021 Act s 6(3)) and Queensland (s 65(3)). WA and Queensland are two states with large and economically critical mining and resources sectors.

161 See, for example, recommendation 86 of the Murray Report (n 12) and recommendation 28 of the Senate Economics References Committee report (n 5).

162 Discussed in the Society of Construction Law Australia's submission to the Senate Economics References Committee, discussed in the Committee's Report (n 5), [9.99] – [9.100].

163 Murray Report (n 12), xiv.

164 Recommendation 23 (see [15.4]ff above).

165 Recommendation 40 (see [15.53]ff above).

166 Recommendation 37 (see [15.39] above).

167 Recommendation 43 (see [15.71]ff above).

not all, of the Australian Acts. Therefore, it should be possible to objectively analyse the effectiveness of these characteristics at achieving the policy aims of the statutory adjudication schemes. The Murray Review noted that each Australian state and territory has its own method of collecting and publishing data in their respective annual reports, and recommended that the jurisdictions cooperate to develop a consistent set of standards for reporting data collected from ANAs and adjudicators.[168]

15.79 Nevertheless, the Murray Review based numerous recommendations upon the data that were available. For example, a sudden and maintained increase of the 'fall-over rate'[169] in Queensland from December 2014 was ascribed in the Murray Review to the enactment of reforms to the forerunner of the Queensland Act that transferred adjudication processing functions from ANAs to the public Queensland Adjudication Registry. This explanation formed the basis of a recommendation that ANAs be retained notwithstanding the perception of bias issues discussed earlier.[170]

15.80 However, the numerous Commonwealth, State and Territory reviews and reports on the Australian Acts tend to be short on objective data analysis, and rather focus on industry submissions, anecdotes and perceptions. Moreover, the 'competitive federalism' which has resulted in fragmented legislation around Australia has tended to hamper attempts to achieve national unification for the foreseeable future. Whilst harmonisation was near the top of the agenda of the Building Ministers' Meeting (comprising state and federal ministers) after the Murray Report was delivered, it has slipped down that agenda as more urgent issues have arisen for the Forum to deal with – primarily, 'rebuilding confidence' in the industry in the wake of high-profile defects-related issues in apartment buildings.[171] Nonetheless, the broad acceptance by Western Australia, via its 2021 Act, of the 'East coast' model keeps the hope alive that national harmonisation may one day be realised.

15.81 As between the UK Act and the Australian Acts, there is differing emphasis on the legislative purpose. The UK Act seeks to create a scheme for the efficient resolution of disputes on construction projects, while the Australian Acts are primarily targeted at achieving prompt cash flow to small and vulnerable subcontractors at the low end of the contracting chain.

15.82 However, the adjudication schemes under the Australian Acts ought not disregard altogether the benefits of effective dispute resolution as part of an adjudication framework. This is reflected in the Murray Review, which tempered some of its conclusions regarding the benefits of quick and efficient adjudication processes with the need to balance procedural fairness. The latter is consonant with the common law principles of natural justice that apply to adjudicators' determinations in the UK and Australia. When used as a cornerstone for legislative reform, focusing on procedural fairness is well suited to adjudication schemes with alternative dispute resolution credentials, such as under the UK Act. The Australian Acts, on the other hand, lack such a clear-cut mandate, and

168 Recommendation 79, Murray Report (n 12) 265–268.

169 This describes an instance of an adjudication claim being voluntarily withdrawn before a determination.

170 Murray Report (n 12) 175–179, and recommendation 37 at 183.

171 See Peter Shergold and Bronwyn Weir, 'Building Confidence: Improving the effectiveness of compliance and enforcement systems for the building and construction industry across Australia' (2018): <https://www.industry.gov.au/sites/default/files/July%202018/document/pdf/building_ministers_forum_expert_assessment_-_building_confidence.pdf>.

seek to balance economic outcomes and political mandates within a fast-tracked dispute resolution framework.

Conclusion and summary

15.83 This chapter has compared the approaches taken by the UK and across the various Australian jurisdictions in respect of five facets of Australian adjudication schemes. The sheer diversity of details across the Australian Acts means that this chapter cannot provide an exhaustive survey of the characteristics of the adjudication schemes in each Australian Act. However, the five topics considered in this chapter provide a 'looking glass' through which can be assessed the unique development of adjudication in Australia under its security of payment legislation.

15.84 In relation to the five aspects providing the focus of this chapter:

- Firstly, the scope of the dispute that may be the subject of an adjudication in Australia is far narrower than under the UK Act. Australian adjudication schemes are targeted towards payment disputes, which aligns with the Australian approach of enacting security of payment legislation that provides a method of independent payment certification, and not general dispute resolution procedures.
- Secondly, reflecting the narrow focus of adjudicable disputes, that the claimant must commence an adjudication promptly upon the dispute arising, and cannot wait until long after the project has ended to bring a claim.
- It was thirdly illustrated that the methods for the appointment of adjudicators are extremely varied. Initial variants allowed the claimant to nominate at its discretion an ANA, which approach aligns with the Australian Acts' intended purpose of providing financial protection to small subcontractors by shifting the relative bargaining power when it comes to determining disputed payment claims. However, this process developed an industry reputation as being unfairly biased in favour of claimants. When the perception of unfairness is coupled with the view in Australia that adjudicators are quasi-public officials performing a public function with quasi-judicial powers, it is unsurprising that some jurisdictions have taken steps to implement a more regulated (and therefore, it is hoped, neutral) process for nominating adjudicators.
- Fourthly, this chapter revealed that, once an adjudicator's determination is obtained, the processes for enforcing that determination provided for under the Australian Acts are efficient and powerful. This also reflects the relatively narrow focus of adjudicable disputes on disputed payment claims and the intended purpose of the Australian Acts, being to promote prompt cash flow.
- Fifthly, judicial recognition in Australia that an adjudicator under the Australian Acts is performing a public function has profoundly influenced the availability and nature of a challenge to adjudicators' determinations. Determinations are interim in nature, but they remain fully enforceable on a summary basis despite not representing a final judicial determination of the parties' legal rights. Therefore, in Australia, adjudicators' determinations can only be challenged for lack of jurisdiction (as jurisdiction is created by legislation, and each of the Australian Acts are different and complex, differentiating between jurisdictional and

non-jurisdictional error can be a difficult exercise) and for a denial of natural justice. The content of natural justice as it applies to Australian adjudicators is broadly similar to associated legal principles in the UK; however, the for-profit nature of ANAs can create peculiar factual scenarios giving rise to apprehended bias.

- Finally, this chapter considered the Australian reform experience over the preceding two decades. This demonstrates above all the need for a clear understanding of the policy goals that the legislation is attempting to achieve, and for objective analysis of the performance of the adjudication schemes measured against those goals. This is the vital lesson which this experience offers to other jurisdictions which are contemplating or implementing similar schemes, especially those – like Canada and the US – which are federal systems like Australia.[172]

Ultimately, this chapter has told a peculiarly Australian story of the development of adjudication. The UK Act is the progenitor legislation; however, it is seldom expressly recognised as such in Australia. This is because the Australian Acts, in both concept and delivery, are so divergent from the UK Act that there seems now little room for the parent legislation to inform the application of its progeny.

172 See, *eg*, Bell and others (n 7), 619. Malaysia offers an example of what can be achieved in this area, with its Construction Industry Payment and Adjudication Act 2012 applicable across its 13 states and three federal territories.

PART VI

CONTRACTING WITH THE STATE IN THE 21ST CENTURY

CHAPTER 16

Achmea

From the judgment to the plurilateral agreement, towards the disappearance of intra-EU bilateral investment protection treaties

Malik Laazouzi

16.1 The *Achmea* ruling has unleashed a storm in the European Union designed to shatter the foundations of investment arbitration under bilateral investment treaties in force between Member States (intra-EU BITs). In just two years, 23 Member States agreed to terminate all intra-EU BITs concluded between them and to remove investment arbitration based on those treaties from the range of legal remedies available to investors who are nationals of a signatory Member State against State measures taken by another signatory Member State where they had invested. We will therefore examine two main aspects of the relationship between EU law and investment arbitration, namely the challenge to the jurisdiction of arbitration tribunals by the *Achmea* ruling and the disappearance of the intra-EU BITs under the Multilateral Agreement, the '*Achmea*' Agreement.

Eradicating the jurisdiction of intra-EU investment arbitral tribunals

16.2 Is it possible for an international arbitral tribunal, ruling on a dispute arising out of an investment transaction carried out in the territory of a Member State by a national of another Member State, to base its jurisdiction on an investment protection treaty concluded between the investment's host Member State and the investor's home Member State? As is well known, the Court of Justice gave a negative answer to this question in the *Achmea* judgment of 6 March 2018,[1] ruling that the BIT provision at issue is contrary to EU law. The follow-up to the *Achmea* judgment is of considerable importance.

The Achmea *judgment*

16.3 Several factors have contributed to the emergence of this difficulty. The accession to the EU of States that had previously concluded BITs with Member States has greatly increased the number of intra-EU BITs. The importance of arbitration based on an investment protection treaty has, furthermore, resulted in a large number of arbitration proceedings under such BITs. Finally, the possible impact of EU law on State measures contested by investors was quickly identified as a factor of friction with the EU legal

1 ECJ, 6 March 2018, *Slowakische Republik v Achmea,* C-284/16, (2008) *Rev arb* 424, obs. S Lemaire; *Rev crit DIP,* 2018.616, note E Gaillard; *Cah. arb.*, 2018.65, note B Siino et A Kirillov; *JDI,* 2018.903, note Y Nouvel.

order.[2] The EU Commission has attempted to have its anti-intra-EU BIT analysis prevail before arbitral tribunals. For example, as early as 2006, in the *Eastern Sugar* dispute between a Dutch investor and the Czech Republic, the European Commission sent a letter[3] supporting the State's position before the arbitral tribunal, highlighting in particular the obstacles to submitting such an intra-EU case to arbitration, but without excluding it. The EU Commission's position subsequently evolved towards the assertion, usually as *amicus curiae*,[4] that the use of arbitration based on an intra-EU BIT was in principle incompatible with EU law. As constant as the EU Commission's position has been since then, so constant has been the indifference of arbitral tribunals to arguments based on EU law to assert their lack of jurisdiction. In the *Achmea* case, the dispute decided by the arbitral tribunal arose between Achmea, a Dutch company, and the Slovak Republic. Achmea had made investments in the private health insurance sector. The Slovak Republic, after acceding to the European Union, opened the national health insurance market to domestic and foreign operators. As a result, Achmea has made an investment in this market. However, as of 2006, the State has taken various measures limiting the liberalization of the private health insurance market. The damage that Achmea considered it had suffered led it to initiate an arbitration proceeding against the State as early as 2008 on the basis of the BIT concluded between the Slovak Republic and the Netherlands. Recourse to arbitration was provided for in Article 8 of this treaty.

16.4 The State invoked the incompatibility of the recourse to arbitration under the BIT with EU law in order to challenge the jurisdiction of the arbitral tribunal. In 2010 the arbitral tribunal issued a partial award admitting its jurisdiction. Since the seat of the arbitration was located in Germany, this first award was subject to the remedies provided by German law, without success for the respondent. Then, the arbitral tribunal ordered the Slovak Republic to compensate Achmea for the damage resulting from the violation of the BIT. After the Slovak Republic brought an action for annulment of this award before the German courts, the *Bundesgerichtshof* finally referred three questions to the Court of Justice for a preliminary ruling. In essence, the referring court wondered whether Article 8 of the BIT providing for recourse to arbitration was compatible with several provisions of the Treaty on the Functioning of the European Union (TFEU): notably Article 344 prohibiting States from submitting their disputes concerning the interpretation or application of the treaties to a method of settlement not provided for therein and Article 267 establishing the jurisdiction of the Court of Justice to interpret EU law. Although the *Bundesgerichtshof* appeared not to be convinced by the arguments raised by the Slovak Republic, the importance of the question in the light of the numerous intra-EU BITs in force and its novelty for the Court of Justice justified the reference for a preliminary ruling. The *Achmea* judgment has indeed shaken the future of investment protection within the European Union.

16.5 The *Achmea* judgment states,

> Articles 267 and 344 TFEU must be interpreted as precluding a provision in an international agreement concluded between Member States ... under which an investor from one of those

2 See: T Fecak, *International Investment Agreements and EU Law* (Wolters Kluwer 2016).

3 Partial Award, 27 March 2007, SCC No 088/2004, p 24.

4 See *J Wirtgen, S Wirtgen, G Wirtgen and JSW Solar (zwei) GmbH & Co KG v Czech Republic,* PCA Case No 2014–03, Award of 11 October 2017, BIT Germany-Czech Republic, pp 65–72.

> Member States may, in the event of a dispute concerning investments in the other Member State, bring proceedings against the latter Member State before an arbitral tribunal whose jurisdiction that Member State has undertaken to accept.

The ECJ indicates that this is the case with Article 8 of the BIT in question, but the scope of the judgment clearly went beyond that sole framework alone and was intended to affect recourse to arbitration in all BITs concluded between Member States.

16.6 In the name of the autonomy of the legal order of the EU, the ECJ has found in the founding treaties a prohibition for the Member States to agree among themselves, by a treaty, to have recourse to a form of justice which, in its view, would not ensure that the interpretation of Union law is respected by arbitral tribunals. The Court of Justice gives undivided precedence to the autonomy of the European legal order. However, this decision has not discouraged investors: the pending arbitration proceedings have continued, while new proceedings have been introduced. The *Achmea* ruling did not impress investment arbitrators either: they refused to decline jurisdiction. First of all, the reasoning of the *Achmea* judgment must be examined in order to assess the role played by the autonomy of the European legal order. Nonetheless, investment arbitrators are still claiming their autonomy in relation to EU law.

16.7 In order to rule on the jurisdiction of the arbitral tribunal, the ECJ had at its disposal the analysis of its Advocate General,[5] who had proposed another approach. Having fully identified the risk of collision between intra-EU investment arbitration and EU law, the Advocate General had suggested to neutralize it by integrating arbitral tribunals that had based their jurisdiction on an intra-EU BIT into the EU's legal system. At the cost of a re-reading of the criteria for defining the concept of jurisdiction of a Member State, the Advocate General's conclusions proposed that such an arbitral tribunal should be considered as a court of each Member State party to the BIT at stake. In that way, the tribunal would be subject to the rules applicable to the interpretation of EU law by the national courts and the Court of Justice. This solution, however interesting, would have saved investment arbitration only in appearance. Since the very purpose of international investment protection treaties is to remove the legal relationship from the legal order of the host State and thus from the grip of its own rules (its rules of law and the decisions of its courts), the idea that investment arbitration tribunals could be considered as courts of the Member States is in fact the very negation of their *raison d'être*. One only has to imagine that the solution of the dispute depends on the interpretation of EU law and its impact on the measures taken by the defendant Member State in the investment arbitration proceedings. In such a case, since EU law forms an integral part of the law of all Member States, it is the interpretation of that part of the law of the defendant State itself, Union law, that would have decided the fate of the investor. The idea, apart from forcing the criteria for identifying Member States' courts, could not flourish. From a practical point of view, it would not even have been certain of achieving its aim since an arbitral tribunal sitting outside the EU could easily have considered itself free not to refer a question to the ECJ for a preliminary ruling, even though it was seized of a dispute on the basis of an intra-EU BIT.

5 Opinion of Advocate General Wathelet delivered on 19 September 2017, *Slowakische Republik v Achmea BV*, Case C-284/16, ECLI:EU:C:2017:699.

16.8 Since the ECJ did not follow the conclusions of its Advocate General, it had to decide the question of the compatibility of intra-EU investment arbitration with Articles 267 and 344 TFEU. The main guide to the Court of Justice's reasoning is 'the autonomy of the EU legal system, observance of which is ensured by the Court' (pt 32), according to Article 344 TFEU. Synthesizing its case law on the 'essential characteristics of the EU and its law' (pt 33), the ECJ highlights 'a set of common values on which the EU is founded' (pt 34) which are shared by the Member States. These values include mutual trust, but also loyal cooperation (sincere cooperation) in order to ensure compliance with EU Member States territory to fulfil their obligations under the treaty (pt 34).

16.9 On the one hand, EU Member States have set up a judicial system capable of preserving the autonomy of the Union's legal order and based on state courts and the ECJ so as to ensure the full application of EU law in all Member States. On the other hand, they have entrusted the power of uniform interpretation of EU law to the Court of Justice through a mechanism of dialogue with domestic courts. The request for a preliminary ruling is the cornerstone of this system. However, according to the Court, to the extent that the investment tribunal is required to take account of the law of the host State of the investment including Union law, a question of interpretation of the latter could arise. The main difficulty then surfaces from the point of view of the ECJ. As these arbitration tribunals are not integrated into the judicial system of the Member States, they cannot refer questions to the ECJ for a preliminary ruling. Consequently, their interpretation of EU law would run the risk of breaking the uniformity guaranteed by the jurisdictional architecture established under the EU Treaties. This consequence would not be a major obstacle if it were possible to review the awards with certainty as regards the interpretation of EU law, if necessary, by means of a reference for a preliminary ruling to the Court of Justice. However, that would not be the case because of the freedom of the arbitral tribunal to choose its 'seat and, consequently the law applicable to the procedure governing judicial review of the validity of the award by which it puts an end to the dispute before it' (pt 51). In other words, the ECJ has highlighted the risk of seeing the fundamental principles of EU law being circumvented by the choice of the seat of investment arbitration tribunals outside the EU. Strikingly though, in the *Achmea* case the seat had been fixed in Germany and the ECJ had been seized of the action for the annulment of the award brought before the German court.

16.10 Moreover, numerous intra-EU BITs offer the possibility to resort to ICSID arbitration, which is subject to an autonomous regime of recourse independent from contracting parties' domestic courts. According to article 54 of ICSID Convention, 'Each Contracting State shall recognize an award rendered pursuant to this Convention as binding and enforce the pecuniary obligations imposed by that award within its territories as if it were a final judgment of a court in that State'[6]. The text adds, 'Execution of the award shall be governed by the laws concerning the execution of judgments in force in the State in whose territories such execution is sought'[7]. It could, however, have been argued that even with an ICSID award the reference for a preliminary ruling would have been made

6 ICSID Convention, Article 54(1).
7 ICSID Convention, Article 54(3).

during the enforcement proceedings before the courts of an EU Member State. However, the validity of the award itself would still have escaped the system of control established by the EU legal order and, not to mention, the absence of enforcement proceedings brought before any EU Member State.

16.11 Besides that, what has triggered the invalidation of the arbitral tribunal's jurisdiction results from the source of the recourse to this type of arbitration. As the ECJ states in a key passage of the judgment:

> arbitration proceedings such as those referred to in Article 8 of the BIT are different from commercial arbitration proceedings. While the latter originate in the freely expressed wishes of the parties, the former derive from a treaty by which Member States agree to remove from the jurisdiction of their own courts, and hence from the system of judicial remedies which the second subparagraph of Article 19(1) TEU requires them to establish in the fields covered by EU law ..., disputes which may concern the application or interpretation of EU law.[8]

16.12 It is therefore less the specific characteristics of international or investment arbitration that are at issue[9] than the source of the jurisdiction of arbitral tribunals. What the ECJ has outlawed is the existence of an international treaty concluded between Member States which undermines the effectiveness of EU law by neutralizing the jurisdictional system established by the founding treaties. Indeed, it is quite clear that Article 267 TFEU cannot on its own be the basis for the invalidity of the bilateral treaty at issue in the *Achmea* case since, precisely, a court of a Member State had implemented the reference for a preliminary ruling in the context of an investment arbitration. Article 267 TFEU is in fact a crutch in support of the main basis of the *Achmea* judgment, Article 344 TFEU. However, a simple reading of this provision convinces that it does not deal with the question of the settlement of disputes between a Member State and a private person who is a national of another Member State. It refers only to disputes between Member States. And even supposing that it also concerns disputes to which only one Member State is a party, is it to be concluded that any arbitration agreement binding a Member State to another party, within the Union, would be contrary to Article 344 TFEU? Any dispute arising out of an arbitration agreement between a Member State and a company from another Member State may give rise to a question of interpretation of Union law. However, the reasoning of the ECJ seeks to distinguish between the fate of international commercial arbitration, which is not under threat, and that of intra-European investment arbitration, which has been wiped out within the legal order of the European Union. The only real distinction between the two results from the source in question: a public international law agreement concluded between Member States outside the scope of Union law and which, according to the Court, undermines the effectiveness of the EU Treaties.

8 ECJ, 6 March 2018, *Slowakische Republik v Achmea*, C-284/16, pt 55.

9 On this alleged obstacle, v. S Lemaire, obs. under ECJ, 6 March 2018, *Slovak Republic v Achmea*, C-284/16, in 'Chronique de jurisprudence arbitrale en droit des investissements', (2018) 2 *Rev arb*, p 432, spec. no. 26.

The aftermath of the Achmea *judgment*

16.13 The consequences of the *Achmea* ruling are diametrically opposed depending on whether we analyze the attitude of investors and arbitral tribunals, on the one hand, or that of the States and the European Union on the other.

16.14 First of all, it should be noted, in a nutshell, that investors have not ceased to submit requests for arbitration in disputes within the EU. While it is true that most of the claims filed since March 2018 have been made under the Energy Charter Treaty[10] (ECT), a multilateral treaty also signed by the European Union, several claims have been filed on the basis of intra-EU BITs.[11] In addition, several dozen arbitration proceedings relating to intra-EU disputes that were initiated before the *Achmea* ruling are still pending,[12] showing that investors have not suddenly abandoned their claims for fear of the arbitral tribunal's lack of jurisdiction.[13]

16.15 On the other hand, with respect to awards rendered after the *Achmea* decision in intra-EU investment arbitration proceedings, the objection to the jurisdiction of arbitral tribunals under EU law has not been found convincing by international arbitrators.[14]

16.16 Recent arbitral awards offer an interesting viewpoint as to the various ways implemented by investment tribunals to deflect the consequences of the *Achmea* judgment. For example, the award in the *Micula* case devoted lengthy passages to the consideration of the objection to jurisdiction based on the *Achmea*[15] judgment. Romania argued that the *Achmea* decision affected the investor's consent as well as its own. On the investor's side, since Swedish law incorporates EU law, the Court of Justice's interpretation of the

10 We have identified 10 cases, all concerning ICSID arbitration: (*EP Wind Project (Rom) Six Ltd v Romania* (ICSID Case No ARB/20/15); *Hamburg Commercial Bank AG v Italian Republic* (ICSID Case No ARB/20/3); *VM Solar Jerez GmbH and others v Kingdom of Spain* (ICSID Case No ARB/19/30); *Strabag SE, Erste Nordsee-Offshore Holding GmbH and Zweite Nordsee-Offshore Holding GmbH v Federal Republic of Germany* (ICSID Case No ARB/19/29); *Sapec, SA v Kingdom of Spain* (ICSID Case No ARB/19/23); *Petrochemical Holding GmbH v Romania* (ICSID Case No ARB/19/21); *Canepa Green Energy Opportunities I, S.á r.l. and Canepa Green Energy Opportunities II, S.á r.l. v Kingdom of Spain* (ICSID Case No ARB/19/4); *European Solar Farms A/S v Kingdom of Spain* (ICSID Case No ARB/18/45); *Veolia Propreté SAS v Italian Republic* (ICSID Case No ARB/18/20); *LSG Building Solutions GmbH and others v Romania* (ICSID Case No ARB/18/19).

11 *Adria Group BV and Adria Group Holding BV v Republic of Croatia* (ICSID Case No ARB/20/6); *Marko Mihaljevic v Republic of Croatia* (ICSID Case No ARB/19/35); *Société Générale SA v Republic of Croatia* (ICSID Case No ARB/19/33); *Alverley Investments Limited and Germen Properties Ltd v Romania* (ICSID Case No ARB/18/30).

12 Of which at least 22 proceedings were brought on the basis of an intra-EU BIT, the majority of the others being brought on the basis of the ECT.

13 An intra-European request for arbitration was abandoned after the *Achmea* judgment in the Airbus-Poland case.

14 With regard to available awards made on the basis of a BIT (and not the ECT) and having addressed the issue of jurisdiction, *Georg Gavrilovic and Gavrilovic d.o.o. v Republic of Croatia* (ICSID Case No ARB/12/39), Award, 26 July 2018; *Ioan Micula, Viorel Micula and others v Romania* (ICSID Case No ARB/14/29), Award, 5 March 2020; *Marfin Investment Group Holdings SA, Alexandros Bakatselos and others v Republic of Cyprus* (ICSID Case No ARB/13/27), Award, 26 July 2018; *WA Investments-Europa Nova Limited v The Czech Republic* (PCA Case No 2014–19), Award, 15 May 2019; *ICW Europe Investments Limited v The Czech Republic* (PCA Case No 2014–22), 15 May 2019; *UP and CD Holding Internationale v Hungary* (ICSID Case No ARB/13/35), Award, 9 October 2018; *United Utilities (Tallinn) BV and Aktsiaselts Tallinna Vesi v Republic of Estonia* (ICSID Case No ARB/14/24), Award, 21 June 2019; *Inicia Zrt, Kintyre Kft and Magyar Farming Company Ltd v Hungary* (ICSID Case No ARB/17/27), Award, 13 November 2019.

15 *Ioan Micula, Viorel Micula and others v Romania* (ICSID Case No ARB/14/29), Award, 5 March 2020, §§ 259–289.

TFEU provisions would have deprived the claimant of the right to consent to arbitration. As regards its own consent, the State considered that, as the TFEU is a treaty subsequent to the BIT, the BIT could only be applied within the limits of its compatibility with the TFEU.

16.17 Both objections have been denied. As to the consent of the claimant, it does not derive from the domestic law of the state of nationality of the investor since the basis for the determination of the jurisdiction by the tribunal is Article 25 of the ICSID Convention.[16] Article 25 does not make the investor's consent to arbitration dependent on the domestic law of the State of nationality. The latter is relevant to the verification of the claimed nationality, but other conditions relating to the status of investors and the existence of an investment fall within the scope of the ICSID Convention (§§ 270–272).

16.18 With regard to the State's consent expressed in the BIT, the tribunal considered that it does not have the same purpose as the TFEU, which does not provide a specific legal remedy allowing an investor from one Member State to sue another Member State. Moreover, as the BIT did not establish a tribunal to interpret EU law, the two treaties do not conflict. In the end, the tribunal considers that it has to deal with the question of the relationship between the BIT and the TFEU as a successor treaty, which is unrelated to the *Achmea* judgment and subsequent events. In particular, at the request of Romania, Sweden had addressed a note to the arbitral tribunal stating that according to the *Achmea* judgment a clause such as the one contained in the BIT at issue was 'contrary to Union law and thus inapplicable' (§ 287). The tribunal refused to take this note into account, considering that it was merely a presentation of the content of EU law. The objections to jurisdiction based on the *Achmea* judgment were thus rejected.

16.19 In the *Marfin*[17] case, the Court stated that it was bound to apply the BIT and principles of customary international law, without having to examine and apply principles of Union law (§ 580). However, the arbitral tribunal noted that the *Achmea* judgment did not take a position on the entry into force or inapplicability of the BIT under public international law. On the contrary, the two Contracting States to the BIT did not denounce it and did not indicate their intention to do so at the date of the award. The tribunal also ruled out any conflict between successive treaties, since they do not have the same object. Finally, the tribunal took note that the enforcement of its award could raise difficulties on the territory of EU Member States, while reaffirming that the tribunal's jurisdiction derives only from the BIT and international law, not from national laws on enforcement.

16.20 In *WA Investments*,[18] the arbitral tribunal also denied any relevance to *Achmea*. But in doing so, it paradoxically confirmed the analysis of the ECJ since it relied on the Swiss location of the seat of the arbitral tribunal to neutralize the relevance of the arguments drawn from EU law. The arbitral tribunal favored an analysis conducted according to the rules of Swiss law on the possible review of the award (§§ 440 *sq*). From the point of view of Swiss law, the tribunal considered Union law 'as public international law between third

16 The domestic law of a claimant's state is relevant to determines some issues (nationality, for example), as is mentioned by the tribunal.

17 *Marfin Investment Group Holdings SA, Alexandros Bakatselos and other v Republic of Cyprus* (ICSID Case No ARB/13/27), Award, 26 July 2018.

18 *WA Investments-Europa Nova Limited v The Czech Republic* (PCA Case No 2014–19), Award, 15 May 2019. The same reasoning has been adopted by the arbitral tribunal in case *ICW Europe Investments Limited v The Czech Republic* (PCA Case No 2014–22), 15 May 2019.

countries' not binding on Switzerland (§ 452). Under Swiss law, however, the objective arbitrability of the dispute did not raise any difficulty, irrespective of the position of Union law in this respect (§§ 455–456). Furthermore, Swiss law 'precludes a State, which is a party to an arbitration agreement, from invoking its own law in order to contest the arbitrability of a dispute covered by such an arbitration agreement', which according to the arbitral tribunal 'applies squarely to the present arbitration' (§ 458).

16.21 In the *UP* case[19], the tribunal emphasized the basis of its jurisdiction under the ICSID Convention, situating it 'in a public international law context and not in a national or regional context' (§ 253). While the *Achmea* award had been rendered by an arbitral tribunal having its seat in Germany, subject to the control of German courts having referred a preliminary question to the Court of Justice, this is not the case of an ICSID arbitration subject to the Washington Convention and which escapes the control of domestic courts. However, the tribunal noted that the *Achmea* judgment contains no reference to ICSID arbitration, which makes it impossible to consider that judgment as terminating the obligations arising for Hungary from being a Contracting State to the ICSID Convention. In substance, the tribunal considered that no provision of EU law affects the obligations of the defendant State under the ICSID Convention and that even if the termination of the BIT or the ICSID Convention were to take place, it could not take effect immediately because of the sunset clause (§§ 261 *sq*).

16.22 Lastly, in the *United Utilities*[20] case, the EU Commission acting as *amicus curiae*, the arbitral tribunal also denied any relevance to the *Achmea* decision. The tribunal based its jurisdiction on the BIT, the ICSID Convention and the consent of the parties. Therefore, it was convinced of the need to approach this issue from a public international law perspective and rejected the EU law stance adopted by the ECJ (§ 539). However, according to the tribunal: the BIT at issue does not refer to the domestic law of the defendant State and therefore does not involve the implementation of Union law; the *Achmea* judgment does not address the case of ICSID arbitration; and it is not convincingly asserted that the ECJ has jurisdiction to intervene where the interpretation and application of EU Treaties are not at issue (§ 540). It also rejected any relevance to the objection based on a possible difficulty in enforcing its award within the EU (§ 541). Finally, the tribunal considered that the accession of the defendant State to the EU did not terminate its obligations under the BIT. In order to make this determination, the tribunal relied on awards rendered prior to the *Achmea* judgment, including the award in the *Achmea* case itself. This is sufficient to emphasize that for arbitral tribunals, as far as their jurisdiction is concerned, the *Achmea* decision is irrelevant.

16.23 The attitude of EU Member States and the European Commission could not have been more different than the stance taken by arbitral tribunals. The EU Commission had quickly drawn the consequences of the *Achmea* judgment with regard to EU law. According to its communication of 19 July 2018,[21] the *Achmea* ruling meant the inapplicability of all

19 *UP and C.D Holding Internationale v Hungary* (ICSID Case No ARB/13/35), Award, 9 October 2018.

20 *United Utilities (Tallinn) BV and Aktsiaselts Tallinna Vesi v Republic of Estonia* (ICSID Case No ARB/14/24), Award, 21 June 2019. See also: *Theodoros Adamakopoulos and other v Republic of Cyprus* (ICSID Case No ARB/15/49), Decision on Jurisdiction, 7 February 2020.

21 Communication from the Commission to the European Parliament and the Council. Protection of intra-EU investment, 19.7.2018 – COM(2018) 547 final.

arbitration clauses in intra-EU BITs, depriving tribunals constituted on the basis of such clauses of any jurisdiction. Consequently, the EU Commission affirmed the obligation of Member States' courts to set aside awards made on the basis of an intra-EU BIT. Finally, the EU Commission considered that Member States were under an obligation to terminate all their intra-EU BITs. Going beyond the scope of intra-EU BIT, the EU Commission also considered that the Energy Charter Treaty should also be considered not to be applicable in intra-EU disputes.

16.24 The Member States quickly made a first step along the lines intended by the European Commission. Twenty-two Member States admitted on 15 January 2019 that the arbitration clauses inserted in the intra-EU BITs and the arbitration offer contained in the ECT for intra-EU disputes were contrary to EU law. They also affirmed their willingness: to ask the courts of third countries not to enforce, or to annul, as the case may be, awards based on these treaties; to inform investors from Member States of the impossibility of introducing any new procedure on the basis of these treaties. Above all, those Member States announced their willingness to terminate all BITs through the conclusion of a multilateral treaty before 6 December 2019, as well as their desire to amend the Energy Charter Treaty. Five other Member States declared the following day, 16 January 2019, their adherence to these principles, with the exception of the arbitration clause in the ECT. Finally, Hungary took the view that proceedings under the ECT should not be affected.

16.25 The multilateral treaty was finally adopted by 23 EU Member States on 5 May 2020 and published in the Official Journal of the European Union on 29 May 2020. Its title is perfectly clear: 'Agreement for the termination of Bilateral Investment Treaties between the Member States of the European Union'. Ireland, Austria, Sweden and Finland are not signatories. This treaty will enter into force 30 days after the date of receipt of the second instrument of ratification, approval or acceptance by the signatory Member States. Once it has entered into force, it will be binding on each Member State that has ratified it 30 days after the date of deposit of that instrument.[22] This treaty will henceforth be referred to as the *Achmea* Agreement, an international treaty concluded between Member States.

The termination of intra-EU BITs by the *Achmea* Agreement

16.26 The *Achmea* Agreement raises certain difficulties.

The Achmea *Agreement against intra-EU BITs*

16.27 The preamble to this plurilateral Agreement sets out the basic elements the signatory Member States have agreed on: investor-state arbitration clauses in BITs between EU Member States are contrary to the EU Treaties; the impossibility to implement those clauses from the day on which the last State party to such a BIT accedes to the Union; the lack of jurisdiction of arbitration tribunals constituted on the basis of such clauses; the indifference of the type of arbitration involved, whether it is ICSID arbitration or not; and the non-application of the *Achmea* Agreement to arbitration proceedings under the Energy Charter Treaty (ECT).

22 Article 16.

16.28 In particular, and even though the signatory Member States have declared in the preamble that this Multilateral Agreement does not concern the compatibility with EU Treaties of the substantive protections offered by the intra-EU BITs, the preamble states that the exercise by investors of one of the fundamental freedoms in the EU places them under the rule of EU law and its protection in the event that a measure taken by a Member State is likely to infringe its provisions. This assertion is, of course, very strongly contested in the light of the repeated positions taken by arbitral tribunals, which consider that the invocation of a violation of a BIT and international law by a Member State does not *per se* bring into question the application or interpretation of EU law. In this Multilateral Agreement, the signatory Member States assert the exact contrary, bearing in mind, of course, the BITs signed with the four Member States which have not signed the Agreement, and also the prospect that arbitral tribunals could simply disregard this plurilateral Agreement.

16.29 What is the content of this Agreement? The core of the *Achmea* Agreement is, of course, the termination of BITs between EU Member States. Article 2(1) states in a sober way that 'Bilateral Investment Treaties listed in Annexe A are terminated according to the terms set out in this Agreement'. But the signatories wanted to guard against the possible survival of their commitments based on these treaties by virtue of the 'sunset clause' that might be stipulated therein. This type of clause is precisely intended to maintain the protection offered to investors for a period of time fixed by the clause, often 10 to 15 years, after the termination of the treaty. The aim is to prevent the State from being too easily released from the commitments made, to the detriment of investors who have been wrong to base their expectations on the BIT. Since the *Achmea* judgment, the signatory Member States have considered that recourse to investment arbitration in intra-EU situations is contrary to EU law. It is therefore of little importance to them whether this arbitration clause is invoked on the basis of a treaty in force or on the basis of a sunset clause. In an attempt to curtail the invocation of sunset clauses, the Member States have asserted, 'For greater certainty, Sunset Clauses of Bilateral Investment Treaties listed in Annexe A are terminated in accordance with paragraph 1 of this Article and shall not produce legal effects'. They extended this position to intra-EU BITs already terminated and for which a sunset clause could have continued to produce effects. Article 3 refers directly to those clauses, being titled 'Termination of possible effects of Sunset Clauses'.

16.30 Article 4 of the Agreement reiterates the statement in the preamble:

> The Contracting Parties hereby confirm that Arbitration Clauses are contrary to the EU Treaties and thus inapplicable. As a result of this incompatibility between Arbitration Clauses and the EU Treaties, as of the date on which the last of the parties to a Bilateral Investment Treaty became a Member State of the European Union, the Arbitration Clause in such a Bilateral Investment Treaty cannot serve as legal basis for Arbitration Proceedings.

And as soon as the Achmea Agreement enters into force for the Contracting State concerned, the BITs listed in Annexe A and the 'sunset clauses' contained in the BITs listed in Annexe B will cease to have effect.

16.31 The 23-signatory Member States having thus doomed all intra-EU BITs concluded between them, they then determined the fate of all arbitration proceedings based on those BITs. They distinguished between past, present and future. As for the past, the States agreed that the *Achmea* Agreement 'shall not affect Concluded Arbitration Proceedings', which 'shall not be reopened'.[23] The definition of the completed proceedings is enlightening as to the crucial importance of the *Achmea* judgment. Indeed, these are the

> arbitration proceedings which ended with a settlement agreement or with a final award issued prior to 6 March 2018 where: (a) the award was duly executed prior to 6 March 2018, even where a related claim for legal costs has not been executed or enforced, and no challenge, review, set-aside, annulment, enforcement, revision or other similar proceedings in relation to such final award was pending on 6 March 2018, or (b) the award was set aside or annulled before the date of entry into force of this Agreement.[24]

16.32 Thus, where the award has been definitively enforced before 6 March 2018, the date of the *Achmea* judgment, without being subject to any remedy of any kind pending at that date, the solution is final. Furthermore, with regard to the existence of a settlement agreement, Article 6(2) states that 'this Agreement shall not affect any agreement to settle amicably a dispute being the subject of Arbitration Proceedings initiated prior to 6 March 2018'. In this case, only the date of the submission of the Request for Arbitration is relevant. The logic of the rule seems intended to favor the amicable settlement of disputes even after the *Achmea* ruling or the entry into force of the Agreement. In this case, therefore, it is not the date of conclusion or execution of the amicable settlement which has to be taken into account. Article 8(4) confirms this by allowing a Member State party to the *Achmea* Agreement to agree with the investor to resolve the dispute, including through Pending Arbitration Proceedings. The only limit will then be that of the compatibility of the content of the settlement agreement with EU law.

16.33 Furthermore, the date to be taken into account for awards that have been set aside, rather than enforced, is different. Proceedings are considered to be completed if the award was 'set aside or annulled' before the date of entry into force of the *Achmea* Agreement. However, where the setting aside of the award results from a defect in the constitution of the arbitral tribunal or in the reasoning of the arbitrators, further arbitral proceedings may be instituted. Four cases must then be distinguished: in the first three cases, the setting aside takes place before the entry into force of the *Achmea* Agreement. The second arbitration proceedings may have been initiated before the *Achmea* ruling (first case), after the *Achmea* ruling but before the entry into force of the *Achmea* Agreement (second case), after the entry into force of this treaty (third case). Finally, in the fourth case, the annulment and the second arbitration proceedings are subsequent to the entry into force of the *Achmea* Agreement.

16.34 According to Article 6(1) and Article 1(4), none of these four cases can be considered concluded, either because the second award was not executed (without recourse) before 6 March 2018 or because its setting aside occurred after the entry into force of the treaty. These post-annulment proceedings must then be paid into the same jar as the *Pending Arbitration Proceedings*. It is the present and the future of intra-EU investment disputes under the *Achmea* Agreement. These pending proceedings, which include all the awards under appeal pending at the date of the *Achmea* judgment, have kept the drafters of the treaty busy. The Member States have devoted three long articles to this

23 Article 6(1).
24 Article 1(4).

issue. According to Article 1(5), '*Pending Arbitration Proceedings*' are those introduced before 6 March 2018, which do not fall under the category of '*Concluded Arbitration Proceedings*'. *New Arbitration Proceedings* are, according to Article 1(6), those introduced on or after 6 March 2018.

16.35 Pending and new proceedings are subject to some common rules. Member States parties to the BIT have to inform the arbitral tribunal of the legal consequences of the *Achmea* judgment (Art 7(a)). Member States also have to exercise all possible recourses against awards made in such proceedings before any competent State Court, including those of third States (Art 7(b)). It should be noted that the *Achmea* Agreement does not, however, require Member States to exercise the same remedies under the mechanisms of the ICSID Convention. This limitation is, however, of very little importance both because States will not hesitate to do so and because Article 7(b) also covers requests to the courts of Member States to refuse enforcement of the award, not excluding awards made under the aegis of the ICSID Convention.

16.36 Two interesting points relate to the 'Structured dialogue for Pending Arbitration Proceedings' provided for in Article 9 and to the access to domestic courts of the States Parties to the *Achmea* Agreement. As to the 'Structured dialogue', Article 9 offers the investor the possibility to request the respondent State, party to the *Achmea* Agreement, 'to enter into a settlement procedure'.[25] However, the Agreement sets out a series of strict conditions. These conditions relate to the status of the pending proceedings, the time limit for filing the claim, and the existence of certain national or EU decisions. As to the status of the proceedings, if no award has been made, the investor must request the suspension of the pending proceedings. If an award has been made but has not yet been enforced, the investor undertakes to refrain from bringing an award before any State court or, if such proceedings are pending, to request a stay of proceedings. Once this condition has been met, another one arises: no more than six months may elapse between the termination of the BIT at stake and the request for a structured dialogue. The aim is to convince as many investors as possible to quickly abandon their interests before the investment arbitration tribunals in favor of an amicable settlement. In addition, the parties to the dispute will have to take into account decisions adopted by State courts, the ECJ or even the EU Commission. Thus, Article 9(3) provides that 'a settlement procedure shall be entered into if the CJEU or a national court has found, in a judgment that has become final, that the State measure being contested in the proceedings referred to in paragraph 1 violates Union law'. The difficulty obviously lies in the fact that the obligation exists only in relation to the violation of Union law, whereas the investor will have invoked before the arbitral tribunal the violation of the BIT and, more often than not, of the principles of international law. Moreover, to the extent that the conditions set for the suspension of the arbitral proceedings or the enforcement of the award remain applicable in this case, the State's willingness to comply with the procedure could easily remain a dead letter. The cornerstone of any settlement procedure being the agreement of the two parties, the investor could easily avoid it.

16.37 The Agreement also prohibits the recourse to a settlement procedure, where the contested State measure has been finally found to comply with Union law, either by the Court of Justice or by a State court. The Commission's final decisions have the same effect in

25 The Respondent State enjoys the same right (Art 9(1), al. 3).

this respect, according to Article 9(4). Finally, when proceedings relating to the conformity of a State measure with Union law are pending, hypothetically before a State court, the Court of Justice or when the European Commission has issued a non-definitive decision, 'the initiation of a settlement procedure shall be suspended until the court proceedings has resulted in a judgment that has become final' (Article 9(5)). According to Article 9(6) the freedom to start or not a settlement procedure exists only 'if a potential violation of Union law caused by the State measure being contested ... can be identified' and the measure has not yet been found to be in conformity or contrary to Union law.

16.38 The Agreement also introduces, as part of the structured dialogue, the intervention of an independent and impartial third party, designated as the facilitator and appointed by the parties to the dispute within one month after the beginning of the settlement procedure.[26] The Agreement goes down to such a level of detail that it sets out a scale of fees for this facilitator. Fortunately, in view of the amounts envisaged, this scale is only indicative. Without delving into the details of the procedure, it should be noted that it is not expected to last for more than approximately 11 months after its activation,[27] unless otherwise agreed by the parties. It should also be noted that the facilitator may, in certain cases, seek the advice of the European Commission on matters relating to EU law. In general, Union law, as implemented by national courts and the Court of Justice, will be of crucial importance. Finally, acceptance of the settlement will imply the waiver by the investor of the enforcement of its outstanding award, the taking into account of the sums already paid, the undertaking not to institute new arbitral proceedings and the waiver of the rights and claims related to the disputed measure.

16.39 Another important provision of the *Achmea* Agreement, Article 10, regulates investors' access to the domestic courts of the Contracting States. The main purpose of these provisions is to persuade investors to seek redress in the courts of the State that enacted the disputed measure. To this end, the Agreement removes the obstacle that the expiry of the time limits for bringing an action could have constituted. Specifically, these periods do not begin to run until the investor meets the conditions for access to domestic courts, as set out in the following. Here again, the conditions are drastic: the investor must waive all rights and claims under the BIT or waive the enforcement of the award already made but not yet finally executed. He must, of course, undertake not to initiate any new arbitration proceedings related to the disputed measure. In addition, no amicable agreement must have been reached. The investor has a period of six months from either the termination of the BIT, where it has not implemented the structured dialogue, or the rejection by the State of its request for a structured dialogue, or the last communication by a party of its position on the proposal for an amicable settlement formulated, as a last resort, by the facilitator. It should be noted that the investor will be able to rely not only on

26 Absent such an agreement, Article 9(8) sets up a complex mechanism: 'the investor or the Contracting Party concerned acting as respondent in the relevant Pending Arbitration Proceedings shall ask the Director General of the Legal Service of the European Commission to designate a former Member of the Court of Justice of the European Union who shall appoint, after having consulted each party to the dispute, a person fulfilling the criteria set out in this paragraph'.

27 A maximum of one month for the appointment of the facilitator, then six months to reach an amicable settlement. Failing that, each party will have to formulate an acceptable proposal within one month, which the other party will have one month to accept or not. Finally, the facilitator will have another month to formulate his final proposal, which the parties will have one month to accept or not.

the violation of EU law but also on the violation of national law (Article 10(1)(b)). On the other hand, the Agreement expressly provides that the terminated BIT cannot be invoked as a basis for the investor's rights.

16.40 All in all, in just over two years, the European Union has managed to get rid of almost all intra-EU BITs. A few comments need to be made on the *Achmea* Agreement.

Future difficulties

16.41 To begin with, the incompatibility asserted by the *Achmea* Agreement between EU Law and each separate intra-EU BIT is deemed to have existed from the accession to the European Union of the last State party to the intra-EU BIT. This defect is deemed to affect the possibility of recourse to arbitration since that date. If such is the case, however, why did the EU Commission not immediately request the Member States to denounce all intra-EU BITs, by systematically bringing infringement proceedings against recalcitrant States? By its lack of action, the EU Commission has allowed EU Member States to maintain these BITs and therefore has let the idea of the stability of the international protection for their intra-EU investments to flourish among European investors.

16.42 Moreover, the mechanism for facilitating a settlement agreement set up by the *Achmea* Agreement is based on the premise that there has been a violation of Union law. Article 9 governs the cases in which the 'Structured dialogue' will either be prohibited, compulsory or possible. Each outcome depends, respectively, on whether no violation of Union law can be established, whether such a violation has been established or whether such a violation is suspected.

16.43 The *Achmea* Agreement makes this mechanism available to parties to investment arbitration only in cases where the violation of EU law is an element of the dispute and not in respect of all parties to arbitration proceedings based on intra-EU BITs. Article 8(4) is very clear in this respect in that it leaves the possibility for the Contracting States of the Agreement and the investors to agree on an alternative dispute resolution scheme, but only if the solution is in conformity with Union law. This limitation of the venues available due to the implication of Union law is self-evident since the core of the Agreement is based on the *Achmea* judgment. Yet the Agreement is an international treaty and not an act of Union law. The difference is significant. For example, Article 10, which seeks to enhance investors' access to the courts of the Member States that are signatories to the Agreement by removing obstacles related to national procedural time limits, is applicable both where investors' claims before national courts are based on the violation of national law and EU law. Clearly, therefore, the contested State measures will not always be challenged – far from it – on the basis of Union law, which has so far not shown how it offers any substantive protection to EU investors in a scale comparable to the one achieved through BITs. Moreover, and this is another shortcoming of the text, it does not mention the possibility that the claim may be based on the contested measure's violation of international law, including the European Convention for the Protection of Human Rights. Could an investor be subject to a procedural time limit in the latter case?

16.44 Finally, with regard to the termination of intra-EU BITs with immediate effect, the question will inevitably arise as to the compatibility of the mechanism adopted with the protection of EU investors' fundamental rights. Indeed, insofar as they could base legitimate expectations on the existence of the international regime for the protection of their investments, the invocation of the right to respect for their property on the basis of Protocol No. 1 of the European Convention on Human Rights is not excluded. To the extent that such protection was in force at the date of the investment, at the date of the contested State measure and, in many cases, at the date of the arbitration claim, it is difficult not to see the termination of the treaties as a possible infringement of these expectations. This is particularly so because the States that signed the defunct BITs had been careful to include a sunset clause specifically designed to protect investors against the termination, including by agreement, of the BIT on the basis of which the investment decision had been taken.[28] By calling into question not only the protection but also the guaranteed temporal scope of that protection, the Member States are likely to see defeated investors invoke the violation of the commitments undertaken through the European Convention on Human Rights and its protocols. Above all, the *Achmea* judgment held that the recourse to arbitration provided for by the intra-EU BITs was contrary to Union law, because of the neutralization of the interpretative competence of the ECJ and the existence of a public international law agreement in the reserved area of Union law. It is therefore solely from the point of view of dispute settlement mechanisms that the intra-EU BITs have been found to be contrary to Union law. Admittedly, as recalled in the preamble to the *Achmea* Agreement, the European Commission has for many years been defending the sufficiency of EU law to protect intra-EU investments and investors. Nevertheless, it remains true that the basis of the *Achmea* ruling did not allow the conclusion to be drawn that the entire content of intra-EU BITs was contrary to EU law, particularly in the case of BITs, which made it possible to refer the matter to national courts for the implementation of the substantive protection. Some investors might thus have wanted to bring a claim before the courts of the host Member State based on a breach of the substantive protection afforded by the BIT. The ECJ could in that case have been requested to answer any question relating to the interpretation of EU law. Absent an ECJ judgment ruling that substantive protection regimes agreed between Member States in intra-EU situations are contrary to Union law, have the Member States not released themselves cheaply and with immediate effect from the guarantees given to investors through intra-EU BITs?

16.45 The attitude of the investments tribunals before which proceedings will still be pending when the *Achmea* Agreement enters into force will be crucial. For the time being, and with regard to the consequences of the *Achmea* ruling, indifference prevails.

Conclusion

16.46 To conclude, a brief mention will be made of the fate of the Energy Charter Treaty (ECT). The EU Commission and the majority of EU Member States considered that the *Achmea* ruling should also apply to investments and intra-EU arbitration where the ECT was invoked as the basis for an arbitral tribunal's jurisdiction and the ground of the investor's claims. However, due to the silence of the *Achmea* ruling and the hostility of other Member States to this assertion, the *Achmea* Agreement has remained silent on this point. The preamble of the *Achmea* Agreement only states that 'it does not cover intra-EU

28 A question that arbitral tribunals have become accustomed to considering from the perspective of investor due diligence in making investment decisions.

proceedings on the basis of Article 26 of the Energy Charter Treaty. The European Union and its Member States will deal with this matter at a later stage'.

16.47 The ECT, signed by all Member States,[29] has also been signed by the European Union and third States, such as Japan. So far, recourse to international arbitration is not contested in relations involving a third State or an investor from a third State.[30] On the other hand, in intra-European situations, the European Commission has affirmed the incompatibility with EU law of recourse to arbitration in this context when the dispute involves Union law.[31] In particular, it has raised the existence of an implicit disconnection clause which would justify the neutralization of recourse to arbitration in relations involving only Member States or their nationals. However, this assertion had been rejected, for example in the *Electrabel* case, where the court ruled that the Union's accession to the ECT guarantees its application even in arbitration proceedings between an investor who is a national of one Member State and another Member State.[32] Prior to the *Achmea* judgment, other courts also ruled out the idea of an implicit disconnection clause.[33] Beyond that, several arbitral tribunals had held that, since the EU negotiated the EC Treaty and is a party to it, it must be presumed that EU law and the EC Treaty are compatible.[34] These analyses in favor of the compatibility of Union law have been reiterated since the *Achmea* ruling. For example, in the *Masdar*[35] case, the arbitral tribunal rejected the objection to its jurisdiction, taking the view that the *Achmea* judgment referred only to the BIT in question and, beyond that, to the agreements concluded by the Member States, without including the agreements concluded by the Union.

16.48 More generally, arbitral tribunals seized on the basis of the EC Treaty in the context of intra-EU disputes do not appear to be prepared to decline jurisdiction on the grounds of alleged infringement of Union law.[36] The confidence placed by investors in

29 Italy, however, withdrew from it.

30 See the Observations of the European Commission in the case of *Eureko BV v Slovak Republic*, Award on Jurisdiction, 26 October 2010, § 177 et seq.

31 See: Communication 'Protection of intra-EU investment', COM(2018) 547 final, 19 July 2018.

32 *Electrabel SA v Hungary* (ICSID No ARB/07/19), Decision on Jurisdiction, Applicable Law and Liability, 30 November 2012, § 4.163–4.164.

33 *Charanne v Spain*, Award of 21 January 2016, §§ 433–439; *RREEF v Spain* (ICSID, No ARB/13/30), Decision on Jurisdiction, 6 June 2016, §§ 81–86; *Isolux v Spain*, Award, SCC V2013/153, 12 July 2016, §§ 646; *Novenergia II v Spain*, Arbitration SCC (2015/063), Award, 15 February 2018, § 454.

34 *RREEF v Spain, cited* in preceding, § 76; *Isolux v Spain*, cited in preceding, § 645; *Novenergia II v Spain*, cited in preceding, § 462.

35 *Masdar Solar & Wind Cooperatief UA v Spain* (ICSID No ARB/14/1), Award of 16 May 2018, spec. §§ 678 et seq.

36 For eg, see: *Belenergia SA v Italian Republic* (ICSID Case No ARB/15/40), Award, 6 August 2019, §§ 288–340; *Photovoltaik Knopf Betriebs-GmbH v The Czech Republic* (PCA Case No 2014–21), 15 May 2019, §§ 337–359; *Voltaic Network GmbH v The Czech Republic* (PCA Case No 2014–20), Award, 15 May 2019, §§ 348–370. Spain has recently seen its claim to have a request for a preliminary ruling sent to the ECJ, in an ECT case, denied by the Svea Court of appeal (*Spain v Novaenergia*, 27 May 2020). In another case, however, the Paris Court of appeal has sent a request for a preliminary ruling to the ECJ as to the interpretation of the notion of investment under the ECT (Paris Court of appeal, 24 September 2019, see Paris Journal of International Arbitration 2019/3, p 523, note P Pedone). *Cube Infrastructure Fund SICAV et a. c/* Espagne, CIRDI, ARB/15/20; aff *Landesbank Baden-Württemberg et a. c/ Espagne*, CIRDI, ARB/15/45; aff *NextEra Energy Global Holdings BV et NextEra Energy Spain Holdings BV c/ Espagne,* CIRDI, ARB/14/11; aff *Eskosol SpA in liquidazione c/ Italie*, ARB/15/50; aff *9REN Holding S.a.r.l c/ Espagne*, CIRDI, ARB/15/1; aff *SolEs Badajoz GmbH c/ Espagne*, CIRDI, ARB/15/38; aff *Belenergia SA c/ Italie*, CIRDI, ARB/15/40; aff *OperaFund Eco-Invest SICAV PLC et Schwab c/ Holding AG*, CIRDI, n° ARB/15/36 + voir ma liste.

the ECT has not waned in the light of the large number of new proceedings initiated[37] since the *Achmea* judgment. Second, the draught of the text recently proposed by the European Commission with a view to reforming this treaty[38] does not even address, for the time being, the question of the jurisdiction of arbitral tribunals in intra-EU disputes. Finally, it should be noted that it is now the European Union itself which, as a party to the EC Treaty, is the subject of claims before an arbitral tribunal based on the EC Treaty and brought by an investor.[39] Thus, after the consequences of the *Achmea* ruling on the jurisdiction of arbitral tribunals, it will no doubt soon be necessary to return to the consequences of EU law on the substantial protection of investors, whether European or from third countries. One current and very important aspect of this matter is obviously the role of the EU illegal state aid regime.[40]

16.49 Ultimately, for the future, the disappearance of intra-EU BITs and the willingness of the majority of Member States and the EU Commission to neutralize the ECT in intra-EU situations will inevitably lead to a restructuring of investments in Europe. In this respect, non-EU countries, including a former UE Member State, which have maintained their BITs with EU Member States, will have a clear comparative advantage. However, investors have to take into account the risk of fraud which could be committed by an investor established on the territory of a Member State in setting up a local structure on the territory of a third State with the (sole?) aim of rendering a BIT concluded with a third State applicable in extra-European relations. No one can say whether the desire to protect the autonomy of the Union's legal order against this sort of corporate restructuring will not go as far as piercing the social veil.

37 *EP Wind Project (Rom) Six Ltd v Romania* (ICSID Case No ARB/20/15); *Hamburg Commercial Bank AG v Italian Republic* (ICSID Case No ARB/20/3); *VM Solar Jerez GmbH and others v Kingdom of Spain* (ICSID Case No ARB/19/30); *Strabag SE, Erste Nordsee-Offshore Holding GmbH and Zweite Nordsee-Offshore Holding GmbH v Federal Republic of Germany* (ICSID Case No ARB/19/29); *Sapec, SA v Kingdom of Spain* (ICSID Case No ARB/19/23); *Petrochemical Holding GmbH v Romania* (ICSID Case No ARB/19/21); *Canepa Green Energy Opportunities I, S.á r.l. and Canepa Green Energy Opportunities II, S.á r.l. v Kingdom of Spain* (ICSID Case No ARB/19/4); *European Solar Farms A/S v Kingdom of Spain* (ICSID Case No ARB/18/45); *Veolia Propreté SAS v Italian Republic* (ICSID Case No ARB/18/20); *LSG Building Solutions GmbH and others v Romania* (ICSID Case No ARB/18/19).

38 EU text proposals for the modernisation of the Energy Charter Treaty, 27 May 2020.

39 *Nord Stream 2 AG v The European Union*, PCA Case 2020–07.

40 See: M Laazouzi, 'Revue de l'arbitrage', (2020) 3, Yearly Column on Investment Arbitration 609–662, spec. pp 639–662; Tim Maxian Rusche, 'State Aid and Arbitration' (2017) 3(1) Competition Law & Policy Debate 70–79, spec. pp 73 *et seq*; L Idot, 'Arbitration and Competition Law – Have We Entered a Fourth Phase in Their Relations?' (2017) 3(1) Competition Law & Policy Debate 38, spec. p 44 *et seq*.

CHAPTER 17

State immunity and its implications when resolving disputes with – and enforcing outcomes against – states

Michael Cottrell[1]

Introduction

17.1 States are a significant presence in the international construction and infrastructure market. By 2025, it is anticipated that worldwide capital project and infrastructure expenditure will reach US$9 trillion,[2] much of which will be procured by states directly, or indirectly through state entities, owing to the public nature of such works and the access states have to the financial resources necessary to fund large-scale projects.

17.2 As a result, many contractors find themselves entering into construction contracts involving states either acting as the direct employer (*ie*, where the relevant government ministry procures the project), or where the employer is a state entity (often referred to as a state-owned entity ('SOE')), such as a corporation which has been formed by the state and in which the state owns a majority shareholding. There is little practical difference, during the execution phase, between contracts involving states and those where the parties are purely private enterprises. The contractor may find itself subject to more burdensome audit requirements in view of the fact that it is receiving public funds, whilst it may also benefit from more readily available tax concessions and less restrictive importation regimes. Nevertheless, fundamentally the contractor must still deliver a completed project in accordance with the contractual specifications for which the employer, which just so happens to be a state or SOE, is contractually bound to pay.

17.3 Where significant differences can and do arise, however, is when the parties to such contracts engage in disputes. When disputes occur between private entities, there is rarely any disagreement as to whether the court has jurisdiction over the parties (*ie*, jurisdiction *rationae personae*),[3] particularly in circumstances where the parties have expressly agreed to submit themselves to the jurisdiction of a specific court system, or, in the absence of a choice, the applicable conflict of laws rules will identify the forum with jurisdiction. However, in disputes involving states and SOEs, the question of a court's jurisdiction – whether in respect of the substantive issues, in proceedings in support of arbitration, or to enforce a judgment or award – must routinely be addressed owing to the

1 The author would like to thank Philippa Webb, Adrian Elliott, and Clotilde Lemarié for their invaluable assistance.

2 *Capital Projects and Infrastructure Spending: Outlook to 2025*, PricewaterhouseCoopers LLP (2014) 6. <https://www.pwc.com/gx/en/capital-projects-infrastructure/publications/cpi-outlook/assets/cpi-outlook-to-2025.pdf>

3 As opposed to jurisdiction over the subject matter of the dispute (*ie*, jurisdiction *rationae materiae*) which gives rise to more frequent jurisdictional challenges.

preclusive effect of state immunity: the principle by which states and their assets may be rendered immune from the jurisdiction of the courts of foreign states.

17.4 A successful plea of state immunity has the effect of denying the court jurisdiction *rationae personae* over a foreign state and, by extension, over its assets. The consequence of this is that the court is prevented from entertaining a claim brought against a foreign state, as an assertion of state immunity must be dealt with before the merits of the underlying claim may be considered.[4] State immunity can also frustrate the enforcement of arbitral awards and foreign court judgments by limiting the pool of assets available to satisfy an award debt.

17.5 However, as this chapter will explore, there are clear limitations to the doctrine of state immunity which prescribe the circumstances in which immunity can be invoked by a state, particularly where a state has agreed to arbitrate its disputes. These limitations reflect the prevailing international approach to state immunity, which has generally developed over the past two centuries from an absolute position which effectively prohibited courts from exercising any jurisdiction at all over sovereign states and their property, to a more restrictive application that accommodates the growing involvement of the state in commercial activity.

17.6 From a practical perspective, parties that contract with states and SOEs need to give consideration to measures that they can put in place at the outset of their engagement in order to minimise the potential adverse consequences that state immunity may have on their ability to enforce their rights. This will involve careful analysis of a variety of factors, including the precise nature of the counterparty in order to determine whether it is truly a state or a separate entity, as well as ascertaining where the counterparty's assets are located in order to establish the potential availability and extent of immunity which the courts of those jurisdictions afford to states and their assets. These considerations arise even where the parties have sought to exclude the involvement of the courts in their disputes by agreeing to arbitration – the typical dispute resolution process for international construction contracts – as ultimately the execution of any arbitral award will necessitate recourse to the courts and their coercive powers.

17.7 The purpose of this chapter is to provide an introduction to certain fundamental concepts of state immunity relevant to understanding how the doctrine is applied by the English courts,[5] before going on to analyse more closely two areas where state immunity

4 See, for example, *Maclaine Watson & Co Ltd v Department of Trade and Industry* [1988] 3 WLR 1033, in which Kerr LJ held that: '*whenever the question arises under the* [State Immunity] *Act of 1978 whether a defendant state is immune by virtue of section 1 or not immune by virtue of one of the exceptions, then this question must be decided as a preliminary issue in favour of the plaintiff, in whatever form and by whatever procedure the court may consider appropriate, before the substantive action can proceed*' (1104 D–E). In the United States, state immunity has been variously described as a defence from liability and a shield '*from trial and the attendant burdens of litigation*' and an immunity '*from the burdens of becoming involved in any part of the litigation process*' (see: *Process And Industrial Developments Limited v Federal Republic of Nigeria and Ministry of Petroleum Resources of the Federal Republic of Nigeria*, US Ct App, DC Circuit, 19 June 2020, pp 5, 11). As a result, the question of whether a state enjoys immunity must be decided at the threshold of every action '*even if that requires jurisdictional discovery and factual resolution of immunity questions to take place before the sovereign is required to defend the merits*', *ibid*, at 11.

5 It would be beyond the scope (and word count) of this chapter to analyse in detail the principles of state immunity and its historical development. However, there are a number of books which provide a detailed exploration of this topic, an excellent example being Hazel Fox & Philippa Webb, *The Law of State Immunity* (Oxford University Press 2015).

most frequently intersects with arbitration. This chapter concludes with a consideration of some of the issues arising from state immunity which will be of relevance to commercial parties when contracting with states.

17.8 This chapter is structured as follows. First, it identifies key principles underlying the modern application of state immunity. Second, it summarises the legislative regime in the UK.[6] Third, it addresses the effect of state immunity on the courts' ability to exercise powers in support of arbitration. Fourth, it considers the impact of state immunity on the ability of a party which has succeeded in arbitration to enforce its award against a state. Finally, conclusions are drawn and practical considerations are developed for identifying and mitigating the potential impact of state immunity in construction and infrastructure disputes.

State immunity: some underlying concepts

17.9 The basic proposition of state immunity is that the courts of one state are prevented, in certain situations, from exercising their jurisdiction over another state or its property in circumstances where they would otherwise be permitted to do so if the state were instead a private entity. The rationale for this doctrine is rooted in classical concepts of the 'state': a legal personality with a centralised power structure, which sits amongst a community of equal and independent states.[7] The natural consequence of these two characteristics – states as sovereign within their own territory whilst co-existing with other states on an equal and independent basis – was that one state could not exercise dominion over another.[8]

17.10 Closely intertwined with this principle, and acting as a further source for the development of state immunity, was the concept of absolute personal immunities that were enjoyed by sovereign heads of state along with their diplomatic envoys.[9] Based on the

6 A comprehensive study of the approach to state immunity adopted by other countries would similarly require more space than circumstances permit. However, given the inherently reciprocal nature of state immunity and the manner in which it has developed at the international level, there is a high degree of comity between nations as to how the principles of state immunity are applied. Moreover, many domestic statutes which address this topic have been drafted so as to implement provisions similar to those found in international treaties, such as the European Convention on State Immunity 1972 and the UN Convention on Jurisdictional Immunities of States and their Property 2004.

7 See: Hazel Fox & Philippa Webb, *The Law of State Immunity* (Oxford University Press 2015) 26.

8 The European Court of Human Rights has described sovereign immunity as '*a concept of international law, developed out of the principle par in parem non habet imperium, by virtue of which one state shall not be subject to the jurisdiction of another state. The grant of sovereign immunity to a state in civil proceedings pursues the legitimate aim of complying with international law to promote comity and good relations between states through the respect of another state's sovereignty*', see: *Jones v United Kingdom* (2014) 59 E.H.R.R. 1, [188]. In that case, which involved an attempt by the appellant to bring proceedings against an official of the Saudi Arabian government alleging torture, the court determined in effect that the rules of state immunity achieved greater international acceptance than the jus cogens prohibition on torture.

9 See, for example, *The Magdalena Steam Navigation Company v Martin* (1859) 2 El & El 94. The case involved non-payment by the defendant of a call made by the liquidator of the claimant company. The defendant, who was a shareholder in the company, asserted immunity on the grounds of his position as Envoy Extraordinary for the Republic of Guatemala and Minister Plenipotentiary for the Republic of New Granada. In finding the defendant immune from what was, on any analysis, a wholly commercial suit, Lord Campbell held that a public minister of a foreign state owes not even a temporary allegiance to the host state and that, '*if he has done nothing to forfeit or to waive his privilege, he is for all juridical purposes supposed still to be in his own country*'. However, during oral argument counsel for the claimant referred to R. Phillimore's *Commentaries upon International Law* to support the assertion that there were exceptions to the absolute immunity of an ambassador, including when

obvious mutual benefit of allowing foreign sovereigns and their agents to enter and stay in a state without fear of being arrested or subjected to judicial process, this immunity was generally recognised as being part of the '*law of nations*' which stretched back to the ancient empires.[10] In fact, so entrenched in the practice of nations was the principle of immunity for sovereigns and their diplomats that it was only following the arrest in England of the Russian ambassador in 1708 for a debt that legislation was considered necessary in the United Kingdom to enshrine the immunity of foreign dignitaries in law.[11]

Acts of a sovereign nature vs acts of a commercial nature

17.11 The interplay between the concepts of sovereign equality and personal immunity was the foundation for what became known as the absolute doctrine of state immunity, by which '*a sovereign or sovereign state was absolutely immune from legal proceedings in foreign national courts, whatever the character of the legal relationship involved, and whatever the type and nature of the legal proceedings*'.[12] This was the prevailing position adopted by most states until the early nineteenth century.[13] Until that point, there was very little need for the courts to consider the scope of state immunity.[14] States rarely, if ever,

---

an ambassador '*becomes a trader or a merchant in the country to which he is sent*', at which point all property belonging to the ambassador in this capacity is liable to seizure '*in the same manner as the property of any other trader or merchant*' (at 100). In support of this argument, reliance was placed on a case from the Hague in 1720, reported in Cornelius van Bynkershoek's treatise *De Foro Legatorum*, when the courts granted a decree of arrest over all of the property belonging to the Envoy Extraordinary of the Duke of Holstein '*with the exception of the moveables, equipages and other things belonging to him in the character of ambassador*' (*ibid*). However, as Lord Campbell noted, the reference to this case was from a chapter in Bynkershoek's text entitled '*De Legato Mercatore*' (the merchant ambassador) which detailed the exception for ambassadors who also engaged in commerce for personal gain. It is therefore apparent that, at the time, certain jurisdictions did recognise limits to the 'absolute' immunity afforded to foreign diplomats based on the nature of their activities (although the English courts recognised no such distinction). As a result, in those jurisdictions the immunity attached to the person of the diplomat only when engaged in diplomatic activities. This exception is recognised in the modern law of diplomatic immunity; see Article 31(c) of the *Vienna Convention on Diplomatic Relations* 1961.

10 See, for example, the Diplomatic Privileges Act 1708, s. 1. See also the judgment of Lord Sumption in *Al-Maliki v Reyes* [2017] UKSC 61; [2019] A.C. 735 where (at [5]) Lord Sumption explained that rules of diplomatic immunity could be traced back to the ancient world, and that Grotius, writing in the seventeenth century, declared that diplomatic immunity '*had been accepted by the nations*'.

11 The Diplomatic Privileges Act 1708 rendered null and void all suits commenced against any ambassador or public minister of a foreign state, along with any proceedings against their property. See Lord Sumption in *Al-Maliki v Reyes* (n 10), at [5].

12 Xiaodong Yang, *State Immunity in International Law* (Cambridge University Press 2012) 7.

13 The absolute doctrine was by no means universally adopted, however. For example, it was never applied in Italy; see the decision in *Typaldos, Console di Grecia a Napoli v Maniomio di Aversa, Giurisprundenzia Italiana* (1886) I, 228 where, at 229, the Italian Corte di Cassazione considered that: '*No one can deny that the foundation of international law is the sovereignty and independence of states; and that in consequence of this principle each state, in the exercise of its powers, is exempted from the jurisdiction of other states. But the fallacy consists in considering the state exclusively and always as a body politic, although its activity as a civil entity cannot be gainsaid when it performs acts acquiring rights and assuming obligations in private relationships, like any other physical or juristic person being capable of exercising civil rights*', referred to by Lord Sumption in *Benkharbouche v Embassy of the Republic of Sudan; Janah v Libya* [2017] UKSC 62; [2019] AC 777, at [49].

14 Xiaodong Yang, *State Immunity in International Law* (Cambridge University Press 2012) 8: '*Absolute immunity was granted in an age when the distinction between sovereign and non-sovereign activities was less manifest, given that state functions were at the time confined to the traditional spheres of, say, legislation, administration, national defence, and the conduct of State-to-State political relations and that, as a result, it was possible and natural to regard 'State' activities as synonymous with 'sovereign' activities*'.

engaged in activities beyond their own territories, and when they did it was either to wage war or conduct diplomacy, both of which were acts of a sovereign nature, with the latter the subject of the personal immunity referred to earlier.[15] On the rare occasions when courts in this period were asked to adjudicate on claims made against foreign states and their property, they were often dismissed on the basis of the absolute immunity enjoyed by sovereigns and their property.[16]

17.12 However, when states started to involve themselves in the realm of international commerce, acting – to all intents and purposes – as private enterprises, the adequacy of the absolute doctrine of state immunity was called into question.[17] One can appreciate the inequity from the perspective of a private trader in the nineteenth century, who would have been bound by the laws of each country they visited, whereas a state engaging competitively in the same market would be immune from the jurisdiction of any foreign courts for liabilities that it might incur. Indeed, it was cases arising out of the arrest of foreign state-owned vessels as a result of claims related to matters such as accidents at sea[18] and salvage liability[19] (matters which would normally have attracted civil liability for private vessel owners) which first tested the boundaries of state immunity in the context of states undertaking activities other than of a sovereign nature.

17.13 In those states which had observed the absolute doctrine of state immunity, the response of many courts was to gradually limit the scope of the immunity afforded to foreign states and their property. The distinction between the matters over which foreign states retained immunity and those over which a court could validly exercise jurisdiction was drawn between the acts of a state in the exercise of its sovereign authority (*acta iure imperii*) on the one hand, and the acts of a state which were commercial in nature (*acta iure gestionis*) on the other.

17.14 It is this distinction between the nature of a state's activities which has become arguably the cornerstone of the modern approach to state immunity.[20] However the English

15 See Lord Sumption in *Benkharbouche v Embassy of the Republic of Sudan; Janah v Libya* [2017] UKSC 62; [2019] AC 777, at [40].

16 See, for example, the decision of the US Supreme Court in *The Schooner Exchange v McFaddon* (1812) 7 Cranch 116. The case involved the attempted seizure of a vessel of the French navy which had been forced to put into port in Philadelphia in bad weather. The decision of Marshall CJ in reinstating the dismissal of the claim was based on the reasoning that the jurisdiction of a state within its own territory is absolute, subject only to the limitations it consents to recognise. Such limitations arise in circumstances where the '*perfect equality and absolute independence of sovereigns*' along with the '*common interest impelling them to mutual discourse, and an interchange of good offices with each other*' compels the state to waive the otherwise complete and exclusive jurisdiction that a state has over its territory (at 137). In respect of warships belonging to a foreign state, the Chief Justice reasoned that the waiver (where not based on an express license to permit foreign ships to enter a state's territory found in the provisions of a treaty) is based on the deemed assent of the host sovereign. In those circumstances, it would be impossible to conceive that a sovereign should '*mean to subject his army or his navy to the jurisdiction of a foreign sovereign*' (at 143). Furthermore, as a warship '*constitutes a part of the military force of her nation; acts under the immediate and direct command of the sovereign; is employed by him in national objects*', any interference by the host state '*cannot take place without affecting his power and his dignity*' (at 144). As a result, the Chief Justice held that the implied licence by which a foreign state's warship enters the host state's port must be construed as containing an exemption from the host state's jurisdiction.

17 Lakshman Marasinghe, *The Modern Law of Sovereign Immunity* (1991) Mod. L. Rev. 54(5) 664, 665.

18 See, for example, *The Parlement Belge* (1880) 5 P. D. 197.

19 See, for example, *The Porto Alexandre* [1920] P. 30.

20 When considering (and eventually allowing) an appeal against a garnishee order in respect of a balance held at a bank account belonging to the Columbian Embassy in London, Lord Diplock in *Alcom Ltd v Republic of Columbia* [1984] AC 580 said of the UK State Immunity Act 1978 that '[t]*he principle of international law that is*

courts were, despite some early indications to the contrary,[21] uncharacteristically slow in adopting what has become known as the restrictive doctrine of state immunity. In *The Parlement Belge*,[22] the Court of Appeal held that a ship owned by the King of the Belgians which was engaged in the delivery of mail between Belgium and England, but which also carried goods and passengers for payment, could not be subjected to proceedings *in rem*.[23] This was followed by a further decision involving a vessel, *The Porto Alexandre*,[24] which was owned by the Portuguese state and was engaged in purely commercial activities, but which the Court of Appeal nevertheless found to be immune from jurisdiction. The court arrived at this decision despite recognising the growing trend of states owning trading ships to engage in ordinary trade, and the difficulties that would entail in allowing such ships to '*wander about without liabilities*'.[25]

17.15 Nevertheless, following the 1938 decision in *The Cristina* in which the House of Lords cast doubt on the status of the absolute doctrine of immunity as both a rule applicable in England and as a matter of international law,[26] the English courts gradually

---

most relevant to the subject matter of the Act is the distinction that has come to be drawn between claims arising out of those activities which a state undertakes jure imperii, i.e., in the exercise of sovereign authority, and those arising out of activities which it undertakes jure gestionis, i.e. transactions of the kind which might appropriately be undertaken by private individuals instead of sovereign states' (at 597–598). Later, Lord Diplock stated that: '*as respects the immunity of foreign states from the jurisdiction of national courts the critical distinction drawn by the existing law, English common law and public international law alike, was between what a state did in the exercise of its sovereign authority and what it did in the course of commercial or trading activities. The former enjoyed immunity; the latter did not*'.

21 See, for example *The Charkieh* (1872–75) L.R. 4 A.&E. 59, in which proceedings *in rem* were brought against the eponymous vessel by the owners of another ship which was lost following a collision in the Thames. The Charkieh was the property of the Khedive (Viceroy) of Egypt and had been in the service of the Ottoman Navy. However, she was at the time of the collision advertised to carry cargo and passengers bound for Alexandria, the money earned from which was to be paid to the Egyptian state. In holding that even if the Khedive could claim immunity generally (which he could not, as Egypt was at the time a province of the Ottoman Empire) he had waived it by putting The Charkieh to commercial use as a trading ship, Sir Robert Phillimore stated that '[n]*o principle of international law, and no decided case, and no dictum of jurists of which I am aware, has gone so far as to authorize a sovereign prince to assume the character of a trader, when it is for his benefit; and when he incurs an obligation to a private subject to throw off, if I may so speak, his disguise, and appear as a sovereign, claiming for his own benefit, and to the injury of a private person, for the first time, all the attributes of his character*' (at 100–101). See also *The Emperor of Brazil v Robinson* (1838) 6 AD. & E. 802, in which the Emperor of Brazil was ordered to give security for costs in an action on a charter-party in circumstances where the Emperor was trading as a merchant.

22 (1880) 5 P. D. 197.

23 Brett LJ held that the public property of foreign states was '*in the same category of immunity from jurisdiction as the person of a sovereign, or of an ambassador, or of ships of war*' and was therefore exempt from the jurisdiction of the courts as the exercise of such jurisdiction was '*inconsistent with the independence of the sovereign authority of the state*'; *ibid*, at 213.

24 [1920] P. 30.

25 [1920] P. 30, per Scrutton LJ at 38–39.

26 [1938] A.C. 485. The case involved an action *in rem* against a vessel which had been requisitioned by the Spanish government to assist in the war effort against the nationalist rebellion in the country. As the decision ultimately rested on a finding that the vessel had been requisitioned for a sovereign purpose (*ie*, defence of the Spanish state) and so was not amenable to the jurisdiction of the English courts, it was unnecessary for the House of Lords to come to a decision on whether the use to which a state's property is put was relevant to the consideration of whether immunity attached. However, Lord Thankerton (at 495–496) noted that the Court of Appeal in *The Porto Alexandre* had found itself bound by the decision in *The Parlement Belge*, but that the decision in *The Parlement Belge* that ships and other property of the sovereign '*destined to public uses*' attracted immunity did not support the conclusion in *The Porto Alexandre* that the immunity applied to all property of the state irrespective of how it was employed. Lord Thankerton stated that a logical inference of Brett LJ's judgment in *The Parlement Belge* was that '*an action in rem against property of the sovereign which is engaged in private*

started to abandon the absolute doctrine. In its place, the courts adopted the restrictive approach, distinguishing between the activities undertaken by states in the discharge of their sovereign authority, and those of a private commercial nature. In a series of cases in the 1950s, statements in obiter and dissenting opinions gradually sought to recognise this distinction, which had been drawn into sharper focus by the increasingly common practice of states delegating their trading functions to separate entities.[27] This head of steam in the English courts in favour of the restrictive doctrine culminated in two decisions in 1977, one of the Privy Council[28] and another in the Court of Appeal,[29] in which the restrictive doctrine was confirmed as applying to both actions against state property and states themselves, so that where the act in question was a commercial act then immunity would not bar

trading, and which is not dedicated to public uses, is not to be regarded as inconsistent with the independence and equality of the state represented by such owner, and that any other view would lead to absolute exemption of all property owned by the sovereign, and not the exemption of some property only'. Lord Maugham also noted (at 519–520) that: '[t]*he judgments in* The Porto Alexandre *seem to me to have omitted any consideration of what I deem to be a vital point – namely, the fact that other countries while they admit the immunity as regards ships of war and other public ships have not been at all agreed that the same immunity ought to be granted to ships and cargoes engaged in ordinary trading voyages*'.

27 See, in respect of trading entities formed by states, the dissenting opinion of Singleton LJ in *Baccus S.R.L. v Servicio Nacional del Trigo* [1957] 1 QB 438, in which the defendant, a separate legal entity established by the Spanish Ministry of Agriculture, succeeded in asserting immunity. His Lordship stated (at 461) that '*I cannot find that it has been almost universally recognized that if a government sets up a legal entity, something which may contract on its own behalf as a limited company does in this country, it can succeed in a claim for sovereign immunity in respect of the activities of that company or entity. The claim goes further than has been generally recognized, and, in the interests of good government, and in the interests of business relationship and business dealings throughout the world, I do not think that the claim ought to be allowed on the material before us*'. However, the majority of the Court of Appeal upheld the claim to immunity, with Jenkins LJ finding that the state did not lose immunity in respect of activities conducted in the public interest simply because it had incorporated a separate legal entity for these purposes, with the distinction as to whether the entity party to the proceedings being a corporate body or an unincorporated body '*purely a matter of governmental machinery*' (at 466). In *Rahimtoola v Nizam of Hyderabad* [1958] AC 379, at 417 Lord Denning referred to *Baccus*, noting that '*I should have thought that a separate legal entity which carried on commercial transactions for a State was an agent, and not an organ, of the Government, and that it was only if it was an 'organ or alter ego' that it could not be impleaded*'. See also: *Sultan of Johore v Abubakar Tunku Aris Bendahar* [1952] AC 318, per Viscount Simon at 343 (in obiter): '*Their Lordships do not consider that there has been finally established in England ... any absolute rule that a foreign independent sovereign cannot be impleaded in our courts in any circumstances*'; a statement which his Lordship considered was '*desirable to say ... having regard to inferences that might be drawn from some parts of the Court of Appeal's judgment in* The Parlement Belge, *and from the speech of Lord Atkin in* The Cristina'.

28 *The Philippine Admiral* [1977] AC 373, in which proceedings *in rem* were permitted to continue against a vessel which was in use as an ordinary trading vessel, despite being owned by a Commission of the Philippine government, and therefore the property of the Philippine state. The Privy Council held that the position adopted by the Court of Appeal in *The Porto Alexandre* should not be followed and that, in respect of the property of a state which was engaged in commercial activities (if not the state itself), immunity could not be asserted. Per Lord Cross (at 402–3): '*the trend of opinion in the world outside the Commonwealth since the last war has been increasingly against the application of the doctrine of sovereign immunity to ordinary trading transactions*'; who also noted that '*the restrictive theory is more consonant with justice*'.

29 *Trendtex Trading Corporation v Central Bank of Nigeria* [1977] QB 529, in which the claimant sought an injunction requiring the Nigerian Central Bank to keep a sum of money within the jurisdiction pending the trial of the underlying action on a letter of credit it had issued. In finding that the bank was a separate entity and not an emanation of the state entitled to immunity, Denning MR noted (at 556) that the Privy Council in *The Philippine Admiral* had accepted the restrictive theory in relation to proceedings against state property, but had considered that the absolute theory still applied to proceedings *in personam* against the state itself. His Lordship considered that the reasoning applied by the Privy Council in restricting immunity in proceedings against state property should also apply to actions against states and that to not do so would be '*an indefensible anomaly*' (at 557).

proceedings. This position at common law was given final judicial assent by the House of Lords in 1983.[30]

17.16 As explored further in the following, the distinction between sovereign acts and commercial acts has been given full statutory force by the State Immunity Act 1978 ('SIA'), which expressly disapplies immunity in proceedings for a wide range of activities (including commercial transactions, broadly defined) which are not sovereign in nature. Whilst this may appear to have created a binary categorisation between sovereign and non-sovereign acts, there are still circumstances where the nature of the acts in question is not entirely clear.[31] However, where such cases occur, the courts have held that it is the act itself, not the state's purpose in performing the act, which determines its nature.[32]

Adjudicative vs enforcement jurisdiction

17.17 Another key concept relevant to understanding the operation of state immunity is the distinction between the adjudicative jurisdiction of the court on the one hand, and the enforcement jurisdiction of the court on the other. In general terms, the former relates to the competence of the court to entertain (or adjudicate) a claim against a putative defendant and render a judgment on the merits of the claim. The latter relates to the power that a court has to order the execution of a court judgment or arbitral award which has previously been rendered, such as granting a charging order over property owned by the judgment debtor to satisfy the award debt, or granting interim relief such as a freezing injunction pending the outcome of substantive proceedings.

17.18 In cases involving private entities, the court's adjudicative jurisdiction is often readily ascertainable by reference to the parties' express agreement to confer jurisdiction on a chosen court, the presence of the defendant within the jurisdictional territory of the court, or the operation of specific rules governing jurisdiction.[33] A court's enforcement jurisdiction is determined by reference to its territorial scope; the defendant or the assets against which enforcement is sought must usually be present within the territorial jurisdiction of the court for the court to be able to grant measures of constraint or execution. The distinction between these two types of jurisdiction is rarely in issue where disputes

30 *I Congreso del Partido* [1983] 1 AC 244. Although a case which post-dated the introduction of the State Immunity Act in 1978, it involved circumstances which pre-dated the Act, and so the common law rules regarding state immunity applied. Lord Wilberforce (at 261) noted that the Privy Council had, in the *Philippine Admiral*, unnecessarily limited application of the restrictive doctrine to actions *in rem* against state property, and confirmed that the departure from the absolute rule should apply to proceedings against states themselves as well.

31 Per Lord Cross in *The Philippine Admiral* [1977] AC 373, at 402: '*There is of course no clear cut dividing line between acts done* jure imperii *and acts done* jure gestionis *and difficult border line cases may arise*.'

32 See the decision of Lord Wilberforce in *I Congreso* (supra, n 30), citing (at 263–4) the 1963 German Federal Constitutional Court decision in *Claim against the Empire of Iran Case*, 45 I.L.R. 57, in which the court stated (at 80): '*As a means for determining the distinction between acts jure imperii and jure gestionis one should rather refer to the nature of the state transaction or the resulting legal relationships, and not to the motive or purpose of the state activity. It thus depends upon whether the foreign state has acted in exercise of its sovereign authority, that is in public law, or like a private person, that is in private law*.'

33 See, for example, Regulation (EU) No. 1215/2012 on Jurisdiction and the Recognition and Enforcement of Judgments in Civil and Commercial Matters (Recast) (the 'Brussels Recast Regulation', which will cease to apply to recognition and enforcement proceedings in the UK commenced after the end of the Brexit transition period); and the Convention on Jurisdiction and the Recognition and Enforcement of Judgments in Civil and Commercial Matters (the 'Lugano Convention', to which the UK is presently seeking to accede).

arise between private entities; where the defendant is amenable to the court's adjudicative jurisdiction then, if it has assets available within the territory of the court to satisfy the judgment debt, the defendant will *prima facie* be amenable to the enforcement jurisdiction of the court.

17.19 However, where the defendant is a foreign state, it does not necessarily follow from a finding that it has no immunity from the court's adjudicative jurisdiction (because, for example it has engaged in a commercial transaction) that the state is also not immune from the court's enforcement jurisdiction. The court is required to address the issue of immunity (and, thus, its own jurisdiction) at each phase of the proceedings,[34] *ie*, once when it is asked to determine a foreign state's liability, and again when it is asked to order enforcement against the foreign state's property.[35]

17.20 The rationale for this is the difference in effect of the exercise of the court's two distinct jurisdictions. A judgment of the court determining that a foreign state has breached a contract and is liable to pay damages has no immediate impact on the state or its ability to discharge its sovereign functions. However, if the court was to subsequently grant an order permitting the judgment debtor to execute the judgment and satisfy the judgment debt by, for example, seizing property belonging to the state, this could constitute a serious interference with a state's exercise of its public functions and pursuit of its sovereign purpose if the property in question was integral to the state's public functions.[36] For example, if a judgment creditor sought enforcement by applying for a third-party debt order over the money standing to the account of a foreign state's embassy,[37] this could impinge upon the embassy's ability to perform its diplomatic activities. Given that the basis of state immunity is the recognition that, as sovereign equals, one state cannot involve itself in another's exercise of sovereign authority, it follows that courts should not be permitted to grant the execution of enforcement proceedings where to do so would have just such an effect. A further reason given by commentators to explain this additional jurisdictional threshold is political expediency.[38] If the courts of one state were to indiscriminately grant

34 In *Alcom Ltd v Colombia* (*supra*, n 20), Lord Diplock stated that the SIA '*draws a clear distinction between the adjudicative jurisdiction and the enforcement jurisdiction of the courts of law in the United Kingdom*' (at 600). As SIA section1(2) provides that the court '*shall give effect to the immunity conferred by this section even though the State does not appear in the proceedings in question*', it follows that this must require a court to satisfy itself that it has jurisdiction at both the adjudicative and enforcement stage of proceedings.

35 The consideration of enforcement as a separate phase from the court's adjudicative jurisdiction has been cited as '*perhaps the single most important aspect of the law of State Immunity that makes judicial proceedings against a foreign state so undeniably different from those against a private individual*'; Xiaodong Yang, *State Immunity in International Law* (Cambridge University Press 2012) 348.

36 Although not argued by the state on these grounds, the situation in *Norsk Hydro ASA v State Property Fund of Ukraine et Ors* [2002] EWHC 2120 (Comm); [2009] Bus LR 558 is demonstrative of the effect that enforcement measures can have on a state. In that case, the Republic of Ukraine sought to set aside an interim third party debt order which had been granted in the claimant's favour in respect of sums standing to Ukraine's account at a bank account in London. The witness evidence submitted by Ukraine in support of its application explained that the sums were intended to pay principal and interest sums on bonds issued by the state as part of its debt restructuring, and that the effect of the interim third party debt order would be to cause an event of default the consequences of which '*would be catastrophic for Ukraine, both politically and economically*' as it would need to reallocate its already limited resources from other areas in order to meet its commitments (per Gross J at [9], quoting from the witness evidence of Ukraine's principal external legal advisor).

37 As was the case in *Alcom* (*supra*, n 20).

38 See, for example: Hazel Fox & Philippa Webb, *The Law of State Immunity* (Oxford University Press 2015) 486. See also: Xiaodong Yang, *State Immunity in International Law* (Cambridge University Press 2012) 362.

injunctions and third party debt orders against another state or its property, it could strain international relations as such conduct could be perceived as hostile.[39]

17.21 As a result, the court must actively consider whether it has jurisdiction to order execution of an award and, in doing so, have regard to the fact that the rules governing the exercise of this jurisdiction are stricter than the more permissive rules governing the court's adjudicative jurisdiction. As will be seen, the SIA expressly prohibits the court from giving injunctive relief against a state unless it is with the state's written consent, whilst enforcement against state property is limited to only that which is in use or destined for use for commercial purposes. The purpose of these restrictions is to prevent the court from taking excessively invasive measures against the dignity of a foreign state itself, or permitting the seizure of state property which is or is intended for use for sovereign purposes.

17.22 The practical effect of this is that it is entirely possible for a claimant to succeed in obtaining a court decision holding a foreign state liable (*ie*, for a breach of contract), but find that the foreign state is able to effectively avoid the adverse practical and financial consequences of the decision by asserting immunity in subsequent execution proceedings. This risk is moderated to a certain extent by the exception of property in use or intended for use for commercial purposes from the exclusion of the court's enforcement jurisdiction.[40]

17.23 However, recognising that the exercise of the court's enforcement jurisdiction over the property of a state *could* infringe on a foreign state's sovereignty, the SIA entitles the state to certify that the property subject to enforcement action is not in or intended to be put to commercial use. The court must accept this certificate as sufficient evidence unless the claimant can prove to the contrary,[41] thereby firmly allocating to the claimant the burden of proving that property is in or is intended for commercial use.

The legislative regime governing state immunity in the UK

17.24 The growing judicial criticism of the absolute doctrine of state immunity led,[42] in part, to the introduction of the State Immunity Bill in January 1978. The impetus for legislative intervention was also driven by the fact that the UK had, earlier in the decade, signed the European Convention on State Immunity 1972 ('ECSI'), which codified the restrictive doctrine at the international level and included obligations to which the UK needed to give effect. A further, and perhaps more pressing, motivation was the risk posed

39 For example, attachment proceedings in the French courts arising out of the long-running *Yukos* arbitrations caused diplomatic tensions with the Russian Federation, which led the Russian government issuing a *note verbale* to the French Embassy stating that the attachments were contrary to international law, and that Russia would retaliate against France and its interests; see: Isabelle Couet, *Emmanuel Gaillard: 'La voie pour effectuer des saisies est déjà très étroite'*, Les Echos, 10 June 2016, available at: www.lesechos.fr/2016/06/emmanuel-gaillard-la-voie-pour-effectuer-des-saisies-est-deja-tres-etroite-224818 (accessed 2 December 2020).

40 SIA section 13(4). This maintains the distinction, explained in the preceding section, between *acta iure imperii* and *acta iure gestionis* by retaining immunity for any property which is not in use or intended for use for commercial purposes (*ie*, that which is to be used in the exercise of sovereign authority) but makes any property which is or will be used for commercial purposes amenable to the enforcement jurisdiction of the court.

41 SIA section 13(5). See the discussion on this point in the section below which addresses the concept of 'commercial use' in the context of executing awards against states.

42 See the comments of Elwyn-Jones LC on introducing the Bill's second reading in the House of Lords, *HL, Hansard*, vol. 388, col. 54.

by the lack of statutory change to the UK's position as a global financial centre, as the adoption of the restrictive doctrine elsewhere made other jurisdictions – notably New York – more attractive.[43]

17.25 Any analysis of the sources of law relating to state immunity (in the UK and elsewhere) will also need to take account of the UN Convention on Jurisdictional Immunities of States and their Property 2004 (the 'UNCSI'), signed by the UK on 30 September 2005. Although not yet in force,[44] the convention has been cited in a number of English and international court decisions as being an authoritative statement of the current status of international law regarding state immunity.[45] However, the English courts have been unwilling to rely on specific provisions of the UNCSI as reflecting customary international law on the points they address,[46] and have refused to use the drafting history of the convention as a means of interpreting the SIA.[47]

43 Andrew Dickinson, Rae Lindsay, James P. Loonam, *State Immunity: Selected Materials and Commentary* (Oxford University Press 2004) 331. The United States enacted the Foreign Sovereign Immunities Act in 1976, however it had formally adopted the restrictive approach to state immunity in 1952, when the acting legal advisor to the US State Department, Jack Tate, wrote a letter to the acting Attorney General (referred to as the 'Tate Letter') in which he confirmed that the State Department would follow the restrictive theory. This was based on the State Department's view that the '*widespread and increasing practice on the part of governments of engaging in commercial activities makes necessary a practice which will enable persons doing business with them to have their rights determined in the courts*'; 'Changing Policy Concerning the Granting of Sovereign Immunity to Foreign Governments,' Letter to US Acting Attorney General, 1952 (1952) *US Department of State Bulletin* 984, at 984–985, in Hazel Fox & Philippa Webb, *The Law of State Immunity* (Oxford University Press 2015) 147.

44 In accordance with Article 30 of the UNCSI, entry into force occurs on the 30th day following the date of deposit of the 30th instrument of ratification, acceptance, approval, or accession with the UN Secretary General. As at November 2020, the UNCSI has been signed by 28 countries, of which 22 have ratified, accepted, approved, or acceded.

45 Hazel Fox & Philippa Webb, *The Law of State Immunity* (Oxford University Press 2015) 294–5. See, for example: *Jones v Ministry of the Interior of the Kingdom of Saudi Arabia and another* [2006] UKHL 26; [2007] 1 AC 270, per Lord Bingham, at [26], where the fact that the UNCSI contained no exception to immunity for civil liability in relation to acts of torture was sufficient to demonstrate that such an exception was not recognised at the international level.

46 See the decision of Lord Mance in *Belhaj and another v Straw and others* [2017] UKSC 3; [2017] AC 964, at [25], where his Lordship noted that Lord Bingham's comments in *Jones* (*supra*, n 45) were concerned with the limits of state immunity, which was a '*fundamental question which the Convention, however embryonic, could be expected to cover*', and could not be used to give binding international status to ambiguous terminology of a specific provision. See also the decision of Lord Sumption in *Benkharbouche* (*supra*, n 13), who noted (at [32]) that: '*In view of the emphasis placed by the European Court of Human Rights on the United Nations Convention and its antecedent drafts, it is right to point out that a treaty may have no effect qua treaty but nevertheless represent customary international law and as such bind non-party states*'. However, '*It would be difficult to say that a treaty such as the United Nations Convention which has never entered into force had led to the "crystallisation" of a rule of customary international law that had started to emerge before it was concluded. For the same reason, it is unlikely that such a treaty could have "given rise to a general practice that is accepted as law". These difficulties are greatly increased in the case of the United Nations Convention by the consideration that in the 13 years which have passed since it was adopted and opened for signature it has received so few accessions.*' After noting that the significance of the UNCSI was in the codification of customary international law, his Lordship stated: '*However, it is not to be assumed that every part of the Convention restates customary international law.*' See also Lord Mance in *Botaş Petroleum Pipeline Corporation v Tepe Insaat Sanayii AS* [2018] UKPC 31, who also noted (at [25]) that the UNCSI was treated in *Jones* as '*an authoritative statement on the then current international understanding of the limits of immunity in respect of torture, the Convention does not have equivalent status on a detailed question such as the present*'.

47 See: *Botaş* (*supra*, n 46), in which the appellant had sought to invoke the *travaux préparatoires* to the UNCSI produced in the late 1980s and early 1990s in support of its interpretation as to the definition of 'property of the state' in the SIA. Somewhat self-evidently, the Board held that '*these drafting discussions on the United*

17.26 There are also key differences between the SIA and the UNCSI, most notably the additional limitations the UNCSI places on the availability of post-judgment measures of constraint.[48] Therefore, integrating the UNCSI into UK law will likely involve either amending the SIA, or else making the UK's ratification subject to declarations and/or reservations. However, the UK may yet ratify the UNCSI; states party to the ECSI have informally indicated their intention to denounce the ECSI once they have ratified the UNCSI and it has entered into force.[49] Should the UK decide to do so, this could lead to substantive changes in the way the courts approach state immunity in the UK.

Structure of the State Immunity Act

17.27 The SIA is divided into three Parts, the first dealing with proceedings involving foreign states in the UK,[50] the second concerning judgments rendered against the UK in states party to the ECSI, with the third covering miscellaneous and supplementary matters. Part 1 is primarily relevant for the purposes of this chapter (although it is worth noting that s. 23 (in Part III) provides that Parts I and II do not apply to '*proceedings in respect of matters that occurred before the date of the coming into force of this Act*').[51]

17.28 The structure of Part I reflects the two overarching concepts addressed earlier. First, the distinction between the court's adjudicative and enforcement jurisdictions is recognised, with sections 1 to 11 broadly dealing with immunity from the former, whilst immunity from the latter is set out in sections 13 and parts of 14.[52] Second, the distinction between sovereign and commercial acts is codified throughout Part I albeit not, as Lord Diplock noted in *Alcom*, in a way which had received general acceptance in public international law.[53] Rather, the SIA starts by granting a general immunity to foreign states before the courts of the UK in section 1, subject to the exceptions to immunity set out in the remainder of Part I (some of which are, in turn, subject to exceptions which reinstate immunity in certain circumstances).

17.29 Whilst it may seem counterintuitive, given the inexorable trend both at the international level and in the English courts towards restricting state immunity, that the

---

Nations Convention post-date the United Kingdom Act by at least ten years; so the Act cannot be construed by reference to them'.

48 Hazel Fox & Philippa Webb, *The Law of State Immunity* (Oxford University Press 2015) 174.

49 *ibid*, at 294.

50 Section 23(7) permits the extension of the SIA by Order in Council to any dependent territory. To date, the provisions of the SIA have been extended by Order in Council to: certain of the British Overseas Territories (by the State Immunity (Overseas Territories) Order 1979); the Isle of Man (by the State Immunity (Isle of Man) Order 1981); Guernsey (by the State Immunity (Guernsey) Order 1981); and Jersey (by the State Immunity (Jersey) Order 1985).

51 SIA section 23(3). In particular, those sections do not apply to any prior agreement that a state may have made to submit to the jurisdiction of the courts of the UK, or any transaction, contract, employment contract, or arbitration agreement entered into before the coming into force of the SIA. The SIA came into force on 22 November 1978 (see: State Immunity Act 1978 (Commencement) Order 1978 (SI 1978/1572), Article 2).

52 Per Lord Diplock in *Alcom Ltd* (*supra*, n 20) at 600[F]. Lord Diplock omits s. 13(1) from his description of the sections which deal with the court's enforcement jurisdiction. However, as this sub-section prohibits the imposition of any penalties by way of committal or fine for failure to produce any documents or evidence in proceedings to which it is a party, this too would appear to touch upon the court's enforcement jurisdiction as it prevents the court from being able to exercise against a state the powers it has to enforce compliance with the procedural rules of court.

53 *ibid*, at 600[D].

SIA should start by granting absolute immunity, this approach reflects the process by which the restrictive doctrine developed prior to legislative intervention through the carving out by the courts of exceptions from absolute immunity. It is therefore understandable that the legislative vehicle giving effect to the concept of restrictive state immunity would begin with an expression of absolute immunity which is then subjected to the limitations which reduce the immunity down to a restrictive core.[54] Furthermore, in listing the ways in which absolute immunity is restricted rather than using the restrictive principle as the starting point, this approach also avoids the need to try and enumerate the types of activities performed in the exercise of sovereign authority. If the SIA were to have opened with a statement of principle that states are *not* immune from the court's jurisdiction except as provided for in the Act, it would have been necessary to list the circumstances in which state immunity could validly be asserted in the exercise of sovereign activity. In view of the tentacular nature of governmental endeavour, such a process could have had the unintended consequence of excluding from the scope of the immunity certain activities which are genuinely sovereign. Given the divergence of views between states as to those activities which constitute the exercise of sovereign authority and those which are non-sovereign, this could result in a politically inexpedient situation whereby a foreign state is subjected to the court's jurisdiction in respect of activities which the foreign state considers sovereign, but which the laws of the court's domestic state hold to be non-sovereign.

17.30 The formulation in the SIA also reflects similar legislative drafting in other common law countries and has since been replicated in the UNCSI.[55]

17.31 The SIA also lays down specific rules for the service of process against states, including the requirement that documents commencing proceedings are to be served on the Ministry of Foreign Affairs of the respondent state via the Foreign, Commonwealth and Development Office.[56] States are also granted a further two months to acknowledge service in response to the commencement of proceedings in addition to the period provided for in the Civil Procedure Rules.[57]

---

54 This is broadly the approach adopted by the ECSI, in which Articles 1 to 14 describe the circumstances in which a state is not entitled to assert immunity, following which Article 15 grants immunity to a contracting state '*if the proceedings do not fall within Articles 1 to 14*'. See also the UNCSI, which grants immunity in Article 5, subject to the provisions of Arts. 7 to 17.

55 Per Lord Sumption in *Benkharbouche* (*supra, n 13*), at [38].

56 SIA section 12(1). This provision only applies to documents which are '*required to be served*', with the effect that where an application may be made without notice, there is no requirement to serve it on the respondent state in accordance with this provision; see: *Gold Reserve Inc v Bolivarian Republic of Venezuela* [2016] EWHC 153 (Comm); [2016] 1 WLR 2829, per Teare J at [58], [64]. It also only applies where the documents are those which commence proceedings, and so does not apply to an order granting permission to enforce an arbitral award; see: see *General Dynamics United Kingdom Ltd v State of Libya* [2019] EWCA Civ 1110; [2019] 1 WLR 6137, at [60], in which the court dispensed with service of the notice owing to the exceptional circumstances in the state at the time, with the effect that neither the arbitration claim form nor the order granting permission to enforce were required to be served (this case is currently the subject of an appeal). However, where a state obstructs service of the claim form which would otherwise be required to be served pursuant to section 12, the court has the power to dispense with service (although it will require that the order dispensing with notice has been notified to the state); see: *Qatar National Bank (QPSC) v Government of Eritrea and State of Eritrea* [2019] EWHC 1601 (Ch), per Master Kaye at [122], [123].

57 SIA section 12(2). The additional two months runs from date on which the documents commencing proceedings are received by the state, following the expiry of which the usual time period for acknowledging service will begin to run. This is '*an acknowledgement of the reality that states do take time to react to legal proceedings*' (*Norsk Hydro ASA v State Property Fund of Ukraine and others* [2002] EWHC 2120 (Comm);

Exceptions to immunity from the court's adjudicative jurisdiction

17.32 The exceptions to the immunity from the adjudicative jurisdiction of the courts are set out in sections 2 to 11. These encompass situations where the state has either submitted to the jurisdiction of the UK courts,[58] or where the subject matter of the proceedings involves acts of a commercial or otherwise non-sovereign nature such as disputes relating to: commercial transactions,[59] contracts of employment,[60] personal injury and property damage,[61] ownership, possession and use of property in the UK,[62] patents and trademarks,[63] membership of bodies corporate,[64] arbitrations,[65] ships in use for commercial purposes,[66] and the foreign state's tax liability.[67] Provisions are also made for proceedings brought against a person other than a state which involve property which is either in the possession or control of a state, or in which a state claims an interest.[68] In such circumstances, the court would have jurisdiction to entertain the claim irrespective of the fact that the property in question belongs to the state, if the state would not have enjoyed immunity had the proceedings been brought against it.

17.33 A detailed analysis of each exception to immunity is beyond the scope of this chapter. However, this chapter addresses the specific exception which arises in the context of arbitration. Given the practical implications of the immunity from enforcement on a party's ability to enforce judgments and awards, the remainder of this section explores in more detail the circumstances in which immunity operates to exclude the court's enforcement jurisdiction.

[2009] Bus LR 558, per Gross J at [25(4)]). Prior to the expiry of this extended period, the court has no jurisdiction to issue an order for summary judgment or other orders for execution of a judgment or award (*Norsk Hydro*, per Gross J at [25(6)]). However, this does not preclude a party from making an application prior to the expiry of the extended period under section 12; see *L R Avionics Technologies Ltd v Federal Republic of Nigeria and another* [2016] EWHC 1761 (Comm), per Males J at [10]: '*the critical date is the date when judgment is given and not the date when an application for such judgment is issued*'.

58 SIA section 2. A state can either actively submit to the jurisdiction before a dispute has arisen or afterwards, or can do so impliedly by either instituting proceedings, or intervening or taking a step in proceedings unless it does so to assert immunity (although the consequences of taking a step in proceedings can be suspended by the court; see: *PAO Tatneft v Ukraine* [2019] EWHC 1543, in which the court ordered that the state's step in proceedings to enforce an arbitral award in relation to one aspect of the award was not to be construed as a step in the proceedings for the other part of the award which remained the subject of appeal proceedings). The head of a state's diplomatic mission to the UK is deemed to have the authority to submit to the jurisdiction on behalf of his or her state, whilst anyone who has entered into a contract on behalf of *and* with the authority of the state is deemed to have had the authority to submit to the jurisdiction on behalf of the state. This is a complete code so far as the circumstances in which a state may be found to have submitted itself to the jurisdiction of the English courts. This is to be contrasted with the position under US law, where the Foreign Sovereign Immunities Act of 1976 simply states that a foreign state is not immune '*in any case in which the foreign state has waived its immunity either explicitly or by implication*'. After exhaustively reviewing the case law which has developed in the US around waiver of immunity, Yang refers to the UK practice regarding waiver as '*just an uneventful, mundane application of the statutory provisions*'; Xiaodong Yang, *State Immunity in International Law* (Cambridge University Press 2012) 338.

59 SIA section 3.

60 SIA section 4.

61 SIA section 5.

62 SIA section 6.

63 SIA section 7.

64 SIA section 8.

65 SIA section 9, as to which, see the detailed discussion below.

66 SIA section 10.

67 SIA section 11.

68 SIA section 6(4).

Exceptions to immunity from the court's enforcement jurisdiction

17.34 The provisions dealing with the court's enforcement jurisdiction are found primarily in section 13. Although entitled '*Other procedural privileges*',[69] this section establishes the limits of what the court can and cannot order when a judgment creditor seeks to enforce a court's judgment or arbitral award, or otherwise compel the state to take or refrain from taking any action. These are often referred to as 'measures of constraint', available at both the pre- and post-judgment stage in proceedings.

17.35 As noted earlier, the nature of enforcement measures and the direct effect they have on a state and its assets means that the court's enforcement jurisdiction is subject to more stringent restrictions, the effect of which is that a state enjoys greater – although not absolute – immunity from measures of enforcement. This section outlines the operation of section 13; a more detailed analysis of these provisions in the context of proceedings related to arbitration is set out later in this chapter.

17.36 The limitations on the court's jurisdiction to order measures of enforcement cascade in section 13 from the most restrictive, *ie*, measures which a court can never grant, to the less restrictive, *ie*, measures which can be granted depending on the circumstances. These are set out in the following.

Measures of constraint involving committal or fines

> 13(1) '*No penalty by way of committal or fine shall be imposed in respect of any failure or refusal by or on behalf of a State to disclose or produce any document or other information for the purposes of proceedings to which it is a party.*'

17.37 Starting with the most restrictive, the court is unable to impose committal orders or fines if a state should fail to disclose or produce documents or information for the purposes of proceedings to which it is a party.[70] This is a restriction on the procedural powers which a court can otherwise exercise to enforce orders made during the course of adjudicative proceedings, rather than a restriction on its powers to ensure compliance with a substantive judgment once the adjudicative proceedings have been completed.

17.38 The exclusion of a committal order from the court's enforcement arsenal is understandable. Who would the committal order be made against in proceedings involving a state? In circumstances where the state is represented in the jurisdiction by the head of its diplomatic mission, she or he would presumably be the responsible individual. However, to order the detention of an ambassador for failing to comply with a disclosure order would be a clear affront to the principle of international comity, not to mention a contravention

69 There is, in reality, no difference between 'immunities' and 'privileges' and any attempt at drawing a distinction between these terms is a '*highly legalistic argument that cannot be accepted*', per Waller LJ in *Sabah Shipyard (Pakistan) Ltd v Islamic Republic of Pakistan & Anor* [2002] EWCA Civ 1643; [2004] CLC 149, at [26], referring to the decision of Saville J in *A Co v Republic of X* [1990] 2 Lloyd's Rep 520, who noted (at 523) that the terms had been used interchangeably in previous court decisions and texts on the subject.

70 SIA section 13(1). In contrast, the US Foreign Sovereign Immunities Act 1976 '*does not abrogate a court's inherent power to impose contempt sanctions on a foreign sovereign*': *FG Hemisphere Associates, LLC v Democratic Republic of Congo* 637 F.3d 373, 380 (D.C. Cir. 2011). This case was recently cited in civil contempt proceedings against Romania for its failure to comply with discovery orders: *Iona Micula et al. v Government of Romania* US District Ct., DC Circuit, 20 November 2020, Case No. 17-cv-02332.

of the individual's inviolable diplomatic immunity,[71] and would likely cause political embarrassment for the states involved.

17.39 However, the rationale for a foreign state's immunity from penalty by way of a fine is somewhat less obvious. Section 13(1) of the SIA does not prevent the levying of fines against foreign states generally. Moreover, non-compliance with an order to disclose documents could be sanctioned through the court's discretion when dealing with costs.[72] The practical effect of a fine prohibited by s. 13(1) could be achieved by an order under CPR Rule 44.11,[73] which permits the court to make an order disallowing a party's costs or ordering it to pay the other party's costs in circumstances where the conduct of the party at fault was unreasonable or improper.[74]

Measures of constraint directed towards the state and its property

> 13(2) '*Subject to subsections (3) and (4) below –*
>
> *(a) relief shall not be given against a State by way of injunction or order for specific performance or for the recovery of land or other property.*'

---

71 Vienna Convention on Diplomatic Relations 1961, Article 31(1): '*A diplomatic agent shall enjoy immunity from the criminal jurisdiction of the receiving State. He shall also enjoy immunity from its civil and administrative jurisdiction.*' See also Article 31(3): '*No measures of execution may be taken in respect of a diplomatic agent except in the cases coming under subparagraphs (a), (b) and (c) of paragraph 1 of this article, and provided that the measures concerned can be taken without infringing the inviolability of his person or of his residence.*'

72 That a court can order a foreign state which is a *bona fide* party to proceedings to pay costs is not in doubt. If the state has submitted to the jurisdiction either by explicit choice or through involvement in non-immune activities, this necessarily encompasses the exercise of the court's procedural powers, which includes the awarding of costs in the proceedings (itself an exercise of the court's adjudicative jurisdiction). There appear to be no reported cases in England on the point since the SIA was enacted, but see, for example, the judgment of the Jersey Court of Appeal in *Re Tantular* [2020] JCA 013, a case in which the Government of Indonesia applied through the Attorney General of Jersey for a *saisie judiciaire* in respect of property owned by an individual who had been convicted of serious crimes in Indonesia. In finding that the proceedings had, with the assistance of the Attorney General, been instituted by the Ministry of Law and Human Rights of Indonesia, the court held that the state had submitted to the jurisdiction of the courts of Jersey ([82] – [93]) and made an order that the state was liable for the appellants' costs ([97]). See also the Australian case of *Eiser Infrastructure Ltd v Kingdom of Spain* [2020] FCA 157, per Stewart J (at [212]) who, after rejecting Spain's objections to enforcement of an award in an ICSID arbitration, awarded the claimant its costs as a claim arising out of arbitration to which the court proceedings related (in accordance with section 10(10) of the Foreign State Immunities Act 1985). Furthermore, the version of s. 13 included in the State Immunity Bill (cl. 14) had originally prohibited orders being made against states for security for costs. However, this was removed during passage of the Bill, with the consequence being that there is no such prohibition, which reflects the position at common law (see *The Emperor of Brazil v Robinson*, *supra* n 21, and Andrew Dickinson, Rae Lindsay, James P. Loonam, *State Immunity: Selected Materials and Commentary* (Oxford University Press 2004) [4.084], [4.092]). It therefore follows that, if the court is permitted to grant an order for security for costs, the court can grant an order for costs in the usual manner at the end of proceedings. See also Article 17 of the ECSI, which permits the granting of orders for security for costs. It also explicitly provides that a state shall pay '*any judicial costs for which it may become liable*', although this only applies where the state appears as a claimant party to proceedings.

73 Describing the previous incarnation of this Rule (which has been re-enacted in substantially the same form), the commentary in the White Book explains that misconduct for the purpose of this Rule can include failures to comply with '*any rule, practice direction or court order*', whilst the latest version extends to conduct before or during the proceedings, *Civil Procedure* (*the White Book*) (Sweet & Maxwell 2020), Vol. 1, [44.11.1].

74 A similar approach is adopted in the UNCSI, Article 24(1) of which prohibits any fine or penalty being levied, or any other consequences as a result of a state's failure to comply with a court's order during the course of proceedings '*other than those which may result from such conduct in relation to the merits of the case*'.

17.40 From the nature of the measures referred to in this second, less restrictive, level of limitation on the court's enforcement jurisdiction, it is apparent that this relates to both pre- and post-judgment measures of enforcement. Therefore, an application for a freezing order to preserve assets belonging to a state pending execution of an arbitration award would, *prima facie*, fall within this limitation,[75] in the same way as an application to injunct a state from breaching a commercial contract.[76]

17.41 However, this provision is stated as being subject to the terms of s. 13(3), which effectively reinstates the court's jurisdiction to issue any such relief *if* the state has consented. The form of such consent is permissibly wide; it can be contained in a prior agreement and can be expressed as applying either to a limited extent or generally. Consent is often given by means of contractual waiver clauses, which do not need to specify the nature of the relief to which consent is being given or refer to section 13(2)(a).[77] Such clauses may therefore be broadly worded,[78] and the courts will construe them in accordance with the normal principles of contractual interpretation.[79] However, as s. 13(3) makes clear, the requirement for consent is not satisfied where the state has merely submitted to the jurisdiction.[80] Furthermore, no matter how widely worded a waiver might be, it is apparent from the fact that s. 13(3) is only directed at the measures in s. 13(2) that it cannot be construed so as to act as a waiver of immunity in respect of any enforcement measures referred to in s. 13(1).

---

75 *ETI Euro Telecom International NV v Republic of Bolivia & Anor* [2008] EWCA Civ 880; [2009] 1 WLR 665, per Lawrence Collins LJ at [113]. See the discussion on ancillary/interlocutory applications later.

76 *ibid.*

77 See: *Pearl Petroleum Co Ltd and others v Kurdistan Regional Government of Iraq* [2015] EWHC 3361 (Comm); [2016] 4 WLR 2, in which a '*concise* [and] *robust*' waiver of '*any claim to immunity for itself and its assets*' would have been sufficient to demonstrate a separate entity's consent to the enforcement of a peremptory order in arbitration. Per Burton J (at [44]) '*I do not conclude that it is necessary for a waiver to spell out consent in respect of section 13(2)(a) relief, which ... extends ... considerably wider, beyond simply injunctive relief, to other kinds of "suit".*'

78 See, for example: *A Company Ltd v Republic of X* [1990] 2 Lloyd's Rep 520, in which a contractual waiver given by a state of '*whatever defence it may have of sovereign immunity for itself or its property*' was sufficient to demonstrate consent to a Mareva injunction. However, not even an express waiver of immunity on such explicit terms could constitute a waiver of the diplomatic immunities conferred on the foreign state by the Vienna Convention on Diplomatic Relations, and so the injunction was discharged to the extent that it included property subject to those immunities. See also: *Sabah Shipyard (Pakistan) Ltd v Pakistan* [2002] EWCA Civ 1643, where an anti-suit injunction was granted restraining proceedings brought by the state in Pakistan in breach of an agreement to submit disputes to the English courts. The waiver provision in the underlying agreement provided that, in respect of any proceedings brought against the state, '*(i) ... no claim of immunity from such proceedings will be claimed by or on behalf of the Guarantor on behalf of itself or any of its assets*', and the state '*(ii) ... waives any right of immunity which it or any of its assets ... now has or may in the future have in any jurisdiction in connection with any such proceedings*'. The court held that the reference to the waiving of immunity 'in connection with any proceedings' was consent to the granting of any relief in relation to the proceedings, such as interim injunctive relief (per Waller J at [20], [25]).

79 Per Saville J in *A Company Ltd v Republic of X* [1990] 2 Lloyd's Rep 520, 523.

80 See, for example, *Arab Banking Corporation v International Tin Council* [1986] 77 Int LR 1, in which the defendant international organisation (which enjoyed certain immunities) was party to an agreement with a very wide provision submitting to the jurisdiction of the English courts, but was held to be immune from a Mareva injunction (cited by Burton J in *Pearl Petroleum* (*supra,* n 77) 4 WLR 2, at [42]). Similarly, a provision in which a state '*irrevocably waives all rights to sovereign immunity*' was found to be insufficient to act as a submission to the jurisdiction for the purposes of section 2 of the SIA (*Svenska Petroleum Exploration AB v Government of the Republic of Lithuania & Anor (No. 2)* [2006] EWCA Civ 1529; [2007] Q.B. 886, per Moore-Bick LJ at [128]).

17.42 Whilst the terms of section 13(2)(a) specifically prevent relief being given '*against a state*', the prohibition has been extended to private entities that act as agents for states and separate entities when exercising sovereign authority. In *Koo Golden East Mongolia v Bank of Nova Scotia and others*,[81] the Court of Appeal allowed an appeal by a commercial bank against a *Norwich Pharmacal* order which sought information regarding the accounts it held in the name of the Mongolian central bank for the purposes of tracing the passage of a quantity of refined gold and the proceeds of sale through the banking system.[82] Finding that the proceedings related to transactions entered into in the exercise of sovereign authority such that the central bank – as a separate entity – would have enjoyed immunity had the application been brought against it, the Court of Appeal held that the claimant could not be permitted to seek relief as against the Bank of Nova Scotia (which was acting as agent to the central bank) which it could not seek against the central bank itself.[83]

17.43 There is an important nuance in the effect of section 13(2)(a) on the court's jurisdiction. Whilst the provision prohibits the granting of measures of constraint against a state, this is only a restriction on the court's exercise of its power to do so; it does not affect the existence of the court's power.[84] As a result of this distinction it has been suggested that, although a court would not be able to exercise its powers to grant an injunction against a state, it would be able to make an award of damages in lieu of an injunction.[85]

Post-judgment measures of execution for judgments and awards

> 13(2)(b) '*(2) Subject to subsections (3) and (4) below –*
>
> *(b) the property of a State shall not be subject to any process for the enforcement of a judgment or arbitration award or, in an action in rem, for its arrest, detention or sale.*'

17.44 There are even fewer restrictions on the court's ability to order measures of execution where judgments or awards have been rendered. Not only will the state's consent under

---

81 [2007] EWCA Civ 1443; [2008] QB 717.

82 The gold in question had been deposited with the Mongolian central bank for safekeeping until, in accordance with their agreement, the claimant was to sell it to the bank. However, prior to the sale and without the claimant's consent, but in performance of its obligations to increase the country's currency reserves, the central bank exported the gold to be refined, much of which had likely been sold on. A quantity of the refined gold had been credited to the central bank's unallocated precious metals account held at the Bank of Nova Scotia, which was bound to account to the central bank for the amount of gold showing in the account. The claimant requested disclosure of the central bank's accounts held with the Bank of Nova Scotia on the basis that it had facilitated the central bank's alleged tortious wrongdoing.

83 *Supra*, n 81, per Clarke MR at [40] – [47], referring to the earlier Court of Appeal decision in *Twycross v Dreyfus* (1877) 5 Ch. D. 605, in which an attempt to sue commercial agents of the Peruvian government was characterised by James LJ as a '*monstrous usurpation of jurisdiction*', and that it '[i]*t really would be indirectly endeavouring to make the foreign government responsible to the jurisdiction of this Court*' (at 618–619).

84 *The London Steam-Ship Owners' Mutual Insurance Association Limited v Spain (The Prestige) (No. 3)* [2020] EWHC 1582 (Comm), per Henshaw J at [188].

85 *ibid*, at [201]: '*it is arguable that a court would have power to award damages in lieu of an injunction even if SIA 1978 section 13 would prevent it from granting an injunction. Section 13, where it applies, prevents the grant of an injunction against a state but does not necessarily deprive the court of its "jurisdiction" to entertain an application for one*'. Section 50 of the Senior Courts Act 1981 grants the court power to award damages in lieu of an injunction where it '*has jurisdiction to entertain an application for an injunction*'.

section 13(3) suffice to permit the court to exercise its enforcement jurisdiction in this regard, but even in the absence of consent, execution against property is permitted where the property in question is in use or intended for use for commercial purposes, pursuant to section 13(4).

17.45 What constitutes 'commercial purposes' is defined by reference to the definition of 'commercial transaction' in the provisions relating to the commercial exception to immunity from the court's adjudicative jurisdiction in s. 3(3).[86] This is explored in more detail later in the section dealing with execution against state property; nevertheless it is worth noting that s. 3(3) casts a wide definition of 'commercial transaction'.[87] The ability to execute against state property which falls within the commercial purpose exception irrespective of whether the state has consented reflects the now entrenched distinction between *acta iure imperii* and *acta iure gestionis*, and recognises that where a state engages in commercial activity, it will be treated as any private commercial entity would. However, as an acknowledgment that the exercise of the court's enforcement jurisdiction involves a more direct judicial interference with a state and its property, s. 13(5) allows the head of the foreign state's diplomatic mission to issue a certificate to the effect that property is not in commercial use or intended for commercial use, which the courts must accept as sufficient evidence to that effect unless the contrary is demonstrated, for which the claimant will bear the burden.[88]

17.46 There is a small but significant distinction between the two subsections which exclude immunity and permit the court to exercise its enforcement jurisdiction when the state has consented or the commercial purpose exception applies.[89] Where the state

86 See SIA section 17(1), which provides that '[i]*n this Part of the Act – ... "commercial purpose" means purposes of such transactions or activities as are mentioned in section 3(3) above*'.

87 This captures: any contract for the supply of goods and services; loans or transactions for the provision of finance; and '*any other transaction or activity (whether of a commercial, industrial, financial, professional or other similar character) into which a State enters or in which it engages otherwise than in the exercise of sovereign authority*'. Arguably the catch-all provision in s. 3(3)(c) is so wide as to make the others otiose. Per Henshaw J in *The London Steam-ship Owners' Mutual Insurance Association Ltd v The Kingdom of Spain* [2020] EWHC 1582 (Comm), at [95]: '*The sweep-up wording in subparagraph (3)(c) is very broadly worded, and in substance is wide enough to cover any non-sovereign activity other than the specifically excluded case of contracts of employment.*' The judge went on to note Lord Goff's observations in *Kuwait Airways Corporation v Iraqi Airways* [1995] 1 W.L.R. 1147 where, at 1159, his Lordship stated that: '*having regard to the very broad definition of "commercial transactions" in section 3(3) of the Act, it is probable that most, if not all, of the actions of a private law character in which a separate entity of a state is likely to engage will fall within that definition*'.

88 In *Orascom Telecom Holding SAE v Republic of Chad & Ors* [2008] EWHC 1841; [2008] 2 CLC 296, at [16(iv)], Burton J noted that the SIA does not provide that a certificate issued under s. 13(5) is '*conclusive evidence, but simply evidence which requires the contrary to be shown*'. This appears to contradict Lord Diplock's finding in *Alcom Ltd v Republic of Columbia* [1984] AC 580 (at 605 [A]) that the certificate of the Colombian ambassador was '*conclusive that the bank account referred to falls outside section 13(4)*' and was therefore immune from the garnishee orders which had been made. However, his Lordship arrived at that decision having analysed the legal status of commercial bank accounts belonging to diplomatic missions, and so it is reasonable to infer that Lord Diplock was referring to the conclusiveness of the certificate in a confirmatory sense, rather than it being – in and of itself – conclusive evidence of the non-commercial nature of the mission's bank account. There is no suggestion that a section 13(5) certificate establishes the non-commercial usage of state property to any higher threshold, or that in order to overturn a certificate, a claimant must establish the commercial use of the property on anything other than the civil standard of proof. The purpose of allowing a state to establish as fact the non-commercial use of its property by way of a certificate avoids the need for the state to appear in proceedings before the court to establish the fact as a litigant, which would be an affront to its dignity if the conclusion was that the state and its property were immune.

89 Hazel Fox & Philippa Webb, *The Law of State Immunity* (Oxford University Press 2015) 215.

consents in accordance with section 13(3), it permits the '*giving of any relief or the issue of any process*', which could be in the form of, for example, pre- or post-judgment injunctive relief (section 13(2)(a)) or the execution of a judgment or arbitration award against the state's property (section 13(2)(b)). However, where the commercial purpose exception in section 13(4) applies, it only permits the issue of process against property falling within this exception for the purposes of enforcing a judgment or arbitration award; the commercial purpose exception does not permit the giving of '*any relief*' against that property. As a result, a claimant cannot rely on the fact that a state's property is in use for commercial purposes as grounds for applying for an interim freezing order to arrest property in the jurisdiction to satisfy a future award if the state has not given its consent in accordance with section 13(3).[90]

17.47 The reason for this appears to turn on the fact that, in order for freezing injunctions and other pre-judgment measures of constraint to have any persuasive effect, they carry with them the threat of imprisonment or a fine for anyone who breaches them.[91] If property belonging to a state and in the state's possession were to be subject to a freezing order, it would involve making orders containing personal sanctions against foreign states and their agents, which could create '*very serious difficulties*' where such orders are enforced via proceedings for contempt.[92]

17.48 However, this rationale does not explain the prohibition against interim measures of constraint where the state's property is in the possession of a third party. The classic example is where the property in question is the balance in a bank account in the name of the state. Interim relief in the form of a freezing injunction would not be addressed to the state as the account owner, but to the bank which will be enjoined from allowing the account to be drawn down on until the injunction is discharged. Therefore, no difficulties in respect of personal sanctions against the state would arise.[93]

90 In this respect, the SIA reversed the previous position at common law which permitted pre-judgment measures of constraint against the assets of a state in commercial use; see: *Trendtex*, (*supra*, n 29) in which Denning MR and Shaw LJ both considered that, even if the Central Bank of Nigeria were a part of the Nigerian State, the fact that it would not have been immune from the underlying claim as a result of the commercial nature of the transaction meant that it was not immune from the injunction proceedings to keep money within the jurisdiction pending trial of the claim (at 561 [B] – [C]; 579 [H] – 580 [B]). Contrast the position under the SIA with the position in Italy, which permits the pre-judgment attachment of state property which is the subject matter of the proceedings, and is connected to a commercial activity, so as to immobilise it in the forum (Hazel Fox & Philippa Webb, *The Law of State Immunity* (Oxford University Press 2015) 491–492).

91 See CPR Rule 81.9(1): '*a judgment or order to do or not do an act may not be enforced under rule 81.4 unless there is prominently displayed, on the front of the copy of the judgment or order served in accordance with this Section, a warning to the person required to do or not do the act in question that disobedience to the order would be a contempt of court punishable by imprisonment, a fine or sequestration of assets*'.

92 See the comments of Elwyn-Jones LC during the House of Lords debate on the Bill, *HL, Hansard (5th series), vol 389, cols. 1936–1937*: '*the Government see very serious difficulties if court orders which are subject to personal sanctions were to be allowed against foreign States. I have a good deal of sympathy with the more limited objectives, but even orders for the detention or preservation of the subject matter of the litigation present, I think, some difficulties. Those orders, although they relate to particular property, nevertheless normally can be enforced only by a contempt process, which noble Lords may think is the kind of sanction which is inappropriate against States*', cited in Hazel Fox & Philippa Webb, *The Law of State Immunity* (Oxford University Press 2015) 215.

93 A point made by Lord Wilberforce who, during the passage of the State Immunity Bill, had sought an amendment to allow injunctions to be given against state property in use for commercial purposes. In response to concerns regarding the ultimate sanctions of contempt for failing to obey remedies of a personal nature, his Lordship stated that it would be possible to '*grant an injunction against someone holding an asset without an*

17.49 An alternative basis for this distinction is that, if the state was found not to be liable in the substantive proceedings, but its property had been subjected to interim measures of constraint pending the final award, it would have constituted an impermissible interference with the state's proprietary and legal interests in its property. This would be the case regardless of whether the state's property was in its own possession or that of a third party. However, the exclusion of immunity for property in commercial use is an implicit recognition that the state – when acting in a commercial capacity – is treated in the same way as a private commercial party, whose property is amenable to interim injunctive relief in anticipation of a final award in an underlying action. The risk of harm complained of by the state – that an interim measure constraining the state's use of its commercial property constitutes interference – is therefore the same as that which would be asserted by a private entity in the same situation.

17.50 Thus, to prohibit measures of interim constraint against the property of a state which is in commercial use is to accord the state greater protection than its private commercial counterparts. There is therefore a case to be made for interim measures of constraint which do not entail *in personam* remedies against the state if breached to be granted against a state's commercial property, particularly in view of the stringent preconditions which apply generally to the exercise of the court's powers in this regard.[94] Nevertheless it remains the case that, absent the state's consent, pre- or post-judgment measures of constraint cannot be granted against the state or its property irrespective of the use to which it is put.

State entities

17.51 Section 14(1) of the SIA defines the 'state' for the purposes of determining which individuals and constituent parts of the state are entitled to assert immunity. These are: (1) the sovereign or other head of state in his or her public capacity; (2) the government of the state; and (3) any department of that government. However, the definition specifically excludes '*any entity (hereafter referred to as a separate entity) which is distinct from the executive organs of the State and capable of suing or being sued*'.[95]

17.52 Whether an entity is an emanation of or separate from the state is a question of fact.[96] Where an entity has been established with separate juridical status, this will be a

order directly against a sovereign State' such as a state trading body and that, as they are not states, '*one has not got the prospect of dragging an ambassador from his coach or arresting a crowned head*'; *HL, Hansard (5th series), vol 389, col. 1528.* In a later debate in which Lord Wilberforce withdrew the proposed amendment, his Lordship noted that an injunction taken out against the Bank of England in a case in which his Lordship appeared as counsel (*Dollfus Mieg et Compagnie SA v Bank of England* [1952] AC 582) '*was very effective and had very beneficial results*', concluding that injunctions were '*not really quite so dangerous*' as had been suggested by the Lord Chancellor earlier in the debate; *HL, Hansard (5th series), vol 389, cols. 1937.*

94 See: Nelson Goh, *Court-Ordered Interim Relief Against States in Aid of Arbitration: Sovereign Immunity, Waiver and Comity* (2017) J. Intl. Arb. 34(4) 679, 701.

95 The broad reference to '*any entity*' has been clarified to mean any entity *of a state*; see the decision of Lord Goff in *Kuwait Airways Corporation v Iraqi Airways Corporation & Anor* [1995] 1 WLR 1147, who considered that section 14 of the SIA was based on Article 27 of the ECSI, which excludes from the definition of 'contracting state' (the nomenclature used in that Convention for the entity entitled to claim immunity) '*any legal entity of a Contracting State which is distinct therefrom and is capable of suing or being sued*' (at 1158 [E] – [H]).

96 This will be primarily (although not exclusively) by reference to the law of the place of the entity's incorporation, see: Andrew Dickinson, Rae Lindsay, James P. Loonam, *State Immunity: Selected Materials and Commentary* (Oxford University Press 2004) [4.102].

significant factor demonstrating that the entity is separate from the state, particularly where the entity has been established for commercial purposes.[97] Although the constitutional arrangements of the entity as well as the degree of control exercised by the state over the entity and its activities may give the impression that the state and the entity are one and the same, the '*strong presumption is that its separate corporate status should be respected*', which would only be displaced in extreme circumstances.[98]

17.53 Even where the state exercises an exceptional level of control over the entity in question, the courts are reluctant to find that an entity which has been created with separate legal status is in fact part of the state. Thus, where the Nigerian state had issued a number of decrees which, it was asserted, had dramatically eroded the independence of the central bank, this had not turned it into an organ of the state.[99] Where the state appointed and removed the entity's board of directors, held the power of veto over decisions to, *inter alia*, acquire and dispose of property and enter into contracts in excess of $20,000, and the entity's assets had originated from the state, this was not considered sufficient to demonstrate that the entity was part of the state.[100] Similarly, where the entity is exempt from tax and receives its funding from a government ministry which '*exercises a close overall supervisory function over the operations and affairs*' of the entity, this too was insufficient to conflate the two.[101]

---

97 *La Générale des Carrières et des Mines v FG Hemisphere Associates LLC* [2012] UKPC 27; [2012] 2 CLC 709 ('*Gécamines*'), per Lord Mance at [28]: '*In the Board's opinion, it is now appropriate in both contexts* [immunity and establishing liability and enforcement] *to have regard to the formulation of the more nuanced principles governing immunity in current international and national law. These, as explained in paras. 10 to 18 above, express the need for full and appropriate recognition of the existence of separate juridical entities established by states, particularly for trading purposes. They do this, even where such entities exercise certain sovereign authority jure imperii, providing them in return (as already noted) with a special functional immunity if and so far as they do exercise such sovereign authority. A similar recognition of their existence and separateness would be expected for purposes of liability and enforcement.*' The status of separate state entities and the treatment accorded them by the English courts predates the SIA. See the dictum of Lord Wilberforce in *I Congreso* (*supra*, n 30), at 258 [F] – [G]: '*State-controlled enterprises, with legal personality, ability to trade and to enter into contracts of private law, though wholly subject to the control of their state, are a well-known feature of the modern commercial scene. The distinction between them, and their governing state, may appear artificial: but it is an accepted distinction in the law of England and other states. ... Quite different considerations apply to a state-controlled enterprise acting on government directions on the one hand, and a state, exercising sovereign functions, on the other.*'

98 *ibid*, at [29]. Lord Mance identified examples of certain 'extremes', including *Kensington International Ltd v Congo* [2005] EWHC 2684 (Comm). In that case Cooke J set out the nature of the entity's relationship with the state at [44] – [55], noting (at [53]) that '[a]*n entity which is constituted in such a way that its purpose is to assist, promote and advance the industrial development, prosperity and economic welfare of the area in which it operates, can be seen as effectively carrying out government policy in the way that a government department does and therefore to assume the position of an organ of government*'. In *Gécamines*, Lord Mance cautioned against taking this statement out of context, noting (at [48]) that the carrying out of government policy '*does not make their activity sovereign activity or make them part of the State*'.

99 *Trendtex* (*supra*, n 29) Per Stephenson LJ (at 565 [F]): '*A hobbled horse is still a horse*'.

100 *Gécamines* (*supra*, n 97) at [53] – [54].

101 *Taurus Petroleum Ltd v State Oil Marketing Co of the Ministry of Oil, Iraq* [2013] EWHC 3494 (Comm); [2013] 2 CLC 835, per Field J at [54] – [59]. Upheld on appeal in Taurus Petroleum Ltd v State Oil Co of the Ministry of Oil, Iraq [2015] EWCA Civ 835; [2015] 2 CLC 284, per Moore-Bick LJ at [45], who (at [43]) cited the decision of Lord Mance in *Gécamines* (referred to *supra*, n 98). The question of the respondent's status was not appealed to the Supreme Court, which overturned the Court of Appeal's decision on other grounds (see: *Taurus Petroleum Ltd v State Oil Marketing Co of the Ministry of Oil, Iraq* [2017] UKSC 64; [2018] AC 690, per Lord Clarke at [28]).

17.54 The default position under section 14 of the SIA is that state entities do not enjoy immunity. However, section 14(2) extends immunity to state entities where the proceedings relate to anything done by them in the exercise of sovereign authority, *and* the state would have been immune had the proceedings been brought against it. Where a state entity is entitled to immunity yet it submits to the court's jurisdiction in respect of proceedings arising out of its immune activity, the state entity will be immune from the court's enforcement jurisdiction to the same extent as the state would have been. For the purposes of determining a state entity's entitlement to immunity in section 14(2), what is relevant is the characterisation of the act performed by the state entity, rather than the purpose for which it was performed.[102] If the act itself is an act *iure imperii*, then the state entity will be immune; if it was an act which could have been performed by a private entity – even if on the direction of the state in the performance of a governmental purpose – the state entity will not be immune.[103]

17.55 Ascertaining whether a party has contracted with a state or a separate state entity is therefore important, as it will determine the extent to which the counterparty in court proceedings will be entitled to claim immunity. The distinction is, in addition, often relevant in the context of enforcing awards (as to which, see the discussion on this topic later).

Central banks and sovereign wealth funds

17.56 As the repository of a state's wealth accumulated from a variety of both sovereign and commercial activities, the accounts and property of a central bank – much of which is often held outside of a bank's home jurisdiction – would be a substantial source of assets from which a state's judgment or award debts could be met. However, in the UK section 14 of the SIA explicitly provides that the property of a state's central bank or other monetary authority '*shall not be regarded for the purposes of subsection (4) of section 13 above as in use or intended for use for commercial purposes*'.[104]

102 Per Lord Goff in *Kuwait Airways Corporation v Iraqi Airways* [1995] 1 W.L.R. 1147, at 1160 [A] – [F]. See also the decision of Lord Wilberforce in *I Congreso* (*supra*, n 30), at 267 [A] – [C]: '*the existence of a governmental purpose or motive will not convert what would otherwise be an act jure gestionis, or an act of private law, into one done jure imperii. ... The conclusion which emerges is that in considering, under the "restrictive" theory whether state immunity should be granted or not, the court must consider the whole context in which the claim against the state is made, with a view to deciding whether the relevant act(s) upon which the claim is based, should, in that context, be considered as fairly within an area of activity, trading or commercial, or otherwise of a private law character, in which the state has chosen to engage, or whether the relevant act(s) should be considered as having been done outside that area, and within the sphere of governmental or sovereign activity*'. See also: *Gécamines* (*supra*, n 97), per Lord Mance (at [54]) who rejected the Royal Court of Jersey's finding that the state entity's involvement in a 'sector of vital importance to the national economy' was relevant to the its decision that the entity was 'an arm of the state': '*There is no doubt that Gécamines had responsibility for operations in a sector of vital importance to the national economy of the DRC, but that may be said of many state-owned corporations in centrally planned or dirigist economies.*'

103 See, for example, *Tsavliris Salvage (International) Ltd v Grain Board of Iraq* [2008] EWHC 612 (Comm); [2008] 1 CLC 592, in which a state entity was bound to a salvage agreement by a third party in respect of a vessel carrying grain it had purchased for public distribution in Iraq. The court held that the underlying motive or purpose which gave rise to the act of entering into the salvage agreement was irrelevant, the character of the act was determinative, and in this case was plainly not a governmental act (per Gross J (as he then was) at [75] – [80]).

104 SIA, section 14(4). This reversed the previous position at common law prior to the introduction of the SIA, which held that the property of central banks was amenable to execution (see, for example, *Trendtex*, *supra* n 29).

17.57 This is important as, although central banks undertake activities of a sovereign nature,[105] they also engage in activities of a commercial nature for which they own assets which are put to use for commercial purposes, and which would therefore be amenable to enforcement. However, the effect of section 14(4) is that all of the property of a central bank is immune, regardless of the purpose to which it is, or is intended to be, put. In this way, a foreign central bank's property is granted even greater immunity that the property of its parent state, which – as noted earlier and considered in more detail later – is not immune if in use or intended for use for commercial purposes.

17.58 Immunity is granted irrespective of whether the central bank is part of the state as defined in section 14(1) of the SIA (and so entitled to immunity by virtue of section 1), or has been constituted as a separate entity. In the case of the latter, whilst a central bank could be found amenable to the adjudicative jurisdiction of the courts in respect of its commercial or other non-immune activities in common with other separate entities pursuant to section 14(2), section 14(4) grants the central bank the immunities from the courts' enforcement jurisdiction set out in subsections 13(1) to (3) irrespective of whether the activity giving rise to the liability was sovereign or commercial. Contrast this with the position of a separate entity which is *not* a central bank or monetary authority, for which the immunity from enforcement in section 13 is only available if the proceedings against it relate to activities in the exercise of sovereign authority (and, if those proceedings had been brought against the state, it would also have been immune).[106]

17.59 This complete and absolute immunity[107] was confirmed by the High Court in *AIC Ltd v The Federal Government of Nigeria & Anor*,[108] in which the claimant sought to enforce an award of the Nigerian courts by way of third party debt orders over accounts held in England by, *inter alia*, the Central Bank of Nigeria. It was argued by AIC that the money held in those accounts belonged beneficially to the Nigerian Federal Government and were used or intended for use for commercial purposes. The court found that, irrespective of whether the sums in a bank account in the name of the central bank were held beneficially for the state or the central bank, the sums were the property of the central bank. As such, Burnton J (as he then was) held that

> *the moneys in a bank account of a central bank with another bank are immune from execution irrespective of the source of the funds of the account or the use of the account or the purpose for which the account is maintained.*[109]

17.60 The same comprehensive approach was endorsed by the High Court when faced with a claim for enforcement over assets in which both the state and the state's central bank were said to have a proprietary interest. In *AIG Capital Partners Inc. and another v Republic of*

105 The key functions of a central bank have been described as '*acting as guardian and regulator of the state's monetary system*', and that '*the most obvious "property" of a central bank, a state's reserves, will be held for governmental or sovereign purposes*', per Aikens J in *AIG Capital Partners Inc and another v Republic of Kazakhstan* [2005] EWHC 2239 (Comm); [2006] 1 WLR 1420, at [58].

106 SIA, s. 14(2).

107 Xiaodong Yang, *State Immunity in International Law* (Cambridge University Press 2012) 415–6.

108 [2003] EWHC 1357.

109 *ibid*, at [47].

Kazakhstan,[110] the claimants attempted to enforce an arbitral award against Kazakhstan by seeking a third party debt order over cash and securities held at a bank in England in the name of the National Bank of Kazakhstan. These sums formed part of the National Fund of Kazakhstan, of which the National Bank of Kazakhstan (the central bank) was the trust manager. It was argued by the claimants that the money in the accounts belonged to the state and that the central bank had no proprietary interest in the sums as Kazakh law did not differentiate between 'legal' and 'beneficial' ownership.

17.61 However, Aikens J (as he then was) held that the central bank had the contractual right to payment of the sums held in the accounts and was recorded as the owner of the securities, which was a sufficient interest to make them the property of the central bank, and that this conclusion was not affected by the fact that the sums in question remained, as a matter of Kazakh law, under the full ownership of the Kazakh government.[111] In articulating the consequences of the '*clear and imperative*' wording of section 14(4) of the SIA, the judge concluded that

> [i]*f the central bank (etc) has an interest in the property concerned, but the state of the central bank has another interest in the same property, then in my view the effect of section 14(4) is that the relevant property is immune from enforcement in respect of a judgment against the state, whether the property concerned is in use or intended for use for commercial purposes or not.*[112]

17.62 Whilst the blanket immunity afforded to the property of central banks under the SIA reflects the position adopted in the UNCSI[113] and by certain other states in their respective immunity legislation,[114] it is by no means a universally accepted approach. Other countries

110 [2005] EWHC 2239 (Comm); [2006] 1 WLR 1420.

111 *ibid*, at [89] – [90].

112 *ibid*, at [57(4)]. It was also immaterial that the securities were actively traded to generate income and that the central bank earned commission for achieving good results. Aikens J held that '*the aim of the exercise, at all times, was and is to enhance the national fund*' which meant that the assets had to be put to use to generate returns to be reinvested in the national fund, '*i.e. to assist the sovereign actions*' (at [92(2)]).

113 Article 21(1): '*The following categories, in particular, of property of a State shall not be considered as property specifically in use or intended for use by the State for other than government non-commercial purposes under article 19, subparagraph (c): ... (c) property of the central bank or other monetary authority of the State.*' In determining whether the immunity afforded to the property of the Kazakh central bank constituted a breach of the claimant's right of access to the courts under Article 6(1) of the European Convention on Human Rights, Aikens J in *AIG Capital* regarded the UNCSI '*as a most important guide on the state of international opinion on what is, and what is not, a legitimate restriction on the right of parties to enforce against state property generally*', and that whilst it did not constitute a *jus cogens* in international law and had, at the time, not been adopted by any states, its existence and adoption by the UN '*powerfully demonstrate international thinking on the point*'; [2005] EWHC 2239 (Comm); [2006] 1 WLR 1420, at [80]. The extent of central bank immunity in customary international was an issue before the International Court of Justice in the *Certain Iranian Assets* case (although the ICJ decided that it did not have jurisdiction to determine the issue: *Certain Iranian Assets (Islamic Republic of Iran v United States of America)*, Preliminary Objections, Judgment, ICJ Reports 2019, 7).

114 The state immunity statutes of Singapore (State Immunity Act 1979, section 16(4)); Pakistan (State Immunity Ordinance 1981, section 15(4)) and South Africa (Foreign State Immunity Act 1981, section 15(3)) duplicate section14(4) of the SIA. The Russian Federation has enacted legislation on foreign state immunity which deems the property of central banks as being in use for the exercise of sovereign powers (Federal Law No. 297-FZ on the Jurisdictional Immunity of a Foreign State and the Property of a Foreign State in the Russian Federation 2015, Article 16(1)(5)), and China has issued a specific law granting immunity to the property of foreign central banks from compulsory measures of property preservation and execution (Law of the People's Republic of China on Judicial Immunity from Compulsory Measures Concerning the Property of Foreign Central

only extend immunity to central bank assets which are held '*for its own account*' (*ie*, assets used for central banking operations),[115] whilst others provide no special protection for central bank assets beyond that which is accorded to the property of the state generally (*ie*, excluding immunity for assets used for commercial activities).[116]

17.63 The basis for the expansive approach adopted by the UK SIA is by no means altruistic. The ability of a state to put beyond reach assets which would otherwise be available to satisfy its liabilities by investing them in the UK via the state's central bank makes the UK an attractive destination for foreign states to invest.[117] This provision of the act, and the motivation behind it, has been the subject of criticism for the all-encompassing nature of the immunity.[118]

17.64 This criticism may prove to be well-founded in light of the growing use of sovereign wealth funds ('SWFs') as vehicles for states to invest commercially their reserves and assets. SWFs, defined as '*special purpose investment funds or arrangements that are owned by the general government*',[119] invest in a diverse range of assets which, given their inherently commercial nature,[120] may well satisfy the commercial exception to immunity and be found amenable to enforcement. However, as has been noted by the OECD, a substantial number of SWFs are either created as part of, or managed by, central banks.[121] At present, following the *ratio* in *AIG Capital*,[122] it is clear that SWFs which

Banks 2005, Article 1), which has been followed by Argentina (Law on Immunity of foreign Central Banks or other Monetary Authorities 2014, Article 1).

115 For example, the USA (Foreign Sovereign Immunities Act, section 1611(b)(1)) and France (Monetary and Financial Code, Article L153–1).

116 For example, Canada (State Immunity Act 1985, section 12(4)); Australia (Foreign State Immunities Act 1985, section 35(1); and Israel (Foreign States Immunity Law 5769–2008, which includes government agencies and separate entities (and thus central banks) within the definition of 'foreign state' (section 1), and withdraws immunity from the commercial assets of a foreign state (section 16(1)). For a comprehensive analysis of the immunities granted by states to foreign central banks and their assets, see: Ingrid Wuerth, *Immunity from Execution of Central Bank Assets* in Tom Ruys, Nicolas Angelet, Luca Ferro, (eds.) *The Cambridge Handbook of Immunities and International Law* (Cambridge University Press 2019).

117 The reason for granting central banks an enhanced immunity beyond that which is granted to states was not made clear during the parliamentary debate on the State Immunity Bill (see: *HC, Hansard (5th series), vol 951, col. 844*). However, the motivation for this was the subject of speculation by the Australian Law Reform Commission in its report on foreign state immunity in 1984 (Australian Law Reform Commission, *Foreign State Immunity* [1984] ALRC 24, at [132]).

118 A motivation which has been described as '*avowedly self-serving*': William Blair, *The Legal Status of Central Bank Investments under English Law* (1998) CLJ 57(2), 374, at 378. In *AIG Capital* (*supra*) counsel for the claimants referred to this as the '*unspoken reason for the width of the immunity granted by section 14(4)*', which Aikens J noted had been criticised in strident terms, citing academic criticism of the provision in the following terms: '*Is it in the true interest of Britain and the City of London to assist foreign states or their central banks in avoiding the discharge of their commercial debts? ... Does principle and financial and commercial probity no longer count?*'; per Aikens J at [40], referring to F A Mann, *The State Immunity Act 1978* (1979) BYIL 43, at 62.

119 International Working Group of Sovereign Wealth Funds, *Sovereign Wealth Funds: Generally Accepted Principles and Practices 'Santiago Principles'* (2008) 3.

120 For example, one of the largest SWF's in the world, the Norwegian Government Pension Fund Global, which was set up for the long-term management of Norway's revenue from its oil and gas resources, is worth approximately US$1.078 trillion dollars and owns on average 1.5% of all listed companies globally (see: www.nbim.no/en/, accessed on 8 November 2020).

121 David Gaukrodger, *Foreign State Immunity and Foreign Government Controlled Investors,* OECD Working Papers on International Investment (OECD Publishing 2010/02), 24.

122 Indeed, Kazakhstan's national fund was in effect a SWF, likened to that of Norway by Aikens J in his judgment: *supra*, n 110 at [11].

form part of a central bank, or the assets of SWFs which are managed or invested by a central bank, would attract absolute immunity from enforcement under the UK SIA.

17.65 The effect of the UK's approach is twofold. First, by operating via SWFs, states are undoubtedly undertaking commercial activity, irrespective of the ultimate – potentially sovereign – purpose to which the investment returns are put. By maintaining immunity for the property of central banks regardless of whether the property is beneficially owned by the state or is put to commercial use, section 14(4) of the SIA effectively reintroduces the doctrine of absolute state immunity for those states who manage their SWFs through their central banks. This gives a level of protection to these assets which is not available to non-state investors.

17.66 Second, despite the potentially enormous value of state assets owned via SWFs, the availability of immunity for SWF assets channelled through central banks makes it harder for award creditors to identify assets which are amenable to enforcement. Therefore, although countries which host significant SWF investments such as the UK may appear to be promising jurisdictions for the execution of awards, the availability of these assets to satisfy a state's liabilities cannot be assumed; thus, ascertaining the ownership structures behind the assets is important.

State immunity and arbitration

17.67 Section 9 of the SIA addresses the exclusion of immunity in the context of arbitrations. The section heading – '*Arbitrations*' – is somewhat misleading; the provision does not deal with any immunity a state may raise as a defence to arbitration proceedings themselves. More accurately, section 9 excludes immunity in respect of court proceedings which relate to arbitrations. The provision states as follows:

> *(1) Where a State has agreed in writing to submit a dispute which has arisen, or may arise, to arbitration, the State is not immune as respects proceedings in the courts of the United Kingdom which relate to the arbitration.*
>
> *(2) This section has effect subject to any contrary provision in the arbitration agreement and does not apply to any arbitration agreement between States.*

Unlike the other exclusions of immunity, which are either based on a state's express submission to the court's jurisdiction or otherwise operate as a consequence of a state's involvement in a non-immune activity, the exclusion of immunity from the court's jurisdiction in proceedings related to arbitration involves neither. The state may not have explicitly consented to the jurisdiction of the English courts in relation to any arbitration-related proceedings,[123] nor is arbitration in and of itself a non-immune activity.[124] The exclusion operates indirectly; as articulated by Fox and Webb, the loss of a state's immunity

123 The arbitration agreement may simply refer disputes to arbitration, either in accordance with a bespoke procedure or by reference to the rules of a specific arbitral institution, and may or may not have identified a seat for the proceedings.

124 The act of agreeing to arbitrate does not carry with it the same irrevocable submission to the court's jurisdiction that flows as a direct consequence of entering into a commercial transaction. It follows from the wording of section 9(2) that a state may agree to arbitrate, but on the explicit basis that it does not submit to the jurisdiction of any national court. It is therefore possible for a state to agree to arbitrate without the act itself of entering into the agreement being an activity which automatically gives rise to a loss of immunity.

in section 9 is not based on its consent to court proceedings, but on its consent to the underlying arbitration out of which court proceedings in support of the arbitration may arise.[125] In other words, the fact that the state has submitted to one jurisdiction (that of an arbitral tribunal) is sufficient – absent any provision to the contrary – to imply a submission to the jurisdiction of the English courts.[126]

17.68 Section 9 differs from the other exclusions of immunity in this part of the Act in two further respects. First, whilst the other exclusions of immunity are directed at specifically non-sovereign activities, section 9 is not limited in its application to arbitrations involving non-sovereign subject matter. The effect of this is that the courts have jurisdiction in proceedings brought in relation to an arbitration even if the subject matter of the underlying dispute is of a sovereign nature.[127] Second, and as will be developed next, although section 9 sits alongside other provisions dealing with the exclusion of immunity from the court's adjudicative jurisdiction, there are certain types of proceedings which relate to arbitration (*ie*, orders for the preservation of evidence, orders relating to property, or injunctive relief) which are, by their nature, part of the court's enforcement jurisdiction.

17.69 Section 9 of the Act can be a powerful tool in arbitrations involving states. It is thus important to analyse the key elements of this provision which regulate the circumstances in which it can be engaged; specifically: (1) the requirement for the state to have agreed in writing to submit a dispute to arbitration; (2) the effect of that consent on a state's ability to assert immunity; and (3) the nature of the arbitration-related proceedings from which immunity is excluded.

The state's agreement to arbitration

17.70 As noted earlier, this exclusion of immunity is implied from a state's agreement to arbitrate. Often, there will be little doubt that a state has agreed to arbitrate in circumstances where the state (via a duly authorised representative such as a minister) has signed a contract containing an arbitration agreement. However, where a state denies that it is party to an arbitration agreement for the purposes of section 9 of the Act, the questions as to whether the state has agreed to arbitrate and, if so, the extent of that agreement, will need to be determined.

17.71 As the issue necessarily arises when proceedings related to the arbitration are brought before the courts, it will be for the court to come to a conclusion as to whether the

---

125 Hazel Fox & Philippa Webb, *The Law of State Immunity* (Oxford University Press 2015) 207.

126 See the Court of Appeal's decision in *Svenska Petroleum Exploration AB v Government of the Republic of Lithuania & Anor (No. 2)* [2006] EWCA Civ 1529; [2007] Q.B. 886, per Moore-Bick LJ at [117]: '*Arbitration is a consensual procedure and the principle underlying section 9 is that, if a state has agreed to submit to arbitration, it has rendered itself amenable to such process as may be necessary to render the arbitration effective.*'

127 The absence of a restriction limiting the operation of section 9 to arbitrations involving disputes arising out of non-sovereign activities was a departure from the equivalent provision in the ECSI which provides, at Article 12(1), that a state may not claim immunity where it has agreed to arbitrate disputes '*of a civil or commercial matter*'. The UNCSI contains a similar limitation in Article 17. However, pursuant to the 'Understandings' annexed to the UNCSI, the term 'commercial transaction' in Article 17 includes '*investment matters*'. The purpose of this clarification is to capture within the ambit of Article 17 disputes which arise in respect of development projects implemented by states: Hazel Fox & Philippa Webb, *The Law of State Immunity* (Oxford University Press 2015) 394.

state has agreed to arbitrate and, as a consequence, submitted to the jurisdiction.[128] Despite the effect such a finding may have on the availability of the immunity defence to the state, the question is determined not by reference to any particular principles specific to states in the context of immunity, but by the rules usually applied for ascertaining the existence, validity, and scope of arbitration agreements in commercial contracts.

17.72 As a result, the courts have readily held that states are bound to arbitration agreements which satisfy the requirements of section 9 of the SIA by reference to the same conditions as private entities would be held as bound.

17.73 This commercially oriented approach to the exclusion of a state's immunity raises questions as to the role of the state's consent in submitting to the court's jurisdiction. As has been seen in other provisions of the SIA, nothing short of an express written agreement, the taking of a step in proceedings,[129] or written consent to measures of constraint, will be sufficient in order to establish a state's consent to submit to the jurisdiction. This reflects the position in international law that consent is an essential element of restrictive state immunity.[130] The International Law Commission's 1991 commentary on the draft of the UNCSI provides that:[131]

> *State immunity applies on the understanding that the State against which jurisdiction is to be exercised does not consent, or is not willing to submit to the jurisdiction. This unwillingness or absence of consent is generally assumed, unless the contrary is indicated. The court exercising jurisdiction against an absent foreign State cannot and does not generally assume or presume that there is consent or willingness to submit to its jurisdiction. There must be proof or evidence of consent to satisfy the exercise of existing jurisdiction or competence against another State.*

The commentary also makes it clear that consent should not be readily implied, and that it should not be implied in the case of '*an unwilling State which has not expressed its consent in a clear and recognizable manner*'.[132]

17.74 However, the English courts' willingness to uphold arbitration agreements in the apparent absence of the foreign state's express and direct consent (as illustrated by the following five examples) reflects a developing trend in state practice to place greater emphasis on the autonomy of arbitration over the immunities granted to states.[133] This is consistent with the treatment of states under the restrictive doctrine of immunity as private entities when engaged in commercial activities.

---

128 *NML Capital Ltd v Republic of Argentina* [2011] UKSC 31; [2011] 2 AC 495, per Lord Mance at [89]: '[t]*his subsection addresses the consequences of submission, and leaves it to the court to determine whether such has occurred*'.

129 SIA, section 2. Not even a provision irrevocably waiving immunity would satisfy the requirements for a submission to the jurisdiction under this provision: *Svenska Petroleum Exploration AB v Government of the Republic of Lithuania & Anor (No. 2)* [2006] EWCA Civ 1529; [2007] Q.B. 886, at [128].

130 International Law Commission, *Draft Articles on Jurisdictional Immunities of States and Their Property, with Commentaries* (1991) YBILC (vol. II), Part 2, 13, 26.

131 *ibid.*

132 *ibid*, at 27.

133 A trend noted by Fox and Webb in the context of the weakening requirement for states to consent separately to the exercise of the court's adjudicative and enforcement jurisdiction (as to which, see the section addressing the effect of the state's consent on its immunity from jurisdiction); Hazel Fox & Philippa Webb, *The Law of State Immunity* (Oxford University Press 2015) 398.

Extension of the arbitration agreement to a non-party state

17.75 A recurrent scenario, particularly in the context of large infrastructure and development projects, is where a state is involved in some capacity in the negotiation or execution of a contract containing an arbitration agreement (including, for example, providing final approval or granting licenses), but the state is not itself a signatory to it. This gives rise to the issue of whether the nature of the state's involvement is such that it should be considered as having implicitly agreed to be bound by the contract, and by extension the arbitration agreement.

17.76 The question of whether a state has agreed to arbitrate will involve ascertaining the law governing the arbitration agreement so as to identify the rules by which the state's involvement or otherwise is to be determined. In the English courts, this involves the court embarking on a process of investigating whether the parties have either expressly or impliedly chosen a law to govern the arbitration agreement by application of English law rules of contractual interpretation (as the law of the forum) or, if no choice has been made, identifying the law of the place with which the agreement is most closely connected.[134]

17.77 Significant divergence exists in state practice regarding the validity requirements for arbitration agreements, and as to whether arbitration agreements can be extended to third-party non-signatories, and if so under what conditions.[135] Differences can also arise in the interpretation of the rules applicable under the governing law of the arbitration agreement.[136] The result is that there are various ways in which a state may be found, applying the law of the arbitration agreement, to have agreed to arbitrate its disputes in circumstances where it has not expressly agreed in writing to do so.[137]

17.78 Although decided on different grounds (as to which, see the final example later), the case of *Svenska Petroleum Exploration AB v Government of the Republic of Lithuania & AB Geonafta*[138] illustrates not only that the courts will apply the law governing the arbitration agreement to determine whether a state has agreed to arbitrate a dispute for the purposes of section 9 of the SIA, but also how doing so can lead to a different result from that which would have been reached under English law.

---

134 *Enka Insaat Ve Sanayi AS v OOO Insurance Company Chubb*; [2020] UKSC 38; [2020] 1 WLR 4117.

135 This is fertile ground for disputes as to whether a state is bound by an arbitration agreement. The involvement (perceived or actual) of the state in the negotiation, execution, performance, and/or termination of the contract is often cited as evidence of an intention on the part of the state to be bound by the arbitration agreement. To illustrate the different approaches adopted in various jurisdictions on this point, see: Eduardo Silva Romero and Luis Miguel Verlarde Saffer, *The Extension of the Arbitral Agreement to Non-Signatories in Europe: A Uniform Approach?* (2015) Am. Bus. Law. Rev. 5(3) 371.

136 See, for example, the conflicting analyses and results in the English and French courts as to the correct approach to the extension of an arbitration agreement governed by French law to a state which was not a signatory to the arbitration agreement: *Dallah Real Estate and Tourism Holding Co v Ministry of Religious Affairs of the Government of Pakistan* [2010] UKSC 46; [2011] 1 AC 763 (England); and *Gouvernement du Pakistan v Societe Dallah Real Estate & Tourism Holding Co*, Cour d'appel de Paris No 09-28533, 17 February 2011 (France). The key distinctions between the conflicting approaches are summarised in: Pierre Mayer, *The Extension of the Arbitration Clause to Non-Signatories – The Irreconcilable Positions of French and English Courts*, (2012) Am. U. Intl. L. Rev. 27(4) 831.

137 As a result, the indirect submission to the court's jurisdiction under section 9 may involve far less formality (or, indeed, intent) than a submission to the court's jurisdiction under section 2 of the SIA (as to which, see *supra* n 58).

138 [2005] EWHC 2437 (Comm); [2006] 1 All E.R. (Comm) 731.

17.79 In this case, Svenska had entered into a joint venture agreement ('JVA') in 1993 with AB Geonafta, the Lithuanian state enterprise responsible for developing oilfields in the country. The JVA included an arbitration agreement for the resolution of disputes between Svenska and Geonafta. Although the Lithuanian state was not identified as a party to the JVA, the state signed the last page of the agreement under wording which stated that the Lithuanian government '*acknowledges itself to be legally and contractually bound as if the government were a signatory to the agreement*'.[139] Svenska commenced arbitration proceedings against the state, alleging that it had been deprived of oilfield development opportunities under the contract. The arbitration resulted in two awards; in the first the tribunal found that the state was a party to the agreement, and in the second Svenska was awarded damages and interest.

17.80 Following Svenska's application for the enforcement of the second award, the state issued Part 11 proceedings disputing the court's jurisdiction and seeking to set aside the order for enforcement. It did so on the basis, *inter alia*, that the state was not a party to the underlying JVA, it was not a party to the arbitration agreement as it only referred to Svenska and AB Geonafta, and that the pre-contractual negotiations did not demonstrate that the arbitration agreement should be extended to it.[140]

17.81 In the first instance decision dismissing the state's challenge, Gloster J (as she then was) applied principles of Lithuanian law (as the law of the arbitration agreement) regarding the validity of arbitration agreements as well as the interpretation of contractual provisions. This included consideration, in accordance with the Lithuanian Civil Code, of the parties' intention regarding the inclusion of the state within the ambit of the arbitration clause,[141] which the judge found by reference to the parties' pre-contractual negotiations and numerous drafts of the JVA.[142] The judge concluded that the state was a party to the arbitration agreement,[143] notwithstanding that the arbitration agreement itself referred to disputes arising between Svenska and AB Geonafta.

17.82 Had English rules of contractual construction been applied,[144] it is arguable that the absence of the state from the express scope of the arbitration agreement would have demonstrated that the parties had not intended for the state to have been a party. However, the judge was bound to apply Lithuanian law to the issue in order to ascertain, for the purposes of the UK SIA, whether the state had in fact agreed (some 12 years prior to the proceedings) to arbitrate disputes with Svenska arising out of the JVA.

---

139 *ibid*, per Gloster J at [13].

140 Summarised in the decision of Gloster J, *ibid* at [84] – [98].

141 [2005] EWHC 2437 (Comm), at [82].

142 [2005] EWHC 2437 (Comm), [99] – [131].

143 On appeal, the Court of Appeal found that there was insufficient evidence to demonstrate that the parties had, from the outset of their negotiations, intended that the government should be bound by the arbitration agreement. However, the addition of the wording between the fourth and fifth drafts of the JVA recording the state's agreement to be bound by the JVA (and the continued inclusion of this wording subsequently) was strong evidence that the parties did intend the state to be bound by the agreement in accordance with its terms. At the time the wording was added, the JVA included a reference to ICSID arbitration thereby demonstrating the parties' intention that the state would undertake obligations which Svenska would be entitled to enforce through arbitration ([2006] EWCA Civ 1529; [2007] Q.B. 886, per Moore-Bick LJ, at [62]; [64]).

144 Including the requirement to interpret the language of the contract '*disregarding subjective evidence of any party' intentions*' (*Arnold v Britton and others* [2015] UKSC 36; [2015] AC 1619, per Lord Neuberger at [15]) and the exclusion of contractual negotiations (*Chartbrook Ltd and another v Persimmon Homes Ltd and another* [2009] UKHL 38; [2009] 1 AC 1101, per Lord Hoffmann at [28] – [41]).

17.83 The judge's finding that, as a party to the arbitration agreement, the state was not entitled to immunity pursuant to section 9 of the SIA demonstrates the willingness of the court to apply general legal and commercial principles to circumstances involving a state in the context of agreements to arbitrate. That is unsurprising given the restrictive approach to immunity and the inherently commercial nature of arbitration as a dispute resolution mechanism.

State bound by arbitration agreement executed by third parties without state's knowledge

17.84 The English courts have also found a binding arbitration agreement existed for the purposes of section 9 of the SIA where the contract in which it was contained was executed by third parties.

17.85 In *Tsavliris Salvage (International) Ltd v Grain Board of Iraq*,[145] the claimant provided maritime salvage services in respect of a vessel which had run aground whilst carrying cargo belonging to the Grain Board of Iraq ('GBI'), a separate state entity. Tsavliris entered into a Lloyds Standard Form of Salvage Agreement ('LOF') with the manager of the vessel, acting as agent on behalf of the vessel owners, and also as agent for the cargo owner. The vessel was re-floated and, following GBI's failure to pay the salvage security and the release of the cargo, Tsavliris commenced arbitration proceedings against GBI for the share of the payment that Tsavliris was entitled to recover from the cargo owner.

17.86 GBI refused to participate in the arbitration, in which Tsavliris was awarded damages and costs. Tsavliris subsequently commenced proceedings in England to have the award recognised and enforced. In response, GBI and the Iraqi Ministry of Trade ('MOT') challenged the arbitral award under section 67 of the Arbitration Act 1996. The bases of the jurisdictional challenge were that GBI was not a party to the LOF, had not been bound by the agents of the owner, and that there was no valid arbitration agreement.[146]

17.87 In dismissing GBI's challenge to the award, Gross J (as he then was) found that GBI, as the owner of the cargo, was bound by the LOF pursuant to Article 6(2) of the International Convention on Salvage (incorporated into English law by the Merchant Shipping Act 1995),[147] by which the vessel's master was given the authority to conclude salvage contracts on behalf of the cargo owners. The LOF contained a written arbitration agreement to which all parties (including those on whose behalf the LOF was entered into) were bound, which satisfied section 9 of the SIA and served to exclude immunity.[148]

17.88 Although the judge found that GBI was a separate entity, and so not part of the state, it is clear from the judgment that the outcome would have been the same had the Iraqi state been the cargo owner, and thus a party to the LOF.[149] The consequence of this

145 [2008] EWHC 612 (Comm); [2008] 1 CLC 592.

146 GBI also contended that the MOT was, in fact the real owner of the cargo, and that GBI was a part of the Iraqi state (hence the involvement of the MOT in the section 67 proceedings). These submissions were rejected by the court at [44] – [50] and [60] – [74] respectively. As a result of the finding that GBI was a separate entity (and thus only entitled to immunity in accordance with section 14(2) of the SIA, the court was required to consider whether GBI had entered into the LOF in the exercise of sovereign authority. Referring to the speech of Lord Goff in *Kuwait Airways* (*supra*, n 102), at 1159–60 and applying the test of whether the act was a governmental act or one which any private citizen could perform, Gross J held (at [70] – [80]) that '*it is plain that the act of entry into the LOF did not have the character of and was not a governmental act*'.

147 s. 224(1).

148 *Supra*, n 145, per Gross J at [56].

149 *ibid*, per Gross J at [55].

is that – in the right circumstances – a state can be bound to an arbitration agreement for the purposes of section 9 of the SIA in the absence of any express agreement and, indeed, in the absence of any direct involvement in the underlying contract containing the arbitration agreement. It was argued by counsel for GBI that the effect of Article 6(2) of the salvage convention, in allowing employees of a vessel manager to bind a state to through to enforcement, would '*ride roughshod over the principle of state immunity*'.[150]

17.89 However, Gross J reconciled the effects of the convention on state immunity on policy grounds. Principally, the judge found that there was a '*strong maritime policy interest in rewarding salvors*'.[151] Additionally, but more subtly, it appears that the judge was concerned with preserving the autonomy of arbitration. In finding that it would be curious for GBI to have been held as bound to the LOF (which included the arbitration agreement) but not as having agreed in writing to submit disputes to arbitration for the purposes of section 9 of the SIA, Gross J gave effect to what he referred to as the '*broad and permissive view of the requirement that an arbitration agreement should be in writing*'.[152]

17.90 Had the Iraqi state been found to be a party to the LOF, this decision would arguably be the clearest example of a state being bound to an arbitration agreement for the purposes of section 9 of the SIA in the apparent absence of express consent. Given that the purpose of immunity is to avoid impermissible interference by one state in the affairs of another, basing a conclusion that the state has agreed to submit to the jurisdiction of the English courts on an agreement to arbitrate to which the foreign state has not given its consent (giving those words their ordinary meaning) would appear to constitute an unwarranted interference with the foreign state's sovereignty.

17.91 However, the decision in *Tsavliris* is in reality the logical consequence of applying the restrictive doctrine of state immunity. Had the Iraqi state been party to the LOF, its consent – although not explicitly affirmed by the state itself – would have been readily capable of implication by viewing the specific contract containing the arbitration agreement in the context of the state's wider participation in the nexus of the commercial arrangements it had entered into. By engaging in the inherently commercial activity of purchasing commodities and having them transported by sea, the state must be taken to have done so on the same basis as private parties. In these circumstances, that must include accepting the possibility that the state could be bound by a third party without its knowledge to an agreement for salvage, the standard terms of which call for the settlement of disputes via arbitration. It therefore follows, as Gross J noted in his judgment, that requiring a state to honour the terms of an arbitration award involved no unfairness towards a state nor (citing the decision in *I Congreso*) was it '*a threat to dignity of that state, nor any interference with its sovereign functions*'.[153] Indeed, the passage referred to by the judge was one of the foundations of the restrictive theory of immunity identified by Lord Wilberforce, which his Lordship said '*arises from the willingness of states to enter into commercial, or other private law, transactions with individuals*'.[154] This willingness

150 *ibid*, as noted by Gross J at [54].
151 *ibid*, At [57].
152 *ibid*, At [56(vi)].
153 *ibid*, at [57], referring to the speech of Lord Wilberforce in *I Congreso*, (*supra*, n 30), at 262 [E].
154 *Supra*, n 30, at 262 [D].

serves as the basis on which the state's consent to arbitrate – and, thus, its consent to submit to the court's jurisdiction – is implied.

State bound to arbitrate when making a claim under an insurance policy containing an arbitration agreement pursuant to the conditional benefit principle

17.92 States have been held to be bound by an arbitration agreement for the purposes of section 9 of the SIA where the agreement was contained in a contract of insurance to which they were not a party, but through which they had brought claims for compensation.

17.93 In *London Steamship Owners' Mutual Insurance Association Ltd v Spain & Anor (The Prestige)*,[155] Spain and France brought claims against, *inter alia*, the insurers of the owners of a vessel which broke up in the Atlantic, polluting stretches of the Spanish and French coast. The claims were brought under the International Convention on Civil Liability for Oil Pollution Damage ('CLC') and provisions of the Spanish Penal Code, both of which permit direct claims by injured parties against a defendant's insurer. The claims were based on the insurers' obligations to not only indemnify the vessel owners against the liability arising under the CLC, (for which they were compulsorily insured), but also the insurers' obligation to indemnify the owners against their liability for the tortious acts of their employees. The insurers acknowledged their strict liability to Spain and France arising under the CLC, but rejected liability for the non-CLC claims, which the insurers asserted the states were obliged to bring in arbitration pursuant to the terms of the insurance contract, which was subject to English law.

17.94 The insurers commenced arbitration seeking – and securing – negative declaratory relief in terms, *inter alia*, that Spain and France were obliged to bring their claims in arbitration as a consequence of the conditional benefit principle.[156] In the insurers' proceedings to enforce the award, France and Spain resisted by asserting state immunity, but also brought their own challenges under sections 67 and/or 72 of the Arbitration Act 1996, alleging that their direct action rights were based on the Spanish statute, and were independent of the insurance contract which contained the arbitration agreement, to which they were therefore not bound.

17.95 The Court of Appeal held that, although a right to bring a direct claim against an insurer may be a statutory creation, the content of the right is defined by the underlying insurance contract.[157] In circumstances where the effect of the Spanish statute was to permit third parties to enforce the terms of the insurance contract, issues relating to the states' ability to recover compensation were issues relating to the insurers' contractual obligations

155 [2015] EWCA Civ 333; [2015] 1 CLC 596.

156 See Gross LJ in Aspen Underwriting Ltd & Ors v Credit Europe Bank NV. [2018] EWCA Civ 2590; [2018] 2 CLC 891, at [57]: '*the principle underlying "conditional benefit" is straightforward. If a party, X, acquires rights arising under a contract between A and B, X can only enforce those rights consistently with the terms of that contract*'. Gross LJ based his formulation of the principle on that of Hobhouse LJ (as he then was) in *Schiffahrtsgesellschaft Detlef Von Appen GmbH v Wiener Allianz Versicherungs AG (The Jay Bola)* [1997] CLC 993, at 1000–1001: '[t]*he insurance company has the right to refer the claim to arbitration, obtain if it can an award in its favour from the arbitrators, and enforce the obligation of the timecharterers to pay that award. Likewise, the insurance company is not entitled to assert its claim inconsistently with the terms of the contract. One of the terms of the contract is that, in the event of dispute, the claim must be referred to arbitration. The insurance company is not entitled to enforce its right without also recognising the obligation to arbitrate*.'

157 *Supra*, n 155, per Moore-Bick LJ, at [24].

which were governed by English law.[158] The insurers' non-payment of the sums claimed in the Spanish proceedings gave rise to a dispute which could be referred to arbitration, which the insurers did when they sought the negative declarations as to the correct forum for the states' claims. In making claims under the insurance agreement,[159] the states had consented not only to arbitrate disputes (such as the insurers' non-payment), but also to submit to the supervisory jurisdiction of the English courts.[160]

17.96 The extent of the states' submission was subject to further analysis when, following the decision in the Court of Appeal, Spain continued its proceedings through to judgment in the Spanish courts, in response to which the insurers commenced further arbitration proceedings seeking a declaration that Spain was in breach of its obligation not to pursue its claims in Spain. The insurers also sought equitable compensation for Spain's breach of its equitable obligation to arbitrate its claims, an anti-suit injunction to restrain the breach of the equitable obligation (or damages in lieu), contractual damages for Spain's breach of the contractual obligation to arbitrate, and an order for the withdrawal of the Spanish claims and preventing Spain from taking any steps to enforce the Spanish judgment. As Spain had refused to engage in the arbitrator appointment process, the insurers sought and obtained an order granting the insurer permission to serve an arbitration claim form out of the jurisdiction seeking the appointment of an arbitrator by the court, which Spain resisted.[161]

17.97 It was argued by Spain that the effect of the Court of Appeal's earlier decision was that Spain's agreement to arbitrate extended only as far as the substantive claims it was pursuing (in the Spanish courts) against the insurers in accordance with the conditional benefit principle and that, as it was not a party to the arbitration agreement in the normal sense, its agreement did not extend to the claims which the insurers were pursuing in the arbitrations. In rejecting Spain's submissions, the court held that, despite the fact that the claims which the insurers were seeking to refer to arbitration were based on Spain's breach

158 *Ibid*, at [30], adopting the same reasoning the judge gave in his earlier decision in *Through Transport Mutual Insurance Association (Eurasia) Ltd v New India Assurance Co Ltd* [2003] EWHC 3158. Whereas the Finnish statutory provision in *Through Transport* expressly stipulated that the right to bring a direct claim was for compensation '*in accordance with the contract*' (*The Prestige*, at [24]), the Spanish statutory provisions giving rise to the direct right in *The Prestige* did not refer directly to the underlying contract, merely an entitlement to demand fulfilment of the entitlement to compensate, and limiting liability to what had been contractually agreed (*The Prestige*, at [19]). Nevertheless, Moore-Bick LJ considered that, as the Spanish law provisions did not materially modify the scope of the contractual obligation and recognised the third party's right to claim against the insurer was to be determined by reference to the contract, this indicated that the effect of the legislation creating the direct claim was '*in substance to enable the claimant to enforce the obligations arising under the contract of insurance*' (at [26]).

159 It was necessary for the states to have actually commenced proceedings in Spain in order to demonstrate consent to arbitrate. Simply acquiring the right under Spanish law to bring a claim would have been insufficient (per Moore-Bick LJ at [65]). On this limit to the conditional benefit principle, see the Supreme Court's decision in *Aspen Underwriting Ltd and others v Credit Europe Bank NV*. [2020] UKSC 11; [2020] 2 WLR 919, at [26] – [30].

160 *ibid*, per Moore-Bick LJ at [66]. The states' conduct also sufficed as an adoption of the arbitration agreement itself, which satisfied the requirement that the arbitration agreement be in writing (at [70]), presumably on the basis that the agreement adopted by the states was contained in the written insurance agreement. Moore-Bick LJ commented that, as there was no requirement under section 5(2) of the Arbitration Act 1996 for the arbitration agreement to be signed, '*it would be surprising if Parliament had intended section 9(1) to apply only in cases where there is a contract containing an arbitration clause formally signed by or on behalf of the state*'.

161 *London Steam-ship Owners' Mutual Insurance Association Ltd v Spain (The Prestige) (No. 3)* [2020] EWHC 1582 (Comm).

of its obligation to arbitrate and not on the substantive claims which Spain had brought in the Spanish courts, this was irrelevant. The arbitration clause (to which Spain had agreed when it pursued its claims through the underlying insurance contract) applied not only to Spain's claims against the insurer, but to any disputes regarding compliance with the obligation to arbitrate. Henshaw J considered that both types of disputes were closely linked, and that

> *it would be highly artificial to conclude that by pursuing its claim Spain has assumed the burden of the arbitration clause insofar as it relates to the substantive issues, but is free of the arbitration clause insofar as it covers disputes arising from a failure to observe the arbitration clause in relation to those same substantive claims.*[162]

In arriving at this conclusion, the judge was influenced by the fact that disputes as to an alleged breach of an arbitration agreement (which did not involve a third party) would fall within the scope of the agreement.[163]

17.98 Four of the insurers' five claims were therefore covered by the arbitration agreement to which Spain was bound. However, the court refused to find that the arbitration agreement extended to the insurers' breach of contract claim. On the insurers' case, Spain's participation in the earlier English court proceedings for the enforcement of the insurers' first arbitral award gave rise to a contract containing an implied agreement to comply with the arbitration clause, the breach of which was also subject to the arbitration agreement. Henshaw J held that, even if taking steps in litigation could constitute a contractual offer to give effect to the court's decision (which was doubtful), this was an allegation of a breach of a free-standing implied contract, to which Spain's agreement to arbitrate in accordance with the insurance contract could not be extended.[164]

17.99 These cases further demonstrate the way in which the English courts will treat states in the same manner as private entities in the context of commercial matters. Finding that the states were bound by the arbitration agreement in respect of the insurers' claim for negative declaratory relief, yet refusing to extend the arbitration agreement to an entirely separate contractual relationship, were conclusions reached following the application of the conditional benefit principle as it would have been applied had the parties claiming under the insurance contract been private entities.

Agreements to arbitrate in international treaties

17.100 The courts have also had little difficulty in finding that states have agreed to arbitrate disputes (and therefore submit to the jurisdiction of the English courts in accordance with article 9 of the SIA) in instances where the 'agreement' is contained in an international treaty, typically a bilateral or multilateral investment treaty which grants certain protections to foreign investors.

---

162 *ibid*, at [82].

163 *ibid*, at [78], referring to Males J in *Nori Holding Ltd v Public Joint-Stock Co Bank Otkritie Financial Corp* [2018] EWHC 1343 (Comm), [2018] 2 All ER (Comm) 1009, at [38], and finding (at [79]) the position to be consistent with the '*broad approach to arbitration clauses*' adopted by the House of Lords in *Fiona Trust & Holding Corp v Privalov (Premium Nafta Products Ltd & Ors v Fili Shipping Co Ltd & Ors)* [2007] UKHL 40, [2007] 4 All ER 951.

164 *ibid*, at [88] – [92].

17.101 However, in reality there is no 'agreement' to arbitrate in the true sense of the word contained in such a treaty. To take an example, the bilateral investment treaty ('BIT') between Turkey and Singapore provides that any dispute between an investor from one contracting party and the other contracting party '*may be submitted*' to either ICSID or UNCITRAL arbitration.[165] There is no wording equivalent to that which one would expect to see in a bilateral contract by which specified parties agree to submit disputes between themselves to arbitration.[166] Arbitration provisions in BITs are simply a statement of what the contracting states agree – as between themselves – will happen should a dispute arise between one state and an investor from the other.

17.102 Nevertheless, the courts have treated the conditional consent of the state expressed in the treaty to arbitrate disputes with investors as a unilateral offer made by the state, which is then accepted by the investor when it commences arbitration proceedings.[167] The rationale for doing so is that the arbitration provisions in a treaty are a

> *deliberate attempt to ensure for private investors the benefits and protection of consensual arbitration; and this is an aim to which national courts should, in an internationalist spirit and because it has been agreed between states at an international level, aspire to give effect.*[168]

17.103 However, arguably as a result of the manner in which the arbitration 'agreements' are formed in the context of BITs, the scope of what can be referred to arbitration may sometimes be unclear. This is relevant because a tribunal's jurisdiction comes from the scope of the agreement to arbitrate. Matters which fall outside the tribunal's subject matter jurisdiction are not matters which the parties can be said to have agreed to arbitrate. In such circumstances, if such matters have been referred then, for the purposes of section 9 of the SIA, there will have been no agreement to submit the specific dispute to arbitration, and so the state's immunity, insofar as that dispute is concerned, will remain intact.

17.104 This was the thrust of the state's argument in *PAO Tatneft v Ukraine*,[169] in which a Russian claimant succeeded in securing an award in damages in arbitral proceedings against Ukraine under the Russia–Ukraine BIT for its failure to afford fair and equitable treatment ('FET') to the claimant's investment of shares in a Ukrainian oil refining company. In seeking to set aside an order for the recognition and enforcement of the award, Ukraine argued that there was no FET obligation in the BIT and that, as such, it

---

165 Article 11(2), Agreement between the Government of the Republic of Turkey and the Government of the Republic of Singapore Concerning the Reciprocal Promotion and Protection of Investments, 19 February 2008.

166 The wording of BIT provisions varies greatly depending on the states party to the agreement and the period in which it was negotiated. Some BITs provide more explicit expressions of consent to arbitrate, *ie*, Article 8 of the United Kingdom – Mozambique BIT ('[e]*ach Contracting Party hereby consents to submit to the International Centre for the Settlement of Investment Disputes ... for settlement by conciliation or arbitration ... any legal dispute arising between that Contracting Party and a National or Company of the other Contracting Party*'), whilst others stipulate that the contracting states' consent expressed in the treaty is an agreement 'in writing' for the purposes of Article 2 of the New York Convention on the Recognition and Enforcement of Foreign Arbitral Awards 1958 (*ie*, Article 12 of the Spain – Mexico BIT).

167 *Gold Reserve Inc. v Bolivarian Republic of Venezuela* [2016] EWHC 153 Comm; [2016] 1 WLR 2829, per Teare J at [17].

168 Per Mance LJ (as he then was) in *Republic of Ecuador v Occidental Exploration and Production Co* [2005] EWCA Civ 1116; [2006] Q.B. 432, at [32].

169 [2018] EWHC 1797 (Comm); [2018] 1 WLR 5947.

had not consented to arbitrate claims of this type.[170] On Ukraine's case, this was a question which went to the jurisdiction of the tribunal. However, Butcher J rejected this submission, finding instead that the question of whether the tribunal had jurisdiction to hear a claim for a breach of an FET obligation was a matter of proper construction of the arbitration provision. In this case, the scope of the arbitration provision in the Russia–Ukraine BIT – which encompassed '*any dispute ... in connection with the investments*' – was found to be wide enough by Butcher J to cover a dispute as to what protections had been conferred by the BIT.[171]

17.105 It follows, therefore, that the requirement in section 9 of the SIA for an agreement in writing to arbitrate a dispute is readily satisfied by the arbitration provisions found in investment treaties. However, parallels can be drawn between the unilateral offer of arbitration made by states in investment treaties and the ability of a state to be bound to arbitration by third parties in the *Tsavliris* case. In both scenarios, the state is subject to a 'floating' obligation to arbitrate disputes: one created when an investor makes an investment pursuant to a treaty, the other when a third party enters into an agreement on behalf of the state, both of which then crystallise when proceedings are commenced. In neither case will the state necessarily be aware that the obligation has been created; investments qualifying for protection under treaties can be of an entirely private nature, whilst in a *Tsavliris*-type situation the agency relationship giving rise to the ability to bind the state is a creature of international convention which can be created at any time.

17.106 In such circumstances, the consent to arbitrate (and, as a result, submission to the jurisdiction of the English courts) can only be implied from the state's participation in commercial activities. However, that implication will be particularly strong where it arises in the context of a unilateral offer to arbitrate made in an investment treaty. States conclude such treaties for the purpose, in part, of facilitating foreign investment for which certain protections, typically enforceable by arbitration, need to be offered. States are therefore willing to trade an element of control over the circumstances in which they will be bound to arbitrate and accept a corresponding loss of immunity in return for the economic benefits that such agreements bring.

A tribunal's award on its own jurisdiction may be sufficient to establish the agreement to arbitrate

17.107 As noted earlier, the reasoning in *Svenska* based on the interpretation of the arbitration agreement in accordance with its governing law was not the primary basis on which the state was found to have consented to arbitrate.

17.108 In response to the state's Part 11 proceedings disputing the court's jurisdiction to grant permission for the enforcement of the arbitral award, Svenska commenced Part 24 proceedings to have the state's application summarily dismissed. Svenska relied, in part, on its submission that the tribunal's first award on jurisdiction gave rise to an issue estoppel which prevented the state from asserting that it was not a party to the arbitration. The court

170 In the arbitration, the tribunal had held that the most favoured nation provision in the Russia–Ukraine BIT permitted the importation of the FET clause from the United Kingdom–Ukraine BIT (per Butcher J at [45]).

171 *Supra*, n 169, at [50]. At the time of writing, there is an appeal outstanding in related proceedings concerning the enforcement of the arbitral award (see: *PAO Tatneft v Ukraine* [2020] EWHC 3161 (Comm); [2021] 1 WLR 1123).

agreed to recognise the first award pursuant to section 101(1) of the Arbitration Act 1996 so that Svenska could rely on it as a defence to the state's Part 11 proceedings,[172] but held that as the first award could still have been challenged at the seat of the arbitration in Denmark, it was not of a final and conclusive nature sufficient to give rise to an issue estoppel.[173] Svenska's summary judgment application was dismissed.

17.109 However, when the state's Part 11 proceedings came to be heard, Gloster J held that such a significant time had passed since the tribunal's award on jurisdiction was rendered and no attempt had been made to challenge it at the seat, that it did in fact give rise to an issue estoppel which prevented the state from arguing that it was not a party to the arbitration agreement.[174]

17.110 In affirming Gloster J's decision on this issue, the Court of Appeal found that, as the tribunal had jurisdiction to determine whether the government had submitted to arbitration, the tribunal's award was '*binding for what it decides, right or wrong*' and that the state could not go behind the decision, concluding that '[t]*he first award therefore establishes that the government agreed in writing to refer disputes to arbitration and is therefore sufficient to bring the case within section 9* [of the SIA]'.[175]

17.111 The effect of this decision is that, where a tribunal's award asserting jurisdiction over a state has become final and binding, the award will be treated as conclusive proof that the state has agreed, for the purposes of section 9 of the SIA, to refer disputes to arbitration with the consequence that the state will not be immune from the court's jurisdiction in respect of related proceedings. Although not expressly stated by the courts in *Svenska*, the underlying rationale for this would appear to derive from the willingness of the English courts to give effect to arbitral decisions and support the process of arbitration generally. In the case, the courts were faced with a decision of a tribunal on its jurisdiction from which no appeal was possible at the seat of the proceedings, and which had been recognised by the court in the Part 24 proceedings for summary judgment when used as a defence by Svenska to the state's Part 11 proceedings challenging jurisdiction. As the state had not subsequently challenged the recognition of the tribunal's award on jurisdiction, the final and conclusive nature of the tribunal's first award could not have been gainsaid. Had the courts refused to permit Svenska to rely on the award as grounds for the estoppel, the effect would have been to allow Lithuania to use section 9 of the SIA as a means to reopen a final

172 *Svenska Petroleum Exploration AB v Government of the Republic of Lithuania & Anor* [2005] EWHC 9 Comm, per Nigel Teare QC (as he then was) at [27].

173 *ibid*, at [36] – [38].

174 [2005] EWHC 2437 (Comm), at [52] – [64]: '*in all the circumstances, the Interim Award gives rise to an issue estoppel and debars the State from arguing before the English court that it was not a party to the arbitration agreement in Article 9 of the JVA. Accordingly, in my judgment, because of the issue estoppel, the State is not entitled to rely on the fact that it alleges that it was not a party to the arbitration agreement in the context of its claim to state immunity.*'

175 *Supra*, n 126 Q.B. 886, per Moore-Bick LJ, at [116]. Counsel for the state had submitted that the fact that the first award had not been challenged at the seat did not prevent it from challenging its recognition and enforcement before the English courts on the grounds set out in section 103(2) of the Arbitration Act 1996. The Court of Appeal agreed, stating that it had always been open to the state to challenge the earlier recognition of the first award and that '*therefore the fact that the award could no longer be challenged in Denmark does not lead inexorably to the conclusion that it can be relied on as giving rise to an issue estoppel*'. However, as the state had not challenged the deputy judge's recognition of the first award when relied on by Svenska in the Part 24 proceedings, the first award had finally disposed of the tribunal's jurisdiction over the state, and could be relied on as grounds for issue estoppel (per Moore-Bick LJ, at [104]).

and binding arbitral decision. The state could have bypassed the mechanisms for appealing awards or resisting enforcement (and the associated time limits), and re-litigate the issues which had already been decided in the tribunal's conclusive decision, an avenue which would not be open to a private commercial entity.

17.112 However, there is arguably some tension between this approach and the court's clear and stand-alone obligation to give effect to the immunity conferred on the state by section 1(1) of the SIA. In *PAO Tatneft*,[176] the claimant objected to the state's case in Part 11 proceedings on the basis, *inter alia*, that the jurisdictional points raised by Ukraine should have been taken in the arbitral proceedings when the state unsuccessfully challenged the tribunal's jurisdiction on other grounds, but were not. Tatneft argued that the court should apply by analogy the approach to challenges to a tribunal's jurisdiction under section 67 of the Arbitration Act 1996 by which, through operation of section 73, a failure to raise an objection during the proceedings precludes a party from raising the objection later. Butcher J found, however, that section 1(1) of the SIA requires the court to give effect to immunity unless an exclusion in the SIA is engaged, which the court must satisfy itself applies.[177] To the argument that the court should adopt the same approach to a state's assertion of immunity as is applied in jurisdictional challenges under the Arbitration Act 1996, the judge held that:

> [t]*here is nothing in the SIA which suggests that there can be a foreclosure of the points which the state may raise as to the applicability of the immunity afforded by the SIA by reason of what may have occurred in front of an arbitral tribunal in a way similar to that provided for by the Arbitration Act. In particular there are no provisions similar to those in section 73 of the Arbitration Act, and I do not consider that such constraints can be read into the SIA.*[178]

It arguably follows from this reasoning that, if the question of immunity should be considered *de novo* by the court irrespective of whether the state had advanced jurisdictional arguments before the tribunal, then this approach should apply regardless of whether the tribunal's decision has become final and binding as it had done in *Svenska*.

17.113 Nevertheless, the approach in *Svenska* is a further example of the courts prioritising the autonomy of arbitration over the immunities granted to states. Yet, the adoption of a tribunal's decision on jurisdiction which has been rendered final and binding gives rise to further implications in the specific context of state immunity. In the first instance, this approach risks forcing states to submit to the jurisdiction of the courts at the seat of the arbitration in order to challenge a tribunal's decision on jurisdiction and prevent it from being used as a basis for establishing the jurisdiction of the court where the substantive award is to be enforced. Although, in England, a state can dispute the court's jurisdiction without submitting to it by applying under Part 11 of the CPR, this is only available where

176 *Supra*, n 169.

177 *ibid*, at [35].

178 *ibid*. Although not referred to in the *ratio* of the judge's decision on this point (at [30] – [37]), it is relevant to note that, in contrast to the situation in *Svenska*, Ukraine had commenced proceedings to set aside the awards on both jurisdiction and merits at the seat of the arbitration in France, and had resisted Tatneft's enforcement proceedings in the USA and Russia (see [19]). Thus, the tribunal's award on jurisdiction had not, it would seem, become final and binding in the same manner as in *Svenska*.

the state is a defendant in enforcement proceedings and, as demonstrated in *Svenska*, will be unsuccessful where the tribunal's award on jurisdiction has become final and binding. All a claimant need therefore do is wait until an appeal can no longer be pursued before relying on the tribunal's decision as conclusive evidence of its jurisdiction (and thus the existence of the agreement to arbitrate) on which to base proceedings to have the award recognised and enforced. As a result, the only way in which a state can avoid an award being rendered final and binding is to appeal it at the seat of the arbitration, which involves a submission to the jurisdiction of the curial courts.[179] Requiring a state to submit to the jurisdiction of a court in such circumstances is, generally speaking, an anathema to the principle of state immunity,[180] and thus the limited circumstances where this may be permitted are regulated by the SIA.[181]

17.114 More fundamentally, this approach creates an artificial distinction between those awards on jurisdiction which have become final and binding and those which may still be appealed. A tribunal may fail to take account of relevant facts or apply the law erroneously when determining that it has jurisdiction. The fact that a decision is not appealed and so becomes final and binding does not correct a deficiency in the award. However, as is apparent from the Court of Appeal's judgment in *Svenska*,[182] a court would be bound to enforce a tribunal's decision as to its jurisdiction over a state irrespective of whether the tribunal's analysis underpinning its decision was right or wrong. If the decision were to be wrong, the court would nevertheless be permitted to exercise its jurisdiction over the state in circumstances where, as a matter of fact, there is no arbitration agreement for the purposes of section 9 of the SIA and, therefore, no grounds on which the state's immunity can be excluded.

179 See the Court of Appeal's decision in *The Prestige* (*supra*, n 155). Spain and France had instigated proceedings under section 67 and 72 of the Arbitration Act 1996 seeking a declaration that the arbitrator did not have substantive jurisdiction as there was no arbitration agreement. In finding that this was a sufficient step in the proceedings so as to demonstrate a submission to the court's jurisdiction for the purposes of section 2(3)(b) of the SIA, Moore-Bick LJ held (at [49]) that '[t]*he application notice, therefore, was directed to the substantive grounds for setting aside the award and had nothing to do with Spain's right to claim immunity from the jurisdiction of the court*'. The judge went on to state (at [50]): '*I accept that a state which wishes to claim immunity is not precluded from taking steps at the same time to resist enforcement, for example, by applying to set aside a default judgment, and that the acid test by which to determine whether it has taken a step in the proceedings otherwise than for the sole purpose of claiming immunity is whether it has acted in such a way as to demonstrate that it is willing to allow the court to determine the substance of the dispute. However, I do not think that it is enough in this case to say that Spain had made clear its intention to claim immunity; it is necessary to consider how it actually conducted itself in relation to the proceedings. The reference to state immunity in Mr Meredith's witness statement did not make it clear that the only purpose of issuing the application under sections 67 and 72 was to claim immunity; indeed, it could hardly do so, given the nature of the relief sought. On the contrary, in the witness statement immunity was said to exist if there was no valid arbitration agreement. It is difficult to resist the conclusion, therefore, that Spain was positively inviting the court to determine whether the arbitrator had jurisdiction, which was the principal issue raised by the Club's application.*'

180 Referred to as indirect impleading, this includes proceedings commenced against a third party in relation to property in which the state has an interest (or proceedings *in rem* against property of the state) which would, but for the availability of immunity in these circumstances, require the state to submit itself to the court's jurisdiction in order to defend its interest. See the decision of Lord Porter in *Dollfus Mieg et Compagnie SA v Bank of England* [1952] AC 582, at 613: '[t]*he object of the rule, it has been said, is that a sovereign may not be compelled either to submit to a foreign jurisdiction or be compelled to go to law to obtain or preserve his right*'.

181 The SIA restricts the court's jurisdiction in proceedings against third parties in relation to state property to matters where the state would not have been immune if the proceedings had been brought against it (section 6(4)), and in actions *in rem* where the property of the state was, at the time of the proceedings, in use or intended for use for commercial purposes (section 10(2)).

182 *Supra*, n 126, per Moore-Bick LJ, at [116].

17.115 It is difficult to reconcile the *prima facie* acceptance of a tribunal's decision with the court's obligation, recognised in *PAO Tatneft*, to satisfy itself that the circumstances exist to justify excluding the immunity accorded to states by the SIA. After all, a tribunal's decision as to whether a state has agreed to arbitrate is a decision as to its own jurisdiction, not a decision as to whether the state has submitted to the jurisdiction of the UK courts.[183] As demonstrated by the examples in this section, there are a number of circumstances in which a state may be deemed, as a matter of private contract and arbitration law, to have agreed to arbitrate, but where it is arguable that the essential ingredient necessary to demonstrate a state's submission to the court's jurisdiction – consent – is not readily apparent.

17.116 It should be noted, however, that in both *Svenska* and *PAO Tatneft* the states had engaged in the proceedings before the respective tribunals from which the awards on jurisdiction were made. The situation is different where a state refuses to participate in the underlying arbitration on the basis that it was not a party to the arbitration agreement; the state is entitled to have the tribunal's decision on jurisdiction fully opened up by the court in the course of enforcement proceedings.[184]

The effect of the state's consent on its immunity from jurisdiction

17.117 Before considering the nature of the court proceedings related to arbitration anticipated by section 9 of the SIA, it is first necessary to ascertain the extent to which immunity can be excluded by an arbitration agreement.

17.118 As discussed earlier, the SIA draws a distinction between the adjudicative and enforcement jurisdiction of the courts, submission to which is governed by separate parts of the SIA. In order for the court to exercise its adjudicative jurisdiction, a state must either have expressly submitted to the court's jurisdiction pursuant to section 2, or otherwise have engaged in a non-immune activity as described in sections 3 to 11 of the SIA. However, in order for a court to be able to grant relief against a state or process in respect of its property (*ie*, exercise its enforcement jurisdiction), the state must have given its written consent in accordance with section 13(3) of the SIA, for which a submission to the court's adjudicative jurisdiction is not sufficient.[185]

17.119 The question therefore arises as to precisely what effect a qualifying arbitration agreement under section 9 of the SIA has on a state's immunity; does it only act as a

183 A point noted by Moore-Bick LJ, *Svenska Petroleum Exploration AB v Government of the Republic of Lithuania & Anor (No. 2)* [2006] EWCA Civ 1529; [2007] Q.B. 886, at [116].

184 See *Dallah Real Estate and Tourism Holding Co v Ministry of Religious Affairs of the Government of Pakistan* [2010] UKSC 46; [2011] 1 AC 763. In the Court of Appeal proceedings ([2009] EWCA Civ 755; [2011] 1 AC 763), Rix LJ (at [88]) distinguished *Svenska* from the case at hand on the basis, *inter alia*, that Lithuania had participated in the arbitration and had waived the right of challenge in the Danish courts, before going on to state that: '*I can conceive that where an estoppel could be proved, the court asked to recognise or enforce would be entitled to say that it need not investigate the defence. Where, however, a defence of no consent is proven, it seems to me much harder to ignore that in the exercise of any discretion. In any event, there is no question in this case of Dallah being able to rely on the interim award as any form of issue estoppel.*' However, the entitlement to have a tribunal's decision on jurisdiction opened up by the court where a party has not participated in the arbitration is not specific to states; it arises by operation of the Arbitration Act 1996. A non-participating party is entitled to challenge an award on jurisdiction without having to have first exhausted arbitral procedures (section 72), and the loss of a right to object under section 73 only applies where the party has taken part in the arbitral proceedings.

185 In order for a general waiver of immunity to operate in respect of both the court's adjudicative and enforcement jurisdiction, the intention must be clearly shown; see: *A Co v Republic of X* [1990] 2 Lloyd's L R 520.

submission to the court's adjudicative jurisdiction, or can it also operate so as to render a state amenable to the court's enforcement jurisdiction so as to permit the granting of measures of constraint against the state?

17.120 The SIA does not specify the extent of a state's submission to the court's jurisdiction consequent on its agreement to arbitrate. However, on the basis of the categorisation of the provisions in the SIA noted by Lord Diplock in *Alcom*,[186] section 9 sits within that part of the SIA which deals with exclusions to the court's adjudicative jurisdiction. Thus, in the same way that participation in a commercial transaction will only serve to prevent a state claiming immunity from the court's adjudicative jurisdiction, an agreement to arbitrate will only exclude immunity in respect of those proceedings 'related to the arbitration' which involve the exercise of the court's adjudicative jurisdiction. As developed in the next section, these proceedings include applications for the recognition and enforcement[187] of an arbitral award, as well as certain proceedings in support of the arbitral process. However, this will not suffice to demonstrate a state's consent (for the purposes of section 13(3)) to pre- or post-award measures of constraint or execution which form part of the court's enforcement jurisdiction.[188]

17.121 This distinction reflects the position had the state agreed to have its disputes settled by the courts instead of arbitration, where the submission to the courts (either expressly or by participating in a non-immune activity) extends only so far as the adjudication of the state's liability in the judgment handed down by the court. However, given the characteristics of arbitration, including the involvement (to a greater or lesser degree) of a state's consent to arbitrate, the question arises as to whether it is somehow inherent in an agreement to arbitrate that a state's consent includes measures of constraint and execution.[189]

17.122 The question is particularly relevant where the agreement to arbitrate incorporates institutional rules which require the parties to give immediate effect to the awards rendered by the tribunal, and include express waivers of any appeal or recourse.[190]

---

186 Per Lord Diplock in *Alcom* (*supra*, n 20), at 600 [F].

187 Reference to 'enforcement' in this context means giving effect to an arbitral award as if it was a domestic court judgment (and adjudicative act) so that it can then be used as a basis for execution proceedings (which are part of the court's enforcement jurisdiction). See the decision in *Svenska* (*supra*, n 126), in which the Court of Appeal held that proceedings to have an arbitral award recognised were proceedings related to the arbitration; per Moore-Bick LJ at [117]: '*The Act itself draws a distinction between proceedings which relate to the arbitration (section 9) and process in respect of property for the enforcement of an award (section 13). In our view an application under section 101(2) of the Arbitration Act 1996 for leave to enforce an award as a judgment is, as subsection (1) recognises, one aspect of its recognition and as such is the final stage in rendering the arbitral procedure effective. Enforcement by execution on property belonging to the state is another matter, as section 13 makes clear*.' See further below.

188 See: *ETI Euro Telecom International NV v Republic of Bolivia & Anor* [2008] EWCA Civ 880; [2009] 1 WLR 665, per Lawrence Collins LJ at [113]: '*it is plain that there is nothing in section 9 which overrides the prohibition* [on the granting of relief against a state] *in section 13*'.

189 Hazel Fox & Philippa Webb, *The Law of State Immunity* (Oxford University Press 2015) 392. See also: Nelson Goh, *Court-Ordered Interim Relief Against States in Aid of Arbitration: Sovereign Immunity, Waiver and Comity* (2017) 34 J. Intl. Arb. 4, 679. Goh posits (at 694) that the consent to arbitration can be extended to execution on the basis that it is necessary in order to allow arbitration – a delocalised form of dispute resolution – to operate effectively. Moreover, he suggests that states are bound, by the principle of *pacta sunt servanda*, to fulfil their promises (here, presumably, the promise to arbitrate) in good faith, which necessitates giving effect to the award.

190 See, for example: ICC Rules of Arbitration 2021, Article 35(6); LCIA Arbitration Rules 2020, Article 26.8; and Arbitration Rules of the Singapore International Arbitration Centre 2016, Rule 32.11.

Where such undertakings are given, it is arguable that a state – in agreeing to honour the award – has impliedly accepted that if it does not, it will be amenable to the court's enforcement jurisdiction.

17.123 This expansive approach to defining the scope of a state's consent has gained traction in jurisdictions such as the USA and Sweden,[191] but has failed so far to find support in England. In *Orascom Telecom Holding SAE v Republic of Chad & Ors*,[192] the High Court was asked to determine (for the first time, it would appear)[193] the effect of Article 35(6) of the ICC Rules on a state's immunity from enforcement.[194] Having considered in outline the position adopted by the French[195] and US courts on the issue, Burton J found himself unable to conclude that the provisions concerning the waiver of immunity from enforcement in the SIA should be expanded to include a waiver on the basis of the state's agreement to give effect to the award.[196] The judge based his view on the fact that neither the USA nor France had at the time a statutory framework governing immunity from the court's enforcement jurisdiction, and so their acceptance of the undertaking in the ICC Rules to give effect to the award as a waiver of immunity had been developed through the courts.[197]

17.124 The judge's consideration of this point was *obiter* and in any event he left the issue unresolved, partly due to the fact that, as the application had been resolved on other grounds, he had not had the benefit of full evidence on the approach taken in foreign jurisdictions.[198] Arguably, however, a case could have been made for the extension of the arbitration agreement to cover measures of enforcement without reference to the foreign law, on the basis of both common law and the SIA.

17.125 In the first instance, English law has long recognised that arbitration agreements contain an implied promise to give effect to the award,[199] breach of which gives rise to a distinct action on the award. As the promise is implied into the arbitration agreement then, unless the arbitration agreement explicitly excludes disputes arising out of the agreement

191 See, for example: *Lliamco v Socialist People's Republic of Libya*, Svea Court of Appeals, 18 June 1980 (Sweden); *Walker International Holdings Ltd v Republic of Congo* 395 F.3d 229 (5th Cir. 2004) (USA). See the discussion in Hazel Fox & Philippa Webb, *The Law of State Immunity* (Oxford University Press 2015) 390–393.

192 [2008] EWHC 1841; [2008] 2 CLC 296.

193 *ibid*, per Burton J, at [33].

194 The provision referred to in the decision is Article 28(6), the equivalent provision under the 1998 Rules.

195 At that time, the French courts recognised the undertaking in Article 35(6) as a waiver of immunity from execution: *Creighton Ltd v Government of Qatar*, France, Ct of Cassation, July 6, 2000, No. 98–19068. The French courts have, however, since resiled from this position with the amendments to the Code of Civil Enforcement Procedures (the 'CCEP') introduced by Law No. 2016-1691 (the *Sapin II* law). Article L-111-1-2 of the CCEP now requires either that the state must have expressly consented to the provisional or execution measure being sought or the state has earmarked the property for the purposes of satisfying the specific claim, or that the property which is the subject of measures to enforce a judgment or arbitral award is in use or intended for use for purposes other than government non-commercial purposes. See also: *Commisimpex v République du Congo*, Ct of Cassation, 10 January 2018, No. 16-22494; *Société Mohamed Abdel Moshen* Al-Kharafi *et Fils c/ société Libyan Investment Authority et al*, Ct of Appeal, Paris, 5 September 2019, No. 18–17592.

196 *ibid*, per Burton J, at [49].

197 *ibid*, per Burton J, at [48].

198 *ibid*, per Burton J, at [49].

199 *Purslow v Bailey* (1704) 2 Ld Raym 1039, per Holt CJ at 1040: '*For the submission is an actual mutual promise to perform the award of the arbitrators*'. The principle has been more recently stated by the Privy Council in *Associated Electric and Gas Insurance Services Ltd v European Reinsurance Co of Zurich* [2003] UKPC 11; [2003] 1 WLR 1041, per Lord Hobhouse at [9]: '*It is an implied term of an arbitration agreement that the parties agree to perform the award.*'

to arbitrate, the state's consent to arbitrate would also encompass a dispute arising out of a breach of the implied undertaking.[200]

17.126 Furthermore, section 13(3) of the SIA recognises that consent to measures of constraint and enforcement can be contained in a prior agreement, which is defined in section 17(2) as including a treaty, convention, or other international agreement. As the debate in the House of Lords during the passage of the Bill makes clear, the purpose of inserting this definition of 'agreement' was to extend the scope of a state's consent beyond a particular transaction or proceedings, and to include instances where a state has undertaken to waive immunity by way of treaty or convention.[201] The SIA therefore anticipates that a state may, in much the same way as an arbitration provision in an investment treaty constitutes a unilateral offer to arbitrate for the purposes of section 9 (and thus submit to the adjudicative jurisdiction of a court competent to hear arbitration related proceedings), make a universal offer to waive immunity from measures of constraint exercised as part of the court's enforcement jurisdiction. If that is the case, then it becomes difficult to reason why a state's agreement to arbitrate in accordance with institutional rules which require the parties to give effect to the award, cannot be an effective consent to measures of constraint in accordance with section 13(3) in the same way as an agreement to do so in a treaty would be.

17.127 The prohibition on the granting of measures of constraint in the absence of consent is a privilege only afforded to states and one which places them at a significant advantage to their non-state counterparties. The ability for a state to avoid its obligation to give effect to an award undermines trust and confidence in transacting with states. Treating the undertaking to give effect to the award as consent to measures of constraint would be a significant step towards avoiding the uncertainty caused by potential state non-compliance, and moreover would be consistent with the court's approach in other respects in giving effect to the restrictive doctrine of state immunity by treating the state as it would treat private commercial entities. As noted by commentators remarking on the missed opportunity represented by *Orascom*:

> [t]*o the reasonable international business person, an undertaking to 'execute' or to 'carry out' an award, together with a promise to waive all waivable challenges, could not possibly be consistent with a claim of immunity from execution, since such a claim is tantamount to a refusal to honour the award.*[202]

200 cf. *The Prestige (No. 3)* (*supra*, n 164). Although Henshaw J held that Spain's consent to arbitrate could not extend to an implied contract to give effect to a court judgment, that was a free-standing implied contract the existence of which was doubted by the judge and to which, in any event, Spain could not have been taken as having consented in accordance with the conditional benefit principle. That case would not, therefore, prevent a claimant from arguing the existence of an implied promise in the case of a direct arbitration agreement with a state.

201 Per Elwyn-Jones LC: '*It is intended that these prior agreements should include not only agreements entered into for the purpose of a particular transaction or litigation by the parties, but also instruments by which the State involved has undertaken to waive its immunity in a manner binding that State in its international relations. The new subsection makes it apparent that not only contracts are involved but also instruments like treaties and Conventions which are binding in public international law*,' *HL, Hansard*, vol. 389, col. 1939.

202 Roger Kennell and Adam Rooney, *The State Immunity act 1978 and Article 28(6) of the ICC Rules: A Missed Opportunity: Orascom v Chad Arbitration* (2010) 76 Arbitration 1 181, 185.

Proceedings 'which relate to the arbitration'

17.128 Where a state has been found to have agreed to arbitration, section 9 excludes immunity in respect of proceedings in the courts of the UK which 'relate to the arbitration'.

17.129 The SIA provides no further guidance as to what this means, but the courts have given this phrase a wide interpretation. In *NML Capital Ltd v Republic of Argentina*,[203] Lord Phillips stated that section 9 '*relates not only to proceedings to enforce an award, but to all proceedings relating to an arbitration to which a state is party, and establishes jurisdiction of the English court in relation to all such proceedings*',[204] whilst Lord Mance found that it '*also covers ancillary or interlocutory applications relating to arbitration, and is not limited to arbitration relating to commercial transactions*'.[205]

17.130 It is important to note, as discussed earlier, that section 9 is concerned with the exclusion of a state's immunity from the adjudicative jurisdiction of the court. It follows from this that proceedings 'related to the arbitration' do not include measures of constraint which fall within the court's enforcement jurisdiction, such as the granting of an interim injunction.[206] As a result, the existence or otherwise of immunity in respect of proceedings for interim relief or to execute against a state's property in satisfaction of an award (even though such proceedings arise out of the underlying arbitration) will be determined by reference to the provisions of section 13.

17.131 The statutory basis for the majority of proceedings which relate to arbitration is Part I of the Arbitration Act 1996 ('AA96'), which sets out the circumstances in which the powers of the court may be invoked in respect of arbitral proceedings. These provisions fall within three broad categories: (1) those for the recognition and enforcement of arbitral awards; (2) those for challenges to arbitral awards; and (3) those which relate to the procedure or conduct of the arbitration.

17.132 Relatively few of these provisions have been given judicial consideration. This is most likely due to the limitations which restrict the scope of the AA96. For instance, much of Part I of the AA96 (which includes the court's powers in support of arbitration) applies only where the seat of the arbitration is England and Wales or Northern Ireland,[207] with only a handful of sections applying to cases irrespective of where the seat is located.[208] Further, as with many other provisions in the Act, certain court powers are non-mandatory, meaning that they can be excluded by agreement between the parties.[209] In addition,

---

203 [2011] UKSC 31; [2011] 2 AC 495. This case was not concerned with proceedings relating to an arbitration, however the question of what constituted proceedings which 'relate to arbitration' in section 9 of the SIA was relevant to ascertaining what was meant by proceedings 'relating to a commercial transaction' in section 3.

204 *ibid*, at [30].

205 *ibid*, at [89].

206 *ETI Euro Telecom International NV v Republic of Bolivia & Anor* [2008] EWCA Civ 880; [2009] 1 WLR 665.

207 Section 2(1).

208 Section 2(2) extends certain provisions such as those relating to the stay of proceedings (section 9) and the enforcement of awards (section 66) to proceedings irrespective of the seat. Section 2(3) does the same for powers in relation to the securing of witness attendance (section 42) and the court's general powers exercisable in support of proceedings (section 44), but subject to the discretion of the court, which may refuse to do so where the fact that the proceedings are seated outside of England and Wales and Northern Ireland makes it inappropriate.

209 Section 4 and Schedule 1. Institutional arbitration rules make provision for matters such as the appointment of arbitrators, extending the time for rendering the award and the assessment of costs which will operate to exclude the court's powers in respect of those matters. However, many institutional rules explicitly permit parties

almost all of the provisions of the Act are expressly disapplied from arbitrations conducted pursuant to the ICSID Convention, and so courts cannot exercise supervisory jurisdiction over these proceedings.[210]

17.133 The remainder of this section outlines the three categories of proceedings which a court may entertain as proceedings 'related to the arbitration' in accordance with section 9 of the SIA.

Recognition and enforcement of an arbitral award

17.134 An issue of nomenclature arises in respect of these proceedings. Despite the reference to 'enforcement' in the phrase 'recognition and enforcement' of awards, enforcement in this context does not involve execution of the award against property by way of, for example, seizure or attachment, and so is not part of the court's enforcement jurisdiction. Instead, enforcement in this context refers to the step prior to the execution of the award and involves the conversion of the award into a judgment of the court (by, for example, ordering the respondent party to pay the sums found due to the claimant by the tribunal), which the claimant can then use as the basis for execution proceedings. Recognition of an award is a step prior to enforcement (but which, in reality, takes place as part of the enforcement process) where the award has been rendered in a foreign jurisdiction by which the court accords the award the same status as an award made in the UK.[211] The process of (where necessary recognising and) enforcing an arbitration award is an exercise of the court's adjudicative jurisdiction,[212] demonstrated by the fact that the eventual order directing, for example, payment of the award sum is equivalent in its effect to the judgment that the court would have given had it been seized of the substantive claim.

17.135 It is well established that proceedings for the recognition and enforcement of arbitral awards against states are proceedings which are 'related to the arbitration' for the

---

to seek interim or conservatory measures from competent judicial authorities (see, for example, Article 28(2) ICC Rules of Arbitration 2021). However, where an arbitration agreement or institutional rules prevent parties from resorting to local courts (or require the parties to have explicitly consented to the availability of measures from local courts in their arbitration agreement, *ie*, Rule 39(6) of the ICSID Rules), such provisions (or the absence of consent) will likely suffice as evidence that the state has not consented to submit to the jurisdiction of the curial court for these purposes.

210 Arbitration (International Investment Disputes) Act 1966, section 3. Only section 9 of the Arbitration Act 1996 (stay of legal proceedings) remains applicable to ICSID arbitrations. Whilst Section 3(1) allows for the Lord Chancellor to order the extension of certain other provisions in the Arbitration Act 1996 (including those in relation to the court's powers in sections 42–44) to ICSID arbitrations, this has not occurred. See: *Republic of Ecuador v Occidental Exploration and Production Co* [2005] EWCA Civ 1116; [2006] Q.B. 432, per Mance LJ at [38]. See also: *ETI Euro Telecom International NV v Republic of Bolivia and Anor* [2008] EWCA Civ 880; [2009] 1 WLR 665, per Lawrence Collins LJ, who commented (at [108]) that Article 39(6) of the ICSID Rules (which permits parties to request provisional measures from any judicial authority where they have stipulated so in the agreement recording their consent to arbitrate) had the effect of excluding the availability of such measures from national courts unless the parties have previously agreed.

211 Where a foreign arbitral award has been recognised, a party is entitled to rely on it by way of defence, set off or otherwise in legal proceedings in the UK. See: section 101(1) AA96 for foreign arbitral awards rendered in states party to the Convention on the Recognition and Enforcement of Foreign Arbitral Awards 1958 (the 'New York Convention'); and section 36(2) of the Arbitration Act 1950 for foreign arbitral awards rendered in states which are not party to the New York Convention.

212 See, by way of analogy: *AIC Limited* (*supra*, n 108), in which Burnton J held (at [21]) that the registration of a judgment against Nigeria under the Administration of Justice Act 1920 was an adjudicative act, as it required the Master to consider the application and exercise the discretion conferred on him as to whether to make the necessary order.

purposes of section 9 of the SIA. It was argued by counsel for Lithuania in *Svenska* that the reference to proceedings in section 9 was limited to proceedings related to the conduct of the arbitration, not proceedings to have the award recognised and enforced.[213] This submission was roundly rejected, with the court finding that the underlying principle of section 9 was that in agreeing to arbitrate, a state '*has rendered itself amenable to such process as may be necessary to render the arbitration effective*'.[214] The court also noted that a provision excluding enforcement proceedings from the ambit of what became section 9 was removed during the passage of the State Immunity Bill.[215] Records of parliamentary debate (as well as a plain text reading of the provision itself) also demonstrate that there is no requirement for a territorial link between the arbitration and the UK in order for immunity to be excluded under section 9.[216] The Supreme Court has also endorsed the inclusion of recognition and enforcement proceedings within the ambit of section 9 of the SIA.[217]

17.136 As a result, proceedings for the recognition and enforcement of all arbitral awards – as an exercise of the court's adjudicative jurisdiction – are proceedings 'related to the arbitration'.

17.137 Different processes of enforcement are available depending on the circumstances in which an arbitral award was rendered.[218] Domestic awards (*ie*, those issued by tribunals seated in England and Wales or Northern Ireland) are enforced in accordance with section 66 of the AA96.[219]

17.138 Awards rendered by tribunals seated outside of the domestic jurisdiction fall into two categories. Those where the proceedings are seated in states party to the New York Convention are enforced by the provisions in Part II of the AA96,[220] which gives effect to the provisions in the New York Convention governing the circumstances in which recognition and enforcement of qualifying awards must be granted, absent grounds for refusal. Where an award is rendered in a foreign jurisdiction which is not a party to the

---

213 *Supra*, n 126, at [112].

214 *ibid*, Per Moore-Bick LJ at [117].

215 *ibid*, at [119].

216 *ibid*, at [120].

217 *NML Capital Ltd v Argentina* [2011] UKSC 31, [2011] 2 A.C. 495, per Lord Mance at [89]: '*a major purpose of section 9 must on any view have been to lift state immunity in respect of the enforcement of arbitration awards against states, including foreign arbitration awards since the subsection is in general terms*'.

218 There does not appear to have been a reported case which has considered whether an action on the award would qualify as a proceeding 'related to the arbitration' for the purposes of section 9 of the SIA. This is likely due to the fact that this is something of a route of last resort, where enforcement is not otherwise available as the arbitration agreement was concluded orally rather than in writing, or the award is somehow deficient which prevents enforcement via a statutory process. Arbitrations with states usually involve experienced arbitrators and counsel and so errors in the award which vitiate its enforceability are unlikely to arise, whilst an oral arbitration agreement would not satisfy the requirements of section 9 of the SIA so as to exclude a state's immunity from enforcement. Nevertheless, it is arguable that an action on the award could constitute proceedings 'related to arbitration'. The cause of action is based on a breach of a term obliging the parties to perform the award (see *supra*, n 199), which is implied into the arbitration agreement itself, not the underlying contract (see *Agromet Motoimport v Maulden Engineering Co. (Beds.) Ltd.* [1985] 1 WLR 762). Thus, the proceedings 'relate to the arbitration' rather than the contract in which the arbitration agreement is contained.

219 The reference to 'domestic' does not preclude awards in arbitrations involving foreign states; see, for example: *London Steamship Owners' Mutual Insurance Association Ltd v Spain & Anor (The Prestige)* [2013] EWHC 3188 (Comm); [2013] 2 CLC 562, in which the claimant sought to enforce an award against Spain and France issued by a London-seated tribunal.

220 Sections 101–103.

New York Convention, enforcement is by means of section 66 of the AA96,[221] the territorial scope of which is extended in the Act for these purposes.[222]

17.139 Irrespective of where an arbitration conducted under the ICSID Rules takes place the resulting awards are enforced in the UK in accordance with sections 1 and 2 of the Arbitration (International Investment Disputes) Act 1966,[223] which gives effect to the obligation in the ICSID Convention for states to recognise and enforce awards.[224]

17.140 Section 9 of the SIA has also been successfully invoked in proceedings for the recognition and enforcement of a foreign court judgment on the basis that the judgment in question ordered the enforcement of an arbitral award at the seat of the arbitration. In *L R Avionics Technologies Ltd v Federal Republic of Nigeria and another*,[225] the claimant succeeded in a Nigerian-seated arbitration against the Nigerian state, but the award did not carry interest. The claimant was granted leave by the Nigerian Federal High Court to enforce the arbitration award, and was awarded interest dating back to the issuance of the award. Subsequently, the claimant brought proceedings in England to enforce both the arbitration award (pursuant to section 101 of the AA96) and the Nigerian judgment (pursuant to section 9 of the Administration of Justice Act 1920),[226] in order to recover the interest awarded by the court. Males J (as he then was) accepted the claimant's submission that, in the same way as an application to enforce an arbitration award is a proceeding related to the arbitration, '*so too is an application to enforce a judgment which is in effect an award which has been converted into a judgment under a foreign statutory provision equivalent to section 66 of the Arbitration Act 1996*'.[227]

Challenges to arbitral awards

17.141 Pursuant to the AA96, awards may be challenged on the grounds that the tribunal lacked substantive jurisdiction,[228] or that there was a serious irregularity affecting the

221 Section 99 of the AA96 maintains in force Part II of the Arbitration Act 1950 for the enforcement of non-New York Convention Awards. Section 36(1) of the Arbitration Act 1950 provides that foreign awards are enforceable in England in the same manner as an award is enforceable under section 66 of the Arbitration Act 1996.

222 Section 2(2)(b).

223 ICSID Awards are subject to a separate enforcement mechanism. It should be noted that the ICSID Convention contains a provision (Article 54(1)) requiring contracting states to recognise an ICSID award as binding '*and enforce the pecuniary obligations imposed by that award within its territories as if it were a final judgment of a court in that state*'. In a recent case, the Federal Court of Australia held that this provision – and the fact that Spain, as a party to the ICSID Convention, had agreed to it – constituted a submission to the court's jurisdiction, and granted leave to the claimants to have their awards against Spain recognised and enforced; see: *Eiser Infrastructure Ltd v Kingdom of Spain* [2020] FCA 157, per Stewart J at [182].

224 Article 54.

225 [2016] EWHC 1761; [2016] 4 WLR 120.

226 The Administration of Justice Act 1920 provides statutory rules for the recognition and enforcement of foreign judgments rendered in certain Commonwealth countries and British Overseas Territories. Provisions for the enforcement of foreign judgments against states generally are found in section 31 of the Civil Jurisdiction and Judgments Act 1982, which permits recognition and enforcement where, *inter alia*, the overseas court would have had jurisdiction had it applied sections 1 to 11 of the SIA, and incorporates the provisions of sections 12, 13 and 14(3) and (4) into the recognition and enforcement proceedings. On to the application of section 31, see: *NML Capital Ltd v Republic of Argentina* [2011] UKSC 31; [2011] 2 AC 495; and *Heiser's Estate v Iran* [2019] EWHC 2074.

227 *Supra*, n 225, at [26] – [27].

228 Section 67.

tribunal,[229] and they may be appealed on a question of law.[230] These proceedings are only available where the tribunal was seated in England and Wales or Northern Ireland.[231]

17.142 As a matter of logic, and in view of the wide definition ascribed to the term 'proceedings' in section 9 of the SIA, it follows that proceedings brought to challenge an award or appeal on a point of law are proceedings which 'relate to the arbitration'. However, as a likely result of the territorial restrictions on the availability of these procedures, there appear to be no reported cases in which the non-state party to an arbitral award has sought to challenge or appeal an award involving a state on these bases before the English courts. Where states have challenged awards on substantive grounds, they have been deemed to have submitted to the jurisdiction of the court for the purposes of section 2(3) of the SIA,[232] and so it would be unnecessary to characterise such proceedings as being 'related to the arbitration' in order to engage the exclusion of jurisdiction under section 9 of the SIA as well.

Ancillary/interlocutory applications

17.143 This category covers the broad range of applications which parties to arbitral proceedings can make, by which the court may be requested to exercise its supervisory powers in support of arbitration. The majority of these powers are conferred by the Arbitration Act 1996, but others may arise under separate enactments.

17.144 Not all of these proceedings fall neatly within the adjudication/enforcement paradigm of the court's jurisdiction. Unlike the proceedings for the recognition and enforcement of and challenges to awards, which are adjudicative in nature, the exercise of the court's supervisory powers does not involve the settlement of substantive disputes; by their nature these applications are incidental to the dispute which has been referred to the underlying arbitration and so are not strictly adjudicative in nature. Yet, with the exception of a few specific types of proceedings, they also do not involve measures of constraint or execution such that they can be characterised as part of the court's enforcement jurisdiction. Nevertheless, to the extent that classification is necessary, the procedures which do not involve measures of constraint are considered as falling within the court's adjudicative jurisdiction.[233] The inclusion of these proceedings within the scope of what a state may be taken to have consented to by virtue of an arbitration agreement can be justified on the grounds that they are necessary to ensure the proper functioning of the arbitral process in which the state has agreed to participate.[234]

---

229 Section 68.

230 Section 69. This is a non-mandatory provision and so may be – and often is – excluded by the operation of institutional arbitration rules.

231 Section 2(1).

232 See: *The Prestige* (*supra* n 179).

233 See: Burnton J in *AIC Limited* (*supra*, n 108 (and see, *supra*, n 212), at [19]): '[t]*he fact that an act does not involve the exercise of judgment by the court does not mean that it is not the exercise of jurisdiction*'. The judge observed that the issue of a claim form against a state may appear to be an administrative act, but it required the court to consider whether the prospective defendant would be immune, and refuse permission for service out of the jurisdiction if immunity existed – an essentially adjudicative act.

234 See: Julian Lew, Loukas Mistelis *et al.*, *Comparative International Commercial Arbitration* (Kluwer Law International 2003) 6. It has been suggested by others that the necessity of interim relief, coupled with the widespread use and acceptance of it as a general principle of international law reflected in the practice of both national courts and international tribunals, justifies the implied waiver of immunity from such proceedings in the

17.145 The principal provisions in the Arbitration Act 1996 through which a party to an arbitration may seek to invoke the court's assistance fall into two categories: (1) those identified as being the 'powers of the court in relation to arbitral proceedings' in sections 42 to 45, which are principally concerned with the substance of the proceedings themselves; and (2) those which concern more procedural issues both before and during the pendency of proceedings, and which are scattered throughout Part 1 of the Act.

• 'Procedural' applications

17.146 Examples of the latter 'procedural' category include: extending time for the commencement of proceedings,[235] excluding periods of time for the calculation of limitation periods,[236] appointing an arbitrator,[237] removing an arbitrator,[238] determining a preliminary point on jurisdiction,[239] extending the time for making an award[240] and determining the recoverability of costs and arbitrator fees.[241]

17.147 With the exception of the court's power to grant a stay of proceedings brought in breach of an arbitration agreement,[242] the availability of these procedural applications is limited to arbitrations seated in England and Wales or Northern Ireland; as a result, there have been few reported cases involving the court's exercise of these powers in the context of arbitrations involving states. Nevertheless, such proceedings are clearly related to the underlying arbitration and – to the extent not precluded by the parties' prior agreement – are proceedings in respect of which the state's immunity is excluded by operation of section 9 of the SIA. Where the court has exercised such powers, it has demonstrated that it will only do so where it is satisfied that the proceedings relate to the arbitration agreement to which the state is a party. Thus, in the application for the appointment of an arbitrator in *The Prestige (No. 3)*, the court analysed whether the various claims which had been identified for submission to arbitration fell within the terms of the arbitration agreement, and ordered that an arbitrator be appointed only in respect of the claims for which Spain was found to have agreed to arbitrate.[243]

• Powers of the court 'in relation to arbitral proceedings'

17.148 Sections 42 to 44 of the AA96 are of greater significance in the context of state immunity, as they are intended to support arbitral proceedings by providing access to certain coercive powers of the court which the tribunal – lacking the necessary judicial character – is unable to exercise. That is not to say, however, that the provisions in these

arbitration agreement: Nelson Goh, *Court-Ordered Interim Relief Against States in Aid of Arbitration: Sovereign Immunity, Waiver and Comity*, (2017) J. Intl. Arb. 34(4) 697–9.

235 Section 12.

236 Section 13.

237 Section 18.

238 Section 24.

239 Section 32.

240 Section 50.

241 Sections 63 and 64.

242 Sections 9–11, extended to foreign-seated arbitrations by section 2(2)(a).

243 *Supra*, n 161. Per Henshaw J (at [168], [213]), excluding the claim for breach of an implied contract (as to which, see, *supra*, n 164), which the claimant could not demonstrate that Spain had agreed to arbitrate.

sections are all measures of constraint which would be prohibited by section 13(2)(a) of the SIA in the absence of the state's consent in appropriate terms under section 13(3).

17.149 For instance, section 42 of the Act permits either the tribunal or a party to the arbitration to apply for an order requiring a party to comply with a peremptory order of the tribunal.[244] In *Pearl Petroleum Co Ltd and others v Kurdistan Regional Government of Iraq*,[245] an arbitral tribunal had issued an interim measure ruling requiring the respondent to pay US$100m in respect of condensate and gas it had purchased under an agreement with the claimants in order to preserve the status quo pending resolution of the substantive disputes. The respondent failed to comply with the order, and so the claimants applied for a peremptory order from the tribunal, which was also not complied with, leading to an application to the court to enforce it. Had the respondent been entitled to immunity,[246] Burton J held that the application for enforcement of the peremptory order – as a simple order for the payment of money from no specified source – was not an application for an injunction as had been contended for by the respondent, and which would have been prohibited by section 13(2)(a) of the SIA.[247]

17.150 Similarly, the provisions concerning the attendance of witnesses and taking of evidence, although coercive in nature, may be directed against non-state parties and thus would not be rendered unavailable on the grounds of immunity, even if deployed in the context of proceedings against a state. An application to secure the attendance of a witness before a tribunal to give oral evidence or produce documents pursuant to section 43 of the AA96 may be entertained when, for example, the request for documents or witness evidence is directed against a non-party to the proceedings where the territorial criteria are met.[248] In addition, by section 44(2)(a) the court may be asked to exercise its general powers in respect of the taking of witness evidence. Although there would appear to be an overlap with section 43, this section is not subject to the same territorial limitations. Thus, the powers exercisable by the court in aid of arbitration include, for example, the taking of evidence from non-parties to the arbitration agreement in respect of foreign-seated arbitral

244 The grounds for issuance of peremptory orders by a tribunal and the consequences of non-compliance are set out in section 41(5) to (7) of the Act.

245 [2015] EWHC 3361; [2016] 4 WLR 2.

246 The respondent was found to be a separate entity which, although it had entered into the agreements for the exploitation of its gas fields in the exercise of its own sovereign authority, was found not to have exercised the sovereign authority of the state of Iraq, and so the respondent was not entitled to immunity pursuant to section 14(2) of the SIA; see Burton J at [36] – [37].

247 *ibid*, at [40(ii)], referring to the Court of Appeal's judgment in *Soleh Boneh International Ltd v Government of the Republic of Uganda* [1993] 2 Lloyd's Rep 208, in which the court held that an order to provide security against the state where it had sought an adjournment of proceedings to enforce an arbitral award, even one with a penal notice directed at the Ugandan High Commissioner in the UK, was not an injunction, and was more akin to a monetary judgment (per Staughton LJ, at 213, who amended the order to remove the penal notice, were his Lordship's decision wrong as to the nature of the order for security). The Court of Appeal recently confirmed that orders for security for costs are not injunctive when it ordered Ukraine to provide security for costs in relation to its attempt to set aside enforcement of the arbitral award obtained by PAO Tatneft (the proceedings analysed *supra*, n 169); see: *Ukraine v PAO Tatneft* [2019] EWCA Civ 763, per Flaux LJ at [15].

248 Section 43 only permits the exercise of the court's powers under CPR Part 34 if the witness is within the United Kingdom and the arbitral proceedings are being conducted in England and Wales or Northern Ireland. See: *Silver Dry Bulk Co Ltd v Homer Hulbert Maritime Co Ltd* [2017] EWHC 44 (Comm); [2017] 1 CLC 1. Note that the requirement that the proceedings be conducted in the court's jurisdiction is not the same as requiring that the proceedings are seated here; it would suffice if a hearing were to be convened in England for the purpose of taking the witness's testimony, even if the proceedings were seated abroad (see section 2(3)(a)).

proceedings,[249] as well as the taking of evidence from foreign non-parties in respect of English-seated arbitrations,[250] but not the power to grant pre-action disclosure.[251]

17.151 However, a witness summons directed at a state will fail as such proceedings would impermissibly require the state to submit to the court's jurisdiction.[252] As a result, an application seeking witness testimony or documentary evidence from a servant or agent of the state is likely to be considered an attempt to circumvent the state's immunity, and will similarly fail.[253] It will therefore be important to understand the nature of the relationship between the state and the non-party from which evidence is sought, and the extent to which the state might be said to have a proprietary interest in the evidence sought.[254]

17.152 The remainder of the proceedings contemplated in section 44(2) are, by their nature, concerned with interim relief involving property or assets belonging to one of the parties to the proceedings.[255] This includes the preservation of evidence;[256] orders for the inspection, photographing, preservation, custody or detention of – or the taking of samples from – property which is the subject of the proceedings (including the granting of authority for any person to enter premises in the possession or control of the parties to carry out said activities);[257] the sale of goods which are the subject of the proceedings;[258] and the granting of interim injunctions or the appointment of a receiver.[259]

17.153 The potential interference with the state or its property to which an order made under this subsection would give rise is clear. Unless the state has given its consent to such measures of constraint, they will not be granted.[260]

---

249 See: *A & Anor v C & Ors* [2020] EWCA Civ 409; [2020] 1 WLR 3504.

250 See: *Silver Dry Bulk Co Ltd v Homer Hulbert Maritime Co Ltd* (*supra*, n 248), per Males J at 49.

251 See: *EDO Corporation v Ultra Electronics Ltd* [2009] EWHC 682 (Ch); [2009] Bus LR 1306, per Bernard Livesey QC at [18], [20].

252 Moreover, were a state to be summoned, any breach of a subsequent order to attend court could not be sanctioned, as the consequences of a failure to comply include committal proceedings, which are explicitly prohibited as against a state pursuant to section 13(1) of the SIA (see, for example, the penal notice on Form N20 (witness summons)).

253 See: *Koo Golden East Mongolia v Bank of Nova Scotia and others* (*supra*, n 81).

254 Consider, for example, a situation where the non-party has been engaged by a state to act as the employer's representative on a construction project. The contract between the state and non-party may include provisions which provide that all documents produced by the employer's representative are the property of the employer (thus the state.) As the state would have immunity were the application to have been made against it on the basis of its contractual right of property in the documents, the employer's representative could not be compelled to disclose them.

255 Following some uncertainty on the matter, it has been held that orders under section 44 of the Act cannot be made against persons who are not party to the arbitration. See: *DTEK Trading S.A. v Mr Sergey Morozov and another* [2017] EWHC 94, per Sara Cockerill QC (as she then was), citing with approval (at [36]) the dictum of Males J in *Cruz City 1 Mauritius Holdings v Unitech Ltd* [2014] EWHC 3704 (Comm) [2015] 1 Lloyd's Rep. 191, at [47] – [50]. Although applications made under section 44 for the taking of evidence from foreign non-parties in respect of English-seated arbitrations (*supra*, n 250) ultimately involve a non-party to the arbitration, the judge in *DTEK* reasoned that these are permitted on the basis that the proceedings are not themselves an order against a third party, but an application for a letter of request to be issued to the foreign court which, if it accepts the request, will be the court which makes the order for the non-party to provide evidence; per Sara Cockerill QC at [47].

256 Section 44(2)(b).

257 Section 44(2)(c).

258 Section 44(2)(d).

259 Section 44(2)(e).

260 The same considerations do not, however, necessarily apply where injunctive relief is given by an arbitrator. In *(The Prestige) (No. 3)* (*supra*, n 84) one of the claims which the claimant sought to refer to arbitration was a claim for an anti-suit injunction to restrain Spain's alleged breach of the equitable obligation to arbitrate the claims it had brought in court proceedings in breach of the arbitration agreement. In holding that the claimant had

17.154 As noted earlier, the Court of Appeal confirmed this position in respect of freezing injunctions in *ETI Euro Telecom International NV v Republic of Bolivia & Anor*.[261] The proceedings in that case involved an application for a freezing injunction related to an order of attachment obtained by the claimant in New York in aid of an extant ICSID arbitration. Although the court rejected the claimant's appeal from the earlier dismissal of the application as there were no grounds on which a freezing order could be made,[262] it also addressed the question of Bolivia's immunity. Lawrence Collins LJ held that nothing in section 9 of the SIA by which Bolivia agreed to arbitrate overrides the prohibition against measures of constraint in section 13, which includes freezing injunctions, and that such proceedings '*are not "proceedings which relate to the arbitration" for the purposes of section 9*'.[263]

17.155 Section 45 of the AA96 stands apart somewhat from the other provisions dealing with the powers of the court in relation to arbitral proceedings. It allows the court, on the application of a party to an arbitration, to determine any question of law which arises during the arbitral proceedings. As this procedure involves the court resolving a matter which goes to ascertaining liability, it is clearly an exercise of the court's adjudicative jurisdiction, rather than being a measure of constraint directed towards the state or its assets prohibited by section 13(2). Furthermore, the requirement that the question of law arises '*in the course of the proceedings*' anticipates that arbitral proceedings are already on foot,[264] and so an application under section 45 clearly arises out of the arbitration, and is thus *prima facie* a proceeding 'which relates to the arbitration' for the purposes of section 9 of the SIA.

17.156 On that analysis, the state's agreement to arbitrate is sufficient to exclude its immunity from proceedings under section 45. However, there is a clear difference between the extent to which the court is required to exercise its adjudicative jurisdiction in respect of a procedural application (discussed earlier), and on an application to determine a question of law. Where the former is concerned, such proceedings are purely facilitative, and the extension of the state's consent to arbitrate to exclude immunity in respect of

---

a good arguable case on the issue (and so it would not be pointless to appoint an arbitrator to hear it), Henshaw J held (at [188]) that whilst an injunction issued by a court '*impinges on the* par in parem *principle by purporting to set up an organ of one state in a position of authority vis à vis another state* ... [s]*uch considerations apply with much less force, if at all, to arbitration, since it is founded on consent (whether actual or, as in the present case, imputed)*'. Although the provision governing the powers of arbitrators in this case was section 48 of the AA96 (which, for the purposes of an award, grants the tribunal the same powers as the court to order a party to do or refrain from doing anything), the reasoning applies equally to interim injunctive relief.

261 *Supra*, n 75.

262 The claimant's case had been advanced on two statutory bases. Its arguments on section 44 of the Arbitration Act 1996 were abandoned at an earlier stage due to the fact that, as the underlying arbitration was subject to the ICSID Rules, section 44 of the Act was inapplicable (see: *supra*, n 210). The other basis was section 25 of the Civil Jurisdiction and Judgments Act 1982, which empowers the court to grant interim relief in respect of certain foreign proceedings. However, as the court explained, an application for the granting of interim relief under this enactment fails as it must be related to substantive proceedings, which the New York proceedings (themselves proceedings in aid of arbitration) were not (per Lawrence Collins LJ, at [62] – [78]); and additionally, section 25 was not applicable to arbitration proceedings ([79] – [98]).

263 *Supra*, n 75, at [113].

264 See: *Taylor Woodrow Holdings Ltd and another v Barnes & Elliott Ltd* [2006] EWHC 1693 in which ascertaining whether the question of law arose '*out of the arbitral proceedings between the Contractor and the Employers*' was one of the '*threshold conditions*' under section 45 of the Act which had to be satisfied, per Jackson J (as he then was) at [54].

these proceedings is justifiable on the grounds that it is necessary to ensure the proper functioning of the arbitration. This reasoning, however, does not apply in respect of an application under section 45, in which the court is being asked to render a judgment[265] which will determine a matter of substance relevant to the underlying dispute referred to arbitration (and which may very well lead to its resolution).[266] Such proceedings require the court to engage with the merits of the dispute in a manner that, for example, appointing an arbitrator or granting an extension of time do not. Moreover, it cannot be said that the determination of a point of law is necessary for the proper functioning of the arbitration; were this procedure to be unavailable it would not prevent an arbitration from continuing as the tribunal could still arrive at a binding award irrespective of whether their determination on the point of law was correct or not.

17.157 If the definition in section 9 of the SIA of proceedings 'related to the arbitration' were to include section 45 of the Act, it would have the paradoxical result that an agreement to arbitrate disputes (the usual effect of which is to exclude a court's jurisdiction) would be treated as being the state's consent to have substantial elements of those disputes determined by the court. As yet, there have been no reported cases in which the courts have considered whether such an application would fall within the ambit of section 9 of the SIA.[267] However, provisions akin to section 45 are rare in other national arbitration legislation.[268] It is therefore questionable whether, if this were to come before the English courts, a sufficient consensus exists in international law to hold that, by agreeing to arbitrate, a state has consented to submit the substance of its disputes to the courts in the same manner as its agreement to arbitrate constitutes its consent to other proceedings which 'relate to the arbitration'.

- Anti-suit injunctions

17.158 Orders restraining foreign proceedings are, by their nature, injunctive, as they are orders directed at the party which has commenced the proceedings to take no further action. As a result, they fall within the parameters of section 13(2)(a) of the SIA and cannot be granted against a state in the absence of its consent. Where such consent has been given, the courts have granted the relief sought,[269] and so it is not necessary in those circumstances to consider whether such proceedings are 'related to the arbitration'.

---

265 Section 45(6), AA96: '*The decision of the court on the question of law shall be treated as a judgment of the court for the purposes of an appeal*'. The court's determination is only appealable in limited circumstances.

266 Section 45(1) requires the court to be satisfied that the question of law '*substantially affects the rights of one or more of the parties*'. In *Taylor Woodrow*, (*supra*, n 264), Jackson J found that this test was satisfied where, on the facts, more than half of the contractor's case turned on the determination of the point of law, but that it was '*not necessary to embark upon any detailed quantification exercise*' (at [54]).

267 Indeed, there have been very few cases involving the use of section 45 generally; see Hew R Dundas, *Questions of Law, Extensions of Time, Injunctions and Bias: Some Recent Cases* (2006) 72 Arbitration 4, 373.

268 Section 45 of the AA96 is the successor in title to the consultative case regime in earlier incarnations of the Arbitration Act; see Donaldson LJ in *Babaneft International v Avant Petroleum* [1982] 1 WLR 871, at 882 [D] (referring to section 2 of the Arbitration Act 1979, which is in similar terms to section 45 of the AA96 Act). The consultative case regime, where either the tribunal could refer a question of law to the court for its opinion, or the court could direct that the question be put to it, has been described as a '*uniquely English concept*'; see: Theodore C Theofrastous, *International Commercial Arbitration in Europe: Subsidiary and Supremacy in Light of the De-Localization Debate* (1999) Case W Res J Intl. L 455, 463.

269 See: *Sabah Shipyard* (*supra*, n 78).

17.159 However, in view of the willingness of the English courts to treat states as commercial entities when they have agreed to arbitrate, coupled with the equivocal comments in *Orascom* (earlier) as to whether a state's undertaking to perform an arbitral award could be construed as consent to measures of constraint under section 13(2)(a), the characterisation of anti-suit injunctions as proceedings which fall within section 9 bears some scrutiny.

17.160 The court's power to grant an anti-suit injunction to restrain foreign proceedings commenced in breach of an arbitration agreement arises not under section 44(2)(e) of the Arbitration Act 1996, but under the general powers of the court to grant injunctive relief under section 37(1) of the Senior Courts Act 1981 ('SCA').[270] The rationale for this, as explained by Lord Mance in *AES Ust-Kamenogorsk Hydropower Plant LLP v Ust-Kamenogorsk Hydropower Plant JSC*, lies in the distinction between the circumstances in which the two provisions can be operated. The latter bestows a general power on the court to grant interim and final injunctive relief, which can be called upon irrespective of whether arbitral proceedings are on foot or proposed; the former is a limited power to grant interim injunctive relief available only where proceedings have either commenced or are pending. An injunction under section 44(2)(e) would therefore be unavailable to a party who has no intention of commencing arbitration, but wishes to restrain its counterparty from commencing proceedings elsewhere in breach of the agreement, and so the correct basis is section 37 of the SCA.

17.161 In distinguishing between anti-suit injunctions and other injunctions which the court may order to preserve the status quo in current or pending arbitral proceedings, Lord Mance observed that an anti-suit injunction is not – as section 44(1) requires – for the purposes of and in relation to arbitral proceedings, '*but for the purposes of and in relation to the negative promise contained in the arbitration agreement not to bring foreign proceedings, which applies and is enforceable regardless of whether or not arbitral proceedings are proposed or on foot*'.[271]

17.162 It is therefore doubtful that an anti-suit injunction could be said to qualify for the purposes of section 9 where the requirement is that proceedings from which immunity is excluded are those which '*relate to the arbitration*'. The use of the definite article denotes that the court proceedings must relate to specific arbitral proceedings. Moreover, if the phrase '*relate to*' in section 9 of the SIA is to be given the same meaning as Lord Mance gave the qualifying phrase '*in relation to*' in section 44(1) of the AA96 as requiring proximity between the orders which a court can make and current or pending arbitration proceedings, then an anti-suit injunction commenced in order to restrain a state from commencing proceedings where no specific arbitration is in process or anticipated cannot be said to relate to the arbitration.

State immunity and the execution of arbitral awards

17.163 Once an arbitral award has been recognised and enforced, and thus has the status of a court judgment, the final stage in implementing its terms is to execute it. Depending on

270 *AES Ust-Kamenogorsk Hydropower Plant LLP v Ust-Kamenogorsk Hydropower Plant JSC* [2013] UKSC 35; [2013] UKSC 35, per Lord Mance at [48].

271 *ibid.*

the nature of the dispute and the relief sought, awards can include a variety of orders which create obligations, including those requiring specific performance, taking or refraining from taking certain actions, or paying sums of money. Where these obligations are not discharged, the award creditor will have recourse to the coercive powers of the court as part of its enforcement jurisdiction in order to compel compliance with the award.

17.164 As set out in the earlier discussion regarding the legislative framework, the provisions of section 13 of the SIA govern the circumstances in which a state is entitled to immunity from the court's enforcement jurisdiction. Where a state has consented to the giving of any measures of constraint pursuant to section 13(3), the court can theoretically make orders for any type of relief available to it.[272] However, where such consent has not been given, an award creditor will only be permitted to issue proceedings for the execution of an award in respect of property subject to the commercial use exception in section 13(4). This has the effect of limiting the categories of reliefs granted in arbitral awards which can be executed via the court, and excludes measures such as orders for specific performance or orders in respect of property which does not fall within the commercial use exception.

17.165 However, where an award orders the payment of money from the state to the award creditor, section 13(4) renders all of the state's property which is currently in use or intended for use for commercial purposes amenable to execution in satisfaction of the award.[273] In order to successfully invoke the court's jurisdiction for these purposes, the award creditor will therefore need to establish that the property it is seeking to execute against is: (1) the property of the state and (2) currently in use or intended for use for commercial purposes. These two elements are addressed below.

Property of the state[274]

17.166 Although ascertaining whether an asset is the 'property of the state' is relevant (as earlier) to the execution of awards against the state, it can also arise when executing awards against state entities or other third parties which may be in possession of assets belonging to the state, and who would be entitled to raise the defence of immunity notwithstanding that the state is not a party to the proceedings. The same considerations as to the ownership and type of property, as well as the nature of the state's interest in the property, will arise in both scenarios.

---

272 The effect of section 13(3) is that a state can consent to '*any relief or ... any process*', which necessarily includes injunctions and other relief requiring a party to do or refrain from doing something. However, the penalty for non-compliance with such orders will involve *in personam* remedies against those responsible for non-compliance, such as proceedings for contempt. Where the non-compliant party is a state, such *in personam* penalties against a state's representatives in the court's jurisdiction are likely to be unavailable as a result of diplomatic immunity. However, in circumstances where a court refuses to exercise its discretion to grant an injunction, damages in lieu of an injunction may be available. See: *The Prestige (No. 3)*, (*supra*, n 84), where it was suggested that damages could be ordered by the court where injunctive relief was prohibited by operation of section 13(2)(a) of the SIA, per Henshaw J at [201] – [202].

273 Equally, as section 13(4) permits the issue of '*any process*', if an arbitral award ordered the delivery up of property in use for or intended for use for commercial purposes, the court could make an order accordingly.

274 The reference to 'property' in section 13(4) is not circumscribed by the words 'of a state'. However, it is evident that these words are to be inferred on the basis that subsection 4 refers back to subsection 2(b), in which the term '*property of a state*' is used. See: *AIG Capital* (*supra*, n 110), per Aikens J at [44]: '*The word "property" in section 13(4) clearly refers to the "property of a state", which is the phrase used in section 13(2)(b). So section 13(2)(b) and (4) set out the rules on immunity from enforcement with respect only to the property of a state*'.

17.167 Again, the SIA is of limited assistance when looking to understand what constitutes the 'property of the state'. However, the English courts have provided guidance as to the limits of what this term will encompass.

Ownership of property

17.168 Evidently, where the term arises in the context of executing the obligations incurred by the state under an award, the property must be that of the state, otherwise the property cannot be executed against. Thus, where a state has created a separate entity, the assets of that entity are not the property of the state and will not be available to satisfy liabilities incurred by the state (and equally do not enjoy immunity so as to be excluded from the pool of assets available for execution to satisfy liabilities incurred by the separate entity). This gives rise to disputes over the status of entities as either an organ of the state or a state entity and thus the availability (or non-availability) of their assets to award creditors.

17.169 In *Gécamines*,[275] the respondent had purchased the assignment of arbitral awards that had been rendered against the Democratic Republic of Congo, which it sought to execute against shares held by – and income due to – Gécamines, a state entity owned by the DRC. Gécamines appealed the decision of the Jersey Court of Appeal which had held that it was an organ of the state, and that its assets were therefore amenable to execution. As set out earlier in the discussion regarding the treatment of state entities under the SIA, the Privy Council found that Gécamines was in fact a separate entity irrespective of the level of control exercised by the state over its affairs. In articulating the correct approach to distinguishing between states and separate entities, Lord Mance held that: '*the strong presumption is that its separate corporate status should be respected, and that it and the State forming it should not have to bear each other's liabilities*'.[276]

17.170 Where property has been found to belong to a state entity confirmed as being separate from the parent state, that determination cannot be displaced by evidence that the property is being used for sovereign rather than commercial purposes so as to render it the property of the state in any event. In *Botaş Petroleum Pipeline Corporation v Tepe Insaat Sanayii AS*,[277] Tepe had prevailed in two arbitrations against Botaş, and sought to execute the awards against shares held by Botaş in two Jersey subsidiaries. Botaş (a state entity) had argued that the question of whether the shares were its property or that of the state should be determined by reference to the commercial purpose test in section 13(4) of the SIA and that, if the assets were used for sovereign purposes, they would be immune.

17.171 In rejecting this submission, the Privy Council held that the words 'property of a state' were a precondition to any consideration of whether the property was in use for sovereign or commercial purposes,[278] such that only if the property is found to belong to the state will the court consider the purpose to which it is put. Lord Mance observed that Botaş's case would '*undermine the evident purpose behind the establishment of separate entities by states and their recognition under section 14 of the* [SIA]', and that embarking on an assessment of whether assets were in use for commercial or sovereign purposes

275 *Supra*, n 97.
276 *ibid*, at [29].
277 [2018] UKPC 31.
278 *ibid*, per Lord Mance at [10].

irrespective of ownership would '*effectively eliminate any difference between assets held by the state and by a separate entity*'.[279]

17.172 Maintaining a clear division between the property of a state on the one hand and the property of a state entity on the other is of significant benefit to third parties when making commercial decisions, particularly as to the risk involved in contracting with state entities (which involves an analysis of the entity's financial position to ascertain whether (and how) it could meet its obligations). It would be considerably more difficult to make any such assessment if assets which, on the face of it, belonged to the entity could nevertheless be found to be property of the state. Not only could this have the effect in certain circumstances of rendering such property immune from execution, but in other cases it could mean that the entity's assets would be available to satisfy obligations incurred by the state which are completely unconnected with the entity's activities.

Types of property and the nature of the state's interest

17.173 As to what constitutes the 'property of the state', the English courts have given the term a wide interpretation which is not limited to real or other physical property, nor does it anticipate that the state holds full title over the property or that it is in the state's physical possession. The formulation which is often cited is that of Aikens J in *AIG Capital* who, in considering that the term should be given a broad scope, stated that:[280]

> *in my view, 'property' will include all real and personal property and will embrace any right or interest, legal, equitable, or contractual in assets that might be held by a state or any 'emanation of the state' ... or central bank or other monetary authority that comes within sections 13 and 14 of the Act.*

The term has been considered sufficiently wide to include the debt owed by a bank to its customer in the form of the credit balance on the account, with the 'property' being the chose in action by which the customer is entitled to withdraw the credit balance.[281] Other contractual rights such as the right to immediate possession under a contract of bailment have also been found to fall within the definition.[282]

17.174 However, the interest must be a 'legal' interest, such as a proprietary interest, against which execution can be levied; anything less, such as control over the use or disposition of the asset in question, will not suffice. The reason for this distinction is that measures of execution can only be levied against legal or proprietary interests, as these are the only interests with realisable value which can be used to satisfy an award or judgment debt. Therefore, the state's legal interest must be threatened in order for an assertion of immunity to be made. To put it another way, as the court cannot make an

279 *ibid.*

280 *Supra*, n 110, at [45]. A definition endorsed by the Privy Council in *Botaş*, (*supra*, n 277) at [17].

281 See: *Alcom* (*supra*, n 20) per Lord Diplock at 602 [D]. His Lordship drew a distinction between the legal nature of the chose in action with the legal nature of cash or currency notes deposited at the bank. See also: *AIC Limited* (*supra*, n 108, at [47]), in which the debts owed by the Bank of England to the Central Bank of Nigeria represented by the credit balance in the accounts held in the name of the central bank were found to be immune.

282 *Dollfus Mieg et Compagnie SA v Bank of England* [1952] AC 582.

order to execute against, for example, the state's right to control an asset, no question of immunity arises.[283]

17.175 In *Botaş*,[284] it was argued by Botaş that the definition of property ought to encompass assets over which the Turkish state exercised significant control,[285] as concepts of possession, use, and control of property are referred to in other sections of the SIA.[286] The Privy Council, however, rejected Botaş's case in this regard, holding that the reference to 'property' in section 13(2)(b) is limited to '*legally ascertainable interests*' for which '[e]*nforcement, in one form or another, can readily be envisaged against them*'.[287] Moreover, the existence of the legal or proprietary interest must be ascertained by the domestic law where the execution proceedings are taking place, as execution can only be performed against property '*recognised as such for the purposes of enforcement under domestic law*'.[288]

17.176 It should be noted, however, that specific measures of constraint may stipulate the nature of the interest against which they can be executed. In *AIG Capital*,[289] although Kazakhstan (the award debtor) had a beneficial interest in the sums held in the bank accounts which rendered the assets the property of the state for the purposes of section 13(2)(b),[290] in order to sustain a third party debt order it was necessary to demonstrate that there was a debt due or accruing from the third party bank to Kazakhstan. The accounts were held in the name of the National Bank of Kazakhstan, which was the entity to which, as a matter

283 See Lord Sumption in *Belhaj* (*supra*, n 46) at [196] where, after considering the line of cases involving state property but in which the states were not direct parties, his Lordship observed that: '[t]*he essential point about the property cases is that they have the potential directly to affect the legal interests of states notwithstanding that they are not formally parties. ... None of this reasoning, however, applies in a case where the foreign state has no legal interest to defend because the court's decision in its absence cannot directly affect its legal interests*'. See also Lord Mance in *Botaş*, (*supra*, n 277 at [20]): '*To the extent that the property is the State's, that suffices for execution, and the State's possession or control will be irrelevant. If all that the State has is mere possession or control without any proprietary interest (such as provided by a lien), enforcement will simply fail for want of any proprietary or legal interest on the part of the State against which to enforce.*'

284 *Supra*, n 277.

285 The control, according to Botaş, was exercised via a 'special legal regime' involving statutory oversight of its activities, restrictions on its ability to dispose of certain assets and state approval for the appointment of personnel (as described in Lord Mance's judgment at [28]). However, the Royal Court of Jersey rejected the contention that this demonstrated control sufficient to render the shares immune from execution by analogy to the approach adopted by the Privy Council in *Gécamines* (n 97) to determining whether the degree of control exercised by a state over a state entity rendered it part of the state; per Lord Mance at [29].

286 See sections 6(1); 6(4); and 10(5).

287 Per Lord Mance, at [17].

288 *ibid.* Botaş had contended that 'property' should be given an autonomous, international definition, and relied on *travaux préparatoires* to the UNCSI which showed that an early draft of Article 19 (prohibiting post-judgment measures of constraint) had indicated a wider definition of 'property' by referring to property in which the state '*has a legally protected interest*'. However, subsequent drafts simply referred to '*measures of constraint against the property of a Foreign State*', which the Board found could not be read as a shorthand for a broader definition of 'property' (at [24]). In any event, the English courts have taken a similarly restrictive view as to the definition of the state '*interests*' to which the UNCSI extends immunity. In *Belhaj* (*supra*, n 46), the Supreme Court held that the reference to a state's '*interests*' in the context of the Article 6(2)(b) (immunity from proceedings where the state is not named as a party, but the proceedings '*in effect seeks to affect the property, rights, interests or activities of that other State*') should be limited to claims which have some legal foundation (per Lord Mance at [26]), and that the scope of the provision was limited by its context to claims in respect of state property (per Lord Sumption at [195]).

289 *Supra*, n 110. See Aikens J at [51].

290 *ibid*, per Aikens J at [91].

of English law, the bank owed the debt.[291] The state's ultimate beneficial interest in the money held in the accounts did not create any contractual relationship between the state and the bank which would have entitled it to demand payment of the sums in the account, and which could be enforced by means of a third party debt order to require payment to be made to the award creditor.[292]

Commercial use

17.177 Once it has been determined that the property in question belongs to the state, in order to render it amenable to execution it is necessary to establish that the property is in use, or intended for use, for commercial purposes.

17.178 As noted earlier in the section addressing post-judgment measures of execution, section 17(1) of the SIA defines 'commercial purposes' by reference to section 3(3). This, in turn, provides a definition of 'commercial transaction' for the purpose of describing the circumstances in which a state will not be immune from the court's adjudicative jurisdiction when it has engaged in commercial activity. It is important to note a nuance in the way in which this tripartite definition is phrased. The first two parts refer to:

> *(a) any contract for the supply of goods and services;*
> *(b) any loan or other transaction for the provision of finance and any guarantee or indemnity in respect of any such transaction or of any other financial obligation.*

However, the third part of the definition refers to:

> *(c) any other transaction or activity (whether of a commercial, industrial, financial, professional or other similar character) into which a State enters or in which it engages <u>otherwise than in the exercise of sovereign authority</u>* (emphasis added).

The absence from parts (a) and (b) of an equivalent exclusion for transactions or activities entered into in the exercise of sovereign authority in part (c) means that property in use or intended for use in a contract for goods or services or a loan or financial arrangement – even if the state does so in the exercise of its sovereign authority – will still be deemed to be in use for commercial purposes in the context of section 13(4).[293]

17.179 If the head of the foreign state's diplomatic mission provides a certificate in accordance with section 13(5) of the SIA stating that property is not in use or intended for use by or on behalf of the state for commercial purposes, this creates a rebuttable presumption to that effect. A claimant must then adduce sufficient evidence to overturn

291 *ibid*, per Aikens J at [30] – [32].

292 However, if both a state and a state entity had proprietary or legal interests in the same asset which were separable (*ie*, money held in a bank account in the joint name of the state and the state entity, into which both had contributed funds), it is arguable that execution could proceed against that portion of the chose in action represented by the sum contributed by the state entity without affecting the state's interest. See the comments of Lord Mance in *Botaş*, (*supra*, n 277): '*If and so far as the separate entity is shown to own or have any other proprietary or legal interest in the shares, that interest will be liable to execution. If the separate entity has only a partial interest, then execution will be limited to that interest – and if the State happens to hold the remaining proprietary or legal interest, no question of enforcement against that remaining interest will arise, and so no need for the State to have or invoke immunity in respect of it.*'

293 See: *Alcom* (*supra*, n, 20), per Donaldson MR in the Court of Appeal at 586 [H] – 587 [E]; per Lord Diplock in the House of Lords at 603 [A] – [D].

the presumption. This creates quite a high barrier for the claimant to overcome as there is no requirement for the certificate to provide any particularisation,[294] and the personal immunity of the ambassador means that she or he cannot be called to give evidence as to the veracity of the certificate.[295] Even in the absence of a certificate, a claimant will still retain the burden (albeit to a lesser degree) of demonstrating the commercial use of the property in question, in view of the court's obligation to give effect to the immunity conferred by the SIA irrespective of whether the state appears in the proceedings.[296]

17.180 Claimants will therefore need to rely on their own evidence to demonstrate the current or intended commercial use of the property.

17.181 For these purposes, evidence as to the origin of the property is not relevant. In *Servaas Inc. v Rafidain Bank*,[297] the claimant had sought to enforce a foreign court judgment against Iraq by way of a third party debt order over a debt payable to Iraq by the respondent bank which was in liquidation. Iraq had previously purchased the assignment of debts owed by the bank to commercial creditors as part of a debt restructuring process. These were submitted as claims for payment from the bank's liquidators as part of the scheme of arrangement, with the claims due to be paid to Iraq as dividends. Iraq's intention was to transfer the proceeds of its claims to the Development Fund for Iraq (which the parties had agreed was a sovereign purpose), and the head of the Iraqi diplomatic mission issued a certificate confirming that the claims under the scheme of arrangement were not in use or intended for use for commercial purposes.

17.182 In dismissing the claimant's appeal, Lord Clarke held that the term 'in use for commercial purposes' should be accorded its ordinary and natural meaning, the result of which being that to describe a debt arising from a transaction as being 'in use' for that transaction would not be the ordinary and natural meaning of the phrase.[298] Moreover, there is a distinction between the phraseology used in the SIA to refer to proceedings 'relating to' a transaction or 'connected with' a ship on the one hand, and property 'in use or intended for use' for commercial purpose, and that the distinction meant that '[i]*t is not sufficient that the property "relates to" or is "connected with" a commercial transaction*'.[299]

17.183 It is also irrelevant that the property is used in commercial transactions if they are collateral to the underlying sovereign purpose. In *AIG Capital*, Aikens J acknowledged that the securities which formed part of the national fund (and were subject to the execution proceedings) were actively traded in order to obtain profit for reinvestment into the national fund. Nevertheless, despite these financial transactions being – in and of themselves – inherently commercial activities, they were not inconsistent with the use of the fund for sovereign purposes.[300] It was necessary, in the judge's view, to set these transactions against

294 See*: AIC Limited* (*supra*, n 108) per Burnton J at [53]. Contrast this with the position taken by the Swiss Federal Supreme Court in *République socialiste du peuple arabe de Lybie-Jamahiriya v Actimon* SA, 24 April 1985, 82 ILR 30, in which the court refused to exempt from enforcement the property of the Libyan central bank held in Switzerland on the basis that the state had failed to provide any details as to the intended purpose of the assets, which could have formed part of the central bank's private fiscal assets (as noted in August Reinisch, *European Court Practice Concerning State Immunity from Enforcement Measures*, (2006) EJIL, 17(4) 803, 827.

295 Hazel Fox & Philippa Webb, *The Law of State Immunity* (Oxford University Press 2015) 216.

296 Section 1(2).

297 [2012] UKSC 40; [2013] 1 AC 595.

298 *ibid*, at [16].

299 *ibid*, at [17].

300 *Supra*, n 110, at [92(2]).

the background of the purpose of the agreement pursuant to which they were traded, which was to assist in running the national fund, thus the dealings with the securities were '*all part of the overall exercise of sovereign authority by Kazakhstan*'.[301]

17.184 Where property is in simultaneous use by a state and a third party, the relevant 'purpose' in order to determine whether it is in commercial or sovereign use is that of the state. In *L R Avionics*,[302] the claimant sought a charging order over premises owned by Nigeria, but leased to a company which provided Nigerian passport and visa services. In support of its position, the claimant relied on various indicia demonstrating that the property was in use for commercial purposes, including the fact that Nigeria was recovering rent from the tenant, which was carrying out its activities for a fee. Males J held that the correct perspective for the purposes of section 13(4) of the SIA was that of the state, which is implicit from the fact that section 13(5) envisages that the state's ambassador may certify the use to which the state is putting or will put the property, and that it is unlikely that she or he could certify the use of a third party.[303] Moreover, in applying the ordinary and natural meaning of the phrase in the SIA, the primary use to which the property was being put was the processing of Nigerian visa and passport applications, which was a sovereign act.[304]

17.185 In view of the burden on the party seeking to demonstrate commercial use, the evidence of use must be sufficiently recent in order to rebut the presumption created by an ambassador's certificate. In *AIC Limited*,[305] the certificate was accompanied by a witness statement describing the purposes for which certain bank accounts were used. Some of them demonstrated a clear commercial use, some were clearly not for commercial use, and for others their use was unclear. However, the accounts had been dormant for 18 months. Burnton J held that, whilst evidence showing recent commercial usage of an account over a significant period of time could be sufficient to demonstrate current or intended use for commercial purposes (thus defeating a certificate issued under section 13(5)), '*the older the use in evidence, the weaker the inference that may be drawn as to the use or intended use of the account*'.[306] On the facts, the judge held that it was not possible to say that an account which had been dormant for 18 months was presently being used for any purpose, and that the previous use to which the accounts had been put was '*weak evidence of the present intention as to its use*'.[307] As a result, the claimants were not able to overturn the presumption of non-commercial use established by the ambassador's certificate.

17.186 However, an example of where evidence of commercial use – no matter how recent or explicit – will be insufficient to dislodge an ambassador's certificate arises in respect of bank accounts belonging to the diplomatic missions of foreign states. In *Alcom*,[308] Lord Diplock recognised that at least some of the money in an account belonging to the Columbian embassy would be used to pay for goods and services for the day-to-day running of the mission which would, as a result of the definition of 'commercial purpose' in

301 *ibid*, at [92(3)].
302 *Supra*, n 225.
303 *ibid*, at [37].
304 *ibid*, at [38].
305 *Supra*, n 108.
306 *ibid*, at [56].
307 *ibid*, at [57].
308 *Supra*, n 20.

section 3 of the SIA (explained earlier) make these *prima facie* commercial transactions,[309] thus rendering the money 'in use or intended for use for commercial purposes'. However, ascertaining the admixture of sums to be used for commercial and non-commercial purposes would necessarily involve the state providing information in the proceedings, which would impermissibly require the state to submit to the court's jurisdiction to defend its interest in its property.[310] Lord Diplock's solution was to hold that the balance in the embassy's account was indivisible, and could not be subjected to '*anticipatory dissection into the various uses to which moneys drawn upon it might have been put*'.[311] Indeed, only if an account could be shown by the claimant as having been earmarked specifically for use in meeting the state's liabilities could it be said to fall within the commercial use exception.[312]

Conclusions

17.187 State immunity is a complex and evolving subject which not only sits at the intersection between public and private law, but also involves the interrelationship between domestic and international law. Nevertheless, what may appear to be a seemingly academic issue can have very real consequences for commercial parties when their rights collide with a state's entitlement to immunity. However, the practical consequences of immunity arise in a commercial context once parties are in dispute and court proceedings are in view. As a result, it is unlikely that questions of state immunity – in common with other dispute-related considerations such as jurisdiction and choice of law clauses for arbitration agreements – will be at the forefront of the minds of those involved in negotiating commercial contracts, for whom the complexities of the contract's subject matter will be of greater significance.

309 *ibid*, at 604 [B] – [C].

310 Although not expressly relied on by the House of Lords in its reasoning, the impermissible interference in the sending state's affairs that would result were it required to provide evidence as to the use of an embassy account was relied on by the German Federal Constitutional Court to deny execution in the *Philippine Embassy Case* (1977) 46 BVerfGE 342 (cited with approval by Lord Diplock at 599 [H]). See: August Reinisch, *European Court Practice Concerning State Immunity from Enforcement Measures*, (2006) EJIL, 17(4) 803, 830.

311 *Supra*, n 20, at 604 [C] – [E]. The wide scope of protection afforded to embassy bank accounts despite the 'commercial' use of certain portions of the amounts they contain to defray running costs is justified on the principle of *ne impediatur legatio*, by which the functioning of foreign state diplomatic missions is granted protection. The treatment of embassy bank accounts as constituting property in use for sovereign purposes irrespective of whether funds may be used for commercial purposes is widely acknowledged internationally. The UNCSI specifically refers to embassy bank accounts within the category of property in use or intended for use in the performance of a diplomatic mission's functions, which is expressly excluded from the definition of state property in use for commercial purposes; see Article 21(1)(a). The Australian Foreign State Immunities Act 1985 grants immunity to diplomatic property which is in use '*predominantly for the purposes of establishing or maintaining a diplomatic or consular mission*'; see sections 3(a) and 32(3)(a). As to the approach adopted by other national legislation and courts, see: Hazel Fox & Philippa Webb, *The Law of State Immunity* (Oxford University Press 2015) 521–526; August Reinisch, *European Court Practice Concerning State Immunity from Enforcement Measures*, (2006) EJIL, 17(4) 803, 827–833.

312 *Supra*, n 20, at 604 [D]. This would appear to apply generally to bank accounts belonging to the state; see: *Orascom* (*supra*, n 192). In that case, funds received by Chad from the sale of oil were separated into accounts in London, one for the repayment of debts to international institutions, another for payment into a Future Generations Fund, with the remainder held in a 'Borrower's Account' for onward transmission to a commercial bank in Chad. The claimant sought to execute only against the Borrower's Account. As the Borrower's Account had been established for the purposes of a commercial transaction (*ie*, to receive the proceeds of contracts for the sale of oil), and any sums which it could have been said were intended for sovereign purposes (*ie*, those invested in the Future Generations Fund, although the court did not address the commercial or non-commercial nature of these sums) had already been separated, no issue of admixture arose; see Burton J at [24].

17.188 In setting out the limits of a foreign state's ability to assert immunity before their courts, state immunity rules enacted by domestic legislatures or set out in treaties provide something of a safety net which prevents states from invoking blanket immunity and avoiding liability entirely. Therefore, a commercial party which gives no consideration to immunity issues prior to contracting with a state is afforded a degree of protection. The exclusion of immunity for commercial transactions will often be wide enough so as to encompass the vast majority of contractual relationships and thus engage the court's adjudicative jurisdiction, whilst the exclusion of assets in use or intended for use for commercial purposes from the ambit of a state's immunity from enforcement will often (but not always) leave a sufficient pool of assets against which an award can be satisfied.

17.189 Nevertheless, the protection afforded by legislation can only go so far and, given the complicated and developing nature of the law in this respect, relying solely on the statutory provisions could lead to lengthy and costly litigation. Therefore, there are a number of practical steps which parties to contracts with states and separate state entities can take in order to manage and mitigate the risk that state immunity may pose.

- Where there is a possibility that the contractual counterparty is either part of a state or a state entity, or the subject matter of the contract may constitute an investment for the purposes of an investment treaty, commercial parties should consider the jurisdictions where it is likely that any proceedings to enforce and execute a judgment or award might take place. Undertaking this analysis will identify the immunity rules which will determine important matters such as: (1) whether the counterparty is characterised as a state or a state entity and, if the latter, the extent to which it is entitled to invoke immunity in respect of the subject matter of the contract;[313] (2) the extent to which immunity is excluded by an agreement to arbitrate;[314] and (3) the restrictions on the categories of assets against which execution may be granted. Indeed, the process of identifying in the first place the jurisdictions where enforcement is likely to succeed requires an understanding of how immunity rules are applied in each instance; countries which host significant volumes of foreign state assets may do so precisely because they afford a higher degree of protection for such assets, even where they are used for wholly commercial purposes,[315] which may limit the scope of assets which are amenable to execution.
- Whilst submission to the court's jurisdiction and waiver of immunity can be implied from the subject matter of a contract or an agreement to arbitrate, the most effective means of excluding immunity is the inclusion of an explicit clause to that effect in a contract with a state or state entity. Such a clause should provide

313 This will also determine the pool of assets available for execution. If the counterparty is a state entity, the pool will be limited to its own assets; if it is state, then the pool will include those belonging to the state generally (subject to any immunity the state is entitled to assert over those assets) but exclude those belonging to separate entities, even if used for ostensibly governmental purposes.

314 Relevant considerations in this respect will include: (1) what constitutes a sufficient agreement to arbitrate; (2) whether an agreement constitutes submission to both the court's adjudicative and enforcement jurisdictions; and (3) connected to that, the nature of the court proceedings from which a state's immunity will be excluded. The latter point will indicate the extent to which the court will be able to support the proceedings and penalise the conduct of a recalcitrant state.

315 For example, see the treatment afforded by the SIA to the property of sovereign wealth funds located in the UK which is channelled through foreign central banks, as set out earlier in this chapter.

for an express submission to the adjudicative and enforcement jurisdiction of the courts of any state with competent jurisdiction (or, where there is an exclusive jurisdiction clause, to the courts of that country),[316] and include an express waiver of immunity in respect of both pre- and post-award measures of constraint and execution, including interim relief. The clause should also stipulate the nature of the state's property in respect of which immunity is waived for the purposes of execution. This could mirror the commercial purposes exception found in many domestic immunity statutes and international conventions, and include any categories of assets (such as embassy bank accounts) which would typically be excluded from measures of execution, or else it could generally waive immunity in respect of all state property but exclude certain categories (such as naval vessels and military aircraft).[317]

- As an alternative to defining the general nature of state property against which an award can be executed, the state may agree as part of the contractual arrangements to earmark specific property (such as money in a specified bank account) from which it agrees to settle any liabilities arising out of the contract, including satisfaction of any award made against it.
- Contractual mechanisms which limit the need to seek redress directly against a state should be considered in order to avoid the issue of immunity arising altogether. These may include stipulating that payment must be effected by means of a letter of credit so that any failure of the state to make payment will entitle the commercial party to seek payment directly from the issuing bank. Similarly, an on-demand bond which guarantees that the state will meet its payment obligations would permit the commercial party to make a call if the state fails to pay. An attempt by the state to injunct payment under a demand and contest the commercial party's entitlement to call would likely be sufficient to demonstrate that the state has submitted to the court's jurisdiction, thereby excluding its immunity for the purposes of any related dispute that may arise.
- Commercial parties should consider engaging in alternative methods of dispute resolution prior to commencing arbitration or litigation. Processes such as conciliation and mediation are effective means of avoiding lengthy and costly formal dispute proceedings in most commercial disputes, particularly on complex construction and infrastructure projects. Arriving at an agreed settlement avoids issues of immunity arising at all as there is no question of a submission to the jurisdiction of foreign courts, and it is more likely that a state will comply with the outcome than it will with an arbitral award. However, it is advisable that any settlement agreement which results from alternative dispute resolution should itself include an express submission and waiver clause to avoid a state frustrating implementation of the settlement agreement by refusing to comply with the terms of the settlement and asserting immunity in subsequent proceedings for breach of its terms.

316 Even where arbitration is the agreed dispute resolution mechanism, a submission to the adjudicative jurisdiction of the competent court(s) will avoid any argument that the state has not consented to proceedings in support of the arbitration or measures for the recognition and enforcement of an award.

317 See, for example, the exclusion of immunity clause in *Sabah Shipyard* (*supra*, n 269, at [18]).

- Where dispute resolution proceedings are necessary, commercial parties should consider the nature of the reliefs they claim. If the counterparty state has not consented to measures of constraint, then reliefs other than those involving the payment of money (*ie*, injunctive relief or specific performance) may not be enforceable by the courts. Therefore, alternative relief for damages in lieu of non-monetary claims should be included if permissible as a means of either compelling the state's compliance with the tribunal's decision on the principal relief sought, or else protecting the commercial party's position financially by enabling it to execute the alternative award in damages if the state does not comply. Similarly, if recourse to the curial courts is necessary in support of an arbitration, an application for measures that may otherwise be denied on the grounds of immunity should be accompanied with an alternative claim for damages in lieu.[318]

318 See: *The Prestige (No. 3)* (*supra*, n 85).

INDEX

Taylor & Francis Group
an **informa** business

Taylor & Francis eBooks

www.taylorfrancis.com

A single destination for eBooks from Taylor & Francis with increased functionality and an improved user experience to meet the needs of our customers.

90,000+ eBooks of award-winning academic content in Humanities, Social Science, Science, Technology, Engineering, and Medical written by a global network of editors and authors.

TAYLOR & FRANCIS EBOOKS OFFERS:

A streamlined experience for our library customers

A single point of discovery for all of our eBook content

Improved search and discovery of content at both book and chapter level

REQUEST A FREE TRIAL

support@taylorfrancis.com

Routledge
Taylor & Francis Group

CRC Press
Taylor & Francis Group

For Product Safety Concerns and Information please contact our EU representative GPSR@taylorandfrancis.com
Taylor & Francis Verlag GmbH, Kaufingerstraße 24, 80331 München, Germany

www.ingramcontent.com/pod-product-compliance
Lightning Source LLC
LaVergne TN
LVHW080804011026
849160LV00015B/1524
* 9 7 8 0 3 6 7 7 4 0 7 4 0 *